HUMANITY

AN INTRODUCTION TO CULTURAL ANTHROPOLOGY

TENTH EDITION

James Peoples
Ohio Wesleyan University

Garrick Bailey
University of Tulsa

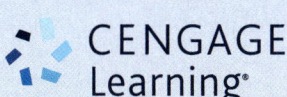

Australia • Brazil • Mexico • Singapore • United Kingdom • United States

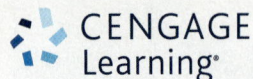

Humanity: An Introduction to Cultural Anthropology, Tenth Edition
James Peoples and Garrick Bailey

Product Manager: Gordon Lee
Content Developer: Robert Jucha
Content Coordinator: Sean Cronin
Product Assistant: Victor Luu
Media Developer: John Chell
Marketing Manager: Molly Felz
Content Project Manager: Cheri Palmer
Art Director: Caryl Gorska
Manufacturing Planner: Judy Inouye
Rights Acquisitions Specialist: Tom McDonough
Production Service: Jill Traut, MPS Limited
Photo Researcher: PreMedia Global
Text Researcher: PreMedia Global
Copy Editor: Laura Larson
Illustrator and Composition: MPS Limited
Text and Cover Designer: Ingalls Design
Cover Image: Strauss/Curtis

© 2015, 2012 Cengage Learning

ALL RIGHTS RESERVED. No part of this work covered by the copyright herein may be reproduced, transmitted, stored, or used in any form or by any means graphic, electronic, or mechanical, including but not limited to photocopying, recording, scanning, digitizing, taping, Web distribution, information networks, or information storage and retrieval systems, except as permitted under Section 107 or 108 of the 1976 United States Copyright Act, without the prior written permission of the publisher.

> For product information and technology assistance, contact us at
> **Cengage Learning Customer & Sales Support, 1-800-354-9706.**
> For permission to use material from this text or product,
> submit all requests online at **www.cengage.com/permissions**
> Further permissions questions can be e-mailed to
> **permissionrequest@cengage.com**

Library of Congress Control Number: 2013940728

ISBN-13: 978-1-285-73337-1

ISBN-10: 1-285-73337-1

Cengage Learning
200 First Stamford Place, 4th Floor
Stamford, CT 06902
USA

Cengage Learning is a leading provider of customized learning solutions with office locations around the globe, including Singapore, the United Kingdom, Australia, Mexico, Brazil, and Japan. Locate your local office at **www.cengage.com/global**

Cengage Learning products are represented in Canada by Nelson Education, Ltd.

To learn more about Cengage Learning Solutions,
visit **www.cengage.com**
Purchase any of our products at your local college store or at our preferred online store **www.cengagebrain.com**

Printed in Canada
1 2 3 4 5 6 7 17 16 15 14 13

BRIEF CONTENTS

1 The Study of Humanity 1

Part I Humanity, Culture, and Language 20

2 Culture 20
3 Culture and Language 46
4 Cultural Diversity and Globalization 66

Part II Theories and Methods of Cultural Anthropology 90

5 The Development of Anthropological Thought 90
6 Methods of Investigation 115

Part III The Diversity of Culture 133

7 Culture and Nature: Interacting with the Environment 133
8 Exchange in Economic Systems 165
9 Marriages and Families 189
10 Kinship and Descent 218
11 Gender in Comparative Perspective 242
12 The Organization of Political Life 271
13 Social Inequality and Stratification 293
14 Religion and Worldview 315
15 Art and the Aesthetic 344

Part IV Anthropology in the Global Community 365

16 Ethnicity and Ethnic Conflict 365
17 World Problems and the Practice of Anthropology 387

CONTENTS

Preface x
About the Authors xvi

1 The Study of Humanity 1

Subfields of Anthropology 2
  Biological/Physical Anthropology 3
  Archaeology 6
  Cultural Anthropology 7
  Anthropological Linguistics 8
Applications of Anthropology 9
  Applied Anthropology 9
  Careers in Anthropology 10
Cultural Anthropology Today 11
Anthropological Perspectives on Cultures 13
  Holistic Perspective 14
  Comparative Perspective 14
  Relativistic Perspective 14
Some Lessons of Anthropology 16
CONCEPT REVIEW Primary Interests of the Five Subfields of Anthropology 3
GLOBAL CHALLENGES AND OPPORTUNITIES The Process of Globalization 12
Summary 18

PART I Humanity, Culture, and Language

2 Culture 20

Introducing Culture 21
Defining Culture 23
  Shared . . . 23
  . . . Socially Learned . . . 25
  . . . Knowledge . . . 28
  . . . and Patterns of Behavior 29
Cultural Knowledge 30
  Norms 30
  Values 31
  Symbols 32
  Classifications and Constructions of Reality 33
  Worldviews 36
The Origins of Culture 37
Culture and Human Life 38
Cultural Knowledge and Individual Behavior 39
  Is Behavior Culturally Determined? 39
  Why Does Behavior Vary? 40
Biology and Cultural Differences 41
Cultural Universals 43
GLOBAL CHALLENGES AND OPPORTUNITIES Is Everyone Becoming a Westerner? 26
CONCEPT REVIEW Components of Cultural Knowledge 31
Summary 44

3 Culture and Language 46

Language and Humanity 47
The Power of Language 48
  Discreteness 48
  Arbitrariness 49

    Productivity 49
    Displacement 49
    Multimedia Potential 49

How Language Works 50
    Sound Systems 51
    Words and Meanings 52

Germanics, Romantics, and Indian Givers 53

Communication and Social Behavior 55
    Nonverbal Communication 55
    Speech and Social Context 56
    The Language of Power 57

Language and Culture 60
    Language as a Reflection of Culture 61
    Language, Perceptions, and Worldview 62

CONCEPT REVIEW Five Properties of Language 50

GLOBAL CHALLENGES AND OPPORTUNITIES Globalization and Language 58

Summary 64

4 Cultural Diversity and Globalization 66

Cultural Change and Diversity 67

The World Before Globalization 68

Globalization 71

Early European Expansion 73
    The Americas 74
    Africa 75
    Asia 75
    Cultural Consequences 76

The Industrial Revolution 78
    Asia 79
    Africa 80
    Oceania 80

Consequences of European Expansion 80

GLOBAL CHALLENGES AND OPPORTUNITIES The Maroons: The New African Peoples of the Americas 84

Summary 87

PART II Theories and Methods of Cultural Anthropology

5 The Development of Anthropological Thought 90

The Emergence of Anthropology 91
    Late-Nineteenth-Century Unilineal Evolutionism 93
    A Science of Culture? 95

Anthropological Thought in the Early Twentieth Century 95
    Historical Particularism in the United States (ca. 1900–1940) 95
    British Functionalism, 1920s–1960s 99
    The Fieldwork Tradition 100

Mid–Twentieth Century: Rebirth of Evolutionism 101

Anthropological Thought Today 103
    Scientific Approaches 104
    Humanistic Approaches 107

Either, Or, or Both? 111

Why Can't All Those Anthropologists Agree? 112

GLOBAL CHALLENGES AND OPPORTUNITIES Global Anthropology 102

CONCEPT REVIEW Main Contrasts Between Scientific and Humanistic Approaches 111

Summary 113

6 Methods of Investigation 115

Ethnographic Methods 116
  Ethnographic Fieldwork 116
  Problems and Issues in Field Research 118
  Fieldwork as a Rite of Passage 124
  Ethnohistory 125

Comparative Methods 126
  Cross-Cultural Comparisons 127
  Controlled Comparisons 128

GLOBAL CHALLENGES AND OPPORTUNITIES The Changing Relationship Between Anthropologists and Indigenous Peoples 120

CONCEPT REVIEW Methods of Investigation 130

Summary 130

PART III — The Diversity of Culture

7 Culture and Nature: Interacting with the Environment 133

Understanding Interactions with Nature 134

Hunting and Gathering 136
  Foraging and Culture 137
  What Happened to Hunters and Gatherers? 140

Domestication of Plants and Animals 142
  Origins of Domestication: Wheres and Whens 142
  Advantages and Costs of Cultivation 145

Horticulture 146
  Varieties of Horticulture 146
  Cultural Consequences of Horticulture 147

Intensive Agriculture 148
  Varieties of Intensive Agriculture 149
  Cultural Consequences of Intensive Agriculture 150

Pastoralism 152

Nature and Culture in Preindustrial Times 155

Industrialism 156
  Energy and Society 156
  Consequences of Industrialism 157

Globalization and the Environment 159

CONCEPT REVIEW Major Forms of Preindustrial Adaptations and Their Cultural Consequences 155

GLOBAL CHALLENGES AND OPPORTUNITIES Who Should Pay to Reduce Global Warming? 160

Summary 163

8 Exchange in Economic Systems 165

Economic Systems 166

Reciprocity 167
  Generalized Reciprocity 168
  Balanced Reciprocity 169
  Negative Reciprocity 171
  Reciprocity and Social Distance 171

Redistribution 172

Market 174
  Money 174
  Market Exchange 175
  Market Economies and Capitalism 176
  Productivity 180

Globalization and Markets 181

CONCEPT REVIEW Three Forms of Exchange in Economic Systems 168

GLOBAL CHALLENGES AND OPPORTUNITIES Globalization of Indigenous Products 184

Summary 187

9 Marriages and Families 189

Some Definitions 190

Incest Taboos 192

Marriage 195
  Defining Marriage 195
  Functions of Marriage 196
  Two Unusual Forms 197

Variations in Marriage Beliefs and Practices 199
   Marriage Rules 199
   How Many Spouses? 200
   Polygyny 201
   Polyandry 205
   Marriage Alliances 206
   Marital Exchanges 207
   Bridewealth 207
   Brideservice 208
   Dowry 208

Same-Sex Marriage and the Culture Wars 209

Postmarital Residence Patterns 211
   Influences on Residence Patterns 212
   Residence and Households 213

Kinship Diagrams 213

Family and Household Forms 214
   Matrifocal Households 214
   Extended Households 215

CONCEPT REVIEW Terms for Groups Formed on the Basis of Kinship Relationships 191

GLOBAL CHALLENGES AND OPPORTUNITIES Marriage and Family in Global Society: The Case of Japan 202

Summary 216

10 Kinship and Descent 218

Introducing Kinship 219
   Why Study Kinship? 219
   Cultural Variations in Kinship 220

Unilineal Descent 221
   Unilineal Descent Groups 223
   Descent Groups in Action 227
   Avunculocality Revisited 229

Nonunilineal Descent 230
   Bilateral 231
   Cognatic 231

Influences on Kinship Systems 233

Cultural Construction of Kinship 234
   Logic of Cultural Constructions 235
   Varieties of Kinship Terminology 236
   Why Do Terminologies Differ? 238

Where's Our Backbone? 240

GLOBAL CHALLENGES AND OPPORTUNITIES Patrilineality and Globalization in China 224

CONCEPT REVIEW Forms of Descent and Kinship 233

Summary 240

11 Gender in Comparative Perspective 242

Sex and Gender 243

Cultural Construction of Gender 244
   The Hua of Papua New Guinea 245
   North American Constructions 246

Multiple-Gender Identities 247
   Native American Two Spirits 247
   Hijra of Hindu India 251

The Gendered Division of Labor 252
   Understanding Major Patterns 253
   Fertility Maintenance 254
   Reproductive Roles 256
   Relative Strength 256
   Compatibility with Child Care 256
   Understanding Variability 257

Gender Stratification 259
   Is Gender Stratification Universal? 261
   Influences on Gender Stratification 264
   Descent and Postmarital Residence 268
   Gender Stratification in Industrial Societies 268

CONCEPT REVIEW Female/Male Differences Affecting Major Patterns in the Gendered Division of Labor 255

GLOBAL CHALLENGES AND OPPORTUNITIES Bridal Photos in Taiwan: Globalization and Localization 266

Summary 269

Contents   vii

12 The Organization of Political Life 271

Forms of Political Organization 272
- Bands 273

CONCEPT REVIEW Political Organization 274
- Tribes 275
- Chiefdoms 277
- States 278
- Inca Empire 279

Social Control and Law 280
- Social Control 280
- Law 281

Legal Systems 281
- Self-Help Systems 281
- Court Systems 287
- Incipient Court Systems 287
- Courts of Mediation 288
- Courts of Regulation 289

GLOBAL CHALLENGES AND OPPORTUNITIES Multinational Corporations Versus the Nation-State 282

CONCEPT REVIEW Legal Systems 290

Summary 291

13 Social Inequality and Stratification 293

Equalities and Inequalities 294

Equalities and Inequalities: Three Systems 294
- Egalitarian Societies 296
- Ranked Societies 297
- Stratified Societies 298

Castes in Traditional India 299

Classes in Industrial Societies: The United States 302

Maintaining Inequality 305
- Ideologies 306
- American Secular Ideologies 307

Theories of Inequality 308
- Functionalist Theory 309
- Conflict Theory 310
- Who Benefits? 312

CONCEPT REVIEW Systems of Equality and Inequality 295

GLOBAL CHALLENGES AND OPPORTUNITIES Globalization and Inequality in China 300

Summary 313

14 Religion and Worldview 315

Defining Religion 316
- Beliefs About Supernatural Powers 316
- Myths and Worldviews 317
- Rituals and Symbols 318

Theories of Religion 319
- Intellectual/Cognitive Approaches 320
- Psychological Approaches 322
- Sociological Approaches 323

Supernatural Explanations of Misfortune 325
- Sorcery 325
- Witchcraft 326
- Interpretations of Sorcery and Witchcraft 327

Varieties of Religious Organization 328
- Individualistic Organizations 329
- Shamanistic Organizations 331
- Communal Organizations 332
- Ecclesiastical Organizations 335

Revitalization Movements 337
- Melanesian Cargo Cults 338
- Native American Movements 338
- Fate of Revitalization Movements 340

CONCEPT REVIEW Varieties of Religious Organization 330

GLOBAL CHALLENGES AND OPPORTUNITIES Religious Diversity in the United States 340

Summary 342

15 Art and the Aesthetic 344

The Pervasiveness of Art 346

Forms of Artistic Expression 347
- Body Arts 347
- Visual Arts 351
- Performance Arts 354

CONCEPT REVIEW Forms of Artistic Expression 356

Art and Culture 356
- Secular and Religious Art 357
- Art and Gender 358
- Social Functions of Art 359

GLOBAL CHALLENGES AND OPPORTUNITIES The Market Economy and Traditional Visual Arts 360

Summary 363

PART IV Anthropology in the Global Community

16 Ethnicity and Ethnic Conflict 365

Ethnic Groups 366
- Situational Nature of Ethnic Identity 367
- Attributes of Ethnic Groups 367
- Fluidity of Ethnic Groups 370
- Types of Ethnic Groups 371

Civilizations 372

The Problem of Stateless Nationalities 372

Responses to Ethnic Conflict 379
- Homogenization 379
- Segregation 381
- Accommodation 382
- Results 383

CONCEPT REVIEW Levels of Ethnic Identity 371

GLOBAL CHALLENGES AND OPPORTUNITIES The Global Economy, Migration, and Transnational Communities 374

CONCEPT REVIEW Responses to Ethnic Differences 382

Summary 385

17 World Problems and the Practice of Anthropology 387

Applied Anthropology 388

Health and Health Care 389
- Medical Anthropology 389
- Scientific Medicine and Traditional Healing 389

Population Growth 391
- Anthropological Perspectives on Population Growth 391
- Costs and Benefits of Children in the LDCs 392

World Hunger 394
- Scarcity or Inequality? 394
- Is Technology Transfer the Answer? 396
- Agricultural Alternatives 398

Anthropologists as Advocates 399
- Indigenous Peoples Today 400
- Vanishing Knowledge 404
- Medicines We Have Learned 405

GLOBAL CHALLENGES AND OPPORTUNITIES The Question of Development 406
- Adaptive Wisdom 407
- Cultural Alternatives 408

Summary 409

Glossary 412
Notes 419
Bibliography 427
People and Cultures Index 439
Subject Index 443

Preface

A textbook titled *Humanity* might seem presumptuous. The authors chose this title back in 1985, when we began working on the first edition. We thought *Humanity* captures the most distinctive feature of the discipline called anthropology: in the social sciences, anthropology alone studies all the world's peoples. Anthropologists are interested in all humans, including those who lived in the prehistoric past, the historic past, and the present day.

As a scholarly field of study, anthropology is very broad in its scope and interests. Several generations of anthropologists have discovered a vast amount of information about humanity. Paleoanthropologists are uncovering fossils and unwinding genetic relationships that are showing how and when the human species originated and evolved into modern *Homo sapiens*. Archaeologists are digging into information about how prehistoric peoples lived their lives.

Another subfield, cultural anthropology, is the main subject of this book. Research done by cultural anthropologists (fieldwork) often involves years of intensive study while living among some human community. Cultural anthropology describes and tries to explain or interpret the fascinating cultural variability of the world's diverse peoples. In this text, we try to convey to students the life-enriching as well as the educational value of discovering this variability. In the process, we hope students and other readers will experience a change in their attitudes about other cultures, about their own lives and nations, and about humanity in general.

We also hope the book leads readers to think about their own identities as individuals, as members of a particular society with its traditions and ways of thinking and acting, and as participants in an increasingly worldwide human community. To achieve this last goal, we discuss anthropological insights into some of the problems that affect the twenty-first century, such as ethnic conflicts, national and global inequalities, hunger, and the survival of indigenous cultures and languages. As we describe the diversity in various dimensions of human life, including relations with the natural world, marriage, gender, and religion, we suggest the implications of such diversity for contemporary people and societies.

Finally, we want newcomers to anthropology to grasp the full significance of the oldest anthropological lesson of all: that their own values, beliefs, and behaviors are a product of their upbringing in a particular human group rather than universal among all peoples. If understood properly and applied seriously, this principle leads us to question unconscious assumptions and to view ourselves as well as other peoples from new perspectives.

As we write the tenth edition in 2012–2013, the United States and its allies remained involved in conflicts in Afghanistan. Iran is alleged to be developing nuclear weapons—or maybe not. In Syria, fighting between a popular movement (or is it?) and the ruling government has killed thousands. The possibility that chemical weapons are used by the Syrian government sharpens a common international dilemma: under what circumstances do humanitarian values outweigh narrow national interests (and budgets)? Such conflicts, perceived threats, and competitions lead some to believe that peoples of different nations, ethnicities, and religions can never live together in peace and security.

In another part of our planet, the People's Republic of China became the world's second-largest economy in August 2010. Offshoring of production to China decreases consumer prices for the people of Europe and North America—but also reduces high-wage factory jobs on those continents. China's factories, massive building projects, and motor vehicles pollute its own air and water. Emissions of greenhouse gases from nations that use fossil fuels in factory production add to the climate change that already has occurred because of fossil fuel–based development in Western nations. Economic competition between nations and international environmental problems lead to dilemmas that are truly global. Will there inevitably be global winners and losers? How should one nation handle environmental problems that are caused partly by other nations?

In the short term, wars and other forms of conflict and competitions separate antagonists from one another. Yet, overall, the world's regions now interact more frequently and intensively than ever before. Words like *multiculturalism* and *multinationalism* have become familiar to most people in the past couple of decades. Anthropology has much to say about these changes. Just as important, anthropology helps us become more aware of how our own lives are affected by such changes.

New to the Tenth Edition

There are many reasons for the growing interdependence of peoples and nations: increased integration of the world's national economies, rises in international travel and migration, educational exchanges between countries and regions, wide availability of the Internet, worldwide spread of consumer culture, and access to international media. The general term for such changes is *globalization*, which has many dimensions: cultural, economic, political, artistic, linguistic, and religious, to name a few. As in the previous two editions, each chapter of *Humanity* includes a feature called Globalization Challenges and Opportunities in this edition, which focuses on the dimensions of globalization that relate to the chapter's subject. Features in various chapters deal with issues such as how globalization affects cultural diversity, language survival, inequality among nations, religious diversity in the United States, production and sale of art, and cultural and religious fundamentalism. Some discussions are mainly factually based, whereas others present anthropological insights into the process or the results of globalization.

Most chapters contain material that explicitly suggests the relevance of the subject for modern North America, such as climate change, exchange forms, and religious accommodation. We have chosen to delete the previous Closer Look boxes, but some of their information is integrated into the main text, such as language survival and same-sex marriage. In most chapters we have rewritten major sections to simplify the style and word use to make the material more engaging. Sections of several chapters have been retitled and reorganized to improve clarity and logical flow.

To those instructors who are previous users of *Humanity*, the following chapter-by-chapter summary highlights the major changes in this edition.

Chapter 1 again introduces the subdisciplines and discusses the importance of anthropological perspectives, methods, and factual knowledge of cultural diversity. We no longer include applied anthropology as a fifth subfield, but the text emphasizes its importance in the field as a whole and for career opportunities for undergraduates. We eliminated the detailed discussion of human biological evolution but do describe the most essential facts and dates. We highlight the change in cultural anthropological field research away from what some call *tribes* toward what some call *modern societies*, including both "mainstream" and immigrant communities. The discussion of relativism retains the distinction between methodological and moral relativism, using female genital mutilation to illustrate the complexity of the relativism issue.

The topical structure and themes of Chapter 2 (culture) are intact. We continue to integrate terms like *cultural identity, subcultures, roles,* and *social learning* into an extended discussion of the concept of culture, with the goal of demonstrating that the concept of culture is more complicated than most people realize. New research findings about toolmaking methods from South Africa are described in the subsection "Origins of Culture," which also covers archaeological and physical evidence for the use of symbols and language. Coverage of the cultural construction of race is moved to a major section of the chapter.

Chapter 3 (language) further condenses the sections on structural linguistics. There is explicit discussion of the use of language to acquire and enhance power, using new examples of political speech. In the section on language and culture, we cover how linguistic words and concepts might affect views of social reality, illustrated by terms like *family, human rights,* and *democracy*. This chapter continues to emphasize relationships among culture, language, thought, and behavior over the technical aspects of linguistics. Information on Native American words that have been incorporated into English now has its own major section.

Chapter 4 (cultural diversity and globalization) is a new chapter. The purpose of this chapter is to provide a context for the chapters that follow, not just the ones concerned with cultural diversity, theories, and methods. After a brief discussion of why and how culture changes, we discuss the broad patterns of culture change that have occurred over the past 150,000 years or so of human history. We end the chapter with a discussion of the global economy.

The focus of Chapter 5 (theory) remains twofold: (1) main historical patterns and early ideas about cultures that gave rise to anthropology today and (2) distinctions between contemporary approaches, which we categorize (broadly) as scientific and humanistic. We try to represent both sides fairly and objectively. Where appropriate, we integrate this distinction into later empirical chapters by stating the interpretations or explanations each broad approach would offer. Relationships between early theorists and modern themes and divisions are explicitly covered, by showing how new ideas were shaped by earlier ones.

In Chapter 6 (methods) we continue to emphasis that anthropological research has two primary objectives: to describe and explain cultural diversity. Cultural research can also focus on the culture of a people at a particular point, or in the changes in their culture over time. The new Global Challenges and Opportunities box addresses the changing relationship between anthropological researchers and peoples being studied. Increasingly these peoples are concerned with the protection of their intellectual properties rights and privacy; thus changing their relationship to the researcher.

In Chapter 7 (environment) we expanded the section on industrialized societies, which includes a new subsection describing how fossil fuels dramatically increased productivity and the social and cultural implications of this increase. Basic facts about the places and dates of domestication are provided in a separate section. The chapter covers how the cultures of industrial societies differ from those of preindustrial times, environmental impacts (especially climate change and pollution), and the globalization of production and resource harvesting. Major themes include the contributions made by China and other emerging economies to climate change, difficulties of the international system in solving the "public bad" problem, how smaller nations (e.g., island countries) are likely to be most affected, and which nations should pay to reduce greenhouse gas emissions (given the globalization of production). New numerical data are added to several topics. Like Chapter 2, this chapter provides information referred to extensively in later chapters.

Chapter 8 (exchange) is extensively revised. We hope the introductory vignette creates student interest in the general topic. Sections on reciprocity, redistribution, and market forms are largely unchanged except for one new example. More than previous editions, we focus on the distinction between market exchanges—which are ancient and culturally widespread—and market economies—which developed since the Industrial Revolution. Thanks to the comments of reviewers, we give explicit attention to capitalism and socialism as ways to organize industrial and postindustrial economies, including the advantages and weaknesses of each, Neoliberalism and social welfare capitalism are covered. We deconstruct the concept of *productivity*, using Karen Ho's research on Wall Street investment bankers as the primary example. There is a new discussion of the complexities of estimating the costs and benefits of the globalization of factory production, including the wider implications of the collapse of a building containing clothing factories in Bangladesh in April 2013.

In Chapter 9 (marriage and family), we streamlined many discussions while retaining the standard textbook structure from previous editions: ideas about incest taboos, problems of defining marriage, marriage forms and their implications, marital transactions, postmarital residence patterns, and household forms. Along the way, we cover fictive kin, matrifocal families, three unusual cases, and descriptions of Old Testament references to levirate, bridewealth, and brideservice to increase student interest. A new section discusses gay marriage and "culture wars" in the United States (including recent events such as the June 2013 Supreme Court decision). We expanded coverage of the relevance of anthropological studies on marriage and family to twenty-first-century issues.

Coverage in Chapter 10 (kinship, descent, and terminology) also remains pretty standard: forms of descent and kinship, influences on these forms, and a minimized description of kinship terminologies to illustrate the cultural construction of kinship. The concluding section of this chapter suggests implications of diversity in marriage, family, and kinship forms for modern life and the future.

In Chapter 11 (gender), we have completed eliminated some old terminologies, using "Two Spirit" rather than "berdache," and "gendered" rather than "sexual" division of labor. Except for streamlining and rewriting several paragraph, this chapter is much the same as in the ninth edition, which added two new ethnographic cases: the hijra for multiple gender identities and the Vanatinai as a possible example of gender equality. We added more suggestions for the relevance of anthropological findings and ideas to modern understandings.

The basic structure of Chapter 12 (political life) has remained unchanged. However, the box entitled "Murder Among the Cheyenne" has been dropped with much of the discussion integrated into the main text. Although the Global Challenges and Opportunities box retains the old title "Multinational Corporations and the Nation-State," the emphasis is now on the global economy and the resultant growing economic power of these corporations and how they are increasingly challenging the authority of national governments.

Chapter 13 (inequality and stratification) continues to contrast egalitarian, ranked, and stratified societies, incorporating many examples. It also discusses the concept of *ideology* (both religious and secular) and the complexities of evaluating it. As in earlier editions, we updated numerical data on the distribution of income and wealth in the United States, including numbers that bring home the extent to which economic inequalities have increased in the last thirty years. In discussing the functionalist and conflict theories of stratification, we used examples (e.g., CEO-to-worker income ratios) to illustrate some ideas.

In Chapter 14 (religion), we rewrote in places to clarify some points. There is a new discussion of the problems of classifications used by anthropologists to compare religions. The subsection on communal religious organizations is expanded to include rites of passage for both genders and seasonal rituals as well as ancestral rituals and totemism. New brief ethnographic examples are the eastern Pueblo, Gebusi of New Guinea, and Hawaiian *mana*. In the globalization feature on religious pluralism, we added new material on European countries.

Chapter 15 (art) is basically the same with the exception of the Global Challenges box. This new box addresses the question of how increased integration into the global economy and less expensive machine-made goods are changing the artistic visual traditions associated with handmade items.

Chapter 16 (ethnicity) has modifications in the defining and describing the attributes of ethnic groups. The discussions of types of ethnic groups have been changed. The discussion of civilizations has been expanded, while transnational groups have been dropped from the list of types of ethnic groups and are now discussed in greater detail in the Global Challenges box. The data on conflicts have been updated and changed.

Chapter 17 (world problems and the practice of anthropology), though modified, still discusses anthropological insights in the issues of health and health care, population growth, and world hunger. The last part on anthropologists as advocates has been modified, expanded, and updated.

Special Features

The boxed features called A Closer Look are eliminated in this edition, in the interest of space and continuity. Each chapter still contains a feature on globalization, titled **Global Challenges and Opportunities**, a label that reflects the focus of most of their content. A photo accompanies each insert.

Several pedagogical aids are intended to help students understand and retain the material they have just read. Each chapter begins with a set of five to eight **Learning Objectives** that focus on the key concepts, ideas, and themes of the chapter. The learning objectives are tied to the end-of-chapter **Summary**. We hope this helps students come away with a solid understanding of the main points of each chapter.

We continue to include at least one **Concept Review** in every chapter to condense ideas and make sharp distinctions in just a few words. A **Glossary** again is included at the end of the book. **Key Terms** in bold are defined immediately at the bottom of the page when students first encounter them in the chapter.

Anthropology is a highly visual discipline, and *Humanity* holds to the highest standards in providing photographs, figures, and maps to illustrate the text. Maps on the inside front cover show the location of peoples and cultures mentioned in the book.

There are two **indexes**, one a traditional subject index and the other a list of peoples and cultures mentioned in the book.

Resources

Student Resources

CourseMate. The CourseMate for Peoples and Bailey's *Humanity*, tenth edition, brings course concepts to life with interactive learning, study, and exam preparation tools that support the printed textbook. Access an integrated MindTap e-book, glossary, quizzes, videos, and more in the CourseMate for *Humanity*, tenth edition. Go to CengageBrain.com to register or purchase access.

Instructor Resources

Online Instructor's Manual with Test Bank. This online supplement offers learning objectives, chapter outlines and summaries, key terms, suggested supplementary lectures, discussion questions, and more. The instructor's manual also includes updated references to relevant news articles, films, and videos for each chapter. The test bank provides approximately 40 multiple-choice, 15 true/false, and 5 essay questions per chapter.

Cengage Learning Testing Powered by Cognero. A flexible, online system, Cognero allows you to author, edit, and manage test bank content from multiple Cengage Learning solutions. Cognero also offers you the ability to create multiple tests in an instant and deliver them from your LMS, your classroom, or wherever you want!

Online PowerPoint Slides. These vibrant, Microsoft® PowerPoint® lecture slides for each chapter will assist you with your lecture by providing concept coverage using images, figures, and tables directly from the textbook.

CourseReader: Anthropology. *CourseReader Anthropology* is a fully customizable online reader that provides access to hundreds of readings and audio and video selections from multiple disciplines. This easy-to-use solution allows you to select exactly the content you need for your courses and is loaded with convenient pedagogical features like highlighting, printing, note taking, and audio downloads. You have the freedom to assign individualized content at an affordable price. The *CourseReader: Anthropology* is the perfect complement to any class.

The Wadsworth Anthropology Video Library Volumes I–IV. Enhance your lectures with new video clips from the BBC® Motion Gallery and CBS® News. Addressing topics from the four fields, these videos are divided into short segments, perfect for introducing key concepts with footage sourced from some of the most remarkable collections in the world.

AIDS in Africa DVD. Expand your students' global perspective of HIV/AIDS with this award-winning documentary series focused on controlling HIV/AIDS in southern Africa. Films focus on caregivers in the faith community; how young people share messages of hope through song and dance; the relationship of HIV/AIDS to gender, poverty, stigma, education, and justice; and the story of two HIV-positive women helping others.

Classic Readings in Cultural Anthropology, Third Edition. Practical and insightful, *Classic Readings in Cultural Anthropology*, third edition, is a concise and accessible reader that presents a core selection of historical and contemporary works that have been instrumental in shaping anthropological thought and research over the past decades. Carefully edited by Dr. Gary Ferraro, the third edition includes five new classic readings from the disciplines of cultural anthropology and linguistics. Readings are organized around eight topics that closely mirror most introductory textbooks and are selected from scholarly works on the basis of their enduring themes and contributions to the discipline. These selections allow students to further explore anthropological perspectives on such key topics as culture, language and communication, ecology and economics, marriage and family, gender, politics and social control, supernatural beliefs, and issues of culture change. The new edition also addresses pressing topics such as globalization, ethnic violence, environmental issues, and more. *Classic Readings in Cultural Anthropology*, third edition, delivers an excellent introduction to the field of anthropology and the contributions it makes to understanding the world around us.

Human–Environment Interactions: New Directions in Human Ecology. This module by Kathy Galvin begins with a brief discussion of the history and core concepts of the field of human ecology and the study of how humans interact with the natural environment. It then looks in-depth at how the environment influences cultural practices (environmental determinism), as well as how aspects of culture, in turn, affect the environment. Human behavioral ecology is presented within the context of natural selection and how ecological factors influence the development of cultural and behavioral traits, and how people subsist in different environments. The module concludes with a discussion of resilience and global change as a result of human–environment interactions. This module, in chapter-like print format, can be packaged for free with the text.

Medical Anthropology in Applied Perspective Module. This free-standing module is actually a complete text chapter, featuring the same quality of pedagogy and written content in Cengage's cultural anthropology texts. See your sales representative for information on bundling the module with this text.

Acknowledgments

Since the first edition was published in 1988, *Humanity* (the book, not the species) has benefited enormously from reviewers. Some reviewers are long-term users of the text, whereas others have never adopted it for their classes. Of course, we have never been able to incorporate all their suggestions for improvement, or the book would be twice as long as it is. But, over the last 25 years, we have added, subtracted, updated, rethought, and reorganized most of the book based on reviewers' comments. We thank all of them.

For the 10th edition, both authors thank the reviewers listed here (their identities were unknown to us until publication):

Lara Braff, San Diego State University
Maureen Sperrazza, Western Connecticut State University
Francine Melia, University of Nevada–Reno
Jeffrey Ratcliffe, Penn State Abington
Micah Soltz, Columbus State Community College

Although we were unable to make all the changes these scholars suggested, many of their comments are incorporated into the text. Their comments that the book needs to be more *explicit* about the relevance of anthropology in today's world were especially influential.

Both authors have benefited from the suggestions of colleagues and friends. Jim is grateful to Thomas Love (Linfield College) for help with the material on energy in Chapter 7 and to Stacia Bensyl (Missouri Western State University) for assistance with Chapter 3. He also thanks Ted Cohen and Mary Howard for their collaboration and support for over twenty-five years (yikes!). Garrick thanks James Faris for his assistance on Nuba body painting, and Robert Canfield for helping to clarify some points on the Pushtun and Afghanistan.

About the Authors

James (Jim) Peoples is currently Professor and Chairperson of Sociology/Anthropology and Director of East Asian Studies at Ohio Wesleyan University in Delaware, Ohio. Peoples has taught at the University of California at Davis and the University of Tulsa in Oklahoma, among other colleges and universities. He received a B.A. from the University of California–Santa Cruz and a PhD from the University of California–Davis. His main research interests are human ecology, cultures of the Pacific Islands, and cultures of East Asia. His first book, *Island in Trust* (1985), describes his fieldwork on the island of Kosrae in the Federated States of Micronesia. His latest project is a coauthored book describing the prehistory, history, and contemporary culture of Kosrae island in Micronesia, to which he most recently returned in July and August 2013. Since joining the faculty of Ohio Wesleyan University in 1988, he has taught courses on East Asia, the Pacific, human ecology, cultural anthropology, the anthropology of religion, world hunger, the prehistory of North America, and Native Americans of the southwestern United States. Since 2010, Peoples has been Secretary of the Japan Studies Association. When not teaching, writing, or attending meetings, he enjoys fly-fishing, traveling, and gardening.

Garrick Bailey received his B.A. in history from the University of Oklahoma and his M.A. and Ph.D. in anthropology from the University of Oregon. His research interests include ethnohistory, world systems theory, and ethnicity and conflict, with a primary focus on the native peoples of North America. His publications include *Navajo: The Reservation Years* (with Roberta Bailey); *Changes in Osage Social Organization 1673–1906; The Osage and the Invisible World;* and *Traditions of the Osage* and *Art of the Osage* (with Dan Swan, John Nunley, and Sean Standingbear). He also was editor of *Indians in Contemporary Society,* Volume 2 of the *Handbook of North American Indians,* Smithsonian Institution. Bailey has been a Senior Fellow in Anthropology at the Smithsonian Institution in Washington and a Weatherhead Resident Scholar at the School of American Research in Santa Fe. Actively engaged in contemporary Native American issues, he has served as a member of the Indian Health Advisory Committee, Department of Health, Education, and Welfare; of the Glen Canyon Environmental Review Committee, National Research Council; and of the Native American Graves Protection and Repatriation Act (NAGPRA) Review Committee, Department of the Interior. Bailey has taught anthropology at the University of Tulsa since 1968.

1 The Study of Humanity

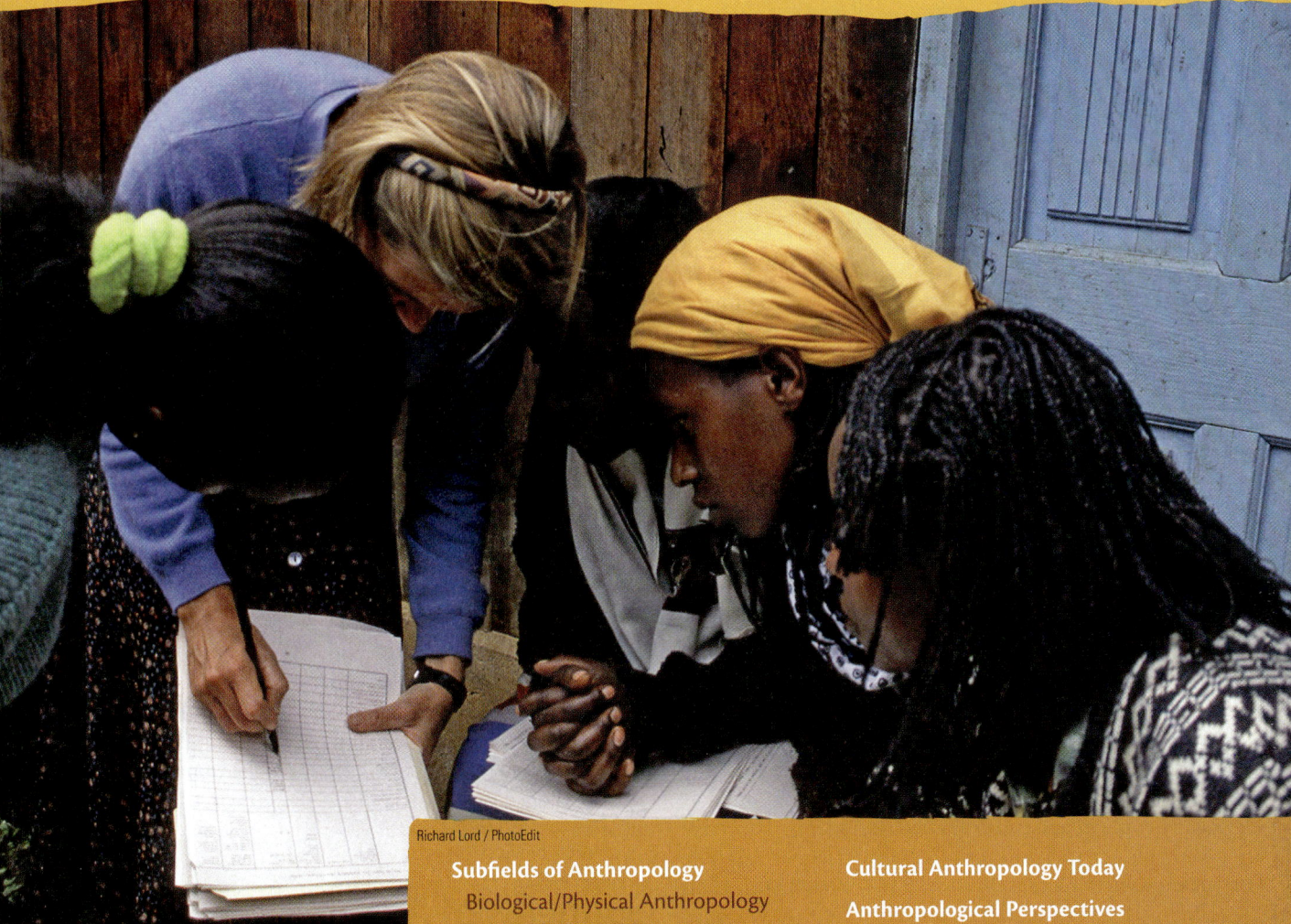

Cultural anthropology is the discipline that studies human cultural diversity, usually by visiting people where they live and interacting with them first-hand. This anthropologist is training Kenyan women to help with her field investigation.

Richard Lord / PhotoEdit

Subfields of Anthropology
  Biological/Physical Anthropology
  Archaeology
  Cultural Anthropology
  Anthropological Linguistics

Applications of Anthropology
  Applied Anthropology
  Careers in Anthropology

Cultural Anthropology Today

Anthropological Perspectives on Cultures
  Holistic Perspective
  Comparative Perspective
  Relativistic Perspective

Some Lessons of Anthropology

LEARNING OBJECTIVES

After reading this chapter, you should be able to:

1. **LIST** the four major subfields of anthropology and describe their primary subject matters.
2. **DISCUSS** how anthropology differs from other disciplines that also study humans.
3. **EXPLAIN** some of the practical uses of anthropology in solving human problems.
4. **DISCUSS** how cultural anthropology has changed in the last several decades.
5. **UNDERSTAND** the meaning and importance of the holistic, comparative, and relativistic perspectives.
6. **DESCRIBE** the wider lessons one can learn from studying anthropology.

What makes humans different from other animals? What is human nature, or is there such a thing? How and why do the peoples of the world differ, both biologically and culturally? Have affluent people in industrialized, urbanized nations sacrificed something important in their quest for the good life? If so, what might we learn from "traditional" or "indigenous" people? What are the implications of living in a world whose diverse peoples have recently become connected by global corporations and international communications? These are some of the questions investigated by **anthropology**, the academic discipline that studies all of humanity.

Almost everything about humanity interests anthropologists. We want to know when, where, and how our species originated and why we evolved into what we are today. Anthropologists try to explain the many differences among the world's cultures, such as why people in one culture believe they get sick because the souls of witches devour their livers, whereas people in another think that illness can result from tarantulas flinging tiny magical darts into their bodies. We want to know why most Argentinians and Australians like beef, which devout Hindus and Buddhists refuse to eat. We are curious about why some New Guinea peoples ritually engorge themselves with pork—the same animal flesh that some religions that began in the Middle East hold to be unclean and prohibited as food. In brief, anthropologists of one kind or another are likely to investigate almost everything about human beings: our biological evolution, cuisines, values, art styles, behaviors, languages, religions, and so forth.

Anthropologists, then, study many different dimensions of humanity. Indeed, the broad scope of anthropology is perhaps the one feature that most distinguishes it from other fields that also study humans, such as psychology and history. Anthropologists are interested in *all* human beings, whether living or dead, Asian or African or European. No people are too isolated to escape the anthropologist's notice. We also are interested in many different *aspects* of humans, including their genetic makeup, family lives, political systems, relations with nature, and emotional responses. No dimension of humankind, from skin color to dance traditions, falls outside the anthropologist's interest.

Subfields of Anthropology

Obviously, no single anthropologist can master all these subjects. Therefore, most modern anthropologists specialize in one of four principal subfields: biological (or physical) anthropology, archaeology, cultural anthropology, or anthropological linguistics. (The Concept Review summarizes the primary interests of each four subfields.) A fifth area, called applied anthropology, uses anthropological methods and insights to help solve real-world problems. Because cultural anthropology is the primary subject of this book, here we briefly summarize the other subfields and describe some of their major findings.

anthropology Academic discipline that studies humanity from a broad biological and cultural perspective.

CONCEPT REVIEW

Primary Interests of the Five Subfields of Anthropology

Physical/Biological — Excavation of material remains in prehistoric sites to reconstruct early human ways of life; study of remains in historic sites to learn more about historic, literate peoples

Archaeology — Comparisons of human anatomy and behavior with other primate species; physical (genetic) variation among human populations; biological evolution of *Homo sapiens*

Cultural — Differences and similarities in contemporary and historically recent cultures; causes and consequences of sociocultural change; impacts of globalization and contacts on the world's peoples

Anthropological Linguistics — Relationships between language and culture; role of language and speaking in social life of various peoples; how language might shape perceptions and thoughts

Biological/Physical Anthropology

Biological (also called **physical**) **anthropology** is closely related to the biological sciences in its goals and methods. It focuses on subjects such as the anatomy and behavior of monkeys and apes, the physical (including genetic) variations between different human populations, and the biological evolution of the human species.

Within biological anthropology, researchers in **primatology** study the evolution, anatomy, adaptation, and social behavior of primates, the taxonomic order to which humans belong. Research on group-living monkeys and apes has added significantly to the scientific understanding of many aspects of human behavior, including tool use, sexuality, parenting, cooperation, male-female differences, and aggression. Field studies of African chimpanzees and gorillas, the two apes genetically most similar to humans, have been especially fruitful sources of hypotheses and knowledge.

In the 1960s, famous British primatologist Jane Goodall was the first to observe toolmaking among African chimpanzees. Chimps intentionally modified sticks to probe entry and exit holes in termite mounds. When termite soldiers attacked the intruding objects, the chimps withdrew the probes and licked off the tasty insects. Goodall observed adult chimps teaching their young how to probe for termites, showing that humanity's closest animal relatives have at least a semblance of cultural tradition. Some chimpanzee groups wave tree branches in aggressive displays against other groups and wad up leaves to use as sponges to soak

One of the most surprising discoveries about the great apes is that they commonly use and even make tools. These two Ugandan chimpanzees are inserting twigs inside termite mounds. When they withdraw the twig, they will eat the insects that have locked their jaws onto it.

biological (physical) anthropology Major subfield of anthropology that studies the biological dimensions of humans and other primates.

primatology Part of biological anthropology that studies primates, including monkeys and apes.

CHAPTER 1 The Study of Humanity

Paleoanthropology is the subfield that specializes in human evolution, using evidence from DNA and fossil discoveries. Here Richard Leakey discusses the evidence for human biological evolution by displaying hominin fossils discovered in the Turkana Basin in Kenya.

up drinking water. Working in West Africa, other researchers have observed some chimp groups using heavy round stones as hammers to crack open hard-shelled nuts. The chimps select stones of the proper shape and weight, control the force of their blows so that the nut does not shatter, and often leave the tools under nut trees for future use.

Other apes also use tools. Using sticks, African gorillas in the wild gauge the depth of water and even lay down tree trunks to cross deep pools. Researchers have seen one young female gorilla use stones to smash open a palm nut to get at the oil inside.

These and other observations dramatically altered our understanding of human–animal differences: prior to such studies, making tools was widely considered to be one of the things humans could do that other animals could not. Also, the ability to make tools reveals a certain amount of mental foresight: the apes must be able to see a natural object as a potential tool that can be used to get something or to solve some problem.

Biological anthropologists who study **human variation** investigate how and why human populations vary physically due to hereditary, genetic factors. All humanity belongs to a single species, which taxonomists call *Homo sapiens*. One of the most important findings of anthropology is that the physical/genetic similarities among the world's peoples far outweigh the differences. Nonetheless, peoples whose ancestral homelands lie in Africa, Asia, Europe, Australia, the Pacific islands, and the Americas were once more isolated than they are today. During this time, they evolved differences in overall body and facial form, height, skin color, blood chemistry, and other genetically determined features. Specialists in human variation measure and try to explain the differences and similarities among the world's peoples in these physical characteristics. (We return to "racial" variation in Chapter 2.)

Often, genetic differences are related to the environment in which a people or their ancestors lived. Consider skin color. When in sunlight, human skin manufactures vitamin D, a necessary nutrient. Melanin is the substance in human skin that produces the color our eyes perceive as dark. High levels of melanin protect skin against sun damage, so melanin usually is beneficial in tropical environments, where sunlight is most intense. However, as humans migrated into more temperate regions tens of thousands of years ago, too much melanin became harmful. In high latitudes, melanin reduces the penetration of sunlight in the skin, reducing its ability to make vitamin D. Thus, dark pigmentation is harmful in high latitudes like Europe and Siberia, and over many centuries skin grew lighter ("whiter") in such regions.

Human populations who live in high altitudes also have evolved physiological adaptations. Andean peoples of South America have relatively large lungs and high levels of hemoglobin. The blood of Tibetans circulates more rapidly than most other people, allowing their muscles and organs to function more efficiently at elevations over 14,000 feet. Such populations evolved physiological adaptations to supply oxygen to their tissues.

Another aim of physical anthropology is understanding when and how the human species evolved from prehuman, apelike ancestors. **Paleoanthropology** investigates human biological evolution. Over decades of searching for fossils and carrying out meticulous

human variation Physical differences among human populations; an interest of physical anthropologists.

paleoanthropology Specialization within biological anthropology that investigates the biological evolution of the human species.

Forensic anthropologists work with governments and international organizations to identify human skeletal remains and to help determine the causes of death. These forensic specialists are examining remains in El Salvador.

laboratory studies, paleoanthropologists have reconstructed the evolution of human anatomy: limbs, feet, hands, skull, and other physical features.

In the late 1970s, paleoanthropologists began to use new methods for investigating human evolution. Scientists in the field of molecular genetics can now sequence DNA—the genetic material by which hereditary traits are transmitted between generations. By comparing DNA sequences, geneticists can estimate how closely different species are related. Studies comparing the genetic sequences of African apes with humans show that humans share 97.7 percent of their DNA with gorillas and 98.7 percent with chimpanzees and bonobos. DNA from modern humans and DNA sampled from bones of the extinct human species *Neanderthal* are about 99.5 percent the same. Similarities in the DNA of two or more species are evidence that they share a common evolutionary ancestor. Also, the more similar the DNA between two or more species, the less time has elapsed since their divergence from a common ancestor. Thus, anthropologists study DNA sequences to estimate how long ago the species separated.

Through discovering and analyzing fossils, comparisons of DNA sequences, and other methods, the outlines of human evolution are becoming clear. Most scholars agree that the evolutionary line leading to modern humans split from the lines leading to modern African apes (chimpanzees and gorillas) at least 6 million years ago.

Most biological anthropologists work in universities or museums as teachers, researchers, writers, and curators. But many also apply their knowledge of human anatomy to practical matters. For instance, specialists in **forensic anthropology** work for or consult with law enforcement agencies, where they help identify human skeletal remains. Among their contributions are determining the age, sex, height, and other physical characteristics of crime or accident victims. Forensic anthropologists gather evidence from bones about old injuries or diseases, which are then compared with medical histories to identify victims. Forensic anthropologists also excavate and analyze mass graves containing the remains of victims of assassination, hoping to identify them and determine the causes of their deaths.

forensic anthropology Specialization within physical anthropology that analyzes and identifies human remains.

Prehistoric archaeologists investigate the remote past by the careful excavation of material remains.

Archaeology

Archaeology investigates the human past through excavating and analyzing material remains. Modern archaeology is divided into two major kinds of studies: prehistoric and historic.

Prehistoric archaeology is the study of prehistoric peoples—that is, those who had no writing to keep records of their activities, customs, and beliefs. Much information about the lives of prehistoric peoples can be recovered from the tools, pottery, ornaments, bones, plant pollen, charcoal, and other materials they left behind, in or on the ground. Through careful excavation and laboratory analysis of such remains, prehistoric archaeologists reconstruct the way people lived in ancient times and trace how human cultures have changed over many centuries and millennia. Contrary to impressions given by many television documentaries and popular films, the main goal of excavating archaeological sites is not to recover valuable treasures and other artifacts, but to understand how people lived long ago. Modern archaeologists seek to reconstruct as fully as possible how prehistoric peoples made their tools, lived in their environments, organized their societies, and practiced their religions.

Over decades of meticulous field excavations and laboratory work, archaeologists have learned that agriculture first developed around 10,000 years ago, when some peoples of the Middle East began planting wheat and barley. For the first time, humans transformed certain edible wild plants into *crops*. A few thousand years later, peoples of China, Southeast Asia, and West Africa also domesticated plants like rice and millet. On the other side of the world, in what we now call the Americas, ancient peoples of southern Mexico, western South America, and the Amazon basin domesticated different plants like corn, squash, beans, tomatoes, potatoes, and manioc. Surprisingly, present evidence shows that these six regions where agriculture developed were independent—meaning that the people of one region domesticated plants on their own, rather than learning the idea of agriculture from other peoples. Similarly, civilization (living in cities) developed in several different regions independently, beginning about 5,000 years ago (see Chapter 6).

> **archaeology** Investigation of past cultures through the excavation of material remains.
>
> **prehistoric archaeology** Field that uses excavations and analysis of material remains to investigate cultures that existed before the development of writing.

To investigate the past of societies in which at least some people could read and write, historians analyze written materials such as diaries, letters, land records, newspapers, and tax collection documents. The growing field of **historic archaeology** supplements historical documents by excavating houses, stores, plantations, factories, and other structures and remains. Historic archaeologists seek to uncover information lacking in old documents about how people lived at a particular time and place.

In early May, 2013, the *New York Times, USA Today*, CNN, and other media reported a startling find by historic archaeologists. In 1607, 104 settlers from England arrived in Jamestown, Virginia, to establish a settlement and make profit for the private company that financed the colony. Only one-third were alive after 9 months in the New World, despite trade with the local Native Americans, the Powhatan. More colonists arrived in the next couple of years. However, in the winter of 1609, the Anglo Jamestown settlers were starving. A drought the previous year had led to low agricultural yields, the fleet of nine ships from England that was supposed to supply the colony had been lost in a hurricane, and relationships with the Powhatan had turned hostile. A letter written in 1625 by the leader of the colony refers to the settlers digging up human corpses to consume their flesh during the Starving Time.

Archaeological excavations in the summer of 2012 led by William Kelso found hard evidence that cannibalism in fact had occurred at Jamestown. The archaeological team unearthed the remains of a girl about 14 years old. After her death, someone had struck the back of the girl's head, and another blow to her left temple split her skull, apparently to remove the brain. Other cuts on the face bones showed that facial tissues had been removed. Douglas Owsley, a well-known forensic anthropologist who studied the skull and the evidence of blows, believes the girl was likely a child of an English gentleman, because analysis of her bones showed a diet high in protein. Excavations in and around Jamestown will continue.

Today, many archaeologists work not in universities but in museums, public agencies, and for-profit corporations. Museums offer jobs as curators and researchers. State highway departments employ archaeologists to conduct surveys of proposed new routes in order to locate and excavate archaeological sites that will be destroyed. The U.S. Forest Service and National Park Service hire archaeologists to find sites on public lands to help make decisions about the preservation of cultural materials. Those who work in *cultural resource management* (CRM) locate sites of prehistoric and historic significance, evaluate their importance, and make recommendations about total or partial preservation.

Since the passage of the National Historic Preservation Act in 1966, private corporations and government agencies that construct factories, apartments, parking lots, shopping malls, and other structures must file a report how the construction will affect historical remains and which steps will be taken to preserve them. Because of this law, the business of *contract archaeology* has boomed in the United States. Contract archaeology companies bid competitively for the privilege of locating, excavating, and reporting on sites affected or destroyed by construction. Hundreds of contract archaeology companies exist, providing jobs for thousands of archaeologists and students.

In 2012, while building a courthouse in Fredericksburg, Virginia, construction workers came across an underground wall. The city government called in contract archaeologist Taft Kiser to lead a team to investigate the wall before the new construction destroyed it. In their hurried excavation (such work used to be called "salvage archaeology"), the team found that the wall was part of an old cellar. The original cellar was from the Civil War period and contained remains of an 1862 battle. The cellar appeared to be a place where Union soldiers sought refuge after a battle. It contained lots of bullets, buttons, pipes, broken pieces from jars and whiskey bottles, and many other everyday objects used by soldiers. The house itself was burned after the 1862 battle, and the cellar was later buried by construction of the city. The cellar was a "time capsule," to use Kiser's words, meaning that it apparently had not been disturbed in the 150 years since the Union soldiers left it.

Cultural Anthropology

Cultural anthropology (also called **sociocultural anthropology** and **social anthropology**) is the study of contemporary and historically recent human societies and cultures. As its name suggests, the main focus of this subfield is culture—the customs and beliefs of some human group. (The concept of culture is discussed at length in Chapter 2.)

---

historic archaeology Field that investigates the past of literate peoples through excavation of sites and analysis of artifacts and other material remains.

cultural anthropology (social anthropology, sociocultural anthropology) Subfield that studies the way of life of contemporary and historically recent peoples.

As we'll see in future chapters, cultural anthropologists study an enormous number of specific subjects, far too many to list here. Here are a few of the main interests of this subfield:

- studying firsthand and reporting about the ways of living of particular human groups, including both indigenous peoples and peoples who live in modernized, industrialized nations;
- comparing diverse cultures in the search for general principles that might explain human ways of living or that might cause cultural differences;
- understanding how various dimensions of human life—economics, family life, religion, art, communication, and so forth—relate to one another in particular cultures and in cultures generally;
- analyzing the causes and consequences of cultural change, including the causes and consequences of what is commonly called globalization;
- enhancing public knowledge and appreciation of cultural differences and multicultural diversity;
- using anthropological methods and insights to aid understanding of life in today's industrialized, capitalistic nations, including the anthropologist's own nations.

The last three objectives are especially important in the twenty-first century, in which individuals with diverse cultural backgrounds regularly come into contact with one another in the rapidly changing global society. Later chapters discuss some of the work cultural anthropologists have done on globalization and in modern nation-states.

To collect information about particular cultures, researchers conduct **fieldwork**. Most fieldworkers leave their own homes and universities, moving into the communities they study and living in close, daily contact with the people. If practical, they communicate in the local language. Daily interaction with the members of a community provides fieldworkers with firsthand experiences that yield insights and information that could not be gained in any other way. Most fieldwork requires at least a year of residence in the field site, and two or more years are common. Fieldworkers usually report the findings of their research in books or scholarly journals, where they are available to other scholars, students, and to the general public. A written account of how a single human population lives is called an **ethnography**, which means "writing about a people." Thus, most ethnographies are reports about the culture of communities where anthropologists have conducted fieldwork. (We have more to say about the processes and problems of fieldwork in Chapter 6.)

To some people, studies of other cultures seem esoteric—"interesting but of little practical value," they often say. Most anthropologists disagree. We think that what we learn by our descriptions, comparisons, and analyses of cultures helps to improve the human condition. For one thing, studies of other cultures help us understand our own way of life. For another, specific studies carried out by cultural anthropologists have helped solve practical problems in real human communities.

Anthropological Linguistics

Defined as the study of human language, linguistics exists as a separate discipline from anthropology. Linguists describe and analyze the sound patterns and combinations, words, meanings, and sentence structures of human languages. The ability to communicate complex messages with great efficiency may be the most important capability of humans that makes us different from primates and other animals. Once we realize how complicated the knowledge of a language is, we realize that the communicative abilities of humans are truly unique. Certainly our ability to speak is a key factor in the evolutionary success of humans.

Cultural anthropologists are interested in language mainly because of how the language and culture of a people affect each other. The subfield of **anthropological linguistics** is concerned with the complex relationships between language and other aspects of human behavior and thought. For example, anthropological linguists are interested in how language is used in various social contexts: What style of speech must one use with people of high status? How do people of various social categories (like genders, ethnicities), classes (ultrarich, middle), and political persuasions (Tea Partiers, environmentalists) use language to promote their social and political agendas? Does the particular language we learned while growing up have any important effects on how we view the world or how we think and feel? (Chapter 3 provides more information about language and social life.)

---

fieldwork Ethnographic research that involves observing and interviewing a community in order to document and describe their way of life.

ethnography Written description of the way of life of some human population.

anthropological linguistics Subfield that focuses on the interrelationships between language and other aspects of a people's culture.

As our brief summary of the four subdisciplines confirms, anthropology is a broad field. Even by itself, cultural anthropology—the main subject of this text—is enormously broad: modern fieldworkers live among and study human communities in all parts of the world, from the mountains of Tibet to the deserts of the American Southwest, from the streets of Chicago to the plains of East Africa.

Today's anthropology is quite different than 30 or 40 years ago. Still, the discipline does have a distinctive focus. More so than other fields, anthropology's focus is *human diversity*. Humankind is diverse in a multitude of ways, but two are most important to anthropologists. First, although all modern humans are members of the same species, human populations differ somewhat in their genetic heritage, making humans diverse *biologically*. Second, the customs and beliefs of one society or ethnic group differ from those of other societies or ethnic groups, reflecting the fact that humans are diverse *culturally*. Archaeologists also investigate diversity in the past, between the world's major regions (e.g., how did the prehistoric peoples of Europe differ from those of East Asia 5,000 years ago?). Archaeologists also trace changes in ways of life over long time spans (e.g., how did human life change in the southeastern United States between 4,000 and 1,000 years ago?). Cultural anthropologists investigate, describe, and try to understand cultural diversity today and in the recent past.

Applications of Anthropology

Not too long ago, most professional anthropologists spent their careers in some form of educational institution, either in colleges and universities or in museums. However, since around 1990, more and more anthropologists have jobs in other kinds of institutions. The American Anthropological Association (AAA, often called "Triple A") is the professional association of anthropologists. In its 2006 *Annual Report*, the AAA reported that more than half of anthropologists work outside academic settings, in government agencies, international organizations, nonprofit groups, or private companies. Hundreds of others make their living as consultants to such organizations and institutions.

Applied Anthropology

Applied anthropology use anthropological methods, theories, concepts, and insights to help public institutions or private enterprises deal with practical, real-world problems. Applied anthropology sometimes is viewed as a fifth subfield, but all applied anthropologists have been trained in one or more of the traditional four fields. In this sense, applied anthropology cuts across the other subfields and individuals in all subfields may also do applied work—that is, work that contributes directly to problem solving in an organization.

We discuss some of the ways applied anthropologists have contributed to the alleviation of human problems in later chapters. For now, a few examples illustrate some of the work they do.

Development anthropology is one area in which anthropologists apply their expertise to the solution of practical human problems, usually in developing countries. Working both as full-time employees and as consultants, development anthropologists provide information about communities that helps agencies adapt projects to local conditions and needs. Examples of agencies and institutions that employ development anthropologists include the U.S. Agency for International Development, the Rockefeller and Ford Foundations, the World Bank, and the United Nations Development Programme. One important role of the anthropologist in such institutions is to provide policymakers with knowledge of local-level ecological and cultural conditions, so that projects will avoid unanticipated problems and minimize negative impacts.

Educational anthropology offers jobs in public agencies and private institutions. Some roles of educational anthropologists include advising in bilingual education, conducting detailed observations of classroom interactions, training personnel in multicultural issues, and adapting teaching styles to local customs and needs. Many modern nations, including those of Europe and the Americas, are becoming more culturally diverse due to immigration. As a response to this trend, an increasingly important role for educational anthropologists working in North America is to help professional educators understand the learning styles and behavior of children from various ethnic and national backgrounds. Persons trained in both linguistic and cultural anthropology are especially likely to work in educational anthropology.

---

applied anthropology Subfield whose practitioners use anthropological methods, theories, and concepts to solve practical, real-world problems; practitioners are often employed by a governmental agency or private organization.

Private companies sometimes employ cultural anthropologists full-time or as consultants, creating a professional opportunity often called *corporate anthropology*. As international trade agreements remove tariffs, quotas, and other barriers to international trade, people of different cultural heritages increasingly conduct business and buy and sell one another's products. The dramatic growth of overseas business activities encourages companies to hire professionals who can advise executives and sales staff on what to expect and how to speak and act when they conduct business in other countries. Because of their training as acute observers and listeners, anthropologists also work in the private sector in many other capacities: they watch how employees interact with one another, analyze how workers understand the capabilities of office machines, study how the attitudes and styles of managers affect worker performance, and perform a variety of other information-gathering and analysis tasks.

A rapidly growing field is **medical anthropology**. Medical anthropologists usually are trained both in biological and cultural anthropology. They investigate the complex interactions among human health, nutrition, social environment, and cultural beliefs and practices. Medical anthropologists with extensive training in human biology and physiology study disease transmission patterns and how particular groups adapt to the presence of diseases like malaria and sleeping sickness. Because the transmission of viruses and bacteria is strongly influenced by people's diets, sanitation, sexual habits, and other behaviors, many medical anthropologists work as a team with epidemiologists to identify cultural practices that affect the spread of disease. Different cultures have different ideas about the causes and symptoms of disease, how best to treat illnesses, the abilities of traditional healers and doctors, and the importance of community involvement in the healing process. By studying how a human community perceives such things, medical anthropologists help hospitals and other agencies deliver health care services more effectively. Language and communication also are important influences on health care delivery, so people trained in linguistic anthropology sometimes work in medical anthropology.

medical anthropology Specialization that researches the connections between cultural beliefs and habits and the spread and treatment of diseases and illnesses.

Careers in Anthropology

People who earn doctoral degrees in anthropology have a variety of career options, as the preceding discussion shows. What opportunities exist for those with an undergraduate degree in anthropology?

A place to start is the website of the American Anthropological Association, which is the professional association of anthropologists. The AAA site has a page titled "Anthropology: Education for the 21st Century" that overviews the importance and some of the main uses of an anthropological education. Another AAA page is titled "Careers in Anthropology," which lists the general kinds of jobs that can be pursued by people with a bachelor's degree. On this page there are links to YouTube videos on topics like an Intel anthropologist who studies how mobile phones are used by Chinese and Indians, using ethnographic methods to help businesses organize workplaces and appeal to customers, and an anthropologist who witnessed the 1997 Japanese financial crisis and realized the same process was occurring in British banks in 2007.

Here are two other useful websites on careers and jobs:

- The National Association for the Practice of Anthropology (NAPA) is the professional association of anthropologists who work predominantly in non-academic jobs. On its website, click the tab "Careers" for job-seeking strategies.

- The Northern Kentucky University website is good for a quick overview of opportunities. Enter "anthropology" in the search box; then scroll down and click on "careers in anthropology."

An Internet search using the phrase "jobs in anthropology" returns many links, including several alternative search phrases.

Generally, in addition to learning to write, analyze, and think critically, students who study cultural anthropology are prepared to examine human life from many alternative perspectives, to study interactions between individuals and groups objectively and insightfully, to adjust to various social situations, to fit into diverse communities by respecting their ways of life, and to be sensitive to the multitude of differences between the world's peoples. Knowledge of the many ways of being human helps thoughtful graduates to have the capacity to consider alternatives that people with other kinds of formal education miss. Of course, along the way, most students master other skills, such as statistical analysis or foreign languages, which demonstrate ability and establish credentials for a variety of career paths.

Cultural Anthropology Today

Because this book deals mainly with the findings and conclusions of cultural (sociocultural) anthropology, from now on when we use the word *anthropology*, we refer to cultural anthropology unless otherwise stated.

In most people's imagination, cultural anthropologists go to far-off places to study "native" peoples. Except for some common but mistaken stereotypes about "natives," this image was reasonably accurate until the 1970s. Until then, cultural anthropology differed from sociology and other disciplines that studied living peoples mainly by the kinds of cultures studied. Anthropologists focused on small-scale, non-Western, preindustrial, subsistence-oriented cultures, whereas sociologists tended to study large Euro-American, industrial, money-and-market countries. Not too long ago, many cultural anthropologists sought untouched tribal cultures to study because living among the "primitives" usually enhanced one's reputation.

All this has changed. As the Internet accelerates global communications, anthropologists publish books with titles like *Dreaming of a Mail-Order Husband: Russian-American Internet Romance* (Johnson, 2007). An anthropologist has done fieldwork among modern Americans who belong to Vineyard churches, an evangelical denomination, showing how they experience God's presence and hear his voice in their everyday lives (Luhrmann, 2012). Changing gender roles and working conditions lead to articles like "Man Enough to Let My Wife Support Me: How Changing Models of Career and Gender Are Reshaping the Experience of Unemployment" (Lane, 2009). In brief, cultural anthropology has widened its investigations well beyond the old idea of Natives. Today we recognize we are all Natives.

Some studies done in the anthropologist's own country are of immigrant communities. Along with Australia, North America is a continent whose people are mostly immigrants. Both continents include people of diverse origins. Some immigrants of the last few decades are largely or partly assimilated, having adopted many of the customs and beliefs of people whose ancestors arrived earlier. In other cases, though, they are only partially assimilated. On the job, they act like they are "mainstreamed." But at home and when among members of their own ancestral communities, they continue their language, cuisine, family relations, wedding and funeral customs, and other practices and beliefs.

For example, in the 1970s, the U.S. government relocated thousands of Hmong, a people of highland Southeast Asia, into places like the central valley of California and the upper Midwest. Even after two or three decades of living in the United States, many elderly Hmong who were first generation immigrants speak little English, have large numbers of relatives living in houses other Americans consider "single-family" dwellings, use their traditional methods of curing, and (allegedly) eat animals that Americans define as pets. Many people with Chinese, Japanese, Korean, and South Asian heritages maintain some traditions of their ancestral homelands to a surprising degree. Some African Americans celebrate their origins with Kwanzaa. A large Somalian community lives in central Ohio. Many Latinos speak "Spanglish" and continue to practice Latin festivals. Citizens whose ancestors came from Italy, Germany, Poland, Greece, and other parts of Europe recognize their national origins. Of course, so do people whose ancestors came from the British Isles, although many of them are not consciously aware that they too have an ethnic heritage and identity.

As anthropologists have focused less on peoples of far away, the boundaries between cultural anthropology and other disciplines (especially sociology) are less clear-cut than they were a few years ago. Most anthropological work, though, is still done in relatively small communities (on the order of a few hundred to a few thousand), where the researcher can interact directly with people and experience their lives firsthand. More than any other single factor, the intense fieldwork experience distinguishes cultural anthropology from other disciplines concerned with humankind.

Increasingly, globalization brings together people of different cultural backgrounds for international travel, education, and business. Learning about other cultures takes on increasing practical and well as intellectual importance in modern global society.

GLOBAL CHALLENGES AND OPPORTUNITIES   The Process of Globalization

The global economy links the world's regions by trade in finished consumer products as well as in raw materials. This plant in Recife, Brazil, produces fabrics to be woven into clothing sold on the global market.

Stories about *globalization* appear almost daily in the news media. The parts (continents, regions, nations, cities, towns, small villages) of the global system are interconnected by flows of technology, overseas transportation of resources and products, communications, short-term travel, long-term migration, and market exchanges of raw materials and finished products. Monthly, huge container ships move billions of dollars' worth of products across the Pacific and Atlantic Oceans. North American consumers benefit from the low labor costs of China, south Asia and other nations when they shop at Walmart, Toys "R" Us, and most clothing and shoe stores. More people than ever before migrate between nations to study and work, affecting their home countries as well as those to which they relocate. The Internet and mobile phones link people together to an unprecedented degree, facilitating the flow of information, ideas, and media between nations.

These interconnections profoundly affect relationships between countries in the twenty-first century. Should the rapidly industrializing countries be forced to enact environmental regulations to curb air pollution and greenhouse gases? If so, by whom and on what authority? What should a democratic government in a developed, free market economy do when its citizens lose jobs from factories located half a world away? Should South Asian, African, and Middle Eastern countries do anything about the flow of information from Western nations to protect their religious heritages? Or should the whole world welcome a "free market" in ideas and beliefs, comparable to the free market in material products? And—perhaps the most important question—who gains and loses the most from the globalization process?

It is important to recognize that globalization is a *process* rather than a *state*. In discussing relationships between parts of a system and the whole system, we often say that the whole affects the parts, which in turn affect the whole. The globalization process impacts nations, so nations respond to globalization, then the process of globalization changes to respond to changes in nations. Thus, as globalization transforms nations it too is transformed. As the global system evolves, some of its parts become more tightly integrated into it, but even localities that most consider isolated or pristine are affected directly or indirectly.

The existence of interconnectedness between world regions is not new, as we will discuss in Chapter 4. Pointing to the half-millennium of contact between regions and peoples,

Also, cultural anthropology remains more comparative in its scope and interests than the other social sciences and humanities. Even today, cultural anthropologists are more likely than sociologists or psychologists to conduct research in a country other than their own.

In the past couple of decades, anthropologists have researched globalization—the process by which citizens of the world's 195 nations participate in a single system that encompasses *all* peoples and nations to varying degrees. Global Challenges and Opportunities presents an overview of the process of globalization in the past several decades.

Disciplines like economics, political science, history, and sociology have done empirical research and much theorizing about globalization. Most of their research concerns the "macro-level," meaning that the unit of study is the nation, region, city within the nation, or—even more "macro"—relationships between nations. Cultural anthropologists occasionally work at this level, but mostly our studies involve intensive, firsthand, prolonged fieldwork in local communities, both rural and urban. We study many dimensions of globalization, including markets, forms of global entertainment, ways of "dating" and getting married, changes in family organizations, how migrant workers adapt to factory life and urban environments, and so on. Such research provides a bottom up view of globalization that complements the top-down view focused on by most of the media and scholars. In later chapters, some say there is nothing new about globalization. If globalization is only about the existence of "contacts" and "interconnections" between peoples, they are correct. However, both the intensity and the form of contacts and interconnections are different in the twenty-first century. By *intensity*, we mean that the number and importance of contacts and interconnections have increased dramatically in the past several decades; today, the lives of more people are affected more thoroughly than, say, 50 years ago. By *form*, we mean that the ways in which the world's peoples are interconnected are different than in the past. Two differences are especially important, each considered in more detail in later chapters.

First, globalization transforms the division of economic activities between nations and regions. Until the mid–twentieth century, some nations and regions specialized mainly in supplying primary products extracted directly from nature, such as food, metals, lumber, and other raw materials in plantations, mines, and forests. For example, there were "banana republics" in Central America, "gold coasts" in West Africa, and "sugar mills" in the Caribbean. Generally, these nations and regions were known as "underdeveloped" or "Third World." Of course, there were exceptions, but the pattern was that "developed" and mostly wealthier countries bought these relatively low-valued raw materials and turned them into higher-valued, profit-making products with their industrial factories and labor force.

Today, factory production itself is rapidly globalizing. In Latin America, Asia, and other regions, hundreds of millions of factory workers produce finished commodities for sale in international markets. More than ever before, there is an *international* market for industrial labor, meaning that factory workers of the countries we used to call "underdeveloped" are competing with the labor force of the "developed" countries. Whole industries have relocated. For example, the American clothing industry has almost disappeared, its factories replaced by those in China, Indonesia, and other countries with far cheaper labor. Other industries that have moved offshore are toys, shoes, and consumer electronics. Some say the globalization of factory production is leading to the decline of incomes among middle-class families in Europe and North America and is largely responsible for the growing disparity of income and wealth in those regions.

Second, international migration, study abroad, tourism and the Internet are increasing two-way cultural exchanges. Most people think the media are rapidly transmitting the "culture" and "tastes" in fashion, music, films, food, and the like of the West to the rest of the world. One concern is that the North American and European culture (the "West") will eventually destroy local traditions. We take up this and other issues about globalization in later chapters.

In sum, although contacts among peoples and nations is not new, the globalization process has transformed the form and intensity of these interconnections in the last two or three decades. In the remainder of this book, we discuss globalization in boxes like this one as well as in the main body of the text itself. We emphasize the effects of globalization on *all* nations and regions, and not just how people like "Us" are affecting people like "Them," or how "They" threaten "Us."

---

we present many examples of such anthropological studies.

Globalization has another consequence for anthropological research: people who used to live in remote villages now migrate to urban areas in their own country and abroad. If an anthropologist wants to conduct fieldwork in a "remote" place, some people from such places will have migrated elsewhere in search of employment or excitement. In the twenty-first century, if an anthropologist wants to study "a people," it is increasingly necessary to study them in all the places on our planet where they now live. Today, globalization and its consequences are one of the most important areas of research. What are its impacts on people of all nations? Is a global megaculture developing that will someday make all human cultures pretty much alike?

Anthropological Perspectives on Cultures

The main difference between anthropology and other social sciences and humanities is not so much the *kinds* of subjects anthropologists investigate as the *approaches* we take to studying human life. We believe it is important to study cultures and communities holistically, comparatively, and relativistically. Taken together, these perspectives also make cultural anthropology distinctive.

Holistic Perspective

To study a subject holistically is to attempt to understand all the factors that influence it and to interpret it in the context of all those factors. In anthropology, the **holistic perspective** means that no single aspect of a human culture can be understood unless its relationships to other aspects of the culture are explored. Holism requires, for example, that a fieldworker studying the rituals of a people must investigate how those rituals are influenced by the people's family life, economic forces, political leadership, relationships between the sexes, and a host of other factors. The attempt to understand a community's customs, beliefs, values, and so forth holistically is one reason ethnographic fieldwork takes so much time and involves close contact with people.

Taken literally, a holistic understanding of a people's customs and beliefs is probably not possible because of the complexity of human societies. But anthropologists have learned that ignoring interrelationships among language, religion, art, economy, family, and other dimensions of life results in distortions and misunderstandings. The essence of the holistic perspective may be stated fairly simply: *look for connections and interrelationships, and try to understand parts in the context of the whole.*

Comparative Perspective

More than most people, anthropologists are aware of the diversity of the world's cultures. The ideas and behaviors learned from upbringing and experience in one's own society may not apply to other peoples with different cultural traditions. This implies that any general theories or ideas scholars might have about humans—about human nature, sexuality, warfare, family relationships, and so on—must take into account information from a wide range of societies. In other words, theoretical ideas about humans or human societies or cultures must be investigated from a **comparative perspective**.

The main reason anthropologists insist on comparison is simple: Many people mistakenly think the customs and beliefs that are familiar to them exist among people everywhere, which is usually not the case. Are humans "innately" aggressive? Are nuclear families "biologically based"? Is pair bonding (the nuclear family) "rooted in our evolutionary past"? Do men "inevitably" seek more sexual variety than women? Is competition "in our genes"? Cultural anthropologists are interested in these and other *general* questions about humanity, but we believe that we must consider *all* of humanity to answer them.

Knowledge of cultural variability makes anthropologists suspicious of any general theoretical idea about humans that is drawn from experience of life in only one nation or community. The idea *might* be valid for all people, but we cannot know until we have looked elsewhere. The beliefs and practices of people living in different times and places are far too diverse for any general theory to be accepted until it has been investigated and tested in a wide range of human groups. To state the comparative perspective concisely: *valid generalizations about humans must take into account the full range of cultural diversity.*

Relativistic Perspective

Fundamentally, **cultural relativism** means that no culture—taken as a whole—is inherently superior or inferior to any other. Anthropologists adopt this perspective because concepts such as superiority require judgments about the relative worthiness of behaviors, beliefs, and other characteristics of a culture. However, such judgments are usually rooted in one's own values; and, by and large, values depend on the culture in which one was raised. (If you think there must be universal standards for judging cultures, you may be right. However, aside from such actions as homicide, people don't agree on what they are.)

To see why a relativistic approach to studying cultures is important, contrast cultural relativism with ethnocentrism. **Ethnocentrism** is the belief that the moral standards, values, beliefs, and so forth of one's own culture are superior to those of other cultures. Most people are ethnocentric, and *some degree* of ethnocentrism is probably essential for individuals to have the sense of belonging needed for personal contentment.

---

holistic perspective Assumption that any aspect of a culture is integrated with other aspects, so that no dimension of culture can be understood in isolation.

comparative perspective Insistence by anthropologists that valid hypotheses and theories about humanity be tested with information from a wide range of cultures.

cultural relativism Notion that one should not judge the behavior of other peoples using the standards of one's own culture.

ethnocentrism Attitude or opinion that the morals, values, and customs of one's own culture are superior to those of other peoples.

It may be necessary for a culture itself to persist. Mild ethnocentrism—meaning that people are committed to certain values but don't insist that everyone else hold and live by those values—is unobjectionable and inevitable. But extreme ethnocentrism—meaning that people believe their values are the only correct ones and that all people everywhere should be judged by how closely they live up to those values—leads to attitudes of intolerance and misunderstandings that anthropologists find objectionable.

Clearly, in their professional role, anthropological fieldworkers should avoid evaluating the behavior of other people according to the standards of their own culture. Ethnocentric attitudes and standards make objectivity difficult while doing fieldwork. Like the holistic and comparative perspectives, the essential point of cultural relativism may be stated simply: *in studying another culture, do not evaluate the behavior of its members by the standards and values of your own culture.*

Unfortunately, many people misunderstand the word *relativism*. To anthropologists, relativism is a *methodological principle* that refers to an outlook that is essential for maximum objectivity and understanding when studying a people whose way of life differs from their own. As a methodological principle, relativism recognizes that behavior viewed as morally wrong (perhaps even sinful) in one society may not be wrong in another. Polygamy, women who go around barebreasted, and sex between unmarried individuals are common practices among the world's diverse peoples. Unqualified condemnations of the actions or beliefs of such people have no place in anthropological research or in anthropological writings.

However, to a great many people, the term *relativism* means "anything goes" with respect to the behavior of individuals. *Moral relativism* (relativism as a *moral principle*) implies that there are no absolute, universal standards by which to evaluate actions in terms such as right and wrong or good and bad.

Some people blame moral relativism for a host of social problems. For example, in the contemporary United States, many worry about the morality and the long-term social effects of gay and lesbian relationships. When gays and lesbians demanded the equal rights they believe only marriage can grant, in the past several years the legislatures of a number of states passed laws defining marriage as a relationship between a man and a woman. Others worry that society's "acceptance" of extramarital sex or "tolerance" for homosexual relationships erodes family values and increases divorce rates. Many believe that public schools should teach patriotism and traditional morality and blame delinquency and crime on public education that has become too secular. Such arguments and policies imply that there *are* absolute standards and clear rules about right and wrong or moral and immoral behavior. But moral relativism *taken to its extreme* says that few such standards or rules exist.

Newcomers to anthropology often confuse the two meanings of *relativism,* mistakenly believing that anthropologists promote both kinds of relativism. Most anthropologists are methodological relativists, but few are moral relativists. Anthropologists are as likely as anyone to consider oppression, slavery, violence, murder, slander, and so forth as morally objectionable. Many anthropologists speak out against the violence that spokespersons for some "cultures" claim are part of their religion, such as stoning of women found guilty of adultery. When a Pakistani teenager was shot in 2012 for promoting the education of girls, anthropologists did not accept the shooting as part of "Pakistani culture." When the Twin Towers in New York were destroyed on September 11, 2001, and when two bombs at the Boston Marathon killed three and injured 264 on April 15, 2013, anthropologists were as horrified as most other people. One way our discipline affects our views on such events is that we seek to understand the historical background and social and cultural context that led to them. Another is that we do not simply blame the culture or religion for the actions of the individuals responsible.

However, the issues are not as simple in practice as the distinction between methodological and moral relativism implies. An example will illustrate. Most people have heard of the custom of *female genital mutilation* (sometimes mislabeled *female circumcision*). The practice is widespread (but far from universal) in some regions of northern Africa. It varies in severity, ranging from removing the clitoris to stitching shut the labia until marriage. Cultural beliefs about the reasons for the custom also vary. Most often the cultural rationale centers on controlling female sexuality and increasing a woman's desirability as a marriage partner. In many places, a majority of older women support the custom, so it is not unambiguously an issue of male control or oppression of women. Sometimes a girl or young woman herself considers it a symbol of her femininity and of her and her family's honor. In instances in which the girl herself consents, the issue of relativism is especially complicated.

How should an anthropologist view this custom? Do we think of it as just another age-old tradition—comparable to people eating with their fingers or men covering their genitals with only penis sheaths—that varies from people to people but is *inherently* neither right nor wrong? Surely not: genital mutilation causes pain, exposes women to the dangers of infection and other complications, and is applied only to women because of their gender. Often, it is forced upon a female at a certain age—even if she objects. Because of its pain, danger, selectivity, and social enforcement, female circumcision is not comparable to customs surrounding foods and clothing styles, which vary from people to people but are generally "harmless."

Then is female genital mutilation a form of oppression? And if so, by whom? Can culture itself oppress people? If it is oppression, does the anthropologist simply learn and write about it, place it in its local cultural context, compare the cultures that practice it with other cultures that do not, develop an idea about its meaning and why it occurs, and then do nothing? That is what many anthropologists believe we should do *as anthropologists*. Others disagree, believing instead that we should speak out against such practices, both as anthropologists and as human beings.

Then again, exactly what counts as "such practices"? Does eating dogs or cats or horses count? Does female footbinding in 1600s China count? Would tightly binding the waists of women in nineteenth-century Europe count? In the twenty-first century, just how different are breast augmentation or reduction surgery, hip and thigh liposuction, face lifts, and nose jobs different from female circumcision? Is it that they seem to be voluntary? If so, then when a North African woman consents to her circumcision, does her consent make the custom acceptable? And if a woman feels constrained by the ideals of beauty as defined by the culture in which she grew up, is it unambiguously true that her liposuction or breast augmentation is voluntary?

Along these same lines, why is there so little international concern over the removal of the foreskin of American male infants, who have absolutely no choice when a physician mutilates their genitals? In 2009 in the Eastern Cape Province of the Republic of South Africa, 91 men died from their circumcisions, considered a rite of passage into manhood. Should we regard male circumcisions as just as morally objectionable as the deaths and suffering caused by female genital mutilation?

Answers to such questions are not entirely obvious, which is our main point. Most anthropologists would probably be satisfied with the following solution. Relativism as a methodological principle is essential to anthropological research because it facilitates fieldwork and leads to greater objectivity. Moral relativism is a separate matter and depends largely on one's personal standards and values. When an anthropologist witnesses customs like female circumcision that clearly cause harm, it is difficult to remain morally neutral. In such cases, we need to examine the custom holistically to place it in its cultural context: perhaps the "victim's" perception of "harm" differs from ours, or perhaps the harm is necessary to achieve some more important objective. We also should consider comparable practices (such as breast augmentation) that might have a similar character or function within our own culture. After doing so, we might note that "we" sometimes do similar things as "them." Perhaps we have trouble recognizing the similarity because it involves "us," so we need also to examine ourselves when we condemn others.

This perspective does not resolve the essential tension between methodological and moral relativism. Do you believe that human rights are universal? If so, then you are *not* a moral relativist. On the other hand, knowledge of cultural diversity leads some anthropologists to wonder about the assumptions implicit in the United Nations Universal Declaration of Human Rights, found at the United Nations website. For example, Article 16(3) states, "The family is the natural and fundamental group unit of society and is entitled to protection by society and the State." Anthropologists are likely to ask questions like "What is meant by *family*?" and anthropologists are skeptical of the assumption that the family is the "*natural* and *fundamental* unit of society."

Some Lessons of Anthropology

In late 2011, the governor of Florida asked whether state-funded universities really need anthropology departments. The governor was interested mainly in saving money for his state. But he specifically targeted anthropology, rather than sociology, literature, economics, or philosophy. Why?

Anthropology does seem esoteric. As we've seen, historically most cultural anthropologists did fieldwork in far-off places, studying "primitive cultures," "tribes," or (more politely) "indigenous peoples." Then we published articles and books that for the most part only anthropologists and their students read—the latter mainly because they were required to. What good is that?

Many political office holders as well as others do not like anthropology for another reason. The field very often adopts a critical perspective on prevalent assumptions, ideas, and practices. We question common assumptions about "human nature." We challenge prevalent beliefs about the causes of inequalities based on socioeconomic and ethnic characteristics. When we hear that families are declining, we look beyond the deterioration of moral standards and alternative sexualities as "the" cause. Most of us even don't apply concepts like *deteriorate* and *decline* when talking about change in families. When environmentalists criticize China and India for their pollution of water and air and their rising contributions to global warming, anthropologists ask how such environmental problems look from the perspective of the Chinese and Indians. As a colleague once said, "Anthropologists think otherwise."

What insights does anthropology offer about humanity? What is the value of the information that anthropologists have gathered about the past and present of humankind? We consider these questions in future chapters. For now, we note some of the most general insights and contributions.

First, anthropology helps us understand the biological, technological, and cultural development of humanity over long time spans. Most of the reliable information available about human biological evolution, prehistoric cultures, and non-Western peoples resulted from anthropological research. This information has become part of our general storehouse of knowledge, recorded in textbooks and taught in schools. We easily forget that someone had to discover these facts and interpret their significance. For example, only in the late nineteenth century did most scientists accept that people are related to apes, and only in the last several decades has the relationship between humans and African apes become clear. Although we *Homo sapiens* (modern humans) share over 98 percent of our genes with *Pan troglydytus* (chimpanzees), many people still do not believe that humans are evolutionarily related to apes—another reason, perhaps, that anthropology is unpopular with some public officials.

Anthropology has contributed more than just facts. Anthropological concepts have been incorporated into the thinking of millions of people. For example, in this chapter, we have used the term *culture*, confidently assuming our readers know the word and its significance. You may not know that the scientific meaning of this word, as used in the phrase *Tibetan culture*, is not very old. Well into the nineteenth century, people did not fully understand the importance of the distinction between a people's culture (the *learned* beliefs and habits that made them distinctive) and their biological makeup (their *inherited* physical characteristics).

Differences we now know are caused largely or entirely by learning were confused with differences caused by biological inheritance. Early twentieth-century anthropologists such as Franz Boas and Alfred Kroeber marshaled empirical evidence showing that biological differences and cultural differences are independent of each other. The writings of Margaret Mead on Samoan girls challenged prevalent beliefs about gender and adolescence. As these examples illustrate, anthropologists have contributed much to our knowledge of the human condition, although most people are not aware how important anthropology was in developing these understandings and insights.

Another value of anthropology is that it teaches the importance of knowing and understanding cultural diversity. Anthropology urges all of us not to be ethnocentric in our attitudes toward other peoples. Mutual respect and understanding among the world's peoples are increasingly important with globalization, with its world travel, international migration, multinational businesses, and conflicts based on ethnic or religious differences. The world's problems will not be solved simply by eliminating ethnocentrism, but a more relativistic outlook on cultural differences might help to alleviate some of the prejudices, misunderstandings, stereotypes, interethnic conflicts, and racism that cause so much trouble among people on all continents. How much can understanding cultural differences help in alleviating international tensions and outright conflicts?

A related point is that anthropology helps to minimize the miscommunications that commonly arise when people from different parts of the world interact with one another. As we shall see in Chapter 2, our upbringing in a particular culture influences us in subtle ways. For instance, English people know how to interpret one another's actions on the basis of speech styles or body language, but these cues do not necessarily mean the same thing to people from different cultures. A Canadian businessperson selling products in Turkey may wonder why her host does not cut the small talk and get down to business, whereas the Turk can't figure out why the salesperson thinks they can do business before they have become better acquainted. A manager from a German firm may be unintentionally offensive when he shoves the business card of his Korean or Japanese counterpart in his pocket without carefully studying it. A Vietnamese student attending a California university may come across as a sycophant to her professors because her culture values learning so highly, which manifests itself as deep respect for teachers. An Anglo tourist visiting the Navajo reservation in Arizona may misinterpret a Navajo's reticence to make eye contact as unfriendliness, when it means something else to the Navajo. Anthropology teaches people to be aware of and sensitive to cultural differences—people's actions may not mean what we take them to mean, and much misunderstanding can be avoided by taking cultural differences into account in our dealings with other people.

Finally, people can use anthropology's comparative perspective to understand their own individual lives. By exposing you to the cultures of people living in other times and places, anthropology helps you see new things about yourself. How does your life compare to the lives of other people around the world? What assumptions do you unconsciously take for granted about people in other places and humanity in general? Do people in other cultures share the same kinds of problems, hopes, motivations, and feelings as you do? Or are individuals raised in other societies completely different? How does the overall quality of your existence—your sense of well-being and happiness, your family life, your emotional states, your feeling that life is meaningful—compare with that of people who live elsewhere? Anthropology offers the chance to compare yourself to other peoples who live in different circumstances. When they learn about others, anthropologists hope that students gain new perspectives on themselves.

SUMMARY

1. **List the four major subfields of anthropology and their primary subject matters.** Anthropologists usually specialize in one of four subdisciplines. Biological/physical anthropology studies the biological dimensions of human beings, including nonhuman primates, the physical variations among contemporary peoples, and human evolution. Archaeology uses the material remains of prehistoric and historic peoples to investigate the past, focusing on the long-term technological and social changes that occurred in particular regions of the world. Cultural anthropology is concerned with the social and cultural life of contemporary and historically recent human societies. Anthropological linguistics concentrates on the interrelationships between language and other elements of social life and culture.

2. **Describe how anthropology differs from other disciplines that also study humans.** The broad scope of anthropology distinguishes it from other disciplines in the social sciences and humanities. The field as a whole is concerned with all human beings of the past and present, living at all levels of technological development. Anthropology is also interested in all aspects of humanity: biology, language, technology, art, religion, and all other dimensions of human life.

3. **Explain some of the practical uses of anthropology in solving human problems.** More and more, anthropologists are applying the insights gained from the concepts, methods, and theories of their field to solve real-world problems in such areas as development, business, education, and health care services. Most people who do applied work are trained in cultural anthropology, but the other three subfields also are represented. As an undergraduate major, anthropology trains people in critical thinking and cultural sensitivity, skills that are increasingly useful as globalization brings diverse people together into larger systems.

4. **Discuss how cultural anthropology has changed in the last several decades.** Until around 1970, cultural anthropology concentrated on cultures known as "tribal" or "indigenous." This is not as true in the globalized world of today. Many anthropologists conduct research in the urbanized, industrialized nations of the developed world. However, firsthand, extended fieldwork in villages or relatively small towns or neighborhoods continues to be a hallmark of cultural anthropology. Also, cultural anthropologists are more comparative and global in their interests and research than other social scientists.

5. **Understand the meaning and importance of the holistic, comparative, and relativistic perspectives.** Cultural anthropologists approach the study of other cultures from three main perspectives. Holism is the attempt to investigate the interrelationships among the customs and beliefs of a particular people. The comparative perspective means that any attempt to understand humanity or explain cultures or behaviors must include information from a wide range of human ways of life. Cultural relativism urges fieldworkers to try to understand people's behaviors on their own terms, not those of the anthropologist's own culture. Most anthropologists consider themselves methodological relativists, but moral relativism is a separate, though related, matter.

6. **Describe the wider lessons one can learn from studying anthropology.** Anthropology has practical value in the modern world. Most existing, reliable knowledge about human evolution, prehistoric populations, and indigenous peoples was discovered by anthropologists. Early anthropologists were instrumental in popularizing the concept of culture and in showing that cultural differences are not caused by racial differences. The value of understanding peoples of different regions and nations is another practical lesson of anthropology, one that is increasingly important as global connections intensify. The information that ethnographers have collected about alternative ways of being human allows individuals to become more aware of their own life circumstances.

2 Culture

Anthropologists usually say that the cultural features of a human group refer to the learned knowledge and behavioral patterns of its members. In most circumstances one peoples' culture should not be considered inferior to another peoples' culture. This tattooed person in a record shop has culture to the same degree as people who regularly go to symphonies and art galleries.

Introducing Culture

Defining Culture
  Shared . . .
  . . . Socially Learned . . .
  . . . Knowledge . . .
  . . . and Patterns of Behavior

Cultural Knowledge
  Norms
  Values
  Symbols
  Classifications and Constructions of Reality
  Worldviews

The Origins of Culture

Culture and Human Life

Cultural Knowledge and Individual Behavior
  Is Behavior Culturally Determined?
  Why Does Behavior Vary?

Biology and Cultural Differences

Cultural Universals

LEARNING OBJECTIVES

After reading this chapter, you should be able to

1. **DEFINE** culture in a way that is useful to compare and contrast different cultures.
2. **UNDERSTAND** the concept of cultural knowledge and five of its key components.
3. **DISCUSS** the evidence for the origins of the human capacity for culture.
4. **ANALYZE** the relationship between cultural knowledge and the behavior of individuals.
5. **DESCRIBE** why cultural and biological differences between human populations vary independently.

The word *culture* is so common that we hear it almost every day. Sometimes we mean that some individuals are "more cultured" than others. For example, some people believe they are more "culturally sophisticated" than other people because they regularly attend symphonies or go to art galleries. Perhaps you have heard someone complain about the "popular culture" of TV reality shows, action-adventure movies, rap music, online gaming, tattoos and other body art, tongue and navel piercings, and the like. Maybe you use people's speech style or personal tastes as a basis for thinking that some persons have "more culture" than others because of their ethnic identity, social class, or where they went to school.

Taken in context, these meanings of the word *culture* are fine. However, anthropologists define and use the term in a different way. In the anthropological conception, it is impossible for one group of people to "have more culture," or to "be more cultured" than another group. Anthropologists believe that judgments about "high culture" and "low culture" are themselves based on cultural assumptions ("high" according to *whom*?) Phrases like "working-class culture" and "popular culture" do have meaning in anthropology, but that meaning usually does not imply judgments about relative quality or sophistication.

In this chapter, we discuss the anthropological conception of culture. After giving the word a fairly precise definition, we cover some of its main elements, introducing some important concepts and terms along the way. We consider how anthropologists think about the relationship between cultural differences and biological heredity.

Introducing Culture

The Englishman E. B. Tylor was one of the founders of the field that was to become cultural anthropology. In Tylor's 1871 book, *Primitive Culture,* he pulled together much of the information available about the "natives" of other lands (that is, places other than Europe). His definition is often considered the earliest modern conception of culture. Tylor (1871, 1) wrote that culture is "that complex whole which includes knowledge, belief, art, morals, law, customs, and any other capabilities and habits acquired by man as a member of society." Notice that this definition is very broad, including almost everything about a particular people's overall way of life, from "knowledge" and "art" to "customs" and "habits." Notice also that culture is something an individual acquires as "a member of society," meaning that people learn their culture from growing up and living among a particular group.

Since Tylor's day, anthropologists have defined culture in hundreds of ways, although the main elements of Tylor's original conception of culture are still with us. Practically all modern definitions share certain key features. Anthropologists agree that culture

- is learned from others while growing up in a particular human society or group;
- is widely shared by the members of that society or group;
- is responsible for most differences in ways of thinking and behaving that exist between human societies or groups;

- is so essential in completing the psychological and social development of individuals that a person who did not learn culture would not be considered normal by other people.

In brief, culture is learned, shared, largely responsible for differences between human groups, and necessary to make human individuals into complete persons.

Cultural anthropologists often use the term *culture* to emphasize the unique or most distinctive aspects of a people's customs and beliefs. When we speak of Japanese culture, for example, we usually mean the beliefs and customs of the Japanese that make them different from other people. How Japanese think and act differs in some ways from how North Americans, Iranians, Chinese, and Indians think and act, and the phrase *Japanese culture* concisely emphasizes these differences. When we speak of the culture of a people we call attention to all the things that make that people distinctive from others.

There are some things that anthropologists do *not* mean by the word *culture*. We do not mean that Japanese culture is inherently better or worse than, say, French or Iranian culture. We mean only that the three differ in certain identifiable ways. Anthropologists also do not mean that Japanese, French, or Iranian culture is unchanging. We mean only that they remain in some ways distinct despite the changes they have experienced over the years from historical contact and globalization. Above all, anthropologists do not mean that Japanese, French, or Iranian cultures are different because of the biological (genetically based) differences between the three peoples. We mean only that children born into the three cultures are exposed to different ways of thinking and acting as they grow up. They *become* Japanese, French, or Iranians because of their upbringing in different social environments.

Notice that individuals do not invent their culture, just as each generation does not invent its own language. Rather, the members of any given generation learn the cultural ideas and beliefs from previous generations. They also transmit that culture to future generations, albeit with some changes. Of course, during their lifetimes some people have more influence on their culture than others, but even very innovative and creative people build on the cultural knowledge their group has learned from previous generations.

How do cultures differ? At the broadest level, they vary in ways of thinking and ways of behaving. *Ways of thinking* means what goes on inside people's heads: how they perceive the world around them, how they feel about particular people and events, what they desire and fear, and so forth. *Ways of behaving* refers to how people commonly act: how they conduct themselves around parents and spouses, how they carry out ceremonies, what they do when they are angry or sad, and so forth. Obviously, thought and behavior are connected. How we act depends, in part, on how we think. In turn, how we think depends, in part, on how people around us behave, because our observations of their actions shape our thoughts.

Ways of thinking and behaving obviously are related. But because neither completely determines the other, anthropologists commonly distinguish between them by using the terms *knowledge* and *behavior*. An analogy with language will help understand why this distinction matters. All the knowledge (information) you have in your head about how to communicate by talking is *language*. What you actually say or talk about in particular situations is *speech*. Although you could not communicate without mastering a language, that knowledge alone does not tell you what to talk about or how to talk about it. That depends on the situation: who is present, your goals at the moment, how you and others define the occasion, and so forth.

Cultural knowledge includes all the information about the world and society that children learn and adults apply during their lives. It is what you know because you were born into a given group at a certain time. Cultural knowledge includes things like

- attitudes about family, friends, enemies, and other kinds of people;
- notions of right and wrong (moral standards);
- conceptions about the proper roles of males and females;
- ideas about appropriate dress, hygiene, and personal ornamentation;
- rules about manners and etiquette;
- beliefs about the supernatural;
- standards for sexual activity;
- notions about the best or proper way to live (values); and
- perceptions of the world, both natural and social.

This list could be expanded greatly to include all other knowledge that the members of a society or other group learn from previous generations. These and other kinds of knowledge largely determine how the members of a culture think, react, and sometimes feel. In this text, we sometimes use words like *beliefs* and *ideas* as synonyms for cultural knowledge.

---

cultural knowledge Information, skills, attitudes, conceptions, beliefs, values, and other mental components of culture that people socially learn during enculturation.

As for *behavior*, it includes all the things people regularly do, or how they habitually act. As the terms *regularly* and *habitually* imply, members of the same culture generally adopt similar behaviors in similar situations (e.g., in church, on the job, at a wedding or funeral, visiting a friend, sitting in a classroom). Anthropologists are usually more interested in these regularities and habits—in what most people do most of the time in similar situations—than in the behavior of particular individuals. That is, we are more interested **patterns of behavior** than in the behaviors of individuals, which might be idiosyncratic. To avoid repetition, we sometimes use the terms *behavior(s)* and *action(s)* as synonyms for *behavioral patterns*.

Defining Culture

The concept of culture is so important that it is useful to have a formal and fairly precise definition of the term:

> The **culture** of a group consists of shared, socially learned knowledge and patterns of behavior.

This definition seems simple and even sounds like "plain common sense," but in fact each part of it is problematic, as we now discuss.

Shared . . .

Culture is a *collective* phenomenon—it is shared. People brought up in a given culture are mostly able to communicate with and interact with one another without serious misunderstandings and without needing to explain what their behavior means. If you are German, other Germans are far less likely than Saudi Arabians to misunderstand your intentions. Individuals who share the same culture usually don't have to explain their intentions or actions to one another so as to avoid "cultural misunderstandings."

Implicit in *shared* is "by some group of people." This is intentionally a vague phrase. The nature of the group that shares culture depends largely on our interests. The people who share a common cultural tradition may be quite numerous and geographically dispersed, as illustrated by phrases like *Western culture* and *African culture*. We use such phrases whenever we want to emphasize differences between Africans and Westerners. However, in this context the hundreds of millions of people to whom *culture* refers are so scattered and diverse that the term *group* has little (if any) meaning. On the other hand, the group that shares a common culture may be small. Some Pacific islands or Amazonian tribes, for instance, had only a couple hundred members, yet the people spoke a unique language and had distinct customs and beliefs.

We often assume that people who share a common culture are members of the same nation-state (country).

The identification of a cultural tradition with a single nation is sometimes convenient because it allows us to use phrases like "Canadian culture" and "Chinese culture." In these and other cases, the people whom we identify as "sharing" culture are the residents of one country. This identification of culture and country is accurate for some countries, like South Korea and Japan—although both these nations have immigrants and foreign residents, and Japan has an indigenous culture, the Ainu.

However, most modern nations contain a lot of cultural diversity within their boundaries. This is especially true for nations with a history of colonialism. For example, the internationally recognized national borders of most African and South Asian countries are a product of their history as colonies, not of their indigenous cultural or ethnic identities. That is, more often than not, colonizing nations created boundaries between "their" colonies to further their own interests rather than to reflect cultural distinctions and ethnic divisions (see Chapters 4 and 16). Thus, modern India has dozens of languages and cultural identities, as do most sub-Saharan African nations like Kenya and Tanzania. The government of the People's Republic of China recognizes 56 minority peoples, some of whom theoretically have traditional homelands labeled *autonomous regions* on maps.

Modern European nations are also multicultural: migrants from North Africa, Turkey, South Asia, and other regions now work in European countries like France, Germany, and Great Britain. The immigrants enrich their host countries with new cuisines, festivals, music, and other cultural practices. But they also take jobs and have different beliefs and behaviors. Some "native" Europeans view immigrants as a political threat and as endangering their own way of life. For example, in 2009, the citizens of Switzerland were so anxious about immigrants from Islamic countries that they voted for a law against building more minarets—the towers that identify (Muslim) mosques.

There are other complexities of the word *shared*. People have a **cultural identity**, meaning that

---

patterns of behavior Within a single culture, the behavior most people perform when they are in certain culturally defined situations.

culture Socially learned knowledge and patterns of behavior shared by some group of people.

cultural identity Cultural tradition a group of people recognize as their own; the shared customs and beliefs that define how a group sees itself as distinctive.

The development of the global economy encourages international migration to seek education, better employment, a more satisfying social life, and even spouses. These men are Muslims praying in the courtyard of the Central Mosque – in London, England.

individuals define themselves partly by the cultural group in which they were born and raised. Your cultural identity helps define who you are, along with your ideas about your gender, race, and other features. Yet cultural identity is actually complicated: if you are an African American, you may feel like you share a common identity with people born and living in Africa or with people of African heritage living in Haiti or Jamaica or parts of Brazil. Although you are far more likely to be like Anglo-Americans in how you think and act, nonetheless you might identify with other persons whose ancestors were Africans. Similar considerations apply to other cultural identities, such as individuals whose parents were born in East Asia and Latin America. Notice that *cultural identity* implies contrast: the traits that define identity such as physical features and historical origins are contrasted with other traits that define alternative identities.

For these reasons, the identification of "culture" with "nation" is simplistic, because many cultural groupings, identities, and traditions coexist within the boundaries of most modern nations. The term *subculture* refers to cultural variations that exist within a single nation. Most obvious are *regional subcultures.* Contrast the American states of Mississippi and Connecticut; the Canadian provinces of Quebec and British Columbia; or the Great Britain regions of Scotland, Wales, Ireland, and England.

Sometimes people extend the concept of subculture to particular groups that recruit their members from the nation at large, as in phrases like *corporate cultures* or *occupational cultures.* Particular religious denominations are sometimes called subcultures to emphasize contrasting worship rituals and values between churches, like Episcopalians and Southern Baptists. The word *subculture* often is applied to people based on sexual orientation, as in gay, lesbian, and straight subcultures. Some people distinguish subcultures based on contrasts like rural and urban, public school and prep school, homemakers and professional women, and even male and female.

These examples show that culture is shared at various levels, which makes the notion of *shared culture* more complicated than it seems: At which level shall we speak of "a" culture or of "the" culture of people X? Generally, the words *culture* and *subculture* are useful if they contrast some group with another of the same kind—for example, West Europe/East Asia, English/French,

subculture Cultural differences characteristic of members of various ethnic groups, regions, religions, and so forth within a single society or country.

Cherokee/Anglo, north/south, Catholic/Methodist. In most cases, the context of the discussion adequately defines the level.

The word *subculture* is often used too loosely, however. It is most useful when it points out distinctions that have many dimensions. For example, if gay subculture refers *only* to sexual orientation, then the word *subculture* is not very useful. It becomes more meaningful if it refers to broader contrasts between straights and gays in values and lifestyles. Also, the more similarities there are between the members of the groups we wish to contrast, the less meaningful the concept of subculture becomes. Not just any difference between groups should be called *subcultural* (otherwise, even families could be subcultures). Distinctions based on criteria like occupation, employment status, or type of school, are so vague that they have limited usefulness.

For all these reasons, in the global society of the twenty-first century, the simple statement "culture is shared among some group of people" has many complexities. In fact, some people think the entire world is headed toward "sharing" a single culture – a monolithic global culture. This possibility is discussed in Global Challenges and Opportunities.

. . . Socially Learned . . .

Individuals acquire their culture in the process of growing up in a society or some other kind of group. The process by which infants and children learn the culture of those around them is called **socialization** or **enculturation**. Learning one's culture, of course, happens as a normal part of childhood. To say that culture is learned from others seems commonsensical, but it has several important implications that are not completely obvious.

To say that culture is *learned* is to say that it is not acquired genetically—that is, through the process of biological reproduction. A people's culture does not grow out of their gene pool or biological makeup, but is something the people born into that group acquire as they grow up. Africans, East Asians, Europeans, and Native Americans do not differ in their cultures because they differ in their genes— they do not differ *culturally* because they differ *biologically*. Any human infant is perfectly capable of learning the culture of any human group or biological population, just as any child can learn the language of whatever group that child is born into. To state the main point in a few words: *Cultural differences and biological differences are largely independent of one another.* (We qualify this statement later in this chapter.)

To say that culture is *socially* learned is to emphasize that people do not learn it primarily by trial and error. The main ways children learn culture are by observation, imitation, communication, and inference. One important way in which humans differ in degree, though not in kind, from other primates is their ability to learn by imitating and communicating with other humans. When you were an infant, you did not learn what is good to eat primarily by trying out a variety of things that might have been edible and then rejecting things that were not edible. Rather, other people taught you what is and is not defined as food. If you are a North American, you probably view some animals (cattle, fish, chicken) as food and others that are equally edible (horses, dogs, guinea pigs) as not food. You did not discover this on your own but by learning from others what is edible, good tasting, or appropriate. This social learning of what is good to eat spared you most of the costs (and possible stomachaches and health hazards) of learning on your own by trial and error.

Relying on social learning rather than trial and error gives humanity many advantages. First, any innovation that one individual makes can be communicated to others in a group, who thus take advantage of someone else's experience. If you recombine the elements of old tools to develop a more effective tool and share your knowledge, other members of your community can also use that better tool.

Second, each generation learns the culture of its ancestors and transmits it to the next generation, and so on to future generations. Thus, any new knowledge or behavior acquired by one generation is potentially available to future generations (although some of it is lost or replaced with each generation). By this process of repeated social learning over many generations, knowledge accumulates. People alive today live largely off the knowledge acquired and transmitted by previous generations. In modern societies, certain kinds of knowledge are transmitted through formal education in schools and colleges as well as through informal teaching by parents, relatives, and community members.

Third, because culture is socially learned, human groups are capable of changing their ideas and behaviors very rapidly. Genetic change (biological evolution) is slow because it relies on biological reproduction. In contrast, no genetic change and no biological evolution need occur for the knowledge and behavior patterns

---

socialization Process of social learning of culture by children.

enculturation (socialization) Transmission (by social learning) of cultural knowledge to the next generation.

GLOBAL CHALLENGES AND OPPORTUNITIES

Is Everyone Becoming a Westerner?

In most modern nations, there are subcultures based on region, ethnic identity, national origin, and many other features that people use to define and themselves as distinctive from others. These Korean-American people of Los Angeles are having a festival that educates others about the Korean culture.

As contacts between the world's nations become more common and intense, people in various places react differently depending on their own culture, the nature of the contacts, and their personal circumstances. The impacts on local cultural traditions therefore differ widely. Those concerned about these impacts have opinions, often strong ones, on what the future holds for cultural diversity on our planet.

First, some fear (while others hope) that the cultures of the most wealthy and militarily powerful regions will eventually become globally dominant, gradually displacing other traditions. This is what many North American travelers to East Asia or India conclude when they see businesses like McDonald's or KFC thriving. It is what many Middle Eastern political and religious leaders fear when they ban movies with scantily clad women. Even some wealthy European countries like Italy and France are concerned that their national traditions are being overwhelmed by the "American consumer culture." Some call the international marketing of products *cultural imperialism*, with companies from the United States usually identified as the main perpetrators—although Nokia (Finland), Nestle (Switzerland), Samsung (South Korea), Panasonic (Japan), De Beers (the South African diamond company), and other companies with global markets and advertising are equally involved.

In short, many believe that what they call Western culture is becoming *the* global culture. Some seem to treat this global cultural future as inevitable—for better or worse.

However, perhaps new forms of culture will arise out of the increased contacts between peoples that result from travel and migration. International travel for tourism or business exposes people to other places and peoples. Many travelers go back home with new understandings and appreciation of the countries that hosted them. Temporary and permanent migration connects peoples and traditions. Most of the richest countries of Europe were formerly colonial powers and many of them are destination countries for migrants. In some, large numbers of people from former colonies have immigrated, as in France (Algerians) and Britain (Pakistanis and Indians). In destination countries like Canada, the United States, and recently Australia, immigrants arriving for jobs bring their traditions along with their labor. Some citizens of destination countries worry about being culturally overwhelmed (and outvoted) by immigrants. They wonder whether "those people" can or even want to be culturally assimilated. Others more sympathetic to diversity enjoy the new choices in food, films, music, and books immigrants bring with them, believing that immigration culturally enriches their nations.

However, globalization also has opposite effects. In some countries, people feel culturally threatened by the frequency and intensity of contacts, which leads them to cling more firmly to what they believe are their traditional values. Globalization can lead to greater attachments to a cultural past perceived as pure or uncorrupted by foreign influences. Outside influences are consciously rejected, sometimes with profound political consequences, including violence. (Most readers will think this paragraph refers to the Middle

of a human population to be utterly transformed. Furthermore, your genetic makeup is fixed at conception. During the course of your life, however, your ideas and actions are likely to change dramatically.

In sum, culture is learned, not inborn, which means that cultural differences cannot be explained by biological/genetic differences between groups of people. The fact that culture is *socially* learned gives humanity some big advantages over other animals: innovations can spread, knowledge can accumulate over time, and peoples' ideas and actions can change rapidly in a single generation.

East, but they should be aware that a similar reaction is occurring in their own nations.)

In countries with large numbers of immigrants, sometimes the newcomers are culturally and linguistically assimilated into the majority or so-called mainstream. Then, future generations may not be recognized as immigrants nor consider themselves such. Alternatively, instead of assimilation, people from a particular national background may establish permanent cultural enclaves in their new homelands. Festivals, cuisines, family and living arrangements, and languages are often preserved in these enclaves, which include various Chinatowns and Koreatowns in North American large cities. Young programmers and software engineers from India work in California's Silicon Valley and other places. To find spouses, many of them use dozens of specially designed websites to connect with people they have never met. They might ask their parents back home to set up meetings with suitable husbands or wives when they go back home. As these examples illustrate, as people of the past and present have migrated from their original countries, they have kept some of their traditions and maintained communities as ethnic enclaves within the larger society.

Not surprisingly, then, globalization has diverse impacts. There is no point in predicting what will happen in the end, mainly because changes will continue in future decades. There will never be an end, in the sense of a final outcome to cultural change once the global system has stabilized—because the global system will never stabilize.

It is worth pointing out, however, that when people discuss the worldwide spread of "Western culture," in most cases they are really talking and worrying about the external manifestations of culture. They are concerned about the observable trappings of culture rather than about *culture* as anthropologists usually use the term. For example, McDonald's originated in the United States, but is its presence in Japan and South Korea a threat to those "cultures"? Is American culture threatened by Honda manufacturing plants in the Midwest? If you are an American citizen, did you feel your "culture" was threatened when a Chinese company bought IBM and started producing computers with the Lenovo label? If you are a Canadian resident of Vancouver, British Columbia, did you worry that your traditions were under attack when thousands of immigrants from Hong Kong settled in your city in the 1990s?

In fact, many things that people now believe are "theirs" originated elsewhere. The "English" alphabet came from the ancient Greeks, who adapted it from the even more ancient Phoenicians. English numerals (1, 2, 3, . . .) are in fact Arabic numerals. The English language originated in northern Europe out of the Germanic subfamily, which is part of the widespread Indo-European language family. Canadian and American staples like bread, steak, and peas originated from other places. At least corn, tomatoes, beans, and chilis originated in North America, but actually those of us whose ancestors were immigrants from Europe learned about them from the original Native Americans.

Finally, it is worth countering the common opinion that the transmission of the material manifestations of culture has been in only one direction—from the West to the Rest. Certainly, Western movies and music are popular in most of the world, as are Western fashions, cosmetics, and a host of other trappings. But similar things have moved in the other direction. Japanese *anime* and *manga*, karaoke, sushi and sushi bars, and horror movies have made it big among North American young people. Indian and Chinese movies, *shisha* smoking from the Middle East, East Asian martial arts and tai chi, tattoos featuring Chinese characters, and salsa dancing and music also are doing well. In Honolulu, you can visit bars that serve kava (a mouth-numbing drink made from the root of a plant from the pepper family, which originated in Polynesia and other Pacific islands like Fiji, Vanuatu, and Pohnpei). In most large North American and European cities, you can visit restaurants that will sell you food from practically anywhere. In late 2012, a Korean singer called Psy set a record for the most hits on YouTube with the music video Gangnam Style. K-Pop was all the rage. Are you feeling threatened yet?

Social learning has a downside, too. For reasons no one fully understands, sometimes ideas and beliefs arise that lead those who believe them to harm or even kill other people. In 1995, in Japan the members of a "cult" called Aum Shinrikyo coordinated the release of a nerve gas in five trains at rush hour, injuring over five thousand and killing twelve persons. In Oklahoma City in April, 1995, Timothy McVeigh bombed the Murrah Federal Building, killing 168 people. McVeigh was influenced by antigovernment, antitax, pro-gun movements. This was the worst terrorist attack on American soil until September 11, 2001. On that date, terrorists influenced

A police lieutenant speaks with reporters about the shooting of 26 people at Sandy Hook Elementary School in Newtown, Connecticut in December 2012. Social learning provides the cultural knowledge essential to get along with other people. However, occasionally some individuals process and interpret that knowledge in harmful ways, especially when the technology needed to do so is readily available.

by Al Qaeda guided an airliner into the Twin Towers of the New York City World Trade Center, the Pentagon, and rural Pennsylvania, killing nearly 3,000 people.

On December 14, 2012, a 20-year-old man killed 20 children and 6 adults at Sandy Hook Elementary School in Newtown, Connecticut. This was only the second-deadliest gun violence in the United States. Even more people died in 2007 when a senior student killed 32 in a mass shooting at Virginia Polytechnic Institute.

None of these individuals simply thought up the beliefs and ideas that led to their violent behavior. They were influenced by the beliefs and ideas of others, perhaps because in their minds these ideas made sense of their life experiences. None of the original beliefs necessarily called for violence, but for some individuals violence was justified for revenge against a generalized Other, or in to achieve some greater good. Individuals react differently to what they have socially acquired from others around them. Sometimes, beliefs not only harm other people, but also the individuals who accept them: the men who guided the 9/11 aircraft died, and the mass murderers at Sandy Hook and Newtown committed suicide.

. . . Knowledge . . .

When anthropologists use the phrase *cultural knowledge*, we do not mean that a people's beliefs, perceptions, rules, standards, and so forth are true in an objective or absolute sense. In our professional role, for the most part anthropologists do not judge the accuracy or worthiness of a group's knowledge. For us, the most important thing about cultural knowledge is not its truth value but that

▌ the members of a culture share enough knowledge that they behave in ways that are meaningful and acceptable to others so that they avoid frequent misunderstandings and usually do not need to explain what they are doing; and

▌ the knowledge guides behavior such that the people can survive, reproduce, and transmit their culture.

In a few words, cultural knowledge generally leads to behavior that is meaningful to others and adaptive to the natural and social environment. We consider some of this knowledge later. Notice what this might mean for your life and your culture: your cultural knowledge leads you to act in acceptable and meaningful ways and allows your culture to persist, but that does not imply that this knowledge is true. Most of us find it much easier to recognize that this applies to Others than to Ourselves.

... and Patterns of Behavior

Even individuals brought up in the same culture differ in their behaviors. The behavior of individuals varies for several reasons. First, individuals have different *social identities:* males and females, old and young, rich and poor, family X and family Y, and so forth. Actions appropriate for people with one identity may not be appropriate for others. Second, the behavior of individuals varies with *context and situation:* a woman acts differently depending on whether she is interacting with her husband, child, priest, or employee. Third, each human individual is in some ways a *unique* human individual: even when brought up in the same society, we all differ in our emotional responses, appetites, interpretations of events, reactions to stimuli, and so forth. Finally, cultural standards for and expectations of behavior are often *ambiguous.* For these and other reasons, the behavior of individuals is not uniform within the same culture.

Despite such complexities, within a single cultural group, behavioral regularities or patterns exist. For instance, into the 1980s had you visited a certain area of the Amazonian rain forest and encountered people known as the Yanomamo, you might have been shocked by some of their actions. By most cultures' standards, the Yanomamo are unusually demanding and aggressive. Slight insults often lead to violent responses. Quarreling men may duel in a chest-pounding contest, during which they take turns beating one another on the chest, alternating one blow at a time. More serious quarrels sometimes call for clubs, with which men bash one another on the head. Fathers sometimes encourage their sons to strike them (and anyone else) by teasing and goading, while praising the child for his fierceness.

If, on the other hand, you visited the Semai, a people of Malaysia, you might be surprised at how seldom they express anger and hostility. Indeed, you might find them *too* docile. One adult should never strike another—"Suppose he hit you back?" they ask. The Semai seldom hit their children—"How would you feel if he or she died?" they ask. When children misbehave, the worst physical punishment they receive is a pinch on the cheek or a pat on the hand. Ethnographer Robert Dentan suggests one reason for the nonviolence of the Semai: children are so seldom exposed to physical punishment that when they grow up, they have an exaggerated impression of the effects of violence.

The contrasting behavioral responses of the Yanomamo and Semai people illustrate an important characteristic of most human behavior: its social nature. Humans are supremely social animals. We seldom do anything alone, and even when we are alone, we rely unconsciously on our cultural upbringing to provide us with the knowledge of what to do and how to act. Relationships between people are therefore enormously important in all cultures. Anthropologists give special attention to the regularities and patterning of these social relationships, including such things as how family members interact, how females and males relate to one another, how political leaders deal with subordinates, and so forth.

The concept of **role** is useful to describe and analyze interactions and relationships. Individuals are often said to have a role or to play a role in some group. Roles usually carry names or labels, such as *mother* in a family, *student* in a classroom, *accountant* in a company, and *headman* of a Yanomamo village. Attached to a role are the group's *expectations* about what people who hold the role should do. Learning to be a member of a group includes learning the expectations of its members. Expectations include rights and duties. The *rights* (or privileges) defined by my role include the benefits the group members agree I should receive as a member. My *duties* (or obligations) include other group members' expectations of my behavior.

Rights and duties are usually *reciprocal:* My right over you is your duty to me, and vice versa. My duties to the group as a whole are the group's rights over me and vice versa. If I adequately perform my duties to the group, then other members reward me, just as I reward them for their own role performance. By occupying and performing a role in a group, I behave in ways that others find valuable, and I hope that some of my own wants and needs will be fulfilled. Conversely, failure to live up to the group's expectations of role performance is likely to bring some sort of informal or formal punishment. Among the Yanomamo, young men who refuse to stand up for themselves by fighting are ridiculed and may never amount to anything. The shared knowledge of roles and expectations is partly responsible for patterns of behavior.

Defining culture as shared and socially learned knowledge and behavior seems pretty inclusive. What else could be "cultural"? Actually, some things most people commonly consider part of culture are not viewed as part of culture by many anthropologists. For example, many anthropologists do not see architecture and art objects

role Rights and duties that individuals receive because of their personal identity or membership in a social group.

such as paintings and sculptures as part of a people's culture. They are, rather, physical representations and material manifestations of cultural knowledge. They are *products* or *expressions* of culture rather than *aspects* of culture. For instance, some think that art expresses a culture's values, ideals of beauty, conflicts, worldviews, and so forth. Houses and public buildings are products of aspects of culture such as family life, sexual practices, political organization, ideas of beauty and symmetry, religious beliefs, and status distinctions.

Similar considerations apply to other kinds of physical objects and material things. For example, tools are physical manifestations of the ideas of their human makers and users, who have a mental template that determines the form of the tool. Even writing is not seen as part of culture by many anthropologists. Rather, writing is a means of storing knowledge, transmitting information, and—in the case of fiction— telling stories that are meaningful in the cultural group. Thus anthropologists do not agree on whether such material objects—often called *material culture*—are "part of culture" or only "material manifestations" of culture.

Notice, though, that these complications depend on how we define culture. Here we consider shared knowledge and behavioral patterns as the essence of culture. We could define *culture* in such a way that it includes material objects (like tools, art, and architecture).

Cultural Knowledge

Cultural knowledge includes beliefs, attitudes, rules, assumptions about the world, and other bits and pieces of information stored in our brains. In this section, we discuss five elements of cultural knowledge: norms, values, symbols, constructions of reality, and worldviews. We cover these elements because they are among the most important components of cultural knowledge and because their anthropological meaning goes beyond that of everyday speech. The Concept Review previews the five major components in just a few words.

Norms

Norms are shared ideals (or rules) about how people ought to act in certain situations, or about how

> **norms** Shared ideals and/or expectations about how certain people ought to act in given situations.

particular people should act toward particular other people. The emphasis is on the words *ideals, rules, ought, should,* and *situations.* To say that norms exist does not mean everyone follows them all the time. Some norms are regularly violated, and what is normative in one situation need not be in other situations. *Norm* thus does not refer to behavior itself. Rather, *norm* implies that (1) there is widespread agreement that people ought to adhere to certain standards of behavior, (2) other people judge the behavior of a person according to how closely it adheres to those standards, and (3) people who repeatedly fail to follow the standards face some kind of negative reaction from other members of the group.

Any culture includes hundreds or thousands of norms. People are not consciously aware of all norms. (For example, the next time you interact with someone, try standing closer than "normal," and observe their reaction.) Borrowing a distinction from sociology, we distinguish *folkways* from *mores* (pronounced "morays"). *Folkways* are norms about how things should be done (properly/improperly) or what behavior is called for (appropriate/inappropriate) in a given situation. Most customs about politeness are folkways, as are greetings, introductions, and table manners. *Mores* are norms about behavior that carry moral connotations, meaning that others judge an individual's character (right/wrong) according to how well she or he adheres to the more. Many collective judgments we make about someone's personal morality or character are based on mores. Many standards about sexual behavior and familial obligations are mores.

Like most dichotomies, the distinction between folkways and mores is clear in theory but not always in practice. How to dress is a folkway when the judgment of others is based on whether your outfit is appropriate for the occasion. Dress also can be a more when others evaluate you negatively if you dress immodestly. Whether to give gifts and what kind of gift to give can be a folkway, if you give too little (inconsiderate) or too much (embarrassing to the recipient). It can also be or a more, if others think you are a slimeball for not living up to your social obligations.

Sometimes people feel that norms are irrational or arbitrary rules that stifle their creativity or keep them from doing what they want for no good reason. In fact, though, norms make social interactions much more predictable and so are quite useful to us as individuals. It is mainly because we agree on norms that we know how to behave toward others and that we have expectations about how others should behave toward us in diverse social situations or settings.

For example, at a party where you do not know many people, you may feel a little nervous. But in your

CONCEPT REVIEW: Components of Cultural Knowledge

Component	Brief Definition	Example
Norms	Standards of propriety and appropriateness	Expected behaviors at weddings and in classrooms
Values	Beliefs about social desirability and worthwhileness	Individual rights
Symbols	Objects and behaviors with conventional meanings	Interpretations of nonverbal behavior
Constructions	Divisions of reality into categories and subcategories	Kinds of persons and natural phenomena
Worldviews	Interpretations of events and experiences	Origin of good and evil

culture people know how to introduce themselves, so soon you are introducing yourself, shaking hands, and asking the other guests what they do, what they are studying, and where they work. Perhaps you even know subtle ways of figuring out whether someone is "available." Here, and in many other cases in everyday life, we do not experience norms as oppressive. Rather, norms are useful instructions on how to do something in such a way that others know what you are doing and accept your actions as "normal."

Values

Values consist of a people's beliefs about the way of life that is desirable for themselves and their society. Values have profound, though partly unconscious, effects on people's behavior. The goals we pursue, as well as our general ideas about the good life, are influenced by the values of the culture into which we were born or raised. Values affect our motivations and thus influence the reasons we do what we do. Values are also critical to the maintenance of culture as a whole because they represent the qualities people believe are essential to continuing their way of life. We may think of values as providing the ultimate standards that people believe must be upheld under most circumstances. People may be deeply attached to their values and, sometimes, are even prepared to sacrifice their lives for them.

Although people may say they cherish their values, it is easy to overemphasize their importance in people's lives. For one thing, to uphold one value sometimes leads us to neglect others (e.g., people "value" career enhancement as well as family life). For another, our personal interests can lead us to ignore or downplay some values in some situations (e.g., people should be "honest" but also should successfully compete). Finally, our fears, loves, hates, and other emotions can lead us to ignore our values in favor of other concerns.

Here are some North American examples that illustrate such complexities. Most people agree that persons accused of crimes have rights to a speedy trial and an attorney. But perceived threats from real and imagined terrorists lead many to agree that these values can justifiably be ignored in some situations. As an abstract moral value, prisoners of war should not be tortured. But national security also is important. What shall we do when national security seems to conflict with upholding human rights? Many disagreements about public policy are based on how much weight people place on one of their values as opposed to other values. To say that values are "shared" does not mean that everyone gives them the same importance.

Then there are conflicting values. For instance, there are *family values*, but what constitutes a family? Many do not think gay and lesbian couples count as families. There are values about *equal opportunity*, but if opportunities are to be truly equal then people should not be allowed to pass much wealth to their children because that would give their children a head start. Yet shouldn't people be allowed to give their wealth to their children if they so choose? It is their *private property* (another value), but children who inherit large amounts of property have done nothing to earn it (which conflicts with many other values).

values Shared ideas or standards about the worthwhileness of goals and lifestyles.

Symbols

A **symbol** is something (like an object or an action) that represents, connotes, or calls to mind something else. Just as we learn norms and values during socialization, so do we learn the meanings that people in our group attach to symbols. And just as norms and values affect patterns of behavior, so do the understandings people share of the meanings of symbols. Our shared understandings of the meanings of actions allow us to interact with one another without the need to explain our intentions. We need not state explicitly what we are doing and why.

For the most part, the understandings that people share about the meanings of actions and objects are unconscious. We can speak to inquiring strangers about many of our values and explain to them why we believe they are important. But it is nearly impossible to tell someone why a particular gesture, a way of walking, a style of dress, or a certain facial expression carries the meaning it does rather than some other meaning. We "just know." "Everyone knows," for such things are common knowledge and maybe even common sense—to people who share the symbols.

Two important properties of symbols are that their meanings are arbitrary and conventional. *Arbitrary* means there are no inherent qualities in the symbol that lead a human group to attribute one meaning to it rather than some other meaning. Thus, the wink of an eye that often means "just kidding" in some cultures is—literally—meaningless in other cultures. *Conventional* refers to the fact that the meanings exist only because people implicitly agree they exist. Thus, at an intersection, a red light means "stop," but only because all drivers agree that it does.

Words provide a familiar example of the arbitrary and conventional nature of symbols. In English, the word for a certain kind of large animal is *horse*, but in Spanish, the same animal is called *caballo,* in German *pferd,* in Arabic *hisanun,* in French *cheval,* and so on for other languages. The meaning "horse" is conveyed equally well by any of these words, which is another way of saying that meanings are arbitrary and conventional.

Often we think of symbols as objects that stand for something important or sacred: a flag, a cross, a wedding ring, a religious text. Other objects have practical uses or functions, in the sense that they are useful in everyday life: expensive cars, enormous houses, expensive jewelry, and clothing styles are status symbols. Even individual persons can be symbols: The queen of England and the emperor of Japan have little formal power in their nation's constitution. Rather, they symbolize their people's history, traditions, and values. Many citizens are emotionally attached to them despite the expense of maintaining the trappings of their offices.

Victor Turner's ideas about symbols have influenced anthropology and other disciplines for decades. Writing about objects used in rituals among the Ndembu, an indigenous people of Zambia, Turner noted that Ndembu ritual symbols have several properties that make them powerful in the minds of people. Turner called two of these properties *multivocality* and *condensation.* Symbols represent many qualities and abstract values simultaneously (multivocality). They do so by expressing their meanings in a material form (condensation) that is easy to represent, think about, and become emotionally attached to. National flags, monuments to soldiers, and religious symbols like statues and crosses are good examples of these two properties. People become emotionally attached to such symbols, which can come to stand for all that is right and valuable. Some feel that flag burning should be illegal and even treasonous. To many, gun ownership is a symbol for individual rights and regulation of guns is an infringement of freedom—heartfelt emotions are expressed when governments want to restrict the right to bear arms. The cross represents more to Christians than just the death of Jesus. Some Japanese continue to revere and their emperor, even though the emperor himself renounced his divinity in 1945.

Behavior as well as objects communicate meanings that are arbitrary and conventional. Our shared understandings of what actions mean allow us to interact with one another without the need to explain our intentions, or to state explicitly what we are doing and why.

The shared understandings that allow people to correctly interpret the meanings of behaviors are enormously important. Because you assume that the people you interact with share your understandings, in most situations you know how to act and what to say so as not to be misunderstood. In other words, cultural knowledge includes common understandings of how to interact with one another appropriately (i.e., according to shared expectations) and meaningfully (i.e., in such a way that other people usually are able to interpret our intentions).

Nonverbal communication provides a fine example of these understandings. When you interact with someone face to face, the two of you are engaged in a continual giving and receiving of messages

---

symbols Objects, behaviors, qualities, and other phenomena whose culturally defined meanings have no necessary relationship to their inherent physical qualities.

communicated by both speech and actions. Spoken messages are intentionally (consciously) sent and received. Other messages—including body language, facial expressions, hand gestures, touching, and the use of physical space—are communicated by nonverbal behavior, much of which is unconscious. Nonverbal messages emphasize, supplement, or complement spoken messages. We are not always conscious of what we are communicating nonverbally, and sometimes our body language even contradicts what we are saying. (Is this how your mother often knew when you were lying?)

The general point is that cultural knowledge conditions social behavior in ways people do not always recognize consciously—at least until someone's behavior violates our understandings. Furthermore, many gestures and other body movements with well-known meanings in one culture have no meaning, or have different meanings, in another culture. On a Micronesian island studied by one of the authors, people may answer "yes" or show agreement by a sharp intake of breath (a "gasp") or by simply raising the eyebrows. One may also answer "yes" by the grunting sound ("uh-uh") that carries exactly the opposite meaning to North Americans. Pointing out a direction is done with the nose, not the finger. You would signal "I don't know" or "I'm not sure" by wrinkling your nose, rather than by shrugging your shoulders. It is rude to walk between two people engaged in conversation; if possible, you walk around them; if not, you say the equivalent of "please excuse me," wait for permission, and then bend at your waist while passing between them.

Aside from showing the social usefulness of shared understandings of symbolic actions, these examples illustrate one way misunderstandings occur when individuals with different cultural upbringings interact. Raised in different cultures in which gestures and sounds carry different meanings, individuals (mis)interpret the actions of others based on their own culture's understandings, often seeing the others as rude, unfriendly, insensitive, overly familiar, and so forth.

Consider some examples. Arabs and Iranians often stand "too close" for the Canadian and American comfort zone. In South Korea, it is common to see two young females holding hands or with their arms around each other while walking. But their touching symbolizes nothing about their sexual orientation, nor does two men holding hands in parts of the Middle East. Japanese are less likely than North Americans to express definite opinions or preferences or to just say no to a request. To outsiders, this reluctance often comes across as uncertainty, tentativeness, or even

Symbols include more than physical objects like religious icons, jewelry, clothing, and cars. When people are socialized they understand the cultural meanings of behavior as well. Most Koreans and Japanese realize that these two young women are just friends.

dishonesty, whereas the Japanese view it as politeness. The common American tendency to be informal and friendly is viewed as inappropriate in many other cultures where outward displays of emotions are not displayed to mere acquaintances.

In a world where the globalization of trade and international travel are commonplace, it is worth knowing that much of what you "know" is not known to members of other cultural traditions, just as what they "know" may be unfamiliar to you. Think before you take offense at their actions. And think before you give it.

Classifications and Constructions of Reality

The members of a cultural tradition share beliefs about what kinds of things and people exist. They have a similar **classification of reality**, meaning they generally share knowledge of the basic kinds of animals, plants, inanimate objects, and humans exist. Another phrase for this is the **cultural construction of reality**: from the multitude of differences and similarities that exist in some phenomena, a culture recognizes (constructs) only some features as relevant in making distinctions. The cultural construction of reality implies that different peoples do not perceive the human and natural worlds in the same ways.

classifications of reality (cultural constructions of reality) Ways the members of a culture divide up the natural and social world into categories, usually linguistically encoded.

Natural Reality

How a people divide up plants, animals, landscape features, seasons, and other dimensions of the natural world is cultural constructed. As just one example, the Hanunoo, a tropical forest people of the Philippines, identify 1,600 kinds of plants. They distinguish 400 more "kinds" of forest plants than a scientific botanist would. The Hanunoo make fine distinctions between flora because of the way they use the forest for slash and burn farming (discussed in Chapter 7). It is not that the botanist is right and the Hanunoo wrong, but that they use different criteria to construct their plant classification.

How people culturally construct natural phenomena influences how they define and use nature. Plants, animals, minerals, waters, and the like are classified not just into various kinds but also into various categories of usefulness. For example, what one group considers *food* is not necessarily defined as *food* by another group. Muslims and Orthodox Jews consider pork unclean. Traditional Hindus refuse to consume the flesh of cattle, their sacred animal. The fact that a given animal or plant is edible does not mean that people *consider* it edible (or else more North Americans would eat dogs, as do many East and Southeast Asians, and horses, as do many French).

Finally, people of different cultures differ in their beliefs about the kinds of things that do and do not exist. Some people believe in witches who use malevolent supernatural powers to harm others. Traditional Navajo believe that witches can change themselves into wolves, bears, and other animals. The Tukano people of the Bolivian rain forest believe that a spirit of the forest controls the animals they depend on for meat. So when meat is scarce, a Tukano shaman makes a supernatural visit to the abode of the forest spirit. He promises to magically kill a certain number of humans and to send their souls to the forest spirit in return for the spirit's releasing the animals so the hunters can find game.

As the Navajo and Tukano examples illustrate, not only do different cultures classify objective reality in different ways, they also differ on what reality *is:* one culture's definition of reality may not be the same as that of another culture.

Social Reality

The preceding discussion of the cultural construction of natural reality reminds us of what used to be called *folk classifications*. As generations of "prescientific" peoples tried to make sense of the world and events based on their experiences, they culturally constructed (probably unconsciously) their perceptions of the natural world. After all, human senses can be misleading: the Earth is not truly flat as once thought; the sun only appears to move across the sky; rocks are not completely solid; life forms change, but too slowly for a human to notice in her or his lifetime. In the last few centuries, systematic observations and experiments have allowed scientists to realize the limitations of our sensory impressions. So "folk classifications" are being replaced by scientific taxonomies based on objective methods. We know so much more about the world than past generations.

True, in general. However, in addition to natural phenomena, human beings also culturally construct human beings, placing them into categories and attributing certain characteristics to those categories. In future chapters, we discuss cultural constructions of families and of gender. Here we consider another cultural construction, that of race.

Race remains a controversial and sometimes even explosive topic in many countries. In the United States, in early 2013 the government of Mississippi attempted to overturn the Voting Rights Act of 1965, which outlawed voting laws that discriminated against blacks in some states. The act specifically forbad literacy tests, for in the past they were the primary means used to make it difficult or impossible for African Americans to vote. Mississippi is now arguing that the era of racial discrimination has passed, and wants the Supreme Court to overturn the Voting Rights Act. More generally, conservatives argue that "race-based" hiring and college admissions practices deny opportunities to qualified white people, many of whom come from socioeconomic backgrounds that are just as deprived as those of many minorities.

Most people assume that race is an objective, natural category into which most individuals can be assigned. If people can't tell which race you are, they probably think of you as "mixed race." *Mixed race* is a tricky concept because people of "mixed racial heritages" are usually assigned to whichever racial category is seen as the minority one. Thus, President Barack Obama is the U.S. first black president, although his mother was white. (The late Ann Dunham Soetoro, incidentally, was a cultural anthropologist who did fieldwork in Pakistan and Indonesia; the latter country is the one that some Americans claim Obama was actually born in.)

Can't we observe racial differences by visiting almost any large city? Race certainly seems natural. Most anthropologists disagree. They argue that race is not, in fact, an objective and natural category, but a cultural construction of people based on perceptions and distinctions that arise more from culture than from biology. What does this mean, and why do most anthropologists believe it?

Figure 2.1 In this portion of the 2010 United States Census Form—sent to all American households—respondents are asked to identify their "race." Question 5. Correctly, does not equate "Hispanic origin" with "race." Notice that there are 12 "races" specifically listed in question 6. Furthermore, if you are a Pacific Islander or Asian, you have lots of "races" with which you can identify yourself. How many of these are "races," in the anthropological meaning?

First, the differences out of which race is constructed are only skin deep. When we place people into racial categories, we generally focus on selected visible physical traits: skin color, facial features, hair characteristics, and so forth. If we looked beyond observable traits to consider other (invisible or less visible) traits, different racial categories would result. For example, a racial classification of the world's people based on blood groups (ABO, rH, and other factors) would yield a different classification than one based on skin color. So would a racial classification based on the shape of teeth or jaws, or on the ability of adults to digest the milk enzyme called lactase. Culturally, we define some physical features as relevant (we consider them significant) whereas others are unrecognized (unperceived) or irrelevant. In short, the sets of traits we use to define races lead to one kind of racial classification, but we would have a different classification if we used different traits.

Second, how many "races" are there? Most elderly people raised in North America would say three, which used to be called Mongoloid, Negroid, and Caucasoid. This threefold classification of humanity is based on the history of contacts between Europeans and certain peoples of Africa and Asia. But why only three? Why not 6 or 13 or 40? The so-called Pygmies of central Africa are quite different physically from their Bantu neighbors, as are the once-widespread Khoisan peoples of southern Africa. The indigenous peoples of New Guinea, Australia, and the surrounding islands are quite different not only from many of their neighbors but also from some Africans whom they outwardly resemble in their skin coloration. Many people of southern Asia have skin as dark as some Africans, although in some other physical characteristics they resemble Europeans. What about Malaysians, Polynesians, and Native Americans? Should they be separate races, or combined with others? If so, which others?

Third, along these same lines, different cultures sometimes develop different racial classifications. Brazil is well known for its history of interbreeding among peoples from different continents. Based on his fieldwork, Conrad Kottak reported that in a single village in northeastern Brazil, 40 different terms were used to refer to "race"! To non-Japanese, Japan appears to be a racially homogeneous country. Yet many "true" Japanese recognize and culturally emphasize the differences between themselves and descendants of immigrants from Korea. Also a few Japanese remain prejudiced against the Burakamin, the modern descendants of groups whose ancestors are believed to have engaged in low-level occupations. Yet Burakamin are so indistinguishable physically that those "pure" Japanese who still care about such things have to investigate the ancestry of potential spouses to be sure they are not Burakamin.

Fourth, racial classifications change over time even within the same cultural tradition. In the Americas, people who are today considered indistinguishable racially once were widely viewed as members of different races. When large numbers of Irish immigrated to the Americas after the potato blight struck Ireland in the mid–nineteenth century, they were considered a race by many other Americans whose ancestors had lived here somewhat longer. Jews were also seen by many as a distinct racial group. Such distinctions sound absurd today—to most North Americans, at any rate. Perhaps present-day racial divisions seem will seem equally absurd in the next century.

In sum, most anthropologists believe that race is culturally constructed for the following reasons:

- Different racial categories can be constructed by applying different criteria.
- There is no objective way to determine whether some population should be considered a separate

CHAPTER 2 Culture 35

race, or grouped with other populations into a single racial type; or how many human races exist.
- Different cultures identify different numbers and kinds of races, raising doubts about the biological reality of any given culture's racial categories.
- Even within a single society or nation, the definition of race changes over time.

So, do some anthropologists deny that there are physical differences between populations whose ancestors originated in different continents? No. To claim that races are culturally constructed is not deny biological/genetic realities. However, it does deny that these differences cluster in such a way that they produce categories of people who consistently differ in the same biological ways (i.e., races). Individual human beings differ from one another physically in a multitude of visible and invisible ways. If races—as most people define them—are real biological entities, then people of African ancestry would share a wide variety of traits while people of European ancestry would share a wide variety of *different* traits. But once we add traits that are less visible than skin coloration, hair texture, and the like, we find that the people we identify as "the same race" are less and less like one another and more and more like people we identify as "different races." Add to this point that the physical features used to identify a person as a representative of some race (e.g., skin coloration) are continuously variable, so that one cannot say where "brown skin" becomes "white skin." Although the physical differences themselves are real, the way we use physical differences to classify people into discrete races is a cultural construction.

For these and other reasons, most anthropologists agree that race is more of a cultural construction than a biological reality. Indeed, the American Anthropological Association recommended (unsuccessfully) eliminating the word *race* from the 2010 American census. The American Anthropological Association has an excellent website that portrays conceptions of human differences. Visit the website and click on the image "RACE: Are We So Different?"

Why does it matter whether race is a cultural construction rather than a biological reality? So long as people can avoid viewing some "races" as inferior to others, why is it so important that we see race as a cultural construct?

worldview Ways people interpret reality and events, including how they see themselves relating to the world around them.

For one thing, once a culture classifies people into kinds or types, it is difficult to avoid ranking the types according to some measure of quality, goodness, or talent. Familiar qualities include intelligence, work ethic, athletic ability, and musical talent. Some people believe Asians are naturally smart and work hard, whereas African Americans are better natural athletes, dancers, and musicians. From such seemingly innocent stereotypes, we too easily conclude that it is natural talent that puts many Asians near the top of their class and explains why so many African Americans succeed in athletics, dance, and music.

Another reason to view race as culturally constructed is that doing so helps to avoid confusing "race" with other kinds of differences that have nothing to do with physical differences. Most North Americans do not distinguish—at least not consistently—differences due to "race" from differences due to language, national origin, or cultural background. The latter differences, of course, are based on culture and/or language, not on physical characteristics. Too easily, *race* is confused with *ethnicity*. For example, many people view Native American and Hispanic as the same kind of identity as race. But Hispanics may be black or white or brown or any other humanly possible color, and many people who identify themselves as Native Americans based on their origins and culture are indistinguishable physically from Americans with European ancestry.

Last, race is currently a part of the way people identify themselves to one another. It is an important part of an individual's social identity. Another person's perception of you—and your perception of yourself—is affected by your assumed membership in some racial category. Such identities often carry a great degree of "racial pride." Racial pride may be a positive force in the lives of people who have suffered the effects of prejudice and discrimination, as older African Americans who were part of the 1960s Black Power movement will appreciate. Yet other "races" also can be proud. Racial pride cuts both ways, as people familiar with the beliefs and activities of the Aryan Nation and other such groups dedicated to maintaining "racial purity" know. Political leaders and opinion shapers in the popular media can and do manipulate the opinions of one "race" about other "races" to further their own political and social agendas.

Worldviews

The **worldview** of a people is the way they interpret reality and events, including their images of themselves and how they relate to the world around them. Worldviews are affected by cultural constructions of reality, which we have just discussed. But worldviews include more than just the way a culture carves up people and nature. People have opinions about the nature of the cosmos and how they fit into it. All cultures include beliefs about spiritual souls and include more beliefs about what happens to souls after bodies are lifeless. People have ideas about the meaning of human existence: how we were put on Earth, who or what put us here, and why. They have notions of evil: where it comes from, why it sometimes happens to good people, and how it can be combated. They have beliefs about what supernatural powers or beings are like, what they can do for (or to) people, and how people can worship or control them. Everywhere we find myths and legends about the origins of living things, objects, and customs. (We have more to say about such topics in Chapter 14.)

These examples all are based in a group's religion. But it is important not to confuse worldview and religion, and especially not to think that *religion* and *worldview* are synonymous. Although religious beliefs do influence the worldview of a people, cultural traditions vary in aspects of worldview that we do not ordinarily think of as religious.

For instance, the way people view their place in nature is part of their worldview: do they see themselves as the masters and conquerors of nature, or as living in harmony with natural forces? The way people view themselves and other people is part of their worldview. Do they see themselves, as many human groups do, as the only true human beings, and all others as essentially animals? Or do they see their way of life as one among many equally human but different ways of life? Most modern scientists share a similar worldview: they believe that all things and events in the universe have natural causes that we can discover through certain formal procedures of observation, experimentation, and systematic logic.

The Origins of Culture

Like so much else about the early past of humanity, when we began to depend on culture is unknown. Most anthropologists think the essence of culture—without which everything else "cultural" could not exist—is the ability to create and understand symbols. If so, then somehow researchers must find a way to date the development of the cognitive capacity needed to understand symbols, the meanings of which are arbitrary and conventional rather than inherent in their physical properties. But how to determine when humanity developed this capacity?

It is difficult to know whether some long-gone people had the ability to create and understand symbols. For example, artifacts like spear points were made for practical purposes—that is, to provide something useful like food or shelter. Tools are not necessarily symbolic, as shown by the fact that other animals make and use them. Their shape or style may have had symbolic components, but often it is difficult to know whether ancient toolmakers chose a particular shape or style because it was "efficient" or because it was "meaningful."

Good material evidence of prehistoric symbolic capacity would be objects that have no obvious or probable use in producing something. There are plenty of such objects in late prehistory. For example, as early as 32,000 years ago, prehistoric people made paintings on the walls of more than 300 caves in France and Spain. Some other objects were clearly produced for their aesthetic/artistic value, like clay, ivory, and stone sculptures of humans and animals, but they too are relatively late.

Archaeologists recently have made discoveries that strongly suggest the existence of symbolic capacity about 80,000 years ago. These discoveries included musical instruments, beads, and evidence of sophisticated transmission of knowledge that suggests language.

In June 2009, a team of archaeologists reported they had found the earliest-known musical instrument. About 35,000 to 40,000 years ago, a prehistoric group living in what is now southwestern Germany made a flute from the wing bone of a vulture. The flute had at least five fingering holds that produced different notes. The makers modified one end of the bone to make it into a better mouthpiece. Two other smaller flute fragments, made of ivory, also were found. The technique for making the flutes seemed highly developed, suggesting that flute-making skills developed even earlier. Why people would make a musical instrument is subject to speculation. One commentator suggests that these early inhabitants of Europe "produced symbolic objects that embodied complex beliefs shared by a larger community of individuals" (Adler 2009, 696). If so, then the instruments, and perhaps music itself, requires the mental ability to create and understand symbols.

In 2007, archaeologists reported even earlier evidence that early *Homo sapiens* from North Africa created objects that carried a meaning beyond their physical properties. An international team of archaeologists excavated marine shell beads that ancient people of Morocco manufactured around 82,000 years ago. Many beads were perforated and had wear patterns indicating that they had been strung and worn on the body. Some were coated with a mineral, red ochre, showing that the makers altered the natural color of the shells. Most likely, people were decorating their bodies with the beads. Bodily decorations imply that others understood the beads as symbols of beauty, status, family or group identity, or the like. The beads communicated meanings that were not determined by their appearance or other physical properties. That is, the beads were symbols. The production of ochre in abalone shells is reported from 100,000 years ago in southern Africa, although the significance of this is not yet clear.

Most recently, in 2012, archaeologists published findings about a site on the South African coast dated from about 71,000 years ago. Here ancient people used fire to heat a mineral called *silcrete*. Heat-treating made it easier to flake stone stools accurately and finely, allowing the manufacture of tiny stone tools called *microliths*, an inch or less in length. Several microliths were attached to a bone or wooden shaft with cords and/or sticky pitch. When thrown or thrust, the sharp edges of the microlith penetrated the hides of animals more efficiently than a single stone point attached only to the tip of a spear. To manufacture microliths, the prehistoric Africans chipped small pieces of stone ("flakes") off a larger piece of stone (the "core"). They then reworked the flakes to make effective cutting edges and attached them to a shaft. Thus, 71,000 years ago, a prehistoric group in South Africa used fire not just for warmth and cooking, but as a part of a manufacturing process. They skillfully struck sharp-edged tiny flakes from heat-treated stone. The final tool was a composite of several stone flakes, cordage, and a shaft. The technology lasted for tens of thousands of years and was thus a toolmaking tradition, passed down over hundreds of generations. All this implies transmission of sophisticated knowledge using language.

Probably culture as we socially learn and experience it today originated earlier than its physical manifestations in the form of instruments, art, beads, or other symbolic objects. But so far, all we can say is that humanity had the capacity for culture by around 80,000 years ago. Perhaps this helps explain why current evidence suggests that *Homo sapiens* did not leave our African homeland until around that time.

Culture and Human Life

Anthropologists believe culture is absolutely essential to human life as it is usually lived—in association with other people, or in social groups. To be sure, living in social groups does not require culture. Many species of termites, bees, ants, and other social insects live in quite complex groups, yet they have no culture. Gorillas, chimpanzees, baboons, macaques, and most other primates are also group-living animals. Primatologists have shown that chimpanzees learn to use and make simple tools, share food, communicate fairly precise messages, have intergroup conflicts in which animals are killed, and form relationships in which two individuals who are physically weaker cooperate to overpower a stronger animal. Yet few anthropologists claim that chimpanzee groups have culture in the same sense as all human groups do. (Some use the term *proto-culture* to emphasize that many animal behaviors are socially learned rather than instinctive.) If other group-living social animals cooperate, communicate, and survive without culture, why do people need culture at all?

The main reason boils down to this: the culture of the society or other group into which people are born or raised provides the knowledge (information) they need to survive in their natural environments and to participate in the life of groups. This knowledge, which infants begin to socially learn soon after birth, is necessary because humans do not come into the world equipped with a detailed set of behavioral instructions inherited genetically from their parents. Rather, people are born with *a propensity to learn the knowledge and behaviors of the group they were born into from observation, interaction, and communication with members of that group.* The title of a 2012 book written by British biologist Mark Pagel phrases the main point concisely: humans are "wired for culture."

Culture is necessary for human existence in at least three specific ways:

1. Culture provides the knowledge by which we adapt to our natural environment by harnessing resources and solving other problems of living in a particular place. As they grow up, children socially learn skills for tracking game, gathering wild plants, making gardens, herding livestock, or finding a job, depending on how people make their living in a particular society. Because most human populations have lived in the same environment for many generations, if not centuries, the current generation is usually wise to take advantage of the adaptive wisdom learned and passed down by its cultural ancestors.

2. Culture is the basis for human social life. It provides ready-made norms, values, expectations, attitudes, symbols, and other knowledge that individuals use to communicate, cooperate, live in families and other groups, relate to people of their own and opposite sex, and establish political and legal systems. As they grow up, people learn what

actions are and are not acceptable, how to win friends, who relatives are, how and whom to court and marry, when to show glee or grief, and so forth.

3. Culture provides our views of reality. We socially learn the concepts by which people perceive, interpret, analyze, and explain events in the world around them. Our culture provides a filter or screen that affects how we perceive the world through our senses. Some objects "out there" in the world are sensed; others are not. Some events are important; others are ignored. Growing up in a given culture thus leads people to develop shared understandings of the world (keep in mind that "shared understandings" do not imply Truth).

In brief, culture is essential to human life as we experience it because it provides us with the means to adapt to our surroundings, form relationships in organized groups, and interpret reality. Adaptation, organization, interpretation—these are three of the main reasons culture is essential to a normal human existence. In later chapters, we look at some of the diverse ways in which various cultures have equipped their members to adapt to their environment, organize their groups, and understand their world.

Cultural Knowledge and Individual Behavior

How are the shared ideas and beliefs of a group of people related to the behavior of individuals? This question is important not only for studying other cultures but also for learning how people think about their own lives and their relationship to society.

Is Behavior Culturally Determined?

Some believe that culture largely determines or dictates behavior, a view known as **cultural determinism**. If this idea is strictly and literally true, then the exercise of free will is an illusion. Perhaps culture is pulling our strings, making us *believe* we have free will. In this view, individuals are carriers and transmitters of their cultural heritage. In fact, the belief we have free will might itself be part of our cultural knowledge, ingrained in us by enculturation.

The cultural determinism view emphasizes some components of culture and deemphasizes others. For example, norms instruct individuals what to do in particular situations: how to act toward friends, co-workers, and mothers-in-law; how to perform roles acceptably; how to settle quarrels; and so forth. The values we socially learn tell us what is important for society as a whole and also provide individuals with a set of goals to pursue. "Deviants" are usually forced to conform, ostracized, or eliminated.

Sometimes the relationship between cultural knowledge and individual behavior is as simple as cultural determinism implies, but not usually. Norms are flexible and usually situational. Values provide only rough and sometimes conflicting guidelines for behavior and can be inconsistent. Culture includes shared symbols with their meanings, constructions of reality, and worldviews. These influence our behavior, but only indirectly (by affecting how we perceive and interpret the world) rather than directly (as instructions). The effects of cultural knowledge on behavior is more complicated than cultural determinism implies.

So although it *could* be true that your mind is mainly a vessel that carries your culture, you probably think you are more than a vessel. Most modern anthropologists agree, rejecting notions of extreme cultural determinism. Culture does shape individuals, but it is also shaped by individuals.

In most situations, individuals calculate, weigh alternatives, and make decisions. For those actions that are important in their own lives or in the lives of others they care about, they plan ahead and consider the possible benefits and costs before they act. In considering the relationship between knowledge and behavior, we must take into account people's ability to think ahead, plan, strategize, and choose.

Notice that formulating plans and making choices involve rational thought and emotional dispositions, both of which occur in the context of cultural knowledge. Planning and choosing involve the following procedures: deciding on one's goals (ends); determining the resources (or means) available to acquire these goals; calculating which specific actions are likely to be most effective; estimating the relative costs (in time and/or resources) and benefits (rewards) of these alternative actions; and, finally, choosing between alternative courses of action.

cultural determinism Notion that the beliefs and behaviors of individuals are programmed by their culture.

Culture affects every step of this choice-making process. Norms force individuals to take into account how others are likely to react to their behavior. Values affect the goals that people have and discourage them from acting in ways that infringe on the rights of others. Choices are affected by the existing cultural constructions of people and things, worldviews, and individuals' anticipation of how others will interpret the meaning of their actions. So important are the effects of cultural knowledge on individual decisions that one influential anthropologist long ago defined culture itself as "standards for deciding what is, . . . what can be, . . . how one feels about it, . . . what to do about it, . . . and how to go about doing it" (Goodenough 1961, 552).

Thus, one important way cultural knowledge affects behavior is by its influences on choices individuals make about what to do in various situations. One way to say this is that cultural knowledge provides "boundaries" for behavior. Within these boundaries, people are free to choose between alternative actions. Most people do not overstep cultural boundaries because they believe in the moral correctness of norms and values, because they fear negative reactions from others, or because doing so would involve actions that others might misinterpret.

Why Does Behavior Vary?

The complexity of the relationship between knowledge and behavior is one reason we distinguish knowledge from behavior. Another is that shared ideas and beliefs sometimes do not predict behavior very well at all, and what is expected is often not what occurs. There are several major reasons the actions of different individuals vary.

The most obvious reason is that no two individuals have exactly the same life experiences, even though they are brought up in the same cultural tradition. Although we often speak of "the" way children are raised, in fact enculturation practices vary from family to family even within the same community. Different childhoods and life experiences make individuals (even siblings, as most people know) different in their reactions and actions.

Other reasons for variations in behavior are more subtle. Norms do not always provide unambiguous guidelines for behavior. Generally, you should not lie, but sometimes a small lie is necessary to preserve a personal relationship, to avoid hurting someone's feelings, or to avoid greater harms. Often, too, small lies are so useful to achieve our personal goals that our private interests take precedence over the norm against lying.

As for values, in many situations pursuing one worthwhile goal or upholding one value conflicts with pursuing another goal or upholding another value, so people must choose between them. You may believe in the work ethic, value success in your career, enjoy sports, and want to be a good parent. You hold these beliefs, values, and goals simultaneously. But holding a job and advancing a career reduces the time we can devote to the pursuit of our "family values," so we must decide how to allocate our scarce time and energy between activities that are all culturally defined as worthwhile.

Also, people find ways to justify (to themselves and to others) violations of norms and accepted moral standards when such norms and standards conflict with their interests. You may rationalize stealing from your employer by your opinion that you are "underpaid." Your boss may justify having you work overtime for no extra pay because he is "pressured" from his own boss. Your company may lay off its workers and move its operations overseas because it must operate in a "highly competitive global environment."

Finally, people receive contradictory messages about what actions are proper and morally right. Sometimes ideal models for behavior are contradicted by the messages and models people receive from the actions of their parents, relatives, friends, political leaders, and the media. Older generations want us to uphold their standards of sexual morality, but when we watch TV and movies or go on the Internet, we are exposed to conflicting messages and values.

The preceding examples are familiar to most readers. Our main point is this: all cultures have abstract public values and norms that distinguish right from wrong, appropriate from inappropriate, and so forth. But real-world situations are complicated. Real-life individuals have personal goals to pursue and sometimes yield to temptation. People have to choose between values and norms that conflict in some circumstances.

In sum, all humans and all groups deal with the complicated conflicts between private interests and public duties. The actions of individuals are often an uneasy compromise between the two. Although our behavior is embedded in the context of cultural knowledge, its relationship to this context is complex and variable. All of us recognize that this applies to ourselves. Rather than simplistically condemning the hypocrisy of others, we should recognize that it applies to them as well.

Members of any "racial" type can and do learn the same culture. Having passed citizenship examinations, these people became American citizens on July 4, 2005.

Biology and Cultural Differences

In many ways, humans are like other mammals. Biologically, we must regulate our body temperatures, balance our energy and liquid intake and expenditures, and so forth. But anthropologists say that humans are special mammals because we rely so heavily on culture for our survival.

Do biological/genetic/physical differences between groups of people have anything to do with the cultural differences between them? To rephrase the question so that its full implications are apparent: is there any correlation between cultural differences and physical differences between groups of people?

Before the twentieth century, many people believed the physical differences between groups of people explained differences in how they thought, felt, and behaved. That is, they believed "racial" differences partly or largely accounted for differences in culture. According to this notion, now called **biological determinism**, cultural differences have a biological basis, meaning that groups of people differ in how they think, feel, and act because they differ in their innate biological makeup.

Biological determinism is a convenient belief about what makes human groups like ethnicities, nations, and "races," differ in their beliefs and actions. It is simple to understand. Often, it is a politically or economically useful idea, especially when combined with ethnocentric attitudes about the superiority of one's own culture. If French or Chinese see their culture as superior to African or Native American cultures, then it might be because the French or Chinese are biologically superior to Africans or Native Americans. Colonialism, expropriation of land and other resources, slavery, and genocides and attempted genocides, often were justified by the idea that groups of people differed in their customs and beliefs—and also in their intelligence—because of their physical differences. If who comes out on top in competition among individuals and groups is biologically determined, then whoever comes out on

biological determinism Idea that biologically (genetically) inherited differences between populations are important influences on cultural differences between them.

top and on bottom is justified—and even inevitable. Competition between individuals and groups produces losers as well as winners *due to the natural or inherent characteristics of both*. This notion is usually called **social Darwinism**, although it is a misapplication of Charles Darwin's theory.

With few exceptions, anthropologists of today reject biological determinism and social Darwinism. The diverse cultures of Africa did not and do not differ from the cultures of Europe or Asia because the peoples of these continents differ biologically. Nor do the cultures of different ethnic groups within a modern nation differ because these ethnic groups differ genetically: African Americans, European Americans, and Asian Americans do not differ in their beliefs and actions because of their different genetic makeup.

To claim that physical differences are largely irrelevant as causes for cultural differences seems like a sweeping overgeneralization. Certainly, it is difficult to prove. But evidence for it is familiar to most people. Consider the following three facts, drawn from everyday life:

1. Individuals of any physical type are equally capable of learning any culture. North America now contains people whose biological ancestors came from all parts of the world. Yet most modern-day African, Korean, South Asian, Irish, and Arab Americans have far more in common in their thoughts and actions than any of them have in common with the peoples of their ancestral homelands.
2. An enormous range of cultural diversity was and is found on all continents and regions. For example, most West Africans are biologically similar, yet they are divided into many dozens of different cultural groupings. The same disjunction between physical characteristics and cultural diversity applies to people of northern Asia, southern Asia, Europe, and other regions. Far too much cultural variability exists within populations that are biologically similar for biological differences to be a *significant* cause of cultural variation.
3. Dramatically different ways of thinking and behaving succeed one another in time within the same biological population and within the same society. Cultures can and regularly do undergo vast changes within a single human generation, as the changes in countries like China, Brazil, and India since the 1980s so clearly reveals.

Because of these and other kinds of evidence, most cultural anthropologists feel justified in reaching the following conclusion: physical (including "racial") differences between human populations are mostly irrelevant in explaining the cultural differences between them. For the most part, if we want to explain the differences between the Kikuyu culture of East Africa and the Vietnamese culture of East Asia, we ignore the physical and genetic differences between the Kikuyu and the Vietnamese.

However, "for the most part" does not mean "totally." There are features in which differences in behavior can be attributed to biological differences between human groups. One well-understood example is the relation between population-level genetic differences and milk drinking. All infants drink milk, but not all human populations retain the ability to continue milk drinking into adulthood. Milk contains lactose, a kind of sugar, but lactose must be broken down in the small intestine by an enzyme called lactase before the body can digest it. Many peoples are lactose-intolerant, meaning that they lose the ability to digest milk as they mature.

For example, most people of eastern Asia and southern Africa cannot digest fresh milk, nor can most Native Americans. But the vast majority of Europeans and people with European ancestry (European Americans and European Australians/New Zealanders) are able to digest lactose, as are most peoples of central Africa. The obvious reason for the difference in "behavior" or even in "taste" is genetic: the ancestors of some peoples were able to drink milk, so milk drinking evolved as a behavioral pattern. This seems to be an example of a biological difference "causing" a difference in behavior between groups of people.

Actually, it is somewhat difficult to disentangle cause and effect in this case. Evidence shows that it is likely that milk drinking and genetic change *coevolved*. After cattle were domesticated several thousand years ago, milk became such a potentially nutritious food that the few people who were able to digest it as adults had more children. Natural selection led more and more people to be able to digest it. So at the group level, milk's food value increased, as did the desire for it. This much is a biological change. People therefore responded by raising more cattle to provide more milk (as well as other resources provided by cattle). This part is the behavioral response to the biological change. As the ability to digest milk increased among the population, more people were able to drink it, so people wanted more cattle,

social Darwinism View that the degree of success in achieving social rewards is determined by the inherent (inborn) characteristics of individuals and groups.

It is not clear whether music somehow helps people survive or performs essential functions for societies and cultures, but it nonetheless is a cultural universal. These Chinese are skilled drummers.

leading cattle to become more valuable and people to breed more cattle, thus further increasing the supply of a food that led lactose tolerant genes to increase in the population. And so on over many centuries.

More briefly, cattle domestication led to a human genetic change, which initiated a cultural response, which led to more genetic changes. This kind of coevolution probably also affected other changes in human diets after people domesticated plants and animals beginning around 10,000 years ago (see Chapter 7).

As lactose tolerance illustrates, in specific cultural features, biological differences do affect behavior—or, at least, behavioral predispositions. It is unlikely that we can explain the difference between milk-averse and milk-drinking cultures without taking genetic differences into account.

Cultural Universals

Biological factors also are relevant to human life in a broader way. Human beings have physiological needs and biological imperatives just like other animals. To persist over many generations, all peoples develop means of meeting biological needs and coping with environmental problems. If any people failed to do so they are no longer around.

Because humans are both cultural and biological beings, much of what we do is oriented around the satisfaction of biological needs for food, shelter, reproduction, disease avoidance, and so forth. It is partly because of such universal problems that anthropologists have discovered **cultural universals**, or elements that exist in all known human cultural groups.

Some cultural universals are obvious because they are requirements for long-term survival in a species that relies on social learning, material technology, and group living. These universals include tools, shelter, methods of communication, patterns of cooperation used in acquiring food and other essential resources, family systems, ways of teaching children, methods of social control, ways of regulating who may have sexual relations with whom, and so forth. There is no great mystery about why all human groups have such things.

cultural universals Elements of culture that exist in all known human groups or societies.

Other cultural universals are not so obvious. They do not seem necessary for the physical survival of individuals or groups, but they are nonetheless present in all cultural traditions. Among these are

- ways of assigning tasks and roles according to age, gender, and skill;
- prohibitions on sexual relations (incest taboos) between certain kinds of relatives;
- organized ways of sharing and exchanging goods;
- games, sports, and other kinds of recreational activities;
- beliefs about supernatural powers and rituals used to communicate with and influence them;
- decorative arts;
- singing and other forms of music;
- standards of modesty;
- customary ways of handling the dead and expressing grief;
- myths, legends, and folklore; and
- rites of passage that publicly recognize the movement of people through certain stages of life.

We could list more cultural universals. Here, our main point is that many cultural universals are not easily explained by the fact that they are necessary for the short- or long-term biological survival of populations. Perhaps many of these universals exist because they are a necessary by-product of a toolmaking, group-living, culture-bearing, language-speaking, symbol-understanding species. For example, singing may bring people together and decorative arts may be related to status or family differences.

Although they are "universal," the precise forms that these and other elements take vary from culture to culture. For instance, all human societies have beliefs about the supernatural, but the nature of these beliefs varies enormously among cultures, as seen in Chapter 14. Likewise, people in all societies have prohibitions against sexual relations with certain kinds of relatives, but which family members are excluded varies from society to society, as discussed in Chapter 9. Male-female differences are important among all peoples but how people culturally construct these differences varies quite a lot, as described in Chapter 11. Most of the rest of this book deals with these and other cultural variations.

Generally, it is important to understand that the peoples of the world are overwhelmingly similar biologically, no matter how different they might appear to our perceptions, which are based in part on our cultural constructions. As we cover cultural variations in future chapters, it is also important to realize that cultures are not infinitely variable.

SUMMARY

1. **Define culture in a way that is useful to compare and contrast different cultures.** *Culture* is here defined as the shared, socially learned knowledge and behavioral patterns characteristic of some group of people. The term *group* may refer to an entire society, an ethnic group, or some kind of subculture, depending on the context of the discussion. To describe and analyze culture, it is useful to distinguish between cultural knowledge and patterns of behavior.

2. **Understand the concept of cultural knowledge and five of its key components.** Cultural knowledge has many components, some of which are norms, values, shared understandings of the meanings of symbolic objects and actions, constructions of reality, and worldviews. Cultural knowledge is not true in any objective sense, but it must at least allow a society to persist in its environment and it must enable people to interact appropriately and meaningfully.

3. **Discuss the evidence for the origins of the human capacity for culture.** How and when the human species first developed culture is uncertain. Because of the centrality of symbols for language and culture, evidence that ancient people used symbols is also evidence for culture. Archaeologists unearthed a musical flute in Germany that is around 35,000 years old. Eighty-thousand-year-old colored beads from southern

Africa were probably strung as jewelry and used as symbols of status of identity. Archaeologists have unearthed indirect evidence of symbolic language from about 71,000 years old.

4. **Analyze the relationship between cultural knowledge and the behavior of individuals.** Cultural determinism is the idea that cultural knowledge determines the actions of individuals, but this view is simplistic. Cultural ideas and beliefs serve as more than just rules or instructions for behavior. A more realistic view is that cultural knowledge affects the choices people make about how to act in particular situations. Cultural knowledge limits and influences behavior but does not determine it in detail because people's actions most of the time are not simply programmed by their culture.

5. **Describe why cultural and biological differences between human populations vary independently.** Biological determinism is the notion that cultural differences between human populations are greatly affected or even determined by the biological differences between them. This idea is generally rejected because convincing evidence exists that biological and cultural differences vary independently. The shared biological heritage of the human species does affect culture, however, because how people meet their biologically given needs is reflected in their culture. The existence of cultural universals also suggests that the shared genetic heritage of all humanity affects the kinds of cultures that are possible in the human species.

3 Culture and Language

People communicate mainly by language, but nonverbal methods also send messages in ways that often vary from people to people, as these Sicilian women illustrate.

Philippe Renault/Hemis/ Terra/Corbis

Language and Humanity

The Power of Language
  Discreteness
  Arbitrariness
  Productivity
  Displacement
  Multimedia Potential

How Language Works
  Sound Systems
  Words and Meanings

Germanics, Romantics, and Indian Givers

Communication and Social Behavior
  Nonverbal Communication
  Speech and Social Context
  The Language of Power

Language and Culture
  Language as a Reflection of Culture
  Language, Perceptions, and Worldview

LEARNING OBJECTIVES

After reading this chapter, you should be able to

1. **EXPLAIN** why language is such a powerful means of communication, using five distinctive properties of human languages.
2. **DESCRIBE** how words are formed from combinations of discrete sounds.
3. **DESCRIBE** how Native American words affected English.
4. **DISCUSS** the modern-day global forces that result in the spread and survival of some languages and the contraction and possible extinction of others.
5. **EXPLAIN** some ways messages are communicated nonverbally and how speech is affected by social context.
6. **DESCRIBE** the Sapir-Whorf hypothesis and some of the controversies surrounding it.

As part of enculturation children socially learn one or more languages of their speech community. **Language** consists of the shared knowledge of sounds, words, meanings, and grammatical rules that people use to send and receive complex messages. Along with our dependence on culture, humanity's ability to communicate complex, precise information is the main mental capability that distinguishes humans from other animals.

Language and Humanity

Although we talk to or text people daily, we seldom consider how remarkable it is that we are able do so. As with culture, language is taken for granted, and most of us do not realize how unusual our communication skills are. (If you were a fish, would you know you are a good swimmer?)

The ability to speak, write, and comprehend the messages of language requires knowledge of an enormous number of linguistic units (sounds, words) and rules for combining them. Language and culture together are critical to the development of human individuals—without them, our psychological and social development is incomplete. In all probability, without them we would be unable to think, as the word *think* is generally understood. The thinking processes itself depend crucially on the knowledge of some language. Indeed, some scholars of language suggest that knowledge and use of a particular language conditions our minds to perceive nature and people in particular ways, thus shaping how we think about the world and things in it.

Not only is *Homo sapiens* the only animal capable of speech but we also are the only animal biologically evolved to speak and understand true language. Other animals certainly communicate. Male birds "sing" to announce territories and attract mates, as do some frogs and toads. Honeybees returning to their hive perform a waggle dance to tell hive mates the direction, distance, and quality of a food source. Other species of social insects like ants and termites have similar capabilities. Elephants, some whales and dolphins, gorillas, bonobos, and chimpanzees likewise perform impressive feats of communication.

However, only humans have language in its fully developed form. To understand what we mean by "fully developed," compare language to the communicative abilities of great apes. With the aid of intensive training from humans, chimpanzees and gorillas have learned to use sign language or to manipulate symbols standing for words and concepts into sentences. With no human interference, one chimp taught sign language to another and later they used it to communicate with one another. Despite these feats, no great ape is capable of answering this simple question: "What are your plans for next week?"

Language shaped humanity's biological evolution. Most obviously, this includes the speech regions of our brain. It also includes our vocal tract. The human *vocal tract* consists of the lungs, trachea (including the vocal cords as well as the "wind pipe"), mouth, and nasal passages. The vocal tract is biologically evolved for speech. It is a remarkable resonating chamber.

> **language** Shared knowledge of sounds, words, meanings, and grammatical rules used to send and receive messages.

Here are a few examples. You make different vowel sounds by raising and lowering the tongue or parts of the tongue. Changing the position of the tongue modifies the shape of the resonating chamber (commonly called the mouth) and produces sounds of different wavelengths which human ears recognize as different sounds. For example, compare where your tongue is for the vowel sounds as you say these words: *sit* and *set*, *far* and *fur*, *did* and *dad*, *teeth* and *tooth*. You pronounce most consonant sounds by interrupting the flow of air through the mouth. The initial sound of the word *tip* is formed by bringing the tip of the tongue into contact with the alveolar ridge just behind the teeth and then releasing the contact suddenly. You change *tip* to *sip* by blowing air through your mouth while almost, but not quite, touching the tip of your tongue to your alveolar ridge, thus making the initial sound a brief hissing noise. Try it and see for yourself.

Your vocal cords interact with your mouth to make distinct sounds. Either they vibrate and produce a buzzy sound (as in "mmmm"), or they remain open and allow air to flow into your mouth freely (contrast the sound *h* in *how* with the first *w* in *wow*). You change *tip* to *dip* by vibrating your vocal cords with the first sound of *dip*. The other vowels and consonants of English and other languages are made by articulating various parts of the vocal tract in contrasting ways.

You move all these parts of your vocal tract unconsciously with astonishing speed and precision. Each sound is possible because the vocal chamber formed by the mouth, throat, nasal passages, and the muscles of the tongue and lips are biologically evolved to allow us to produce it. There is a good reason chimpanzees cannot speak human words: their vocal tract is not evolved to do so. Yet, with training, any human can utter the sounds found in any language.

Language allows people to communicate about concrete persons, places, things, actions, and events. It allows communication and thought about abstract concepts as well. Among such abstractions are *truth, evil, god, masculinity, values, humanity, zero, law, jihad, universal, democracy, space,* and *hatred*. Humans all understand such abstractions. Indeed, without the ability to conceptualize such abstractions, culture as we experience it could not exist. Furthermore, our everyday behavior is greatly affected by contrasts that are abstract, such as *friend* and *enemy, beautiful* and *ugly, play* and *work*.

The social learning by which children acquire culture would be impossible without language. Because people share language, much of the knowledge in one person's mind can be transmitted into the mind of another person. During enculturation, not only do we learn "facts" and "lessons" about the world, but we also hear and stories and myths, whose lessons often are only implicit. These stories, myths, and other narratives become part of our identity, shape our relationships with other people, and help formulate the cultural constructions and worldviews of a people.

The Power of Language

Language is the most powerful known means of communication. This means that all languages have properties that allow *novel* and *complex* messages to be communicated *quickly*, *precisely*, in *several mediums*, and even if the people or events under discussion are *far away in space or time*.

Way back in 1960, linguist Charles Hockett identified 13 properties that distinguish language from the communication abilities of other animals. Five of Hockett's properties are especially important to demonstrate the power of language.

Discreteness

Discreteness means that when speaking people combine units (sounds and words) according to conventional rules. Knowing a language means knowing both the units and the rules for combining them. Words are composed of discrete units of sound (e.g., *j, u, m, p*) that are combined to communicate a meaning (*jump*). Similarly, we apply rules to combine units of meanings (words) to form sentences.

Discrete sounds are the essential units (metaphorically, they are the building blocks) of language. Discreteness makes alphabets possible. In alphabetic writing, people combine the letters of their alphabet to form printed words. Originally, each sound of the English alphabet was pronounced in a similar way in all the words in which it appeared. For example, the letter (sound) *t* appears in *student, textbook, eat,* and *today*.

In English writing, most letters no longer represent a single sound. The letter *a*, for example, is pronounced differently in the words *act, father, warden, assume,* and *nature*. Some single sounds in English are rendered in spelling as two letters, such as *th, ng,* and the *gh* in *rough* and *ghoul*. Why doesn't English spelling always reflect the way words are pronounced? Basically, because since the widespread use of the printing press, changes in English pronunciation have occurred faster than changes in spelling.

By themselves, most sounds carry no meaning. The three sounds in *cat*, for example, carry meaning only when strung together. When combined differently, they mean *act* and *tack*. Words, then, are composed of sound combinations that a speech community recognizes as conveying standardized meanings. Not all combinations of sounds are possible in a given language. For instance, in English, *mp, nt,* and *ld* are all possible combinations, but *pm, tn,* and *dl* are not (although these combinations are used by other languages).

Just as all languages use a small number of sounds to make a large number of words, so words are combined according to grammatical rules to convey the messages carried by sentences. By mastering their language's words and meanings, and the rules for combining words into sentences, speakers and listeners can send and receive messages of great complexity with amazing precision (e.g., "From that bowl of apples on your left, hand me the reddest one on the bottom").

Arbitrariness

The relationship between the sound combinations that make up words and the meanings these words communicate is *arbitrary*. The words and combinations of words (sentences) are symbols (see Chapter 2). Children learn to match certain sound combinations (words) with their meanings. By the age of one or two, most children have learned the meanings of dozens of words. They have mastered words that refer to objects (*ball*), animals (*doggie*), people (*mama*), sensory experiences (*hot*), qualities (*blue, hard*), actions (*eat, run*), commands (*no, come here*), emotions (*love*), and so forth. The child learns to associate meanings with words, even though the specific sound combinations that convey these various meanings have no inherent relationship to the things themselves. Because of the arbitrary relationship between meanings and words, our ability to communicate linguistic messages is based on shared conventions. As symbols, words can carry factual meanings ("look at trees") or meanings that are charged with emotion ("save the trees"), as discussed later.

Productivity

Productivity refers to a speaker's ability to create totally novel sentences and to a listener's ability to comprehend them. Productivity means that a language's finite number of words can be combined into an infinite number of meaningful sentences. The sentences are meaningful because the speaker and listener know what each word means individually and the rules by which they may be combined to convey messages. Although people routinely apply them each time they speak and hear, most people are not consciously aware of their knowledge of these rules. Unless you have linguistic training, you probably do not know that you form an English plural by adding one of *two* sounds (either *-z* or *-s*) to the end of a noun. For example, contrast the last sounds of *beans* and *beats*.

Displacement

Displacement refers to our ability to talk about objects, people, things, and events that are remote in time and space. Because language uses symbols (words and sentences) to transmit meanings, things and people do not have to be immediately visible for us to communicate about them. We can discuss someone who is out of sight because the symbols of language (in this case, a name) call that person to mind, allowing us to think about him or her. We can speculate about the future because, although its events may never happen, our language has symbols that stand for future time, and more symbols that allow us to form a mental image of possible events. We can learn about events that happened before we were born, such as wars in Korea and Vietnam. People can learn of events and things far away in space, such as fighting in Afghanistan, factories in China and India, oil spills in the Gulf of Mexico, tsunamis in Japan, mass homicides in Colorado and Connecticut, and explosions at the Boston Marathon.

The displacement property also makes it possible to describe things (like ghosts and zombies) and places (like Avatar and The Shire) that do not even exist. We can share stories about events that might not have really happened and thus create myths, fiction, legends, fairy tales, and folklore. Political leaders can mislead citizens, and be misled themselves, about weapons of mass destruction and terrorist connections in distant lands. Much that is familiar in human life depends on this important property—including the ability to lie.

Multimedia Potential

Unlike most other ways of communicating, language has *multimedia potential*, meaning that linguistic messages can be transmitted through a variety of media. When you speak, the medium for your message is speech, transmitted to the ears of your listeners by sound waves. Writing is the medium in which the messages of this book are transmitted. When you text relatives and friends, software converts the letters on your phone's keypad into a digital form that is transmitted in cyberspace into letters that another person can read and understand. Gestures and bodily movements are communications media that are received by the sense of sight rather than hearing. Hand and finger gestures media for the hearing impaired, as illustrated

CONCEPT REVIEW

Five Properties of Language

Discreteness — Units of sound and meaning are combined in various ways to communicate messages.

Arbitrariness — Meanings cannot be understood by people who do not know the language.

Productivity — A finite number of words are combined into an infinite number of sentences.

Displacement — Language allows the ability to discuss things, persons, and events remote in time and space.

Multimedia potential — Messages can be transmitted through many media (sound, print, sight, electronic).

---

by American Sign Language. Even touching and the resulting nerve signals can be a medium for language. Helen Keller, both blind and deaf, communicated and received linguistic messages by touch.

Of course, speech was the original medium for language. Beginning about 5,000 years ago, the ancient Sumerians developed writing. Egyptians developed their hieroglyphic system shortly afterwards. Chinese writing grew out of symbols incised into cattle scapula and the underside of tortoise shells. The ancient Mesoamerican peoples known as Zapotecs and Mayans carved meaningful symbols into stone pillars and walls, now recognized as yet another development of writing. In various ancient civilizations, writing was used to keep records of taxes, labor, oracles, the passage of time (calendars), and military conquests. Over several centuries, writing techniques spread to other regions such as the Greek islands, South Asia, Korea, Japan, and Western Europe. We take writing so much for granted that it is hard to imagine life without books and magazines, computers and the Internet, street signs and billboards, cell phones and texting, and various other "media."

The Concept Review summarizes these five important properties of language. Together, discreteness, arbitrariness, productivity, displacement, and multimedia potential make language the most precise and complete system of communication known among living things.

In brief, language is powerful. It makes abstract thought possible. It allows the fast and precise transmission of information from one individual and generation to another. It makes it possible to speculate about events that could possibly happen tomorrow if another set of events should happen to occur. We can learn about events that happened far away and long ago and events that didn't really happen at all. Language allows us to text, to say "I love you" when we don't mean it, to write and read fictional stories and novels, and to understand myths and legends. All these are things humans do so routinely that we consider them ordinary. But they are not ordinary: they are a human capacity that makes us distinctive from other animals.

How Language Works

When children learn language, they master an enormous amount of information. **Grammar** refers to all the knowledge shared by those who speak and understand a language: the sounds of the language, rules for combining sounds into sequences, meanings conveyed by these sequences, and how sentences are constructed by stringing words together according to precise rules.

Grammatical knowledge is *unconscious:* those who share a language cannot verbalize the knowledge that allows them to communicate with one another. It also is *intuitive:* speaking and understanding are automatic, and we ordinarily do not need to think about how to speak or understand linguistic messages.

This scientific use *of grammar* differs from the everyday use of the term. In everyday speech, some people judge others partly on the basis of whether others use "proper" grammar. In the English language and most others spoken by large numbers of people, there are several **dialects**, or variations in speech patterns, including in pronunciation and vocabulary. Dialects may be based on factors like region (e.g., England, Wales, the American South, Australia, Jamaica) or ethnic identification (e.g., Louisiana Creole, Black English,

---

grammar Total system of linguistic knowledge that allows speakers of a language to send messages that communicate messages to hearers.

dialects Variations in a single language based on factors such as region, subculture, ethnic identity, and socioeconomic class.

"Spanglish"). But speakers of English all understand one another, although sometimes with difficulty. In the United States, one American dialect, called *Standard American English* (SAE)—and it *is* a dialect, the one common in the national news media—is culturally accepted as most proper. Some of those whose dialect is SAE look down on those with other dialects, often based on differences in class, race, or educational levels.

Members of various ethnic and "racial" categories often have their own ways of pronouncing words or styles of speaking. Children learn dialects based on ethnic identity at a young age from family and friends. But there may be more to speaking a dialect than simply speaking the way you learned while growing up. In Canada and the United States, many African and Hispanic Americans adopt a speech style as a symbol of pride in their identity. To show they are cool, some young Anglos adopt phrases they hear from the media or from persons with African or Hispanic heritages. Hip-hop and rap have become mainstreamed because of their use of language as well as rhythm. In Hawaii, some Haoles use the word *brudda* to address native Hawaiians, thus demonstrating they know the local lingo.

Notice that there is no such thing as a superior and inferior dialect (or language) *in the linguistic sense.* That is, each language, and each dialect, is equally capable of serving as a vehicle for communicating the messages its speakers need to send and receive. So long as a person successfully communicates, there is no such thing as "bad grammar" or people who "don't know proper grammar." If Jennifer says, "I ain't got no shoes," you will have a different impression of her than if she says, "I have no shoes." But the first Jennifer's speech is perfectly good English— to members of certain subcultures who speak one English dialect. If speakers communicate their intended meaning to listeners, then the words they use or the ways they construct their sentences are as valid linguistically as any other. The evaluations we make of someone else's grammar or overall style of speech, then, are *cultural* evaluations. They are based on some people's cultural norms of correct grammar, conceptions about the kinds of people who speak in a certain way, and so forth.

With this point about the equality of languages and dialects in mind, here we briefly cover two aspects of grammar: (1) sounds and their patterning, and (2) sound combinations and their meanings.

Sound Systems

When we speak, our vocal tract emits a string of sounds. The sounds of a language, together with the way these sounds occur in regular and consistent patterns, make up the *phonological system* of the language. The study of sound systems is called **phonology**.

The particular sounds that speakers of a language recognize as distinct from other sounds are called **phonemes**. Phonemes are individual sounds that make a difference in the meanings of words. Linguists use slash marks / / to show that a particular sound is a phoneme in a given language. Thus, a few English consonants are /f/, /t/, /b/, /n/, /z/, and /1/. Some English vowels are /a/, /i/ (pronounced "ee"), /o/, and /u/. Thus, words consist of a string of phonemes, like /mi/ and /yu/ (although there is an *o* in the way we spell *you*, phonologically the "o" is absent).

Of course, languages have different phonemes, and the phonemes of some do not appear in others. If you know Spanish, then you know that /v/ does not exist in that language, which is why native speakers of Spanish may pronounce *very* as *berry*. Japanese has no /l/ or /r/ sound, which is why Japanese people have trouble distinguishing them when they speak English. On the other hand, the Japanese language distinguishes sounds that English does not. Japanese has double consonant sounds that make a difference in the meanings of words, like /t/ versus /tt/ or /p/ versus /pp/. Thus (using English spelling), *kite* means "come" and *kitte* means "stamp," which is one reason Japanese can be hard for many foreigners to pronounce correctly.

Furthermore, differences that one language recognizes in sounds are not always recognized in other languages. English speakers hear differences between consonants that are voiced (your vocal cords vibrate to make a buzzy sound, as in /v/) and voiceless (your vocal cords do not vibrate, as in /f/). Thus, in English, *vat* and *fat* are different words, as are *bat* and *pat.* But in Kosraen, a language of Micronesia, the sound differences between /v/ and /f/, /d/ and /t/ , /b/ and /p/, and /g/ and /k/ make no difference in meaning. It is as if English speakers could not distinguish between *veal* and *feel*, between *dan* and *tan*, between *big* and *pig,* and between *got* and *cot.* In English, whether a consonant is voiced or voiceless makes a different in the meanings of words in which they occur; in Kosraen, it does not.

One of the most interesting ways languages differ in phonology is using the pitch of the voice to convey

---

phonology Study of the sound system of language.

phoneme Smallest unit of sound that speakers unconsciously recognize as distinctive from other sounds; when one phoneme is substituted for another in a morpheme, the meaning of the morpheme alters.

As they are growing up, these children are learning the four tones of their native language, Chinese.

meaning. (The *pitch* of a voice depends on how fast the vocal cords vibrate: the higher the frequency of vibration, the higher the pitch of the voice.) English speakers use pitch to convey different meanings, as you can see by contrasting the following sentences:

She's going home.

She's going home?

The first statement is turned into a question by altering the pitch of the voice. In the question, the pitch rises with the word *home*.

Speakers of English use pitch changes over the whole sentence to communicate a message; that is, the voice pitch falls or rises mainly between words, rather than within a word. There are many other languages in which a high, medium, or low pitch used within an individual word, or even in a syllable, changes the fundamental meaning of the word.

Languages in which the pitch (or tone) with which a word is said (or changes in the voice pitch during its pronunciation) affects the meaning of a word are known as **tone languages**. Tone languages are widespread in Africa and in southeastern and eastern Asia. Chinese, Thai, Burmese, and Vietnamese are all tone languages (Japanese and Korean are not), which is one more reason most Canadians, French, and Germans have trouble mastering these languages. As an example of how pitch can affect meaning, consider these words from Nupe, an African tone language:

bá (high tone) to be sour

bā (mid tone) to cut

bà (low tone) to count

Here, whether *ba* is pronounced with a high, mid, or low tone changes its meaning. Because the tone with which a word is pronounced changes its meaning, the pitch of the voice is a kind of phoneme in tone languages. It has the same effect as adding /s/ in front of the English word *pot*, which totally alters its meaning to *spot*.

Words and Meanings

Words are combinations of phonemes to which people attach conventional meanings. Any language contains a finite number of words, each matched to one or more meanings.

Morphology is the study of meaningful sound sequences and the rules by which they are formed. Any

---

tone languages Languages in which changing voice pitch within a word alters the meaning of the word.

morphology Study of the units of meaning in language.

sequence of phonemes that carries meaning is known as a **morpheme**. Why not just call them "words"? Because in analyzing meanings, morphologists need a more precise concept than *word*. For example, you know the meanings of the following sound sequences, none of which is itself a word:

un	ed
pre	s
non	ing
anti	ist

Both the prefixes in the first column and the suffixes in the second alter the meaning of certain other morphemes when they are attached to them.

Sound sequences like these are "detachable" from particular words. For instance, adding the suffix *-ist* to *art* and *novel* creates new meanings: "a person who creates art" and "one who writes novels." That *-ist* has a similar meaning whenever it is a suffix is shown by the made up word *crim*; by adding *-ist* to it, you instantly know that a *crimmist* is "a person who crims."

To analyze such compound words and their meanings, linguists have a concept that includes prefixes and suffixes such as *uni-, -ing,* and *-ly*. There are two kinds of morphemes in all languages. **Free morphemes** are any morphemes that can stand alone as words—for example, *desire, possible, health, complete, anthropology,* and *establish*. **Bound morphemes** are attached to free morphemes to modify their meanings in predictable ways—for example, *dis-, bi-, un-, -er, -ly,* and *-ed*. Thus, by adding bound morphemes to the free morphemes in our examples, we get the following:

desires	desirable	undesirable
possible	impossible	impossibility
healthy	healthful	unhealthy
completed	incomplete	uncompleted
establishing	establishment	antiestablishment
anthropologist	anthropologically	nonanthropologist

Just as phonemes are a language's minimal units of sound, morphemes are the minimal units of meaning. Thus, we cannot break down the free morphemes *friend, vocabulary, linguistics,* and *soccer* into any smaller units that carry meaning in modern English. Nor can we break down the bound morphemes *non-, -ish,* and *tri-* into any smaller meaningful units.

We make new compound words by applying a rule of compound-word formation, not by learning each compound word separately. For instance, take the English rule for forming a plural noun from a singular noun. It is usually done by adding either the bound morpheme /z/, as in *beads, colors,* and *eggs*; or /s/, as in *lamps, steaks,* and *pots*—all meaning "more than one." Children learn the rule for plural formation at an early age, but it takes them a while longer to learn the many exceptions. Adults think it's cute when children apply the morphological rules of English consistently to all words, saying "childs," "mans," "foots," "mouses," and "deers" for plurals and using "goed," "runned," "bringed," and "doed" to make a present-tense verb into a past-tense verb. But children are born with the mental capability to deduce rules of sound and word combinations from their speech community, so are merely applying the rules they have deduced from many other words.

Of all linguistic elements, free morphemes are most easily transmissible across different languages. Speakers often do not know how much of their native vocabulary is more mutt-like rather than purebred. For example, English has taken lots of words that did not exist in its Germanic origins, as the next section discusses.

Germanics, Romantics, and Indian Givers

When peoples who speak different languages come into contact, one or both groups often incorporate ("borrow") foreign words. Incorporation is especially likely to happen if one language's words have no counterparts in the other, as is often the case for nouns and verbs. Because of the spread of world trade and political systems during the last five centuries, English words have spread widely into other languages. Japanese and Korean have incorporated hundreds of English words, many from the realm of technology and commodities. In France, the use of English words became such a hot political issue that the government outlawed the "importation" of further English words.

However, English speakers should not become too proud of the spread of "their" words. English itself is a member of the Germanic subfamily of languages, along with Dutch, German, Norwegian, Icelandic, Swedish, Danish, and Afrikaans. Between two and

---

morpheme Combination of phonemes that communicates a standardized meaning.

free morphemes Morphemes that can be used alone.

bound morphemes Morphemes attached to a free morpheme to alter its meaning.

three thousand years ago, all these languages were a single language, which linguists call proto-Germanic. As the Germanic peoples migrated to different regions, the proto-Germanic languages diverged until separate languages existed. As a result of the divergence modern speakers of the various modern Germanic languages can no longer understand one another. Although classified in the Germanic subfamily, over the centuries English adopted hundreds of words from the Romance languages, which include French, Spanish, Portuguese, Italian, and Romanian. These languages originated out of Latin. As the Roman Empire spread throughout much of Europe, people who spoke Germanic or other local languages incorporated words from their Roman overlords. Many of these words are cognates, as English speakers who study modern languages like Spanish and French recognize.

Far less recognized is the fact that early English colonists who settled in the Americas adopted lots of words from Native Americans—words that are now "English."

The earliest European settlers of eastern North America came from the British Isles. Except for French-speaking Quebec and parts of California, Texas, and the Southwest, most citizens of Canada and the United States speak English as their native language. Few of us know about the influence of the original native languages—those spoken by Native Americans—on English vocabulary. Many familiar English words, phrases, and place names are derived from one or another Native American language.

The earliest Spanish and Portuguese explorers were surprised at how many of the plants and animals in the "New World" (North and South America and the Caribbean) were unknown to them. A few animals, such as deer and wolves, were enough like familiar European fauna that European words were applied to them. Others, however, had no European counterparts. Terms taken from North American Indian languages were adopted for many of these, including *cougar, caribou, condor, moose, raccoon, chipmunk, opossum, skunk, woodchuck,* and *chigger.* Other "English" terms for animals are taken from the languages of South American peoples: *condor, piranha, tapir, toucan, jaguar, alpaca, vicuna,* and *llama.* Plants, too, were unfamiliar, and Native American words were adopted for *saguaro, yucca, mesquite, persimmon, hickory,* and *pecan,* to name only some of the most common derivatives.

As we discuss in Chapter 7, Indians of the Americas were the first to domesticate numerous food plants that now have worldwide importance. All the following crop names have Native American origins: *squash, maize, guava, hominy, avocado, tapioca* (also called *manioc* and *cassava,* both words also taken from native languages), *pawpaw, succotash, tomato,* and *potato.* Indian words for natural features other than plants and animals also were adopted by European immigrants: *bayou, muskeg, savanna, pampas, hurricane,* and *chinook.* Terms in various Native American languages for clothing, housing, and other material objects have made it into English: *igloo, tepee, wigwam, moccasin, parka, poncho, toboggan, husky, canoe, kayak,* and *tomahawk. Caucus* and *powwow,* for meetings, are two other English words with native origins. If you still smoke, it's good to know that the plant *tobacco* is from the New World, as is the name.

People everywhere name geographical locations. The earliest European settlers often named American places to honor important people in their home countries—for example, Charleston, Albuquerque, Columbus, Carolina, and Virginia (the latter named after the supposed condition of England's Queen Elizabeth I). Other American place names are derived from European geography—Nova Scotia (new Scotland), New Hampshire, Maine (a province in France), and, of course, New York and New England.

Native American peoples had their own names for places and landscape features, and often these names were the ones that endured and appear on modem maps. River names with Indian origins include Mississippi, Ohio, Yukon, Missouri, Arkansas, Wabash, Potomac, Klamath, Minnesota, and Mohawk, to mention just a few of the most familiar. The lakes called Huron, Ontario, Michigan, Oneida, Tahoe, and Slave have Indian names, as do hundreds of other bodies of water in Canada and the United States. Whole states are named after Indian peoples, such as the Illini, Massachuset, Ute, Kansa, and Dakota, whereas names of other states and provinces are derived from native words, such as Manitoba, Ontario, Saskatchewan, Texas, Oklahoma, Ohio, Minnesota, Iowa, and Nebraska. A few large cities with names derived from Indian languages are Tuscaloosa, Tallahassee, Natchez, Tulsa, Cheyenne, Miami, Chicago, Saskatoon, Ottawa, and Omaha. Seattle was named after a particular Indian leader, Seal'th, of the West Coast. Finally, the names of two whole countries on the North American continent have Indian roots *Kanata* (Canada) is an Iroquoian word meaning "village" (although it now is applied to a much larger community). The area formerly known as New Spain took the word the rulers of the Aztec civilization used for themselves—*Mexica*—after winning its independence in 1823.

In sum, many "English" words and place names have "Indian" origins. More generally, the languages people consider *native* to their region or country usually are a product of historical contacts and interactions. Our time perspectives—how far into the past we go when we think about language—are too short to recognize connections between our "native" tongue and other tongues.

Growth in the intensity of economic globalization and global contacts in the last several decades have had a multitude of impacts on the world's languages and their survival, as discussed in Global Challenges and Opportunities (pp. 58–59).

Communication and Social Behavior

Anthropological linguists are interested in how language is related to a people's way of life—their cultural knowledge and behavioral patterns. One topic is how language is *used* when people with different roles interact with one another. Even when our voices are silent, we send messages by body language and facial expressions, both of which are enormously important in conveying emotions and intentions. Also, language itself is only one way people send messages to one another. We begin with this topic: nonverbal communication.

Nonverbal Communication

People send and receive messages using more than just phonemes, morphemes, and sentences. Facial expressions allow people to read one another. We also routinely send both conscious (intentional) and unconscious (implicit) messages by how we move our bodies or parts of our bodies. *Kinesics* studies the role of bodily motions in communication. We also can convey feelings and other emotions and messages by touching another person.

Some nonverbal facial expressions convey the same messages among all peoples, so presumably are part of *Homo sapiens'* biological heritage. Pleasure, sadness, anger, puzzlement, and some other emotional responses are shown by similar facial expressions everywhere and convey similar meanings universally. Notice, though, that people sometimes use facial expressions to deceive, as with phony smiles and feigned anger. Also, frequently a given facial expression is normatively appropriate (like a smile in greeting someone), so the expression occurs regardless of the actual internal emotional state of the person.

People also communicate nonverbally by using space, here meaning how closely persons who are interacting space themselves apart when standing or sitting or walking. *Proxemics* studies the meanings conveyed by space and distance. Edward Hall, who pioneered the field of proxemics with his books *The Silent Language* and *The Hidden Dimension,* noted that in the United States people communicate messages by how far apart they stand or sit while interacting. There is intimate distance (up to about 18 inches), personal distance (more than 2 feet to 4 feet), and social distance (over 4 feet), the latter applying mainly to formal situations. (Try violating these conventions by standing a bit too close to an acquaintance; just be sure to do so in an area where the person can back away from you.) It is usually offensive or a sign of aggression "to get in someone's face," as illustrated by barroom quarrels and player-umpire altercations.

Like speech, most forms of nonverbal communication are symbolic: a particular bodily motion or distance does not inherently convey a certain message but does so only because of conventions, or common understandings. Because much nonverbal communication is arbitrary and conventional, there is great potential for misunderstanding when people do not share understandings about nonverbal messages—that is, when people have learned different conventions. Probably the potential for misunderstanding is even greater with nonverbal messages than for spoken language. When "foreigners" converse, both people generally know that they don't understand the other's language, so at least they are aware of their ignorance. However, both are more likely to think they understand nonverbal messages, so they might give or take offense when none is intended.

Miscommunication is especially likely with touching, the unspoken rules for which vary greatly from people to people and even from individual to individual. On one Micronesian island, married, engaged, or romantically involved couples rarely walk hand in hand in public, although close friends of the same sex frequently do so (carrying no implication of sexual preference). Touching someone on the head—including what North Americans consider an affectionate rub or friendly pat—is offensive. In Korea and Japan, women often affectionately walk holding hands or with their arms around one another.

Some scholars who study nonverbal communication distinguish "low-touch" and "high-touch" cultures. Such dichotomies are usually simplistic, but it is true that cultures vary greatly in how they define situations in which touching is normatively desirable or appropriate. There is often an implicit power dimension to physical contact as well: high-status people are much more likely to affectionately touch subordinates than the reverse—affectionate (or "phony affectionate") touching symbolizes familiarity, and touching by lower-status individuals is often seen as "too familiar."

Similar ideas apply to the use of space. Again, the possibilities for miscommunication are great when people with different cultural upbringings interact. Sometimes Middle Easterners or Latin Americans stand too close for North Americans' comfort zones. Simply becoming aware that cultural norms about body motions, touching, distance, and so forth differ from people to people can help us all avoid taking offense when none is intended. In a world where international migration, tourism, global business, and other forms of intercultural contact are exploding, awareness of such differences is both personally useful and socially valuable.

Speech and Social Context

During enculturation, children learn how to communicate appropriately in given social situations. Different situations require different verbal and nonverbal behavior because how you speak and act varies with whom you are talking to, who else is listening, and the overall situation in which the interaction is occurring. Much speech behavior is an aspect of the role a person takes on relative to other people such as friends, bosses, children, siblings, and teachers. When you want to make a good impression at a job or admissions interview, what you say and how you say it might matter greatly.

To speak appropriately, people must take the total context into account. First, they must know the various situations, or social scenes, of their culture: which are solemn, which are celebrations, which are formal versus informal, which are argumentative, and so on. Cultural knowledge includes knowing how to alter one's total (including verbal) behavior to fit these situations. Second, individuals must recognize the kinds of interactions they are expected to have with others with whom they have particular relationships, which is connected to their social roles. Should they act lovingly, jokingly, contemptuously, or respectfully and deferentially toward someone else?

sociolinguistics Specialty within cultural anthropology that studies how language is related to culture and the social uses of speech.

These two elements—the particular culturally defined situation and the specific individuals who are parties to the interaction—make up the *social context* of verbal and nonverbal behavior. The field of **sociolinguistics** studies how speech behavior is affected by social context.

Terms of address are a familiar example of how speech both reveals and reinforces the nature of a social relationship. Calling someone by a first name or a title like "doctor" varies with the social context. Higher-ranking people are more likely to address lower-ranking individuals by their first name, or even by their last name used alone. Not only does this nonreciprocal use of address terms reflect social inequality, but it also reminds people of it each time they speak. Spanish speakers have a similar understanding with polite address terms such as *Don* or *Señora*. They also have to choose between two words for *you:* the formal (*usted*) or the informal (*tu*), depending mainly on relative status.

Speech style and habits depend on status and rank in other ways. For example, in the old days there were greater differences between the speech of men and women in North America than today, as in the use of profanity and words like *adorable* and *lovely*. In modern times, there are fewer differences between women's and men's vocabularies, largely as a consequence of the women's movement and the influence of popular media. Even today, though, some people make judgments about a stranger's class background or sexual orientation by how he or she speaks.

Other cultures exhibit customs in speech behavior with which most English-speaking people are unfamiliar. Here are just three examples:

- In parts of Polynesia and Micronesia, there used to be a special *respect language,* with which common people had to address members of the noble class. On some islands, the respect language had not only a different speech style but also different words. Often there were severe penalties for commoners who erred in addressing a noble, including beatings or worse if the offender was judged to have been intentionally disrespectful or challenging.

- In Korean and Japanese, a complicated set of contextual norms (called *honorifics*) governs the degree of formality and politeness people normally use to show respect to those of higher social position. For instance, verbs and personal pronouns have alternative forms that speakers must choose between in addressing others.

Relative status is the main determinant of which form to use. In Japanese, one verb form is used when the speaker is of higher status than the listener, another form when the two are of roughly equal status, and yet another when the speaker is a social inferior. Japanese and Koreans use different forms of personal pronouns (like *I* and *you*) to reflect the relative status of the parties. For example, when a social superior is addressing an inferior, he or she often does not use the pronoun *I* as a self-reference but instead refers to his or her status relative to the person being addressed. For instance, a higher-status person may say "Look at teacher" instead of "Look at me," or "Listen to father" instead of "Listen to me." Reciprocally, one usually does not use the pronoun *you* with one of higher status but replaces it with a term denoting the superior's social position—for example, "What would teacher like me to do now?" and "Would father like me to visit?" Confused foreigners trying to learn the subtleties of Korean and Japanese speech etiquette are usually advised to use the honorific forms to avoid giving offense unintentionally. Today, to a large extent, knowing how to speak is a matter of politeness and decorum, but in traditional Korea and Japan, honorific speech was socially and even legally enforced.

- All societies have customs of taboo, meaning that some behavior is prohibited for religious reasons or because it is culturally regarded as immoral, improper, or offensive. There are linguistic taboos also. For instance, the Yanomamö of the Venezuelan rain forest have a custom known as *name taboo*. It is an insult to utter the names of important people and of deceased relatives in the presence of their living kinfolk. So the Yanomamö sometimes give names like "toenail of sloth" or "whisker of howler monkey" to children, so that when the person dies, people will not have to watch their language so closely. Other name taboos are enforced only against specific individuals. Among the Zulu of southern Africa, for example, a woman was once forbidden to use the name of her husband's father or any of his brothers.

Norms partly explain why people's use of language varies with social context—you are not expected to act and speak the same way at a party as you do in church or at work, for instance, and you are enculturated to know intuitively and unconsciously how to adjust your behavior to these different contexts.

The choice of speech style, words, and phrases is governed by more than just norms, however. People have personal goals, and speaking in a certain way can help them get what they want. In everyday life, we strive to present the image of ourselves that we want someone else to perceive. The opinions that employers, friends, lovers and hoped-for lovers, coworkers, roommates, and even parents have of us depend partly on how we speak—our use of certain words and avoidance of others, the degree of formality of our style, whether we try to hide or to accentuate regional dialects, and so forth. How we speak is an important part of what social scientists call our *presentation of self*. It is part of how we try to control other people's opinions of us.

Like other ways we present ourselves—including the jewelry we wear, how we sit and walk, how we design our hair or shave our head, where and what tattoos to place on our bodies—the way we speak is part of the way we tell others what kind of a person we are. Almost without knowing it, we adjust our speech style, mannerisms, and body language to manage the impressions other people have of us. Our cultural knowledge of these adjustments is mostly routine and usually unconscious—except perhaps at events like job interviews or public speeches.

The Language of Power

We noted earlier that language is "powerful," allowing people to communicate complex messages precisely and efficiently. Used strategically, language is powerful in another sense, that of influence or persuasion. By controlling *discourse*—what is talked about and how it is discussed in the public arena—individuals and groups attempt to control opinions. Those who control the content of messages potentially control the information available to other people. Because human emotional reactions, thought processes, and behavioral responses depend largely on information, language potentially is an instrument of power.

Political speech obviously employs language of power. Professional consultants advise politicians on what (and what not) to say and how to say it to increase political advantage. Here are a few recent examples of language use in an attempt to control political discourse:

- On abortion: Is it "murder," or does a woman have "the right to choose," and how much does this answer depend on whether "human life begins at conception" or somewhere later in pregnancy?

GLOBAL CHALLENGES AND OPPORTUNITIES

Globalization and Language

Commercial relations, international travel, entertainment media, and other connections increase contacts between nations. Learning a language other than one's native tongue is increasingly useful—and economically valuable.

Migration is one of the most important patterns in humanity's past. When people move to a new region, they carry lots of "baggage"—not just their possessions, but also their genes, cultures, and languages. Until several hundred years ago, migration was the main way languages spread to new regions.

Among the largest-scale migrations are those that brought the bodies, cultures, and languages of western Europeans to the Americas, which to the Europeans was a New World. As a consequence of this migration, a large number of the several hundred indigenous languages of North and South America disappeared between the 1500s and the 1900s. The people who spoke them either died out from new diseases and violence or became linguistically assimilated into whichever European ethnic group came into political and economic dominance. Today, the vast majority of people who live in the Americas speak English, Spanish, Portuguese, or French. Most of those born into some indigenous Native American community also speak one of these four languages as their first or second language.

At the global level, no one knows how many of the languages that existed a few hundred years ago are extinct today. A recent estimate is that between 4,000 and 9,000 languages have disappeared since the fifteenth century. In some cases, as among Native North Americans and many Australian aborigines, the main reason for linguistic extinction was the biological extinction of the speakers from disease and violence. In other cases, although the people whose ancestors once spoke their own language are alive today, the languages have died as the groups became assimilated culturally and linguistically into their nation's majority. For example, in the late nineteenth and early twentieth century in the United States, the federal government opened dozens of "Indian Schools." Native American children were removed from their families and reservations (forcefully, if "necessary") and placed in Anglo educational surroundings where they usually were forbidden from speaking in their Native tongues.

To see how a language can wither away over several generations, consider the languages of immigrants. Some second- and third-generation immigrants continue to know the language of their ancestral land, but after that few descendants are likely to speak it. Once a language is no longer spoken in the home, it takes a conscious and dedicated effort to learn it, and over time fewer and fewer children will do so. If children are exposed to only the majority language in formal school settings as well as in their peer groups, their chances of learning the language of their ancestors dwindles. Only if there is an entire community of speakers—who use the language among themselves, who serve as linguistic models for young children, and who reward youngsters for speaking it well—is a language likely to survive. In present-day North America, the Amish are one such community, as are various big-city Chinatowns, Koreatowns, and numerous Latino, Persian, and Arab communities. Cities like Vancouver, San Francisco, and Los Angeles include tens of thousands of Chinese who form enclaves where Cantonese or Mandarin is spoken as the first language. There are other less well known linguistic communities, such as the Hmong (refugees from Southeast Asia who were resettled in the United States in the 1980s), South Asians (in California's Silicon Valley and many other cities), and Somalis (in central Ohio).

A rich source of statistical information on the world's language is SIL International's Ethnologue. com. According to Ethnologue's 2013 website, there are about 7,100 languages in existence, of which nearly 4,500 are spoken in Asia and Africa. The Asian continent—which contains two-fifths of the Earth's land surface and three-fifths of its people—has thousands of languages, but most are very localized. In fact, more than half of Asia's languages have fewer than 10,000 speakers. In Canada and the United States, about 300 indigenous (Native American) languages are still spoken. This sounds like a high number, but almost 100 of them have only a few elderly speakers and so are likely to be gone soon. Ethnologue reports that 377 languages have become extinct just since 1950—a rate of 6 languages per year.

Ethnologue breaks down endangered languages into categories, according the degree to which they are endangered. One category is languages "In Trouble," meaning that parents still speak it but increasingly do not teach it to their children. About 1,500 (21 percent) of world languages are in this category. Another category is "dying" languages, those in which the only living speakers are older than childbearing age. More than 900 (13 percent) of languages fall into this category. It is likely that one-fifth or even one-fourth of languages will disappear in the next 50 years if the history of languages repeats itself.

Unlike in the past, few people today are actually forced to give up their indigenous language. However, modern-day globalization affects the survival of languages. When representatives from companies speaking different languages make deals, either they need to use translators or someone has to learn the other's language. When people on remote Pacific islands or in mountain villages of Southeast Asia rent DVDs or search the Internet, they are exposed to new languages. Globalization thus promotes the success of a few languages—namely, those used for communication in the global arena. Over time, communication in one of these languages becomes more and more useful. If, at the same time, the linguistic community that once sustained the local language is disintegrating, the local language is likely to become endangered.

Today Mandarin has more native speakers than any other language, around 850 million. Spanish has the second-most native speakers (406 million), followed by English (335 million), Hindi (260 million), and Arabic (223 million). However, English is now the language most widely used in worldwide commerce, the international mass media, and globally popular culture. More than any other single language, English is learned as a second language in diverse countries from Japan to Mexico. In fact, far more people now speak English as their second language than as their first language. In places like southern Asia and the Pacific, where there are many hundreds of localized indigenous languages, English is usually the *lingua franca*—the language that people learn as their second language so that they can communicate widely with one another. And English nouns are commonly used for modern objects and technology.

Although English is the language most commonly used in international politics and marketing, the English-speaking world also is responding to global changes. In the 1970s and 1980s, the West feared competition from "Japan, Inc.," and American colleges hired Japanese language teachers. The global reach of Japanese popular culture—*anime, manga, sushi,* horror films—continues to make Japanese "cool" to many young people. In the 1990s and 2000s, China's annual economic growth rate of around 10 percent and its rising importance in international affairs led to the expansion of Chinese language programs in North America and Europe. In many American colleges, German and French instruction withered as enrollments in Chinese boomed. In 2012, the Korean pop star Psy released a music video that has received over 1.6 billion views on YouTube. "K-pop" is big in Japan, China, North America, and Europe. Perhaps Korean will soon become a hot second language.

That English is so widely spoken as a second language is a result of the history of British colonialism and the twentieth-century economic and political dominance of the United States in world affairs. It is certainly not because English is a superior language or because it is easy to learn as a second language. Some countries known for their strong national identity resent the influx of English words—notably France, which actually has laws against the use of certain English words.

Some think that eventually the world's peoples will all speak only a few languages. For example, in his 2003 book *Language in Danger,* Andrew Dalby predicted that within the next couple hundred years, only about 200 languages will survive. Surviving languages will include those like English and Spanish that are now in global use as well as others that are or will become the national languages of their countries. All indigenous languages will be gone, including languages like Irish and Welsh.

But perhaps not. In many regions, people want to reaffirm their national or ethnic identities, and learning to speak the ancestral language of their homelands is one symbolic means of doing so. Schools in Wales now require Welsh. The desire to preserve the language of one's native land is a mark of national or ethnic identity. It is a symbol of a political or social commitment to the broader goal of preserving identities.

Thus, speaking a particular language can do more than send the messages encoded in words and sentences. With the spread of globalization, speaking a native tongue can tell people that you are proud to be who you are. In Europe, many people learn several languages because languages are emphasized in schools and because so many Europeans travel widely on their continent. Such multilingualism is almost certainly a positive force in the world. Perhaps more American school districts should realize that learning "foreign languages" is not a costly luxury in today's world.

- On immigrants: You can tell how a politician feels by whether she talks about "no amnesty for illegal immigrants," or wants to provide "a path to citizenship for undocumented workers."
- On steep inheritance taxes: Those who oppose taxing the enormous estates of wealthy people are not in favor of the "death tax," while those who favor taxation speak of "equal opportunities."
- On gun control: Opposing groups speak of the "right to bear arms" guaranteed by the "Second Amendment," contrasted to massacres such as those in Colorado and Connecticut for which the "gun lobby" bears "partial responsibility." The Second Amendment to the U.S. Constitution reads, "A well-regulated militia, being necessary to the existence of a free State, the right of the people to keep and bear arms shall not be infringed." Should the "well-regulated" phrase be emphasized over the "right . . . shall not be infringed"?

Strategic use of speech happens most intensively during elections. Candidates and parties choose words that arouse positive emotions and attachments to themselves and their programs. In the United States, phrases like "socialist" and "socialized medicine," "tax and spend," "big government," "national security," and "personal freedom" resonate with most conservatives, who say that increasing taxes on the wealthiest is to tax "job creators." Liberal leaders favor "working people," "environmental protection," and "universal health coverage." They speak of "giant corporations" with their "fat cat CEOs." Both parties use the phrase "the American people want (need)" as often as possible, although in reality few Americans want and need precisely the same things as the rest of Americans. Every leader uses phrases like "strengthen the middle class," "protect families," "grow the economy," and "jobs, jobs, jobs." Climate change legislation is a "job killer" for some and a "surefire job creator" to others.

During primary elections, competing candidates often try to capture their party's most extreme voters, reasoning that party moderates will vote for them anyway. In the 2012 Republican presidential primaries, Mitt Romney's advisors worried that the candidate was too moderate to win enough votes from Republican religious and social conservatives. Mr. Romney emphasized that his Mormon faith was a mainstream Christian denomination and firmed up his opposition to emotional issues abortion and gay marriage in his speeches and debates.

However, such strategies are hazardous when the general election rolls around. Words and phrases that win primaries by appealing to the left or right wing at

Japanese honorifics include rules about formality and politeness, many of which are related to the relative status of the individuals interacting.

state primaries are then used to portray a candidate as "too extreme." One reason people mistrust politicians is their double-speak. They say one thing to one group, something else to another group. They back off from their primary statements during the general election campaign. Of course they do: in order to win, they must appeal to one constituency during the primaries and to a broader constituency during the general.

Why is the strategic use of words, phrases, slogans, and the like so important to politicians and their campaigns? The simplest answer is correct but is only part of the story: they must counter the appeal of their rivals and get enough of their own supporters to the polls to win elections. The rest of the story, though, is that effective language use—the kind that arouses emotions, plays to differences, emphasizes values, calls on patriotic impulses, and the like—saves them from having to reveal details of what they will actually do should they be elected. Solving a complicated country's complicated problems is a tough job. If failure occurs, though, "we inherited this mess from the other party," which "wants us to fail" (which, by the way, was actually stated by the leader of the Senate soon after Barack Obama's election in 2008).

Language and Culture

Another interest of anthropological linguists is how the culture a people share is connected to the language they speak. This topic can be technical, so in this section we focus on only two areas that might tie language and culture together. First, some parts of language reflect social relationships and the importance people culturally attach to different things or categories. Second, it is possible that language shapes a people's perception of reality and even their entire worldview.

Language as a Reflection of Culture

Most anthropological fieldworkers try to learn the language of the community in which they work. For one thing, speaking in the local language facilitates interaction and may help create relationships of trust. But fieldworkers also know that learning language helps them understand the local culture because many aspects of a people's language reflect their culture.

For instance, a complex classification tends to develop around things that are especially important to a community. If people frequently communicate about objects, qualities, actions, or persons, they are likely to have many names or labels for them and to divide and subdivide them into many detailed categories. Occupational differences illustrate the point. A professional mechanic or carpenter identifies hundreds of different tools, whereas the Saturday-afternoon home mechanic or handy spouse identifies several dozen. Attorneys must master a complex vocabulary that other people sometimes call *legalese*. Numerous other examples could be cited, but there are no surprises here.

What about differences *between* whole languages, spoken by members of *different* cultures? Similar ideas apply. To understand them, the concept of **semantic domain** is useful. A semantic domain is a set of words that belongs to an inclusive class. For example, *chair, table, ottoman,* and *china cabinet* belong to the semantic domain of "furniture."

In a similar way, different languages vary in the semantic domains they identify, in how finely they carve up these domains, and in how they make distinctions between different members of a domain. Some differences are obvious. For instance, tropical lowland peoples are not likely to have semantic domains like "snow" or "ice" in their native language, whereas some Arctic peoples have an elaborate vocabulary about snow and ice conditions. Furthermore, the degree to which some semantic domain has a multilevel hierarchical structure depends on the importance of the objects or actions in people's lives: island, coastal, or riverine people dependent on fish are likely to have many categories and subcategories of aquatic life, fishing methods, and flood and tide stages, for instance. Can we go beyond such fairly obvious statements?

For some domains, we can. Some things or qualities seem "natural," meaning that the elements in the semantic domain appear obvious to anyone. Distinctions even seem inherent in the things themselves. We therefore expect that people everywhere would construct these domains in similar ways. For instance, the wavelength and amount of light reflected from an object determine its color, so color is an inherent (natural) quality of a thing. Blue, green, and other colors reflect different wavelengths, but not every language recognizes the same wavelengths with names for colors.

Likewise, biological kinship is a natural relationship, in the sense that who an infant's parents are determines who will and will not be the baby's genetic relatives.

"Obviously" aunts and uncles are different kinds of relatives from parents. But not all peoples recognize such differences and make them culturally significant, which means that "relatives" is not entirely a natural semantic domain.

Consider the relatives that English-speaking people call *aunt, first cousin,* and *brother*. An aunt is a sister of your mother or father; a first cousin is a child of any of your aunts and uncles; and a brother is a male child of your parents. These individuals are all biologically related to you differently, so "naturally" you place them into different categories and call them by different terms.

But other distinctions are possible that you do not recognize as distinctions and that are not reflected in the kinship terms you use. Not all your aunts are related to you in the same way: some are sisters of your mother; others are sisters of your father. Why not recognize this difference by giving them each their own term? Similarly, your first cousins could be subdivided into finer categories and given special terms, such as terms meaning *child of my father's sister, child of my mother's brother,* and so on. And since we distinguish most other categories of relatives by whether they are male or female (e.g., brother versus sister, aunt versus uncle), why don't we apply the sex distinction to our cousins?

How do we know that the way a people divide the domain of relatives into different categories is cultural rather than natural? Because different cultures divide the domain in different ways. People in many societies, for instance, call their mother's sister by one term and their father's sister by another term. It is also common for people to distinguish between the children of their father's sister and their father's brother, calling the first by a term we translate as "cousin," the second by the same term they use for their own brothers and sisters. Even stranger, from the English language's perspective, are peoples who call the daughters of their

semantic domain Class of things or properties perceived as alike in some fundamental respect; hierarchically organized.

maternal uncles by the term *mother* (just like their "real mother"), but not the daughters of their paternal uncles, for whom they use the term *sister*. (These various ways of categorizing kin, by the way, are not random; such labels are related to other aspects of a people's kinship system—see Chapter 10.) Obviously, the way various peoples divide the seemingly "natural domain" of biological relatives is not the same the world over.

We could provide other examples, but the overall point is clear. A language reflects how the members of a culture divide up the world. Cultures often divide the world differently, constructing various categories of reality out of the "natural" properties of things and people.

The implications of this point are more important than it seems at first glance. If a language has a word for something—an object, a kind of person, an emotion, a natural feature of the landscape—then those who know the language tend to think it is real. Giving something a label tends to make us think of it as a "thing." These "things" are real in one sense: the word refers to *something* in the mind of the speaker, even if only to emotions or abstractions. But this reality might differ for someone who speaks a language that reflects a different culture.

Language, Perceptions, and Worldview

We've seen that many aspects of a language reflect the culture of the people who speak it. Could the converse also be true? Is it possible that knowing a given language predisposes its speakers to view the world in certain ways? Could the categories and rules of language condition people's perceptions of reality and perhaps even their worldview?

Language could shape perceptions and worldviews both by its vocabulary and by the way it leads people to communicate about subjects such as space and time. Any language's vocabulary assigns labels to only certain things, qualities, and actions. It is easy to see how this might encourage people to perceive the real world selectively. For instance, as we grow up, we learn that some plants are "trees." So we come to think of *tree* as a single kind of thing, although there are so many kinds of trees that there is no necessary reason to collapse all this arboreal variety into a single label. In such cases, language affects our cultural constructions of reality.

Also, language might force people to communicate about time and space in a certain kind of way. The words and rules of language could condition relationships between individuals and between people and nature. Potentially, linguistic constraints on the way people must speak to be understood by others can shape their views of what the world is like.

The idea that language influences the perceptions and thought patterns of those who speak it, and thus conditions their worldview, is known as the **Sapir-Whorf hypothesis** (or the **linguistic relativity hypothesis**), after the two anthropological linguists who proposed it. One of the most widely quoted of all anthropological passages is Edward Sapir's statement, originally written in 1929:

> [Language] powerfully conditions all our thinking about social problems and processes. Human beings do not live in the objective world alone, nor alone in the world of social activity as ordinarily understood but are very much at the mercy of the particular language which has become the medium of expression for their society.... The fact of the matter is that the "real world" is to a large extent unconsciously built up on the language habits of the group.... The worlds in which different societies live are distinct worlds, not merely the same world with different labels attached.
>
> (Sapir 1964, 68–69)

Sapir and Whorf believed that language helps define the worldview of its speakers. It does so, in part, by providing labels for certain kinds of phenomena (things, concepts, qualities, and actions), which different languages define according to different criteria. Language thus makes some phenomena easier to think about than others. The attributes that define them as different from other things become more important than other attributes. These attributes provide a filter that biases our perceptions.

In brief, the linguistic relativity hypothesis holds that people's perceptions, the verbal categories they use to think about reality, and perhaps their entire worldview, are related to the language they learn while growing up.

The units of time sequence of the English language are a good example: seconds, minutes, hours, days, weeks, months, years, decades, centuries, millennia. Of these, only days, months, and years are in any sense "natural," meaning they are based on natural occurrences (sunrises and sunsets, moon phases, annual cycles of the seasons).

Even these natural occurrences do not correspond with the English language's units of time. Days do not run from sunrise to sunrise but begin at midnight. Months no longer reflect lunar phases. New years begin

---

Sapir-Whorf hypothesis (linguistic relativity hypothesis) Idea that language significantly shapes the perceptions and worldview of its speakers.

in January rather than at solstices or equinoxes. Decades, centuries, and millennia are purely linguistic categories with no natural basis. Units used on watches—seconds, minutes, and hours—are linguistic units as well.

The Aztecs of central Mexico used two calendars simultaneously. When the day names of both calendars matched each other once every 52 years, a ceremony called "New Fire" occurred. All fires in the empire were extinguished. The high priests sacrificed a human by removing his heart and then tried to rekindle a fire inside the chest cavity. If the fire burned, all was well for another 52 years; if it went out, the world would end in a cataclysm.

How much is our perception of time affected by such arbitrary divisions imposed on our minds by language? Do the time units of calendars and watches "create" our views of time?

In the 1930s and 1940s, Benjamin Whorf suggested that language does indeed condition a people's conceptions of time. He noted that English encourages its speakers to think about time using spatial metaphors. For example, we say "a long time" and "a long distance," although time is not really "long" or "short" in the same sense as distance. Also, English-speaking people talk about units of time using the same concepts with which they talk about numbers of objects. We say "four days" and "four apples," although it is possible to see four objects at once but not four units of time. Finally, English-speaking people classify events by when they occurred: those that have happened, those that are happening, and those that will happen.

Whorf suggested that the Native American Hopi speak and think about time and events differently, because of their language. With no tenses equivalent to English's past, present, and future and no way to express time in terms of spatial metaphors, Hopi speak of events as continuously unfolding, rather than happening in so many days or weeks. Whorf argued that the Hopi language led the Hopi people to a different perception of the passage of time.

Notice some implications of linguistic relativity. If true, it implies that without knowing it, our perceptions and thought processes are shaped by the language community into which we happen to have been born. Therefore, the world is not *directly* perceptible through our ordinary senses because the categories of our language bias our interpretations of sensory inputs. Potentially, this "fact" makes it difficult for anyone to know anything for sure. Taken truly seriously, it would mean that human rational thought and reason are partially an illusion because individuals can reason only with the subjective concepts and patterns their language provides.

What shall we make of the Sapir-Whorf hypothesis? Certainly, none of us as individuals creates the labels our language assigns to reality, nor do we create the constraints our grammar places on the way we talk about time and space. Rather, we learn them from our linguistic ancestors, and we must adhere to these labels and rules if we are to be understood. Surely, this necessity biases our perceptions *to some degree.* The question is, how much? More precisely, how important is language as opposed to other influences on perceptions and views of reality?

For decades, the Sapir-Whorf hypothesis was not generally accepted, although most scholars were intrigued by the idea that language shapes thought. One reason for skepticism is that if language significantly shapes the way its speakers perceive and think about the world, then we would expect a people's perceptions and worldviews to change only at a rate roughly comparable to the rate at which their language changes. But worldviews typically change much more rapidly than language. In the past century, the English language has changed little compared with the dramatic alteration in the worldviews of most of its speakers. Despite the enormous economic, political, and ideological changes that have swept Asia in the past several decades, Chinese, Japanese, Korean, Hindi, Vietnamese, and other languages have changed little. The fact that linguistic change or replacement is usually far slower than changes in worldviews suggests that language and worldview are not tightly integrated.

Despite such weaknesses, recent empirical research has led to reconsideration of the Sapir-Whorf hypothesis. Researchers at the Max Planck Institute for Psycholinguistics have investigated how speakers of different languages talk about space and location. (Here, we simplify their complicated and technical findings.) English speakers talk about space in multiple ways. Space can be relative to the location of the speaker or hearer—for example, "on my left" or "above you." We also talk about space using absolute locations, especially when we discuss long distances—for example, "head north to get there" and "south of town." These "cardinal directions" do not depend on which way an individual is now facing. When we provide someone with directions, we often combine relative and absolute references—for example, "turn left on Main Street and go west for about 2 miles."

Other languages speak about directions differently. In southern Mexico, there is a Mayan community who speak a language called Tzeltal. In their language, the important spatial references are "uphill" and "downhill." These are more like cardinal directions to them because the overall slope of the land is consistent and they are seldom on the other side of the mountaintop or ridge. Tzeltal speakers

Australian aborigines are the indigenous people of Australia, who lived on the continent at the time of English settlement during the early 1800s. These indigenous Guugu Yimithirr are well-known to linguists and anthropologists because they use cardinal directions in indicating location.

describe movements in terms of "ascending," "descending," or "going across." If an object is on the ground, a person might say it is "uphill of us." They make no distinction between left and right, so a translation of the location of a house might be "to the downhill of you." Apparently, the Tzeltal language does affect perceptions: when shown two mirror-image photographs, Tzeltal speakers usually say they are exactly the same.

Also interesting is an Australian aboriginal language called Guugu Yimithirr. It uses only absolute references, comparable to English's cardinal directions. Thus, they might say, "There's a fly on your northern knee" (P. Brown 2006, 109). They have no equivalent to "right," "left," "front," or "behind." A Guugu Yimithirr warned a linguist who was filming him to "look out for that big ant just north of your foot" (Deutscher 2010, 166). If they ask you to move over so they can sit down, they might tell you to move to the west. When some older Guugu Yimithirr were watching a TV with a screen facing south, they said that a man on the screen moving toward them was walking northward.

Whether languages like Tzeltal or Guugu Yimithirr cause or even predispose their speakers to perceive the world in certain ways is not proven, of course. However, the Guugu Yimithirr seem always to know their directions even when they are in unfamiliar surroundings, suggesting that they are more attuned to four directions than other people. From wherever you are reading this, can you point to the east?

SUMMARY

1. **Explain why language is such a powerful means of communication, using five distinctive properties of human languages.** Along with culture, language is the most important mental characteristic of humanity that distinguishes us from other animals. Language shaped the evolution of our vocal tract, allows us to communicate abstract concepts, is necessary for complete social learning, and enables us to rapidly and precisely send and receive complicated messages. Five properties differentiate language from other systems of communication. It is composed of discrete units (sounds, words)

combined in different sequences to convey different meanings. It relies on the shared, conventional understanding of arbitrary and meaningful symbols. Language is productive, allowing us to intuitively and unconsciously combine sounds and words creatively to send an infinite number of messages. Displacement enables humans to communicate about things, events, and persons that are remote in time and space. Language's multimedia potential allows communication in writing and movements (e.g., signing).

2. **Describe how words are formed from combinations of discrete sounds.** Phonology is the study of the sounds and sound patterns of language. When we speak, we combine sounds in patterned ways to articulate meaningful sound sequences (words). Knowing a language includes mastery of its discrete phonemes, based on the features of sounds that speakers recognize as making a difference in the meanings of words in which they occur. Among many other phonological differences, languages vary in the way they use voice pitch to convey meanings, as illustrated by tone languages.

3. **Describe how Native American words affected English.** As English settlers visited and colonized North America, they encountered animals, plants, and crops that did not exist in Europe. In many cases, the word they adopted for these unfamiliar life forms was taken from a Native American language. Native words were also adopted to refer to locations, means of transportation, articles of clothing, and many other objects unknown to European settlers.

4. **Discuss the modern-day global forces that result in the spread and survival of some languages and the contraction and possible extinction of others.** Languages spread or contract geographically, or disappear altogether, for many reasons. Population gains or losses and assimilation by more powerful societies historically were the most widespread reasons. With globalization, communication in the world arena is causing language change. Economic trade, popular media, international education, and other forces that create new relationships lead to the favoring of some languages over others. However, national and ethnic pride can counteract such global forces if a language itself becomes a symbol of some larger objective.

5. **Explain some ways messages are communicated nonverbally and how speech is affected by social context.** The meanings of body language and facial expressions used in nonverbal communication vary from people to people and are an important source of cultural misunderstandings. Sociolinguists study how speech is influenced by cultural factors, including culturally defined contexts and situations, and the presence of other parties, Speech styles mark differences in rank and status, as between ethnic groups, classes or statuses, and males and females. Speech formality and overall style are parts of a person's presentation of self, so speaking communicates many meanings beyond the words themselves. Language is a strategic tool in competitions over political power and government policies.

6. **Describe the Sapir-Whorf hypothesis and some of the controversies surrounding it.** The Sapir-Whorf hypothesis proposes that the language a people speak shapes their perceptions of reality and thus predisposes them to view the world in a certain way. Vocabulary might influence perceptions by leading its speakers unconsciously to filter out some properties of reality in favor of other properties. The conventions of language also might force individuals to talk about subjects such as time and space in certain ways. The notion that language significantly shapes perceptions and thought processes is not accepted by most modern scholars. Recent research concentrates on how particular language constraints affect perception and thought in specific areas of culture, as illustrated by directional labels among the Tzeltal and Guugu Yimithirr.

4 Cultural Diversity and Globalization

One obvious cultural consequence of globalization is in urban architecture. Although this is a photo of Mumbai in India, the buildings could easily be in any major city in the world.

Dinodia Photos/Alamy

Cultural Change and Diversity

The World Before Globalization

Globalization

Early European Expansion
 The Americas
 Africa
 Asia
 Cultural Consequences

The Industrial Revolution
 Europe and the Americas
 Asia
 Africa
 Oceania

Consequences of European Expansion

LEARNING OBJECTIVES

After reading this chapter, you should be able to:

1 EXPLAIN why society is dynamic.

2 DISCUSS how the present diversity of human culture came about.

3 ELABORATE on the development and spread of globalization.

4 DESCRIBE how the Industrial Revolution gave European powers dominance in the world.

5 ANALYZE the third and most recent stage of globalization and the global economy.

Humans are social animals; we live in groups. We do this not simply out of desire but out of necessity. We cannot survive as individuals—at least not indefinitely. Thus, we live in groups—societies. A **society** is a group of people who share a common language and culture. The two most critical purposes of a society's **culture** are to provide its members with the means to gain adequate food and shelter while protecting them from the members of other societies with whom they might be in competition. To accomplish these ends, its members have to act collectively and maintain group social cohesion over time. The culture of a society functions, among other things, to organize the behavior of individuals not only to accomplish these necessary economic and political ends, but also to reinforce interdependence of individuals within the society while minimizing personal conflicts that might disrupt or destroy the group's cohesiveness. Every society has an organizational structure that defines the rights and obligations of the individual members of the society in regard to their behavior in economic, family, political, religious, and other group activities.

Cultural Change and Diversity

Neither the membership boundaries of a society nor its culture are stable over time. The members of a society may, and frequently do, become geographically separated, usually through migrations. The cultures of these separate groups will change independently. The result will be two or more groups that are increasingly culturally distinct from one another; new societies. For example, starting in the seventeenth century, French settlers came to North America. Today there are the Quebecois (primarily in Quebec), the Acadians (in the Maritime Provinces of Canada), and the Cajuns (in Louisiana). Over the last three centuries, they have become increasingly culturally distinct from each other as well as from the peoples of France. In other cases, the members of two or more societies may come into contact, combining cultural traditions of both. The people of Haiti are an example in that their culture blends the cultural traditions of various African peoples and also the French. In the case of smaller societies, they might be totally absorbed, socially and culturally, by more dominant societies.

Why does the culture of a society change over time? Culture is a dynamic dimension that allows us, both individually and collectively as groups, to adapt to new natural and social environments. This capacity is critical to our survival as human beings because, directly or indirectly from our natural environment, we acquire those things we need to meet our most basic biological needs—food, clothing, and shelter—while at the same time we are usually in contact and frequently competition with other human groups for survival—our social environment. Since over time both our natural and social environments change, through environmental change, migrations of people, or other factors, our culture also has to change to meet new challenges. While all aspects of culture are dynamic and subject to change, changes in technology have the most basic effect on our culture in that they can profoundly redefine our relationship to our natural environment as well as

---

society Socially distinct group of people who share a common language and culture.

culture The socially learned knowledge and patterns of behavior shared by some group of people.

with the other peoples with whom we are in contact. However, this still does not answer the question of *how* the culture of a society changes.

Two major processes are involved in culture change: (1) members of the society independently discover new knowledge or create new behaviors or technologies; and (2) they borrow knowledge, behaviors, or technology from some other group. Of the two processes, internally generated changes are the slowest in that they depend on the size of the group and the existing cultural complexity of the society. Changes within a society usually take the form of recombining two or more existing culture elements to produce something new. The simplest example is when some individual or individuals (it may have occurred independently more than once) took a stone point and mounted it on a wooden club to produce a stone-headed ax. The same is true for most other internally generated changes: a society builds on what it has. Contact with other societies, particularly culturally more complex societies, produces more rapid culture change. In some cases, the members of a society see the cultural alternatives presented by another society, judge them to be superior to their own, and voluntarily borrow and adapt them. This pattern is particularly true in technology. In other cases, a society becomes politically dominated by another society that physically forces them to adopt new cultural behaviors to conform to the standards of the dominant group. An example is when the Spanish, starting in the sixteenth century, forced Native American peoples under their control to become Catholics.

Finally, it is important to realize that the culture of a society is an integrated system. The introduction of some new cultural element has to be accommodated within the existing culture, thus resulting in the modification or replacement of others aspects of the culture. In the case of Native Americans under Spanish rule, they usually retained many of their preexisting religious traditions and practices while also adopting and modifying many Catholic religious practices. The result was a unique mix, a new religious tradition.

For most of human history, culture change has progressed slowly since most societies were geographically isolated, and the possibility for learning and borrowing knowledge, behavior, and technology from other societies was limited by geography. That is not true today. Globalization ended the geographic and cultural isolation of people and allowed for the first time the diffusion of culture between virtually all of the peoples of the world. As a result, we live in a time of rapid cultural change unparalleled in human history. Not only is culture rapidly changing, but the rate of change is accelerating.

We sometimes speak of globalization and the global economy as if they are the same, but they're not. *Globalization* refers to the spread of culture between all of the peoples of the world; this started 500 years ago with European expansion. The first phase, which started in about 1500 and ended in about 1800, saw the European conquest of the Americas and establishment of direct trade with Asia and Africa. The second phase, which began in about 1800 with the Industrial Revolution in Europe, ultimately resulted in the division of Asia, Africa, and Oceania into European-controlled empires. The global economy, an integrated world economic system, started only about 60 years ago with the collapse of these empires, and it is the third phase of globalization.

The World Before Globalization

Contrary to many commonly held beliefs, all contemporary humans are fully modern *Homo sapiens*, meaning (among other things) that they all possess the same intellectual capabilities for the learning and development of culture. The present diversity in human culture is the product of 150,000 years or more of localized histories of human groups as new societies and technologies developed and each adapted to unique social and natural environments. Thus, to more fully understand cultural diversity, we have to start with the broad patterns of human culture change. Over time, the basic economic activities of people have changed dramatically, necessitating the development of new social cultural institutions to organize and direct their behaviors.

Modern humans evolved in Africa about 200,000 B.P. (Before Present); and between 125,000 and 60,000 B.P., some migrated to Asia and Europe. About 50,000 B.P., the first humans arrived in Australia. Humans started arriving in the Americas by at least 15,000 B.P. By 10,000 B.P., if not earlier, humans had occupied all major lands masses except for Antarctica and a few isolated islands. They had accomplished this as

---

globalization Flow of cultural knowledge, directly or indirectly, between the different peoples of the world.

As small groups of nomadic foragers, like the San pictured in this photo, humans spread throughout the world.

hunters and gatherers, with the same basic stone, bone, horn, and wood tool technology; living off wild animals, fish, eatable plants, and other naturally occurring food sources. In doing so, their cultures changed as they migrated and adapted to new natural environmental settings—from the arctic to the tropics, from mountains to plains and islands; to grasslands, deserts, temperate forests, rain forests, and swamps. With each migration, they had had to learn the behaviors of new animals and modify their basic technology and hunting techniques to successfully hunt them. For people who settled along the coasts, lakes, rivers, and streams, they had to gain knowledge of the different species of fish, shellfish, or marine animals and how to acquire them. Similarly, they learned about new floral resources available to them, which ones were eatable, when and where they could be found, and which ones were best suited for making tools, shelters, as well as fuel for fires, and curing diseases and injuries. In addition, they had to adapt their clothing styles and dwellings to meet the different climatic conditions. Finally, they had to modify their social behavior and movements to adapt to the seasonal and geographic variability in the availability of critical food resources and other needs. Localized knowledge of critical natural resources was the key element to human survival during this early period. Thus, although there were broad similarities in basic technologies, in the application and modifications of these technologies, in specialized cultural knowledge, and in social behaviors, there was also increasingly localized cultural diversity among the world's peoples.

Starting about 10,000 B.P., people began domesticating wild plants. Plant domestication occurred independently in many scattered regions of the world, in each case involving the domestication of different plants. Crops such as wheat and barley were domesticated in the Middle East, wet rice and millet in Asia, dry rice and sorghum in West Africa, corn and beans in Mesoamerica, and potatoes and manioc in South America. Each of these crops required a somewhat different technology for cultivation and was limited to only certain environmental settings. Domestication meant that humans were now food producers and able to some degree to control both the location and the quantity of food available to them. No longer were they totally dependent on the whims of nature for their food. These first food producers planted only small gardens to supplement

CHAPTER 4 Cultural Diversity and Globalization 69

their primary source of subsistence: hunting, gathering, and sometimes fishing. Over time, foraging activities declined as the size of gardens and their dependence on food production increased. Associated with this early raising of crops were a rapid growth in population and an increase in size and permanence of settlements. Even in the regions where these plants were domesticated, only a small portion of the land was actually suitable for their cultivation. This led to a new migrations as the now more numerous farming peoples began expanding out of their original areas in search of new land—changing, displacing, or absorbing many, but not all, of the neighboring foraging societies. However, it is important to note that most of the regions of the world were still occupied by foraging peoples. Domestication only added a new level of cultural diversity. Later, in Chapter 7, we will discuss hunters and gatherers, which we term *foragers*, and these first agriculturalists, which we term *horticulturalists*, in more detail. Here we are going to note just a few characteristics.

Among foragers, land was usually collectively owned by the group, all families had equal access to natural resources, and group leadership was informal. Among horticulturalists, land was still communally owned, but individuals or families now had "use rights" to the land they cleared for gardens. Living in larger social groups, leadership became more formalized and structured. However, although all of the horticultural societies were confronting the same basic issues, each developed its own distinct cultural solutions. Thus, between the different horticultural societies, there was localized cultural diversity as well.

Sometime after the domestication of plants, people began domesticating animals. In Europe, Asia, and Africa, such animals as cattle, horses, asses, camels, sheep, goats, and water buffalo were domesticated. The Americas had few animals suitable for domestication, and thus few were domesticated, with llamas, alpacas, turkeys, and guinea pigs being the most important. In both cases, domestication of animals gave local populations a new and more reliable source of meat. However, in Europe, Asia, Africa, and South America, it resulted in a new form of economic adaption: herding. We will discuss these people, *pastoralists*, in more detail in Chapter 7. Here it is important to note that herd animals gave some people the ability to move into grassland and desert regions, regions unsuitable for growing crops. These migrations resulted in the changing, replacement, or absorption of many foraging peoples. Although the land was still usually owned communally, individuals and families now had "use rights" to particular grazing areas and water sources. However, the most important change was in personal property, as herd animals were owned individually or by families. These animals were portable, transferable, and inheritable wealth. Significant inequalities in wealth appeared. Once again, new localized differences in cultural institutions appeared.

In many but not all parts of the world, horticulture evolved into intensive agriculture, which allowed for the support of even greater numbers of people. In Europe, Asia, and Africa, domestic animals were critical because of their physical strength and ability to pull plows—a new technological development. Lacking suitable animals for plowing, in the Americas intensive agriculture was dependent on still other new technologies, such as terraced fields, raised fields, and irrigation. Regardless, the cultural effects were basically similar. Fields now became inheritable private property being worked generation after generation. Villages now became permanent, with houses occupied for multiple generations. Inequalities in wealth became greater and inheritable, resulting in the development of class and caste systems. Leadership became increasing formalized and centralized.

Intensive agriculture resulted in increasing the land area suitable farming as well as a rising productivity of the land under cultivation. As a result, there was a dramatic increase in the population of intensive agricultural peoples and a territorial expansion at the expense primarily of small horticultural populations, but also of some foraging and pastoral peoples. Intensive agriculture was the basis for the independent emergence of cities and localized civilizations in the Americas, Europe, Asia, and Africa. Each of these civilizations emerged with its own distinctive cultural traditions—in art and architecture, crafts, religious practices, technologies, and frequently, but not always, writing systems. With the emergence of cities and civilizations, new cultural diversity began to appear: craft specialization, markets and market exchange, ecclesiastical religious organization, and state-level political organization.

In sum, early human culture history was characterized by the migration of foraging peoples, followed by scattered independent localized cultural developments associated with horticulture, intensive agriculture, and pastoralism. Trade between groups was limited, and diffusion of cultural knowledge minimal. This began to change with the emergence of civilizations. Civilizations were much larger, politically organized aggregates of peoples. Because of their far more complex technologies and economies, they needed a broader range of natural resources than they usually controlled. This led to expansionist warfare, the creation of multisocietal empires, and the development of long-distance trade, which resulted in ever-increasing contact between regional civilizations as well as neighboring foraging, horticultural and pastoral peoples.

In the **Old World**, most these regional civilizations had come into contact with each other by early in the ancient period when they formed an almost continuous band from the western Mediterranean through the Middle East to South and Southeast Asia to China and the Far East. Another group of civilizations were found in sub-Saharan Africa. Although members of these civilizations had extremely little, if any, personal contact with individuals from more distant civilizations, they usually had a vague knowledge of their existence and, indirectly, exchange of some cultural knowledge and technologies with them through a series of middlemen. Similarly, in the Americas, each regional civilization had its own distinct cultural traditions, forming an almost continuous band from Mesoamerica south into the Andes.

Thus, prior to 1492, two different more or less interconnected groups of civilizations had developed: one in the Old World and the other in the **New World**. While most of the world's population at this time was in some way incorporated into one or another of these civilizations, most of the land surface of the world was still occupied by scattered groups of foragers, pastoralists, and horticulturalists. The general pattern of human cultural development up to this point in history had been one of ever-increasing, highly localized cultural diversity.

One of the defining characteristics of civilization was the development of monumental architecture such as seen in the Parthenon of ancient Athens.

Globalization

Since globalization was the result of European expansion, and the relative wealth and power of European peoples have changed more dramatically during this period than any other region, let us start this discussion with Europe. In the late fifteenth century, Europe was a relatively isolated, politically fragment region with a population of only about 60 million (see Figure 4.1). Agrarian-dependent, its people relied on farming oats, rye, wheat, barley, other crops, and domesticated animals. With most of the population consisting of self-sufficient peasants, specialized craftspeople and artisans were relatively few. Trade both within Europe and with other civilizations was limited, and thus Europe's trade centers and cities were few and small. Compared to the civilizations of Asia, its technology was relatively limited.

Asia at this time is best seen as a series of culturally distinct, more or less adjacent civilizations stretching from North Africa east to China. With a population of about 300 million, collectively Asia was the most technologically and politically developed portion of the Old World. The three main centers of Asia civilization were the Islamic Middle East (which included North Africa); South Asia, or India, which was basically Hindu; and China. In addition, there were many smaller secondary centers. In contrast to Europe, the cities and trade centers of Asia were large, and highly skilled craftspeople and artisans numerous. A series of land and maritime trade routes connect the major centers of Asia, and some cultural knowledge, behaviors, and technology diffused between them. Land routes such as the Silk Road connected China and the Middle East. The maritime routes were controlled by Omani Arabs whose ships traveled between the ports of China, Southeast Asia, India, the Middle East, and eastern Africa. The western-most of these Asian civilizations and the one directly bordering Europe was Islamic. The conflict between the Muslims and the Christian peoples that started in the seventh century C.E. (Common Era) was primarily responsible for the economic isolation and relative technological backwardness of Europe.

South of the Sahara were the scattered kingdoms of the African civilizations. Except for those kingdoms bordering the Sahara, most lacked indigenous writing

Old World Landmasses of Europe, Asia, and Africa.

New World Landmasses of North and South America.

Figure 4.1 Major States and Regions of Europe, Asia, and Africa (ca. 1500).

systems; thus, relatively little is known about these peoples. Their agriculture was based on the growing of millet, sorghum, dry rice, melons, and other crops, some of which had been domesticated locally. Although covering a larger land area than Europe, the population of sub-Saharan Africa was not as dense, probably between 35 and 60 million. Some of the coastal peoples of east Africa traded with the Omani, while the trade of the western kingdoms was by trade routes across the Sahara. There were cities, such as Timbuktu and Gao, but they were fewer and smaller than those of Asia and Europe. Although they were metal workers in iron and bronze, African craftspeople and artisans were fewer. The civilizations of sub-Saharan Africa, though not far behind Europe, were the least technologically developed of those of the Old World.

The vast majority of Old World peoples were by 1500 members of the politically organized states associated with one or another of these agriculturally based civilizations. However, in the arctic, northern woodlands, deserts, grasslands, tropical rain forests, swamps, and rocky or forested mountains of Europe, Africa, and Asia were still other peoples—foragers relying on hunting or fishing, horticulturalists, and pastoralists. Some of these peoples were in direct contact with members of one or more of these civilizations, but most were not.

In the Americas, the major civilizations were in Mesoamerica and in the Andes. Here were the largest cities, the most skilled craftspeople and artisans, and the largest politically organized empires and armies. In 1500, the largest empires were the Aztecs in Mexico, with about 25 million, and the Inca in the Andes, with about 12 million. Both were multisocietal empires, meaning that there was cultural diversity within as well as between the two. The Mesoamerican civilizations were based primarily on the cultivation of corn, whereas the Andean civilizations heavily dependent on the potato. While both had writing or records systems, they were also very different. In Mesoamerica, they used symbolic glyphs; in the Andes, they used the *quipu* or knotted strings—systems very different from those of the Old World. Although they had some knowledge of metallurgy, working gold, silver, copper, and bronze, in most cases it was used for ritual items or ornaments. For most purposes, even the most technologically advanced Native Americans relied on a stone and wood tool technology.

Other regions were populated with other well-developed horticultural societies: the eastern portion of what eventually became the United States, islands of the Caribbean, and lowland South America. However, most of the Americas were occupied by foragers dependent on hunting, fishing, and/or gathering. Unlike in the Old World, few animals were suitable for domestication in the New World, and only in a small portion of South America were there any herding societies. Altogether, the population of Native America was probable between 80 and 120 million in 1492, with the majority of this population concentrated in Mesoamerica and the Andes. In comparison, the population of the Americas was about the same as Europe and sub-Saharan Africa combined. However, the comparison of the size of states shows a greater difference. The Aztec Empire was far larger in population than any country in Europe at that time—the largest, France, having a population of only about 15 million. The Inca Empire was larger than any European country other than France. Spain, soon to conquer both the Aztecs and the Inca, had a population of only about 6.5 million.

The smallest of these major world regions, with a population of only a few million, and the most culturally isolated was Oceania: Australia and the islands of the Pacific. Geographically, it was divided into four distinct areas: Australia and Tasmania, Melanesia, Micronesia, and Polynesia. Linguistically and culturally, the peoples of Australia and Tasmania were distinct from neighboring peoples. Nomadic foragers dependent on hunting and gathering, they had the least complex technology of any people in the world, even lacking the bow and arrow. Politically, they were organized into small groups usually with informal leaders.

To the north and east were island peoples of Melanesia, Micronesia, and Polynesia. Melanesia consisted of New Guinea and several large, mountainous island groups as far east as Fiji. To the north were the islands of Micronesia, a mix of small volcanic islands and scattered coral atolls. To the east, in the central Pacific, was Polynesia, which except for New Zealand consisted mainly of widely scattered volcanic island groups. The peoples of all three of these regions were horticulturalists, with a heavy dependence on fishing for the coastal and island populations. Although they varied regionally, their main crops were either root crops such as taro or tree crops such as sago, breadfruit, bananas, and coconuts. They also raised pigs. With only indirect contact with the peoples of Asia, they had only a stone (or shell) tool technology, but it was far more highly developed than that of the peoples of Australia and Tasmania. All of the coastal and island peoples made highly sophisticated outrigger and hulled canoes with sails. With these canoes and well-developed navigational skills, these peoples, particularly the Micronesians and Polynesians, were able to travel hundreds, if not thousands, of miles over the open Pacific between islands and island groups. Although they varied politically, most of these peoples were formally organized with hereditary leaders. The islands of the central Pacific were the last land areas settled by humans, with Easter Island and the Hawaiian Islands being discovered and settled sometime after 300 C.E. With the settlement of these islands, the first stage of human expansion had come to an end.

Prior to 1492, there had been two major independent lines of cultural development: the Old World and the New World. However, even within the Old World and the New World, the diffusion of new technologies, ideologies, and cultural knowledge between the major centers of civilization was usually indirect, extraordinarily slow, and limited by geography. Thus, each of these centers retained its own distinctively different cultural traditions. European expansion was going to end this isolation. First, it would bring the peoples of the Old and New worlds into contact, resulting in what Alfred Cosby termed the "Columbian Exchange" (discussed in the next section). Just as important, European explorers would provide a conduit that would greatly increase the directness and the speed through which technologies, ideologies, and other forms of cultural knowledge and behaviors could diffuse among all of the regions of the world.

Early European Expansion

European contact with other civilizations had been blocked by Islamic expansion during the seventh century. From ancient literature, they knew of other civilizations to the east: India and China. Some luxury goods, such as silks, cottons, porcelains, and spices, came into Europe via Islamic middlemen. However, they were extremely limited and expensive. In the fifteenth century, first the Portuguese and later the Spanish attempted to make direct contact with the eastern-most civilizations of the Old World, India, and China.

In the 1430s, the Portuguese began charting the Atlantic Coast of Africa. The Portuguese moved slowly and cautiously down what was initially the dry coastline of the western Sahara Desert. By the 1450s, they had reached the tropics, making contact with non-Islamic coastal kingdoms. Treaties and trade agreements were made with these kingdoms by which the Portuguese acquired gold, ivory, and other local products. They still proceeded slowly, and it was not until 1488 that they reach the Cape of Good Hope, the southern tip of Africa.

In the 1490s, two world-changing events occurred. In 1492, Christopher Columbus, sponsored by Spain, sailed west across the Atlantic hoping to reach India. Instead, he found the Americas. In 1498, the Portuguese explorer and trader, Vasco Da Gama, sailed around the Cape of Good Hope and landed in India. The era of globalization had started. The initial cultural consequences of European contact differed qualitatively from one region to the next, so we will discuss the Americas, Africa, Asia, and Oceania separately.

The Americas

The earliest Spanish settlement in the Americas was on the island of Hispaniola, present-day Haiti and the Dominican Republic. Their initial discovery was disappointing: there were small gold deposits, but little else of interest. Still looking for India or China, Spanish explorers and settlers quickly spread to other islands in the West Indies: Cuba, Jamaica, and Puerto Rico. In 1513, Balboa crossed the narrow Isthmus of Panama and discovered the Pacific. The Spanish were beginning to realize that the world was larger than they had thought, discovering a previously unknown world. In 1519, Hernán Cortés landed on the coast of Mexico and by 1521 had completed the conquest of the Aztec Empire. Cortés sent vast quantities gold and silver back to Spain, which encouraged others to search for wealth and plunder. In 1532–1534, Francisco Pizarro discovered, conquered, and plundered the Inca Empire. By the late 1500s, Spanish conquistadores had explored much of the Americas, from the lower Mississippi valley to the Amazon and the La Plata, and had located and conquered every major indigenous American state.

Columbian Exchange Exchange of people, diseases, domesticated animals and plants, and other cultural knowledge between the peoples of the Old World and the New World.

In little more than half a century, the Spaniards had gained control of the richest and most populous portions of the Americas: the West Indies, Mesoamerica, and the Andes. More than half of the native population of the Americas had fallen under Spanish political and cultural domination. The relative ease with which the Spanish came to conquer and control such vast land areas and large indigenous populations with so few people is best explained by the Columbian Exchange and its consequences.

The term *Columbian Exchange* refers to the diffusion of cultural knowledge, people, and diseases between the peoples of Old World and the New World. This exchange resulted in the massive destruction of indigenous American peoples and their cultures, while ultimately changing the political and economic balance of power among the peoples of the Old World. In the centuries that followed, the culture of virtually every society in the world would either directly or indirectly be changed to some degree by what occurred.

The Spanish conquests, and the later conquests of other indigenous Americans by other Europeans, were not the result of the superiority of their steel weapons and guns over stone weapons and bow and arrows. European conquest was primarily the result of the introduction of Old World diseases for which indigenous Americans had no natural immunities: smallpox, measles, influenza, bubonic plague, diphtheria, typhus, cholera, malaria, and scarlet fever. The rapid decline in the Native American population started almost immediately at contact. When Cortés landed in Mexico in 1519, there was an estimated population of over 25 million. The Spanish were aided in their war by a smallpox epidemic that destroyed or incapacitated most of the Aztecs. Similarly, smallpox destroyed or incapacitated much of the Incan army, making possible Pizarro's conquest of Peru in the 1530s.

Following these conquests, the native populations collapsed even more. By 1568, the native population of Mexico had dropped to 2,650,000; and by 1605, to slightly more than 1 million. In Peru, the native population of about 12 million in 1532 had declined to only about 1 million by the late 1550s. Highly contagious, these epidemics also spread to indigenous populations well beyond the area of Spanish control and contact. Particularly vulnerable were the powerful and populous farming peoples of the eastern portion of what was to become the United States and in South America. It was not a single epidemic of one disease that killed off the native populations, but a series of epidemics of different diseases. In the first two centuries following European contact, the population of Native America had probably declined by 90 percent or more.

The Spanish had taken control of the richest resources of the Americas: gold and silver deposits as well as lands for farming and ranching. At the same time, the Portuguese had taken control of the easternmost portion of South America: Brazil. From the very beginning the Spanish and the Portuguese faced a dilemma: few Europeans were willing to settle in the Americas, and the collapsing native population was inadequate to supply the labor needed to economically develop them. This labor shortage would result in the African slave trade.

Africa

During the sixteenth century, the Portuguese had a virtual monopoly on the European trade with Africa. Slavery had existed in Spain and Portugal before 1492; however, the number of slaves was extremely limited. A new source had to be found to supply labor needs of their colonies in the Americas, and Africa was going to become that source. Slavery also existed in Africa, and initially the Portuguese traded for these individuals. However, as the demand for slaves increased, this source was quickly depleted, and the Portuguese then began encouraging the leaders of the coastal kingdoms to raid other, usually interior groups for slaves.

The magnitude of the African slave trade cannot be determined with any exactness. We know that the slave trade grew steadily during the sixteenth and seventeenth centuries as the English, French, and Dutch established ports along the coast of Africa and also became involved in the trade to supply their new colonies in the Americas. It reached its height in the last decades of the eighteenth century and only ended about 1870. Estimates of the total number of African slaves sent to the Americas range from 10 million to 50 million, but the actual number was probably closer to 10 million. The vast majority of these individuals were captured in slave wars. In exchange for slaves, ever-increasing numbers of guns were traded in Africa. During the early eighteenth century, 180,000 guns were annually being traded; and by the late eighteenth century, at the height of the trade, between 300,000 and 400,000. As a result, warfare became endemic through most of western and central Africa.

Little is directly known concerning the nature and the consequences of the slave wars on the peoples of Africa during the three centuries between 1500 and 1800 since most African peoples did not have writing systems, and Europeans restricted their movements to the ports where they traded for slaves. We can only surmise that there must have been a significant displacement of people and that several individuals died for every slave sold.

Asia

The Portuguese faced a problem in Asia. The population of Asia far surpassed that of Europe and was divided into numerous highly developed, wealthy, and militarily powerful states. In almost every aspect of technology, Asian peoples were equal to if not more advanced than Europeans. In economic terms, Asia was a self-sufficient region with only limited interest in outside trade. Asians had highly desirable goods such silk and cotton textiles, spices, coffee, tea, and porcelain, but the Portuguese had little to offer in exchange. Realizing that the only significant role they could play in Asia was as middlemen in the inter-Asian trade, particularly between India and China, they turned to the only advantage they had: superiority in naval warfare. In 1509, they defeated the Arab fleet and took control of the Indian Ocean from the Omani traders. Then, by entering into agreements with local rulers, between 1509 and 1557, they established a series of trading ports along the coast of southern and eastern Asia. With profits from the Asian trade, during the 1500s an average of 10 ships per year returned to Portugal with goods from Asia to be then traded in Europe.

In 1564, the Spanish established a trading port at Manila in the Philippines to trade with Chinese merchants; and Spanish ships, Manila galleons, sailed between Manila and Acapulco in Mexico. From Acapulco, goods were transported over land to Vera Cruz and from there shipped to Spain. Unlike the Portuguese, the Spanish had nothing to exchange for goods except silver and gold from their mines in the Americas.

Starting in the 1600s, Dutch, English, and French merchants began sailing around the Cape of Good Hope and establishing small fortified trading ports in India, Ceylon, and the islands of the East Indies. The ports were fortified to protect them not from local rulers, with whom they had trade agreements, but from rival European powers. After Ivan the Terrible fused the Russians into a centralized state in the 1550s, Russia began expanding overland across northern Asia, conquering the small nomadic pastoral and foraging peoples of Siberia. By the 1630s, the Russians had reached the Pacific coast of Asia and in 1640 signed a treaty with the Chinese allowing them to trade gold and furs for tea.

The introduction of New World crops greatly changed the lives of many of Africa's farming peoples.

Cultural Consequences

By the late 1700s, the first phase of European expansion—the initial conquest of the Americas and the establishment of trade with Africa and Asia—was coming to an end. The cultural consequences of European expansion, both direct and indirect, varied greatly from one region of the world to the other. The vast majority of the peoples of Oceania had experienced no effects. The Manila galleons avoided the scattered islands, except for Guam, in Micronesia, where the galleon made its only stop. Otherwise, the peoples of Oceania were as unknown to Europeans as Europeans were to them. While the Asian trade was extraordinarily valuable and important to Europeans, it was relatively insignificant to the economy of Asia. Whatever cultural effects Europeans had on the peoples of Asia were highly localized and insignificant.

Although direct contact between Europeans and the peoples of sub-Saharan Africa had been limited to a few coastal areas, the slave trade had greatly changed most of the region. Prior to the slave trade, firearms, if known at all, would have been extremely rare. During the seventeenth and eighteenth centuries, Europeans were trading African peoples for muskets of ever-increasing sophistication and in ever-increasing quantities. The slave-for-gun trade shifted trade networks and disrupted the existing balance of power among the African societies. As slave-related warfare escalated, new states emerged, and many of the older kingdoms declined. In West Africa, the Songhai Empire disintegrated, and Kanen-Bornu weakened considerably. At the same time, along the coast, many of the small kingdoms and city-states such as Oyo, Aboney, Ashanti, and Benin were rapidly expanding due to the slave trade. In central Africa, the Kongo kingdom, refusing to participate in the slave wars, disintegrated, and new slave-raiding states such as Lunda emerged.

At the same time, New World crops introduced by the Portuguese were dramatically changing African farming. In the early 1500s, corn, manioc, sweet potatoes, pineapples, peanuts, papayas, and some lesser crops were introduced. In savannas and grasslands in portions of West Africa, central Angola, and the northern and southern extremes of the Congo basin, corn became the dominant staple, greatly increasing the productivity of their farming. In the tropical forest regions, manioc was far superior to existing starchy crops. Few details are known about the effects of these new crops. Some scholars have suggested that the introduction of corn resulted in a population explosion that minimized the demographic impact of the slave trade. It is also clear that corn and manioc allowed for the expansion of farming populations into regions that had been occupied by foragers and pastoralists.

Conversion of native peoples to Christianity was one of the primary interests of the Spanish in the Americas.

The two regions of the world most directly and dramatically affected during this first stage were the Americas and Europe. After the initial occupation of the major islands in the West Indies and the conquest of the main Indian states and empires of Mesoamerica and the Andes, Spanish expansion slowed. After 1600, the Spanish extended their control to only a few small adjacent areas of the Americas. In the West Indies, due to epidemics of Old World diseases and absorption by European immigrants and African slaves, with few exceptions, Native Americans had vanished. The few survivors were absorbed into the now more numerous European and African populations. Among the highly civilized peoples of Mesoamerica and the Andes, several things had occurred. The vast majority of native people had died in epidemics, taking with them most of their hereditary political leadership, priests, and other cultural leaders. The Spanish reduced the surviving native population to illiterate agrarian peasants who were forced to at least seasonally work in the Spanish-owned mines and on their farms and ranches. They forced upon all of these people at least a veneer of Catholicism, destroying temples, while building churches and assigning priests to their communities. In addition, they introduced Western technology as well as crops and animals: plows, steel tools, wheat, oats, horses, donkeys, cattle, sheep, and goats. In spite of these changes, most surviving communities still retained their social and cultural distinctiveness: languages, most of their cultural institutions, many of their religious beliefs and practices, and their traditional crafts.

The greater portion of the Americas remained beyond direct Spanish control. However, even among the still politically autonomous groups of Native Americans, dramatic cultural changes had already occurred. The epidemic diseases had also affected these peoples. Most of the populous, highly organized agricultural peoples of the eastern United States and lowland South America had been destroyed by disease. Much of the cultural knowledge of these peoples had died with their former political and religious leaders. The remaining population survived as small politically fragmented groups of widely scattered horticulturists. The peoples least affected by the early Spanish were the scattered foraging peoples who still occupied much of North America and South America.

The Spanish conquest of the West Indies, Mesoamerica, and the Andes effectively cut the Americas in two: the part north of Mesoamerica, and the region east of the Andes, the lowland tropical forests, and grasslands of eastern South America. The Atlantic coast of South America was going to be colonized first, by the Portuguese, while the Atlantic coast of North America was going to be settled somewhat later, mainly by the English and French.

Change came most rapidly for the still autonomous **indigenous peoples** of the tropical forests and grasslands of lowland South America. Having a tradition of keeping domesticated animals, llamas, and alpacas, by the mid–sixteenth century the peoples of the grasslands of southern South America started adopting horses, donkeys, cattle, sheep, and goats from the Spanish. By the seventeenth century, many of these groups had become pastoralists, while others had become horse-mounted foragers. In the 1530s, the Portuguese began establishing sugarcane plantations along the coast of Brazil. While areas of settlement would be limited to the coast for the next three centuries, their effects on native peoples extended well into the interior. Africa was the source of most of the slave labor to work their sugarcane plantations, but the Portuguese enslaved Native Americans as well. By the last decades of the sixteenth century, Portuguese slave raiders were ranging into the interior in search of villages to attack. As the surviving groups withdrew, the slave raiders went ever farther into the interior, even attacking Jesuit-controlled Indian mission communities in Spanish territory. In the late 1600s, these slave raiders also began prospecting for gold, diamonds, and other minerals; by the late 1700s, they had penetrated virtually every portion of the Amazon basin.

It was not until the early seventeenth century that the relative isolation of the North American peoples started changing with the establishment of colonies by the English, French, and, for a short period, the Dutch along the Atlantic coast. Most of these settlers, particularly the English, were not interested in conquering the native people, but rather dispossessing them of their land. However, some Europeans became traders, exchanging guns and metal tools for hides and furs. By the mid-1700s, virtually all of the woodland peoples from Hudson Bay to the Gulf of Mexico were actively involved in this trade. In the last decades of the seventeenth century, horses from the Spanish settlements in New Mexico started diffusing among the foraging peoples of the Great Plains and Rocky Mountains. By the eighteenth century, these indigenous peoples had become horse-mounted foragers. Also during the same period, the Navajo in the Southwest became pastoralist; keeping herds of sheep and goats. During the eighteenth century, the Spanish extended their mission settlements of Indians up the California coast, while Russians began trading with the peoples of Alaska and the Northwest Coast in the 1780s.

By 1800, the indigenous civilizations of the Americas had been virtually eliminated. Little remained of their cultural achievements other than the ruins of what had been their cities. Their population, once reduced by 90 percent or more, was now recovering. However, they were still under the political control of resident Europeans. The Indian population of most of the Caribbean and Atlantic coastal areas had vanished. Even though most of the land area of the Americas was still occupied by small communities of autonomous foragers and horticulturalists, even the lives and cultures of these scattered peoples had, to varying degrees, been changed either directly or indirectly by European expansion.

The Industrial Revolution

The establishment of overseas colonies and trade ended European isolation and dramatically increased their knowledge of both the natural and human world. Intellectually, Europe entered what some have called the "Age of Enlightenment," with major advancement in philosophy, science, and technology. In the last decades of the eighteenth century, two events dramatically changed not only the relationship between Europe and the other regions of the world, but Europe itself.

Starting in 1775, in the English colonies of North America, the resident European population revolted, establishing the United States. This revolution soon spread to the Spanish colonies; and by the 1820s, the resident Europeans in these colonies had established independent countries. In 1804, the African slaves revolted in Haiti and drove out French. Although some colonies remained, by the 1820s, the English, French, and Spanish had lost their most valuable colonies in the Americas.

> **indigenous people** Culturally distinct peoples who have occupied a region longer than peoples who have colonized or immigrated to the region.

During this same period, machine-made goods began replacing handcrafted items—the start of the Industrial Revolution. At first, textiles were produced using water wheels to power the machinery in the mills. However, this technology soon changed to coal-fired, steam-driven machinery producing other goods. The steam engine allowed for the production of much greater quantities of goods with less human labor. Thus, they were less costly than handmade goods.

This basic change in the production of goods resulted in a wide range of other technological innovations, particularly in the transportation of goods and people. Steam-powered locomotives replaced horse-drawn wagons for long-distance land transport. Wooden sailing ships were first replaced by steam-driven wooden paddlewheel boats and ships only to be replaced by steel-hulled, propeller-driven ships by the last decades of the nineteenth century. Whether by land or sea, greater quantities of goods, products, and people could be moved much faster and cheaper.

What truly changed the balance of power in the world, however, were the advances in military technology. In the first decades of the 1800s, European armies were still armed with slow, inaccurate, single-shot, muzzle-loading muskets. Before the end of the century, these armies were armed with rapid-firing, highly accurate, cartridge-loading rifles, and even machine guns. Similarly, the old muzzle-loading cannons were replaced by breach-loading artillery pieces with exploding shells.

During the same period, European navies changed. Wooden sailing ships armed with muzzle-loading cannons were replaced by steel-hulled, steam-powered ships armed with breach-loading cannons. Europeans now had overwhelming military superiority over the other peoples of the world on both land and sea.

The industrializing countries of Europe needed markets for the ever-increasing quantities of goods being produced by their factories, as well as new sources of raw materials and food to maintain the production of these industries and feed their workers. Initially, the colonies or former colonies in the Americas were the primary overseas markets and sources of raw materials, resulting in increased economic expansion even after independence. The United States was the main beneficiary. At first a source of timber, cotton, tobacco, whale oil, and a variety of food crops, the United States soon experienced its own industrial revolution while increasing exports of commodities.

The economic expansion of the United States was accompanied by rising numbers of immigrants from Europe. In 1776, the settled area of the United States was limited to the coastal fringe, east of the Appalachian Mountains. By the 1880s, the entire region from the Atlantic to the Pacific had been settled and the indigenous peoples defeated and placed on small reservations. The change was not as dramatic in Latin America; many of the countries there were still relying on gold, silver, and other mineral production as well as plantation crops to pay for imports. There were exceptions; Argentina, for example, became a major supplier of grain and cattle to feed industrial Europe. As a result, the resident European population expanded into the grasslands of the Pampas and Patagonia, displacing the native peoples.

Asia

During the early 1800s, European powers, particularly England, France, and the Netherlands, started expanding their areas of control in Asia. China had successfully resisted making trade concessions. In the Opium War with England (1839–1842) and in a second war with England and France between 1856 and 1858, China saw its navy and army badly defeated and was forced to make humiliating land and trading concessions.

During the late 1700s and early 1800s, the British East India Company had expanded its territorial control in parts of India. The crushing of the Sepoy Mutiny (1857–1858), a native uprising, ended any question about the English political domination in India. However, there was still the problem of distance: all shipping to and from Europe and Asia had to pass around the tip of Africa—a long and costly journey.

In 1859, a French company began construction on the Suez Canal, connecting the Mediterranean and Red seas. Open to the ships of all countries, the canal was completed in 1869, cutting the shipping distance between Europe and Asia by more than half and greatly increasing the European presence in Asia. By the end of the nineteenth century, most of Asia had been brought under the direct or indirect of European powers. England had India, Burma, Malaya, Sarawak, Hong Kong, and Ceylon. The French held Indochina; the Dutch had extended their control over the islands of East Indies; while Russia controlled most of central Asia, Siberia, and part of Manchuria. Although still technically independent countries, China, Nepal, Afghanistan, Thailand, and Persia (Iran) were so strongly dominated by one or another European powers that some have termed them *semicolonial* regions. Only two countries truly retained their autonomy: the Ottoman Empire, which included at this time Turkey, Iraq, Syria, Lebanon,

Palestine, Jordan, and most of the Arabian Peninsula; and Japan. Japan, adopting a European model, was creating its own empire, including Korea and Formosa.

Africa

The initial impact of European industrialization on Africa was an intensification of the slave trade as plantations in the Americas increased their production of sugarcane, cotton, and other commodities. However, as opposition to slavery and the slave trade increased, during the early and mid–nineteenth century, the slave trade declined, only ending in the 1870s. Africa had potential as both a supplier of raw materials and a market for manufactured goods—a potential that could not be realized under the existing conditions. The slave trade and resulting warfare had destroyed the political stability of much of the region, and as a result Europeans saw sub-Saharan Africa as a dangerous place in need of control. As late as the 1870s, the French, English, Spanish, and Portuguese claimed and controlled only a few scattered coastal areas. However, other European powers coveted portions of the region, most of which was still unmapped and unknown to Europeans. In 1884–1885, the Berlin Conference was held in which Britain, France, Germany, Belgium, Italy, Spain, and Portugal unilaterally divided up the peoples and resources of sub-Saharan Africa among themselves. The geographic boundaries now agreed on among themselves, they quickly proceeded to bring the peoples of their new territories under their physical control and developed their resources. With overwhelming military power, they quickly crushed the few native peoples who attempted armed resistance. Although policies varied greatly from colony to colony, now under the control of Europeans, the peoples of sub-Saharan had their political organizations and economies restructured, while Christian missionaries traveled widely in search of converts.

Oceania

The extension of European domination over the peoples of Oceania was sporadic and slow. The Spanish had established the first European colony in 1668 in Oceania on Guam. However, it was over a hundred years later that the English established the second, a penal colony, at Botany Bay in Australia in 1785. The pattern of English expansion in Australia and the nearby islands of Tasmania and New Zealand basically followed the pattern of the earlier English expansion in North America. The initially small colony of Europeans grew through continued migration, as the native population declined due to disease and/or warfare. By the mid-1800s, Europeans outnumbered native populations who had or would soon be given small reserves. Of little economic value, European countries had little incentive to extend their empires to include the other islands of Polynesia, Melanesia, and Micronesia.

By the mid–nineteenth century, American and European missionaries, whalers, traders, and sailors were frequenting the islands of the still independent peoples of the Pacific. The effects of contact varied greatly from island group to island group. Epidemics destroyed much of the population on some island groups but had no lasting effects on others. Islands such as Fiji, Hawaii, and New Caledonia with valuable resources to be developed found their populations displaced by immigrant workers. The largest numbers of these immigrants were not Europeans but Asians from India, Japan, China, Indo-China, and the East Indies. However, most islands saw no influx of immigrants.

The French and English began to slowly incorporate some the island groups into their empires in the mid–nineteenth century, usually through agreements with local leaders. In the 1880s, Germany began incorporating others into its new overseas empire: portions of Micronesia, western Samoa, and part of New Guinea. During the Spanish-American War in 1898, the United States took control of Guam and the following year annexed Hawaii and American Samoa. Finally, in 1900, the Tonga Islands became a British protectorate. The political division of Oceania among the Dutch, British, French, German, and Americans was virtually complete.

Consequences of European Expansion

By the beginning of the twentieth century, European peoples virtually dominated the world, politically and economically. The Americas were politically controlled by resident Europeans, the only exception being Haiti, which was African American. Sub-Saharan Africa, with minor exceptions, was divided into European colonial processions. Most Asian countries were under either the direct or indirect control of one or another European country. The same was now true of Oceania as well.

The social and cultural consequence of 400 years European expansion differed greatly from one region of the world to the next. Europe itself had changed dramatically. In 1500, Europe was still basically a feudal society, with a hereditary and land-owning nobility supported by peasants who worked on their estates. Towns with merchants and craftspeople were small and few.

With the conquest of the Americas and the expansion of **global trade**, this landscape began to change.

While the nobility of these countries profited most from this expansion, other elements of the society also profited. Towns began to grow, and a rising wealthy middle class of merchants and artisans began to emerge. The overseas colonies and possibility for migration presented an opportunity that many of the poorer people and religious dissidents took advantage of.

However, it was not until the Industrial Revolution that European society, particularly in Western Europe, began to change. While the nobility continued to live off the income from their agricultural estates, the middle class expanded dramatically with the emergence of the industrialists—the owners of the new textile mills, coal mines, and manufacturing plants. Many of these industrialists quickly accumulated fortunes that far exceeded those of most of the landed nobility. Associated with industrialization was a rapid growth of urban manufacturing and trade centers and a massive migration of families from rural farms to cities. Most workers were now wage workers, in manufacturing, mining, or commerce, and not tenant farmers or laborers on the estates of the nobility. A modern capitalist economy had emerged with it increasing demands for political and other social rights, not just by the now economically power middle class, but by the factory workers and miners, too. In addition to the changes in technology and material wealth, socially the most readily apparent change was increasingly democratic political institutions and the erosion of the nobility's rights and privileges.

The Americas had changed more than other regions of world. Now resident were three major distinctly different populations: Native Americans, Europeans, and Africans. This resident European population was far from homogeneous. During the colonial period, Spanish, Portuguese, English, French, Scots, Scots-Irish, Irish, and Germans had settled in various regions of the Americas. The nineteenth century had seen the arrival of immigrants from still other parts of Europe. African slaves, primarily but not exclusively from Western and Central Africa, had been brought to the Americas. This African population arrived speaking many different languages and representing a wide diversity of cultural backgrounds. All of these various groups of people had experienced changes in their cultures, to varying degrees, by the others. Scattered groups of Native Americans still existed from the arctic to the tip of South America. All had to some degree been culturally influenced by Europeans, while many had been influenced by Africans as well. This influence varied greatly from one part of the Americas to another. There were some regions where the Native Americans constituted the vast majority of the population. There were others regions where Native population had disappeared altogether, and there were regions where surviving native groups had been reduced to small minority populations. The vast majority were under the control of the dominant European population; however, there were some still autonomous groups, particularly in South Americas. Some were still foragers, others were farmers, and some lived on support from their national governments.

Originally, the major European groups differed from each other in language and culture. However, residence in the Americas forced new regionalized adaptations. They had to adopt economic behaviors and technologies suitable to environmental conditions frequently very different from those of Europe. Depending on where they lived, they came into cultural contact with other groups of Europeans, Native American, and/or Africans. As slaves, Africans were usually settled in communities of individuals of mixed African cultural heritage. While all Africans were forced to conform to certain cultural practices imposed by their European owners, what those new cultural practices were and how stringently they were imposed varied greatly from region to region. As a result, the culture that developed among the slave population was partly European and to varying degrees African or even Native American in origin.

In addition, even in colonial times there were free black communities. In some cases, these individuals had gained their freedom and lived among the dominant European population, usually adopting the cultural practices of the dominant community. In many other cases, escaped slaves, particular in South America and the Caribbean, formed their own separate communities. In some cases, the cultures of these communities were basically derived from African traditions. In other cases, they adopted Native American language and a culture that was both African and Native American in origin. Thus, these new "African American" cultures showed an extremely high degree of localized diversity. In addition, through intermarriage, a large number of mixed societies emerged that combined varying degrees of Native American, European, and/or African ancestry and cultural heritage. Although all had greatly changed, by 1900, the peoples of the Americas were far more socially and culturally diverse in 1900 than they had been in 1492.

global trade Economic exchange of goods and other products between the different peoples of the world via established trade networks.

The effects of European expansion on the peoples of Oceania had been mixed. The suffering and cultural change of the indigenous peoples of Australia, Tasmania, and New Zealand paralleled what had happened to the native peoples of the Americas. At the other extreme were several hundred thousand or more horticultural peoples of highland New Guinea who had yet to have any direct contact with Europeans and would not until the 1930s. In between were the other peoples whose experience varied greatly from one island group to another.

The direct and indirect cultural effect of European contact and colonial subjugation varied greatly from one area to another in sub-Saharan Africa. The four centuries of the slave trade and internal slave raiding undoubtedly affected the cultures of people throughout much of sub-Saharan Africa. The colonial period also had some affects, but they varied greatly from region to region and colony to colony. In the Congo Free State (later the Belgium Congo), the ruthless exploitation of resources and people had resulted in the deaths of over half the population within the first 20 years. However, African peoples who had little if anything that European colonialist wanted barely, if at all, felt the European presence. In the Kalahari Desert and other isolated regions, there were still foraging peoples, such as the San, whose lives had been little touched by Europeans. Throughout the grasslands and desert regions there were traditional pastoral communities, while in the woodlands and jungle regions most of the farming communities had only indirectly felt the influence of European colonial domination.

Asia was less affected by European expansion than another other region of the world. With highly organized political, social, economic, and religious institutions, the European colonial officials attempted only to modify and manipulate them to economically benefit the empires, not destroy or replace them. European influence in Asia was greatest, not in the countries they directly or indirectly controlled, but rather in one of the few that fully retained it autonomy: Japan. In the last decades of the nineteenth century, Japanese leaders began to systematical adopt the latest European technology. While minimizing the effects of this new technology on other aspects of Japanese culture, Japan was developing an industrial economy competitive with Europe and the United States by the early twentieth century.

This is the way the world would basically remain for the next half century. Residence Europeans would control the independent countries of the Americas, while most of the countries of Africa, Asia, and Oceania were dominated by one or another of the imperial European powers. There was an increased diffusion of cultural practices. However, it was not balanced. While Europeans attempted to impost their cultural beliefs and ideas, particularly Christianity, on other indigenous peoples, they were highly protective of their manufacturing technology, wanting to sell only finished products. There was global trade, but not an integrated global economy. The independent countries of the Americas imposed tariffs and quotas on imported and exported goods to protect their local markets and industries. The European empires had been created for the economic benefit of the "home country," as protected markets for manufactured goods and as sources of raw materials. Trade both within and between empires and independent countries was strongly regulated. It was not until after World War II and the collapse of the European empires that the global economy would start to emerge with free trade.

By *global economy*, we are referring to an integrated global market in which goods and services are exchanged globally, with their prices determined by supply and demand and with minimal interference or control of national governments. Before this global exchange could develop, the colonial empires had to disintegrate. In 1945, there were about 60 fully independent countries in the world. Between 1946 and 1980, 88 newly independent countries were created out of the old colonial empires. In the 1990s, the Soviet Union (the old Russian Empire) and Yugoslavia collapsed, resulting in the creation of 18 new countries. Today there are about 200 countries in the world. However, independence alone did not result in free trade with other countries. Taxes (tariffs) and quotas on the importing and exporting of goods of was not only an important source of revenue for most countries; they also served to protect local markets for domestic producers and consumers. In 1947, 23 countries signed the General Agreement on Tariffs and Trade (GATT). This agreement lowered or eliminated tariffs on thousands of goods traded between these countries. Over the last half century, still other agreements involving still other goods and countries have been signed. In 1995, GATT was replaced by the World Trade Organization (WTO), which today has 158 member countries. There are still tariffs and quotas on the importing and exporting of some goods, but they are minimal.

> **global economy** Integrated global market in which goods and services are bought and sold globally with prices determined by supply and demand.

Container shipping has greatly lowered the cost of shipping of manufactured goods and has played a key role in the development of the global economy over the past 30 years.

This same period has seen major advances in shipping and communications. Most of the international shipping of goods, about 90 percent, is carried by ocean-going ships. As late as the 1960s, cargo was usually packed in small boxes and loaded and stored on ships, piecemeal, by hand. Unloading was done in the same manner. Starting in the 1960s, a new method using standardized containers, usually 20 to 40 feet in length, and ships designed to carry these containers started being used. Goods were loaded in these containers at the factory, taken to the port, and loaded by cranes onto ships, to later be unloaded by cranes usually on to trucks or trains. Today it takes one-tenth the amount of time to load and unload cargo ships that it did in 1960. This change has greatly decreased the amount of labor needed, and thus cost, to handle shipments. It has also greatly reduced the amount of time cargo ships spend in port to load or unload, once again reducing cost.

In the early 1960s, international communication usually took the form of letters or packages sent by post or voice communication by radio or telephones using land line or transoceanic cables. Both were slow and costly. Today, thanks to communication satellites, communication is both instantaneous and cheap. One can e-mail a letter or even a whole database to almost any place in the world. With modern smart phones, one can talk with other individuals almost anywhere in the world. For businesses, these advances mean that goods can be produced and marketed anywhere in the world. For a company, they mean that it does not make any difference whether their supplier or branch office is on the other side of town or in some other country or another continent. For the production and marketing of goods, geographic locale has become increasing irrelevant.

The consequences of the emergence of the global economy were not just economic but cultural as well. As we noted earlier, contact between culturally difference peoples results in various types of cultural exchange—cultural knowledge as well as technology. Ever-accelerating cultural exchange is both a direct and indirect consequence of the global economy. This exchange is occurring simultaneously in many

GLOBAL CHALLENGES AND OPPORTUNITIES

The Maroons: The New African Peoples of the Americas

The survival of African cultural traditions among the maroon peoples of Suriname is readily apparent in this painted Djuka house front.

African slaves began escaping almost immediately after having been brought to the Americas. Many found refuge among the Native American peoples. Still others escaped in small groups and formed their own distinct societies. During the colonial period, large numbers of free African communities were established in the southern portion of the United States, the West Indies, Mexico, and Central and South America. In language and culture, these new African societies were highly diverse and distinct from each other, their African ancestors, and the slave populations from which they had fled. Here we are going to discuss just two of these groups.

Black Carib

The Garifuna, or Black Carib, are predominantly African in ancestry, with a high degree of Native American ancestry. In 1675, a slave ship was wrecked on a small island near St. Vincent in the West Indies. The surviving Africans, Ibibio men from what is today Nigeria, were rescued by the Caribs, who brought them to St. Vincent. The Spanish had avoided these smaller islands, the Lesser Antilles, in part because the Caribs were a highly aggressive and warlike people. The words *Caribbean* and *cannibal* are derived from Carib. The Ibibio men intermarried with Carib women. The descendants of these couples spoke the Carib language, with male and female dialects, practiced Carib-style skull deformation of infants, and in their material culture and most other aspects of their culture were indistinguishable from the Caribs. Like the Caribs, they also relied on hunting, fishing, and the cultivation of manioc. This assimilation of Native American culture occurred in spite of the fact that increasing numbers of other escaped African slaves were joining the community. This mixed African/Native American community, the "Black Caribs," quickly came into conflict and separated from the Native American community, occupying the windward side of the island, while "Red Caribs" lived on the leeward side.

In the late 1600s, the French and the British began occupying the Lesser Antilles, both claiming St. Vincent. The French first settled on the leeward or "Red Carib" side of the island and developed plantations worked by African slave labor. The Black Caribs were extremely hostile to Europeans, and they defeated a French military force in 1719. In the Peace of Paris, signed in 1763 to end the Seven Years War, the French ceded St. Vincent to the British. The new British governor of the island, wanting to expand the sugarcane plantations, was faced with a problem: two-thirds of the richest land on the island was on the windward side belonging to the Black Caribs. The British were conflicted over how they should be dealt with. Although some referred to them as "Indians" and argued that they had an "aboriginal claim" to their lands, others saw them as "usurpers of . . . Carib heritage" who should be transported back to Africa. No one seems to have suggested that they be reenslaved; they were considered far too dangerous for that. Attempts to negotiate land sales from the Black Caribs failed. A British attempt to build a road on the windward side resulted in armed resistance, and the First Carib War broke out. Lasting from 1769 to 1773, this war consisted primarily of skirmishes and ended in a peace agreement in which the Black Caribs ceded a very small portion of

---

different ways, some explicit and some implicit. Here we are going to discuss five of the main ways this is occurring: academic knowledge, popular culture, migration, technology, and restructuring of economic behavior.

Universities and colleges are becoming globalized as both faculties and students are increasingly drawn from countries around the world. Academic conferences and journals are more and more global in scope, not just in subject matter but also in participants. This globalization of academic knowledge is most evident in, but not limited to, engineering and the sciences. Fifty years ago, no one would have thought that Iran might be able to develop nuclear weapons or that India would be a leader their land. However, conflict between the British planters and the Black Carib continued. In 1795, with French support, the Black Caribs attacked the British plantations. The following year, the British defeated the Black Carib and took about 5,000 captive. About half died in captivity before, in 1797, the surviving Black Caribs were taken to Roatan Island off the coast of Honduras. From Roatan, the Black Carib were removed by the Spanish to the mainland where they became known as the Garifuna or "Cassava (manioc) eaters." Today there are about 200,000 Gurifuna occupying 43 communities along the Caribbean coast from Belize to Nicaragua.

The Saramaka of the Guianas

The Guianas refers to the northern coast of South America between the Orinoco and Amazon rivers. Both the Spanish and Portuguese ignored this resource poor region. In 1605, the Dutch established a small settlement and in the 1620s began importing African slaves and developing sugar and cotton plantations. Starting in the mid-1600s, the English and French also began completing with the Dutch for the Guianas, a rivalry that would last for 200 years.

The Guianas never became an important region for sugar, cotton, and other plantation crops and thus never attracted many European settlers nor had large numbers of African slaves. Most of the Native American population died during the seventeenth century due to Old World diseases, and thus the vast jungle areas back from the coast were lightly inhabited and of little value or interest to the European colonist on the coast. As early as the 1620s, escaped slaves from the coastal plantations began forming communities along isolated river valleys in the interior. Due to their relative isolation from each other, during the colonial period, at least six new African societies would emerge, each with its own distinctive language and generic African-derived culture. The two largest of these groups were the Saramaka (Saramacca) and the Djuka (Ndjuka).

From their isolated communities in the interior, these African communities would raid the coastal plantations for weapons, tools, and supplies, freeing other slaves to join them. Europeans would periodically mount military expeditions to travel into the interior to attempt to destroy these communities and reenslave their inhabitants. Finally, in 1762, the Dutch negotiated a treaty with the Saramaka and the Djuka, which formally recognized their independence and allowed them peaceful trade with the European settlers. However, they could no longer give refuge to escaped slaves.

The Saramaka live on the Suriname River in what is today Suriname, formerly Dutch Guiana. Their language is a mixed English-Portuguese Creole with a few words from Dutch and African languages. The traditional economy is based on hunting, fishing, and gardening. They have collective ownership of their land and "use rights" to the gardens they clear. They live in small, scattered permanent villages and also have smaller farming villages. Descent is matrilineal (through the mother's line), and the core of every village is a group of matrilineal families. They have paramount chief as well as other formal officials. Their religion is a syncretic blending of various African-derived deities and ritual practices reflecting their diverse African origins. They practice scarification, the African practice of creating designs on the skin by scarring. However, it is in their art where the strength of their African heritage becomes most overtly apparent. Even common domestic items, wooden bowls, combs, spoons, house doors, drums, canoe paddles, and prows are frequently carved with highly elaborate designs.

For over 300 years, the Saramaka remained relatively isolated and independent of the other peoples of Suriname. In 1975, Suriname became an independent country; and in 1986, fighting broke out between government troops and members of the six maroon tribes. Many Saramaka fled to French Guiana. A peace agreement ended the war in 1992, but the Maroons lost title to their lands. In the 1990s, the government began granting logging and mining concessions to multinational corporations, some of which are to land in the traditional territory used by Saramaka. The Saramaka filed a case against the government in the Inter-American Court of Human Rights. In November 2007, the court found in their favor, ruling among other things that the Saramaka are a "tribal community" and have the same legal status as "indigenous" peoples. However, the government of Suriname has ignored this ruling.

in information technology. However, more is involved that merely the dissemination of knowledge. The global academic world is structured on a Western academic model. This is a Western cultural model that defines how academic institutions are structured as well as how research is conducted and findings are evaluated and disseminated. Thus, implicit in becoming part of the global academic community is the adoption of certain Western cultural behaviors. This change, however, directly affects only a small portion of the global population.

The globalization of popular culture, primarily movies and television, has a far more pervasive reach in the global populations. In fact, few peoples in the world are so isolated today that they are uninfluenced

Human migration is resulting in increasing socially and culturally diversity in urban population. Here Muslims pray outside the mosque in the Barbès-Rochechouart district of Paris.

by global popular culture. While most such pop culture is Western in origin, non-Western peoples are also increasingly producing movies and television programming. However, even when produced by non-Western peoples, they are usually produced by highly urbanized populations reflecting their cultural interest.

It is difficult to overestimate the potential influence of popular movies and television. Being both visual and aural, they transport the individual into other worlds. Individuals in even remote farming villages in Latin America, Africa, and Asia today can "visit," thanks to the media, New York, London, Tokyo, and other great cities of the world. They can see their homes, their ways of life and behaviors. They can see and hear of ways of behaving that are so removed and different from their own personal experience that even in their wildest imagination they could not have conceived of them. For the vast majority of people, movies and television are the primary means of education for the world beyond their experience. They are also the major marketing tool for the products of the global economy, creating ever-growing "need" for material goods.

The global economy has greatly benefited the peoples of the world. Today more people are better fed and clothed than ever before. However, some individuals, countries, and regions within countries have materially benefited far more than others, and many have not benefited at all. Economic inequalities in the world are growing, and at the same time, the peoples of the world are increasingly aware of these inequalities due to the popular media. Over the past 50 years, the population of the world has grown from 2.5 to over 7 billion. That growth plus the combination of economic inequalities and heightened awareness of these inequalities have resulted in the greatest migration in human history. In search of economic opportunities, people are moving from less developed to more developed regions and countries. The greatest movement has been within countries, as people move from rural areas to cities. Still others, about 200 million, have moved to other countries. Both cities and countries are become increasingly mixed with peoples from highly diverse social and cultural backgrounds. For urban dwellers today, one does not have to travel to some remote region or another country or even another continent to find to "strange" and "exotic" other people. In more and more cities throughout the world, those "other" peoples whose norms, values, and beliefs are very different from the "natives" are living nearby and interacting with them every day.

For the first time in human history, all of the peoples of the world have potential access to the latest basic technological innovations. This is most evident at the individual level in communications and transportation technology. Growing numbers of people have access to cell phones, smart phones, computers, and television. As of March 2013, the number of Facebook subscribers alone totaled over 1.1 billion. The number of registered motor vehicles in the world surpassed 1 billion in 2010 and is still rapidly growing. While the adoption of modern technology is most evident in urban populations, lives of rural peoples are also being transformed. Farming peoples are increasingly adopting mechanized farming equipment and using pesticides, synthetic fertilizers, and genetically modified seed. Inuit hunters in arctic Canada now use snowmobiles, and Mongolian herders travel by motorcycle. The major factor limiting the adoption of modern technology is the ability of individuals to purchase it.

Noting that there are many forms of capitalism, implicit in the global economy is the modern Western capitalist model. This model disproportionally rewards individual economic behavior over collective or group economic behavior or interest. Individuals are placed in competition with all other individuals in pursuit of material gain. In this system, if an individual does not attempt to maximize economic gain, then he or she is disadvantaged in this competition with others who are maximizing their gain. Some have referred to this as a "winner take all" system. The big get bigger at the expense of the "losers." This is most evident in the multinational corporations who are growing ever larger by the destruction and absorption of smaller companies and corporations. As more and more individuals are drawn to and integrated into the global economy, by necessity their economic and social behaviors are changed.

Traditional cultural behaviors, by which we mean preexisting cultural behaviors (which are the focus of most of the following chapters), are being challenged directly and indirectly by the growing and expanding global economy. What is going to be the final result? Is a common global culture going to be the result? That is highly doubtful. All we can say with any certainty is that the cultures of the peoples of the world are going to change significantly—some far more than others.

SUMMARY

1. **Explain why society is dynamic.** The culture of a society is always changing. Our culture allows us to attempt to change our natural and social environments; it is our adaptive dimension. We act in groups to acquire the food, shelter, and other things we need from the natural environment and to protect ourselves from groups of competing humans. While all aspects of a people's culture change over time, changes in technology have the greatest effect in that a new technology can profoundly change our relationship to our natural environment as well as our social environment. The two main sources of cultural change are (1) the independent inventions, discoveries, and creations of a society's members and (2) the borrowing of cultural knowledge from members of other societies with whom they are in contact.

2. **Discuss how the present diversity of human culture came about.** At first all peoples were foragers sharing the same basic technology. As they migrated to different regions of the world, they modified their technology and other cultural behaviors as they adapted to new natural and social environments—from the arctic to the tropics, and from jungles and woodlands to deserts and grasslands. Later, independently of one another, peoples in widely scattered regions of the both the Old and New worlds domesticated plants and animals. As they became farmers and herders, their cultures became increasingly diverse and localized. However, farming and herding were not suitable for all areas of the world, and foragers continued to flourish. Later, new farming technologies (intensive agriculture)

developed that could support growing numbers of people and required greater cooperation between people. The result was the emergence of civilizations with, among other things, cities, metallurgy, and highly centralized governments. These civilizations developed independently in different regions of the Old World and New World, adding still another level of localized cultural diversity. Eventually, the civilizations of the Old World came into contact with each other, exchanging some but not all cultural knowledge and remaining distinct from one another. In the New World, a similar process occurred. Thus, in the 1400s, there were still two totally independent lines, and also numerous distinct secondary regional lines, of cultural development, each with its own domesticated plants and animals, technologies, writing systems, religious beliefs, and other cultural knowledge.

3. **Elaborate on the development and spread of globalization.** Globalization began in 1492 with Columbus and can be divided into three stages. The first stage was the conquest of the Americas and the development of a global maritime trade network. During the next three centuries, Europeans dramatically changed the world. The Spanish and later the Portuguese, English, French, and Dutch invaded the Americas, conquering or displacing most of the native peoples and gaining control of most of the land and resources. At the same time, these same European peoples were establishing a global maritime trade network that soon brought all of the peoples of the world into contact with one another, directly or indirectly. The establishment of this global trade network resulted in the Columbian Exchange—the exchange of peoples, diseases, and cultural knowledge between the Old World and the New. Initially, the single-most important consequence was in the New World. Europeans introduced Old World diseases such as smallpox, malaria, influenza, and cholera for which the indigenous peoples of the Americas had no nature immunities. The result was a massive population collapse. On one hand, this collapse greatly facilitated the conquest of the rich natural resources of the Americas by Europeans; but on the other hand, it created a labor shortage. The conquering Europeans solved this labor problem by bringing in slave labor from sub-Saharan Africa to work in their mining and on their plantations. The slave trade result in slave wars throughout most of western and central Africa. These wars politically destabilized most of Africa. At the same time, the introduction of New World crops, primarily corn and manioc, greatly expanded agriculture in Africa, resulting in a growth in population. Contact with Asia was limited to trade. To Europeans, the trade for Asian luxury goods, silks, cottons, porcelains, tea, and spices was important and desirable. To Asians, this trade was insignificant, and the vast majorities were not affected at all by Europeans. Until 1785, European contact with the people of Oceania was limited to a single island group: Guam. Thus, while the cultures of many of the peoples of the world were directly or indirectly affected by European expansion during this period, the impact differed greatly from one region to another.

4. **Describe how the Industrial Revolution gave European powers dominance in the world.** The Industrial Revolution in Europe, starting in the last decades of eighteenth century, dramatically changed the balance of power among the world's peoples. For the first time Europeans became the most technologically advanced people in the world. At the same time, the resident European populations in the Americas were becoming politically independent of Europe. In search of new sources of raw materials for their industry and new markets for the growing quantities of manufactured goods they were producing, they turned to Asia, Africa, and Oceania. During the mid–nineteenth century, Britain, France, and the Netherlands expanded their political and economic control in Asia. By the end of the century, almost every country in Asia was either a colonial possession or under the political control of one of these countries. In the 1880s, Germany, Britain, France, Portugal,

and Belgium unilaterally divided Africa between their empires. Also in the last decades of the nineteenth century, Germany, Britain, France, the Netherlands, and the United States claimed dominion over the last remaining independent peoples of Oceania. The dominance of European peoples in the world was complete.

5. **Analyze the third and most recent stage of globalization and the global economy.** At the beginning of the twentieth century, most of the peoples of Africa, Asia, and Oceania were under the direct or indirect control of one or another European empire. The purpose of these empires was to economically benefit the "home country." The colonial possessions served as controlled markets for their industrial production and sources of raw materials for their industries. Trade within and between these empires was regulated by the home country by tariffs (taxes) and quota on goods. Global trade was thus highly fragmented. While there was global trade, the global economy—meaning an integrated global market in which goods and services are sold at prices determined by supply and demand—did not and could not exist. Following World War II, the European empires started to disintegrate. Starting in 1947, a group of countries began negotiating agreements to eliminate tariffs and quotas on imports and exports of goods: free trade. This evolved into the World Trade Organization, which today involves the vast majority of the world's countries. At the same time, technological advances in shipping drastically lowered the cost of shipping goods, while developments in communications technology allowed for virtually instantaneous communication between people throughout the world. Associated with the emergence of the global economy has been the globalization of knowledge, particularly in engineering and science; popular culture; and technology. In addition, there have massive migrations of people, both within and between countries, and the increasing integration of people into a Western capitalist economic system. The eventual cultural consequences of these dramatic changes are yet seen.

5 The Development of Anthropological Thought

North Wind / North Wind Picture Archives

The discipline now called anthropology arose out of the encounter of Western Europeans with the indigenous peoples of Africa, Asia, the Americas, and the islands of the Pacific. This woodcut portrays the conquest of the Aztec civilization of central Mexico by the Spaniard Hernando Cortez.

The Emergence of Anthropology
  Late Nineteenth-Century Unilineal Evolutionism
  A Science of Culture?

Anthropological Thought in the Early Twentieth Century
  Historical Particularism in the United States (ca. 1900–1940)
  British Functionalism, 1920s–1960s
  The Fieldwork Tradition

Mid–Twentieth Century: Rebirth of Evolutionism

Anthropological Thought Today
  Scientific Approaches
    Evolutionary Psychology
    Materialism
  Humanistic Approaches
    Interpretive Anthropology
    Postmodernism

Either, Or, or Both?

Why Can't All Those Anthropologists Agree?

LEARNING OBJECTIVES

After reading this chapter, you should be able to

1 DISCUSS the global forces that contributed to the emergence of anthropology.

2 DESCRIBE the main ideas of the nineteenth-century unilineal evolutionists.

3 UNDERSTAND the ways American historical particularism and British functionalism challenged unilineal evolutionism.

4 DESCRIBE the mid-twentieth-century rebirth of evolutionary interests (neoevolutionism).

5 DISCUSS the main differences between the scientific and the humanistic approaches to modern anthropological thought.

6 DESCRIBE evolutionary psychology, materialism, interpretive anthropology, and postmodernism.

7 ANALYZE why contemporary anthropology has no single unifying theoretical orientation.

The field of anthropology developed out of the contact between Europeans and the rest of the world. Even before the voyages of Columbus in the early 1490s, horses and camels took a few Europeans to the Middle East and parts of Asia. After Columbus's voyages, ships carried Spaniards, Portuguese, English, French, and Russians to the two Americas and to remote islands of the Pacific Ocean. There Europeans contacted people who did not look, act, and think in familiar ways.

Some European intellectuals struggled to understand these peoples and their exotic and "primitive" ways of living. Between the 1500s and 1800s, most European interpretations were based on their Judeo-Christian worldview. By the last few decades of the nineteenth century, advances in knowledge and the emergence of the scientific worldview resulted in new ways of understanding humanity in all its variability. Only then did anthropology become an independent field of academic study.

When it began, cultural anthropology was distinct from other fields because of its focus on the peoples and cultures of other (non-European) lands and with other (non-Western) traditions. Increasing contacts between Europeans and other peoples brought new knowledge and curiosities, but this alone did not lead to the formation of a new discipline. In the 1800s, the expansion of European colonies in Africa and parts of Asia produced practical reasons to learn about and understand cultural differences. Many anthropologists call faraway peoples with diverse ways of living "the Other" in contrast to Ourselves—the cultures of the West, as we say. Although the word is problematic (*Other* is a bit ethnocentric—Other to whom? to Us, of course), we use it in this chapter because it is a convenient shorthand for the non-Western peoples on which anthropology used to concentrate.

The Emergence of Anthropology

Until a few centuries ago, the vast majority of Earth's people had no knowledge of any people or any culture other than the one into which they themselves were born. Of course, there were some exceptions. In the fifth century B.P., the Greek historian Herodotus wrote about the peoples of Persia, northern Africa, and nearby regions. Much later, in the 1200s, the Venetian trader Marco Polo reached China (then called "Cathay") via the ancient Silk Road that connected Rome and China since before the time of Christ. Marco Polo's descriptions of his adventures in China made his book popular among the European literary elite. However, descriptions like those of Herodotus and Marco Polo were rare and often treated skeptically. Some parts of Marco Polo's account were so surprising to his European readers that many of them did not believe his tales, such as the one about the Chinese burning black rocks as fuel.

In the 1500s, the nations of Europe began to send large numbers of explorers, traders, missionaries, and military personnel to other continents. During the next 400 years, Spain, Portugal, Britain, France, and other European nations established formal colonies in large parts of Africa and Asia and in most of the Americas. European visitors produced hundreds of written descriptions about the customs and beliefs of Native Americans, Asians, Africans, and Pacific Islanders.

From such books, articles, and letters sent back home, Europeans learned that previously unknown continents and regions were populated by people who were definitely Other in their customs and beliefs.

Between around 1500 and the mid-1800s, most Western scholars believed in the essential accuracy of the story of creation recounted in the Judeo-Christian Bible. In the biblical account, Earth was only a few thousand years old; one biblical scholar claimed that Earth was created in 4004 B.P. Because God created everything in only 6 days, humanity was the same age as Earth itself. Furthermore, the biblical creation story contained no explicit reference to any land occupied by the kinds of Others that Europeans were encountering. Who were all these people of the Americas and Africa? How could Western thinkers make sense of these "primitives" and their ways of living? Did their existence challenge the worldview derived from Judeo-Christian teachings?

The discovery of two unknown civilizations in the New World across the Atlantic Ocean caused debates. In 1521, Hernán Cortés encountered the Aztec civilization of southern Mexico. He and later Spaniards were awed by temples placed atop steep-sided pyramids, by broad plazas, by complicated agricultural fields, and, of course, by all the gold and other riches of the Aztec elite classes. Farther south, the civilization known as the Inka existed along most of the length of the Andes mountains. When Spaniard Francisco Pizarro and soldiers entered the Inka capital in the early 1530s, he met a ruler whom people treated like a god. These two civilizations might have challenged ideas that Europeans had about their own superiority, except that both were soon conquered, the Aztec by Cortés in 1521, the Inka by Pizarro in 1535.

By the mid-1800s, other puzzles had sprung up. For example, people in Europe discovered human bones and stone tools and other evidence suggesting that ancient people had lived on these continents. In Germany's Neander Valley, a partial skeleton of a humanlike creature was unearthed. Were the Neanderthal bones human, and, if so, what did they mean? From such finds, archaeology soon emerged.

European archaeologists in the 1800s noted that many tools were made of chipped stone. They later noticed a regular sequence of toolmaking: the earliest were made of stone, some later tools were smelted of bronze, and still later iron was used. This sequence came to be known as the Three Ages: the Stone Age, Bronze Age, and Iron Age. Each age had a greater variety of tools than the preceding age, and the materials used in each stage seemed superior to those of the earlier age. It looked like the lands where Western civilization now existed once contained "simpler, more primitive" peoples.

In North America, in the early 1800s Anglo settlers of Ohio and surrounding states commented on the existence of large earthen mounds, wondering who could have constructed these ancient monuments—certainly not the ancestors of the "Indians" who then lived in these regions! (Of course, future work showed conclusively that the mounds were made by "Indians," whose cultures later proved to be about as complicated as those of Europe itself.)

Until the mid-1800s, the Judeo-Christian worldview framed most interpretations of contemporary primitives and archaeological remains. Perhaps the "savages" of other lands were the descendants of Noah's wayward son, Ham. Maybe they were remnants of one of the lost tribes of Israel, as some scholars claimed about the Polynesians. Possibly, the Devil buried the Neander bones and prehistoric artifacts to undermine believers' faith. Whatever the specific explanation, the customs and beliefs of people who lived long ago or far away generally were interpreted in terms of the biblical account of world creation and human history.

In the mid–nineteenth century, in geology and biology a new set of beliefs about how to understand the world emerged. The findings of geology and biology led to a whole new worldview about Earth, life in general, and human life in particular, which is now accepted by the majority of scholars from all continents. Geology and biology helped bring humanity within the grasp of the *scientific* worldview, in which human beings and human cultures are understood to be the result of some process that is entirely natural.

In geology, James Hutton and Charles Lyell demonstrated that Earth itself was not merely thousands but many millions of years old (today, geologists believe our planet is about 4.5 billion years old). In biology, Charles Darwin revolutionized popular ideas about life. Rather than each plant and animal being separately made by a Creator, Darwin proposed that one species arose out of another by an entirely natural process. He documented this process in his 1859 book, *On the Origin of Species*.

Darwin's natural process is *evolution*. Evolution means that over long periods of time, one species changes into a new species or into several new species. Some species die out altogether, leaving no descendant species. But often, before its own extinction, a species changes (evolves) into one or more new species. Thus, multiple new species evolve, and they eventually change into even more species. Given enough time, all the diversity of life on Earth can be explained by this process of natural transformation. From simple beginnings, the natural process of evolution created all the forms of life that surround us today. All it takes are the slow accumulation of changes and time—millions and millions of years of time. When geology demonstrated the age of Earth, it showed that our world was old enough for diverse and complicated life forms to evolve from simple beginnings.

Darwin's main impact was on biology and the field now called *paleoanthropology*. Darwin established the possibility that the human species evolved from an apelike ancestor, and his idea was confirmed in the twentieth century (see Chapter 1).

Darwin's ideas about origins and changes in the natural world also influenced how Western intellectuals viewed human *cultural* existence as well as *biological* existence. If biological life forms could evolve, then could cultural forms also have arisen through a process of change? Simple forms of organic life had transformed into more complex forms of life. Analogously, in human cultural existence, some scholars reasoned that more complex ways of life had developed out of earlier, simpler ways of life.

During these same centuries in Europe and North America, the Enlightenment (Age of Reason) and the Industrial Revolution led to belief in progress—the notion that human life has gotten better and better over the course of many centuries. The idea of progress in the realms of technology and ideas led to optimism about the human future.

In summary, by the nineteenth century scholars who wanted to understand human cultures had access to two major kinds of information: (1) written accounts left by Westerners who visited other lands, including colonies of European nations; and (2) tools that ancient, long-disappeared peoples from Europe and North America had left in the earth. Influenced by Darwin's theories and the intellectual climate of the Enlightenment, scholars assimilated ideas about origins, evolution, and progress. They reasoned that there is a relationship between the various peoples in the written accounts and the ancient people who made the prehistoric tools and monuments. The long-disappeared prehistoric peoples of Europe and the Americas were similar to the peoples described in the accounts of Western visitors to other continents. Just as stone tools were the earliest form of technology, so "primitive" peoples still alive in the nineteenth century were living representatives of the earliest forms of culture. American "Indians" and many of the Others were still living in the Stone Age!

Late-Nineteenth-Century Unilineal Evolutionism

In the late nineteenth century, scholars became interested in how and why cultures had changed over the course of many centuries and millennia. Like plants and animals, cultures had evolved. The earliest simple ("primitive") cultures had given rise to ever more complex ("advanced") cultures. This cultural evolution represented progress or development: later cultures were, in some *objective* sense, superior to earlier cultures. (Here, *objective* means that there is a universal standard by which superiority can be judged, an assumption that later anthropologists questioned.)

The approach of these early anthropologists is called **unilineal evolutionism**. At the time, founders of this approach could not have known that future generations of anthropologists would challenge most of their goals and methods.

Briefly stated: As human cultures evolved, they passed through a series of stages. Examples of each stage could be found in the peoples described in all those written accounts and also in the artifacts that prehistoric people had left behind, in or on the ground. Although nineteenth-century Western civilization represented the highest stage of cultural evolution, on other continents lived peoples whose cultures remained in earlier stages. The cultures of these peoples had survived into the present because they had evolved at slower rates than the cultures of more advanced peoples. Such peoples were living relics from humanity's distant past, or "survivals" of earlier cultural stages.

For example, the evolutionists thought that survivals of the earliest stages of cultural evolution still existed in remote places, like Australia and Polynesia. In 1877, American Lewis Henry Morgan published *Ancient Society*, a book that integrated information compiled from written accounts of peoples from all continents. Morgan identified and labeled the stages. He placed the Australian aborigines and the Polynesians in *Savagery*, the earliest stage. Remnants of later, intermediate stages can be found in the Fiji islands of the Pacific and also existed among the Iroquois Indians. Both are living representatives of the middle stage of cultural evolution, which Morgan called *Barbarism*. Elsewhere, later evolutionary stages exist: the Inkas of the Andes, the Aztecs of Mexico, the Chinese, Koreans, and Japanese all represent *Civilization*. Thus, Morgan reasoned, very early cultures were like the Australians and Polynesians, later ones resembled contemporary Fijians and Iroquois, and the later stages were known from Inkas, Chinese, and

> **unilineal evolutionism** Nineteenth-century theoretical orientation that held that all human ways of life pass through a similar sequence of stages in their development.

AUSTRALIAN ABORIGINES, PREPARING A MEAL.

Unilineal evolutionists believed that the world's cultures evolved through sequential stages, with peoples from various regions arrayed along a continuum from simple to more complex cultures. To document and explain their evolutionary stages, they searched documentary records for survivors of the earliest stages, imagining that people like Australian aborigines were in the earliest stage of "savagery."

some other ancient civilizations. The highest stage was Western civilization. By carefully comparing peoples exemplified all the stages, evolutionists believed they could reconstruct the nature of the various stages and figure out what had led one stage to progress to the next.

The unilineal evolutionists are usually considered the first true cultural anthropologists. They had a subject matter that was by and large separate from that of other disciplines—the cultures and societies of peoples who lived in foreign lands (the "Others"). They had a reasonably coherent objective: to reconstruct and understand the stages through which human cultures had traveled along the narrow road to civilization. They used a methodology that was then in its infancy—comparing and contrasting diverse peoples to discover the nature of the stages and the relationships between them. In brief, cultural anthropology became an academic discipline because it had its own subject matter, objectives, and methods.

As another example of unilineal evolutionism, in 1871 the Englishman E. B. Tylor published the landmark book *Primitive Culture*. In it, he investigated the origins and development of religious beliefs. Tylor argued that religious beliefs originated out of peoples' attempts to explain certain experiences. For example, immediately after someone dies, the physical body still exists even though the life of the person has ended. What explains the difference between a living and a dead person? Being ignorant of the actual causes of death, early humans reasoned that living people have a spiritual essence (a "soul") that animates or gives life to the physical body. When the soul leaves the body, the person stops breathing and moving and, hence, dies. Also, people have dreams, trances, and visions in which they see images of all kinds of things and events. Reasoning logically, but falsely, early peoples concluded that the things are real and that the events actually occurred. Tylor called the form of religion that this reasoning produces *animism*. Peoples with animistic religions believe in spiritual beings, including nature spirits living in mountains, trees, water, heavenly bodies, and animals; spirits of deceased persons (ghosts); spirits that cause illness; spirits that possess someone and make them insane; and a multitude of other spirits.

Tylor thought animism was the earliest (primeval) form of religion from which all others arose. He reasoned that living peoples who still had animistic beliefs represent survivals of this earliest stage of religion. Therefore, scholars could learn about the earliest form of religion by studying living peoples who were still animistic. How did animism evolve into its later forms? Over time, early peoples reasoned that some spirits were more important or influential than others. Eventually, such spirits were elevated to higher positions. They became gods of various things and activities such as gods of sun, moon, sky, rain, earth, clans, war, agriculture, love, fertility, and so forth. There were many such gods, as well known from Greek and Roman mythology and writings of the Hindu of ancient India. This stage of religion is called *polytheism*, meaning religions that include a belief in many gods, each with his, hers, or its own sphere of influence.

What about *monotheism*? This form of religious belief was represented by the Judeo-Christian heritage of the West. It was also familiar from Islam, which had been known to Europeans for more than a millennium. Tylor argued that monotheism evolved when one of the gods of polytheism acquired dominance over other gods. Eventually, over centuries, the other gods came to be seen as false gods or not to exist at all. Not surprisingly, Tylor believed that monotheism was the most evolved form of religion.

Morgan's and Tylor's stages illustrate the main ideas of the unilineal evolutionists. Examples of each stage survived in many scattered places—in fact, on all continents. One stage evolved into another, not just in one region or continent, but in many. For example, animistic religions evolved into polytheistic religions among many peoples, and, in turn, polytheism evolved into monotheism several times. The fact that the same sequence of stages occurred again and again among widely scattered peoples seemed to imply that human cultures developed in regular, recurrent patterns. If so, then human cultural evolution followed some sort of "law," meaning that similar processes were resulting in similar changes, analogous to Darwinian evolution.

A Science of Culture?

Following this logic, most unilineal evolutionists thought that the new field of anthropology could and should be a science. They believed the development of culture could be explained much as biology explains the evolution of living organisms. Tylor (1871, 2) wrote that human "thoughts, wills, and actions accord with laws as definite as those which govern the motion of waves, the combinations of acids and bases, and the growth of plants and animals."

Few anthropologists of today agree with this statement because, unlike waves and chemicals, humans have active minds of their own. Many contemporary thinkers do not believe that Tylor's "science of culture" is possible at all. Some do not think it is desirable, because one kind of human should not treat other kinds of humans as objects for study.

The unilineal evolutionists made significant contributions to the development of anthropology. Thanks largely to their writings, by the early twentieth century, anthropology became a full-fledged academic discipline. Scholarly fields that investigate various aspects of humankind were already established in European and American universities as departments or schools of religion, theology, art, philosophy, classics, history, anatomy, and so forth. But a discipline whose focus was the physical and cultural diversity of humanity was not recognized until the last decades of the 1800s. In the United States, the first anthropology course was taught in 1879 at the University of Rochester. In 1886, the first anthropology department was founded at the University of Pennsylvania. It was followed near the turn of the century by university departments at Columbia, Harvard, Chicago, and California (Berkeley).

Anthropological Thought in the Early Twentieth Century

Despite their contributions, many assumptions that the unilineal evolutionists seemed to take for granted were questionable. In the early decades of the twentieth century, their ideas were largely rejected, partly because their methods were flawed and much of their information was erroneous. In the English-speaking countries, anthropologists in America and Great Britain set out in different directions, as we now discuss.

Historical Particularism in the United States (ca. 1900–1940)

At the end of the 1800s and for the next three or four decades, the American anthropologist Franz Boas and his students questioned the methods and the findings of unilineal evolutionism. Boas was so influential in the United States that he is often called the "father of American anthropology." In his view, each and every culture has its own separate past and each culture is unique. Because each culture was affected by almost everything that had happened to it in the past, and because different things had happened to different cultures, each culture is different from all others.

This approach is usually called **historical particularism** (or **historicism**). Notice that if it is true that each culture is the *distinctive* product of its *unique* history, then it is difficult to identify any general principles that affect all cultures. Rather, each culture must be studied on its own terms.

Clearly, the unilineal evolutionists did not study each culture "on its own terms." In making their comparisons and formulating their stages, they imposed their own "terms" (e.g., complexity, progress, stages) on other cultures. Take the notion of complexity, for example. In the realm of technology, most people might agree that guns and bullets are more complex than bows and arrows, which, in turn, are more complex than spears and throwing sticks. But what can *complex* mean when applied to other customs and beliefs, like those about marriage, political organization, or religion? In what sense is the religion Tylor called monotheism more complex than animism? Boas held that such features are merely *different* from culture to culture. By any *objective* criterion, one form of religion does not represent "progress" over another.

There were other problems also. Japan clearly was a civilization, but its indigenous religion was Shinto, which would be considered animistic. In a similar fashion, Polynesians had a pretty complex system of governance, but Morgan placed them in Savagery because of the names they called their relatives and their marriage practices. The coexistence of "low-stage" traits in "high-stage" cultures, and vice versa, suggests that there was more than one line of cultural evolution.

Furthermore, Boas realized that the stages of the nineteenth-century evolutionists derived from ethnocentric assumptions. Evolutionists placed their own cultural existence at the top of the (imaginary) cultural ladder, searched writings to find many Others whose cultures represented "earlier stages" gave the stages labels like "savagery," slotted particular cultures into their preconceived classifications, and then concluded that they were discovering the laws of cultural development using the methods of science.

As an example of Boas's point, consider Lewis Henry Morgan, who labeled various peoples "savages," "barbarians," and "civilized." But many literate, civilized people, including Japanese, Koreans, and Chinese

historical particularism (historicism) Theoretical orientation emphasizing that each culture is the unique product of all the influences to which it was subjected in its past, making cross-cultural generalizations questionable.

Often considered the "father of American anthropology," Franz Boas challenged the unilineal evolutionists' concept of stages. In doing so, he made many lasting contributions, including popularizing the notion of cultural relativism and marshaling evidence that cultural differences and biological differences are largely independent of each other.

labeled Morgan's own people as "barbarians." Is monotheism more "evolved" than animism or polytheism? Perhaps, but you are more likely to think so if your own religion is monotheistic. If your criteria for defining evolution are ethnocentric, then your concept of "evolutionary stages" is almost useless.

These arguments seemed to mean that the unilineal evolutionists were wrong: cultures do not develop along a single series of progressive stages, culminating in nineteenth-century Western civilization. Instead, each culture changes along its own unique path, depending on the particular influences that affect it. To understand a culture, therefore, we must study it *individually*, not as a representative of some hypothetical stage, which Boas thought existed only in the minds of the evolutionists. Anthropologists must free themselves from preconceived ideas and assumptions and give up speculative schemes of evolution and ethnocentric definitions of progress.

The historical particularists also claimed that it is very difficult to place the customs and beliefs of *different* peoples into the *same* stage of progress. In most cases, the customs and beliefs of widely scattered peoples only *appear* to be similar. For example, in Tylor's scheme the ancient religions of both Greece and Polynesia had many gods and so would be classified as polytheistic. Tylor *defined* a stage of religion, polytheism, and placed peoples who believed in many gods into that stage. What would the ancient Greeks and Polynesians have said about such comparisons? Muslims, Jews, and Christians are all monotheistic, but is this single feature of their religions enough to place them into the same "stage"?

In short, to say that the customs and beliefs of two or more Other cultures are the "same" or "similar" because they look the same to Us is to ignore a host of differences between these cultures. The Greeks and Polynesians had different gods, who did different kinds of things to and for people. For the historicists, this is enough to consider them different forms of religion. (Carried to its extreme, of course, this means that every religion has a different form from every other religion, which makes *every* religion unique.) The only way to get a valid notion of stage would be to study the development of each religion separately, which might lead to the discovery of the stages of evolution for each religion. But these stages, if found, would probably not be universal. The same applies to other elements of culture, Boas thought.

Boas believed the basic assumptions of the evolutionists were flawed, mainly because their ideas about progress and stages were ethnocentric. But he also noted that the ways the evolutionists investigated other cultures—their methods—led them to errors. Today, nineteenth-century evolutionists often are called "armchair anthropologists" because they themselves had not lived among any of those "savages" and "barbarians" (with a few exceptions like Morgan, who actually studied the Iroquois firsthand). Instead, for the most part, they relied on descriptive accounts written by people who too often were untrained, who presented their "impressions" rather than "hard facts," and who were biased in their perceptions of Others.

Boas thought that professional anthropologists must abandon the comforts of their office armchairs and engage in firsthand interactions with members of other cultures. The main need of the young field of anthropology was more factual information about other cultures, not unsupported speculations in faculty offices and classrooms. Anthropologists themselves must conduct *ethnographic fieldwork*. This was the only way they can be somewhat confident that they have their facts correct. And only after anthropologists are sure that their facts are correct should they begin to even try to make general statements or to theorize about cultures. Boas, in brief, wanted more and better descriptions of more cultures.

Boas thought it essential that fieldworkers remain objective as they observe and record the customs and beliefs of other cultures. Fieldworkers must enter the communities and lives of Others with an open mind. Above all, they should not be ethnocentric because ethnocentrism inevitably leads to errors. If a fieldworker visits another people with an attitude of superiority, he or she is not likely to come away with accurate information. Fieldworkers who go into the field with preconceived notions are likely to observe and report on things consistent with their own preconceptions and not notice or report on contradictory things.

According to Boas, fieldworkers need to be cultural relativists (Chapter 2). While living among Others, we must temporarily suspend our own values, morality, standards of hygiene, ways of interpreting actions, and so forth. Not only does a relativistic attitude help us fit into the community, but it also minimizes the chances that we will misinterpret or misunderstand people just because we see them through the filter of our own culture's perceptions and biases.

Boas himself conducted firsthand fieldwork among two Native American peoples, the Inuit ("Eskimo") and the Kwakiutl. He sent many of his students at Columbia University out for fieldwork experiences, including Margaret Mead, who became famous for her 1928 book, *Coming of Age in Samoa*. For decades, Margaret Mead was the one anthropologist most people knew about. Again and again, she discussed how different the various peoples of the world are, so much so that the idea that there was a Human Nature became widely questioned. Mead also was one of the intellectual founders of modern feminism, because she emphasized the multitude of differences in how cultures regard relations between the sexes.

Because of the influence of Boas and his students, in anthropology today living among and participating in the lives of the people under study is the main method by which one becomes a professional and acquires a positive reputation in the discipline. The tradition of fieldwork is one of Boas's lasting legacies.

In addition to learning more about cultures, firsthand fieldwork has another benefit. The traditional customs, beliefs, and languages of many of the world's peoples had already disappeared because of diseases, genocide, assimilation, and other effects of global contacts. Surviving cultures and languages were vanishing or changing rapidly. Boas believed it was the duty of anthropologists to record disappearing traditions before they were gone forever. Many students of Boas, like A. L. Kroeber and Robert Lowie, did fieldwork among Native American peoples, whose cultures they believed were especially endangered.

Finally, Boas and his students conducted a lot of research to show that biological differences and cultural differences are largely independent of each other, that is, the culture of a human group is a product of social learning and tradition, not of genetic heritage (see Chapter 2).

In sum, historical particularism made four enduring contributions to modern anthropology: (1) it discredited the overly speculative schemes of the unilineal evolutionists; (2) it insisted that fieldwork is the primary means of acquiring reliable information; (3) it imparted the idea that cultural relativism as a methodological principle is essential for the most accurate understanding of another culture; and (4) it demonstrated and popularized the notion that cultural differences and biological differences have little to do with each other. These contributions helped to shape modern cultural anthropology.

Historical particularism gave rise to other movements in the first half of the twentieth century. One of the most influential is called **configurationalism**. One of Boas's students was Ruth Benedict, whose 1934 book *Patterns of Culture,* is considered a classic. Benedict argued that, from the vast array of humanly possible cultures, each particular culture develops only a limited number of "patterns" or "configurations" that dominate the thinking and responses of its members. Each culture develops a distinctive set of feelings and motivations that orients the thoughts and behaviors of its members. These configurations give each culture a distinctive style, and the thoughts and actions of its members reflect its configurations. *Patterns of Culture* emphasized both the uniqueness of particular cultures and cultural relativism.

For example, Benedict wrote that the Kwakiutl of the Northwest Coast of North America are individualistic, competitive, and intemperate. This cultural configuration affects Kwakiutl customs. They stage ceremonies known as *potlatches,* in which one kin group gives away enormous quantities of goods to another. The aim is to shame the rival group, for if the rival is unable to return the presentations on certain occasions, its members suffer a loss of prestige. To avoid losing prestige, the recipient group is obliged to return gifts of even greater value. The whole complex of behaviors connected to the potlatch reflects the cultural configuration of the Kwakiutl—the Kwakiutl are so caught up by the prestige motivation that groups will give away large quantities of material wealth achieve prestige. To describe the Kwakiutl, Benedict used the term *Dionysian*, after the Greek god known for his drinking, partying, and other excesses.

Benedict contrasted the Kwakiutl configuration to the Zuni of the North American Southwest. Zuni control their emotions, she claimed. They are moderate, modest, stoical, orderly, and restrained in their behavior. They do not boast or attempt to rise above their peers but are social and cooperative. This "Apollonian" cultural theme, as Benedict called it, permeates all of Zuni life. Unlike a Kwakiutl leader, a Zuni man does not seek status; indeed, a leadership role practically has to be forced on him. So, according to Benedict, each culture has its unique patterns and themes, which makes it possible for a megalomaniac in culture A to be a model citizen in culture B.

Although modern anthropologists agree that different cultures emphasize different themes or patterns, most believe Benedict overemphasized the effect of culture on the thoughts, feelings, and actions of its members. It is misleading to characterize cultures in such simple terms, such as that Kwakiutl are prone to excess, whereas Zuni are moderate in all things. Rather, the personality and character of the members of a culture are highly variable, and the relationship between cultural knowledge and the individual behavior is complicated (see Chapter 2).

Historical particularism changed the way anthropologists thought about culture and conducted research, but it has limitations. Think about the claim that each culture is unique—like no other. Certainly, if we are most interested in cultural differences we will easily find them. We can legitimately claim that no two cultures are alike. So at some level, the view that "each culture is unique" is correct. However, so is the claim that no two individuals brought up within the same culture are exactly alike. Yet they *are* alike in some ways. It is true that in *some ways,* cultures are unique. But also, *in some ways,* a given culture does have things in common with some other cultures. More generally speaking, there are similarities as well as differences between ways of life. Historical particularists tended to overlook the similarities and to neglect the investigation of factors that might explain them.

Consider also the claim that, because each culture is the product of its particular history, one cannot generalize about the causes of cultural differences. According to historicism, there are no "general causes" of cultures. Rather, there are multiple causes, whose relative importance is difficult to disentangle. Besides, causation varies from people to people, depending on their particular history.

Others disagree. To say that the natural environment is important in culture X, religion in Y, values in Z, and so forth, is to say little more than that everything is related to most everything else. However, it is possible that some influences are more important than

---

configurationalism Theoretical idea that each culture historically develops its own unique thematic patterns around which beliefs, values, and behaviors are oriented.

other influences in all or most human populations. For example, some scholars claim that how people interact with their natural environment is *generally* more important than religion or values in causing people to live the way they do.

By the 1940s and 1950s, the interests of many American anthropologists returned to discovering the general principles of human cultural existence. Meanwhile, another way of studying human societies and cultural diversity developed in Europe.

British Functionalism, 1920s–1960s

At about the same time that historicism was popular in the United States, a very different approach developed in Great Britain. Generally called **functionalism**, its main tenet was that social and cultural features should be explained mainly by their useful functions to the people and to the society—that is, by the benefits they confer on individuals and groups. Because humans are social beings who live in families, communities, and other kinds of organized groups, most aspects of their culture and society serve to help individuals meet their needs and/or to contribute to the maintenance of the society itself.

Bronislaw Malinowski was a leading British functionalist. He emphasized the needs of individuals. To Malinowski, the main purpose of culture is to serve human biological, psychological, and social needs. What are these needs? Most biological needs are rather obvious: nutrition, shelter, protection from enemies, maintenance of health and—if the society is to persist—biological reproduction. Humans also have psychological and social needs such as love and affection, security, self-expression, and a sense of belonging. The purpose of culture is to fulfill these needs. Unlike other animals, humans have few inborn instructions or instincts that tell us how to meet our needs. Instead, as we grow up in our culture, we learn the behaviors, social rules, values, and ways of perceiving the world that guide our actions and our thoughts (see Chapter 2).

Some parts of culture meet individual needs directly, such as knowledge of how to acquire food or make shelter. Other aspects function to raise and socialize new generations of group members, such as enculturation practices and family life. Still others encourage people to adhere to group values and rules that make cooperation possible, such as religious beliefs and practices and creative arts. Thus, even if a given cultural feature does not *directly* serve individual needs, it still *indirectly* contributes to the maintenance of the entire cultural system without which human survival would be difficult.

It is hard to deny that an important function of culture is to help people meet their "needs." However, in some kinds of societies, some individuals and groups have their needs (and wants) met more completely than others. Furthermore, culture itself can create perceived needs (you can think you need something when you merely desire it). And the social and economic conditions under which people live make them need some things that people of other times and places did not need. If you were an attorney in Britain or a college student in India in the 1970s, you would not need a computer, but you would today, if you are to be successful. Finally, it is likely that perceived "needs" grow as the capacity for meeting them increases, as all economists know. Thus, the idea of "needs" is more of a problem than it appears: "needs" do vary from place to place and time to time.

Also, if we are interested in cultural differences, then the idea that the main function of culture is to satisfy needs does not take us very far. If *needs* do not include *wants*—what we'd *like* to have to make us content, such as material wealth and social status—then needs are pretty much the same among all peoples. People living in different times and places satisfy their needs in a wide variety of ways. By themselves, universal needs cannot explain cultural differences.

For example, eating beef will satisfy the nutritional need for protein. However, many devout Hindus and Buddhists not only refuse to consume cattle flesh but maintain an entirely vegetarian diet because of their religious beliefs. Most contemporary vegetarians and vegans do not consume meat because of health or moral considerations, or because their diet is an important part of their self-identity. A human body does not need meat to maintain health, so the universal need for protein cannot explain the many ways in which people acquire protein. To generalize this point: The basic needs of humans are the same everywhere and can be satisfied in such a variety of ways that needs alone cannot explain cultural diversity. At the very least, differences in the natural environment that provides need-satisfying resources must be taken into account.

A. R. Radcliffe-Brown was another influential British functionalist. Instead of emphasizing the needs of individuals, Radcliffe-Brown focused on the needs of societies. For him, maintaining orderly social relationships—between family members, friends, members of the same

---

functionalism Theoretical orientation that analyzes cultural elements in terms of their useful effects to individuals or to the persistence of the whole society.

CHAPTER 5 The Development of Anthropological Thought 99

Bronislaw Malinowski was an influential British functionalist. He is best known for his ethnographies about the Trobriand Islanders. Like the American Franz Boas, Malinowski insisted that cultural anthropologists conduct firsthand fieldwork themselves.

village or town, leaders and followers, and the like—is the main function that must be met if societies are to exist and persist. He imagined that a human society is like a living organism in which each organ has a function to fulfill that contributes to the life of the whole body. In studying a body, a physiologist not only looks at each organ individually but also considers its role in the life process of the whole organism. Just as organisms cannot stay alive for long unless their organs function properly, so a society cannot persist unless its various institutions play their proper roles in social life. Radcliffe-Brown felt that most customs and beliefs a people share help their society remain in *equilibrium* (a steady state, with not too much conflict or rapid change).

From today's perspective, it is clear that societies are not very much like living organisms. Individuals have minds and motives of their own, unlike cells and organs. And few societies are in equilibrium for very long. Societies change constantly. The rate of change and the direction of change vary, and functionalism had relatively little of lasting value to say about change.

Despite various shortcomings, British functionalists made lasting contributions to anthropology. Emphasizing the importance of social relationships between individuals and of living in organized groups leads us to pay more attention to how groups are organized and how they relate to one another. Radcliffe-Brown's emphasis on social equilibrium led us to pay more attention to how the parts of a society and culture fit together, and therefore made us pay more attention to cultural integration.

The Fieldwork Tradition

Like the American historicists, the British functionalists helped establish the tradition of firsthand fieldwork. Malinowski is famous mainly because of his fieldwork and ethnographic writings about the Trobriand Islanders of the western Pacific. Some of his books, like *Argonauts of the Western Pacific* and *The Sexual Life of Savages*, are ethnographic classics. Not only is fieldwork the best means of obtaining reliable information about a people, but it is also a necessary part of the training of anthropologists, Malinowski believed. We cannot claim to understand people, or the diverse cultures in which people of various places grow up, until we have immersed ourselves in the experience of some culture other than our own.

Malinowski thought the main objective of fieldwork is to see the culture as an insider to the culture sees it. In an often-quoted passage from his famous 1922 ethnography *Argonauts of the Western Pacific*, Malinowski (1922, 25) wrote:

> [T]he final goal, of which an Ethnographer [*sic*] should never lose sight . . . is, briefly, to grasp the native's point of view, his relation to life, to realize *his* vision of *his* world.

This idea of what fieldwork is all about remains influential—though controversial—today.

To "grasp the native's point of view," fieldworkers usually make visits that last at least a year, and they often return to the community many times. Also, fieldwork involves deep involvement in the daily lives of the people. Where possible, fieldworkers should master the local language, live with the local people, participate in games and voyages, become familiar with how members of families relate to one another, observe lots of ceremonies and rituals, record myths and legends, and—generally—learn all they can about a culture from interacting with people and participating in their lives. This way of learning about another culture is generally called *participant observation*, and it is the most important method for many fieldworkers (Chapter 6).

Because of the influence of early twentieth-century anthropologists like Boas and Malinowski, today the fieldwork experience is an essential part of the graduate training of almost all cultural anthropologists. Fieldwork demonstrates that you can *do* anthropology yourself as well as *study* the anthropological research and theories of your teachers and other scholars. It demonstrates that you can contribute original knowledge about some group of Others; and in most colleges and universities, making new contributions is essential for success in one's academic career.

Until 20 or 30 years ago, most fieldworkers were from either North America or Western Europe. As a consequence, most ethnographies describing the ways of life of diverse peoples were written by Western anthropologists, who for the most part were trained in Western universities. But anthropology today has gone global. People of many nationalities representing many cultures are now anthropologists, interested in writing about the very people whom Western ethnographers used to monopolize. This has led to new issues, and in the future new ways of representing Other cultures are likely to emerge (see Globalization Challenges and Opportunities).

For many anthropologists, fieldwork transforms them as persons. Even anthropologists have trouble overcoming their own biases and looking at Others relativistically instead of through ethnocentric lenses. After being intensively exposed to another way of living, we often come away with a different perspective on Ourselves. Fieldwork is the closest most of us come to dissolving the differences between Us and Others. This is another reason most professional anthropologists conduct fieldwork. That, and the fact that most of us like it.

Mid–Twentieth Century: Rebirth of Evolutionism

The objections of Boas to unilineal evolutionism were powerful ones, but other evolutionary approaches came back into fashion in the 1940s and endure today. The problems with the "old" (unilineal) evolutionism were its flawed assumptions and inadequate methods. Some mid-twentieth-century scholars thought they corrected the assumptions and adopted more sophisticated methods. They developed a "new evolutionism," or **neoevolutionism**, so called because their objectives were much the same as the objectives of the nineteenth-century evolutionists, but their methods and specific theories were different. Two North American anthropologists were especially influential.

Writing mostly in the 1940s–1960s, Leslie White thought that the nineteenth-century evolutionists got some things right after all. The technologies (tools, technical knowledge, skills) that people use to acquire nature's resources have, in fact, improved over the centuries. Improved in what respect? Improved in the sense that people with better technologies are able to harness more energy per person per year. That is, some technologies are more productive or efficient than others, so people can produce more useful products with them. Cultural evolution is an *objective* fact, White argued. It occurs as the amount of energy harnessed from the natural environment increases. In principle, cultural evolution can be defined without resorting to ethnocentric assumptions. It true, White overcame one of historical particularism's objections.

White went further. Over long periods of time, as humans discovered and invented new technologies that increased the quantity of energy captured, changes in the organization of societies and in the ideas and beliefs of their members followed. To use White's own terminology, improvements in the "technological system" drive changes in the "social system" and the "ideological system." Generally speaking, over time, human social and ideological systems have grown more complex. What does *complex* mean? It means that the scale (size) of societies increases dramatically, occupational specialization develops, large-scale trade and long-distance exchange grow,

---

neoevolutionism "New evolutionism," or the mid-twentieth-century rebirth of evolutionary approaches to studying and explaining culture.

GLOBAL CHALLENGES AND OPPORTUNITIES

Global Anthropology

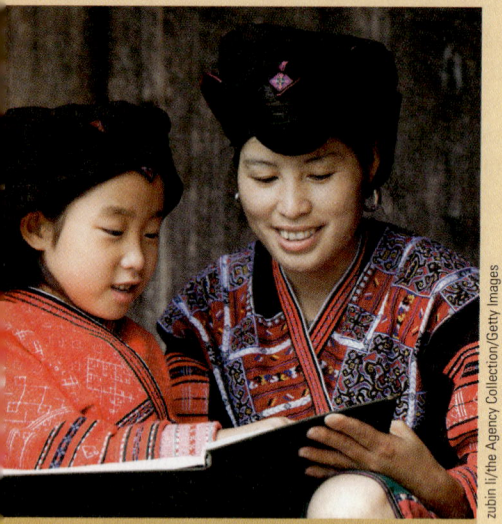

Globalization affects anthropological teaching, research, and writing in many ways. As more and more of the world's people become literate and more conscious of their cultural traditions, they read ethnographies and other anthropological writings. How should this affect the field work and writing of anthropologists?

As we've seen, anthropology arose after Western Europeans contacted Other peoples of Africa, Asia, Australia, the Americas, and the Pacific. For nearly a century, the theoretical and field research of most Western anthropologists occurred with little regard for how the Natives would react to the research and its publication. For the most part, the neglect of local reactions was not because researchers did not care about the people, but because so few of them were literate enough to read our writings. Most fieldworkers were interested in what Malinowski called the "native's point of view," but they did not worry too much about the Natives' views of the scholarly books and articles anthropologists wrote about them.

Today, anthropology itself has globalized. Countries whose peoples we study have universities with their own anthropologists who write about their own country or their own people. National or regional governments are sometimes reluctant to allow Western fieldworkers to come in. Many people who appear in our ethnographies now read what we write and are often critical of our findings and, occasionally, of how they are used. Some are resentful because their customs, beliefs, opinions, and voices are represented by outsiders rather than by themselves. Some believe (usually mistakenly) that anthropologists grow wealthy by writing about them, while they are paid relatively little when they assist us.

One issue for a global anthropology is *who benefits*? Until 20 or 30 years ago, the main readership of much anthropological writing was other anthropologists or students. Anthropology was mainly the study of Others, and such study was valuable for its own sake. Ideally, it taught values of mutual understanding between peoples as well as educating people about cultural variations in time and space. This remains an important goal of anthropology today. However, more anthropologists believe that the benefits of their research

political centralization occurs, and inequality between classes increases.

White believed that improvements in technology and the resulting increase in the ability of people to harness energy *caused* most important changes in human cultures. For example, he argued that the transition to agriculture *caused* civilization to develop in some regions, and the discovery of how to harness the energy of coal *caused* the rise of industrial society in Great Britain. For this reason, White is often called a *technological determinist*, meaning he believed that technology causes ("determines") almost everything else in culture that is important. What causes changes in aspects of culture like family organization and political structures? To White, these were part of the "social system" and largely responded to changes in technology. What about aspects of culture like religion, philosophy, worldview, and art? To White, these were part of the "ideological system," and by and large they changed to reflect and justify changes in the social system.

In summary, White boldly generalized that as technology develops, the social system evolves to take advantage of the increased energy available and new ideologies arise to explain and justify the new technological and social arrangements. So, cultural evolution is in fact a regular, patterned process about which anthropologists can generalize by making objective comparisons and contrasts. Each culture is *not* entirely unique, and we can legitimately provide explanations that do not depend on the "native's point of view." White agreed with E. B. Tylor that anthropology should be "the science of culture," and White made this the title of a book he published in 1949.

Julian Steward was a contemporary of White who agreed that how a people acquire natural resources and cope with their environment is the most important part of their way of life. But, more than White, Steward's theory emphasized the natural environment, which should be more widespread and should filter out to those whose lives and cultures we research and write about. Among other things, this desire argues for clearer and more jargon-free writing, and too often such writing is undervalued in the colleges and universities in which most research-oriented anthropologists work. Also, more work should be translated into more languages, which is very expensive.

Another issue for a global anthropology is *representation:* who is best qualified to describe the culture of a people, to translate their customs and beliefs into a form that is intelligible to outsiders? Some anthropological scholars from the West are reluctant to give up their claim to represent the Others, even when educated Others challenge their findings. In his 2004 book *Native Anthropology,* Takami Kuwayama notes that because the most well-endowed and prestigious universities are in Western Europe and North America, the representation that prevails may be based on political concerns rather than accuracy or completeness.

Kuwayama offers a solution to the dilemma of writing about cultures in an increasingly global community. He proposes that anthropology develop a forum in which all opinions about an issue of fact or interpretation can be aired on an equal footing. At present, if you are to speak authoritatively (i.e., have others take your views seriously), you must publish. You must write scholarly books and find someone to publish them. Better, you must get your articles published in scholarly journals that are peer reviewed (i.e., the article is critically analyzed by others who are recognized experts in the subject, who decide whether your article is meritorious enough to be published). Many Native anthropologists have less access to the world of publishing than most scholars in the major universities. Therefore, the information they gather and the opinions they offer may be underrepresented in the global community of anthropological scholars. The fact that English has become the primary language of discussion does not help the situation. Finally, in publishing as in other realms of life, sometimes it's whom you know rather than what you say that determines whether something you write appears in print.

Kuwayama suggests that more people be given an opportunity to have their voices heard. Exactly how this opportunity will be offered is unclear, even to Kuwayama. But he notes that worldwide access to the Internet is increasing dramatically and that it is more inclusive than other forums because anyone can post to it. (Interestingly, this is exactly the reason so many scholars mistrust the Internet: except for the restrictions placed on content from countries such as China, there are few controls over it, so "anyone can post to it," which is why so much of it is "garbage.") Someday, there may be a wiki-anthropology.

---

provided food, fuel, water, and other necessary resources. In his study of the Western Shoshone of the Great Basin, Steward investigated how food resources were distributed seasonally and geographically. He argued that much of Shoshone culture could be explained by how people schedule their work and movements to take advantage of the availability of food. Steward's ideas eventually gave rise to the modern field of ecological anthropology, which studies how humans relate to the environment. We discuss the general results of such studies in Chapter 7.

Men like White and Steward made attempts to explain culture in scientific terms respectable again. For White, the general principle needed to explain cultural evolution is technological determinism. For Steward, the complicated interactions between humans and the natural environments are the most important causes of cultural differences and similarities. White and Steward are two of the most important intellectual ancestors of the various scientific approaches in Western anthropology today.

Anthropological Thought Today

Boas's early criticisms of the unilineal evolutionists illustrate a controversy that continues to this day. First, the unilineal evolutionists thought that anthropology should be like the natural sciences in its goals. Their goal was to discover the general principles ("laws") that governed cultural development. In contrast, the historicists mistrusted most generalizations, especially broad and sweeping ones like "all cultures pass through similar stages." The closer you come to getting inside another culture, they argued, the more details you perceive and, hence, the more different it looks from other cultures. Most similarities are only superficial, like the "similarity" between polytheism in ancient Polynesia and Greece.

Second, the evolutionists uncritically placed similar cultures in the same stage of progress (like the Iroquois and the Fijians, both placed in "barbarism"). But the historicists insisted that the evolutionists' idea of progress was ethnocentric and that therefore stages were artificial creations. If there are no universal stages, or even widespread stages, then the "regularities of cultural development" that the nineteenth-century scholars perceived were not real, but only the result of their ethnocentric assumptions and faulty methods.

Third, the evolutionists compared and contrasted cultures from all parts of the world and found customs they considered the "same" among widely scattered peoples. But the historicists reasoned that because each culture's history is different from the history of every other culture, it follows that each culture is unique and distinctive. This means that it is very misleading to place customs and beliefs from several cultures into the same category because there are always differences between them. For example, if you say that the ancient Polynesians and Greeks have the "same form" of religion, which *you* label as polytheism, that label is *yours*, not theirs. To call the two religions the same is to misrepresent and distort them. It denies the religions, and the people who believe and practice them, their distinctiveness. It denies the Others their own Voices. It privileges the voice of the anthropologist, meaning that it assumes the anthropologist's ideas are more valid than the ideas of Others about what they do and how they think.

It is impossible here to discuss all the issues that concern cultural anthropologists in the twenty-first century. Instead, we concentrate on a few major but related questions. Can and should cultural anthropology be a science, in the same sense that biology is a science? What are the most useful concepts and theoretical orientations to use in studying human cultural diversity? When we conduct fieldwork another culture during fieldwork, should the fieldworker decide what's important—that is, should anthropologists define the questions and propose the answers? Or, should the views of the Others themselves take precedence—that is, should the Native point of view take priority?

scientific approaches General approaches suggesting that human cultural differences and similarities can be explained in the same sense as biologists explain life and its evolution.

evolutionary psychology (sociobiology) Scientific approach emphasizing that humans are subject to similar evolutionary forces as other animals; associated with the hypothesis that human behavior patterns enhance genetic fitness.

One important division today is between cultural anthropologists whose interests and methods are more similar to science and those whose interests and methods are more humanistic. These two generalized approaches provide a focus for discussing anthropological thought in the twenty-first century.

Scientific Approaches

Those who adopt one of the **scientific approaches** seek to discover the general forces that make cultures the way they are; that is, they want to *explain* human ways of life. As well as researching specific Others, scientifically oriented anthropologists are interested in human culture in general, meaning they want to discover whether there are any general principles ("laws," E. B. Tylor called them) that affect all peoples. They are interested in big questions: What are the primary causes of social and cultural differences and similarities? What makes societies and cultures change and/or change at different rates? What are the relationships among the major components of a people's way of life such as resource acquisition, family organization, political structure, and religious beliefs and rituals? When two cultures come into contact, what kinds of forces affect the outcome?

Given the complexity of humanity, and even of a single culture, the answer is always going to be "It all depends." Scientifically oriented scholars ask, "On what, mainly?" If the answer turns out to be "On everything else," then the scientific approach probably will not be able to achieve its goals. There can never be a "general theory" that answers their big questions because the word *theory* implies that only a small number of general principles are responsible for most of the important differences, changes, relationships, and other phenomena. *Theory* implies only a few underlying causes, principles, or forces. However, if cultures are indeed products of "everything that happened in the past," then there are not a few processes that operate widely and that are *generally* important in *most* societies *most* of the time. Human existence would be too chaotic and random to be explained by any general theory.

Scientifically oriented anthropologists agree that cultures are complicated and subject to random forces, but they hold that the most *important* forces are not random but operate widely and powerfully. In this respect, they follow the tradition of the unilineal evolutionists and the neoevolutionists.

Here we consider only two scientific approaches.

Evolutionary Psychology

In the late 1970s, some anthropologists adopted a theory then known as **sociobiology**. Social scientists now usually call it **evolutionary psychology**. It emphasizes the similarities between humans and other animals, arguing that humans are subject to the same kinds of processes that operate in other mammals. Harvard biologist Edward O. Wilson was instrumental in the development of this theoretical framework in the biological sciences. Wilson was interested in animal social behavior. For example, why do so many animals (e.g., lions, ants, many ungulates) live in herds or other groups whose members help one another by cooperating in hunting or emitting alarm calls that warn the group of a nearby predator?

Why are such behaviors puzzling? Most biologists have long believed that natural selection usually produces organisms that are genetically *selfish*, meaning that unselfish (*altruistic*) behavior in animals is rare, existing only under very special circumstances. For instance, most cooperative social behaviors such as alarm calls are costly to the individual animal, yet the benefits accrue to the entire group. A prairie dog calling to alert its neighbors to a predator might call the predator's attention to itself and thus stand a greater chance of getting eaten. How could natural selection produce animals that act altruistically, when altruistic behavior is so costly to the altruistic animal? Natural selection should select against altruism because an altruistic animal will have less chance of survival and reproduction than the selfish ones.

Wilson, along with other biologists such as Richard Dawkins and William Hamilton, solved this puzzle by noting that the beneficiaries of altruistic behaviors are not individual organisms but genes. Because genes are the units that are transmitted to offspring through reproduction, only genes that (re)produce more copies of themselves in the next generation can survive. Sociobiologists argue that genes tend to program the bodies that temporarily house them to act in ways that improve their biological *fitness*—that is, in ways that increase their frequencies in the next generation. To paraphrase Dawkins, a body and its behavior are a gene's way of making more copies of itself. Some evolutionary psychologists claim that this statement applies to humans as well as to other animals. If taken seriously and applied to humans, potentially this means that *your* body and behavior are your genes' ways of making more copies of themselves. (Here you can understand why some find sociobiology less than enlightening.)

The main contribution of evolutionary psychology is the insight that the fitness of an individual animal is enhanced if it aids a relative that shares the gene for altruism. This principle is most apparent in parents aiding (feeding, protecting, teaching) their offspring. However, it also applies to other relatives. For example, a female can potentially increase her fitness if she aids her brother, if that brother carries the same gene. By helping her brother, she herself may reproduce less, but this cost can be more than offset if her help improves her brother's chances of transmitting that gene to his offspring.

Thus, natural selection increases the survival of any gene that programs its body to help a relative if the cost in fitness (to the gene) is lower than the benefit to the same gene housed in the relative's body. So, an individual animal can behave altruistically, but only if the benefit of the altruism helps a relative more than it costs the "altruist" (note that the behavior is not truly altruistic because it increases the fitness of the *gene* that causes it).

Some anthropologists believe that such ideas contribute to explaining human social behavior. For example, you and I have a genetic interest in the welfare of our relatives. All else equal, the more closely related we are, the more we care for them, and people care most for those individuals who are the main vehicles for transmitting their genes—their own offspring and offspring's offspring. We care little, or less, for nonrelatives and will assist them only if they somehow return benefits to us or to our relatives. They do this mainly by reciprocity; that is, they return our help immediately or at some later time *if* we can count on their presence and help in the future. Evolutionary psychologists claim that selfishness motivates most human actions, although the selfish motive is sometimes disguised when we help family members or friends in expectation of future returns.

More generally, evolutionary psychologists note that, for most of human history, the most important human groups (bands, discussed in later chapters) were largely composed of relatives who cooperated in foraging, food sharing, child care, and other activities. They also point out that far more human societies allow a man to have several wives than allow a woman to have several husbands, which is consistent with sociobiology. They claim that evolutionary psychology helps explain many of the following widespread human mental and behavioral predispositions:

- Xenophobia—We may hate or mistrust strangers who belong to other "races" or cultures because, as obvious nonrelatives, we cannot trust them, and any help we give them is unlikely to be reciprocated.

- Warfare—Braver men who protect the group are more likely to attract more wives and/or have more sex and hence more offspring.

- Male unfaithfulness to wives—Extramarital sexual relationships allow males to have more children and therefore more fitness without the costs of raising the children.

- Female preference for marrying high-status/wealthy males—Women get access to more resources through such marriages, thus improving the survival chances and ultimately the fitness of their offspring.

Critics of such ideas charge that these and other so-called predispositions are more the product of socialization than of genes because they vary markedly from people to people. Even if evolutionary psychology "helps" in understanding such widespread patterns, critics say that it tells us little or nothing about the reasons different peoples exhibit them strongly, only weakly, or not at all. So the "help" is minimal at best. It may even be harmful if it makes us falsely believe we now understand something. And, at any rate, the insights of sociobiology apply mainly if "all else is equal," which it never is in human societies. Finally, many self-sacrificial acts of devotion by individuals, such as suicide bombers and *kamikaze* pilots who kill themselves because of devotion to their faith, values, or homelands, are problematic for evolutionary psychology (unless their families receive some benefits in fitness).

Numerous other arguments exist both for and against evolutionary psychology, some of which we cover in later chapters. For now, note that it is an excellent example of the scientific side of cultural anthropology: it holds that people are subject to the same principles and pressures as other animals—most important, to the forces of natural selection.

Materialism

Another modern scientific approach—more popular than evolutionary psychology—is **materialism** (also called **cultural materialism**). It claims that the satisfaction of human material needs and desires is the most important influence on how societies are organized and on what people think and believe. People face the same kinds of material needs as all mammals: we must receive adequate intakes of food and water, regulate our body temperature (by building shelters and wearing clothing), reproduce, cope with organisms that cause disease, compete successfully, and so forth. To satisfy these needs efficiently, people have to organize their societies in certain ways

> **materialism (cultural materialism)** Scientific theoretical orientation claiming that the main influences on cultural differences and similarities are technology, environment, and how people produce and distribute resources.

to cooperate or to succeed in competition with other societies. Many other elements of a people's culture are determined by or are greatly influenced by how people organize their activities to survive and persist in their environments.

In essence, materialists think that how a people make their living in their environment is the most important influence on the rest of their cultural existence. If one thinks that relationships with the environment and acquisition of material resources are primary, then those aspects of culture that help people acquire resources will strongly affect all other aspects. More than any other animal, people depend on *technology* to exploit resources, compete, and cope with other problems of environmental adaptation. Technology includes not just the physical *instruments* (the tools) used to produce food, provide shelter, and generally manipulate the environment. Equally important, technology includes the *knowledge* (skills) about the environment, about resources, and about the manufacture and effective use of tools that people have acquired by learning from previous generations.

Because humans rely on tools and knowledge to acquire food and harness other resources, technology is among the most important aspects of culture everywhere. Materialists believe a people's technology strongly affects other parts of their culture, including family life, political organization, values, and even worldviews, much as White argued in the 1940s. Yet most materialists of today disagree with White's view that increased energy capture made possible by technological improvements has generally made human life better, leading to cultural progress. In contrast to White, most modern materialists believe technological changes have improved the lives of *some* people in *some* respects, but that changes in technology have had mixed results overall.

By emphasizing the importance of physical/biological needs, technology, environment, and population size, modern materialists resemble earlier thinkers such as Malinowski, White, and Steward. However, modern materialists emphasize interrelationships between people and environments. For the most part, early theories about causation were *linear,* meaning that one thing makes another thing the way it is; thus, A "causes" B, or A "determines" B. But modern materialists are more likely to view technology, environment, population, and culture as having *feedback* relationships with one another. That is, as their numbers increase and people interact with their environment, they change the environment, which in turn changes the way the people live, and so on over long time periods. An important process for many materialists is *intensification:* as human numbers grow in a region, people modify more and more of the natural environment in order to produce greater quantities of food and other material needs. Usually intensification involves greater and/or more extensive modification and/or destruction of the natural environment. For example, as people exploit a resource, they may deplete its supply. Future generations must then work harder to acquire the same resource, develop a new method of acquiring it, or switch to an alternative resource. Other cultural changes accompany this long-term process of intensification, if the process is not halted or reversed.

We discuss some of these processes in later chapters. For now, note three of the main arguments of materialists: (1) many customs and beliefs of a particular culture can be explained by how they help people live in the natural world; (2) population growth and intensification are major factors that lead to cultural change; and (3) generally, and *in the long run*, material forces like the natural environment, resources, technologies, and population densities are more important than aspects of cultural knowledge (ideas and beliefs), such as values, symbols, and worldviews.

Humanistic Approaches

Many ideas of both evolutionary psychology and materialism are not seriously questioned. Most people do transmit their genes by having children, and most of us are more likely to help relatives than strangers. But whether the biologically determined "predispositions" identified by evolutionary psychology really are important causes is debatable. Some deny that such universal human predispositions exist at all. Some say that even if such predispositions do exist, then explaining them has the effect of "justifying" (in the guise of science) racial hatreds, violence, sexual inequalities, and the like. The very notion that human beings are innately selfish is odious to many anthropologists.

Likewise, no one denies that people have material needs. But whether such needs are "basic" and "shape" all of human existence is debatable. Some think humans differ from other animals in that these needs can be satisfied in such a multitude of ways that cultural differences cannot plausibly be reduced to material need and want satisfaction. They deny that material factors cause cultural differences and similarities and long-term changes. In fact, they doubt that culture has any *general* explanation. Many believe that any scholar who tries to "explain" culture or cultures dehumanizes people by treating them as objects.

Most scholars who adopt the **humanistic approach** doubt or deny that any general theory can "explain" culture in the same way that evolutionary theory explains life or that Einstein's relativity theory explains the physical world. Humanistic anthropologists are skeptical of general theories for many reasons. One is that humanity's social and cultural worlds are just too complicated for one theory to explain them. All those cultures of all those Others cannot be reduced to a single formula, they claim.

Humanistic scholars say that another reason for rejecting general theories is that humans are unique. *Homo sapiens* is such a special kind of animal that the methods and analysis that biology uses to explain other life forms do not apply to us in any significant respect. Human uniqueness lies mainly in our heavy dependence on social learning and our capacity for complex communication—that is, in both culture and language.

Other animals live in the natural world, with its food sources, predators, mates and potential mates, and so forth. Of course, humans also eat, drink, sleep, and engage in sex. But, humanists point out, we also live in a *cultural* world: what, when, and how we eat, drink, sleep, and have sex are largely determined by the culture into which each of us happens to have been born. People live in the natural world, but they also "culturally construct" the natural world and have a "worldview" (Chapter 2). Their constructions and worldviews are about as important in affecting their behaviors, thoughts, and feelings as living the real world itself.

Language also makes us unique, humanists say. Language provides words with which we classify and categorize objects, people, events, actions, qualities, and so forth. Because of language, we construct categories of events, people, groups, objects, plants, and so on, which vary from culture to culture. Because of its displacement property (see Chapter 3), language even provides us with words for things that have no material existence at all, such as ghosts and demons. If the Sapir-Whorf hypothesis has any validity and generality, then our language conditions our perceptions of the world itself, so every people exist in a perceived world that is like that of no other people. These features of language are all unique to humanity, and because of them we create our own reality as well as respond to actual reality.

All of this means that human reactions to the natural environment and human beliefs about the world are products of culture and language. To humanists,

humanistic approach Orientation that mistrusts attempts to explain cultural differences and similarities and cultural changes in favor of achieving an empathetic understanding of particular cultures.

Humanistically inclined anthropologists point out weaknesses of the materialist orientation. For example, because a natural resource used by one people is not a resource for other people or is used for other cultural purposes. Traditional higher caste Hindus do not eat beef, but revere cattle and use them in rituals and festivals around temples.

this implies that, at most, material factors like environment, technology, and population affect culture only by *limiting* (constraining) how a people act, think, and feel. Material factors cannot *determine* (cause) actions, thoughts, and feelings because these factors themselves are in part products of actions, thoughts, and feelings. Neither causes or "explains" the other, which makes untangling causes and effects pretty much impossible, humanistically inclined anthropologists argue.

When materialists claim that nature's resources are important influences on cultures and societies, a critical humanist may respond that resources are not entirely natural. Consider food resources, for instance, which materialists believe are among the most important influences on cultures. Based on religious prohibitions and cultural notions of what's edible and what's not, various peoples refuse to eat cattle, pigs, dogs, horses, and insect larvae. These (including the larvae) are the same flesh considered so delicious by many other peoples. Cultures have food taboos that are based on something besides nutritional considerations. For example, in 2012 the British people were outraged when it was discovered that some beef products also contained horsemeat, although their fellow Westerners, the French, freely buy horsemeat. If food and other resources are culturally defined and culturally meaningful as well as biologically nutritious, then in human life food is culturally defined, not "given" by the environment. Long ago, our cultural ancestors built (culturally constructed) the cultural world in which we live our lives. We live within this cultural world as well as within the natural one, humanists point out.

Thus, some humanistic anthropologists think that Tylor's and White's "science of culture" is not possible: humans and their societies are too complex and too diverse, and humans live partly in worlds that their language and culture construct for them.

Other humanists do not believe that anthropology should even *try* to be scientific. In their view, scientific anthropology "objectifies" cultures; that is, in its efforts to generalize, science places cultural features into categories (e.g., forms of marriage, types of religions) that are the categories of the anthropologist, not those of the people themselves. Humanists often make this point by saying that scientifically oriented

108   PART II   Theories and Methods of Cultural Anthropology

anthropologists "rob people of their voices." They mean that scientific anthropologists are arrogant to the extent that they believe they know better than the Other people themselves what is important in their lives and what was important in shaping their culture.

A similar objection is that scientific approaches "deny that people are agents." Humanists charge that scientific anthropologists by and large view people and groups largely as *responding* (in predictable ways) to conditions, not as *actively* trying to come up with new ways of responding to conditions. Materialists treat people, and especially "Other" people, as automatons who pretty much act in ways that are determined by their natural environment and other people around them.

Thus, some humanistic anthropologists believe that the scientific perspective is not only mistaken but also not desirable. It treats Others as mere objects, often ignoring their views of what they are doing and falsely treating them as automatons rather than agents. At least, these are some things that many humanistic anthropologists *claim* is true for materialists and other scientific anthropologists.

Humanistic anthropologists point out that fieldworkers carry their own culture with them into their research experiences. This culture affects their interactions with the community, whose stories they believe, their perceptions of what is important, and so forth. Conversely, individuals in the community have their own perceptions, opinions, and biases about the fieldworker. Among the many factors that affect how the community reacts are the fieldworker's physical characteristics, gender, and personality, as well as the historical experience of the community with individuals of the anthropologist's own society. Although most fieldworkers attempt to overcome their own cultural biases and to fit into the community, complete objectivity is impossible. In fact, many humanists think that any ethnography is not a simple report on "facts" about a given group. Rather, it is a "construction," meaning that an ethnography is a product of interactions that another fieldworker would not experience.

You might well wonder, *If* all this is true, how is it that materialist scholars have been so misguided about the importance of environment, technology, adaptation, and so forth? Some humanistic anthropologists claim that materialist thinking is a product of Western cultural values and beliefs. Because the West places such high value on material welfare and consumption, materialists mistakenly impose these same values and beliefs on other cultures. Living in a competitive and capitalistic society predisposes materialists to see "economic man" in cultures where he does not exist. Materialist theory is a kind of ethnocentrism, they claim.

Some materialists respond in kind. They point out that most academics are members of the privileged class, in status, wealth, or both. Because most academics (including humanistic anthropologists) so seldom have to worry about filling their stomachs, or sheltering themselves from heat, snow, and rain, or protecting themselves from enemies, it is easy for them to believe that such concerns are not important in other cultures either. The humanists' failure to realize the broad importance of material factors is related to their own wealth and privilege. The humanistic approach is a kind of ethnocentrism, some claim.

Even more than the scientific approach, it is difficult or impossible to collapse humanistic anthropology into a few schools or ways of approaching Others. Here, we discuss only two. Interpretive anthropology has been around for several decades, whereas postmodernism has become popular in anthropology only since the 1980s.

Interpretive Anthropology

Interpretive anthropologists emphasize the uniqueness and individuality of each human culture. Every culture has its own ways of doing things, its own worldview, its own values, and so forth. Even if two or more cultures look similar, close examination usually shows that the meanings they attach to behaviors, objects, and concepts are different. This uniqueness makes comparisons between different cultures misleading. In this and other respects, interpretive anthropology is similar to historical particularism. And because science attempts to generalize through comparisons and contrasts, it follows that anthropology is more of a humanistic discipline than a scientific one. It has more in common with literature and art than with biology or psychology, according to the interpretive approach.

Interpretive anthropologists emphasize the symbolic dimensions of culture. All social behavior has a symbolic component, in the sense that participants constantly must behave in ways that others will understand. All social interaction, therefore, is symbolic and meaningful. Meanings exist only by virtue of common agreement among the parties to the interaction—whether the interaction involves making conversation, making change in a store, or making bumpers in an auto plant. Neither participant can tell an observer how he or she knows what the other participant "means" by this or that behavior. Yet participants

interpretive anthropologists Contemporary theorists who analyze cultural elements by explicating their meanings to people and understanding them in their local context; generally emphasize cultural diversity and the unique qualities of particular cultures.

consistently behave in ways that others understand, and they consistently interpret the behavior of others correctly.

The job of the anthropologist is not to explain elements of a culture but to *explicate* one element through others. That is, the anthropologist shows how one thing in a cultural system makes sense in terms of other things in the same system, because interpretation *is* seeing how things make sense when understood in their context. (Analogously, a dictionary explicates the meanings of words in terms of other words. Only if one knows the meanings of many words in the dictionary can one use them to decipher the meanings of unknown words.) We seek to understand a people's way of life as they understand it. In the words of the late Clifford Geertz (1983, 58), who shaped the entire approach, we seek to grasp "the native's point of view," "to figure out what the devil they think they are up to." This involves acquiring intimate knowledge of a particular culture so that the ethnographer can make sense of the culture for those who do not know it.

According to many interpretive anthropologists, the search for generalized explanations of human ways of life is futile. So many factors contributed to the formation of a culture, and these factors interacted in such complex and unpredictable ways, that we must concentrate on understanding the unique elements of each way of life. In this respect, interpretive anthropologists exemplify the humanistic perspective.

Postmodernism

Postmodernists generally believe that the methods and assumptions of all science—including fields such as biology—are themselves culturally situated and culture bound. This means that science, as most people understand it, is not objective in its theories and even in its facts ("data"). Rather, it is carried out by scientists who are products of a particular cultural upbringing. Like all knowledge, scientific theories are affected by conditions in the scientists' own culture.

For example, a postmodernist might say that evolutionary psychologists are enculturation into a culture that practically celebrates selfishness. In free-market economies, everyone is supposed to be looking out for themselves and consuming commodities and competing. So the evolutionary psychologists raised in this economic system think people everywhere act this way and claim that these alleged biological imperatives apply to humanity in general. Such theories are culture bound, in the same way Boas showed that unilineal evolutionism was culture bound (ethnocentric).

How can the proponents of science be so misguided? Postmodernists point out that scientific thinking and methods became prominent during the Enlightenment period (also called the Age of Reason) of late eighteenth- and nineteenth-century Western Europe. Enlightenment philosophers emphasized rational thought as the key to advancing knowledge about the world, from the solar system to humanity. Tradition and especially religion were viewed as impediments to discovering Truth. Emotions could also get in the way, especially if they keep otherwise rational thinkers from accepting the reality of a fact or principle just because they don't like it or its implications.

For example, you might refuse to accept evidence showing that not all societies are patriarchal. You reject or discount the evidence because it is not consistent with what you learned while growing up so or what you think your religion teaches. Your refusal to accept the evidence is not "rational," so it gets in the way of improving your knowledge. This would not matter very much for your society unless, of course, men hold the power in that society and most of them feel and believe as you do. Enlightenment thinkers tried to free thought from the shackles of religion and emotion, so that Reason and Science could reveal the world to us as it really is.

Postmodernists do not think there is anything very special about the Enlightenment version of rational thought. They say that human knowledge originates in a particular social, economic, and political context. *Scientific* knowledge is no exception. Science is a product of a particular cultural tradition—that of the West—and therefore reflects the economy, family organization, political ideology, worldview, and so forth of Western society. Science is just one among hundreds of other systems of cultural knowledge. At the extreme, postmodernists hold that science has little more claim to absolute Truth than the ideas and beliefs of other peoples. All are valid on their own terms, but none is "privileged" or has any exclusive claim to objectivity. If scientists themselves don't realize this, it is because they are inside their own knowledge system and so do not grasp the implicit assumptions of their rationalistic and mechanistic worldview.

Postmodernists also think the most important thing about the context of knowledge is power relationships. Prevalent beliefs and ideas in a community reflect lines of power, largely because those with power have the most influence on which ideas and beliefs become "prevalent." To illustrate with a modern example, most North Americans attach positive value to abstractions

---

postmodernists Followers of the philosophical viewpoint emphasizing the relativity of all knowledge, including science; focus on how the knowledge of a particular time and place is constructed, especially on how power relations affect the creation and spread of ideas and beliefs.

CONCEPT REVIEW: Main Contrasts Between Scientific and Humanistic Approaches

	Scientific	Humanistic
Overall goals of anthropology	Explain cultural differences and similarities and how and why cultures change.	Describe and interpret particular cultures.
Human uniqueness	As an animal species, all humans share core motivations, emotions, and behavioral predispositions; food, shelter, security, and reproduction are primary needs.	As a culture-dependent and and language-using species, human motivations and behavioral predispositions vary enormously; constructions and symbolic meanings are important.
Role of comparison	Discover patterns and relationships that apply broadly.	Distort the cultures compared and ignore the complexities of particular cultures.
Objectivity	Systematic observations and cross-checking of individual and group patterns of behavior make objectivity attainable.	Descriptions emerge from interactions between fieldworkers and local people; knowledge of cultures is constructed, not objective.
Fieldwork emphasis	Research topics are chosen for their relevance to wide issues in the scientific community.	Achieve an insider's view and/or represent the Voices of the people themselves.

like private property, free-market capitalism, democracy, and various individual rights and freedoms. These values reflect, and support, the interests of some people over other people. Much scholarly knowledge—including much of what is taught in colleges and universities—is like this, postmodernists claim. For example, evolutionary psychology is often taught as a credible or even correct theory in biology courses, although many postmodernists believe its theories support sexism and patriarchy.

In anthropological fieldwork, there is often a power dimension to the relationship between the fieldworker and the local people. Most fieldworkers are able to command more resources and thus can influence people to talk about things they'd rather not discuss (although there are ethical standards in fieldwork, covered in Chapter 6). Postmodernists tend to mistrust most older ethnographies, and generally they prefer accounts in which the fieldworkers openly discuss their personal relationships with members of the community. They also prefer ethnographies in which the ethnographer gives her or his readers access to the local voices.

As mentioned, postmodernism penetrated anthropology in the 1980s and has attracted more converts in our discipline than in any other social science. One reason for the popularity of this perspective in anthropology is its apparent consistency with cultural relativism. However, critics of the approach became vocal in the late 1990s. Do postmodernists adopt the tenets of their own ideas in their personal lives? If science is "just another" kind of knowledge, do postmodernists refuse to ride in airplanes or use microwaves? How have their own ideas escaped the influence of power relationships? Why wouldn't *their* ideas be culture bound as well?

Postmodernism reminds us that rationality and science do not provide all the answers and do not ask all the necessary questions. It leads us to ask where our ideas come from and who might gain and lose from them. Perhaps most important, it warns anthropological thinkers of the dangers of becoming arrogant about our objectivity. Scientifically oriented theorists can easily forget that they are cultural beings and that their own ideas about the human world are culturally conditioned.

The Concept Review sharply contrasts some of the main differences between the scientific and the humanistic approaches. Notice that they differ in their conceptions of the primary goals of anthropology, in the significance of humanity's mammalian biology for anthropological research and findings, in the validity of conducting cross-cultural comparisons, in whether anthropological research among humans can be objective, and in the appropriate aims of conducting fieldwork. Like most contrasts, the ones in the Concept Review are presented starkly, and there is more overlap between the two approaches than shown.

Either, Or, or Both?

The differences between the scientific and humanistic orientations are sometimes presented as conflicting: Humanists often accuse scientists of dehumanizing people in their vain effort to explain them, whereas scientists claim that humanists are deceiving themselves if they think they can get inside some Other culture.

A recent controversy illustrates that many anthropologists continue to have contrasting views of what their discipline is or should be. Until 2010, the American Anthropological Association stated that its long-range plan is "to advance anthropology as the science that studies humankind in all its aspects." At the 2010 annual meeting of the AAA, however, the Executive Board revised the plan to state its purpose as "to advance public understanding of humankind in all its aspects." The replacement of *science* with *public understanding* led to strong reactions from scientifically oriented anthropologists, who felt the official statement undermined their perspective.

To some extent, different approaches exist because of the differing interests of anthropologists. For example, scholars whose research areas include subjects such as human–environment relationships, economic systems, or long-term changes in societies are likely to find a materialist approach useful. Those who study dimensions such as mythology, art, oral traditions, or worldviews are more likely to fall into the humanistic camp. So, in part, the diversity of modern approaches reflects the fact that human beings and their cultures are complex and multifaceted, so the orientation most useful to understand one facet (e.g., subsistence) may not prove very useful to understand another (e.g., worldview).

In the interest of balance, in the remainder of this book, we try to avoid choosing between the two orientations by taking the following approach. Like evolutionary psychologists and cultural materialists, we think *it is important* that people are part of nature. But we recognize that different elements of a culture are influenced to different degrees by material conditions. The way an economy is organized is greatly influenced by the local environment, climate, technology, and the size and density of the human population. But the ways the members of a culture resolve their disputes, raise their children, perform their rituals, or act toward their fathers-in-law are less influenced by material conditions or are influenced by them only indirectly. Details of the legends they recite, the specific objects they use as religious symbols, and the way they decorate their bodies may have little to do with material forces. Such elements of a cultural system are only loosely tied to the natural world and to material needs and wants. We cannot account for them without considering people's desires for a meaningful existence, an emotionally gratifying social life, an intellectually satisfying worldview, creative self-expression, and so forth.

So, different orientations are useful for studying different dimensions of culture. Still, people who are new to anthropology are often puzzled by the diversity of approaches within the field. We therefore conclude this chapter by suggesting answers to the question posed in the following section.

Why Can't All Those Anthropologists Agree?

Most fields in the natural sciences generally agree on a set of laws or principles that govern the world. In geology, for example, processes such as sedimentation, plate tectonics, volcanic eruptions, fossilization, and so forth are fairly well understood and account for the main geological features of our planet. Biologists, likewise, believe that the process of evolution produced the diversity of all life on Earth, although the relative importance of natural selection and random events in this process remains uncertain.

Cultural anthropology lacks a comparable set of general principles. Consider one basic question of the scientific orientation: what are the main causes of differences and similarities among the world's known cultures? If you asked 100 anthropologists this question, you would get a multitude of answers. Materialists would mention forces such as climate, resources, population sizes, and technology. Humanistically oriented scholars would say the question itself is wrongheaded because anthropologists should be trying to interact with members of particular cultures and gain an insider's view of them—not to "explain" them. Many would respond that there is no generalized explanation because cultures are so complex and diverse that the most important causes in culture X are not at all important in culture Y. Still others would hold that the question is ethnocentric because it reduces people in other cultures to the status of "objects" of our explanations.

Why don't anthropologists agree about the answer to this question and numerous other basic questions about humanity? Several factors contribute to the absence of consensus.

First, we humans are conscious and self-aware beings who state a variety of reasons for why we do and think what we do and think. The zoologist studying an animal's behavior observes and records the behavior, and then typically tries to identify the elements of the natural and social environment to which the behavior is adapted. But the anthropologist must listen to the reasons people themselves give for their behavior. People talk back, and anthropologists must take their talk as well as their actions, into account.

Second, for ethical reasons, anthropologists do not set up controlled experiments to study how people respond. Suppose—following Steward's lead—we want to study how the natural environment affects cultures. We cannot hold everything constant except the supply of food, water, or shelter and then see how people react when the supply of food, water, or shelter is varied. The only way the anthropologist can "control" conditions is by looking around the world for "natural experiments"—places where the natural environment is similar and peoples with different histories live. We can choose a sample of peoples who live in environments that appear to be similar and then see whether the peoples who live in these places have similar cultures. For example, we might compare indigenous peoples who live in the world's deserts: the Sahara of northern Africa, the Kalahari of southern Africa, the American Southwest, the Gobi of Central Asia, and so forth. To conduct such a comparative study, we would have to rely on the ethnographic reports written by a multitude of earlier ethnographers, whose reports resulted from their observations and discussions with peoples in the various deserts.

Suppose our comparative study finds, as it will, that the cultures are similar in some respects but different in others. Then other problems arise: Natural environments are only similar, never identical. Did we fail to detect a small but critical difference in the environment that might explain the cultural differences? Or, are the differences due to nonenvironmental factors? Likewise, shall we call customs and beliefs that differ in minor ways between the cultures the "same," or are the subtle differences between them sufficient to call them "different"? Suppose we decide that some behavior, like sharing food within a village, is the "same" behavior in the cultures. But then we discover that people in several of the cultures give different reasons for the behavior—in culture X, people say they want to help one another, whereas in culture Y, they say they give only because they expect to get something back later. Are both of these behaviors still "sharing food"? Or, should we consider them different because people's stated motivations differ? Such questions are *inherently* difficult to answer when dealing with human beings, and anthropologists cannot sort them out in laboratories or other experimental settings.

Quite likely a third reason anthropology lacks a common theoretical orientation and an agreed-upon set of principles is because people become anthropologists for a wider variety of reasons than people become, say, physicists. Some of us study anthropology because of our curiosity about why the human species is so diverse culturally. Others go into the field to further the cause of social justice—by educating themselves and others about racism, ethnocentrism, colonialism, or sexism, for example. Some want to immerse themselves in travel and interaction with people who are different from themselves, and they become anthropologists because the field provides them with such opportunities. The very broad scope of anthropology (see Chapter 1) helps account for the variety of reasons people choose it as a career: you can study agriculture, family life, political organization, medicine, art, religion, folklore, and almost anything else having to do with humankind. Naturally, people who study topics as diverse as these are unlikely to agree on their theoretical orientations to the field as a whole. Indeed, many of them consciously reject any form of theoretical orientation, preferring to concentrate on researching particular cultures.

In sum, there are at least three major reasons modern cultural anthropologists have such varied orientations to the study of culture:

1. Our subjects—other human beings—are conscious beings who are aware of their own behavior and state their own reasons for why they do what they do. Human subjects talk back.
2. Anthropologists cannot set up experiments that enable them to control the conditions under which people live, allowing their behavior to be manipulated. Anthropologists observe people as they live their everyday lives.
3. The broad scope of the field and the enormous diversity of reasons people study anthropology make it unlikely that consensus will emerge. Cultural anthropologists are among the most diverse of scholars.

SUMMARY

1. **Discuss the global forces that contributed to the emergence of anthropology.** Anthropology originated as a distinct academic discipline in the late nineteenth century, after colonialism intensified contact between peoples of European ancestry and the indigenous peoples of Africa, Asia, the Americas, and the Pacific. Darwin's theory of evolution was one of the main notions that allowed Western intellectuals to make sense of the peoples and cultures of other lands.

2. **Describe the main ideas of the nineteenth-century unilineal evolutionists.** Unilineal evolutionists applied

the notion of evolution to cultures. Using written accounts as their main source of information about Other cultures, they arranged cultures into a sequence of progressive stages, from simple to complex, with Western civilization at the pinnacle. Anthropology thus began as the academic field that studied how humankind progressed out of rude beginnings into a more "civilized" cultural existence.

3. **Understand the ways American historical particularism and British functionalism challenged unilineal evolutionism.** In the early twentieth century, both American and British anthropologists developed new approaches. The American historical particularists, led by Boas, demolished the speculative schemes of the unilineal evolutionists by arguing that concepts such as "complexity" depend on one's point of view and so have little objective meaning. Boas popularized the notion of cultural relativism that remains a hallmark of anthropology today. In Great Britain, functionalists such as Malinowski and Radcliffe-Brown tried to show how the various parts of a culture and a social system serve to meet the needs of individuals and society. Both the historical particularists and the functionalists emphasized the importance of firsthand fieldwork as the surest path to accurate descriptions of a people and as essential for the training of anthropologists.

4. **Describe the mid-twentieth-century rebirth of evolutionary interests (neoevolutionism).** In the middle decades of the twentieth century, neoevolutionists like White and Steward returned to cultural evolution, avoiding most mistakes of the nineteenth-century scholars. White emphasized the importance of technology, Steward of adaptation to the local environment, in making cultures the way they are. Both men thought that a people's methods of acquiring resources (energy, food, and so forth) from nature are the main influences on culture. Both also believed that anthropology should and can be a science.

5. **Discuss the main differences between the scientific and the humanistic approaches to modern anthropological thought.** One broad controversy among modern cultural anthropologists is whether their field is primarily a scientific enterprise or a humanistic study. Scientifically oriented scholars believe that people are subjected to the same kinds of natural forces as other animals and that genuine explanations of differences and similarities and long-term changes are possible and desirable. Humanistically inclined anthropologists believe that humanity is such a very unique kind of animal that special tools are required to understand our species and that attempts to explain humans are futile and dehumanizing.

6. **Describe evolutionary psychology, materialism, interpretive anthropology, and postmodernism.** Evolutionary psychology (sociobiology) and materialism are examples of scientific approaches. Evolutionary psychology emphasizes that humans are like other animals in that most of our behavior helps us transmit our genes to future generations. Materialists argue that how a given people organize their groups and pattern their activities to acquire energy and materials from their natural environment is the major explanation for other aspects of their cultural system. In contrast, humanistically oriented anthropologists mistrust all generalized explanations of cultural phenomena. Interpretive anthropologists emphasize the uniqueness of each culture and favor studying, appreciating, and interpreting each culture individually. Postmodernists think that science in general has no particular claim to Truth and that many scientific ideas taught by schools and colleges reflect power relationships in the wider social and cultural context.

7. **Analyze why contemporary anthropology has no single unifying theoretical orientation.** Contemporary anthropologists do not agree among themselves on many fundamental questions, including even the major objectives of their field. Their lack of consensus is understandable, given that their (human) subjects are self-conscious and willful beings; that anthropologists cannot experiment with people's lives; and that anthropology studies such diverse subjects that a single theoretical orientation is unlikely to be able to encompass all of them.

6 Methods of Investigation

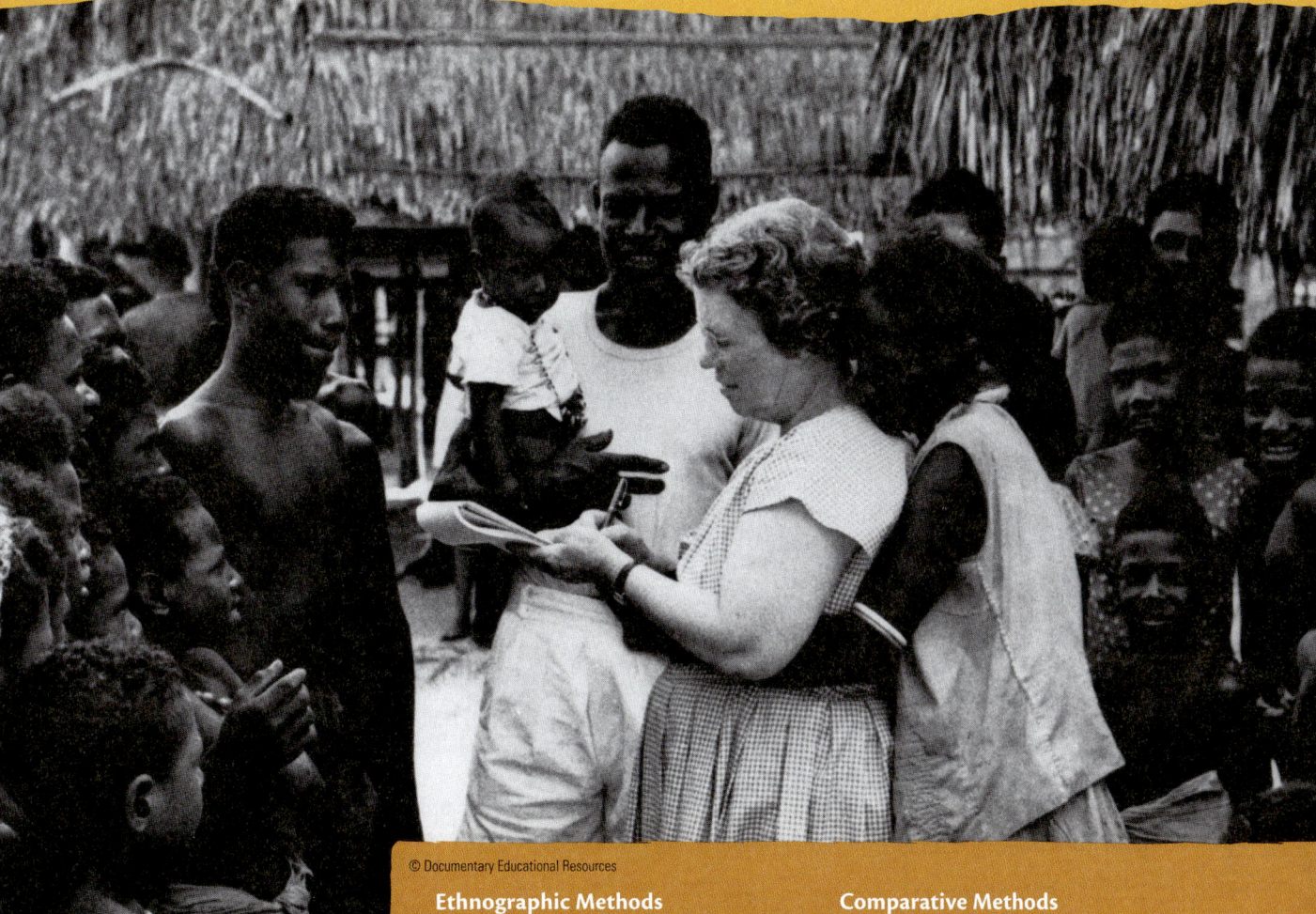

© Documentary Educational Resources

Ethnographic Methods
Ethnographic Fieldwork
Problems and Issues in Field Research
Fieldwork as a Rite of Passage
Ethnohistory

Comparative Methods
Cross-Cultural Comparisons
Controlled Comparisons

Margaret Mead's highly innovative field studies in Samoa and New Guinea made her one of the most widely read anthropologists of the twentieth century.

LEARNING OBJECTIVES

After reading this chapter, you should be able to

1. **DISCUSS** the major objectives of cultural research.
2. **UNDERSTAND** that research requires different methods.
3. **DESCRIBE** the methods used to study the culture of a contemporary or living society.
4. **DESCRIBE** the method used to study the past culture of a society.
5. **UNDERSTAND** the purpose of comparative research.
6. **EXPLAIN** cross-cultural comparisons.
7. **DESCRIBE** controlled comparative studies.

Anthropological research has two purposes: (1) to collect and record descriptive data about the cultures of specific peoples (**ethnography**), and (2) to explain the past and present diversity found in cultural systems in the world (**ethnology**). We discussed culture change in Chapter 4. Recognizing that the culture of a society is constantly changing, we further divide research into studies that describe a culture at one period in time (**synchronic**) and research that studies the changes in culture of a people over time (**diachronic**). As a result, research can be grouped into four broad categories, each with its own methodologies (see Table 6.1). However, it is important to note that any particular study may actually involve the use of two or more methodologies. For example, it is very common for ethnographic studies to combine both ethnographic field research and ethnohistoric research, as seen in Table 6.1.

TABLE 6-1 Research Methodologies

Ethnography	Ethnology
Synchronic ethnographic fieldwork	Cross-cultural comparisons
Diachronic ethnohistoric research	Controlled comparisons

Ethnographic Methods

There are two sources of cultural data about a particular people: the living members of the society and written accounts or other records about that group of people. Collecting cultural data by studying and interviewing living members of a society is called **ethnographic fieldwork**. Studying a people's culture using written accounts and other records is termed **ethnohistoric research**.

Ethnographic Fieldwork

Ethnographic fieldwork, the most commonly used research method, involves the collection of cultural data from living individuals. The researcher lives with or close to the people being studied and interacts with them on a day-to-day basis for a long period, usually a year or more. Not infrequently, the anthropologist has to learn the group's language and behave according to the group's social norms. By its very nature, fieldwork fosters a close personal relationship between the researcher and members of the society being studied. This social closeness between researchers and the people they study distinguishes anthropologists from other social scientists.

Anthropologists have always used fieldwork as the primary method for collecting cultural information.

---

ethnography Description of a specific culture.

ethnology Study of human cultures from a comparative perspective.

synchronic Describing a culture at one period in time.

diachronic Describing changes in a culture over time.

ethnographic fieldwork Collection of information from living people about their way of life; *see also* fieldwork.

ethnohistoric research Study of past cultures using written accounts and other documents.

Over the past century, the objectives of fieldwork have changed and with it the data-gathering techniques. Today, a number of techniques are used in the course of any research project.

Interviewing is the most basic method of collecting cultural data. The anthropologist asks questions and elicits answers from members of the society being studied. Interviews may be structured or unstructured. A *structured interview* consists of a limited number of specific questions. It may take the form of a questionnaire the researcher fills in as the questions are answered. This type of interview is best suited for collecting general quantitative data about the group. For example, most research begins with a census of the community: the number of people in each family, their ages and relationships, and basic economic information about the family. In this manner, the researcher constructs demographic and economic profiles of the group. Structured interviews are also used to create genealogies. Most research requires a clear knowledge of how group members are related to one another. Genealogies are important in understanding the social and economic behavior of individuals beyond the immediate family. There are, however, limits to the utility of structured interviews.

In *unstructured interviews,* the researcher asks open-ended questions, hoping that the respondent will elaborate on the answers. The questions may be general, about family life, marriage, a particular religious ritual, or economic activity. Most cultural data are collected through unstructured interviews. In these interviews, the researcher learns the cultural explanations for information collected in the structured interviews.

Although it is the source of most cultural data, interviewing has severe limitations. The problem usually is not with the answers given by the members of the group, but rather with the questions asked by the researcher. What is relevant or irrelevant to the proper understanding of a particular cultural phenomenon depends on the culture of the individuals involved. Initially, the researcher does not understand the cultural context of the data and thus does not know what questions need to be asked and answered. The early stages of a research project are often characterized by "shotgun" questioning as the anthropologist seeks to learn enough about the culture to ask the right questions. Through interviewing, a researcher can gain a good basic knowledge of a culture's major structural features. However, no matter how knowledgeable and willing the respondents might be, verbal descriptions in themselves are incomplete and do not enable the researcher to gain an in-depth knowledge of the people or an understanding of the true dynamics of their culture.

To understand the limitations of interviewing, ask yourself this question: If an anthropologist from another culture asked you to describe a baseball game, what would you say? How complete would your description be? Chances are, if you are an avid fan, you could relate enough information for the anthropologist to gain a basic understanding of the game. You could tell how many players are on each side and explain the basic rules about balls, strikes, runs, errors, and innings. However, from memory alone, it would be impossible to explain everything that might occur during a game. Every baseball game, like every other cultural event, is to some degree unique. From memory alone, it is impossible for you to explain everything that might actually occur during a game. The best you could do is give the researcher an idealized model of a baseball game. Certain facts would be left untold, not because you were hiding them but because they are either so commonplace or so unusual that they are not part of your consciousness concerning the game. Interviews alone can give the researcher only a simplified overview of a particular cultural phenomenon, an idealized model.

If researchers want to truly understand baseball, they cannot simply talk to someone about it; they need to see a game. In fact, researchers should observe several games and discuss what occurred with a knowledgeable person. It would be even better for researchers to participate, at least in a minor way, in some games. Only by combining interviewing with observing and participating can one begin to more fully understand the rules and dynamics of the game. So it is with the study of any cultural phenomenon.

During the late nineteenth and early twentieth centuries, anthropologists relied primarily on interviews alone to collect cultural data. This technique was well suited to the anthropological objectives of that time. The traditional lifestyles of non-Western peoples were rapidly changing in many parts of the world, and anthropologists were concerned about collecting as much cultural data as possible before knowledge of these ways of life disappeared. This was particularly true in North America, where Native American groups had already been placed on reservations, and their economies and cultures had drastically changed. Anthropologists wanted to learn about earlier Native American lifestyles before all knowledge of the prereservation period was lost. Researchers could not observe, let alone

---

interviewing Collecting cultural data by systematic questioning; may be structured (using questionnaires) or unstructured (open-ended).

participate in, a bison hunt or the organizing of a war party. The only way the prereservation culture of these peoples could be studied was by interviewing individuals who had grown to adulthood before the reservations were created. Today, we refer to this early use of interviewing alone as **recall ethnography**. In a relatively short period, anthropologists were able to collect, and thus preserve, a vast body of general descriptive data on pre-reservation Native American cultures.

In the 1920s, anthropologists' interest began to shift from just recording descriptions of the general culture of a society to attempting to understand the basic dynamics of cultural systems. In other words, anthropologists wanted to see how these systems worked and how their parts fit together. A leader in this change was Bronislaw Malinowski, mentioned in the discussion of functionalism in Chapter 5, who popularized a new data collection technique called **participant observation**. Anthropologists no longer merely recorded interviews and analyzed people's statements. To a greater or lesser extent, they took up residence with the people they were studying and began trying to learn about the culture by observing people in their daily lives and participating in their daily activities.

Participant observation has often been misinterpreted, even by some anthropologists who have taken it too literally. It does not mean becoming a full participant in the activities of the people—in other words, "going native." The emphasis of this technique is more on observation than on participation. Participant observation usually does require that one live in the community because only by doing so can one observe and record the behavior of individuals as they go about their daily work, visit their friends, interact with their relatives, participate in rituals, and so on. These observations of behavior serve to generate new questions. Why does a man share food with some families but not with others? Why do some women wear their hair in a particular style? Does a particular color of clothing have any meaning? Some behaviors have significance; others do not. For example, variations in hairstyles may be merely the result of personal preferences, or they may reflect status differences. Color may or may not have special significance. In American society, black symbolizes mourning; but in other societies, covering one's body with white clay symbolizes the same emotion. Participant observation allows the researcher to collect more detailed data than does interviewing alone, and thus it makes possible a deeper understanding of interrelationships among cultural phenomena.

Firsthand observations of the members of a society also enable the researcher to see how people diverge from the culturally defined, idealized model of behavior. An incident that occurred while Malinowski was working in the Trobriand Islands illustrates the divergence between cultural norms—the way people say they ought to behave and the way they actually behave. One day, Malinowski heard a commotion in the village and discovered that a young boy in a neighboring village had committed suicide by climbing a palm tree and flinging himself onto the beach. In his earlier questioning of the islanders, Malinowski had been told that sexual relations between a man and his mother's sister's daughters were prohibited. On inquiring into the suicide of the young boy, Malinowski found that the boy had been sexually involved with his mother's sister's daughter and that such incestuous relationships were not rare. So long as such liaisons were not mentioned in public, they were ignored. In this particular case, the girl's ex-boyfriend had become angry and publicly exposed the transgression. Although everyone in the village already knew of this incestuous relationship, by making it public the ex-boyfriend exposed his rival to ridicule, thus causing him to commit suicide. It is doubtful that such behavior could have been discovered by only interviewing individuals.

Problems and Issues in Field Research

Every fieldwork experience is unique. Thus, specific problems differ, depending on the personal characteristics of the researcher, the nature of the community, and the particular questions being studied. There are, however, three difficulties that, to varying degrees and in different ways, affect virtually every field research situation: (1) stereotyping, (2) defining the fieldworker's role in the community and developing rapport, and (3) identifying and interviewing consultants.

Ethnic Stereotyping

When we think of stereotypes—preconceived generalizations concerning a particular group of people—we usually think only of their effects on the perceptions of one party of a relationship. Anthropologists ask themselves how they can overcome their own stereotypes and cultural biases about the people they study. Stereotyping,

---

recall ethnography Attempt to reconstruct a cultural system at a slightly earlier period by interviewing older individuals who lived during that period.

participant observation Main technique used in conducting ethnographic fieldwork, involving living among a people and participating in their daily activities.

however, is a two-way street. Every society has beliefs or stereotypes concerning members of other societies and of ethnic and racial groups. Thus, although the goal is for anthropologists to put aside their personal stereotypes sufficiently to research the cultural system of another people with some degree of objectivity, those with whom the ethnographer will be living and studying will not have put aside their own biases and beliefs about other people. The situation is rapidly changing, but most anthropologists have been and still are of European ancestry, while most subjects of anthropological research are non-European peoples. Even if a particular anthropologist is of Asian, African, or Native American ancestry, a similar problem exists because anthropologists seldom belong to the local community they study and thus are outsiders. As a result, an anthropologist who enters another community must contend with local stereotypes about the ethnic or racial group with which the anthropologist is identified.

During World War II, many Navajos served as "code talkers" for the Marine Corps in the Pacific, sending and receiving coded messages in Navajo for field communication. The Japanese were never able to break the code since they were unfamiliar with the language. Tom Sasaki, a Japanese American anthropologist, arrived on the reservation in 1948 to begin his research on the Navajo. The rumor spread that he was possibly a Japanese spy wanting to learn the language so they could break the code. As a result, he did not attempt to learn the language. Even still, mistrusting his motives, many of the Navajo veterans initially avoided him.

In the case of anthropologists of European ancestry, local stereotyping has most frequently been derived from contact with only a limited range of individuals such as missionaries, soldiers, government officials, tourists, or people involved in economic development projects. Regardless of the nature and intensity of this contact, most non-Western peoples have well-developed ideas about the expected behavior of such individuals. The tendency of local people to attempt to fit the ethnographer into one of their existing stereotypical categories can at times prove a burden for fieldworkers. Anthropologists' behavior seldom conforms to the model that the local people have developed. Thus, an anthropologist attempting to gain social acceptance in such a society is typically met with suspicion, if not at times with hostility. The types of questions anthropologists ask about behavior and beliefs frequently arouse suspicions further and elicit guarded answers. Why does this researcher want to know about our family structure, political organization, and ritual secrets? What is the person going to do with this information? While the anthropologist is trying to understand the community, the members of the community are attempting to understand the anthropologist's motives. Depending on the nature of previous contacts, some types of questions may provoke more suspicion than others. For example, a minority or tribal group involved in some illegal or illicit activity—such as smuggling, poaching, or growing drugs—may wonder whether the anthropologist will inform government authorities. Members of groups that have been exposed to Western culture frequently assume that the ethnographer's objective is to make money and that researchers become wealthy by publishing books.

In other cases, members of the community may be aware that Europeans and Euro-Americans do not approve of or believe in certain types of behaviors, and few people will disclose information on topics they think will be met with disapproval or scorn. This reticence is particularly evident for certain types of religious beliefs and practices. As a result of the extensive activities of Christian missionaries, most non-Western peoples are well aware that Westerners usually deny the validity of witchcraft and the existence of werewolves. Members of societies that hold such beliefs are usually hesitant about discussing these subjects with Westerners. They are understandably reluctant to talk openly about an uncle who they believe can turn himself into a deer or a snake with someone who will probably view what they say as ridiculous. Likewise, they probably would hesitate to say that their father had been killed by a witch if they thought the researcher did not believe in witchcraft. Clyde Kluckhohn found Navajos to be highly reluctant to formally discuss witchcraft in interviews. In his book *Navaho Witchcraft*, he noted that over half of the individuals he "interviewed" for the book were Navajo hitch-hikers he picked up driving around the reservation or friends who he talked to while driving them to town or a government agency. In private casual conversations while driving, they were more far likely to discuss witchcraft.

Developing a Role and Rapport

Often against a background of suspicion and distrust, an anthropologist has to develop a rapport with the members of the community. *Rapport* in this sense means acceptance to the degree that a working relationship is possible. Although ethnographers are rarely totally accepted by the people among whom they work, over a period of time, most anthropologists succeed in gaining some degree of trust and friendship among members of the group.

The particular role or roles that anthropologists eventually define for themselves within a society vary

GLOBAL CHALLENGES AND OPPORTUNITIES

The Changing Relationship Between Anthropologists and Indigenous Peoples

In 1897 an invading British military force took over 900 brass plaques from the royal palace of the Kingdom of Benin (now part of Nigeria) and sold them at auction to help cover the cost of the expedition. Today they are scattered among museums in Europe and North America. As early as 1936, the Oba of Benin requested their return. More recently the Nigerian parliament has requested repatriation.

From the very beginnings of European expansion, individual scholars thought that it was important to create a record of the peoples whose cultures they were in the process of destroying. Four years after the conquest of Mexico, in 1529, Father Bernardino de Sahagún arrived as a Franciscan missionary. His interest in Aztec culture eventually resulted in what some have termed the first ethnography of a Native American society. In 1549, Diego de Landa became the Bishop of Yucatán. While aggressively pursuing a policy of converting the Maya to Catholicism, he also wrote an account of the Maya religious and cultural practices he was attempting to destroy. In 1609, Garcilaso de la Vega, the son of a Spanish conquistador and a member of the Incan nobility, published an account of the Inca in Peru. Other Spaniards recorded similar accounts, and in the centuries that followed, still other Europeans thought it important to do likewise. By the seventeenth century, members of the European nobility and wealthy merchants had begun collecting exotic ethnography items from around the world, creating what were called curiosity cabinets. However, these early ethnographic accounts and collections were not done in a systematic manner.

It was not until the mid-1800s, with the creation of public museums, that the systematic study and collecting of anthropological materials began to emerge, and it would not be until the beginning of the twentieth century that anthropology would become an academic discipline within universities. What originally distinguished anthropological collecting in museums and anthropology from other disciplines within universities was its focus on non-Western peoples, particularly smaller preliterate, indigenous hunting, gathering, herding, and farming societies. It was widely believed that these smaller indigenous peoples could not become modern or "civilized" and survive. They were doomed to extinction—if not biologically, then certainly culturally. In regard to the native peoples of the United States and Canada, this view became expressed in the myth of the "vanishing Indian," although the same belief was held concerning similar smaller peoples throughout the world. To the academic world, it was important to preserve a permanent record of these peoples, since they represented an earlier vanishing stage of human cultural development.

To anthropologists, the idea that within a few generations these peoples would be gone meant that in the study of these peoples, they could disregard their cultural sensitivities in collecting and recording their cultures. Archaeologists could excavate their burials. Physical anthropologists could collect and study the remains of their ancestors. Museum curators could collect their most sacred religious objects, even the ones still in use. Cultural anthropologists could research the most private and sacred aspects of their lives and record them in text, photographs, and drawings as well as on film and audio recordings.

Early cultural anthropologists approached their research and collecting with an almost religious zeal. In regard to their cultural behavior both past and still existing, they had no rights, and many anthropologists went to great lengths to secure cultural data. Leslie White, in his introduction to his study of the Zia Pueblo in New Mexico, notes, "The pueblo . . . takes a firm stand on the question of secrecy [in regard to religious practices]." However, "there are occasional individuals . . . who feel that a record of it [meaning religious practices] should be made and preserved. It is the ethnographer's task to 'scent out' such individuals" (White 1967, 17). He further stated that these individuals had to be interviewed secretly to protect them. To anthropologists, it was critical to preserve a complete a record of the culture of these peoples before they were gone—not for the use of their descendants, if there were any, but for civilized peoples to have a better understanding of their own, uncivilized past. This is not to say that anthropologists totally disregarded their human rights. In fact, anthropologists were among the earliest and most vocal supporters of individual and economic rights for these peoples at a time when most Europeans argued that they had no rights.

This relationship between anthropological researchers/collectors and the indigenous peoples remained basically unchanged until the last decades of the twentieth century. Early anthropologists were correct, in part. Globalization eventually changed the lives of these peoples—some more than others. Collectively, they have become increasingly educated and literate, with rising numbers even attending universities to become lawyers, doctors, and other professionals. In other words, many members of these societies have become "modernized." However, early anthropologists were incorrect in their assumption that these descendants would lose their identities and their cultural heritage. As they became more integrated into and aware of the "modern" world, they became increasing hostile not only to the economic and political domination and exploitation by the societies that controlled them, but to the cultural exploitation by members of these societies as well.

Initially, their concern was with the repatriation of their tangible cultural properties: human remains, burial goods, sacred objects, and objects of cultural patrimony. Western societies had applied a different legal standard to the properties of indigenous peoples. Had these same properties belonged to members of the dominant society, there would have been no question as to illegality of having taken them. Anthropologists and museums had in fact "stolen" them.

Many governments have adopted laws and policies in attempts to remedy this situation. In 1984, Australia passed the Aboriginal and Torres Straits Islander Heritage Act, which gave protection to indigenous areas and objects of significance. In 1990, the U.S. Congress passed the Native American Grave Protection and Repatriation Act (NAGPRA), which called for the repatriation of human remains, funerary objects, sacred objects, and objects of cultural patrimony to Native American groups, including Native Hawaiians, held by museums and federal agencies. In the 1990s, Canada adopted a policy, not a law, to encourage the repatriation of cultural properties to its native peoples, and many Canadian museums have voluntarily done so. In 2000, the Working Group on Human Remains, a governmental advisory committee, was established in Great Britain to study the issue of human remains in publicly funded museums. Many British museums have already repatriated human remains. In 2007, the United Nations passed the Declaration on the Rights of Indigenous People. Among other things, the declaration states that indigenous peoples have the right to "the access and/or the repatriation of ceremonial objects and human remains." However, this policy is not legally binding. Regardless, the repatriation of the tangible cultural properties of indigenous people has increasingly become a global issue.

The question of tangible cultural properties only affects some forms of cultural anthropological research. However, it is the related issue of intellectual property rights that is most directly relevant to cultural anthropologists' research. Most developed countries in the world today have laws protecting intellectual property rights. Literature, songs, music, art, logos, and knowledge are or can be the property of individuals or groups in the form of copyrights, patents, or trademarks. Also legally recognized, but not as clearly defined, are the rights of individuals and groups to privacy and even secrecy as well as protection against slander and libel. The earliest anthropologists recognized that individuals and groups within these indigenous societies owned and controlled the use of certain oral traditions, songs, music, artistic designs, and knowledge. They also noted that certain (usually religious) activities were not public but private, the knowledge of them being restricted to certain groups within these societies. Yet they, like White, worked diligently to record them, in writing, in photographs, and on film and tape recordings. Even worse still, other members of the dominant society ignored the intellectual property rights of indigenous peoples, freely using them for commercial purposes in popular literature, movies, television programs, advertising, and countless other ways, while frequently demeaning the members of the society as being childlike, savages, or worse.

Near the time of his death in 1976, Charles Mountford, an Australian anthropologist, published *Nomads of the Australian Desert,* using photographs of and other materials he had collected from the Pitjantjatjara people in the 1930s and early 1940s. The Pitjantjatjara sued, claiming a "breach of confidence" and that the publication had made available to uninitiated men as well as women and children information that harmed the social and religious stability of the Pitjantjatjara. The Australian courts agreed, blocking sales of the book in the Northern Territory where they live. In 1982, Mountford's photographic collection was to be sold at auction. However, the Pitjantjatjara Council again sued in court and was able to remove those photographs that its members considered potentially harmful from the auction.

Intellectual property rights, the rights of privacy, and control of public images have become increasingly contentious issues. The 2007 UN Declaration states that indigenous peoples "have the right to maintain, control, protect and develop their intellectual property over . . . cultural heritage, traditional knowledge, and traditional cultural expressions" as well as "privacy to their religious and cultural sites." However, this is a moral position that lacks the force of law.

Increasingly, indigenous peoples throughout the world are themselves attempting to control cultural access to members of their societies, related archival materials, and the public

continues on next page

dissemination of information relative to their cultural heritage. In 1997, the Working Group of Indigenous Minorities in South Africa (WIMSA) announced that from now on they would require payments from the media and from researchers wishing to document or study San life and that legal action would be taken against companies for the unauthorized use of San photographs in books, postcards, advertisements, and tourist promotions. However, the San were concerned about other intellectual properties as well. Based on traditional San knowledge and use, the South African government agency the Council for Scientific and Industrial Research (CSIR) was able to study and isolate the active chemical properties of the hoodia cactus. CSIR sold their now patented discovery to a pharmaceutical company to be used in diet pills. The San sued in court, and in 2003 the CSIR agreed to share in the royalties.

In 2006, a group of Native and non–Native American academics drafted a set of "Protocols for Native American Archival Materials," which, among other things, calls for the restricting of access to and use of certain culturally "sensitive" materials in library archives.

Many indigenous groups and societies throughout the world have developed their own formal protocols for the researching and recording of members of their society. Probably none are as comprehensive as the one adopted by the Hopi in Arizona, entitled "Protocol for Research, Publication and Recordings: Motion, Visual, Sound, Multimedia and Other Mechanical Devices." The stated reason and purpose of this policy is to protect the Hopi people's rights to privacy and to intellectual property, due to the continued abuse, misrepresentation, and exploitation of the Hopi. All projects or activities involving intellectual property have to be reviewed and approved by the Hopi Cultural Preservation Office. It further defines "projects" or "activity" as, "but not limited to, research, publications recording-motion, visual sound whether oral, written, via multimedia or other mechanical devices discovered or yet to be discovered." Research is defined as including, "but not limited to, ethnology, history, biogenetic, medical, behavioral, ethno-botany, agronomy, ecology, anthropology, archaeology, and microbiology." The Hopi tribe furthermore "reserves the right to: 1) Prevent publication of intellectual resources which is unauthorized, sensitive, misrepresentatives or stereotypical of the Hopi people. . . . 2) May require deposit of raw materials or data, working papers or products in a tribally designated repository, with specific safeguards to preserve confidentiality." Finally, it states that the Hopi tribe will "review and have input into the product or results before publication. The purpose of this step is to assure that sensitive information is not divulged to the public or misrepresentations can be corrected."

The importance of the Hopi statement on protocols is that they are voicing the concerns that indigenous peoples throughout the world have. Survival of a people depends on being able to have some control over their own cultural traditions and the outside world's perceptions of those traditions—an almost impossible task for smaller, relatively powerless peoples alone.

Globalization has changed all peoples in the world, including smaller indigenous societies. All peoples have become increasingly aware of other societies and their cultural differences, particularly over the past 100 years. This has dramatically changed the relationship between cultural researchers and the people they study. Anthropologists have long held that their research should "do no harm" to the people they study, either individually or collectively. It was implicit in the first formal Code of Ethics adopted by the American Anthropological Association (AAA) and explicitly stated in later codes, together with the recognition of their rights to "privacy." In 2009, the AAA code specifically recognized the need to "protect cultural heritage or tangible or intangible cultural or intellectual property." However, the new Code of Ethics, adopted in 2012, dropped the term "intellectual property," using the terms "intangible heritage" and "privacy" and emphasizing "do no harm" and "freely granted consent." The difficulty is that "harm" is a culturally relative term. Mountford did not think that publishing photographs and descriptions of rituals would "harm" the Pitjantjatjara, but they saw that these things could. Only the people themselves can or should judge what is or might be harmful. As to a society's right to privacy, as White discovered, a researcher can always find someone who will "freely grant consent."

In large part, the changes in the AAA's Code of Ethics are a public acknowledgment that a professional organization does not have the authority to control its members' behavior. Indigenous peoples have to protect themselves by developing formal or at least informal protocols for research, such as those of the Hopi tribe. Increasingly, out of necessity, cultural research will focus on the study of issues that both the researcher and the people being studied see as being of mutual value, not just of some abstract "academic" importance. Thus, cultural research during the twenty-first century will be very different from that of the late eighteenth and twentieth centuries, and both cultural anthropology as a discipline and the peoples we study will greatly benefit from the change.

Among the earliest anthropological researchers and writers was Francis LaFlesche (1857–1932), an Omaha Indian from Nebraska.

greatly with the circumstances of the particular situation. Depending on the amount and nature of research funding, an anthropologist may be an important economic resource for the community, paying wages to interpreters and assistants or distributing desirable goods as gifts. Anthropologists who have a car, truck, or other means of transportation frequently find themselves providing needed transportation for members of the community. Ethnographers may also provide comic relief by asking "silly questions," behaving in a funny manner, making childlike errors in speaking the language, and generally being amusing to have around. Researchers may also be a source of information about the outside world, disclosing information to which local people would not otherwise have access. Sometimes community members are as curious about the anthropologist's society as the anthropologist is about theirs. Or the anthropologist may be considered just a harmless nuisance. During the course of research, the typical fieldworker adopts most of these roles, plus many others.

Identifying and Interviewing Consultants

Ethnographers learn a good deal about people simply by living among them and observing and participating in many of their activities. However, observation and participation alone are insufficient. We want to know not only what people are doing but also why they are doing it. Because certain realms of culture are not observable (e.g., religious beliefs, myths, stories, and social values), the researcher has to interview members of the group.

An individual who supplies the ethnographer with information is called a **consultant (informant)**. Field research involves the help of many consultants, who sometimes are paid for their services. Just as no one individual is equally well informed about every aspect of our own cultural system, so no single individual in another society is equally knowledgeable about every aspect of that society's way of life. Women are more knowledgeable than men concerning certain things, and vice versa. Shamans and priests know more about religious rituals than other people. The elderly members of the community are usually most knowledgeable about myths, stories, and histories. Thus, the anthropologist has to attempt to identify and interview those most knowledgeable about the particular subject or subjects being studied. Individuals whom the local community considers to be expert in some particular area are known as **key consultants**, or **key informants**.

A number of factors affect the quality and accuracy of the data collected through interviewing. It is important to always remember that the members of the community are just like any other group of people. Whether they are fully cooperative or not, individuals differ in their abilities to recall specific facts. Still other individuals are actually misinformed, or for various reasons they deliberately misinform the researcher. There is a widespread belief among many younger Native Americans that their "ancestors" frequently and deliberately gave anthropologists misinformation about their culture. Did this happen? It undoubtedly did occur. Also, Native American people in particular love to joke, and a naive researcher would be a likely victim of their humor. The first summer I was working on the Navajo reservation, I was interviewing a talkative local man who suddenly remarked that the valley in back of his house was called "No Fat Valley" after a cow they had butchered there was found to have no fat on it. I had never met the man before and he seemed to have good sense of humor and liked to joke. Although

consultant (informant) Member of a society who provides information to a fieldworker, often through formal interviews or surveys.

key consultant (key informant) Member of a society who is especially knowledgeable about some subject and who supplies information to a fieldworker.

I made a note of his remark, I was thinking that he was joking with a naïve anthropologist and forgot about it. Several years later I was driving by this valley with another local man with whom I had become a close friend. To pass the time, I casually asked if the Navajo had a name for this valley. He told me that in the 1930s he was working on digging the irrigation ditch near the mouth of the valley. There had been a bad drought on the mesa and the workers saw a skinny stray cow coming down the valley. The workers caught it and killed it. When they were butchering it, they were surprised. It was so skinny that it had no fat on it, so they started calling the valley "No Fat." In this case I was initially wrong. However, undoubtedly in others cases many cultural researchers have probably been "victims" of local humor.

Cultural barriers also make it difficult to collect certain types of data. For example, collecting genealogies is not always as easy as it might seem because in many societies, it is customary not to speak the names of the dead. Among the Yanomamö in Venezuela and Brazil, not only is it taboo to speak the names of the dead, but it is also considered discourteous to speak the names of prominent living men, for whom kinship terms are used whenever possible. When ethnographer Napoleon Chagnon persisted in his attempts to collect genealogies, the Yanomamö responded by inventing a series of fictitious genealogical relationships. Only after 5 months of intensive research did Chagnon discover the hoax. When he mentioned some of the names he had collected during a visit to a neighboring village, the people responded with "uncontrollable laughter" because his informants had made up names such as "hairy rectum" and "eagle shit" to avoid speaking the real names. Some of this misinformation has probably worked it is way into the ethnographic literature. However, to avoid these and other difficulties, anthropologists try to interview a number of individuals separately about specific points to gain independent verifications.

Fieldwork as a Rite of Passage

Fieldwork is important to cultural anthropologists not just because it is our primary source of data on human cultures but also because it is a key aspect of the anthropologist's education. It is one thing to read ethnographies about other ways of life, but it is something quite different to live among and interact with individuals from another cultural tradition daily for a year or longer.

As we have seen, anthropologists usually live in the native community, submerging themselves in the social life of the people, living in native dwellings, eating local foods, learning the language, and participating as fully as an outsider is allowed in daily activities. Living as social minorities, usually for the first time in their lives, anthropologists depend on the goodwill of people whose norms and values they neither totally understand nor completely accept. Under these conditions, the researcher has to adjust his or her behavior to fit the norms and behavior patterns of the people under study. This modification of the fieldworker's own behavior is a necessary part of learning about the community. During the course of their research, anthropologists will violate, or at least be perceived as violating, some of the societal norms of behavior. Such incidents may destroy the rapport gained with some key consultants or result in the researcher being ostracized. In serious cases, the fieldworker may become the target of physical violence.

When in the field, except on rare occasions, the anthropologist is the uninvited guest of the community. Regardless of how researchers may rationalize their work as being for the long-term good of the community, science, or humanity in general, they are basically there to serve their own needs and interests. If a serious problem develops between the anthropologist and members of the community, the fieldworker must bear the primary responsibility and blame.

The fieldwork experience tests and taxes the attitude of cultural relativity (as discussed in Chapter 1) that anthropologists teach in their classrooms. It is easy to discuss the concept of cultural relativity in a university setting, but it is more difficult to apply this concept when actually living with another group of people. Regardless of which society it is, certain cultural aspects will offend one's own cultural norms and values. For example, according to the anthropologist's own social norms, some local people might "abuse" certain family members or certain powerful leaders might "exploit" lower-ranking members of the society. As the fieldworker develops friendships, this "abuse" or "exploitation" frequently becomes personalized. Under what circumstances, if ever, an anthropologist should attempt to intervene and try to impose her or his cultural standards on the members of another society poses a real and personal dilemma. In theory, such intervention is never permissible, but in real-life situations, the answer is not always so clear.

Many people experience a kind of psychological trauma when surrounded by people speaking a language they cannot fully understand and can speak only imperfectly, eating foods that are strange, seeing architecture that is alien, and observing people using gestures and behaving in ways they either do not comprehend or do not approve of. The strange sounds, smells, tastes, sights, and behaviors result in disorientation. Out of their normal cultural context, fieldworkers do not understand what is happening around them, yet realize that their own actions are often misunderstood. The symptoms of **culture shock** are psychological and sometimes even physiological: paranoia, anxiety, longing for the folks back home, nausea, hypochondria, and, frequently, diarrhea.

The attempts by ethnographers to maintain their relativistic perspective and objectivity in their daily interaction with members of the other society usually compound the normal trauma of culture shock. Socially isolated and unable to release their frustrations and anxieties through conversations with sympathetic others, they often have to cope with their psychological difficulties alone.

For many anthropologists, much of their time in the field is extremely traumatic, and as a result, most anthropologists view fieldwork as a rite of passage. More than any other aspect of their training, fieldwork transforms students of anthropology into professional anthropologists. Although many overemphasize the importance of fieldwork, it is undeniably a significant educational experience. Most individuals return from their fieldwork with a different perspective on themselves and their own culture. Fieldwork often teaches us as much about ourselves and our own culture as about the culture of the peoples we are studying.

Ethnohistory

The study of past cultural systems through the use of written records is called **ethnohistory**. Since the late nineteenth century, anthropologists have used historic written materials in their studies, but the importance of this research has been widely recognized only since the 1970s. The growing interest in ethnohistory had come with the realization that non-Western societies have changed far more dramatically over the past few hundred years than had previously been thought.

Like historians who study their society's past, ethnohistorians make use of such materials as published books and articles, newspapers, archival documents, diaries, journals, maps, drawings, and photographs. Not surprisingly, many scholars treat history and ethnohistory as if they were synonymous. There are, however, critical—yet frequently overlooked—differences between ethnohistory and history.

▮ An ethnohistorian is primarily interested in reconstructing the cultural system of the people. The actual historical events themselves are of interest only because they cast light on the cultural system or changes in the system.

▮ Historical events have little significance outside the cultural context of the peoples involved. Ethnohistorians study nonliterate peoples. Thus, whereas historians can use accounts recorded by members of the society being studied, ethnohistorians have to use accounts recorded by members of other literate societies. As a result, the problem of interpreting accounts is far more difficult for the ethnohistorian than for the historian.

The problem of interpretation raises an additional question about the validity of particular reports. Not only do we have to ask about the accuracy of the account, but we also have to ask how knowledgeable the recorder was about the cultural context of the events. Ethnohistorians use certain criteria to evaluate the potential validity of an account. How long did the writer live among these people? Did the observer speak the language? What was the observer's role? Soldiers, missionaries, traders, and government officials have different views, biases, and access to information.

The difficulty with ethnohistory is that no hard-and-fast rules can be used in evaluating these data. The longer an individual lived among members of a particular society and the better the person spoke the language, the more reliable the account should be; however, this cannot be automatically assumed. In some cases, the writer may have had little interest in the people, perhaps because the contacts were only job related. This attitude is evident in the accounts of many traders and government officials. In other cases, the account may be self-serving, with individuals attempting to enhance their careers. Thus, sometimes soldiers and government officials falsified their official reports.

Ethnocentrism is still another factor. Missionary accounts, in particular, often demonstrate overt bias against local customs and beliefs; one has to remember that individuals become missionaries because they are avid believers. Nevertheless, some of the most objective accounts of other societies were written by missionaries who were scholars themselves.

Thus, in ethnohistoric research, there is no simple way to evaluate a particular document or account. At best, a single event may be recorded in several independent accounts that can each be used to

---

culture shock Feeling of uncertainty and anxiety an individual experiences when placed in a strange cultural setting.

ethnohistory See ethnohistoric research.

verify the accuracy and interpretation of the others. Unfortunately, multiple observations are the exception, not the rule.

A good example of the problem of the cultural interpretations of historic events is the case of Captain James Cook. In January 1778, Cook discovered the Hawaii Islands. He stayed for only 3 days before sailing for the North Pacific. The next winter he returned and sailed among the islands for 7 weeks before landing on the large island in January 19, 1779. This second landing was greeted by thousands of Hawaiians, including King Kalani'opu'u. Cook was presented with a feathered cloak and cap while thousands of people prostrated themselves chanting the name "Lono," a Polynesian god. On February 4, he left with a great celebration by the people. However, problems with one of his ships forced him to return. On this third landfall he was killed on the beach. Why?

For a long time scholars have argued that Cook was identified as the god Lono. Studying the written accounts of English seamen who accompanied Cook and ethnographic descriptions of Hawaiian religious beliefs and practices, Marshall Sahlins reexamined the case. Lono was a mythical god-king who periodically returned to the islands and ruled in human form, usurping the power of earthly kings who were representatives of the rival god Ku. Every year a series of rituals were performed dedicated to Lono's symbolic returns. Cook movements and his first two landings in 1778 and 1779 corresponded with the timing of these rituals. However, his third landing did not. It was interpreted as Lono's return to take the power of the earthly kings and the priests of the god Ku. Thus, the priest of Ku killed Cook, viewing his killing as sacrifice of the rival god-king Lono, a ritual that they reenacted every year. Is Sahlins correct in his interpretation?

Gananath Obeyesekere, a Sri Lankan anthropologist, challenged Sahlins's analysis. He could not think of a single example of Sri Lankans or any other South Asian people seeing the newly arrived Europeans as gods. To him this was an example of European myth building in which the European explorer/civilizer becomes a "god" to the natives and of the implicit assumption among Western academics (meaning Sahlins) that non-Western peoples are prelogical or mystical. However, neither Sahlins, Obeyesekere, nor the early English who accompanied Cook were Hawaiians. Ethnocentric bias is a problem not just with interpreting ethnohistoric accounts but in the academic interpretations of these accounts as well.

A final limitation on the use of ethnohistoric materials is that seldom are all aspects of a particular society evenly reported. For example, data on economic activities may be the most abundant, whereas information on religious ceremonies and beliefs may be absent or limited. As a result, ethnographic studies based on ethnohistoric research alone usually lack the depth and balance of studies gained from field research. Despite its problems and limitations, ethnohistoric research provides us with the only clues we have to the past culture of many societies, as well as the key to a vast store of cultural data hitherto untapped.

Comparative Methods

So far, we have discussed only how anthropologists collect cultural data on peoples, past and present, using fieldwork and historical materials. We have some cultural data available on more than 1,200 societies. As shown in the following chapters, anthropologists have used these data to demonstrate a wide range of cultural variability among human populations. However, we are not interested in merely describing particular cultural systems and the range of variability they display. We are also interested in attempting to explain why these differences exist. In other words, anthropologists want to make generalizations concerning cultural systems. Generalizations cannot be made based on the study of a single society; we need methods by which many societies can be compared in a systematic way. The objective of comparative studies is to test hypotheses.

Comparative research dates back to the earliest day of anthropology. The research of the unilineal evolutionists of the late of the nineteenth century, Tylor and Morgan (discussed in Chapter 5), was based on comparative studies. However, there were some serious methodological problems in this early comparative research that resulted in the abandonment of this approach. In 1937, a group of social scientists at Yale University led by George Peter Murdock produced the Outline of Cultural Materials, the first universal systematic scheme to topically classify cultural variables. This led to the establishment of the Human Relations Area Files (HRAF) in 1949. HRAF created the "Collection of Ethnography," mainly published books and articles on about 400 different societies in the world, which are indexed for 710 subject categories. This setup allows for quick retrieval of relevant cultural material on specific topics. Later, between 1962 and 1967, Murdock complied his *Ethnographic Atlas*, in which he coded cultural variables on 100 topics for 1,167 different societies, allowing researchers to analyze the correlations between a limited range of cultural variables without consulting the ethnographic literature. HRAF and the *Ethnographic Atlas* revolutionized comparative studies (see www.yale.edu/hraf).

Cross-Cultural Comparisons

By far, the most frequently used comparative method is **cross-cultural comparisons**. In this method, hypotheses are tested by examining the statistical correlations between particular cultural variables, using synchronic data drawn from a number of societies. Historical changes in the societies examined are ignored; the societies are compared at whatever period they were studied or on which relevant cultural data exist. The HRAF, for example, allows one to compare variables not just between twentieth-century peoples throughout the world, but with imperial Romans, sixteenth-century Aztecs, and many other earlier societies as well.

This research method involves three steps. First, the researcher must state the idea as a hypothesis—that is, state it in such a way that it can be supported or not supported ("tested") by data drawn from a large number of human populations. Second, the ethnologist chooses a sample of societies (usually randomly) and studies the ethnographies that describe their way of life. Third, the data collected from these ethnographies are classified and grouped in such a manner that the correlations between variables may be shown statistically. What the researcher is attempting to find is the pattern of association: do two or more cultural variables consistently occur together or not? In most cases, these tasks are far more difficult than they may sound.

To illustrate how the cross-cultural method is used to test a hypothesis, we shall examine the relationship between sorcery and legal systems within a group of societies. Sorcery is discussed in some detail in Chapter 13. Here, it is sufficient to know that sorcery is the belief that certain people (sorcerers) have power, either supernatural or magical, to cause harm to others. Some anthropologists believe that sorcery serves as a means of social control in societies that lack a formalized legal apparatus—courts, police, and so forth—to punish wrongdoers. They argue that people will be reluctant to cause trouble if they believe that a victim of their troublemaking has the ability to use supernatural power to retaliate against them. Overall, societies without a formal legal system should have a greater need for a mechanism such as sorcery to control behavior. So, if the hypothesis that sorcery is a mechanism for social control is correct, we ought to find that sorcery is more important in societies that have no formal means of punishment than in societies with a specialized legal system.

To see whether this hypothesis is true across a variety of societies, we use the cross-cultural method. We determine for many societies (1) the relative degree of importance of sorcery and (2) whether the society has a formal apparatus for punishing wrongdoing. We make a table in which all the possible combinations of the two cultural elements are recorded:

Sorcery	Specialized Legal Apparatus Absent	Specialized Legal Apparatus Present
Important	A	B
Unimportant	C	D

In the cells of the table, we record the number of societies in which the four possible combinations are found. If the hypothesis is supported, we should find that cells A and D contain the greatest number of societies. If the hypothesis is not supported, we should find that the distribution of societies in the cells is random, or that cells B and C contain the greatest number of societies, or some other distribution.

In 1950, Beatrice Whiting conducted such a study by surveying the ethnographic literature for 50 societies. Her results were as follows (Whiting 1950, 87):

Sorcery	Specialized Legal Apparatus Absent	Specialized Legal Apparatus Present
Important	30	5
Unimportant	3	12

On the basis of this comparison, we might conclude that the hypothesis is supported because most of the societies fall into the cells predicted by our hypothesis. We would not worry about the eight societies (the "exceptions") that appear in cells B and C. The hypothesis did not claim that social control was the *only* function of sorcery, so the importance of sorcery in the five societies in cell B might be explained by some other factor. Nor did we claim that sorcery was the *only* way that societies lacking a specialized legal apparatus had to control their members, so the three societies in cell C might have developed some alternative means of social control. (Although outside the scope of this text, statistical tests are available that show how confident a researcher can be that such associations did not occur by chance.)

Some confusion is caused by cross-cultural tabulations such as this. One of the most common is to mistake correlation for causation: simply because two

cross-cultural comparisons A methodology for testing a hypothesis using a sample of societies drawn from around the world.

cultural elements (X and Y) are usually found together does not mean that one (X) has caused the other (Y). Y could have caused X, or both X and Y could have been caused by some third element, W. In the preceding example, it was assumed that the absence of formal legal punishments "caused" many societies to need some other social control mechanism, and that sorcery became important to meet this need. On the basis of the data in the table, we might also conclude that societies in which sorcery is important have little need for a formal legal apparatus, so they fail to develop one.

This approach suffers from several disadvantages, the most important of which is the problem of bias by the researcher, who must decide, for example, whether sorcery should be considered "important" or "unimportant" among some people. Borderline cases might get lumped into the category that supports the researcher's hypothesis.

Using cross-cultural methods to see whether some specific hypothesis applies to a large number of societies is thus easier today than ever before, but some difficulties still exist. One seems to be inherent in the method itself, which dissects whole cultures into parts ("variables," as we called them) and assigns a value (or "state") to each part. In the preceding example, the variables were sorcery, which had two states (important, unimportant) and specialized legal apparatus, which also had two states (present, absent). To test the hypothesis that the states of these two cultural elements are consistently related, we ignored everything else about them. We also ignored everything else about the societies in the sample, such as their family systems and their economies.

A more familiar example makes the point clearly. One element of cultural systems is the number of gods in whom people believe. For purposes of some specific hypothesis, the possible states of this variable might be monotheism (belief in one god), polytheism (belief in many gods), and no gods. Any researcher who included modern North America in the sample would probably consider our primary religion—Christianity—as monotheistic. Most of the Middle East also would be considered monotheistic. The problem is, Can North American monotheism be considered equivalent to Middle Eastern monotheisms? If we consider them the same, we ignore the differences between the worship of the Christian God, the Jewish Yahweh, and the Islamic Allah. When we lump these three varieties of monotheism together into a single kind of religion, we distort them to some degree.

Cross-cultural studies examine data ahistorically, or without reference to time. In other words, the cultural system of a particular society is treated as timeless or unchanging. Thus, in cross-cultural studies and the *Ethnographic Atlas,* there is "a" cultural system coded for the Cheyenne: Cheyenne cultural system circa 1850. However, the culture of a society is constantly changing. For example, today the Cheyenne live in houses, drive cars and tracks, and participate in a wage-money economy. In 1850, the Cheyenne lived in hide-covered tepees, rode horses, and hunted buffalo. In 1650, the Cheyenne lived in permanent earth lodge villages, traveled by foot or canoe, and depended on farming and hunting for their subsistence. Although Cheyenne cultural systems have continuity, all aspects of their culture have changed, to some degree, over the period just described. Thus, in reality, there is no "Cheyenne culture" but an ever-changing system. The ahistorical studies used in cross-cultural research create an artificially static picture of the cultural system of a society.

Controlled Comparisons

In contrast to cross-cultural comparisons, controlled comparisons make use of diachronic data, comparisons of known changes in certain cultural variables, while controlling for historical and environmental factors. This allows the researcher to define general cultural patterns and test hypotheses. Although a number of early researchers produced such studies, it was not until 1954 that Fred Eggan formally defined controlled comparisons as a distinct research method. Since then, as ethnohistoric research became an important ethnographic research tool, these studies have become far more common. Controlled comparisons, like cross-cultural studies, can be extremely complex. We illustrate this method with a simple example.

As we discuss in Chapter 9, people organize their family lives in various ways. Two common ways are matrilineal descent and patrilineal descent. In matrilineal societies, family group membership is inherited through your mother; you belong to your mother's family. In patrilineal societies, group membership is inherited through your father; you belong to your father's family. Anthropologists have long attempted to explain why some societies are matrilineal and others patrilineal. Cross-cultural research has shown that a relationship exists between matrilineality and patrilineality and the relative economic importance of males and females in the society. However, cross-cultural studies can show us only correlations between descent and other synchronic aspects of the cultural system. For example, these studies can tell us what types of economic systems are most frequently found with matrilineal or patrilineal societies. Cross-cultural studies cannot measure the long-term effects of external changes on matrilineal or patrilineal societies. Is matrilineality or patrilineality

Christianity, Judaism, and Islam are all monotheistic and have common historical roots. But Christians and Jews do not pray by prostrating themselves toward Mecca, as these Muslims are doing. Should cross-cultural researchers consider all of them one kind of religion, or not?

more adaptive in some situations than in others? If so, what types of situations favor matrilineal societies, and which favor patrilineal societies? To examine this question, we must turn to controlled historical comparisons.

Michael Allen (1984) has asserted that matrilineal societies in the Pacific were more successful than patrilineal societies in adapting to European contact. Is there a way to test Allen's assertion? First, we must restructure this statement as a testable hypothesis. What do we mean by success? The term *success* is subjective and cannot be directly measured. We have to convert this term into some measurable quantity. One quantifiable measure of the success of a particular system is the relative ability of a society to maintain or expand its population over time. Thus, our hypothesis would be "Given the same disruptive external pressures, matrilineal societies maintain their population levels better over time than patrilineal societies." Now we need to find groups of matrilineal societies and patrilineal societies that experienced a comparable intensity of external contact over a period of time and compare their relative populations at the beginning and end of the period. If Allen is correct, the matrilineal societies should have a larger population at the end of the period than the patrilineal societies.

The farming Native American tribes of the eastern United States present an almost ideal case for testing Allen's assertion. They had similar cultural systems, except that some were matrilineal and others were patrilineal. Their collective histories of contact with Europeans were also basically the same. During the historical period, all these societies suffered the effects of epidemic diseases, warfare (with Europeans as well as each other), severe territorial dislocation, political domination by Europeans, and social discrimination.

Now the problem is determining an appropriate time frame to examine and finding comparable population data. One problem with ethnohistoric research is that the researcher is forced to use the data available in the records. It is not until about 1775 that sufficient population data are available in missionary, military, and explorer accounts to estimate the populations of all these tribes with any accuracy. In 1910, the U.S. Bureau of the Census conducted a special Native American census, which was the first truly comprehensive census of Native American societies in the United States. Thus, the time frame we will use is from 1775 to 1910. Using ethnographic data, we can then classify particular societies as either matrilineal or patrilineal and determine their populations at the beginning and end of this period:

	1775	1910	Percent
Matrilineal societies	88,590	82,714	93
Patrilineal societies	36,400	13,463	37
Totals	124,990	96,177	77

CHAPTER 6 Methods of Investigation   129

CONCEPT REVIEW: Methods of Investigation

Ethnographic methods	The collection of cultural data on a particular society or group of societies. The primary purpose is the collection of descriptive data.
Ethnographic fieldwork	The collection of cultural data from living individuals. This usually requires that the researcher live with or close to the people being studied.
Ethnohistoric research	The study of the past cultural system of a people through the use of written records.
Comparative methods	The comparative study of the cultural systems of a number of different societies. The objective is to test hypotheses so that we can explain why differences exist.
Cross-cultural comparisons	The testing of hypotheses by using synchronic data drawn from a number of different societies.
Controlled comparisons	The comparative use of historically documented changes in particular groupings of societies over time to define general cultural patterning and to test hypotheses.

From this table, we can see that during this 135-year period, the matrilineal societies declined by only about 7 percent of their total population, whereas patrilineal societies lost 63 percent of their population. If maintenance of population is a measure of a society's success, then matrilineal societies in the eastern United States were more successful than patrilineal societies.

As is the case with all comparative studies, findings such as these raise more questions than they answer. Are these population figures and the historical experiences of these societies truly comparable? If they are comparable, is the significant factor differences in descent form, or is it some other cultural factor we have not considered? We need to add at this point that not all matrilineal societies in this study were equally successful in maintaining their population levels, and that a few patrilineal societies studied increased in population during this period. There is room, then, for argument. If, in the final analysis, however, we decide that our findings are valid and that matrilineal societies are, under certain conditions, more adaptive than patrilineal societies, we still cannot directly say why.

Cross-cultural comparisons and controlled comparisons give us distinctly different measures of cultural phenomena. They address different questions and test different hypotheses. They are complementary, not competitive, methodologies.

Some anthropologists believe that both types of comparative studies distort each cultural system in the sample so much that the whole method is invalid. They think that ripping each element out of the particular context in which it is embedded robs it of its significance because each element acquires its meaning only in its unique historical and cultural context.

Despite these and other problems, comparative methods are the only practical means available for determining whether a hypothesis is valid among human cultural systems. Those who use these methods are aware of the difficulties, yet they believe that the advantage of being able to process information on large numbers of societies outweighs the problems.

SUMMARY

1. **Discuss the major objectives of cultural research.** Cultural research has two objectives. One objective is to record as complete a description of the culture of a particular society as possible. These descriptive studies are termed *ethnographies*. As you will discover in the following chapters, there is tremendous cultural diversity among the world peoples. Why? The

other objective, therefore, is to attempt to explain this diversity in cultural behavior. These studies are called *ethnologies*. Not surprisingly, the research methods used differ greatly.

2. **Understand that ethnographic research requires different methods of study.** Remembering that the culture of a society changes over time, there are two sources of cultural data: the living members of the group and historical materials, such as earlier published accounts, manuscripts, drawings, maps, photographs, and the like describing or relating to their past culture. The ethnographic method used by researchers depends on whether they are studying the contemporary culture or the past culture of the society. Studies of the past culture of a society can be either *synchronic*, a description of their culture at a particular time in their past, such as during the 1700s or in the 1870s; or *diachronic*, a description of the changes in their culture over time, such as from 1700 to 1890. These two different approaches to the study of a particular culture involve the use of very different methods and very different research problems.

3. **Describe the methods used to study the culture of a contemporary or living society.** Fieldwork—or, more correctly, ethnographic field research—is the primary method of collecting data concerning the culture of a living people. Fieldworkers usually live among those they study for at least a year, conducting formal interviews and surveys and engaging in participant observation. The difficulties of conducting fieldwork vary with the personality and gender of the fieldworker and with the people and specific topic being studied. All fieldworkers must address four problems. First, not only must fieldworkers fight against their own ethnocentrism and tendencies to stereotype the people they study, but they must also overcome the stereotypes local people have developed about outsiders. Second, it is often difficult to establish a rapport with local people because they may have had no previous experience with the kinds of questions fieldworkers ask. Third, identifying reliable consultants/informants and finding people willing to participate in intensive study may pose a serious problem. Fourth, sometimes people deliberately deceive anthropologists because they mistrust their motives, do not want certain facts to become public, or are culturally forbidden to give away secrets of their religion. Thus, researchers have to attempt to interview several members of the society to gain independent verification of the interpretation or description of a particular event or behavior.

4. **Describe the method used to study the past culture of a society.** Research into the past way of life of a people involves the analysis of written accounts, published and unpublished, and any other materials that shed light on their past culture. This research is called *ethnohistoric research*. This method requires considerable interpretation by the researcher. In almost all cases, the materials used in ethnohistoric research were recorded by individuals who, because they belonged to different societies and came from different cultural backgrounds and traditions, had at best an imperfect understanding of the cultural traditions they were describing. How well did they understand what they were describing? Do they know the language, or did they depend on interpreters? How long did they live there, and in what capacity? In addition, the contents of these accounts are to some degree affected by the ethnocentrism as well as by the personal interests of their authors. Just as in the case of ethnographic fieldwork, the research has to attempt to find two or more sources to independently verify a particular cultural interpretation or description of an event.

5. **Understand the purpose of comparative research.** The purpose of comparative research is to test hypotheses in order to attempt to explain cultural diversity. Comparative methods involve ways of systematically and reliably comparing massive amounts of ethnographic information. The use of comparative methods presents many difficulties, including stating the research hypothesis in such a way that is testable, reliably defining and measuring the variables of interest for many societies, deciding whether similar cultural elements from two or more societies are the "same" or "different," and contending with unintentional researcher bias. The results of

comparative studies can be difficult to interpret. Correlation is often confused with causation.

6. **Explain cross-cultural comparisons.** Cross-cultural comparisons involve the systematic comparisons of synchronic cultural data to determine correlations between particular cultural variables. By "synchronic," we do not mean that the cultures of all of the peoples compared were contemporaneous, but only that these descriptions were for a single period of time in the history of a particular people. What the researcher is attempting to do is discover correlations between different aspects of cultural behavior. The only important factor is that they occurred within the same society at the same time.

7. **Describe controlled comparative studies.** Controlled comparisons involve the systematic comparisons of documented changes in a limited number of cultural variables and societies over time. In addition to the problems noted with comparative studies in general, the ethnographic literature needed for these studies is extremely limited.

7 Culture and Nature: Interacting with the Environment

Meogia/Shutterstock.com.

Scientifically-oriented anthropologists believe that the way people harness nature's resources for food, drink, shelter, fuel, and other uses are the most important influences on their way of life. These wet rice terraces in Vietnam illustrate one form of intensive agriculture, which led to dramatic changes in human existence.

Understanding Interactions with Nature

Hunting and Gathering
 Foraging and Culture
 What Happened to Hunters and Gatherers?

Domestication of Plants and Animals
 Origins of Domestication: Wheres and Whens
 Advantages and Costs of Cultivation

Horticulture
 Varieties of Horticulture
 Cultural Consequences of Horticulture

Intensive Agriculture
 Varieties of Intensive Agriculture
 Cultural Consequences of Intensive Agriculture

Pastoralism

Nature and Culture in Preindustrial Times

Industrialism
 Energy and Society
 Consequences of Industrialism

Globalization and the Environment

LEARNING OBJECTIVES

After reading this chapter, you should be able to

1. **DISCUSS** how relationships between humans and the environment differ from those of other animals.
2. **DESCRIBE** hunting and gathering and analyze its major impacts on cultures.
3. **DESCRIBE** horticulture and analyze its major consequences for cultures.
4. **DISCUSS** how intensive agriculture led to the emergence of civilization.
5. **DISCUSS** nomadic pastoralism and its benefits in certain environments.
6. **ANALYZE** industrialization and how it affects human lives, globalization, and worldwide environmental problems.

In this chapter, we describe the major ways human groups interact with the natural environment. Anthropologists who follow the materialist orientation (Chapter 5) believe that how people interact with their environment is a primary cause of cultural differences and similarities. Materialists also argue that changes in human–environment relationships are the prime mover of long-term cultural changes. Following the materialist orientation in this chapter, in addition to describing interactions between humans and nature, we also cover their main cultural consequences and show how changing interactions between humans and nature affected long-term changes in human cultures. Later chapters deal with other dimensions of cultural diversity: forms of exchange, marriage and family life, kinship systems, gender relationships, political organization, religion and worldview, and artistic expression.

Understanding Interactions with Nature

In the biological sciences, *adaptation* refers to how organisms survive and reproduce in their environments. Humans also adapt to their natural surroundings. However, to emphasize that human groups—to greater or lesser degrees—alter their environments in the process of living in them, for humans the term *interaction* is more accurate than *adaptation*. Of course, other animals also alter their environments, as when beavers construct dams, birds build nests, prairie dogs dig burrows, and earthworms aerate and create new soil with their "casings." However, humans sometimes extensively modify nature as they interact with it, as when farmers clear land for crops, families cut forests for houses and fires, and civilizations build cities. Both prehistorically and historically, humans altered nature in the process of adjusting to it. *Interaction* both emphasizes these alterations and calls attention to how humans and nature mutually affect one another.

As with other species, the environment affects humans physiologically and genetically. For example, bacteria, viruses, and parasites kill or sicken susceptible individuals, but those who are genetically resistant survive, reproduce, and pass more of their genes along to the next generation. By means of natural selection, over many generations human populations become more resistant to the life-threatening microorganisms to which they are exposed—even as the microorganisms evolve better means of attacking us. Natural selection acting on our genes helps us to adjust to the environments in which we live.

However, the most important way humanity differs from other species is that we adjust and adapt to changes in our environments *mainly*—not exclusively—by cultural rather than biological/genetic means. If the climate grows colder or if a group migrates to a colder area, humans cope mainly by lighting fires, constructing shelters, and making warm clothing, not mainly by evolving physiological adaptations to cold. Humans hunt animals by making weapons and mastering techniques of cooperative stalking and killing, not by biologically evolving the ability to run faster than game. Group cooperation and technology (including both the tools themselves and the knowledge required to make and use them) allow humans to adapt to a wide range of environments without undergoing major alterations in their genetic makeup.

The transmission of socially learned knowledge and behavior (that is, culture) enabled humanity to colonize all of Earth's terrestrial habitats, from tropical rain forests to Arctic tundra, from the vast grassy plains of central Asia to tiny Pacific atolls. Our ability to live in diverse habitats by means of technology and group living is mainly responsible for the secrets of the success of the human species—in 2013, over 7 billion humans live on Earth, and our numbers continue to grow.

Of the many dimensions to human–environment relationships, two are most important for our purposes. First, the natural environment in which a people live provides *resources* that they extract in meeting their material needs and wants. From their natural surroundings, people harness energy to nourish their bodies (food), to keep themselves warm and cook their foods (fuel), and to put to other uses. People mine raw materials like stone and metals to make tools and cut trees to provide shelter. Harnessing energy and harvesting materials takes technology (tools and skills) and requires that people expend their own time and energy (in labor, or work). As they use their technology and expend their labor, people transform resources into *products* that help meet their needs and wants.

Second, the environment poses certain *problems* that people strive to solve or overcome: resource scarcity, excessively high or low temperatures, parasites and diseases, rainfall variability, deficient soils, and so forth. Solving these and other problems of living in a particular time and place sometimes leads a group to modify their surroundings. For example, hunters can set fire to woodlands or grasslands to attract more game animals to their territories. Farmers can produce more food by clearing new lands, fertilizing soils, or irrigating their crops. Industrialized nations construct highways, shopping malls, factories, and housing developments.

There are other dimensions to human–nature interactions. Humans are social animals (see Chapter 2) who live in groups of various sizes and compositions. Groups have to organize their members to acquire resources and solve problems efficiently. First, individuals have to know what to do and what they can expect others to do. So groups allocate different tasks to different people, resulting in the *division of labor*. Second, many tasks are more efficient if people work together for common goals. For example, several hunters will have a better chance of spotting, tracking, and killing large game than a single hunter. Net fishing may be more productive if people work together. Because cooperation is often more efficient (and enjoyable) than working alone, human groups develop *patterns of cooperation*. Third, it is helpful if people know when and where to apply technology and labor so they do not come into conflict with others or get in one another's way. Groups therefore develop patterned *ways of allocating resources* among individuals, families, and other kinds of social units.

Materialists give priority to human–environment interactions in their efforts to explain cultural differences and to account for long-term cultural changes in our species. In this chapter, we explore this idea by describing and comparing some of the major ways various peoples interact with their environments. Humanistic anthropologists tend to disagree that material factors have "priority," for reasons described in Chapter 5. Even if materialists are correct, always keep in mind that the ways a people interact with nature has greater effects on some aspects of their way of life than on other aspects.

At the broadest level, anthropologists categorize human–environment relationships into four major categories, based largely on how people acquire products—especially food—to meet their material needs and wants:

1. **Hunting and gathering** (also called **foraging**), in which people exploit the *wild* plants and animals of their territory for food
2. **Agriculture** (or **cultivation**), in which people intentionally plant, care for, and harvest *crops* (domesticated plants) for food and other uses
3. **Herding** (or **pastoralism**), in which people tend, breed, and harvest products of *livestock* (domesticated animals) for food, trade, and other uses
4. **Industrialism**, in which people discovered ways of harnessing the energy in *fossil fuels* (coal, oil, natural gas), resulting in a dramatic increase in levels of material consumption and profits for private industries.

---

hunting and gathering (foraging) Harvest of wild (undomesticated) plants and animals.

agriculture (cultivation) Purposeful planting, cultivation, care, and harvest of domesticated food plants (crops).

herding (pastoralism) Tending, breeding, and harvesting the products of livestock, which are taken to seasonally available pasturelands and water.

industrialism Development of technology to harness the energy of fossil fuels to increase productivity, profits, and the availability of consumer commodities.

Figure 7.1 Principal Regions of Foragers at the Time of First Contact with Europeans.

The first three categories are *preindustrial*, applying to how all of humanity acquired food before the Industrial Revolution of the late 1700s. Even after the origins and spread of industrialism, many of the world's people remained preindustrial, which does not mean that they remained unaffected by what happened in Europe. "Preindustrial" thus refers to a *condition* more than to a specific time.

Anthropologists use these four categories to distinguish major differences. Like other categories, these do not faithfully depict the complex realities of human–environment interactions. It is *very* important to recognize that the categories are not mutually exclusive. For example, before contact with Europeans, many Native Americans cultivated crops like corn and squash, but they relied on wild game for most of their meat supply because most people kept no livestock. Many African people today farm some of their lands, but they also raise cattle and other livestock on lands less suitable for agriculture. Since agriculture began several thousand years ago, most peoples have adopted a combination of production strategies, depending on their technologies, local environments, and what their neighbors are doing. Finally, although we speak of today's *industrialized nations*, hunting, fishing, agriculture, and livestock husbandry are carried out by various occupations. However, people pursue these occupations for wages and profits rather than for their own subsistence.

Hunting and Gathering

Hunter-gatherers—also called *foragers*—acquire food from collecting (gathering) the wild plants and hunting (and/or fishing for) the animals that live in their regions. On current evidence, *Homo sapiens* has existed as a separate species for less than 100,000 years. But none of Earth's peoples farmed crops or herded livestock until about 10,000 years ago, and most people continued to live off wild plants and animals until a few thousand years ago. Hunting and gathering thus supported humanity for the first 80 to 90 percent of our existence as a unique species. Figure 7.1 shows roughly where hunters and gatherers lived at the time of their first contact with Europeans. After Western exploration and colonialism brought so many indigenous people into larger systems, many hunters and gatherers survived in a few places even into the twentieth century.

Although foragers do not attempt to grow crops or keep livestock for meat and other products, many attempt to increase the supply of food in other ways. For example, some Native Americans periodically burned forests and grasslands to attract game or increase the supply of sun-loving wild berries or other plants. However, compared to farmers and herders, hunters and gatherers do not modify their natural environments very much but instead take what nature offers. If edible wild plants are available only in particular places during particular seasons, foragers move to those places at those times to harvest them. If major game animals live in large migratory herds, hunters must follow them or else hunt other animals when the game herds have left their region. A brief principle helps understand the foraging way of life: to acquire resources efficiently, foragers must organize themselves to be in the right place at the right time with the right numbers of people.

Foraging and Culture

Anthropologists classify hunting and gathering as a single "type" of adaptation, and in the minds of many people, all foragers seem pretty much alike. (This is why you may have heard "When humans were hunters and gatherers on the African savannah….") But foragers living in different habitats differ, partly because environments vary in the kinds and quality of food resources they contain. For example, fishing peoples of the resource-rich environment of the American Northwest Coast lived a fairly sedentary existence in large permanent settlements, whereas the Shoshone of the arid and resource-sparse American Great Basin roamed in small bands or individual families. In spite of such differences, most—but not all—foraging peoples share certain cultural similarities. Our main goal in this section is to describe how the ways hunters and gatherers interact with their environments affect their cultures.

Division of Labor by Age and Sex

Among foraging peoples, sex and age are the major basis for the division of labor. Of course, in any group, special knowledge and skill also are a basis for assigning tasks. In the vast majority of foraging peoples, men do almost all hunting and women most of the gathering of plants. However, it is not unusual for either sex to lend a hand with the activities of the other. For example, among the BaMbuti of the tropical forest of central Africa, the women and children help the men with hunting by driving game animals into nets. However, in general, hunting is men's work.

Seasonal Mobility

Most foragers move across the landscape to cope with seasonal changes. None of Earth's environments offers the same kinds and quantities of resources year-round. Most places experience seasonal differences in precipitation. Outside the tropics, marked seasonal variations in temperature occur as well. Ordinarily, game animals are available in some places and not others at different seasons, and nuts and fruits tend to be available at only certain times of the year.

Foragers migrate to where food or water is most plentiful or easiest to acquire during a given season. For example, the Hadzabe people of Tanzania lived in an arid region with distinct wet and dry seasons. In the rainy months, the Hadzabe dispersed around the many temporary water holes that formed, living on the wild plants and animals in the immediate vicinity. At another time of the year, when these ponds evaporated, they lived in large camps clustered around the few relatively permanent water sources.

Seasonal Congregation and Dispersal

To gather plants and hunt animals efficiently, foragers adjust the sizes of their living groups to adapt to the seasonal availability and abundance of their food

Gathering plant foods is mainly women's work among foraging peoples. This Ju/'hoansi woman is bagging mongongo nuts, a nourishing staple.

CHAPTER 7 Culture and Nature: Interacting with the Environment 137

supply. At some times of the year, it is most efficient to disperse into small groups, which cooperate in the search for food. During other seasons, these groups come together in larger congregations.

The Western Shoshone live in the arid Great Basin of what is now Nevada and Utah. Until white settlers disrupted their indigenous way of life in the mid–nineteenth century, the Shoshone lived off wild plants and animals. Most of their meat came from deer, antelope, and small mammals such as rabbits and squirrels. Plant foods included roots and seasonally available seeds, berries, pine nuts, and other wild products.

For most of the year, the Shoshone roamed the dry valleys and slopes of the Great Basin in tiny bands consisting of a few families or even single families. Families occasionally gathered for cooperative hunting of antelopes and rabbits, which they drove into corrals and nets. But a more permanent aggregation of families was difficult because a local area did not have enough resources to support large numbers of people for more than a few days.

Around October, the cones of the piñon trees on the high mountains ripened and produced large, nourishing pine nuts. During their travels in late summer, Shoshone families noticed which specific mountain areas had the most promising pine nut harvest. They arranged their movements to arrive at these productive areas in the early fall. Ten to 20 families arrived in the same region, harvesting and storing pine nuts, which sometimes lasted throughout most of the winter. In spring the families split up again, reliving the pattern of dispersal into tiny groups until the next fall.

Bands

To hunt and gather efficiently, in most environments foragers live in small, mobile groups of 50 or fewer. To distinguish these living groups from the settled hamlets, villages, towns, and cities found among other peoples, anthropologists call these mobile living groups *bands*. (Chapter 12 discusses the political aspects of band life.) All or most members of a single band are relatives or are married into the band. Kinfolk or not, members cooperate in acquiring the wild resources of a given territory. In most foraging communities, the size of bands is flexible, with the numbers adjusted to the availability of the food supply.

The Ju/'hoansi (also known as the !Kung) of southern Africa illustrate band organization. Living in what is now southeast Angola, northeast Namibia, and northwest Botswana, the Ju/'hoansi are the most thoroughly studied of all hunter-gatherers. The

The Ju/'hoansi (also known as the !Kung) are among the most well-known hunter and gatherers. These Ju/'hoansi men are discussing the hunt. The meat will shared by all band families.

northern part of their environment is an arid tropical savanna, which turns into the Kalahari Desert in the south. Until the twentieth century, most Ju/'hoansi exploited this habitat entirely by foraging. They gathered more than 100 species of plants and hunted over 50 kinds of animals, including mammals, birds, and reptiles. Plant foods consisted of nuts, fruits, berries, melons, roots, and greenery. A particularly important and nourishing food was the mongongo nut, which ripens in April and provided about half the people's caloric intake.

Because their habitat received so little rainfall and then only seasonally, the availability of water greatly affected the annual rhythm of Ju/'hoansi lives. From about April to October (winter in the Southern Hemisphere), there was little precipitation. Practically no rain fell between June and September. During this dry season, water for people and animals was available only at a few permanent water holes, around which many families congregated into relatively large settlements of 50 or more individuals. When summer rainstorms created temporary water holes between November and March, Ju/'hoansi traveled in smaller camps to exploit the more widely distributed wild resources. But rainfall in this part of southern Africa is not reliable from year to year or place to place. In some years, up to 40 inches of rain falls during the wet months; in other years, as little as 6 inches. Precipitation is also spatially unpredictable: one local area may receive severe thunderstorms, while 20 miles away there is no rain at all.

The aridity, seasonality, and variability in precipitation influenced how the Ju/'hoansi organized their bands. During wet months, people spread out among the temporary water holes in camps numbering about 10 to 30. When they moved to a water hole that had not been occupied recently, game was relatively plentiful and a wide variety of plant foods were easily available. But the longer a band remained, the more its members exhausted the resources surrounding the water hole. The men had to roam farther away from their camps while hunting, and the women had to travel longer distances while collecting plants. After several weeks, a camp reached the point at which its members judged that the costs of continuing to forage in the area were not bringing adequate returns in food. They then moved to a new wet-season camp. One ethnographer, Richard Lee (1969, 60), succinctly noted that the Ju/'hoansi "typically occupy a camp for a period of weeks or months and eat their way out of it." If the Ju/'hoansi stayed in larger groups during the dry months, they would have had to move more often, consuming more time and energy. As the months passed and the land dried up, people made their way back to the permanent water holes, where several dozen people congregated and food scarcity made life a bit harder.

Reciprocal Sharing

It is mutually beneficial for foragers to share food and other possessions, both within and between families. The sharing is more or less on the basis of need: those who have more than they can immediately use share with others. For example, among the Ju/'hoansi, on any given day only some people actually go out gathering and hunting. Sharing applies especially to meat. Successful hunters returning to camp share the kill with other families, including those who have not participated in the day's hunt. One reason for the special emphasis on the sharing of meat is the uncertain returns of hunting compared to gathering. Among the Ju/'hoansi, on most days women return to camp with their carrying bags full of nuts, roots, fruits, and other wild plants. Men's chances of capturing game, however, are smaller: only about two out of five hunting trips capture animals large enough to take back to camp. Men who are successful one day may be unsuccessful the next, so they give today in expectation of receiving tomorrow.

Sharing is *normatively expected* behavior: people who regularly fail to share are subjected to ridicule or other kinds of social pressures. Going along with the expectation of sharing is a positive cultural value placed on equality of personal possessions (property) and even of social status. Families who attempt to hoard food or other products may be ostracized. Men who try to place themselves above others socially by boasting about their hunting skills or other accomplishments are soon put in their place. The result is that—compared to many other peoples—there is both economic and social equality between the families of most hunting and gathering bands.

Resource Allocation

It is useful to have familiar, patterned ways of allocating natural resources among individuals, families, and other kinds of groups—"property rights," in some form. Many hunters and gatherers have developed similar ways of allocating such rights: who can harvest which resources, where, and when.

One possible way to allocate rights over a territory and its resources is for each group to establish and maintain *exclusive* claims to particular territories. Cultural ideas about the relationship between people and territory might be, for example, that this area is *mine* or *ours*, whereas that area is *yours* or *theirs*. Among foragers, exclusive access would mean that each band has rights to remain in a specific area during a particular season. One benefit of allocating rights in this way is that the members of each band would know they alone can harvest the foods found in particular places at definite times. Another advantage is that bands would not interfere in each other's hunting and gathering activities.

Despite these (apparent) benefits, most foragers allocate rights to resources differently. Among the Shoshone during the hot months when nuclear or extended families were sparsely distributed, rights to resources were "first come, first served," meaning that whichever group arrived at an area first was free to harvest its plants and animals. No family had exclusive access to any particular territory in any season.

Among the Ju/'hoansi, rights were better defined. People recognized particular individuals as the "owners" of places where food and water resources were found. Commonly, the reliable water holes together with the wild resources around them were "owned" by a set of siblings whose rights grew stronger as they grew older. But by merely asking permission—seldom refused—anyone with a kinship relationship to one of the "owners" could come and visit and use the area's food and water. Because most Ju/'hoansi had many relatives and in-laws who were "owners" of various places, each family had many options about where and with whom they would live, work, relax, and socialize.

Thus, who was living and foraging together fluctuated radically and each band received visitors several times a year. Instead of establishing exclusive claims to particular places, Ju/'hoansi families were attached loosely to territories and for the most part came and went according to their preferences and circumstances. If a quarrel or dispute occurred, one of the parties could simply leave to join another group temporarily. Most other known hunter-gatherers had similar ways of allocating rights to resources.

To sum up, most foraging peoples were similar in the following respects:

- Division of labor based mainly on sex and age
- High mobility between areas
- Congregation and dispersal of groups, especially from season to season
- Life in bands of varying size and flexible composition
- Strong values of reciprocal sharing and of equality in personal possessions and social status
- Loose attachment of people to territory and flexible rights to resources

You can see how these similarities helped foragers harness resources and cope with problems. But, although these characteristics describe most hunter-gatherers reasonably well, we must keep in mind that foragers are diverse. Not all have these cultural features.

In fact, in some environments, foragers lived quite differently. Along the Northwest Coast of North America (roughly from the northernmost California coast into the Alaskan panhandle), food resources—especially fish—were exceptionally abundant, and the Native Americans who lived there were able to smoke and preserve a supply of fish that lasted for many months. Also, salmon and other fish were more reliably abundant on the Northwest Coast than in most other environments where foragers lived—in most years, people could count on fish swimming up the rivers to breed in the fall, and in the bays and estuaries year-round. Because of abundance, reliability, and long-term food storage, there was not much need for seasonal mobility or small living groups. Most Northwest Coast people settled in villages, where many families lived in spacious and often elaborately decorated wood-plank houses. Resource abundance and reliability also affected property notions along the coast. If a food resource is so abundant and reliable that you can usually count on its availability, then it makes sense for you to stay close to it and defend it against other groups that might desire it as well. So, people of the Northwest Coast developed more defined property rights: particular groups were more closely associated with particular locations than were people such as the Hadzabe, Shoshone, or Ju/'hoansi.

Foraging cultures also varied on the North American Great Plains after about 1700, when the Native Americans acquired horses. Plains peoples were hunters and gatherers—they did not farm—but the horses introduced by Europeans allowed them to effectively hunt the tens of millions of bison that once grazed North America's tall grass prairies. Although they hunted antelope and other mammals, bison was Plains peoples' main food resource. During the spring and summer, the bison gathered in huge herds that were most effectively hunted cooperatively by dozens of mounted men. In most areas of the Plains, grasses grew luxuriantly in the spring and early summer, leading the bison to congregate in herds of tens of thousands. As the summer progressed, the land became drier and the grass patchier, so the bison broke up into smaller herds for the fall and succeeding winter months.

The Cheyenne are one Plains people. After acquiring the horse in the late 1700s, until around 1850 the Cheyenne lived mainly on bison meat. On horseback, they followed the seasonal movements of their principal food source. From June until late summer, as the bison gathered in huge herds, the people lived as a single tribe in an enormous camp of several thousand. Men on horseback used bows and arrows and, later, rifles to hunt the animals for their meat and hides. As the bison herds split up in the fall, so did the tribe because it was too difficult for the people to remain together as a single enormous camp when their food supply was so widely scattered. By breaking up into smaller bands during the fall and winter, each with its own name and identity, the Cheyenne gained other advantages. Their numerous horses, which were their main source of wealth and pride, had more grass to graze on. Fuel for fires during the freezing winter was easier to acquire, for dried animal dung was the primary fuel in tall grass prairies with few trees.

What Happened to Hunters and Gatherers?

For tens of thousands of years, living exclusively from wild foods worked well enough to allow the human population to grow to several million. Furthermore, foraging is a flexible strategy to acquire food that historically has supported people in rain forests, grasslands, savannahs, high mountains, and northern tundras. For example, the Netsilik are an Inuit (formerly called "Eskimo") people who traditionally spent the winters in igloos erected on the surface of arctic ice in the Hudson's Bay region. Here in their winter camps, Netsilik lived largely on the meat and blubber of seals that they captured by ingenious methods. As the seasons changed, Netsilik moved to rivers and lived off fish and in summer and in fall off migratory herds of caribou. Ingenuity and rapid communication by social learning allowed hunter-gatherers to migrate into all the continents except Antarctica by around 13,000 years ago. Even by that early date, humanity was a successful species.

In fact, most research suggests that hunter-gatherers enjoyed a relatively high quality of life. Richard Lee's quantitative studies of the Ju/'hoansi in the 1960s show that they worked only about two and a half days per week to acquire their food supply. Even adding in time spent in other kinds of work, such as toolmaking and housework, the Ju/'hoansi worked only about 42 hours per week. Most adults in modern industrial nations would be happy with such a short workweek! Furthermore, the Ju/'hoansi's relatively modest work efforts were sufficient to keep them well fed most of the time: adults consumed an average of 2,355 calories and 96 grams of protein per day, more than sufficient for their bodily needs. Robert Kelly compared figures on other foragers living in various environments. He found that working hours about like those of the Ju/'hoansi were common in reasonably productive environments, but quantitative studies are few and have uncertain reliability.

Most evidence also indicates that foraging peoples enjoyed a diverse diet and were healthy compared to farmers. Hunters and gatherers live from plants and animals that naturally occur in their habitats and that are well adapted to periodic droughts and other hazards. In most places, their diets were diverse compared to those of farmers and herders, who focused their attention and efforts on only a few crops and livestock. Foraging bands were small and moved often, which reduced the incidence and spread of infectious diseases. There are, of course, exceptions, but generally hunter-gatherers did not have a particularly hard life.

Once plant and animal domestication developed, however, agricultural and herding peoples increased in numbers and expanded their territories. Over several millennia of expansion, cultivators and herders pushed most foraging peoples into regions that were ill suited to crops and livestock. As a result, when European contact with people of other continents intensified after about 1500, hunters and gatherers lived primarily in regions too cold or arid to support agriculture (see Figure 7.1). In the last two or three centuries, even more foragers have lost their lands as they died from diseases and warfare, yielded their territories to outsiders for plantations and mines, relocated onto reservations, and/or gave up foraging voluntarily for the attractions of introduced ways of making a living.

By the beginning of the twentieth century, most foragers had died out altogether or had become assimilated into some other society. Contact was especially hard on Native Americans, who lived on lands highly coveted by Spanish, French, Anglo, and Portuguese settlers. Because of their isolation from Old World populations, Native Americans were susceptible to a host of diseases brought by Europeans and the Africans they enslaved. Most scholars who have looked seriously at the impact of diseases on Native Americans estimate that 80 to 90 percent of Indians died from epidemics. Europeans did indeed conquer and subdue many Native peoples, but not in the way most people imagine: bacteria and viruses were more important than guns and bullets. The indigenous foraging peoples of Australia and Tasmania suffered in similar ways and degrees.

Only a few foragers preserved their way of life into the twentieth century. In the twenty-first century, the hunting and gathering way of life is almost gone. The Ju/'hoansi were surrounded by herders, and many had taken up raising livestock. Governments curtailed their old freedom of movement by fencing off lands. Some left the Kalahari to work for wages in mines or, in the 1960s and 1970s, to serve as trackers for the military in South Africa. Some voluntarily settled down at government-funded stations, where they began eating large quantities of corn porridge, drinking alcohol, and catching new diseases (including HIV). Recently, governments realized they could earn money from tourists by turning much of the Ju/'hoansi territory into game parks. Even the people themselves have become tourist attractions: outsiders come to watch them perform "traditional" dances and curing ceremonies.

The Hadzabe, discussed earlier, are one of the few remaining East African people who still get a lot of their food from foraging. In 2006, the royal family of the United Arab Emirates offered large payments to the government of Tanzania to lease part of Hadzabe land for hunting safaris. The international press publicized the lease offering and international pressure led the U.A.E. to cancel the plan, but the Hadzabe had already lost some of their hunting grounds to another game park and to encroachments by neighboring peoples. Just as foragers lost numbers and territories in the past, so today forces arising from the global economy endanger their ways of living.

Some Native peoples of the Americas continue to hunt and gather. Ojibwas in Minnesota harvest wild rice in lakes. Inuits hunt sea mammals in Alaska and the Canadian Arctic. Northwest Coast peoples still fish for salmon and other fish along the coast and in rivers. Some Native Americans of the Great Plains and Southwest still hunt bison for ceremonial purposes. However, none of these Natives make their living off the land. Too much of their land and resources have been lost. Incorporation into nations has led them to make new adaptations. They coped with new problems brought about by contacts with wealthier and more powerful people. By force and/or choice, Natives now live from new resources, such as jobs and market sales. The total environment in which they live is more a product of their historical interactions with other peoples than of the natural world.

Domestication of Plants and Animals

Domestication is the purposeful planting, cultivation, and harvest of selected plants and the taming and breeding of certain species of animals. People who live by domestication of plants ("farmers") increase the supply of their foods by replacement of the natural vegetation with edible or useful crops. Those who make part of their living from livestock ("herders," but also many farmers) control their location, breeding, and numbers. Controlling part of the environment for farming requires new technologies and, in most circumstances, additional labor inputs compared to foraging.

With respect to plants, in this book we are concerned with *food crops*, or those species that people intentionally select, plant, care for, harvest, and propagate for purposes of eating. People also grow plants for other purposes, such as for fibers (cotton, flax, hemp) or for drugs (tobacco, coca leaf, opium poppy). With animals, we are concerned with *livestock*, or those species that

people raise, control, and breed to provide food (meat, dairy products) or other useful products (hides, wool), or for performing work (pulling plows and wagons, carrying people and possessions). People also keep animals for other reasons, such as companionship (pets).

Origins of Domestication: Wheres and Whens

Extensive coverage of the origins of plant and animal domestication is outside the scope of this text. The "wheres and whens" of domestication are fairly well established by archaeologists, botanists, and other scholars. Most people alive today do not know that many or most of their meals contain foods that were domesticated in other continents. A Canadian meal consisting only of potatoes, squash, and beef contains foods that originated in three continents. Spicy dishes in Sichuan province of China might contain tofu, green beans, chili peppers, sweet potato, and noodles made from wheat. Only one of these was domesticated in China. Knowing the original places where the food on our plates was domesticated perhaps will help us appreciate the contributions of our long-dead ancestors to how we live.

Domestication of both plants and animals occurred independently in the Old World (Europe, Asia, and Africa) and the New World (North and South America and the Caribbean). Before Columbus's voyages initiated contact between the two worlds, the crops grown in the two hemispheres were completely different.

Old World Crops

The earliest plant domestication occurred about 10,000 years ago in the region around what is now Jordan, Israel, Syria, eastern Turkey, western Iran, and Iraq. This region is known to prehistorians as the Fertile Crescent. Wheat, barley, lentils, peas, carrots, figs, almonds, pistachios, dates, and grapes were first grown here. Oats, cabbages, lettuce, and olives were first domesticated along the Mediterranean fringe. West African peoples domesticated sorghum, finger millet, watermelons, and African rice between 6,000 and 4,000 years ago. Sorghum and finger millet still feed millions of people on the African continent. Eggplants, cucumbers, bananas, and coconuts originated in southern Asia and Southeast Asia. Soybeans, Oriental rice, two varieties of millet, citrus fruits, and tea were domesticated in ancient China at various times, rice around 7,000 years ago and millets as early as 10,000 years ago. Taro and Pacific yams (root crops widely grown in Southeast Asia and the Pacific) and bananas were probably first cultivated

---

domestication Process by which people control the distribution, abundance, and biological features of certain plants and animals in order to increase their usefulness to humans.

142 PART III The Diversity of Culture

in New Guinea or the islands around it, perhaps as early as 9,000 years ago. Sugar cane may have originated in the same area. We get our morning caffeine from coffee, first domesticated in the Ethiopian highlands.

New World Crops

Maize (corn), tomatoes, several varieties of beans, peppers, avocados, and cacao (now used in the making of chocolate) originated in Central America and Mexico, in either the highlands or the coastal lowlands, or both. Various members of the squash family (squash, pumpkins, and gourds) were first intentionally grown in the same region, although squashes probably also were grown in eastern North America. The earliest evidence for domestication of these crops is between 10,000 (for maize and squash) and 4,000 (for common beans) years ago. From northern and western South America came numerous crops that are still important to the region and to the world, including potatoes, sweet potatoes, and lima bean dating about 6,000 years ago. Between 8,000 and 6,000 years ago, lowland South Americans peoples were planting manioc (cassava), peanuts, and pineapple. Chili peppers originated in South America also, but Europeans took them back to the Old World and then to Asia during the colonial era. Chilis spiced up food in southern China, India, Thailand, and other parts of the Old World.

In the 1980s, researchers discovered that the Native Americans who inhabited the eastern United States 5,000 to 4,000 years ago domesticated several crops, including sunflower, gourds and squash, marshelder, and goosefoot. The Native peoples apparently abandoned the last two, grown for their tiny seeds, when maize and beans from Mesoamerica became available, with their larger seeds and better yields. A couple of crops that were important in the diet of other Indians at the time of contact with the Spanish were amaranth

The chili peppers used in southern Chinese cooking were domesticated by prehistoric Native Americans of southern Mexico. After contact with Europeans, chilis and many other foods that originated in the Americas spread to other continents, where many people are unaware of their origins.

and quinoa, but the Spanish outlawed them because of their use in "pagan" ceremonies.

Some plants were domesticated not just once but several times in various parts of the world. Squash may have had independent origins in Mesoamerica, the Andes, and eastern North America. Separate species of rice were domesticated in Africa and Asia, apparently independently. Cotton was domesticated independently in three places: South America, Central America, and either India or Africa. Three yam species were grown in West Africa, Southeast Asia, and tropical South America. Apparently, when conditions were right, peoples of all world regions were quite capable of transforming wild plants into domesticated crops—a good point to keep in mind when next you hear someone claim that some cultures (usually their own) are more inventive or creative than others.

Old World Livestock

In the Old World, the earliest animals were domesticated at about the same times and in the same places as crops were first grown. Dogs probably were the earliest domesticated animals. Genetic studies comparing dogs with grey wolves (their wild ancestors) suggest that people first domesticated dogs about 20,000 years ago, probably in the Middle East and/or in East Asia. In the Middle East, the wild ancestors of the most important livestock lived in large herds, including sheep, goats, and cattle. These animals were and are kept for their hides, wool, meat, and milk. Another large mammal, the horse, was first domesticated and ridden on the Asian grasslands around 3,500 years ago.

New World Livestock

Compared to ancient Old World peoples, Native Americans domesticated few livestock. In the Andes, llamas, and alpacas (related to camels) were used for meat and transportation. Their thick, long hair was also woven into beautiful clothing by weavers of the ancient Andean civilizations. In South America, people still raise guinea pigs for their meat. Elsewhere in the Americas, turkeys and Muscovy ducks were the only animals domesticated for food, and these only in a few areas. Dogs, present also in the Old World, were used in hunting and often as food.

Why did American Indians domesticate so few animals compared to Middle Easterners and Asians? The answer is uncertain, but one important reason may be that so many of the large herd animal species in the Americas became extinct shortly after the end of the Pleistocene epoch, about 11,000 years ago. Members of the horse and camel family, in particular, all disappeared (except in the Andes). Horses did not return to the Americas until the Spanish brought them in the 1500s. Jared Diamond argues that the large herd mammals such as bison and caribou that remained after the New World extinctions were not amenable to human control. Certainly, it was not the capabilities or the intelligence of the prehistoric Indians that explains why they domesticated so few animals.

What's for Dinner?

Soon after Spain, Portugal, France, Britain, and the Netherlands began exploring and establishing colonies on other continents, crops and livestock spread from continent to continent. Many New World crops were taken to various parts of the Old World, where they became important foods for millions of people. Manioc (or cassava, as it is commonly known) from Amazonia became a staple in tropical Africa and Asia. Mexican corn spread widely, especially in Africa, Mediterranean Europe, and eastern Asia. In China, corn and South American sweet potatoes grew well in lands and climates that were marginal for other crops and probably alleviated or even prevented some famines. After initial resistance, the Andean potato became a staple food in Russia, northern Europe, and—especially—Ireland. Imagine modern Italian food without the Mexican tomato! Over the centuries, Native American cultivators had become master farmers, and food crops are one of the greatest gifts they bestowed upon the rest of the world.

Crops and livestock also moved across the Atlantic Ocean in the other direction. European colonists took Old World wheat, oats, barley, grapes, and other crops to temperate zones of the Americas. In parts of the Americas with more tropical climates, rice, bananas, and coconuts became important foods.

Livestock were the most important foods taken from the Old World to the New. Pigs, cattle, sheep, and horses were introduced very soon after the European encounter with the Americas. Over the next couple of centuries, they multiplied rapidly and spread widely, becoming feral in many places. Pigs and cattle thrived and multiplied in the Americas and became enormously abundant by the time European settlers began spreading over the landscape. Abundant and familiar cattle, pigs, and sheep helped attract European colonists to the Americas in the 1700s and 1800s. Plows pulled by horses, mules, and oxen turned over heavy soils and broke up the matted roots of grasses, enabling settlers to farm the rich earth of the American Midwest and Plains for the first time and making this region the breadbasket for the rest of the country.

Too few of us alive today recognize our debt to the prehistoric Middle Easterners, Asians, Africans,

Andeans, and Mexicans who domesticated the plants and animals we eat daily. Yet most North American meals include foods brought to the New World centuries ago from other continents. If you're an all-American person who likes steak, potatoes with sour cream or butter, broccoli, and spinach or lettuce salad, only the potatoes are truly American—and they came from well south of the border. If you live in southwest China or southern India, your cuisine would be much different without the chili peppers and sweet potatoes that originated in South America.

Today, there is an ecological movement to "eat local" because a lot of energy can be saved from transportation costs if people in New York eat, say, apples from their own state rather than those grown in Washington. Eating local is something we should do more often. But in doing so, remember many locally grown foods originally came from other parts of our planet. The next time you enjoy bread and beef, think of the Middle East. As you bite into the corn cob or relish the tomato in the salad, remember the ancient Mexicans.

Advantages and Costs of Cultivation

Once plants and animals were domesticated in these various region, over the next several thousand years many foraging peoples took up cultivating crops and raising livestock. Most people who lived in European, African, and Asian environments that could support farming and in which it was reliable became farmers by 3,000 or 4,000 years ago. This was probably not primarily because hunters and gatherers realized the benefits of farming and seized the opportunity to work less and be better nourished. For one thing, farming people lived in denser settlements and outnumbered foragers, so they tended to spread into regions suitable for cultivation. For another, in several of Earth's regions, civilizations developed and civilized societies tried to expand to acquire more territory, resources, and wealth for their elite classes.

As we've seen, most prehistoric hunters and gatherers lived fairly well, so why humans took up farming does not have a self-evident answer. In trying to account for why agriculture developed at all, most archaeologists point to two factors that led prehistoric foragers to gradually begin cultivating crops. The first is climate change: in the eastern Mediterranean, where agriculture developed earliest—about 10,000 years ago when the last Ice Age ended—the climate became warmer at about the same time people began domesticating plants and animals.

The second factor is growing human populations. Although prehistoric hunters and gatherers lived well, once their numbers began to increase substantially, wild plants and animals could no longer support the population size in a region. Growing crops gives a group greater control over the numbers of *edible* plants that exist in their environment, raising the ability of the land to support people. If a field is planted in wheat, or rice, or corn, then nearly all the plants growing there produce foods that humans can digest. If the field is left in its natural state, only a fraction of the wild plants are digestible and, hence, edible. Thus, agriculture nearly always supports far more people per unit of territory.

How these two factors interacted, and the importance of other factors, is one of the most controversial issues in modern archaeology. However, most agree the single greatest and most widespread advantage of agriculture over foraging is that agriculture supports far more people—10 or even a 100 times more than gathering and hunting.

Farming the land does entail costs, however. Creating and maintaining the community of plants that make up a garden or farm requires labor, time, and energy. First, the plot must be prepared for planting by removing at least some of the natural vegetation, whether it be forest or grasses. In some kinds of agriculture, people modify the landscape itself by constructing furrows, dikes, ditches, terraces, or other artificial landforms. Second, the crops must be planted, requiring an investment of labor that foragers do not make. Third, natural processes continually invade the artificial plant community and landscape that people have created: weeds invade and compete for light and soil nutrients, animal pests are attracted to the densely growing crops, and floods may wash away physical improvements. Periodically, cultivators must "beat back nature" by removing weeds, protecting against pests, rebuilding earthworks, and so forth. Fourth, the act of farming itself reduces the suitability of a site for future harvests, by reducing soil fertility if nothing else. In future years, the farmers must somehow restore their plots to a usable condition or their yields will fall. All these necessities require labor and other kinds of energy expenditures.

So, farming is a lot of work, and much evidence suggests that most preindustrial people who make their living by agriculture work longer and harder than most foragers. Cultivation also led to other changes—in settlement size and permanence, in ownership of resources, in political organization, and in many other dimensions of life—that culminated in the evolution of whole new forms of culture, as we shall see.

In parts of the Old World, livestock were an efficient complement to farming. Their availability meant that most men eventually gave up hunting, putting their labor into farming, crafts, warfare, metallurgy, ruling, and other activities instead. When mounted, horses greatly increased the speed of long-distance travel and, of course, increased the mobility of warriors and soldiers. Horses, donkeys, South Asian yaks, and camels enabled people to carry heavy loads long distances, increasing the possibilities and profits of trade, especially when the animals pulled wagons and carts. For thousands of years, camels made it possible for people and products to cross vast stretches of arid lands in Central Asia and North Africa's Sahara. When harnessed to plows, cattle, horses, mules, and Asian water buffalos supplemented human labor in farming. Their dung added nutrients to agricultural fields and gardens. Finally, pigs—first brought under human control in Southwest Asia and perhaps eastern Asia—are an outstanding source of protein and today remain the major source of meat in China and non-Muslim Southeast Asia.

In the New World, except for residents of the Andes, farming peoples continued to acquire all or most of their meat from deer, antelope, small mammals, fish, and other wild animals. Most New World peoples got the bulk of their meat from wild, not domesticated, animals, even though many of them were farmers.

Plant and animal domestication probably had more long-lasting and dramatic effects on cultures than any other single set of changes in peoples' relationship with nature—except industrialization. For example, once certain plants evolved by human selection into crops, people produced more food in a given area of land. Increased production allowed them to remain in one place for long periods—over time, groups became more *sedentary*. They could also live in much larger settlements than the bands of most foragers— groups settled in *villages* and, later in some places, in *towns* and *cities*.

Preindustrial farming systems are conveniently divided into two overall forms, based partly on the energy source used in farming and on how often a garden or field is cultivated. The forms are usually called *horticulture* and *intensive agriculture*. Both have many, many varieties—far too many for us to even mention most of them.

> **horticulture** Methods of cultivation using hand tools powered by human muscles and in which land use is extensive.

Horticulture

In **horticulture**, people use mainly or entirely the energy (power) of their own muscles to clear land, turn the soil, plant, weed, and harvest crops. There are no plows pulled by horses, oxen, or other draft animals to help prepare the soil. Instead, hand tools such as digging sticks, shovels, and hoes are used for most tasks. Some people clear new fields by burning the natural vegetation and fertilize their gardens with animal or human wastes or with other kinds of organic matter. If irrigation is necessary, horticulturalists usually hand-carry water from nearby rivers or streams. Figure 7.2 shows the most important regions where the horticultural adaptation existed at the time of contact by the West.

Varieties of Horticulture

One type of horticulture is *shifting cultivation* (also called *slash and burn*). Once very widespread, in the modern era it is found in pockets of remote tropical rain forests in Central and South America, Southeast Asia, and Central Africa. Shifting cultivators farm the forest in a cycle. Using axes, knives, and other hand tools, they first remove a small area of forest. After the wood and leaves dry out, they burn the refuse to recycle some valuable plant nutrients in the form of ash. Generally, a given garden plot is cultivated for only 2 or 3 years before its fertility declines and it is gradually abandoned. Then a plot is cleared in another place; a new garden is planted, tended, and harvested until its productivity declines. It, too, is abandoned, until its natural vegetation regrows and it recovers its ability to produce an adequate harvest, which typically takes 10 or more years.

Shifting cultivation works well so long as population density (the number of people who live in an area of a given size) does not grow too large. For every plot of land under cultivation at any given time, several plots are *fallowed*—they have been left alone for the forest to regrow and the land to recover. If, for every acre of land being cultivated, 10 acres are under fallow, then far fewer people could be supported per acre than if only half the land were fallowed at any one time.

Environmentalists often blame shifting cultivators for cutting and burning the tropical forests that are carbon sinks and protect the land from erosion. To some extent, this is true. However, shifting cultivation has been practiced for many centuries, whereas the large-scale deforestation is a more recent phenomenon. Perhaps the blame for deforestation lies elsewhere.

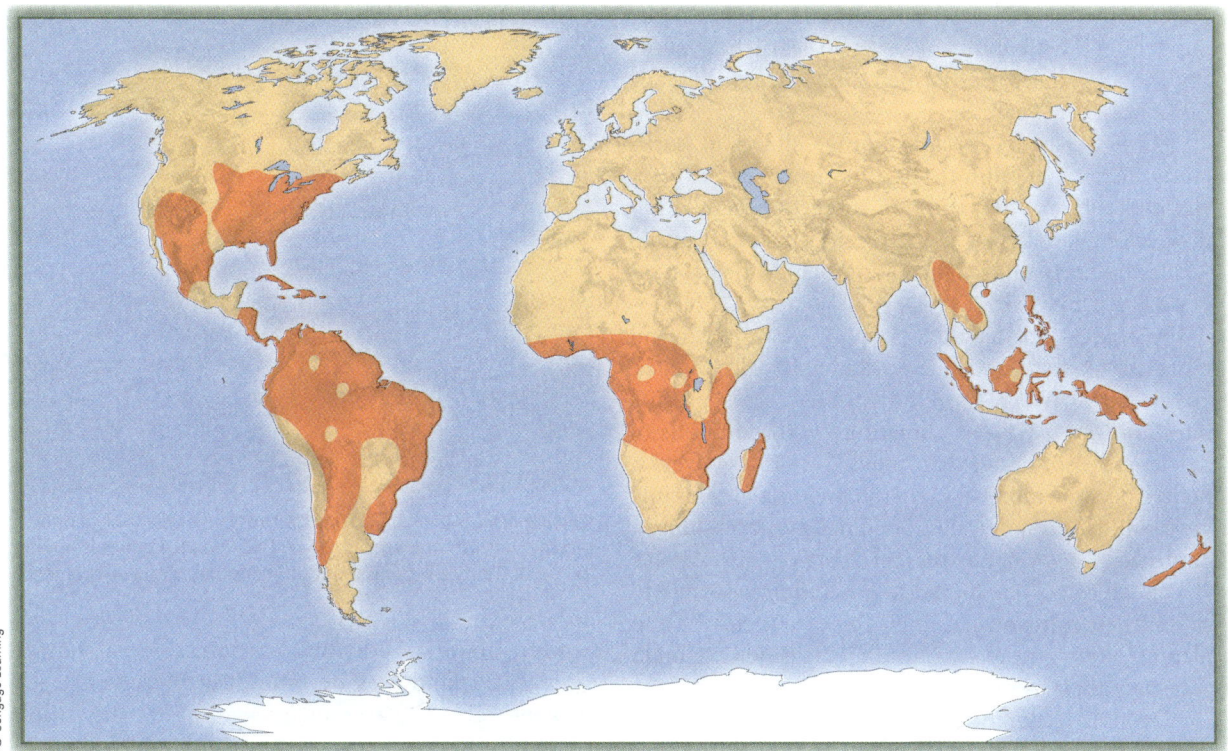

Figure 7.2 Principal Regions of Horticulture at the Contact Period.

Dry land gardening is another form of horticulture. It is defined by the main climatic factor with which cultivators have to cope: low, erratic, and unpredictable rainfall. Dry land gardening occurs in the American Southwest, in arid parts of Mexico, in some of the Middle East, and in much of sub-Saharan Africa. In the more arid regions of Africa where rainfall is too low and unpredictable for people to depend entirely on their crops, dry land gardening is complemented by livestock such as cattle and goats.

Cultivation in arid lands is risky: even if rainfall and harvests are adequate in most years, there is a chance that in any given year not enough rain will fall. Therefore, people who cultivate in dry regions have developed various gardening strategies and techniques to cope with the possibility of drought.

In most parts of the American Southwest, annual rainfall averages only about 10 inches, concentrated in the spring and late summer. Furthermore, in this high country, the growing season for corn—the major food—is only about 4 months long. Over centuries, Western Pueblo peoples such as the Zuni, Hopi, and Acoma learned to cope with risk by planting some of their crops in those areas most likely to retain soil moisture, as around seeps and springs. Yet, in some years, the unpredictable rains are so torrential that runoff washes away the crops. To cope with such natural hazards, Pueblo diversify both the place and the time of their planting. They plant the seeds of corn, squash, beans, and other crops in several locations so that, no matter what the weather, some fields usually produce a harvest. Staggering the time of planting likewise lowers the risk of cultivation: by planting crops weeks apart, the risk of losing all of a planting because of an untimely frost is reduced. Thus, by mixing up where and when they plant, Pueblo peoples reduce the risk of cultivation in an arid, highly seasonal environment. In favorable years, they stored corn in ceramic pots placed inside adobe and wood houses.

Cultural Consequences of Horticulture

The productivity (yield for a given amount of land) of various horticultural methods is much greater than that of foragers. To some people, horticulture seems like "rudimentary" agriculture because the physical tools are so simple. However, horticultural peoples developed sophisticated knowledge of what, when, and where to plant to handle environmental problems. Their tools may be simple, but their knowledge is not at all "rudimentary." In fact, agricultural scientists study indigenous horticultural systems to learn how some traditional peoples have farmed their lands sustainably for hundreds of years.

At very basic levels, how do the cultures of horticulturalists differ from those of foragers? Subsequent chapters address this question more thoroughly. For now, we note only two of the most important ways in which the horticultural adaptation shapes the cultures of people who live by it.

First, most horticultural peoples live in larger and more permanent settlements. Rather than bands or camps of 20 to 50, most horticulturalists aggregate into *hamlets* or *villages,* sometimes with hundreds of residents. Also, rather than moving every few weeks, people become more *sedentary,* remaining in the same location for years, decades, or sometimes even longer. Settlements are more permanent for two main reasons: (1) effective adaptation does not require people to move frequently, and (2) families who have cleared and planted plots want to stay around at least long enough to recoup their labor investment.

Second, resource allocation differs from most hunter-gatherers: particular individuals, families, and other groups are more attached to specific, fairly bounded places where they or their ancestors established a claim. Among most groups, some kind of nuclear or extended family cooperates in food production. When a family invests its labor in clearing, planting, and improving plots or fields, over time that investment establishes the family's *claim* to the land. Families pass those claims (rights) on to their children, most of whom transmit the rights to their own children. Over several generations, families—and/or "family lines"—become the recognized owners of particular plots of land.

In sum, two major ways the cultures of horticulturalists differ from those of foragers are (1) living groups (hamlets, villages) are larger and more permanently settled, and (2) families have more definite rights of ownership over particular pieces of land.

In turn, these two factors have other effects. For example, when people become more sedentary, they can store possessions, raising the potential for wealth accumulation. More definite land rights raise the possibility that some families will inherit or otherwise

Getting food is perhaps the most important way that people interact with their environments. This Somali woman is hoeing her field. Cultivating the soil is only one way of producing food.

acquire more productive resources than others. Because the land itself becomes valuable, *within* a settlement rights to parcels may be disputed and people who cultivate the land are not likely to be willing to abandon their ancestral lands without some kind of argument or conflict. *Between* settlements, potentially some larger, stronger village will want to take over the lands of smaller, militarily weaker groups. Intergroup violent conflict is more likely among horticulturalists than foragers.

Intensive Agriculture

In the farming system known as **intensive agriculture**, farmers keep their fields under cultivation far longer than horticulturalists. Indeed, some intensive agriculturalists have their lands under almost continuous cultivation—the same fields are farmed year after year, with only brief fallow periods. This is what is meant by using land more *intensively:* to produce higher yields, farmers work the land (and usually themselves) harder. (Figure 7.3 shows the major regions where intensive agriculturalists lived at the time of contact with Europeans.)

With shifting cultivation, people rely mainly on natural processes to restore land productivity, which works but takes a long time. Intensification is possible only if people use their own labor and knowledge to maintain the yields of their land for long periods. In various regions, people fertilize (generally with the dung of livestock), rotate crops, weed carefully, turn over the soil prior to planting, add compost (organic matter) to the

---

intensive agriculture Systems of cultivation in which plots are planted annually or semiannually; usually uses irrigation, natural fertilizers, and (in the Old World) plows powered by animals.

148 PART III The Diversity of Culture

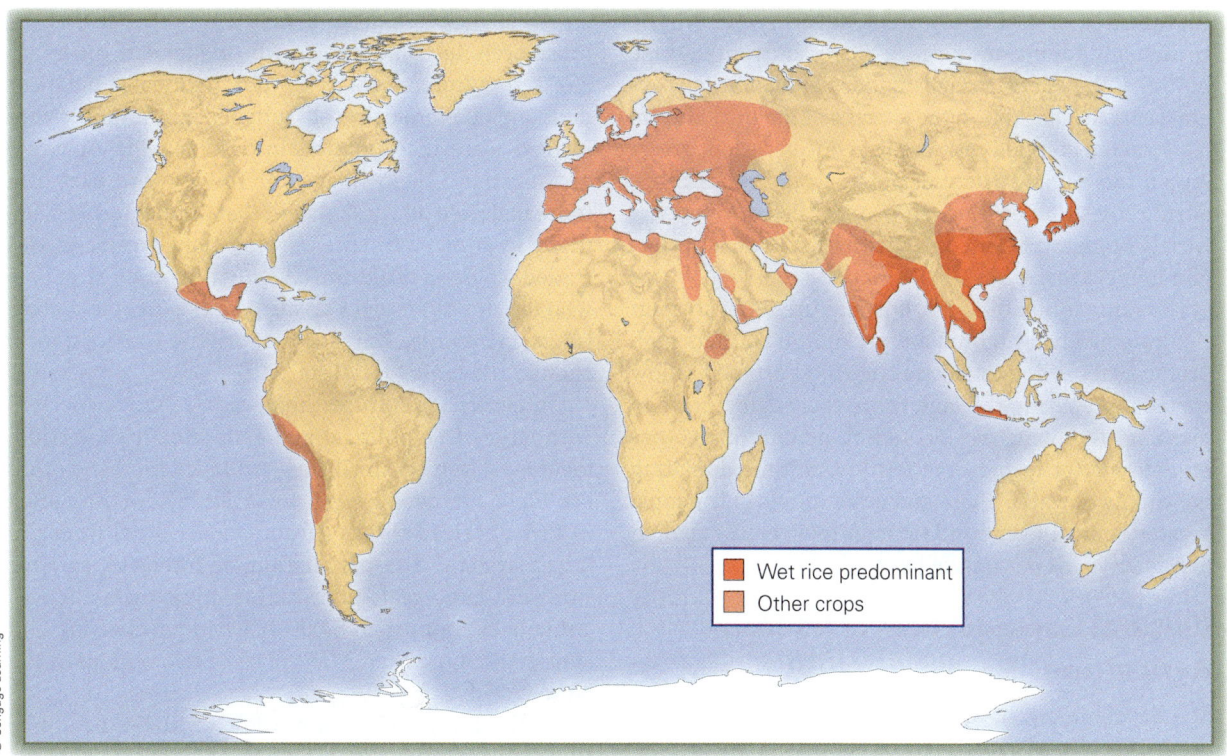

Figure 7.3 Principal Regions of Intensive Agriculture at the Contact Period.

soil, and irrigate their crops. For some of these tasks, a new tool, the plow, and a new source of energy (power), draft animals, are useful. Using plows pulled by horses, mules, oxen, water buffalo, or other draft animals, a farmer can more quickly prepare the soil. In addition to traction for the plow, livestock provide many other useful products: meat, milk and other dairy products, manure, hides, and transportation. After harvest, livestock may be turned loose to graze on the residue of crops, fertilizing fields with their dung.

For all these reasons, intensive agriculture is substantially more productive per area of land than horticulture. An acre of land produces greater yields; hence, it is capable of supporting far more people—5, 10, and even 20 times the numbers of most horticultural peoples. Supporting more people is probably the main advantage of intensive agriculture over horticulture.

Varieties of Intensive Agriculture

In the Old World, especially in parts of Asia and Europe, intensive agriculturalists plowed the land by harnessing oxen, horses, or other draft animals to plows. This allowed them to farm more land than if they used only human labor. Another method of increasing yields is to augment the water supply by artificial means. Farmers around the world use many ingenious irrigation methods. Some construct dams along streams and rivers to conserve runoff and dig ditches to transport water to the fields. In many Asian river valleys, ditches transport water and fertile silt to fields during the annual monsoons, when rivers overrun their banks. In many mountainous regions of Southeast Asia and China, the level of water in hillside rice fields is controlled with an elaborate system of terraces. Rice is produced through a highly coordinated system to supply water in these *wet rice* regions. Along China's northeastern plain, the emperor controlled floods along the Yellow River by organizing citizens to construct and maintain levees. Visitors to the region may be surprised to find the river level is higher than the surrounding plain, thanks to the labor of millions of Chinese peasants over many centuries.

Although New World peoples had no animals suitable for plow agriculture, they found other ways of improving yields and keeping land under prolonged cultivation. Native Americans in places such as the valley of Mexico (land of the Aztecs) and the Andes found ways of increasing yields by intensifying their work. In the valley of Mexico, for example, people transformed swamps and the margins of lakes into productive fields called *chinampas* by constructing raised fields in which they planted crops like tomatoes, squash, and corn. By continually adding new organic materials from the lake bottoms, they kept gardens under cultivation for several years. In the Andes, the citizens of the Inca Empire constructed stepped terraces to reduce erosion, growing an incredible variety of potatoes and other crops during the summer. Andean peoples also developed a variety of methods for coping with frost in their mountain homelands.

In sum, compared with horticulture, intensive agriculture produces more food per unit of land. Its high productivity is due to factors such as shortened fallow periods, preparing the land more thoroughly prior to planting, removing weeds, adding manure and other organic matter to preserve fertility, and manipulating the supply of water. These and other inputs give people greater control over conditions in their fields, leading to higher yields per unit of land.

Cultural Consequences of Intensive Agriculture

The development of intensive farming eventually had dramatic cultural consequences in many regions, most of which resulted from relatively high productivity. A single farm family using intensive methods can usually feed many more people than just its own members. Intensive farmers can produce a **surplus** over and above their own subsistence (food) requirements. This surplus can be used to feed other people, families, and groups, who no longer need to produce their own food.

What happens to this surplus? Many things, depending on circumstances. Farmers trade excess food for other useful products like pottery, tools, wood, and clothing. If the community uses money (see Chapter 8), families may produce surplus food to sell and use the money to buy other goods. If the village or other settlement has a strong political leader, such as a chief, he can collect the surplus from his subjects and use the food to pay laborers who work on public projects such as trails, temples, and irrigation works. If the community is part of a larger, more encompassing political system, with a ruler and a governmental bureaucracy, then the government may collect part of the surplus as a tax. Political officials then use the tax for public purposes (e.g., support of armies, the judiciary, and the religious hierarchy) and/or to further its own political interests.

surplus Amount of food (or other goods) a worker produces in excess of the consumption of herself or himself and her or his dependents.

All these possibilities illustrate a central fact about most preindustrial peoples who depended on intensive agriculture: most were not politically independent and economically self-sufficient communities but instead were incorporated into some kind of larger organization. Their villages or towns were part of a more inclusive political system that dominated or ruled them in some way. The surplus they produced was traded, sold, or taxed (or all three) to support people who did not themselves do farm work—people such as rulers, aristocrats, bureaucrats, priests, warriors, merchants, and craft specialists.

Intensive agriculture, then, was strongly associated with large-scale political and economic organization: local-level farmers in villages produced food and other products for people who lived elsewhere, and they in turn received things (products, services) from the larger system. The association of intensive agriculture with large-scale political organization is ancient, going back more than 5,000 years in parts of the Old World and more than 3,000 years in two regions of the New World.

In these regions, within a few centuries or a millennium after the development of intensive agriculture, the socially and politically complex society we call *civilization* (including, among other things, the first cities) emerged. Civilizations have a form of government known as the *state* (discussed further in Chapter 12), which contrasted markedly with the egalitarian groups of foragers. *States* are large-scale political units that include a ruler, a governing bureaucracy, class distinctions between the elite and common people, and methods of extracting labor and surplus products from those responsible for farming the land.

In ancient times, intensive farmers were incorporated into the four major civilizations of the Old World: the valley formed by the Tigris and Euphrates rivers of Mesopotamia, the Nile valley of Egypt, the Indus River valley of Pakistan, and the vast empire of China. In the New World, too, agricultural peoples were part of large-scale political units, such as the Mayans, Toltecs, and Aztecs of Mesoamerica, and the Incas of the Andean coast and highlands (see Figure 7.4).

All these early civilizations were supported by intensive agriculture based on large-scale irrigation and water control facilities. Intensive farmers produced the food supply and paid tribute or taxes to support the rulers, priests, armies, and officials who staffed the government, protected the city, organized the worship of gods, and performed other roles that had now become necessary. So far as we know, intensive agriculture is virtually a prerequisite for civilization. No

Figure 7.4 Ancient Civilizations.

civilization ever developed out of a foraging or horticultural adaptation.

By about 2,000 years ago, other states developed in Old World places like Korea and Japan (both influenced by China), southern India, much of Southeast Asia, parts of Africa, and most of Europe. In later centuries, the entire world was dramatically affected by states, which tended to expand to incorporate more people and resources to supply necessities for ordinary citizens and luxury goods for elite classes.

Intensive farming methods survive even in the twenty-first century—especially in the developing regions of southern Asia and Southeast Asia, Latin America, and Africa. Economically, farming communities often fit into their nations as **peasants**, a term anthropologists use for rural people who live by a combination of subsistence agriculture and market sale. Peasants are integrated into a larger society both politically (i.e., they are subject to laws and governments imposed by their nations) and economically (i.e., they exchange products of their own labor for products produced elsewhere). In many developing countries, peasants are a numerical majority of the population and produce much of the food consumed by town and city dwellers. Peasants produce goods that are sold for money, traded or bartered, paid to a landlord as rent, and rendered to a central government as taxes.

So far as we know, there were no peasant classes until the emergence of the ancient civilizations, so one by-product of civilization was the development of peasant classes. The farm work of prehistoric and historic peasants fed the craft workers, the merchants, the state-sponsored priests, the political elite, the warriors, and the builders of palaces and temples. Peasants paid tribute or tax (in food, crafts, labor, and/or money), and these resources provided for the maintenance of the society as a whole as well as of the elite classes. The peasantry of medieval Europe, for example, eked out a meager living, paying a substantial portion of their annual harvest to their lords or working many days a year on their lord's estate.

Civilization is usually viewed as a good thing, leading to progress as it spread around to other world regions. True, the high productivity of intensive agriculture allowed the specialized division of labor that

peasants Rural people integrated into a larger society politically and economically.

CHAPTER 7 Culture and Nature: Interacting with the Environment 151

led to writing, metallurgy, monumental architecture, cities, and the great religious and artistic traditions we associate with civilization. But what happened to peasants who produced the food that made "progress" possible? For them, writing meant that more accurate records could be kept of their taxes or the number of days they worked for overlords. Iron and other metals meant that peasants had better farming tools; yet for the most part they were not allowed to use them to ease their own work but instead only to produce more surplus for others to appropriate. Metal also meant that weapons became more deadly and armies more dangerous, allowing one state to make war against other states more effectively. Most peasant families continued to live in hovels, even while engineers designed great palaces, religious structures, and walled cities and towns that were built using peasant tax-labor. Throughout history, most peasants the world over were denied the benefits offered by technological progress, although the food they produced made much of this progress possible.

In his 2007 book *The End of Alms*, economic historian Gregory Clark argues that agriculture and civilization did not improve human life for the majority of people at all. Only well after the Industrial Revolution of the late 1700s did the quality of life for most ordinary people improve, as measured by nutrition, longevity, health status, and consumption levels. The situation is more diverse than Clark implies, but for decades anthropologists have questioned the notion that human life has steadily improved since the "discovery" of agriculture. Agriculture *could* have improved human life, and sometimes it did. But often the secondary effects of agriculture on societies and polities made the majority of people worse off: surpluses benefited elite classes, not those who actually produced the food.

Pastoralism

Most farmers also keep domesticated animals. Southeast Asian and Pacific horticulturalists raise many pigs and chickens. Intensive agriculturalists raise livestock like horses, mules, oxen, water buffalo, and cattle. Livestock pull their plows, fertilize their fields, yield leather and wool, and provide meat and dairy products (milk, cheese, yogurt, and other nutritious foods). Livestock do not merely "supplement" farming: because of the meat, eggs, milk, hides, wool, transportation, fertilizer, and horsepower they provide, domestic animals are usually critical to the nutritional and economic welfare of cultivators. The income earned by selling livestock or their products is often the main source of cash for many peasants and other farmers in developing countries.

However, cultivators do not depend on their livestock to the same extent or in the same way as *pastoralists,* or herders. Herders acquire much of their food by raising, caring for, and subsisting on the products of domesticated animals. With few exceptions, the livestock are gregarious (herd) animals. Cattle, camels, sheep, goats, reindeer, horses, llamas, alpacas, and yaks are the common animals kept by herders in various parts of the world.

Agriculture and pastoralism are not mutually exclusive ways of living on the land. Many pastoral peoples also farm. In saying a people are "pastoralists," we do not mean simply that they keep livestock. More important, the needs of their animals for naturally occurring food and water greatly influence the seasonal rhythms of their lives.

When farmers raise livestock, they generally grow crops especially for their animals or maintain fallowed fields on which their animals graze. In contrast, among pastoral peoples, livestock rely on grassy pasturelands that grow naturally in their territories. The key phrase is "grow naturally." Most often, the best natural grasslands are seasonally available, either because of altitudes (generally more grasslands exist in the mountains during summers) or because the herds themselves deplete the grasses by feeding on them. So most pastoralists migrate two or more times a year. This seasonal mobility, called **nomadism**, is one of the defining features of the pastoral way of life.

Contrary to what some people think, pastoralists do not wander aimlessly, but migrate in organized seasonal and spatial patterns. Most herders take their livestock to highland areas or mountain pastures to graze during the hottest season of the year. Seasonal movements up- and down-slope according to the productivity of pasturelands is called **transhumance**.

For the most part, herders live in only certain kinds of environments (see Figure 7.5 for the main areas where pastoralists lived prior to European expansion). Pastoralists live mainly in deserts, grasslands, savannas,

---

nomadism Seasonal mobility, often involving migration to high-altitude areas during the hottest and driest parts of the year.

transhumance Pastoral pattern involving migration to different elevations to respond to seasonal differences in the availability of pasturelands.

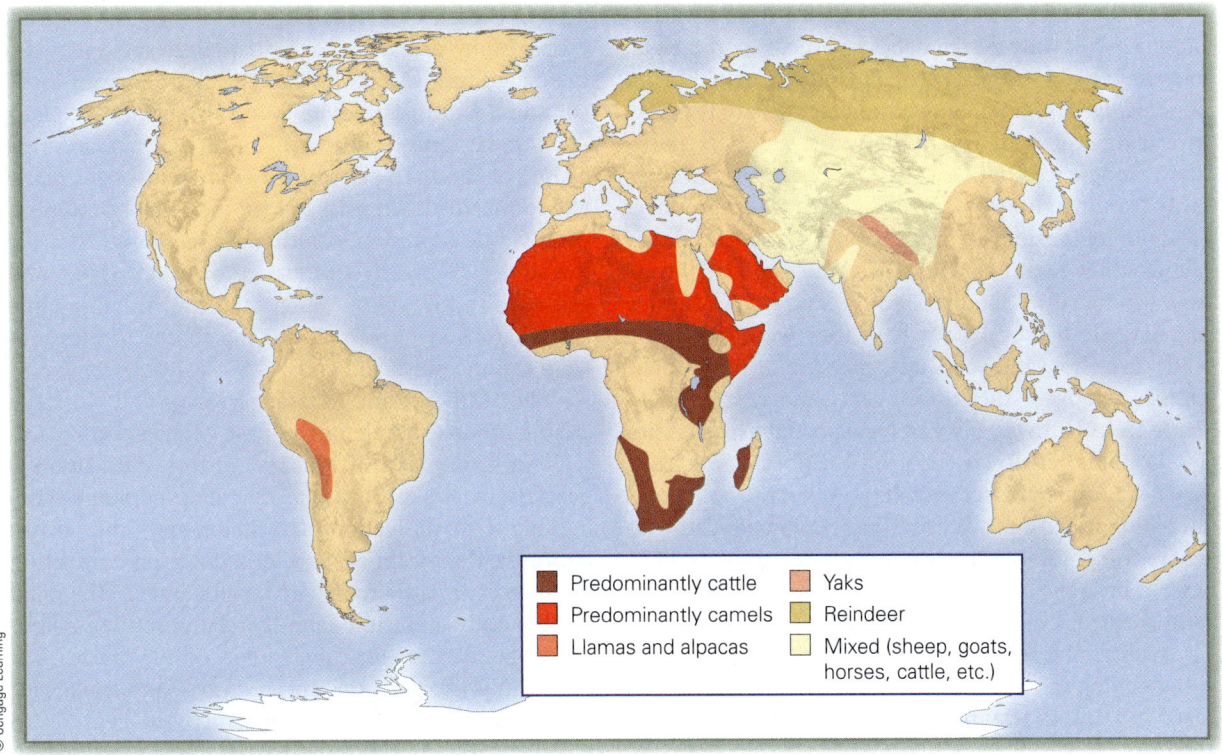

Figure 7.5 Principal Regions of Pastoralism at the Contact Period.

mountains, and arctic tundras. Although diverse, these environments do share a common feature: cultivation is impossible, extremely difficult, or highly risky because of inadequate or great yearly fluctuations in rainfall (as in deserts or savannas) or very short growing seasons (as in mountains and tundras). As always, there are exceptions to our generalizations, but most pastoralists live in regions not well suited to cultivation.

In such arid or cold environments, keeping livestock offers several advantages. First, most vegetation of grasslands and arid savannas (grasses and shrubs) and tundras (lichens, willows, and sedges) is indigestible by humans. Livestock such as cattle, sheep, goats, and reindeer can digest this vegetation and transform it into milk, blood, fat, and muscle, all of which are drunk or eaten by various pastoral peoples. The Sami people (formerly called the Lapps) of northern Europe keep reindeer that eat the sparse tundra vegetation and transform it into flesh and milk that is eaten by their owners. The Turkana of Kenya and many other East African peoples who live in arid lands maintain enormous herds of cattle, drinking their milk and blood almost daily and eating their flesh only on special occasions. A cow, after all, is worth more alive than dead. As these examples illustrate, in some regions livestock allow people to exploit indirectly certain wild plant resources not directly available to them. In brief, livestock convert inedible plants into edible products.

A related advantage of herding is subsistence risk reduction. In areas of low and unreliable rainfall, in some years crop yields are inadequate because of drought. In high-altitude or high-latitude regions, crops may fail because of low temperatures or short growing seasons. Livestock provide insurance against fluctuations in the food supply from an unpredictable droughts and cold periods. The Karimojong of Uganda traditionally lived by a combination of horticulture and cattle herding. In the central, wetter part of their lands, Karimojong women tended gardens of sorghum (an African grain) and a few other crops. Crop yields fluctuated unpredictably with rainfall. Boys and young men took the family's cattle to pasturelands away from where the women lived and worked. While living in these small mobile "cattle camps," the men lived largely by drinking the milk and blood of their herds, supplemented by the sorghum beer that the women sometimes brought when they visited. Not only did cattle add animal products to the Karimojong diet, but they provided insurance against low sorghum yields. In brief, livestock help people cope with risky environments.

CHAPTER 7 Culture and Nature: Interacting with the Environment

Another advantage of keeping livestock is their mobility. Not only do animals store meat on the hoof, but they also can be traded or sold to neighboring peoples. Herds can be moved to areas where the pasture is most lush or where the water supply is abundant. People can move their herds and themselves away from neighbors who have grown too aggressive. In some regions, like Africa's Sahara or Central Asia's ancient Silk Road, caravans of camels moved products produced in one place across hundreds of miles of relatively barren land, where they were traded or sold. Two thousand years ago, the elite of the Roman Empire enjoyed the translucent, flimsy garments made from Chinese silk and transported across Asia. The Romans had no idea that the fine fibers came from larval stage of an insect we call the silk moth. All along the cold, arid route were trading stations and towns where traders were serviced and where products were sold to be transported and sold again at the next station or town.

Aridity, temperature, short growing seasons, and other ecological and climatic factors go a long way toward explaining why pastoralists live where and how they do. However, the natural environment does not totally explain the geographic distribution of pastoral peoples. Some herders live in areas where the environment can support crops, and they certainly know how to cultivate the soil, but they choose not to grow crops. Many decades ago, British anthropologists defined a culture area known as the "East African cattle complex." In this complex, found throughout the East African savannas, cattle are more than an ordinary source of food. The East African man loves his cattle like some North Americans love their SUVs and minivans. Cattle represent wealth and manliness. They are the source of prestige, influence in tribal affairs, and bridewealth for wives. When sacrificed ritually, cattle are religious symbols and are the source of blessings from the ancestors and gods.

The cattle-herding Maasai of Kenya and Tanzania are a famous example of the East African cattle complex. In some parts of Maasai territory, cultivation is possible; in fact, most Maasai neighbors combine cattle herding with cultivation of sorghum and other crops. However, the proud Maasai look down on cultivation because their cattle represent wealth and are the main symbol of their cultural identity relative to their neighbors. Maasai, therefore, live largely off the products of their cattle—blood, milk, meat, curds—and trade with their neighbors for cultivated foods. The reasons so many Maasai continue their pastoral way of life are, therefore, "cultural" as well as "ecological." Their pastoral way of life helps define their cultural identity relative to neighboring peoples.

Nomadic pastoralists move their herds and themselves to areas of fresh pasture, usually following seasonal variations in rainfall and heat. The Massai of Kenya and Tanzania are among the most famous African cattle herders.

CONCEPT REVIEW: Major Forms of Preindustrial Adaptations and Their Cultural Consequences

Form of Adaptation	Food Acquired by Means of	Basic Organization of Communities	Rights to Resources	Internal Differentiation
Hunting/gathering	Collection/gathering of wild plants; hunting of animals; sometimes fishing	Small, mobile bands of 10–50, usually varying in size according to season	Flexible access to resources over large territories	Division of labor based on sex and age; social equality based on sharing
Horticulture	Cultivation of crops using hand tools and mainly human muscle power	Scattered hamlets or villages of 100 or more, largely but variably sedentary	Ownership of land and productive resources by kin groups and/or residential groups	Variable social differentiation, but little specialization and inequality
Intensive agriculture	Cultivation of crops with animal-powered plows or other means of using land intensively	Central administrative places, with cities and towns surrounded by rural "peasant" communities	Rights vested in or controlled by multilevel administrative officials responsible to the "state"	Craft and service specialization with social distinctions and major inequalities
Pastoralism	Tending of livestock that provide products (meat, milk, hides, wool) to eat, trade, and sell	Seasonally nomadic living units of varying size and composition	Grazing rights based on membership in families, kin groups, or the tribe itself	Variably complex differentiation based on age, sex, and often hereditary distinctions

The main benefit of pastoralism is that it allows large numbers of people to live well in regions unsuitable or marginal for farming. It therefore is informative to compare how most herders raise and feed livestock with how livestock are raised and fattened in nations with an industrialized food system. Pastoral peoples might teach the world that livestock are most efficiently used as converters of inedible plants into edible meat and other animal products. If you feed foods that people can eat to livestock, you lose most of the energy, vitamins, and protein to the bodily functions of the animal.

Yet consider livestock use in North America and other nations where agricultural production is mechanized. In such nations, government policies provide subsidies to certain farmers, high yields produce an excess of low-priced agricultural commodities, and most citizens have little knowledge of livestock (what farm animal has life stages called *gilt* and *shoat?*) or about how their food is produced. In North America, most soybeans and corn are grown as fodder for cattle, pigs, and fowl. When you eat a pound of flesh, indirectly you consume several pounds of corn and soy. You also consume (and pay for) the energy used to grow and process the corn and soy into animal fodder. You support the industries that produce the fertilizers, herbicides, and insecticides used to produce the crops that make grocery-bought meats so tender and juicy—that is, so fatty.

Nature and Culture in Preindustrial Times

In this chapter, we have synthesized an enormous amount of information, although we have not covered many complications and exceptions because of space limitations. Recognizing these, we emphasize one major point: *the ways a people harness the resources and cope with the problems of living in a particular environment are important influences on many dimensions of the group's culture.* (See the Concept Review for a summary of these influences.)

Just how important these "influences" are, of course, is debatable, as the theoretical approaches known as scientific and humanistic illustrate (see Chapter 5). Nonetheless, few anthropologists question the following generalizations about the relationship between the main forms of human interaction with nature and cultural systems:

▪ In most environments, foraging is most efficient when people live in small, seasonally mobile groups that maintain flexible rights to the natural resources of large territories.

- Horticultural people settle in hamlets or villages in which land and other productive resources are owned by families or other kinship or residential groups.
- Intensive agriculture resulted in the development of towns and cities occupied by elites and specialists and surrounded by rural peasant communities that contribute labor, tribute, and/or tax to support the government and public projects.
- Pastoral peoples are seasonally nomadic, with grazing rights to pasture lands vested in families or other kin groups or in the tribe as a whole.

In future chapters, as we cover various aspects of culture, we sometimes discuss the ways in which human–environment interactions affect family life, gender relationships, political organization, and other dimensions of cultural systems.

Industrialism

Thus far, we have focused on preindustrial peoples. Before the domestication of animals and the development of plow farming in parts of Asia, Africa, and Europe, humans used their own muscle power and hand tools to interact with their environments. Once intensive agriculture developed in some regions, farmers took advantage of the muscle power of their cattle, oxen, horses, and other livestock. In addition using their own energy to do agricultural work, humans worked their livestock to acquire additional energy. Notice that both these energy sources were living organisms. Another source of energy was dead trees (wood), which provided fuel for warmth and cooking, but those trees had died pretty recently.

Industrialism is the most recent—although not necessarily the final—major way in which humans interact with nature. Industrialism shelters the world's more affluent persons from the environment and provides them with their means of survival without them having to engage nature directly—except under tightly controlled conditions like sea cruises, hunting trips, and fishing vacations. Heating and air conditioning keep us warm or cool indoors, and we no longer need to butcher our own meat or gather firewood for cooking. Machines and the energy needed to power them substitute for human labor, allowing people who 300 years ago would have been producing food, wood, pottery, metals, and other material things to find other jobs in factories and services. In fact, one of the hallmarks of industrialization is that few people work in activities that extract natural resources like farming, fishing, lumbering, and mining. This is a new condition in human history.

Energy and Society

The essence of industrialism is that nonliving resources supply the overwhelming amount of energy that humans use to satisfy their material needs and wants. Industrialization began in Great Britain in the late 1700s and in the next several decades spread to the rest of Europe and North America. At first, British textile mills (and later those in New England) were powered by falling water. Around 1800, efficient ways were found to burn coal to produce compressed steam, which powered looms that could turn out textiles of cotton and wool in massive quantities. Later, people figured out ways to harness the energy stored in oil and natural gas.

There is a reason that coal, oil, and natural gas are called *fossil fuels*—each of these energy sources derives ultimately from long-dead plants and animals. While alive, these organisms took in carbon from the atmosphere, concentrating it in their bodies, where most of it still exists in the form of mineral deposits or natural gas released by decay. Once combusted, coal, oil, and natural gas release enormous quantities of energy. Physicists often say that energy is the capacity to do work. With vast quantities of energy, vast quantities of "work" can be done—thanks to machinery and fossil fuels more than to human work. Therefore, vast quantities of products can be manufactured. Electricity generated from coal- or oil-fired power plants, falling water (hydroelectric), and most recently nuclear sources provides power for private industries and private homes. In the long time frame of human prehistory and history, these are all very recent developments, no matter how normal they seem to people alive today.

In the 1940s, the neoevolutionist Leslie White (Chapter 6) theorized that energy capture is the most important factor in powering cultural change. Whether White was correct or not, some numbers he would find important are worth mentioning. Kilowatt hours are one measure of power, or the rate at which energy is converted to work; we use it here merely for comparison. Every week, the muscles of a man who is fairly fit can generate about 3 kilowatt hours of power. A gallon of gasoline contains about 12.3 kilowatt hours of power, which is equivalent to about 4 weeks of human muscle power. If gas costs $3.50 per gallon, then $3.50 buys about 4 weeks of equivalent human power.

In terms of ability to get work done without having to do it with our own muscle power, think of energy from fossil fuels as comparable to the human power that slaves provided to their "masters." One slave provided power (work), two slaves about twice as much power, and so on. Metaphorically, fossil fuels are our *energy slaves*: the energy output of $3.50 worth of gasoline is equivalent to having one slave working for us for 4 weeks.

Except during periodic energy crises, citizens of industrialized nation-states take the energy derived from fossil fuels for granted, seldom thinking about what happens when they turn on light switches, car engines, air conditioners, and stoves. When the global price of crude oil rises to over $100 per barrel, we become aware of the monetary costs of energy. Although we might complain about oil-producing countries and oil companies, we continue to pay at the pump even though we are sure "they" are gouging us. Energy to move around as we wish and to heat and cool our living space is so important that we usually give up something else if its price increases.

But fossil fuels actually are cheap, contrary to popular opinion. If you drink bottled water, you pay more per gallon to slake your thirst than you do to power your car when the price of gasoline skyrockets to $4.00 per gallon. Giving up bottled water will help you weather the next energy crisis—and save the oil used to manufacture the container.

Consequences of Industrialism

Acquiring energy from fossil fuels was the key development of the **Industrial Revolution**. It was more than just a revolution in how products were made. As just one component of the dramatic consequences for human life, consider what happened to food production and distribution. As factories developed, over time more and more people migrated to cities to work for wages. Urban factory workers and their families needed food, and industrial products had to be moved around, so roads and transportation networks became more extensive. Markets expanded to supply food to city people and factory products like clothing and tools to farmers. Some farmers out in the countryside continued to grow their own food but eventually most farmers specialized in selling food to others. The more farmers can produce, the more they can sell, so farmers were motivated to invest in technology that made their land more productive. By the early twentieth century new companies specialized in supplying the demands of farmers for equipment (e.g., tractors), chemicals (e.g., fertilizers, insecticides), water (e.g., pumps), and similar products. By the mid–twentieth century, *factory farming* was common in the developed world: with very little labor, a factory farmer could produce enough to supply food for 20 or 30 nonfarmers. In 2010, that ratio was closer to 50.

This very brief summary is only one aspect of the changes brought about by the Industrial Revolution. Because most people take their lifestyle for granted, think about just a few implications of industrialism for your life. Most of our readers would go hungry or even starve without supermarkets or some other kind of retail outlets that used to be called *grocery stores*. Even if you know how to hunt, fish, and garden, you probably don't have access to enough land to support yourself. Most likely, your individual workday is (or someday will be) tightly scheduled. The same applies to your week—but at least there's the weekend. Perhaps you think you are "burning up" when you go outside into 95-degree heat, and "freezing" if your living space goes down to 55 degrees. If you are not already a homeowner, someday you hope to become one. You will feel lucky to have your own place and probably do not know that most people in history have had access to a place to live without having to buy it at all. You are far more likely to have one or two children than six or seven. Your family size won't matter much because you don't need children to help around the farm, and you trust that Social Security and other forms of public assistance will still be there when you retire. Chances are you will live long after your retirement, at least if you have enough discipline to control your diet and exercise more often.

If none of this seems like the result of a "revolution," contrast how we live with the ethnographic examples of foragers, farmers, and pastoralists described earlier in this chapter. Remember also that industrialism has lasted only about two and half centuries.

Industrial technology opened up all kinds of possibilities for humanity. It has improved the material living standards of two to three billion people in the last two or so centuries. Like other ways of extracting nature's resources, industrialism has social and cultural consequences. Like the others, it is not free of costs.

Transportation provides an example of these "possibilities" and "costs." By the mid-1800s, steam

Industrial Revolution Process by which fossil fuels provide most of the energy used in production, dramatically increasing the quantity of products that can be produced.

engines powered the locomotives that made train transportation both rapid and cheap. One cost of this progress was that most wagon makers had to find new ways of making a living. Trains greatly facilitated the settlement of the American West. Box cars moved western products east, and vice versa, helping integrate the American economy and eventually forming a single market where the beef from cattle grazed in Colorado sold at about the same price in Oregon and North Carolina.

Later, when a way was found to manufacture internal combustion engines powered by gasoline, automobiles were invented. After Henry Ford introduced the assembly-line production of automobiles in the early decades of the twentieth century, increased efficiency of production led the costs of autos to fall so much that ordinary families could afford one. In the United States in the 1950s, the federal government responded by constructing tens of thousands of miles of new roads, including the interstate highway system. By using income tax revenues to do so, the feds subsidized the auto industry and car owners. (This is ironic given the present widespread outcry over proposed federal and state subsidies for public transportation!) Passenger travel and freight transport by rail declined as a consequence, even though trains are far more efficient in energy terms than cars and trucks. By the late 1900s, middle-class families could afford two, three, or more motor vehicles, including the minivans that facilitated hauling kids and purchases.

In the last half of the twentieth century, two new methods of freight transportation grew rapidly: trucks and container ships. Both modes of transporting freight had worldwide consequences and caused rapid changes in how millions of people live their everyday lives.

The long-haul trucking industry moves products rapidly and cheaply from factories and fields to retail stores and supermarkets. In January, residents of Ontario and North Dakota enjoy produce grown on irrigated mega-farms in Southern California's Imperial Valley and tomato fields in northwest Mexico. Should global energy prices increase significantly, increased costs for growing and transporting the veggies will rise, and northerners will pay more for southern foods. The same will occur should the federal government eliminate the huge subsidies it now pays for the irrigation water necessary to transform the Imperial Valley from semidesert to agricultural paradise. If you like fresh fruits and vegetables in January, stop complaining about the feds subsidizing western farmers—you benefit also.

By lowering costs of transporting freight to overseas destinations, giant container ships helped integrate the *global* economy. The places and people that produce manufactured commodities are different places and people than where the company is registered and where most of its stockholders reside. Of course, profits are the reason so many manufacturing jobs have moved "offshore." If production and shipping costs are low enough, then market forces encourage companies to move at least some manufacturing operations to low-cost regions. It is cost-effective for American companies to ship computer components to China where Chinese workers assemble them into a Mac or PC, then send them back to the United States. Many computer parts cross the Pacific Ocean *twice*, so companies pay two-way shipping costs. But computer makers still make more profits and consumers enjoy lower costs than if computers were assembled by American or Canadian workers. Should global energy prices rise enough, then higher shipping costs will curtail or slow the globalization of production. The consequences of such a slowdown would be global and serious.

Most people explain the relocation of assembly and other production facilities to newly industrialized countries in Asia and other continents by low labor costs. Labor is inexpensive in countries like China and India for several reasons. They have millions of people migrating to cities looking for factory jobs, so the labor supply is plentiful. (Chinese factories, though, began complaining about "labor shortages" in 2012.) For many reasons, most unskilled labor is not organized by unions. One reason is that governments and local managers want to keep wages low so their workforce is competitive in the global labor market. Another is that there are plenty of unskilled laborers to accept work that others refuse because of its low wages.

Also, India and China are often said to be overpopulated, meaning they allegedly have too many to be supported by their nation's resource and economic base. Globalization of factory production provides their people with more resources—mainly with jobs, which have become the "resources" (no longer "natural" ones) that most people in industrialized nations need for survival and well-being. Conversely, factory globalization has taken away resource from many factory workers in North America, Japan, and Europe. At the same time, globalization indirectly has increased the resources for consumers in the wealthier nations whose corporations have exported jobs overseas. If you pay much lower prices for electronics, clothing, shoes, and a host of other goods because they are produced in countries with low wages, your money will buy more commodities. In effect, you now have more "resources."

Globalization and the Environment

Low labor costs alone do not account for the explosive growth of what some call the *global factory* since the 1980s. Other costs of offshore production for corporations also are low, because factory health and safety and environmental regulations are more relaxed than in the corporations' home countries. When European, Japanese, North American, and Australian governments passed serious environmental regulations in the 1970s, they increased the production costs of their industries. But to the extent that governments applied the regulations evenly and fairly, no particular company in an industry received a competitive advantage. Companies adjusted by lowering expenses in other areas and increasing what they charged consumers. They "adapted" to the new "regulatory environment."

However, few consistent, enforceable environmental regulations operate at the global level. This fact leads to global environmental problems that are very difficult to solve, because there is no global organization to solve them.

Most scientists and ordinary citizens recognize the heavy environmental costs of industrialization. Natural resources are harvested from all over the world to supply raw materials for factories. Extracting resources leads to depletions, landscape destruction, soil erosion, and other deteriorations of environmental quality. As a by-product of burning fossil fuels like coal and oil, factories pollute the air, making government regulation mandatory for environmental and health reasons. Coal mines dig out earth and rock to uncover seams of coal. If there were not laws to curtail them, factories would release toxic chemicals that pollute waterways. Modern agriculture usually is more factory-like than farm-like, relying on machinery for most operations and consequently consuming more total energy than the food energy of the products. Runoff from agricultural chemicals and modern livestock feedlots pollutes rivers and streams.

These people in Guangdong province of China are manufacturing toys that accompany McDonalds' Happy Meals. As globalization provides resources ("jobs") for some workers in the world economy, it removes resources from other workers. What, therefore, are the net benefits of the globalization of factory production?

CHAPTER 7 Culture and Nature: Interacting with the Environment 159

GLOBAL CHALLENGES AND OPPORTUNITIES
Who Should Pay to Reduce Global Warming?

As these cement factories illustrate, China's rapid growth in the last 30 years has led to serious pollution of air and water.

One environmental problem has been recognized widely only in the past 20 years: climate change, most of which is caused by global warming. Combustion of fossil fuels releases carbon dioxide into the atmosphere, which traps solar radiation, leading to global warming, changes in rainfall patterns, and other results. Some believe that climate change is not a serious problem and, even if it is, doubt that human activities are its main causes. (Cattle do indeed "pass" methane, a potent global warming gas.) However, there is very broad consensus among credible scientists that climate change is real and is a *global* problem, meaning that the carbon dioxide that one country puts into the atmosphere harms or will harm all other countries. Global warming therefore requires international agreements and cooperation.

However, agreements at the global level are difficult to reach. In July 2009, there was a meeting in Italy of the 17 nations that generate about 80 percent of Earth's greenhouse gases. In a draft agreement, the wealthiest eight nations offered to reduce their emissions by 80 percent by 2050, primarily by means of government mandates and regulations. Unfortunately, India, China, Brazil, Mexico, and the other less developed countries refused to agree to even the indefinite goal of reducing their emissions "significantly" to achieve a worldwide greenhouse gas reduction of 50 percent by 2050. In December 2009, representatives of 193 nations met in Denmark, aiming to reach a binding agreement on reductions in greenhouse gas emissions. Environmentalists hoped countries would agree to cut emissions by a certain percentage, depending on their level of development, by a given date like 2030 or 2050. However, there was no international agreement because countries could not agree on issues like the scale of reduction, the timetable, or financing. Subsequent meetings were equally unfruitful.

Why haven't international agreements about climate change been made? Greenhouse gases are "public bads." It does no good if richer countries cut their emissions by half if the less rich nations continue to increase their emissions of greenhouse gases. Citizens of richer nations would pay the costs of reducing their emissions only to have their efforts undone by other nations that refused to agree. By 2008, China emitted more carbon dioxide and other greenhouse gases than the United States, becoming the world's largest single contributor to global warming (although not in per capita terms). Without cooperation from the Chinese and other emerging industrial economies, any agreement on global warming would not matter. An agreement between all major emitters is necessary. Why don't the leaders of emerging nations sign agreements that are in the global interest?

Political leaders in some countries claim—understandably and truthfully—that industrialization in the West historically caused the most depletions and pollutions and brought the planet dangerously close to irreversible climate change. Among large nations that are growing rapidly are Brazil, Russia, India, and China, which are commonly referred

Government regulation of mines, industries, farms, auto emissions, and the like have significantly reduced many environmental impacts in Japan, Australia, North America, and Europe. If it were not for these regulations and their enforcement, the environmental consequences of industrialism would certainly be worse than they are. Anyone who lived in the Los Angeles basin in the 1960s and 1970s has experienced these consequences. Anyone living today in Beijing, Rio de Janeiro, or Mumbai is experiencing them now.

Why don't farms and businesses just act in environmentally responsible ways? Some do, of course. However, in a market economy, if an environmentally responsible company voluntarily decides to clean up its wastes and reduce its harmful emissions, then that company will suffer in the competitive marketplace to as BRIC nations. Why should the citizens of BRIC countries be forced to pay the costs of damage already done by the countries that became wealthy by not attending to the environmental damage their economies caused? Why should their people have to sacrifice their recently rising standards of living to protect the global environment? Their citizens still consume far less than those of the rich nations and contribute less to climate change than the developed world.

Leaders of many newly industrialized countries also point out that European and North American companies have relocated some of their most hazardous and polluting industries in poorer regions in order to avoid costly government regulations in their home countries. Western companies and governments therefore are responsible for part of the pollution generated by global factories that produce commodities for export to highly developed countries. The richer countries export some of their dirtiest industries to the newly industrialized countries and then expect those countries to clean up their pollution and reduce their harmful emissions. Consumers in Europe and North America also benefit from the global factory by significantly lowered retail prices of clothing, shoes, consumer electronics, and other offshore products. Therefore, consumers in the developed countries should do their part to reduce global warming by paying the higher prices that tighter and enforced regulations would bring.

These are some of the arguments of those who think it is unreasonable for newly industrialized nations to pay the costs of reducing greenhouse gas emissions. Richer countries point out that there is nothing they can do about their past environmental records and that cooperation from all nations is needed. The issue is one of equity: which countries should reduce their emissions by how much?

Perhaps it will help if people realize that there are nations whose people contribute almost nothing to climate change, yet will be most affected by them. Two such impacts are rises in sea levels and changes in temperature and precipitation.

Thermal expansion of sea water and melting glaciers led to a rise in sea level of about 2 inches between 1993 and 2009. This rise appears to be accelerating as glaciers melt faster. By 2100, sea levels are likely to increase by 1 to 6 feet, depending on the rate of glacial melting. North Americans hear that low-lying areas like southern Louisiana and much of Florida will be seriously affected by land losses and storm surges if sea levels rise only 8 to 20 inches in this century. This would be a tragedy that should be avoided. But theoretically most Florida and Louisiana people can be relocated. The United States now emits about one-fourth of the world's greenhouse gases. Factories in low-lying Bangladesh produce a lot of clothing for export. Yet Bangladesh contributes only about 0.1 percent of all greenhouse gases. A sea-level rise of 20 inches would inundate the living space of about 20 million mostly impoverished people. In densely populated Bangladesh, there are few other places for people to move. How will they cope with a global problem not of their own making?

Other regions would be even more affected by climate change. We seldom hear about the fate of Pacific island nations composed entirely of low atolls, such as Kiribati, Tuvalu, and the Republic of the Marshall Islands. The *highest* elevation of most atoll nations is around 20 to 30 feet. A significant rise in the sea level would flood most of their living spaces. Equally seriously, their staple crops, like taro (an edible root) and breadfruit (a tree crop), are intolerant of salt water and are already being killed as ocean water that lies just below the land surface reaches their roots through the permeable limestone. The coral reefs on which coral atoll people depend for fish are already affected by bleaching and acidification, which dissolves the calcium carbonate of shells and reefs. Again, atoll peoples contribute essentially nothing to climate change, but their lives may be most seriously affected.

because its production costs will rise. That would be economically foolish, and competitive markets do not reward this kind of foolishness.

Ever since factory production boomed in countries like Brazil, India, and China, their citizens also experienced the negative environmental effects of factory production. Consider the People's Republic of China. With several hundred million rural peasants and relatively low factory wage rates, China is still not a rich country. China has a huge population of 1.4 billion (four times that of the United States), a government that seems committed to development, a cultural tradition infused with a work ethic, and a large pool of workers. In August 2010, China surpassed Japan as the world's second-largest economy, now trailing only the United States.

China's industries have grown so rapidly since the 1980s that it now has serious air and water pollution problems. China uses about half of the world's cement for its new roads and buildings. It imports about half of the world's iron ore, which it manufactures into steel for use in construction and in products like motor vehicles and ships. Tap water is unsafe to drink in most large Chinese cities. Three-fourths of China's energy comes from coal, burnt to heat Chinese homes and combusted to produce electricity in power plants. According to the World Bank in 2007, China had 16 of the world's 20 most polluted cities. One day in January 2013, the air pollution index in Beijing was 755—measured on a scale of 0 to 500! In late 2012, 16,000 dead pigs were found floating in the river that supplies water to Shanghai, the PRC's largest city. For 2010, a ministry of the Chinese government estimated the monetary cost of the environmental damage caused by rapid industrialization at $230 billion, which is 3.5 percent of China's gross domestic product.

China and India together have about 2.6 billion people, or 40 percent of the world's total population. When countries this large pollute, other countries notice because some kinds of pollution easily cross national borders. Air pollution from Chinese factories wafts over to the Koreas and Japan. Sometimes, upper atmospheric winds carry the sulphur dioxide from China's coal-burning clear over to North America's west coast. Countries like India and China are experiencing car booms, which raises global oil prices and hastens the time when the price of oil will rise high enough to really threaten the standard of living of the middle class in many countries. The newly industrializing regions also contribute significantly to global warming, raising world issues such as who should pay most to reduce greenhouse gas emissions in the interest of future generations. Globalization Challenges and Opportunities discusses this issue.

Rising sea levels caused by global warming receive a lot of media attention because coastal and island people might be affected most seriously. However, greenhouse gases alter worldwide precipitation patterns as well as temperature. Climate scientists cannot predict the severity or location of the most serious impacts. Some regions will experience a more favorable climate for crop production than at present because the length of growing seasons will increase, or more rainfall will occur. Some climate models suggest that the tropics and subtropics will experience the most severe agricultural impacts. About 3 or 4 billion people still get most of their food from subsistence farming. For many of them, global warming will reduce their ability to support themselves.

Because future net impacts on the food supply will be mixed and thus cannot be predicted, the recent past might help estimate the future. A 2011 statistical study in the prestigious academic journal *Science* studied the impact of climate change (including the effects of both temperature and precipitation) on net yields of wheat, rice, corn, and soy between 1980 and 2008. These four crops together account for around three-fourths of the calories consumed by humans on the planet, either as direct consumption or through the products of animals fed on crops rather than pasture. Controlling for fertilization and other technological inputs, in these 28 years global wheat production declined by 5.5 percent and maize production by 3.8 percent. The impacts on soy and rice production varied by country, with no global generalization possible.

The advantage the recently industrializing nations have is their ability to deliver products to the global market at extremely low costs. If they do not do so, other countries will. Viewed in this context, serious and enforced environmental and safety regulations like those adopted by the present rich countries would threaten the constant creation of new jobs and the rise in consumption. Should China impose costly regulations on its factories, prices for their products would rise, and the continual growth of Chinese employment and living standards would be threatened. International corporations will outsource factory work somewhere else. The Chinese government is legitimately worried about the impacts on social stability and what Chinese leaders call a "harmonious society." China has an active environmental movement, and its national government is making efforts to clean up its manufacturing, but officials at the local level too often profit by not enforcing regulations.

All the above is not meant to "excuse" Brazil, India, China, and other rapidly industrializing nations for their inability or unwillingness to pass and enforce environmental regulations. Rather, our point is to propose that environmentalists and self-righteous citizens in the more affluent parts of the world make more of an effort to "grasp the native's point of view," to quote Bronislaw Malinowski (Chapter 4). How much harm would be done to the ordinary citizens of the newly industrializing nations if their production costs rose substantially? China already is offshoring some of its own production to still poorer nations, who in their turn are likely to contribute to global environmental problems. If the Chinese central government should lose control because the country cannot provide jobs for 200 or 300 million people, what would be the global consequences? If the richer nations enjoy cleaner air and water partly because they shipped some of their most polluting industries overseas, what are their obligations in regard to environmental protection in the overseas nations?

One consequence of globalization is the globalization of consequences. When industrial production globalizes, so do its negative environmental impacts. We began this chapter by saying that two of the most important dimensions of human–nature interactions are extracting resources and handling environmental problems. Industrialism extracts resources from all over the world, and these resources are bought and sold on the world market. The scale of this buying and selling is new.

Global industrialism has created environmental problems that are worldwide in scale. That also is new. In the last few decades, new international institutions have been created, such as the Organization of American States, the Association of Southeast Asian Nations, the Organization of African Unity, and the European Union. Nations have signed agreements that promote free trade, such as the North American Free Trade Agreement. Members of the European Union buy and sell to one another using a new currency, the euro. Countries seem to find ways of negotiating and enforcing agreements when it is in their economic interest. Perhaps it's time to do the same for the global environment.

SUMMARY

1. **Discuss how relationships between humans and the environment differ from those of other animals.** Humans adjust to their environments by cultural changes in technology and organization more than by changes in their genes. One important way people interact with nature is by productive activities, which require labor, technology, natural resources, and group organization. People also find ways to cope with the problems of living in a particular habitat, which occurs mainly by means of group-level accumulated experiences.

2. **Describe hunting and gathering and analyze its major impacts on cultures.** Hunters and gatherers, or foragers, live exclusively from the wild plants and animals available in their habitats. Foragers organized their activities so that at the proper season, they could be at the places where wild foods were naturally available. Most exhibited the following characteristics: (1) a division of labor based mainly on sex and age; (2) high mobility; (3) congregation and dispersal of groups, usually based on seasonal changes; (4) small living groups or bands; (5) reciprocal sharing; and (6) loose and flexible rights to the resources of a given territory. These features are well illustrated by cultures such as the Hadzabe, Shoshone, and Ju/'hoansi. However, there are many exceptions to these generalizations such as fishers of the Northwest Coast and the Cheyenne of the Great Plains.

3. **Describe horticulture and analyze its major consequences for cultures.** Domestication increases the productivity of an environment by planting and cultivating selected plants (crops) and taming and breeding certain animals (livestock). Horticulture is one form of plant domestication. Horticulturalists use only hand tools in planting, cultivating, and harvesting their plots or gardens, as illustrated by shifting cultivation and dry land gardening. Horticulture produces more food per acre than foraging, and it requires that people make a labor investment in particular pieces of land (their plots). Broadly, this lead to two cultural consequences: (1) people remained in one place for a long time (sedentism) and the size of their settlements increased (villages), and (2) particular families established their own claims to certain pieces of land, producing cultural beliefs that land is the property of specific groups.

4. **Discuss how intensive agriculture led to the emergence of civilization.** Intensive agriculturalists use various methods to keep yields high, including fertilization and irrigation. Intensive farming eventually raised productivity enough that a single farm family was able to

produce a surplus over and above its own food needs. Out of this surplus potential a new form of culture, called *civilization*, arose in several regions of both the Old World and the New World. Supported by intensive agriculture, civilization changed human life profoundly, leading to new developments such as writing, specialization, huge architectural structures, roads, and familiar artistic traditions. But whether the class of peasants enjoyed very many of these benefits is doubtful.

5. **Discuss nomadic pastoralism and its benefits in certain environments.** Nomadic pastoralism is most beneficial in regions unsuitable for agriculture due to aridity, extreme temperature, or inadequate growing seasons for crops. In these kinds of habitats, herding offers several advantages. It allows people to convert indigestible grasses and other vegetation into edible flesh and dairy products. It reduces the risk of living in an unreliable environment, both because livestock provide a way of storing food on the hoof and because the food supply (herds) can be moved to more favorable places when times are hard.

6. **Analyze industrialization and how it affects human lives, globalization, and worldwide environmental problems.** Industrialism exploits the energy contained in fossil fuels like coal, oil, and natural gas. By vastly increasing the amount of energy available to humanity, industrialism transformed most aspects of human life, from the number of people working in extractive industries to family sizes. To reduce the costs of production, corporations in the richer nations relocated many factories overseas, providing jobs for citizens there and greatly impacting the work force and consumers in their own nations. Because of the globalization of production, environmental problems like water and air pollution and climate change have accelerated, generating international issues about which nations should bear the costs of environmental cleanup.

8 Exchange in Economic Systems

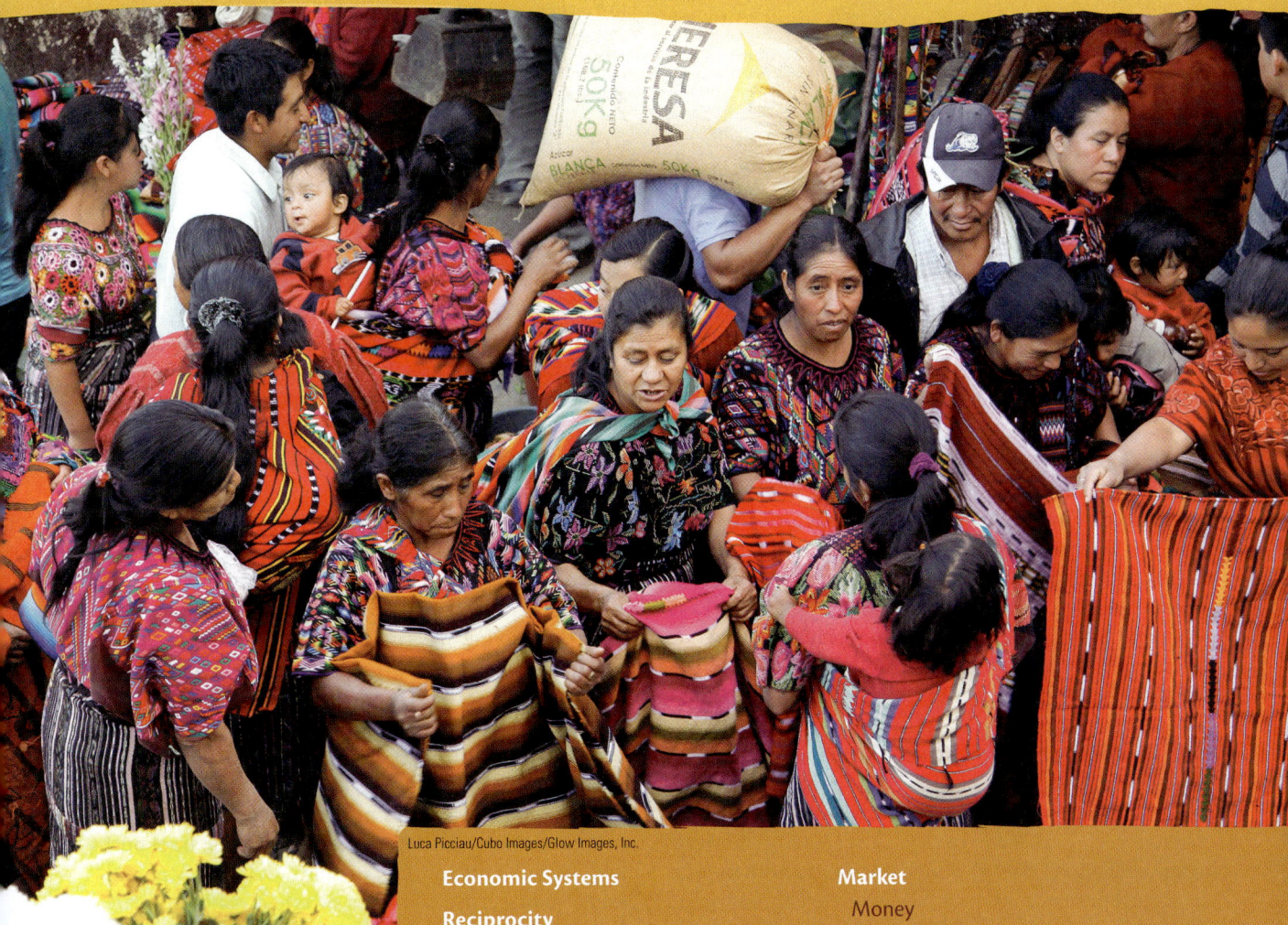

- **Economic Systems**
- **Reciprocity**
  - Generalized Reciprocity
  - Balanced Reciprocity
  - Negative Reciprocity
  - Reciprocity and Social Distance
- **Redistribution**
- **Market**
  - Money
  - Market Exchange
  - Market Economies and Capitalism
  - Productivity
- **Globalization and Markets**

Peasants and other classes who sell products at market places like this one in Chici, Guatemala, make money, but they do not depend on market sales for their entire livelihood. In this and other ways, their lives contrast with those of people who live and work in countries with fully market economies.

LEARNING OBJECTIVES

After reading this chapter, you should be able to

1 **DESCRIBE** the three main forms of exchange in economic systems.

2 **ANALYZE** how the form of reciprocity between people varies with social distance.

3 **DISCUSS** the relationship between redistribution and political organization.

4 **DESCRIBE** the properties of money.

5 **DISCUSS** the distinction between market exchange and market economies (capitalism) and the differences between neoliberalism and social welfare capitalism.

6 **DISCUSS** the globalization of markets and its impacts on workers, consumers, corporations, and cultural preservation.

East Liverpool is an Appalachian town of about 13,000 in southeast Ohio. The heading on its 2013 website is "The Pottery Capital of the World." Indeed, there used to be four dozen pottery factories here. Its workers made off-white, generic-looking coffee mugs for coffee shops and small diners as well dinnerware for households. Today, only two pottery factories remain in East Liverpool, which is about half its size in the 1950s. American pottery manufacturing globalized in recent decades, sending pottery jobs overseas to East Asia and other places. Many town residents now work in services at West Virginia casinos, just across the Ohio River, at the airport in Pittsburgh, Pennsylvania, or for the local school district.

However, pottery is making a small comeback in East Liverpool. On June 12, 2012, Starbucks began marketing a new $10 coffee mug labeled with the word "Indivisible." It is made by East Liverpool's American Mug and Stein Company, which was able to keep its four specialist pottery makers and even hire eight new ones. The workers at American Mug produced 20,000 mugs for Starbucks, casting the mugs in molds, firing them in a 30-year old kiln, and finishing and glazing them by hand. Despite its back-in-the-day technology, American Mug has two advantages over Chinese factories: it can supply the mugs to Starbucks in only 4 days, and Chinese suppliers usually require orders in the hundreds of thousands, potentially sticking Starbucks with a large inventory of unsold mugs.

Does the "rebirth" of pottery making in East Liverpool illustrate reverse globalization? No, because when Starbucks' sells the mugs, the proceeds support Starbuck's Create Jobs for USA Fund, which aids small businesses. Starbucks coffee shops are not selling American Mugs' mugs to make profit for Starbucks. Its motivation is a mixture of altruism and public relations. Fortunately for Starbucks, as a corporation, most of its business is more profit centered. If it weren't, there would be no Starbucks.

Economic Systems

The word *economics* has many meanings, but here we use its everyday meaning: economics is how people make their living by satisfying needs and wants. At the societal level, three processes are involved in making a living. First, people work and use technology to transform nature's resources into useful *products*. In modern *postindustrial* economies, most people do not produce any tangible (material) product but work in *services*. For example, they produce or process or transmit information, sell something to someone else, post blogs, nurse or doctor their patients, wait on restaurant diners, manage the activities of others, and so forth. Service industry workers do not produce any material products with their own labor, but their jobs allow them to earn money that satisfies their own material wants and needs.

Second, someone *consumes* the products. We consume material products by eating them, living in them, driving them, wearing them, and so forth. Many material products are valued for their practical use: food nourishes, houses shelter, motor vehicles transport, and clothes cover. In addition to their material usefulness, many products also are valued *symbolically.* For example, in addition to their practical value, food choices may express identity, houses demonstrate wealth, motor vehicles show status, clothes flatter. These products send social messages about who we are as well as satisfying our material needs and wants. Many products and services are bought largely or entirely for their symbolic significance, such as jewelry, cosmetics, haircuts, athletic shoes, and sometimes club and fitness center memberships.

Third, between the time they are produced and consumed, many material products are *exchanged*. In economies like those of foragers or horticulturalists, often the producers and the consumers are the same people (usually, family members), but nonetheless exchange exists in these and in all economies. In modern market economies, the producers and the consumers are nearly always different people or groups, so practically every product is exchanged (marketed) before it is consumed. Most people make their living by working for firms or public agencies in exchange for money in wages, salaries, tips, commissions, and the like.

In market economies, most products are produced entirely for sale. Once the value (money) acquired from the market exchange has been gained, the companies or persons who produce and sell the product have little further economic interest in it, except insofar as its quality affects future sales or reputation. However, markets are only one way of organizing exchange. In subsistence-based economies, families or other kinds of kinship groups produce mainly for their own needs, not for sale on the market. And rather than exchanges based on supply, demand, and prices, exchanges are organized around other principles.

Anthropologists usually classify various forms of exchange into three major modes or types:

- **Reciprocity**, in which individuals or groups pass products back and forth, with the aim of helping someone in need by sharing with him or her; creating, maintaining, or strengthening social relationships; or obtaining products made by others for oneself.
- **Redistribution**, in which the members of an organized group contribute products or money to a common pool or fund that is divided (reallocated) among the group as a whole by a central authority.
- **Market**, in which products are produced and sold for money, which in turn is used to purchase other products, with the ultimate goal of acquiring more money that can be spent on more products, or saved, or invested.

The Concept Review illustrates the three forms of exchanges. Notice the key differences. With reciprocity, generally speaking products pass between individuals who already know one another or wish to establish or strengthen a relationship. With redistribution, all contributors to a central pool or fund may or may not have relationships with one another, but all have a relationship to the authorities who collect and reallocate. With markets, no party needs to know any of the others outside the context of the exchange itself. With some qualifications, market transactions are *impersonal*, and one person's money is worth the same as anyone else's.

Most products (including land and labor) are exchanged through the market mode in modern industrial economies, but reciprocity and redistribution also exist. Examples of reciprocity are various gifts we give and receive on holidays, birthdays, weddings, baby showers, and other culturally special occasions. If you are employed, every pay period you participate in redistribution because federal, state, and local governments collect a portion of your wage or salary as taxes. They spend these public monies on public purposes, like wars or roads, or transfer money to other members of society, like the elderly, the poor, and subsidies for corporations.

All these exchange forms thus exist in modern societies, but not all preindustrial peoples have all three. Reciprocity in one form or another occurs in all human populations. But redistribution implies a central leader(s) whose role(s) carries authority to organize the collection of resources from the group and to make decisions about how they will be reallocated. Redistribution, therefore, is an insignificant exchange mode in societies that lack strong leaders who make decisions on behalf of the group. The market mode of exchange requires money, private property, and certain other features that are absent in nonmarket economies.

Reciprocity

In subsistence-oriented economies such as those based on foraging, horticulture, and pastoralism, most families and households are capable of producing most of the food and other products they consume. That is,

---

reciprocity Exchange of products or objects between two or more individuals or groups.

redistribution Collection of products or money from an organized group or society, followed by a reallocation to the group by a central authority.

market Exchange by means of buying and selling, using money.

CONCEPT REVIEW: Three Forms of Exchange in Economic Systems

Reciprocity — Back-and-forth exchange of products, gifts, and objects; symbolizes relationships as well as satisfies material needs and wants.

Redistributions — Collection of products and valuables by a central authority, followed by distribution according to some normative or legal principle.

Market — Free exchange of products (P_1, P_2) and services (S_1, S_2) for money ($) at prices determined by impersonal forces of supply and demand.

most families are *potentially* self-sufficient in the sense that they own or have access to the land, labor, tools, and other resources necessary for survival.

However, in no known society are families, households, or other kinds of social groups self-sufficient *in fact*. Everywhere, such groups exchange products with other groups. Most anthropologists say this is because families and other groups need or want to maintain relationships with other families and groups, and exchange is necessary to create and sustain these relationships. For one thing, most groups need help from time to time, so they keep up relationships with others to increase long-term economic security. Other reasons include acquiring spouses, maintaining political ties, strengthening military alliances, and having new social contacts.

The form of exchange used for such purposes is *reciprocity,* defined as the transaction of objects without the use of money or other media of exchange. Reciprocity takes several forms, including sharing with those in need, providing hospitality, giving gifts, engaging in mutual feasting, and bartering. Various forms are motivated by different considerations and values, so anthropologists distinguish three forms of reciprocity: generalized, balanced, and negative.

Generalized Reciprocity

The defining feature of **generalized reciprocity** is that those who give objects do not expect the recipient to make a return at any definite time in the future. Generalized reciprocity occurs between individuals who are (or at least are normatively expected to be) emotionally attached to one another and therefore have an obligation to help one another on the basis of relative need. Parents who provide their children with shelter, food, vehicles, and college educations are practicing generalized reciprocity that sustains younger generations. Giving without expectation of definite return also should occur between parties to certain other kinds of social relationships, such as wives and husbands, siblings, and sometimes close friends. Other familiar forms include donating objects to Goodwill and Salvation Army and giving money to United Way or your alma mater. However, in these latter cases the possibility of taking tax deductions for your gift complicates the concept of generalized reciprocity.

---

generalized reciprocity Giving of products or service without expectation of a return of equal value at any definite future time.

Each member of this Inuit ("Eskimo") whaling crew will receive a share of the whale meat and blubber. Sharing the fruits of cooperative efforts is one form of generalized reciprocity.

Because it includes various forms of sharing with relatives and other people whom cultural norms define as close, generalized reciprocity is found in all societies. However, among some peoples it is the dominant form of exchange, meaning that more resources are distributed using this form than any other form.

For example, most hunter-gatherers expect their band mates to share food and be generous with their possessions, partly because most members of a band are relatives of some kind (see Chapter 7). Among the Ju/'hoansi, the band is a social group within which food sharing is culturally expected or even mandatory. Those who are stingy with possessions or who fail to share food with others are ridiculed or socially punished in some other way. Generalized reciprocity ensures an equitable—if not entirely equal—distribution of food among the band's families.

Balanced Reciprocity

In **balanced reciprocity**, products are transferred to the recipient and the donor expects a return in products of roughly equal value. Over the long run, the value of the products exchanged should be roughly equivalent. The return may be expected soon, or whenever the donor demands it, or by some specified time in the future. With generalized reciprocity, the giver continues to provide assistance even when the receiver is unable to return anything for a long time, if ever. With balanced reciprocity, the giver tries to apply some kind of sanction against the receiver if the latter does not reciprocate within the appropriate time period. Donors may become angry if there is no reciprocation, may complain or gossip to others, may try to force a return, or may suspend all relations until things of appropriate value are returned.

Although the value of the objects exchanged is supposed to be about equal, balanced reciprocity is characterized by the absence of bargaining between the parties. In some preindustrial economies, the exchange of objects without having to negotiate for each transaction frequently is organized by a special relationship between two individuals known as a *trade partnership.* Individuals of one tribe or village pair off with specific individuals (their "partners") from other regions with whom they establish long-lasting trade relationships.

For instance, in the Trobriand Islands off the eastern tip of the island of New Guinea, there was a form of balanced reciprocity called *wasi.* Residents of coastal villages traded fish for yams and other garden crops

balanced reciprocity Exchange of products or services considered to have roughly equal value; social interests or goals usually motivate the exchange.

CHAPTER 8 Exchange in Economic Systems 169

produced in the mountainous interior. The exchange was formalized: a coastal village paired off with an interior village, and within each village individuals formed trade partnerships. The rates at which garden produce was exchanged for fish were established by custom, so there was no haggling at any particular transaction.

In *wasi*, each trade partner received foods not readily available locally, so parties to the transaction gained a material benefit. In other cases, trade partnerships have social as well as material benefits. For example, the Ju/'hoansi have a gift exchange custom called *hxaro*. In hxaro, the gift exchange is delayed—those who receive an object are not expected to return anything for an indefinite and often long period of time. Hxaro partners rely on one another for mutual support in other contexts, such as when one partner asks to forage in the territory of another. The social relationship created and reinforced by hxaro matters more to people than the objects given and received.

In hxaro, gifts make friends and vice versa, illustrating that gifts have *symbolic value*. More generally, when two people exchange gifts, ideally both gain something more than the sum total of the economic worth of the objects. On your friend's birthday, instead of giving her earrings in exchange for a gift of about equal value on your own birthday, you both could save the cost of wrapping paper and cards by buying the objects yourselves. However, neither of you would gain the symbolic value added when the exchange of "objects" becomes an exchange of "gifts" on culturally appropriate occasions. As material symbols of good relations, gifts both create and sustain feelings of solidarity and relations of mutual aid between individuals and groups.

Gifts show that the giver has expended some resources and taken some trouble because she or he cares about the recipient. Perhaps this is one reason why so many people do not like giving or receiving cash or gift cards: cash and gift cards take too little effort, are too generic to be personal, and the nature of the gift does not express the character of the relationship. To many people, gifts of cash or cards dilute the symbolic value of the gift.

Gift exchange communicates warm feelings, perhaps even better than words, both because talk is cheap and because some of us never know the right words to say. Conversely, failure to present objects of the socially appropriate value also can communicate feelings, although less warm ones.

However, gifts are also used to create social bonds that are useful to the giver, and to obligate people from whom the giver wants something. Giving a gift tends to make someone feel indebted and therefore can be used to create an obligation to return a favor if not a material object. Political lobbyists and sales representatives know that balanced reciprocity can serve one's self-interest.

Among many preindustrial peoples, balanced reciprocity takes the form of mutual exchanges of gifts or invitations for political purposes. The Maring are a horticultural people of the mountainous interior of Papua New Guinea. In the 1960s, when Roy Rappaport worked among them, the Maring lived in settlements composed of clusters of kin groups. Each settlement engaged in periodic warfare with some of its neighbors. Unless a settlement was unusually large, its members formed a political alliance with one or more nearby settlements. When warfare occurred, the warriors of each settlement relied on their allies for military support and, in the case of defeat, for refuge.

An important expression of continued goodwill between allied settlements was periodic invitations to feasts, accompanied by exchanges of pigs and wealth objects. Every few years, whenever they accumulated enough pigs, the members of a settlement invited their allies to an enormous feast, appropriately called a *pig feast*. At the pig feast, which was attended by hundreds of people, allies brought large quantities of wealth objects to exchange and pay off debts; they consumed enormous quantities of pork provided by their hosts; they were on the lookout for potential spouses and sexual partners; and they aided the host settlement in the ceremonial dancing that the Maring believed ritually necessary for success in the fighting that soon occurred. The host group also used their pig feast to gauge the amount of military support they could expect from their allies: the more people who attended the feast, the more warriors the host settlement could put on the battleground. Later, the guests accumulated enough pigs to reciprocate by hosting a pig feast of their own.

Reciprocal feasting was essential to the military success and continued survival of a Maring community. Here, and among many other peoples, the back-and-forth flow of products, invitations and return invitations, and other forms of give-and-take are essential for well-being and even military survival.

In the contemporary world, too, balanced reciprocity in the form of foreign aid creates and sustains relationships between "communities"—in this example, between nations. In anthropological jargon, foreign aid seems like more of an example of generalized reciprocity conducted on a massive scale. However, to the extent that it influences relationships between donors and recipients it is more than "aid." American aid promotes political stability in another country (Egypt, Afghanistan and Egypt until August, 2013), maintains potential sites for military operations (Pakistan), and assists allies in warding off perceived or actual enemies (Israel, South Korea). Moreover, foreign aid is a relatively cheap way to look out for the interests of one's own nation. In a 2001 American survey about foreign aid, on average Americans believed that 20 percent of the U.S. federal budget went to foreign aid. The actual percentage is less than 1 percent of the annual budget.

Negative Reciprocity

In **negative reciprocity**, the third form, both parties attempt to gain all they can from the exchange while giving up as little as possible. Negative reciprocity is usually motivated largely by the desire to obtain material goods at minimal cost. Insofar as it is motivated by the desire for material goods, negative reciprocity is like market exchange; it is different mainly because no money changes hands.

In economies with no money, negative reciprocity is an important way for individuals and groups to acquire products that they do not produce themselves. Few communities are entirely self-sufficient: some foods they like to eat are not found where they live, some materials they need to make tools are not found locally, or they lack the skill to produce some of the objects they use. To acquire these things, people produce other goods to exchange for "imports."

Barter is the most common form of negative reciprocity. In the interior highlands of Papua New Guinea, many indigenous peoples manufactured money or wealth objects by stringing shells together into long chains or belts. Because these shells did not occur naturally in the interior, they were traded from people to people until they reached their final destination. Salt was also a trade object because it was found in only a few areas. Similarly, in western North America, the obsidian (volcanic glass) used to make stone tools was found in only a few areas; other peoples acquired it through trade. In some cases, these trade routes stretched for hundreds of miles, with the obsidian passing through the hands of numerous middlemen before finally being made into a tool.

Reciprocity and Social Distance

Each type of reciprocity tends to be associated with certain kinds of social relationships. As Marshall Sahlins, who first distinguished the three varieties, noted, the kind of reciprocity that occurs between individuals or groups depends on the **social distance** between them. Social distance is the degree to which cultural norms specify persons should be intimate with or emotionally attached to one another. A given mode of reciprocal exchange is normatively appropriate only with certain kinds of social relationships.

North American social norms illustrate the concept. We expect people to practice generalized reciprocity with children and perhaps with siblings and elderly parents. All else equal others may judge those who refuse to offer to help family members as uncaring or selfish. Well-off grandparents may help with their grandkids' higher education, with cars or down payments on a house. But middle-income persons who repeatedly give or "lend" money to a deadbeat cousin might be seen as a bit foolish.

As our social relationships with other people change, so does the kind of reciprocity we practice with them. For example, as we mature, our increasing independence from parents is manifested by a change in the way we exchange goods with them. We go from being the recipients of generalized reciprocity to more of a balanced reciprocity as we become more independent. Near the end of our parents' lives, we are providers of generalized reciprocity, for most people need or appreciate the assistance in spite of government aid by Social Security and Medicare.

Finally, changing one form of reciprocity into another can be a way of changing the nature of a social relationship. Because the form of reciprocity two people practice is related to the degree of social distance between them, one party can increase or decrease the social distance by initiating a new form of exchange. Or someone can signal his or her wish to draw another person closer by tentatively initiating a relationship of balanced reciprocity.

If we are work colleagues, I can let you know that I want to become more friendly by giving you an unexpected gift or inviting you to dinner. In turn, you let me know whether you share my feelings by whether you return my gift on an appropriate occasion, repeatedly find reasons to refuse my dinner invitation, or come to dinner several times at my place without reciprocating.

---

negative reciprocity Reciprocal exchange motivated largely by the desire to obtain products or services.

social distance Degree to which cultural norms specify that two individuals or groups should be helpful to, intimate with, or emotionally attached to one another.

Gift exchange is a familiar form of reciprocity. Here in Narita, Japan, two men formally exchange gifts before an important festival.

If we both use this "strategy of reciprocity," neither of us needs to be put in a potentially embarrassing position of verbalizing our feelings. I signal my wish by my initial gift or invitation, and you decline or accept my offer of friendship by your response. Here again reciprocity is symbolic, conveying messages about ideal social relationships, hoped-for relationships, and even rejected relationships. Because we routinely use reciprocity as a way of conveying feelings and sending social messages, anthropologists commonly view reciprocal exchanges as a form of communication.

Redistribution

The major difference between reciprocity and redistribution—the second major form of exchange—is how the transfer of products and other resources is organized. With reciprocity, resources pass back and forth between two participants, with no third party to act as intermediary. With redistribution, resources collected from many individuals or groups are taken to a central place or put into a common pool or fund. Some overarching authority (empowered to make decisions on behalf of those who contributed) later draws from this pool or fund and returns public goods and services to allegedly benefit the group as a whole.

In modern nations, the main resource (money, in this case) that is collected is taxes on wages, profits, retail sales, property, interest, and other income and assets. Consider how national tax systems are supposed to operate in most modern nations. The national government redistributes tax revenues in two main ways. First, revenues are distributed in such a way as to benefit the whole country. Citizens receive police protection, law enforcement, national defense, infrastructure (e.g., dams, roads, airports), regulation of polluting industries, and so forth. Here, resources collected from the citizenry are expended on public goods and services. Second, taxes provide assistance for individuals in need. In the United States, these are "transfer payments" in the form of Social Security, Medicaid and Medicare, disaster relief, children's services, and so forth. Such public expenditures are based on moral norms and cultural values about social justice, equal opportunity, and helping those in need. Redistribution systems around the world are used for similar purposes: to provide public goods and services and to provide assistance to individuals and groups in need.

There is another side to redistribution, a side that also is familiar. First, there is often conflict over who should provide the public resources, how the resources should be expended, and how much of a share should be given to those who collect and distribute them. One common social and political problem with redistribution is political disagreement: when many individuals have contributed to the public pool or fund, not everyone is likely to agree on how the "public resources" should be spent for the "public good." Much of the conflict between political parties in modern industrial democracies is rooted in disagreements over who should be taxed and how much and over how government revenues should be spent. Parties and various interest groups are, in many cases, quarreling over redistribution: Who pays? Who gets what? And how much?

Second, elected officials and other officeholders who make important decisions about redistribution sometimes use public resources to further their own interests and ambitions, rather than to benefit the entire country or to help those in greatest need. In the United States, for instance, elected officials make "pork barrel" deals to allocate federal tax dollars to finance highway construction in their districts. Congestion might be reduced for a while, but the real purpose is to provide jobs for their constituencies or to serve special-interest groups who contribute to their reelection. Balanced reciprocity between members of Congress often integrates well with redistribution: "You vote for my district's highway project; I'll vote for your wetlands reclamation." Speaking more generally, political interests—in addition to concern for the public welfare—enter into decision making about redistribution. Many politicians oppose subsidies to special interests—at least, those that are in someone else's state or district or constituency.

For over a decade in the U.S. political conflict over health care has existed. It is widely agreed that American health care is both too expensive and too unequally distributed and so should be reformed. Around 18 percent of the U.S. gross domestic product is spent in the health care industry, far more than any other industrialized nation, and costs are expected to increase further. The United States is nearly alone among developed nations in not providing coverage for all its citizens. Reforming health care is difficult because it raises so many issues about redistribution over which there is no agreement: Is health care a "right" that all should have? Is providing health care a legitimate function of government; that is, should the government redistribute tax dollars to provide health care? If the federal government does offer health insurance for citizens who prefer it or who have no other source of health insurance, will this put many private insurers out of business? Will universal health coverage lead the country down the slippery path to the dreaded European-style socialism? Even though most people believe that American health care needs "reform," issues of redistribution—who should pay how much, to whom, and what is the proper role of government—are among the most difficult obstacles to political action.

In the preindustrial world a common form of redistribution is **tribute**. The subjects of a chief or other title holder contribute products (usually including food) into a common pool under the control of the central authority. Often the tribute is culturally viewed as a material symbol that the subjects continue to acknowledge the chief's sacred authority. Some of the accumulated products are consumed by the chiefs and their relatives, some are distributed to support the work of crafts specialists (e.g., weavers and potters), and some are redistributed to the whole population at public feasts, celebrations, and ceremonies.

Examples of redistribution systems using tribute payments exist on many of the islands of Polynesia and Micronesia in the Pacific. On many islands, the entire population was divided traditionally into two ranks or classes, noble and commoner (Chapter 13 has more about rank and class). Members of the nobility did little agricultural or other manual work, but instead managed the political system and organized religious ceremonies. Commoners produced the food for themselves and their families and performed most physical labor, giving products and services to nobles.

On some islands, the king or principal chief was culturally perceived as the ultimate owner of the land and its resources. Nobles generally had ritual functions, including prayers and sacrifices to deities and ancestors. On most islands, commoners paid periodic tribute to families of noble rank, whether in return for their use of the land or as a sacred obligation, or both. Tribute fed the nobility and their families and supported specialists. The tribute rendered by commoners was used partly for public purposes, such as feeding people who worked on trails and public buildings, providing relief from temporary food shortages, and publicly celebrating special events. On a few of the larger, resource-rich islands such as Hawaii and Tahiti, the nobles were sufficiently powerful to become materially wealthy from tribute: they lived in the best houses, slept on the softest woven mats, wore special clothing, had numerous servants, and ate only the finest foods.

tribute Rendering of products (usually including food) to an authority such as a chief.

Market

For our purposes, the word *market* has two uses. In one usage, market is one of the main forms of exchange, alongside reciprocity and redistribution. In another, market is a set of organizing principles, as in the phrase *market economies.* The two uses are related but not identical. Market exchange can exist even in economies that are not based on the market's organizing principles. Here we define market exchange as requiring a medium of exchange, so we begin with money.

Money

Money is another of those things we take for granted—so much so that it seems like a simple thing. However, the idea of money presupposes a lot of other ideas and institutions, so money actually is rather complicated.

At root, money is objects that serve as *media of exchange* in a wide range of transactions of goods, services (perhaps including labor), or both. With money, person A can acquire something from person B without having to return an object desired by B—that is, without having to barter. B can then use the money to buy a chosen object or service. If people sell their time and skills for money, the value of the labor is expressed in terms of money ("wages" and "salaries"). This facilitation of exchange is the main function of money.

Other characteristics of money are derived from its function as a medium of exchange. For example, money serves as a *standard of value:* we can compare the values of the goods and services because money serves as a common measure of how much things are worth. Having a common standard makes it a lot easier to compare the values of alternative products; for example, if you buy that new HDTV, you can calculate what you are foregoing by your purchase.

Money is also a *store of value:* because you can use it any time to purchase a wide range of goods, it stores your wealth, often in a portable form that can be carried in pouches or pockets. If you want to defer immediate consumption so that you can get something really expensive later, just save your money, since it stores your resources indefinitely. If inflation is high, though, and you store your wealth in a low-yielding bank account, then your money becomes worth less without you doing anything at all.

Money has *symbolic significance.* Money is one way to evaluate people, especially if we don't already know them. Clothing, jewelry, cars, houses, and so forth are not indicators of moral worthiness, but they are still signals about how much individuals or families are "worth." How you spend your money also tells others a lot about you. Money can even symbolize national identity or independence: citizens of England still resist adopting the pan-European currency (the euro) because they see it as a threat to their sovereignty.

These and other characteristics mean that not just any object is suitable to be used as money. Obviously, money objects must be *durable.* This is why hard objects such as modified stones, shells, and metals often serve as currency.

Money is more useful as an exchange medium if it is *divisible,* so sometimes different kinds of objects serve as denominations of money—equivalent to nickels, quarters, dollar bills, and thousand-dollar bills. Among the Kapauku, a people of the rugged interior of Papua province, Indonesia, small cowrie shells imported from the coast serve as money. As the shells circulate, their natural polish wears off. Because the older ones are more scarce, they are worth more than the newer ones. Among Kapauku, the "age" of the money serves as a kind of denomination.

The supply of the money object must be *controllable* because if people can get all they want of it, its value inflates and it becomes worthless as an exchange medium: who would give you anything in exchange for it? The monetary supply can be controlled by a government, which manufactures the only "legal tender" in the society. Or the supply can be controlled by using only imported or rare objects as money. Shells imported from far away frequently serve as money because of their scarcity and durability. The money supply can also be controlled by using a currency that requires a lot of labor to make. Minerals or shells can be ground into precise shapes, drilled with holes, and strung into necklaces. In such cases, money remains scarce because it takes a lot of time to make it.

For convenience, most money is *portable.* In different cultures, you can stick it in your pocket, carry it around your neck or waist, wrap it in a bundle, roll it up, or wear it around your arm. Chinese and Korean coins had holes in the center so the owner could store them on a cord. On the island of Yap in Micronesia, however, huge stone disks weighing hundreds of pounds serve as a kind of money. Yapese stone money is seldom moved; rather, the ownership of it is transacted so that the money stays in one place even when its owner changes.

As the stone money of Yap illustrates, an enormous variety of objects serve as money in one or another region of the world. In preindustrial economies, the kinds

---

money Objects that serve as media of exchange in a wide range of transactions of goods, services (including labor), or both.

One of the more unusual forms of money is the stone money of Yap in the Federated States of Micronesia.

of monetary objects are surprisingly diverse. In Africa, for example, the following objects served as money in some part of the continent: iron, salt, beads, cowrie shells, cloth, gin, gold dust, metal rods, brass bracelets, and livestock. Among the ancient Aztecs, cacao beans served as currency.

The range of goods that can be acquired with money varies greatly. In some economies, the range is broad. Many kinds of resources and goods can be bought and sold, including labor, land, tools, and sometimes even people (slaves). In these systems, money serves as a *generalized medium of exchange*; that is, it can be used to acquire many kinds of goods and services. Of course, there are always some things that money just can't buy. Love is the classic example, but if you have enough money, it might be easier for you to *think* everyone loves you.

In many preindustrial economies, the range of money uses is relatively narrow. Only a few categories of products may be purchased. For example, it may be possible to buy food, clothing, and a few other goods; but land is not available for sale at any price, and labor is rarely for sale. One reason for such limitations on the use of money is that something (like land) must have a price to be transacted for money. In many cultures, people rarely give up or acquire land, so it has no monetary price.

Market Exchange

To say that objects or services are exchanged by markets means they are bought and sold at a price measured in money. Person A possesses products that person B wants to acquire; B acquires the products by giving A whatever amount of money both A and B agree on; A then uses the money to acquire more products from other people.

Most readers are so familiar with money and markets that the preceding sentence is just a convoluted way of stating common sense. If it seems that way to you, perhaps it is because you are making assumptions about the conditions that market exchange requires, forgetting that these conditions did not exist in the past or even in the present of many peoples. Market exchange requires three conditions:

- Some object(s) that serves as a medium of exchange, as *money*. Notice that money itself potentially earns more money, as when it is lent for interest (the price of money).
- Rates at which particular products and services exchange for money or at which money itself can be purchased for a fee, that is, *prices* and *interest* that are determined by *supply and demand*.

CHAPTER 8 Exchange in Economic Systems 175

▌ Parties to exchanges have choices about alternative buyers or sellers and are free to make the best deal they can. Market exchange implies the absence of coercion: neither party to a transaction can be forced to buy or sell from the other party. This is the *free market*. No third party (a government, for example) sets prices or forces anyone to buy or sell from anyone else. No single supplier of a good (a monopolist) controls enough of the market to force people to buy from him, her, or it (in the case of firms).

Some people don't grasp the full significance of differences between market exchanges and balanced reciprocal exchanges. There is often an element of selfishness in balanced reciprocity, making some think that reciprocal exchanges would become market exchanges if only the people had a form of money. If only they had money, they would have markets, goes the logic. Although balanced reciprocity does not involve monetary exchanges, in a sense there are implicit "prices" of reciprocity (otherwise, how would a person know what to give and what to expect back?).

However, the difference is real and significant. It lies in the form and degree of selfishness in the total context of the exchange. Acting in your own self-interest is not merely culturally "tolerated" in markets. In the free market context, selfish acts are expected and positively valued because selfish choice making leads to an efficient economy. Selfish behavior is a *market norm*, so in the market context lawful selfishness rarely is criticized. With balanced reciprocity, the two parties expect something from one another, but the return cannot be precisely judged to be equivalent and can be largely symbolic. Returns can be material objects, mutual help when needed, invitations and hospitality, or even just a well-communicated sense of gratitude. It is crass to measure such returns in money. Reciprocity is a *social norm*.

This difference between market and social norms is why you might worry or feel anxious about buying a used car from a friend, as will your friend. If the car is a lemon, how will it affect our friendship? In contrast, when you buy a used car from a dealership, your purchase makes you worry about other things besides damaging your relationship with the salesperson.

> **market economy** Economy organized by market principles: prices determined by supply and demand; individuals and families rely on the market for livelihood; free market allocation of resources, products, and services; self-regulation and decentralization of decision making.

To clarify the difference, consider this example. When you go to a friend's house for dinner, to be polite and show gratitude you might take a small gift, like a drink, a dessert, or a plant. Alternatively you might invite your friend over for a meal to reciprocate. Next time, show up empty handed. At the end of the meal, pull out your wallet and tell your friend that you estimate the cost of the meal at about $15 and you'd like to pay your share now rather than inviting your friend over to your place later. Or, the next time you exchange gifts, if someone has clearly shorted you, tell the person that she owes you about $6, your estimate of how much more your gift cost than hers. If doing this makes you uncomfortable or if the very idea of doing it seems wacko, then you recognize the difference between social norms and market norms. On the popular TV show *The Big Bang Theory*, one of the many reasons Sheldon Cooper's behavior is humorous is that he seems oblivious to this distinction, often treating other people as means to his own ends.

Market Economies and Capitalism

Some societies have money and markets without also having a market economy. For centuries, peasant classes in various places have sold foods they produce themselves at local markets. People make baskets, pottery, leather goods, art objects, cloth and clothing, and other goods sold locally or, sometimes, in distant places. The Aztec civilization of Mexico had enormous marketplaces and even had traveling merchants who went around buying and selling products. The ancient silk routes connected the civilizations of China and the Middle East along trading stations and towns in Central Asia, where traders bought and sold Western and Eastern products like glass and silk. Even today, peasant marketplaces remain important in West Africa, southern and Southeast Asia, the Caribbean, and Central and South America.

However, marketing products and going to marketplaces does not imply that the entire economy is organized by market exchanges. Most peasants and other indigenous peoples grow most of their food using family labor and are not employed for wages in the impersonal labor market. They go to the market (in the sense of *place*) to buy something they need but can't or don't want to produce themselves, but they do not depend on the market (in the sense of *system*) for their livelihood.

A **market economy** is one organized on *market principles*. Briefly, here are the most important of these principles and a short example of each:

▌ *Practically all privately owned goods and services have a monetary price and can be bought and sold*

Market economies require monetary prices determined by supply and demand, widespread dependence on the market for livelihood, market allocation of the factors of production, and decentralized self regulation of economic activity. Buying and selling shares on the New York Stock Exchange illustrates these features.

on the free market. Families live in houses and the land on which they are built. This kind of property is the main "asset" of most families. Many move from house to house every few years, depending on the local housing market.

- *Most people make their living by selling something on the market.* Some people make a living by selling goods or services to consumers. But most people are workers: they make their living by selling their labor to a group (such as a firm or public agency). Workers have to do this because most of them do not own the natural resources and capital with which to make their own living.

- *The market allocates productive resources, such as labor, land, equipment, and technology.* The supply of and demand for these resources determine the uses to which they are put. If some company is producing products consumers aren't interested in or is charging prices consumers refuse to pay, the company will go out of business, or change what it produces, or find ways to lower prices by lowering its production costs. All companies adjust to "market realities." In the 1970s, the American auto industry adjusted to Japanese competition and rising global oil prices by reducing car sizes and improving gas mileage. Resources were reallocated toward smaller cars because car companies made new choices.

- *The economy is self-regulating.* The impersonal forces of supply and demand set prices and therefore regulate the kinds of economic activity that occur. No individual, corporation, industry, or other entity regulates a market economy because it is inherently decentralized. The Invisible Hand, as economist Adam Smith called this principle of self-regulation, is impersonal.

Capitalism is organized on these same four market principles, but this term emphasizes profits and the accumulation of capital. As companies produce products or services, they earn profit through sales. Profits may be distributed to owners (often dividends to shareholders), saved in a financial institution, given as bonuses

> **capitalism** Market economy; emphasizes capital accumulation through profit making as the key to economic growth and maximum material welfare.

CHAPTER 8 Exchange in Economic Systems 177

to top managers or workers, and/or reinvested in the company in hope of future profits to make the company grow. Through capital accumulation, companies expand and hire more workers, benefitting them. If a company is profitable, its profits go to owners and investors, who may save or spend them, creating additional demand for goods and services and thus stimulating more business activity. Capitalism is the economic growth engine.

If you remember economic systems based on other exchange principles such as reciprocity and redistribution, you can see how unusual capitalism is. Be careful, though, not to confuse *capitalism* with *market exchange*. Lots of past societies had markets, but capitalism existed only after the Industrial Revolution.

Between the economic systems of industrial nations, capitalism and socialism are often contrasted. Ignoring many complications, in essence **socialism** means that the government makes decisions about product prices, wages and employment, what is produced and how, and the accumulation of income and wealth. Under socialism, the government sets prices for products and wages, which means that product prices and wages are not determined by supply and demand. The government, not market forces, decides what and how much is produced and thus allocates productive resources.

Each economic system has strengths and weaknesses. Again setting aside numerous complexities, it is commonly said that the strength of capitalism over socialism is *efficiency*: overall, capitalist economies outperform socialist ones in the quantity of goods and services produced per person. This is because the incentives built into capitalism encourage and reward hard work and training. (Notice that if one is an evolutionary psychologist, one might claim that capitalism is more consistent with "human nature.") On the other hand, capitalism automatically and regularly produces losers as well as winners: some individuals are better off than others, often because of inheritance from parents or because of educational and other advantages they have from living in a particular place. It also has business cycles (booms and recessions), which occasionally are economically disastrous for workers and businesses (the Great Depression) and often require government bailouts (the 2007–2011 financial crisis).

socialism Economy in which government makes decisions about product prices, wages and employment, what is produced, and accumulation of income and wealth.

Finally, capitalism automatically produces *social and economic inequalities*, further discussed in Chapter 13.

It is both easy and convenient for someone who believes in capitalism to give credit to the winners and disparage the talents and efforts of the losers. (Notice that if you are a postmodernist, you are likely to believe that such common beliefs reflect wealth inequalities and power relationships.) It is especially easy for someone to believe this if that person is winning—unless that person later becomes a loser. Then previously unsuspected complications become apparent.

The ideas justifying socialism are that it provides better for the poor by heavy taxation on the well-off and thus produces greater equality and more of what some call *social justice*. However, this has not always happened in real socialist economies, which critics of socialism say is why so few socialist economies remain today. Socialism is friendlier to workers than capitalism with respect to wage laws, regulations about factory conditions, parental leave, unemployment compensation, and similar policies.

Economies organized by market principles have many advantages for individuals. You can shop around until you find the best deal available, now especially easy with your smartphone. You can change jobs if you are dissatisfied with the work or your employer. In the twenty-first century, many people carry hardly any money but have deposited "it" somewhere and use small cards that are a promise to pay when they want to buy something—not only a convenient practice, but one that allows people to spend money they have not yet earned and thus invites indebtedness. Furthermore, an economy organized on free-market principles is tremendously productive, as Karl Marx—the nineteenth-century archenemy of capitalism—recognized. The People's Republic of China has experienced tremendous economic growth since its government introduced market reforms in 1978.

After the Industrial Revolution (Chapter 7), capitalism took hold and expanded in Western Europe and North America. Its philosophical basis—the cultural ideas that provide its legitimacy—was and is that free markets lead to what has been called "the greatest good for the greatest number in the long run." For example, to say that the market "allocates resources" means that if some industry is declining (like textiles or shoes), then the profit made by companies in that industry fall. Companies in that industry will go bankrupt or choose to go into some other industry. As a result, companies that produce products (like computer software) or services (like Internet advertising) will profit and grow, producing value for their owners. This process can be hard on the families of workers in declining industries but benefits those in growth industries, so people shouldn't be too concerned if the local businesses in their town go out of business when a large retail store moves in or an upscale mall develops. Market principles are operating: consumer demand, prices, market allocation of resources, relative profits and wages, and other market forces.

Capitalism is a "system," not a "thing," and how its principles operate vary from place to place and time to time. People—including economists—have different ideas about which version of capitalism works best. One set of ideas is called **neoliberalism** (or *laissez-faire*, roughly translated as "leave them alone"). People who believe in it are not liberal in the political sense. Rather, they believe in what they call *economic freedom:* in market situations, leave people and corporations alone to do what they think is best for themselves and those they care about. This results in the best results for society as a whole. Governments can interfere with free markets with the best of intentions, but usually there are consequences they do not intend that result in less growth and public benefit than would otherwise occur.

For example, when governments intervene to protect workers, they interfere with the workings of free markets. Examples of intervention are minimum wage laws, safety regulations, requiring employers to provide health insurance, and allowing labor unions to require workers to pay union dues. These kinds of government interference might help the few (the workers in a given industry) but hurt the economy overall, because government interference reduces the efficiency of the overall economy.

Neoliberals argue that similar consequences follow when governments pass regulations to reduce the negative environmental or social effects of external costs. Examples include heavy pollution regulations, favoring companies that manufacture solar cells with subsidies or tax breaks, and heavy taxation of the profits of companies. These, too, affect the operation of free markets, leading to losses in efficiency and, eventually, a net lowering of benefit to society as a whole.

In short, neoliberals place a lot of trust in free markets. But even they agree that various levels of government have legitimate roles in the market. It should protect property, construct infrastructure (e.g., roads, ports), and provide defense, police, and some form of public schools. It should regulate industries by minimizing external costs, which are things companies do that harm individuals, communities, or the environment. Forcing factories to reduce the amount of air and water pollution is a familiar example. Mandating auto safety equipment is another. However, neoliberals argue against other kinds of government actions. Governments should not give tax breaks or subsidies to companies that government officials judge are in the public interest (e.g., solar technology, electric cars) because then it is the government that is allocating resources rather than the market. Governments should not impose heavy taxes on corporate profits, because then corporations are less motivated to make as much profit as they can, which reduces growth and ultimately harms everyone. Governments should be only minimally involved in redistribution of income from wealthier people to poorer people, both because the wealthy have earned their income, and because redistribution discourages work effort. Governments should not force companies or individuals to reduce their carbon emissions to reduce climate change, because even if climate change is real, it might not be caused by human activity.

Social welfare capitalism is another form, justified by different ideas. This form and these ideas also are based on free markets, although many people incorrectly consider social welfare capitalism to be a form of socialism. People who champion social welfare capitalism point out that free markets generate a lot of "bads" along with their "goods." One important task of elected governments is to minimize the negative consequences of capitalism without seriously compromising the value of free markets and the capitalist system. This involves heavy regulation of external costs ("heavy handed," neoliberals believe); extensive legal or regulatory requirements about worker safety, wages, and benefits; and taxation of the wealth and income of individuals to fund social programs benefitting the poor and unemployed. When North American political candidates and officeholders talk about "European-style socialism," they actually are referring to social welfare capitalism, because no European country remains socialistic.

However, most European countries do have socialized medicine: governments pay for preventative medical care and for treating the sick and injured. To neoliberal thinkers, this is not a legitimate function of government

---

neoliberalism (*laissez-faire*) Belief that economic freedom results in the best results for society as a whole; mistrust in government interference with free markets.

social welfare capitalism Capitalist economy in which a legitimate function of government is protection of workers and society from the harmful impacts of free markets; involves extensive regulations of business and worker protections.

and results in long waits for treatments and high costs. Neoliberals believe that governments are inefficient because they are not subject to the "discipline of the market." However, American health care costs are the highest of any developed nation at 18 percent of GDP, partly because the medical profession is compensated by the number and kinds of tests and procedures rather than by patient outcomes.

Productivity

For a society or nation as a whole, then, the number one benefit of a market economy is *productivity:* compared to socialism, market economies allocate resources more efficiently, which leads to higher productivity.

Think about the cultural meaning of the word *productivity*. When you say have a productive day, you mean you have done a lot of work in some period of time. In economics, though, factory productivity is measured by the cost of producing goods compared to the market value of the goods when they are sold. Costs are measured by money, as is the GDP of a nation. Many economists worry when factory productivity falls, because it means that factories are using more "input" to produce the same level of "output." Because labor is a cost, companies can reduce their costs by finding ways to employ less labor by automation, reorganizations, or moving production to places where labor costs are lower. This leads to layoffs and firings, which is good for the company's productivity, however hard it is on unemployed workers and their families.

In a capitalist economy in which neoliberal ideas are influential, companies do not and should not care about such things as whether firings and layoffs harm their workers or the general economy. By "companies," we do not mean the individuals in the company or even its managers or board, all of whom have a diversity of ethical and moral views. We mean what is in the interest of the company, or what it should do to maximize its . . . what?

Most readers will answer "profit." In her 2009 book *Liquidated: An Ethnography of Wall Street*, anthropologist Karen Ho provides a slightly different answer: *shareholder value*. On the basis of her detailed ethnographic interviews in 1998–1999 with investment bankers working for Wall Street firms, Ho describes the *corporate culture* of the financial industry. One thing investment bankers do is use money (much of it borrowed) to buy stock in underperforming ("undervalued") companies. Typically, they then break the company up and sell parts of it to other companies, thus "liquidating" the company. Ho's study is too complex to summarize in its entirety, so here we present some of her main findings.

First, investment bankers judge the success of a company by shareholder value (roughly, the price of its stock). According to Ho's interviews, in the culture of Wall Street, a company owes nothing to its employees aside from the provisions of their contract. Nor is it obligated to consider the impacts of its actions on the national welfare. For example, in a great many cases, soon after a company has fired or laid off a large number of its "excess" employees, its stock price rises. This increases its shareholder value because it has shed excess capacity. The management is responsible to the company's shareholders, so if shareholder value increases after layoffs and firings, management has done what it is supposed to do: increase the wealth of its shareholders.

Second, Ho writes, the high-level employees of Wall Street firms consider themselves as among the smartest people around. Most have degrees from Harvard or Princeton and rarely underestimate their own abilities. This does not imply they think their decisions are perfect, but a relative lack of humility makes them more likely to allocate money—usually the money of other people who are looking to achieve high returns on investments—toward risky investments because they think they have the brainpower and skill to assess risks accurately. Once hired, they work very long hours, often 70 or 80 hours a week, and are under constant stress because of pressures to perform.

Third, in addition to salaries, investment bankers earn annual bonuses, often far exceeding their salaries. Usually, senior managers make decisions about bonuses in secret and without justifying them to their subordinates. More often than one might expect, midlevel analysts themselves are "liquidated"—fired. The world of finance changes so rapidly that a division of a firm that was profitable last year may not be this year, so whole divisions are often let go. Wall Street culture instills the belief that that most assets must be "liquid"—they must be able to be reallocated very quickly. Labor is such an asset. Because of bonuses and the real possibility of not working for a company very long, employees are "incentivized" to raise the shareholder values of companies they buy and sell as rapidly as they can.

Like you and I, investment bankers are natives. To grasp their point of view, suppose you work as an investment banker in a Wall Street firm. Your compensation is tied to your performance, which depends on what happens to the shareholder value of the companies you advise your firm to invest in or take money out of. You are not always sure whether your performance meets expectations, which makes you work even harder to become more productive. Your firm believes that the financial sector changes so often that not you and your entire division might be liquidated at any time. You had better make all the money you can right now. You, and your colleagues, can play it safe and allocate money in relatively safe but low-return investments. But you and your colleagues are the smartest of the smart, so you are able to evaluate the risks of investments. If the future works out, you will make loads of money for the company and for yourself at annual bonuses. If not, you might be downsized, but that could happen anyway.

Karen Ho's Wall Street research has many implications for understanding financial markets in market economies. Here we call attention to only one. Many people blame "greedy bankers" for the financial collapse that began in 2007. They seem to assume that the crisis was caused by the actions of individuals who were so intent on making money that they set aside their ethical standards or morality or found some other ways of justifying their actions. Ho's work provides an alternative: it was not greed but the way that the financial industry is "structured"—the corporate culture that guides decisions, how rewards are allocated, expectations placed on people working in a highly competitive industry, and the like. Without a change in industry structure and corporate culture, a new group of less greedy bankers would soon appear to be equally greedy.

Remember the difference between market norms and social norms? In a capitalist economy, a corporation that acts altruistically toward its own workers or the general society raises its own costs and thus reduces its competitiveness. Because of globalization, in the twenty-first century the companies of one nation's economy are competing with the companies of other nations, whose governments impose fewer or different regulations. There are few enforceable international regulations that level the playing field for corporations active in the global economy.

Therefore, the desire/need to remain "globally competitive" becomes an argument for a political strategy. A nation's industries or other kinds of companies claim that things like "government overregulation" and the "unreasonable demands of labor unions" are reducing their international competitiveness. In this and other ways, the global economy affects national elections, political debates, and programs that are enacted or not enacted. Public policies in all nations are affected by how nations are integrated into the global economy. So are ideas about the optimal form of capitalism. In the United States, neoliberal ideas have been around for a long time but have become more influential in the last several years with the emergence of the Tea Party. Perhaps globalization has promoted the influence of the neoliberal agenda in politics.

Globalization and Markets

Between May 2011 and May 2012, the world price of oil hovered between $100 and $118 per barrel. During those months, the price of gasoline in some parts of the United States exceeded $4.00 per gallon. This led to the latest American realization of overdependence on foreign oil, some of which is produced in nations that "hate us." Private industry and the government point to alternatives sources of energy that potentially reduce foreign dependence. The most recent large-scale energy industry is hydraulic fracturing, or "fracking," the controversial technology that supplies petroleum and natural gas by forcing water and chemicals into underground shale deposits. Fracking has become a major industry in Pennsylvania, eastern Ohio, North Dakota, and Wyoming. Although it has driven down consumer costs of natural gas considerably since about 2010, there are concerns about its impact on ground water supplies and health.

Ethanol is another fuel source. In the United States, ethanol is made mainly from maize (corn). American family farmers and giant agricultural corporations produce a lot of corn—so much that corn and its many products cost remarkably little to produce. Once processed into ethanol, mixed with actual petroleum, and pumped into automobile fuel tanks, corn can both reduce prices at the pump and free North Americans from becoming too dependent on people who don't like them, and vice versa. Everyone benefits.

Actually, not everyone. The federal government subsidizes both corn production and ethanol processing plants, to reduce foreign energy dependence. By 2008, about 30 percent of the corn produced in the United States was processed into ethanol. Rising demand from ethanol plants contributed to the near tripling of the market price of corn between the end of 2005 and mid-2008. Corn products are used in lots of processed foods, so when corn prices rise, the price paid by consumers for other foods increases. Corn syrup (fructose) is used to sweeten such a large number of products that there was a generalized increase in food and soft drink prices. People saved some money on fuel for their cars from ethanol but lost most or all of the savings in increased prices for their snack foods, soft drinks, and many other fructose-loaded products. Furthermore, at most ethanol yields only about 30 percent more energy than the energy needed to produce it, and some researchers claim its energy balance is negative. Most researchers doubt that ethanol will reduce our dependence on foreign oil, despite its political popularity.

There is a global market for corn. Increased American demand for corn made into ethanol contributed to a global rise in the price of corn. In a 3-week period in early 2007, the price of corn tortillas in Mexico rose by a third. When there are shortages and anticipated shortages, speculators on commodities tend to bid on them, and competition between them further drives up prices—as seen repeatedly in world petroleum prices. Distributors and processors also publicly justify price increases to consumers by citing their own rising costs—as seen repeatedly in pump prices for motor fuels. Poor Mexicans eat a lot of corn tortillas and beans, which for many are staples of their diet. They had to pay more for their major dietary staple because Americans diverted part of their production of a food (and feed) crop to energy. Popular protests in 2007 against high prices were later called the "corn riots."

Corn continues to supply a large portion of food for rural Mexican people—about 40 percent of the caloric intake in many parts of the countryside. The Mayans and other prehistoric Mesoamericans invented the process called *nixtamal* or *nixtamalización*. Derived from the language of the Aztec, nixtamalización involves boiling maize kernels with calcium hydroxide ("lime" as in limestone, not citrus) and ash (sometimes volcanic). After soaking in this alkaline solution, the kernels absorb valuable nutrients, and the soaking makes the niacin available for absorption by digestion. When the processed kernels are ground into tortillas and eaten with beans as tamales or another food, a nearly complete diet results. The form of protein deficiency called *pellagra* is prevented, and the added calcium prevents the disease called *rickets*. One Mexican nutritionist reported that rising corn prices led many poor Mexicans to switch to eating instant noodles, a much cheaper but far less nourishing food than the maize and beans that have nourished them for centuries.

Maize also is intimately tied into Mexico's history and culture. Corn was first domesticated in southern Mexico. It is a meaningful as well as nutritional food, like rice in Japan or lamb in Iran, and a symbol of Mexico's national identity.

The impact of American ethanol on Mexican corn prices is an example of **market globalization**. The entire world is increasingly integrated into a single system organized by market principles. Labor, capital, technology, consumer products, and services move with few restraints across national boundaries.

> **market globalization** Process through which the world's national economies become integrated into a single exchange system organized by market principles.

Market globalization affects almost everyone to some degree, including people who seem remote and relatively isolated from global forces. In the last five centuries, indigenous peoples (see Chapter 17) were dramatically affected by colonialism, diseases, resource extraction from their lands, and (in some cases) slavery. In the modern global economy, many of them have found their own market niche (see Globalization Challenges and Opportunities).

Global markets go back to the colonial centuries beginning about 1500 (see Chapter 4). However, their size and geographic reach expanded dramatically in the last half of the twentieth century. In the 1960s, for example, an agreement between the United States and Mexico allowed U.S. corporations to set up factories (called *maquiladoras*) in Mexico along the Texas border region. The plants produced clothing and consumer electronics for American consumers. American garment companies sent cloth to the maquiladoras to be cut and sewn into clothing sold to American consumers. Electronic firms sent components south to be soldered and assembled. Products were then brought back to the United States for final finishing and sale. There were no tariffs (import taxes) on the finished products, and Mexico allowed North American companies to retain ownership of assembly plants on its soil in return for the jobs and training received by its citizens. Most Mexican employees of these multinational firms were unmarried women. American and European corporations made similar arrangements with Asian countries like Taiwan, Singapore, and South Korea.

Since the 1980s, wage levels in the countries mentioned above have climbed, and their governments have instituted more workplace and environmental regulations. To remain competitive by controlling labor and other production costs, corporations relocated production facilities to other countries that had even fewer regulations and lower prevailing wages. In addition to India, China, and Brazil, countries in Southeast Asia (like Malaysia, Indonesia, and the Philippines), the Caribbean, and Africa invited foreign companies to establish factories to provide jobs for their people and tax revenues for their governments.

The impacts of market globalization are debated by news media, government officials, labor unions, corporations, and consumers. The most important questions focus on its costs and benefits, especially the question of who loses and who gains. Four main metaphorical "interests" participate in globalization: corporations who lower costs by outsourcing production, consumers in the more developed nations, workers in the more developed nations, and workers who hold jobs in the lesser developed regions and countries.

Corporations

Nearly everyone agrees that corporations in the richer countries win from globalization, mainly because of reduced labor costs and less restrictive environmental and workplace regulations. The owners and managers of businesses in what we used to call the Third World also gain new income by producing for the export market.

Consumers

Consumers in the richer nations mostly benefit from lower prices because so many of the products they purchase are made so cheaply. Go to your closet and try to find a garment or pair of shoes manufactured in your own country. Check out your gaming console, TV, smartphone, tablet computer, and other electronic equipment. What do you suppose you would have paid for such products if they were manufactured in Toronto, London, Tokyo, or Chicago?

On the down side, in recent years Mattel's Chinese-made toys were found to contain too much lead, some pet foods imported from China contained an additive that harmed animals, and Chinese-made drywall contained toxic chemicals and often disintegrated. A favorite phrase of economists is "There is no such thing as a free lunch," so if retail prices are lower, then the costs are borne by someone else.

Workers in Richer Countries

Other players in the global market are workers who used to work in the factories in the developed countries, whose formerly high-paying jobs were replaced by people who live half a world away. In market terms, many are the victims of "restructuring" and "increasing efficiency" because their employers must "lower costs" to "compete in the global market" in order to "be responsible to their stockholders" and increase "shareholder value." Kannapolis, North Carolina, was once the home of Cannon Mills, the company that supplied a large percentage of textile products like sheets and towels. Cannon's buildings were demolished into enormous piles of brick rubble, and the American workers were "let go."

Those who favor globalization point out that most laid-off and fired North American workers have found other jobs. At any rate, in their role as consumers, workers benefit from the lower prices made possible by lowered overseas production costs. Critics of globalization claim that most of these new jobs are lower paid jobs in various service industries and that the alleged decline of the American middle class and increasing economic inequalities (Chapter 13) are due largely to globalization. Thus, the global labor market forces millions of workers—most of whom do not have higher education or professional training—to compete in a wider, global arena.

Workers in Developing Countries and Regions

Views also diverge on the welfare of these workers. Critics of globalization claim that these workers are exploited. Rich foreign and domestic companies take advantage of their poverty and lack of alternative economic opportunities by offering low wages and deplorable working conditions in terms of working hours, health, and safety.

Those who favor the expansion of global markets respond that these workers are being paid more than they would otherwise be paid, they are getting job experience and training, their governments receive the taxes paid on their wages, and their local businesses receive the capital needed for investment and future growth. In China, India, and many other countries, tens of millions of rural people who would otherwise remain peasants migrate to cities to work in factories. Do we think they are too ignorant to judge whether they and their families are better off taking wage work in cities?

It is difficult for most people to decide which opinion is correct about workers in the "global factory." Compared to wages, safety regulations, and general labor welfare standards in Western nations, no doubt the critics are right. Yet compared to the living conditions many factory workers would otherwise face, those who claim that offshore production helps those who work in factory production for export have a case.

Wage rates can be argued either way: if factory workers choose factory work, perhaps outside critics whose life conditions are different should not be so quick to second-guess their choices. However, whether workers suffer health effects from their jobs—or die—is about as clear a criterion as can exist. In November 2012, a fire at a garment factory in Bangladesh killed 112 workers. International companies that subcontracted for clothing produced at the factory said they would work to improve working and safety conditions in the country's poorly regulated industries.

Factories located in Bangladesh produce more clothing for global markets than any other nation except China. In 2013, international businesses outsource production to about 5,000 garment factories in Bangladesh, employing 3.2 million workers. Bangladesh citizens working in the garment industry have the world's lowest minimum wage rates, $37 per month (many make more than this, of course). Because the labor market is increasingly global, low wages in one country tend to

GLOBAL CHALLENGES AND OPPORTUNITIES
Globalization of Indigenous Products

By moving people as well as things and messages around more than ever before, globalization makes it easier for this Western woman to buy a tapestry from someone on the island of Sulawesi, Indonesia.

Indigenous peoples are groups whose ancestors lived in a particular region until they came into contact with outsiders who were more powerful and wealthy than themselves. Most often, the indigenous peoples lost land, population, and resources as a result of the contact. Nearly always, their traditional ways of living were affected due to exposure to new beliefs and customs as well as loss of resources, land, and participation in a wider economic system. In the Americas, Australia, New Zealand, and most of the Pacific, the indigenous peoples suffered from Old World diseases that resulted in population declines, usually estimated at 80 to 90 percent.

Technically, peoples like the French and Germans are also indigenous, in these cases to Europe. However, the common use of *indigenous* implies peoples whose ancestors were conquered and who therefore became part of a larger nation state and/or global empire. As we use the phrase, *indigenous* refers to peoples like Native Americans, Pacific Islanders, native Africans, and Asians who are ethnic minorities (Chapter 17).

Today's worldwide economic system affects indigenous peoples in many ways. One way is that the global market connects consumers in the more affluent nations and regions with producers of indigenous arts and crafts. Most large world cities have small stores that sell "tribal" products made by the world's diverse indigenous peoples. Here, you can buy things marketed on the basis that they are indigenous. They are handmade (rather than mass-produced), traditional ("just like their ancestors used to make it," although usually this is not the case), authentic (made by an indigenous person who is "Other"), and different (few people you know have anything like it). The object's appeal is further enhanced if buyers can become the expert among their family and friends, because the object traditionally was used in a cultural context that the educated buyer has taken the time to master.

In the North American Southwest, stores in cities like Santa Fe, Albuquerque, Gallup, and Phoenix sell Native American products. Pottery made by Pueblo peoples sell for hundreds or even thousands of dollars. Navajo, Hopi, Zuni, and other Native peoples make bracelets, necklaces, belt buckles, conchos, and other jewelry from silver and turquoise. Thousands of members of the Navajo nation in the four corners region maintain herds of sheep, whose wool they dye and hand-weave into rugs sold to Anglo and European tourists. Visitors who travel on to one of the more than two dozen Southwest reservations have the opportunity to buy pots, jewelry, rugs, and other crafts directly from the Indians, enhancing their sense of an authentic experience.

Most pastoral peoples (Chapter 7) have marketed their products for centuries, relying on such exchanges for much of their livelihood. They sell or trade wool, hides and leather, milk, and meat to neighboring farmers or at local marketplaces. Many use the hair of their animals to make carpets, garments, carrying bags, and other kinds of tapestries. Herders in Persia (Iran) and many Arab countries shear the wool of sheep, dye it in beautiful colors, and use the fibers to weave carpets, bags, and clothing on hand looms. Ethnic groups in northwestern China and Tibet, of the Caucacus in Europe, of parts of South Asia, and in northern Africa do the same.

Outsiders have long recognized the craftsmanship and beauty of such woven products. The expansion of global markets in recent decades has increased consumer demand for pastoral products, which have become global commodities that fetch high prices among more affluent people of the herders' own country and others. To cover their floors or hang on their walls, people in the richer countries with enough money can buy carpets—both new and antique—that are hand-woven by herding peoples.

Carpets, hats, coats, tapestries, and other woven products sell for high prices on global markets because they are certified to be "authentic," meaning they were hand-woven by an indigenous ethnic group using fibers sheared from local livestock. The price may be even higher if the dyes are made from local plants and minerals rather than chemically manufactured in factories. If you can't make it to Amsterdam, London, Vancouver, or New York, you can find one on eBay, perhaps even offered by the indigenous person who made it. If you live in Asia you can buy almost anything in Seoul, Shanghai, Tokyo, Mumbai, Karachi, Kualu Lumpur, or Manila. In all the world's cities, beware of knockoffs and counterfeits. You don't want to buy a rug or serape that looks indigenous but isn't really.

Buying material products is only one way to make a connection to indigenous peoples. For a fee, small companies organize groups of tourists to visit "primitive" places like New Guinea and Vanuatu where native peoples allegedly still follow the ways of their ancestors. Like its companion known as *ecological tourism*, cultural tourism has become popular as an alternative way to visit and learn about other places without so many modern amenities.

Sometimes, people who feel their nations are sacrificing their values and traditions as they grow richer seek connections with a more unadulterated, authentic cultural past. The government of the People's Republic of China has built roads and provided public services that have opened up many of the nation's remote mountainous southwest regions, making it easier for China's emerging middle class to spend a few days in the "backward" areas where minority peoples live. This is one way to transfer money from China's more affluent citizens to regions that have not experienced the boom in the export economy. In Yunnan province in the far southwest, there is actually a cultural park where Chinese and foreign tourists can witness traditional dances and other "authentic" practices.

In Western as in other countries, many people have houses full of things but feel their lives are empty of meaning. They long for authentic experiences, feelings of belonging and identity, spirituality in their lives, and other intangibles. Most people find these within their own cultural traditions. However, some prefer to connect more directly with "native cultures." Familiar examples include Eastern practices like Zen, yoga, meditation, tai chi, and prophylactic acupuncture.

In their quest for meaning and identity, some Anglo Americans turn to Native American cultures. They think they know enough about shamanistic worldviews (Chapter 14), vision quests, holistic healing, and sweat baths to believe such Native beliefs and customs will help them in their search for meaning and for their own spiritual path. Santa Fe, New Mexico, and Sedona, Arizona, are among their favored destinations. Entrepreneurs have established businesses to provide metaphysical services in return for fees in the thousands of dollars. Among other issues, such practices raise questions about whether it is disrespectful to borrow just a little bit of someone else's religious traditions during a week-long sojourn to acquire meaning or spiritual power.

Occasionally, tragedies result. In October 2009, two men died and three people were hospitalized during a "sweat lodge ceremony" held near West Sedona, a place where multitudes of vortexes release spiritual energies with healing powers. According to the *New York Times,* the overcrowded sweat lodge was wrapped in blankets and plastic tarps; then water was poured over hot rocks to release the heat and steam needed for the experience. A member of the Klamath-Modoc Native American tribe—who organizes such events—commented, "We would never use plastic to cover our lodges. The lodge has to breathe, that steam has to go someplace." A man who is part Mescalero Apache noted that this event was a good example of "why it is extremely dangerous to conduct sweat lodge ceremonies without proper training."

The costs and benefits of market globalization are difficult to determine, because whether workers gain and/or lose depends on complicated circumstances. However, the 2013 deaths of 1,127 factory workers due to the collapse of five factories in a single unsafe building in Bangladesh leaves no debate over "losers."

drive down the cost of labor in other countries. Since the early 2000s as wage rates in China have risen, clothing companies from rich nations have relocated factories to countries with lower production costs to stay globally competitive and/or to make still higher profits. Bangladesh clothing factories receive credit for helping to lift some families out of poverty. At the national level, factories provide foreign exchange, helping Bangladesh earn money to buy products like oil and technology from other countries.

In an industrial suburb of Dhaka, the capital of Bangladesh, there was an eight-story building called Rana Plaza. Garment factories owned by five separate Bangladeshi owners and employing about 2,500 people were housed on the four upper floors of the building. Investigation showed that the top four stories had been constructed with no building permits and with substandard materials and disregard for building codes. Because of frequent power failures, to keep machines operating, factory owners installed large electric generators in the upper stories, which shook the whole building when switched on. A visit by inspectors the day before revealed large cracks in the walls. For safety's sake, a bank and several retail shops on the first floor closed, but managers of the garment factories on the upper stories ordered their workers to show up the next day.

On April 24, 2013, a generator turned on and Rana Plaza collapsed. For several days rescue personnel and ordinary citizens worked to free trapped persons and clear away the rubble to search for more. After more than a week of rescue attempts, it was determined that 1,127 people died, the deadliest disaster in the known history of the garment industry.

In explaining this and other human tragedies, many people blame national- or local-level owners, managers, and officials. Local building codes are too lax or are not enforced. Corrupt officials are often bribed to ignore violations. Greedy owners don't care about their employees. Such factors certainly contribute. However, the responsibilities of corporations and consumers in richer nations should not be underestimated. If a global corporation is searching for a place with low production costs to remain competitive, then it should be assumed that suppliers in a place know that a lower bid is more likely to win a contract than a higher one. They know that large international corporations are able to look elsewhere, whereas their own options are more limited. What do you think those suppliers are likely to do to earn the contract?

Odds are, you own some garments that say "Made in Bangladesh" on their labels. Perhaps you don't even know where Bangladesh is. Probably you have no knowledge of conditions in its garment factories, because it would take a lot of moral commitment to do the research necessary to find out. "Supply chains" in a global economy are very complex, and you cannot see how your choices as a consumer impact workers on the other side of the planet. Consumer demand for a particular product is typically a combination of price and perceived quality, as affected by advertising. Is it too much to ask global companies to tell us more about a product than where it was made? Suppose you could use your smartphone to scan the QR code that now accompanies many products sold at retail stores. But instead of finding out more about the nature of the product itself from the website that appears on your phone, you could learn whether the company stands behind the working conditions that produced it. Would you do that?

SUMMARY

1. **Describe the three main forms of exchange in economic systems.** Anthropologists classify exchange into three major modes or forms: reciprocity, redistribution, and market. Reciprocity is the giving and receiving of objects or services without the transfer of money. There are three subtypes, distinguished by motivations and social effects: generalized reciprocity, balanced reciprocity, and negative reciprocity. In redistribution, the members of a group contribute products, objects, or money into a pool or fund, which a central authority reallocates or uses for public purposes, as exemplified by taxes and tribute. Market exchange involves buying and selling commodities and requires money, prices determined by supply and demand, and privately owned property.

2. **Analyze how the form of reciprocity between people varies with social distance.** The kind of reciprocity that exists between individuals and groups depends on the normatively appropriate social distance between them. Exchange relationships alter as social relationships change. Conversely, one party can attempt to alter a relationship by offering an object (or invitation), and the other party can signal acceptance or rejection by a particular response. Reciprocal exchanges can communicate messages about feelings and relationships, so they often have symbolic as well as material content.

3. **Discuss the relationship between redistribution and political organization.** Redistribution is a major form of exchange in societies that have formal political leaders, who in preindustrial cultures are most commonly called chiefs. As part of their status, chiefs have the right to receive tribute from their subjects, in the form of labor or products. Chiefs organize labor for public projects and reallocate the products among the community. Chiefdoms vary in the proportion of tribute kept by the chief's family versus redistributed back to the community.

4. **Describe the properties of money.** Money makes the exchange of goods and services more convenient and facilitates the making of profit and accumulation of wealth. Money functions as a medium of exchange, a standard of value, and a store of value. These functions mean that money objects usually have the characteristics of durability, divisibility, limited supply, and portability.

5. **Discuss the distinction between market exchange and market economies (capitalism) and the differences between neoliberalism and social welfare capitalism.** Market as a form of exchange involves the buying and selling of products or services using money. Market economies exist wherever market principles organize the entire economy of a people. Capitalism refers to economic growth by the accumulation and investment of capital. Neoliberals place great trust in the Invisible Hand of markets to regulate economic activity and produce optimal outcomes. In social welfare capitalist economies, governments exercise a lot of control over the free market to benefit workers and the poor.

6. **Discuss the globalization of markets and its impacts on workers, consumers, corporations, and cultural preservation.** Because of market globalization, most of the world is integrated into a single-market system. Global markets impact all categories of people. There is wide agreement that corporations who export production facilities benefit from lowered production costs and generally make more profit. Consumers also benefit from prices that are lower than they otherwise would be. The impacts on working-class people in all countries are more complicated, variable, and debated. However, worker health and safety is one issue on which both critics and promoters of globalization agree.

9 Marriages and Families

Kim Kulish/Corbis News/Corbis

Popular ideas about whether legal marriage should be limited to opposite sex persons are changing very rapidly in many nations. Anthropology has some insights on this issue.

Some Definitions

Incest Taboos

Marriage
 Defining Marriage
 Functions of Marriage
 Two Unusual Forms

Variations in Marriage Beliefs and Practices
 Marriage Rules
 How Many Spouses?
 Polygyny
 Polyandry
 Marriage Alliances

 Marital Exchanges
 Bridewealth
 Brideservice
 Dowry

Same-Sex Marriage and the Culture Wars

Postmarital Residence Patterns
 Influences on Residence Patterns
 Residence and Households

Kinship Diagrams

Family and Household Forms
 Matrifocal Households
 Extended Households

LEARNING OBJECTIVES

After reading this chapter, you should be able to

1. **DISCUSS** the main theories of the culturally universal incest taboo.
2. **ANALYZE** why marriage is difficult to define cross-culturally.
3. **DESCRIBE** the forms of marriage and some of the ways cultures use marriage relationships for wider purposes.
4. **LIST** the main patterns of marriage exchanges and the cultural rationales behind them.
5. **EVALUATE** changes in attitudes toward same-sex marriage and why the issue is so controversial.
6. **DISCUSS** patterns of postmarital residence and some major influences on them.
7. **EXPLAIN** why household forms are important in a human community.

When politicians proclaim that "the family is the backbone of our nation" and that their own policies promote "family values," they can hardly go wrong. How many voters see themselves as antifamily? However, when most politicians call families the nation's backbone, they mean the "traditional" nuclear family, consisting of a married couple and their unmarried children. They do not mean families like the gay couple with the adopted daughter on the TV show *Modern Family*. These are not real families. What is a *family*, anyway?

It is true that the bonds of marriage and family are among the central social relationships of most societies. For one thing, a married couple, aided by some of their relatives, is usually the social group that nourishes and socializes new generations. For another, some kind of kin ties are the basis of residential groups that not only live together but often own property together, work together, and venerate ancestors together.

Families do a lot of things that are helpful to their members and to society at large. So, when close to half of American marriages end in divorce and about a third of children live in households with only one parent present, people tend to think that something is amiss. Will "broken homes" and single-parent families cause harm to children, communities, and even the whole nation? Worrying that marriage between people of the same sex will erode the "sacred institution" of marriage, in 2004 the American president and some members of Congress attempted (unsuccessfully) to amend the Constitution to enforce the one man–one woman marital norm.

Ethnographic studies and anthropological ideas have something to contribute to such contemporary issues. We look at some of the main ways cultures differ in their marriage practices and in the organization of their families and households. Before doing so, though, we need to define some terms used in this and later chapters.

Some Definitions

An organized, cooperative group based on kinship relationships between the members is what anthropologists call a **kin group**. The **nuclear family**, which consists of a married couple together with their unmarried children, is one kind of kin group. Typically its members live together, share the use of family wealth and property, rely on one another for emotional support, pool their labor and resources to support the family, and so on.

Among their many functions, nuclear families usually have primary responsibility for nurturing and enculturating children. North Americans usually think of each nuclear family as living in its own dwelling such as an apartment, condo, townhouse, or their own house. In fact, some Euro-Americans look down on immigrants from Latin America, Africa, and Southeast Asia for housing too many nuclear families in one "single-family" dwelling.

---

kin group Group of people who culturally view themselves as relatives, cooperate in certain activities, and share a sense of identity as kinfolk.

nuclear family Family consisting of a married couple and their offspring.

CONCEPT REVIEW

Terms for Groups Formed on the Basis of Kinship Relationships

Term	Meaning
Kin group	A social group formed on the basis of recognized (including fictive) kin relationships between its members
Nuclear family	A married couple and their unmarried children
Extended family	Culturally recognized relatives of varying degrees of distance
Household	A domestic group, or people who live in the same place and share assets and certain responsibilities

People everywhere keep track of distant relatives who are part of their **extended family**. In North America, cousins, aunts and uncles, and other distant relatives gather periodically for holidays, family reunions, weddings, and funerals. However, we recognize how hard it can be to "get the whole family" together for such events. Extended families do not have clear social boundaries; rather, people's recognition of relationships wither and disappear as relatives become more and more distant. You may know and occasionally interact with your first and second cousins, but beyond that range, whether you even know their names depends mostly on circumstances such as whether they live in your town or state.

In contrast, in many preindustrial societies, most important relationships in people's lives are defined by extended kinship ties. Extended families are far more important in the lives of individuals: members live in the same household, rely on one another for help with work and access to resources, share religious duties, and so forth. Some of these groups are enormously large, consisting of hundreds of members, as we see in the next chapter.

A **household** refers to people who reside in the same physical location. In the United States, most people continue to believe that typical households consist of a married couple plus any children still living with them. Yet the 2010 census revealed that only 48 percent of households were "husband wife households," either with or without children. A third were "nonfamily households," meaning that no family members lived in the same space. Popular ideas about what families and households are like often are inaccurate, partly because people tend to confuse their cultural norms with social realities.

In some societies, nuclear families live in separate dwellings on land they own jointly with families who are related to them. For example, women who are sisters may live on land given to them by their parents and bring their husbands to live there also. So long as the families use common property like land and tools, cooperate in work, share income or wealth, and recognize themselves as having distinctive identities, they belong to a single *household* even though they live in separate *houses*.

The preceding terms referring to groupings based on family and kinship seem simple enough. But it is easy to use one term when technically you mean another, which can lead to confusion. The Concept Review may provide some help.

Households are not always formed exclusively by family or marital ties, as gay and lesbian couples, heterosexual unmarried couples living together, and various other roommates and housemates illustrate. In a great many societies, people incorporate unrelated people into their household, acting and feeling toward them in the same way as they do biological relatives. This practice is widespread enough that there is a phrase for it: **fictive kinship**, in which individuals who are not actually biological relatives act toward one another as if they were kin. Adoption is a familiar example. In many islands of the Pacific, it is very common for a couple to adopt (or foster) one or more children, whether or not they have parented children themselves. Unlike in

---

extended family Set of nuclear families related through culturally variable kinship ties.

household Dwelling or compound inhabited by biological relatives or fictive kin who cooperate and share resources; in some contexts, a kin group of one or more nuclear families living in the same physical space.

fictive kinship Condition in which people who are not biologically related behave as if they are relatives.

most Western nations, usually adopted children in the Pacific also maintain relationships with their biological parents, who are often relatives of their adopted parents. For many purposes, such children in effect have two sets of parents to support them emotionally and economically.

This chapter mainly concerns the diversity in marriage and family among humanity. We begin with the point that every people have rules that govern who may and may not marry. The most universal of these rules is the *incest taboo*, which is so basic that we discuss it first.

Incest Taboos

Rules against sexual intercourse between relatives are called **incest taboos**. Although incest taboos are cultural universals (see Chapter 2), there are many complexities. For one thing, the specific relatives to whom the taboos apply vary from people to people. Some societies prohibit sex and marriage between all first cousins, whereas others not only allow but prefer marriage among certain cousins. We cover such cases later.

For another thing, nearly every society prohibits sex between nuclear family members. However, there are three documented cases in which sexual intercourse between siblings was permitted: the ancient Hawaiians, the prehistoric Incas, and the civilization of Egypt. Among the Hawaiians and Incas, incest was allowed only to members of the royal family and existed to preserve the purity and exclusiveness of the royal ancestral bloodline. In ancient Egypt, even common people sometimes married (and presumably had sex with) their own siblings. Everywhere else in the known world, sexual intercourse between siblings and between parents and children is culturally forbidden (which is not the same as saying it does not occur). In most cultures, the incest taboo is extended beyond the nuclear family to prohibit sex between uncles and nieces, aunts and nephews, and some kinds of cousins. Other than the widespread extension to these relatives, cultures vary in the categories of kinfolk with whom sex is taboo.

Anthropologists have wondered a lot about why nuclear family incest is almost universally taboo. This wonder sometimes surprises people who are not anthropologists, who usually think that intercourse within the family is universally prohibited because inbreeding

incest taboo Prohibition against sexual intercourse between certain kinds of relatives.

is genetically harmful to the children. Indeed, in Euro-American societies, incest is illegal because science has demonstrated that the offspring of incestuous matings have a significantly higher chance of exhibiting harmful recessive alleles. But human societies had laws or norms against incest long before genetic science even existed, so clearly biomedical knowledge is not the primary explanation for the universality of the incest taboo.

What, then, are some other reasons for the nuclear family incest taboo? There are four major explanations.

The first two explanations begin with the assumption that many or most people have sexual desire for their close relatives. Because acting on these desires would somehow harm others in their family or other group, the incest taboo exists to help groups control such behavior. In many cultures, adults teach children that incest is one of the most reprehensible crimes, and this culturally imposed prohibition discourages people from acting out their desire. Several specific hypotheses make these assumptions, but we discuss only two of the most credible.

"Marry Out or Die Out" is the idea first proposed by E. B. Tylor, one of the nineteenth-century evolutionists mentioned in Chapter 6. Tylor noted that a rule prohibiting marriage between close relatives forces people to seek their mates outside their domestic groups. Such marriages force families to establish relationships with one another—relationships that widen the scale of economic and political cooperation. Over time, groups that marry out had an advantage over those that did not, so eventually all groups developed incest taboos.

As we note later, Tylor's idea contains an important insight: outmarriage offers advantages to those family groups that practice it. Unfortunately, this insight does not pertain to the incest taboo. There is no necessary reason a successful family could not allow sexual relations between its members but forbid them to marry one another. This hypothesis thus confuses the incest taboo ("Thou shalt not have sexual intercourse within thine own domestic group") with outmarriage rules ("Thou shalt not marry within thine own domestic group").

The "Peace in the Family" hypothesis, also called the *family disruption hypothesis*, argues that nuclear family incest would lead to sexual rivalry and competition within the family unit. It would interfere with the normal and essential functions of the family, such as economic cooperation and enculturation. It also might undermine the authority of the parental generation, who would often be challenged by their children. Brothers might be brought to blows over their sisters, and vice versa. Imagine the status and role confusions: for example, if a man had children by his daughter, the daughter's children would also be her half-siblings, and the father's children would simultaneously be his grandchildren.

This hypothesis is certainly plausible but difficult to evaluate. We do not know whether sexual relations in the family would threaten the "family peace" because the nuclear family incest taboo is nearly universal. Most likely, families would be seriously "disrupted," but we have no way of testing the hypothesis. At any rate, the incest taboo is sometimes extended to very distant relatives who hardly know one another, and family disruption cannot explain these extensions.

The other two explanations both assume that the majority of people have little sexual desire for their close relatives. The two hypotheses are closely related and, indeed, complementary. Also, the same objection applies to both: if there is so little sexual desire between close relatives, then why do people need a taboo at all?

"Inbreeding Avoidance" is the cultural rationale for the taboo familiar to most readers. Both genetic theory and animal experimentation have established that offspring of sexual unions between close relatives have a significantly higher probability of inheriting homozygously recessive harmful alleles that show up phenotypically; that is, incest is bad for the children and the "gene pool." The inbreeding avoidance explanation simply states that the incest taboo exists to reduce the incidence of mating between close relatives.

Why, then, are many anthropologists not completely satisfied with this explanation? One reason has already been mentioned: many peoples are unaware of these harmful genetic effects, so these effects cannot consciously be the reason for the taboo. This objection, however, does not invalidate the inbreeding-avoidance idea because the hypothesis does not require conscious awareness that inbreeding is potentially harmful. Nonhuman primates do not "know" that inbreeding increases the expression of harmful alleles, but they act "as if they know": they generally do not mate with close genetic relatives. We need only assume that throughout humanity's evolutionary history, those individuals who mated with their close relatives left fewer surviving and reproducing offspring than those who did not. The genes of those who did not interbreed with their close relatives would have spread within the population. Evolution thus "built in" a lack of sexual desire for close relatives over a long time span. If so, our knowledge is instinctive rather than conscious. This idea about the incest taboo is consistent with evolutionary psychology (see Chapter 5), the general theory that humanity's behavior has been shaped by genetic evolution. (Notice that evolution would also have had to build in knowledge of who one's close relatives are, or who they are most likely to be.)

Another objection to the inbreeding avoidance hypothesis is more serious: many peoples do not apply the taboo to the kinds of relatives that the hypothesis predicts they should. For example, some peoples allow or encourage marriage between one set of cousins but prohibit both marriage and sexual intercourse with another set of cousins who are equally closely related genetically. Among certain populations, it is quite common for a man to marry his mother's brother's daughter, but for his father's brother's daughter to be prohibited as both a sexual and marriage partner. Yet among other peoples, a man is encouraged to marry his father's brother's daughter. Now why should some populations prohibit sex with one kind of cousin and others encourage it? In other words, the inbreeding-avoidance theory alone does not explain the cross-cultural variability in the kinds of relatives to whom the taboo applies. It predicts (or seems to predict) that all peoples ought to prohibit the same relatives.

The "Familiarity Breeds Disinterest" explanation holds that males and females who are closely associated during childhood have little sexual desire for one another when they grow up. Also called the *childhood familiarity hypothesis,* this hypothesis was first proposed by a nineteenth-century scholar named Edward Westermarck. It was rejected for decades but became popular again in the 1970s because of some ethnographic studies that seem to support it.

One study is from the *kibbutzim,* the agricultural collectives first established in Israel in the 1950s. Most kibbutzim have disbanded, but in the past children were not raised by their parents but in communal peer groups by specialists in child care. Several infants of similar age were placed in a common nursery soon after birth. They were nourished and enculturated as a group, with more children joining them later around five or six years of age. A peer group of 10 to 20 children was raised together until adolescence, more or less as if they were siblings. Boys and girls raised in the same peer group were not forbidden to marry and in fact adults often encouraged them to get together. But people raised together almost never married, although they had lots of opportunities to get to know one another. Their behavior seems to support the "familiarity breeds disinterest" idea.

Arthur Wolf's 1960s study of marriage in Taiwan also supports the childhood-familiarity theory. Some Taiwanese couples with male children took girls to be

On the kibbutzim of Israel, children raised in communal nurseries tended not to be interested in one another sexually, supporting the "familiarity breeds disinterest" theory of the incest taboo. Here four kibbutz children are getting ready for bed after their baths.

reared and trained in their households as future wives for their sons. In such families, a boy and girl grew up together in the same household—in most respects just like brother and sister—and were expected to marry. If it is true that children raised together have little sexual interest in one another, then there should be less sexual activity and greater marital difficulties for these couples than for other Taiwanese. Wolf found that these couples had fewer children, higher rates of divorce, and more extramarital sexual activity than other couples.

Evidence from an Arab village in Lebanon studied by Justin McCabe also supports Westermarck's hypothesis. For a variety of reasons, it is fairly common in the Middle East for a man to marry one of his father's brother's daughters. In the village McCabe studied, about 20 percent of all marriages were between men and women whose fathers were brothers. These cousins were in constant childhood association with one another because of the sibling relationship between their fathers. If childhood familiarity does indeed produce adult sexual disinterest, then it should be revealed in these marriages. In fact, it is: these cousin marriages had three times the divorce rate and produced fewer children than other kinds of marriage.

So, some ethnographic research suggests that individuals who experience intimate childhood associations tend not be interested in one another as sexual partners. This sexual disinterest cannot be universal, or there would never be any nuclear family incest, but such incest is likely more common than publicly recognized. However, the childhood-familiarity hypothesis does explain why most people do not commit incest within the nuclear family—they have little sexual desire for one another.

Furthermore, if childhood familiarity leads to erotic disinterest as adults, then the inbreeding-avoidance explanation is also supported. To avoid inbreeding, people must have some way of recognizing their close relatives. In general, my close relatives are likely to be those with whom I was raised, so if I avoid mating with my childhood associates, I generally will not be inbreeding. Both these hypotheses taken together are capable of explaining why nuclear family incest is uncommon.

Some scholars have used the very existence of a taboo on incest to argue against both the inbreeding-avoidance and childhood-familiarity explanations. Their argument is that if people generally do not have erotic feelings toward close relatives, then cultures do not need a taboo. The fact that there is a taboo at all proves there is sexual desire for close kin, for why prohibit an action that people have no desire to commit? But this objection is unfair because neither explanation denies that some people desire close relatives sexually. There is merely evidence suggesting that *most* people do not. We can see why this objection is unfair with an analogous legal prohibition: few people argue that laws against murder or assault prove that most people would commit these acts without the laws.

To conclude, notice that three of the four hypotheses account mainly for the incest prohibitions within the nuclear family. They therefore cannot explain everything about incest taboos because in most human populations incest prohibitions are extended to more distant relations. For example, in a great many societies, members of the same clan (discussed in Chapter 10) are subject to the taboo, and clanmates are often very distantly related. Therefore, it is plausible to conclude that the incest taboo has a biological basis, but that some peoples extend it beyond close relatives to achieve other social and cultural objectives.

Marriage

Biologically speaking, procreation creates the family relationships of an individual: who your parents are determines your grandparents, your aunts and uncles, your cousins, and so forth. Assuming the woman and man are married, marriage and its resulting family relationships seem pretty basic. How many ways can people marry and have families? Quite a few, it turns out. We begin with marriage.

Defining Marriage

What is marriage? Westerners with little knowledge of cultural diversity might say that marriage is a relationship between a woman and a man involving romantic love, sexual activity, cohabitation, child rearing, and shared joys and burdens of life. People trained in law might also note that marriage has legal aspects, such as joint property rights and obligations to share support of children. Religious people may want to include their beliefs that marriage is a relationship sanctioned by God, a relationship that should last until the parties are separated by death. Gay, lesbian, and bisexual people will add their own provisions, which we address later.

These provisions are broadly applicable in many modern nations. However, they obscure the diversity in marriages that anthropologists have uncovered. For example, choosing one's spouse is not always a private matter decided by the couple. In many cultures, marriage is likely to be a *public* matter that involves a broad range of relatives who must consent to or even arrange the marriage.

Also, as often as not romantic love is not considered necessary for marriage, and sometimes it is not even relevant to the relationship. Couples do not marry because they "fall in love." For example, in traditional China, Korea, and Japan, a man and a woman seldom had a chance to fall in love before they married because they usually hardly knew each other and often had not even met. Sometimes boys and girls were betrothed at birth or as children. Even when couples married as adults, the marriage was arranged by their parents with the aid of a matchmaker, usually a female relative of the groom's family or a woman hired by them. She tried to find a woman of suitable age, wealth, status, and disposition to become a wife for the young man. The matchmaker would "match" not only the couple to each other, but also the woman to the husband's parents. This was important because the new wife would be incorporated into her husband's family. Her labor would be under the control of her husband's parents, especially her mother-in-law. She was expected to revere the ancestors of her husband's family more than those of her own parents. Her behavior would be closely watched lest she disgrace her husband and in-laws; often she would stay inside the family compound and not be allowed to interact with outsiders without supervision. Her children would become members of her husband's family, not her own. Love and affection might come after a marriage, but duty and procreation were more important than romantic love in China, Korea, Japan, as among many other peoples.

Even cohabitation in the same house does not universally accompany marriage. In many villages in Melanesia, Southeast Asia, and Africa, the men sleep and spend much of their time in a communal house (called, appropriately, the *men's house*), while their wives and young children live and sleep in a separate dwelling.

Other Western cultural notions of and customs about marriage do not apply elsewhere. Sex is not always confined to the marriage bed (or mat). There may or may not be a formal ceremony (wedding) recognizing or validating a new marriage. The marital tie may be fragile or temporary, with individuals expecting to have several spouses during the course of their lives. Or the tie may be so strong that even death does not end it. For example, in parts of old India, there were strict rules against the remarriage of a higher-caste widow, and such a widow often followed her husband to the grave by throwing herself onto his cremation fire (a practice now illegal in India).

Finally, there are culturally legitimate marital relationships that are not between a man and a woman. Among the Nuer of south Sudan, sometimes an older, well-off woman pays the bridewealth needed to marry a girl. The girl then takes male lovers and bears children, who are incorporated into the kin group of the older woman. The pastoral and horticultural Nandi of Kenya allow marriage between women. Some men have more than one wife, and at her husband's death surviving wives normally receive a share of his cattle, which they, in turn, pass along to their own sons. When a married woman grows too old to bear children and happens to have no sons to inherit the cattle given her by her husband, she may take a younger woman as her wife, thus becoming a "female husband." She picks a sexual partner for her young wife, whose male children then become the heirs of the "female husband." The two women, however, are not supposed to be sexually active after the birth, with other men as well as with each other. Regina Smith Oboler, who worked among the Nandi, reported that the relationship was almost identical to that between a married woman and a man.

Because of such diversity, defining marriage to encompass all the cross-cultural variations in the relationship is hard because there will always be some people who do not fit the definition. As you can imagine, numerous definitions have been offered, but there is still no agreement on the "best" one. Most anthropologists agree, however, that marriage in *most* human societies involves the following:

- A culturally defined and variable relationship between a man and a woman from different families, which regulates sexual intercourse and legitimizes children
- A set of rights the couple and their families obtain over each other, including rights over children born to the woman
- An assignment of responsibility for nurturing and enculturating children to the spouses and/or to one or both sets of their relatives
- A creation of variably important bonds and relationships between the families of the couple that have social, economic, political, and sometimes ritual dimensions

If we define marriage in this way, do all societies have some form of marriage?

This question is tricky, and not just because the definition above is problematic. However, the answer appears to be no. Consider the Musuo (also called Na and Naxi) an ethnic group of Yunnan Province in the south of China. The Musuo are ethnically distinct from the Han, who are the cultural and linguistic majority in China. Among traditional Musuo, a typical adult woman remains at the home of her mother and siblings. Men visit her at night for sexual intercourse, but such visits carry no commitment or obligation. Both people have multiple sexual partners without stigma, normatively speaking. The man does not spend the night and seems to have no obligation to his children, or even to recognize them as his. Children are raised by their mother and her own family, which means that Musuo have no nuclear families. Either the woman or her male visitor may initiate the communication that leads to their sexual relationship, but it is always the man who visits at night. The Musuo thus lack all four aspects of the definition of marriage given earlier. Therefore, they have no marriage as we define the term, nor do they have marriage as most people understand it. Cai Hua, the Han Chinese ethnographer, says that the Musuo show that marriage and nuclear families are not universal human institutions. (Where, we might wonder, is the "backbone" of Musuo society?)

Some Han find Musuo so different that many of them visit Yunnan province to see them. Han people often view Musuo women as promiscuous and the Musuo people as matriarchal. (If this were true, in these two respects, Musuo would contrast strongly with traditional Han practices, which perhaps is why so many Han are interested.) The Chinese central government has a policy of speeding the development of the country's more remote, poorer regions, including the rural areas of Yunnan province. So the government encourages Han visits and has even helped establish "parks" where Musuo perform their allegedly traditional songs and dances.

However, the Musuo are very unusual. Nearly all other peoples have some institution that is recognizably "marriage."

Functions of Marriage

The near-universality of marriage suggests that marriage does important and useful things for individuals, families, and/or society at large. Four functions are among the most important:

1. Marriage creates the social relationships that provide for the material needs, social support, and enculturation of children. Most cultures recognize

that forming a (variably) stable bond between a woman and her husband is an important reason to marry. In the human species, one reason the tie between mothers and fathers is more important than in most other animals is the lengthy dependence of children on adults. Until age 10 or older, children are largely dependent on adults for food, shelter, protection, and other bodily needs. Equally important, children need adults for the social learning that is crucial to complete their psychological and social development. It is theoretically possible that children *need* only one adult, the mother. But generally children benefit from multiple caretakers and supporters, and marriage helps to create and expand relationships that help children.

2. The marriage bond reduces (but does not eliminate) potential conflicts over sexual access by defining culturally approved sexual activity and constraining adult sexual access. Of course, extramarital sex is not prohibited to the same degree in all cultures, but some kind of limitations are placed on it, often varying by gender. In the vast majority of societies, the nurturing and care of young infants are entrusted mainly to mothers, so it is beneficial for mothers to receive material and social support for some period after childbirth by their relatives, usually including their husbands.

3. All known societies divide up work like getting food and household tasks according to age and gender (Chapters 7 and 11). Men do some kinds of tasks, women other kinds. Although the work usually overlaps, there is enough differentiation in most communities that the products and services produced by women must be shared with men, and vice versa. Marriage helps define these rights and duties and establishes the household within which family members do things for one another. The division of labor also means that most mothers need the assistance of *some* male to help provide food and other necessities to her young children. Commonly, this male is her husband.

4. Marriage creates new relationships between families and other kinds of kin groups. In a few societies, nuclear families are physically able to produce what they need to survive with their own labor and resources. But the incest taboo forces individuals to marry someone other than their immediate relatives. Every such marriage creates a potential new set of relationships between the relatives of the couple. The importance attached to these relationships varies from people to people. At the very least, the families of the wife and husband have a common interest in the children. In addition, a great many societies use the relationships created by intermarriage to establish important trade relationships or political alliances, as we see later.

Because marriage—and the new nuclear family each marriage creates—is useful to individuals and to societies in these and other ways, a relationship like marriage and a group like the family are almost universal among the world's cultures. However, no particular *form* of marriage or *type* of family is universal. Cultures evolved various marriage and family forms to perform these functions. To illustrate the diversity of these forms, we now describe two unusual systems.

Two Unusual Forms

"Marriage" Among the Nayar of Southern India

Before Great Britain assumed colonial control over their part of India in 1792, the Nayar were a warrior caste (see Chapter 13). Because so many Nayar men

Human children are dependent on adult care for many years, as this photo of a Laotian woman and her children reminds us. Providing for the physical and emotional needs of children is everywhere a major function of families.

served as soldiers for surrounding Indian kingdoms, they were away from their homes and villages much of the time. Frequent male absence affected marriage and family life. The Nayar lacked nuclear families, in the sense of a couple and their offspring living together and sharing responsibilities. Depending on how we define marriage, they may have had no marriage either. Yet Nayar people managed all the "functions" of marriage listed earlier. How did sexuality and provision for children work in such circumstances?

Each Nayar village contained several kin groups. At birth, most children became members of the kin group of their mother. Each group was linked for certain ceremonial purposes to several other groups, either from its own or from neighboring villages. Nayar women and men who engaged in sexual relations with anyone in their own kin group were put to death because such behavior was considered incest. Restrictions on Nayar women were even more severe: in addition to upholding the incest taboo, under penalty of death or ostracism, women had to confine their sexual activity to men of their own or a higher subcaste.

Every few years, all the girls of a kin group who were nearing puberty gathered for a large ceremony, the purpose of which was to ceremonially "marry" these girls to selected men from the linked kin groups. At the ceremony, each "groom" tied a gold ornament around the neck of his "bride." Each couple then went to a secluded place for three days, where they sometimes had sexual relations. Afterward, the "grooms" left the village, and none had any further responsibilities to his "bride." He might never even see her again. For her part, the "bride" and the children she would later bear had only to perform a certain ritual for her ceremonial "husband" when he died. The ritual tying of the ornament by a man of a linked kin group served to establish a girl as an adult, able to have sexual liaisons with other men when she matured.

After her "marriage," each girl continued to live with her own family. When she reached menarche, she received nighttime male visitors from other kin groups. She established long-lasting relationships with some of her partners, who gave her small luxury gifts periodically but did not live with her. None of her partners supported her or her children in any way other than these occasional gifts. In fact, they also visited other women and fathered other children. The food, clothing, and other needs of a woman and her children were supplied by her brothers and other members of her own family.

A Nayar woman's early "marriage," then, did not establish a nuclear family, nor did her later sexual partners live with her or support her children. There was only one other thing a woman required from her partners: when she got pregnant, one of them had to admit that he could have been the father of her child by paying the fees for the midwife who helped deliver the baby. If none of her partners did so, it was assumed that she had sexual intercourse with someone of a lower caste. She, and sometimes her child, would be expelled from her kin group or killed.

Cross-generational Marriage Among the Tiwi of Northern Australia

In most societies, people who marry are comparable in age. Often the husband is older, sometimes significantly older. The Tiwi, who traditionally lived on the Bathurst Islands just off the coast of northern Australia, were unusual because both sexes frequently married people of markedly different ages—in fact, most spouses belonged to different generations. Ethnographer C. W. M. Hart worked among the Tiwi in the late 1920s, and Arnold Pilling worked there in the early 1950s. Jane Goodale's later work in the 1960s focused on Tiwi women.

Like other aboriginal peoples of Australia, the Tiwi were hunters and gatherers. Male elders made most of the important decisions in a band, including decisions about foraging activities and the distribution of food. Many elderly men were polygynous—that is, they had more than one wife. Polygynous men had access to lots of food from their wives' gathering and fishing, and they could acquire prestige and allies by distributing the food widely to other families. Tiwi prized meat, but as men reached their 50s and 60s, they were unable to hunt effectively. To hunt meat for food and distributions, they needed sons, which they generally had, and sons-in-law, which they could get by marrying off their daughters.

Tiwi marriage was unusual because of two rare customs. First, when a girl was born, she was almost immediately promised as a wife to some other man. This is "infant betrothal," with the girl's husband selected by her father. Second, Tiwi norms required that all females be married virtually all their lives. So after she was betrothed, an infant girl was considered already married. And when a woman's husband died, she remarried almost immediately, called "widow remarriage."

An astute Tiwi father did not marry his infant daughter to just anyone. He used her marriage to win friends and gain allies. The allies who were most valuable were men of about his own age, so naturally he tended to marry his daughters to these men. But the relationship created by one such marriage was often reciprocated: if you married your daughter to a friend, you would likely receive his daughter, sooner or later. So a man might gain a wife in return for a daughter.

If a man's wives had daughters when he was in his 40s and 50s (which was common because wives were so young), then he married some of them to men his own age. Not all of them, though, because a man also wanted young sons-in-law to come live in his band and help supply meat. An elder would look around for a man in his 20s who seemed like a diligent and skillful hunter and a promising ally. He married some of his daughters to these younger men. When his daughters grew up, his sons-in-law would supply him and his household with meat.

A girl growing into womanhood would already have a husband, most likely one who was perhaps 20 or 30 years older than herself. Of course, this meant that most wives outlived their husbands but did have children by them. By Tiwi custom, widows had to remarry. But to whom? Some young men in their 20s had failed to attract the notice of elders and therefore had no wives of their own. But they still could be friends and useful allies of the sons of these widowed women. So at the death of a man, her sons (usually with her consent and approval) married their mother to a man 20 or 30 years her junior. That way, she would have the support of a strong hunter as she aged, and her sons would strengthen a friendship and gain an ally. (Incidentally, Tiwi wives might seem like "pawns," but in fact they were active participants in marital machinations, as Jane Goodale documented in her book *Tiwi Wives*.)

If you had visited the Tiwi during their traditional life, roughly here's what you would have observed: Many elderly men had several wives, most of whom were 20 to 30 years younger than themselves. Young men had either no wife at all or only one wife, and that one wife was probably at least 20 years older than her husband. Elderly men were married to women in the prime of their lives, whereas many younger men in their "prime" had wives who were old enough to be their mother. Looked at from the point of view of a typical female's life cycle, she was first married to a much older man. Then after he died, she married a man who was young enough to be her son.

We emphasize again that both the Nayar and the Tiwi had unusual marriage systems. (Both systems are no longer operating.) Of course, neither people viewed their own marriage practices as "unusual." It was just what they did. Perhaps they even thought it was only natural. Maybe they even considered it the backbone of their societies.

Variations in Marriage Beliefs and Practices

As suggested by Nayar and Tiwi, the marriage relationship varies enormously among cultures. For one thing, most traditional cultures allow multiple spouses. For another, the nature of the marital relationship—living arrangements, what wives and husbands expect from each other, who decides who marries whom, authority patterns, how the relatives of the couple relate to one another, and so forth—differs from people to people.

Marriage Rules

Everywhere, norms identify members of some social groups or categories as potential spouses and specify members of other groups or categories as not eligible for marriage. One set of rules is **exogamous rules**. Exogamy ("outmarriage") means that a person is prohibited from marrying within her or his own family or other kin group or, less commonly, village or settlement. (Recall that the incest taboo prohibits *sex*, whereas rules of exogamy forbid *intermarriage*.) Because the incest taboo applies to those people whom the local culture defines as close relatives, members of one's own nuclear family and other close kin are almost everywhere prohibited as spouses.

Other kinds of marriage rules are **endogamous rules**. Endogamy ("inmarriage") means that an individual must marry someone in his or her own social group. The classic example of an endogamous group is the caste in traditional Hindu India (see Chapter 13). Other kinds of endogamous categories are found in orthodox Jews, races in the American South during slavery, and noble classes in many ancient civilizations and states.

Endogamous rules have the effect of maintaining social barriers between groups of people culturally defined as having different social statuses or ranks. Rules of endogamy maintain the exclusiveness of the endogamous group in two ways. First, they reduce

---

exogamous rules Marriage rules prohibiting individuals from marrying a member of their own social group or category.

endogamous rules Marriage rules requiring individuals to marry some member of their own social group or category.

social contacts and interactions between individuals who are culturally believed (often, by widely accepted world views) to belong to distinct social categories. Intermarriage creates new relationships between the families of the wife and husband and potentially is a means of raising the status or rank of oneself or one's offspring. Endogamy keeps marriage within the caste, class, ethnic group, race, or whatever. Over generations, this reinforces ties *within* the endogamous groups and decreases interactions *between* the groups.

Second, endogamy symbolically expresses and strengthens the exclusiveness of the higher ranking endogamous group by preventing its "contamination" by outsiders. This is most apparent with Indian castes because the cultural rationale for caste endogamy is to avoid ritual pollution: the Hindu religion holds that physical contact with members of lower castes places high-caste individuals in a state of spiritual danger, precluding the possibility of marriage between them.

Technically, *endogamy* applies only to cultural rules (or even laws) about confining marriage to those within one's own group. But it is important to note the existence of *de facto endogamy*, meaning that although no formal rules or laws require inmarriage, most people marry people like themselves. De facto social class endogamy exists in most modern nations, including North America, partly because opportunities for members of different classes to get to know one another are often limited. For instance, members of different classes often go to different kinds of schools and hang out with different sets of friends. Such practices decrease social interactions between classes and thus reduce the possibility that people of different classes will meet and fall in love.

De facto endogamy also exists because of beliefs about the dangers of marrying outside one's own "kind." Members of elite classes (and parents and other relatives of young people) may worry that would-be spouses of lower-class standing would not fit in with their social circle (to phrase their objection politely). Likewise, interracial couples are warned about the social stigma attached to their relationship and about the "problems" they and their children will encounter. Of course, these problems exist largely because some people continue to think that interracial marriages are problematic.

Racial, ethnic, and even religious barriers to intermarriage are breaking down in many regions due to improved education and increased interactions between peoples due to globalization. By expanding the range of nationalities people get to know, international and intercultural marriages are becoming commonplace. Globalization is changing popular attitudes and affecting marriage and family in this obvious way but also in more subtle ways (see Globalization Challenges and Opportunities).

How Many Spouses?

One way cultures vary in marriage practices is in the number of spouses an individual is allowed to have at a time. There are four logical possibilities:

1. **Monogamy**, in which every individual is allowed only one spouse
2. **Polygyny**, in which one man is allowed multiple wives
3. **Polyandry**, in which one woman is allowed multiple husbands
4. **Group marriage**, in which several women and men are allowed to be married simultaneously to one another

The last three possibilities are all varieties of **polygamy**—"plural spouses." It is important to recognize that the three types of polygamy refer to the number of spouses *allowed* to a person, not necessarily to how many spouses most people have. For example, in polygynous cultures, men are permitted more than one wife, but only a minority of men actually have more than one.

It may surprise members of monogamous societies to learn that most of the world's cultures historically allowed polygyny. In the past, before colonialism affected most of the world's peoples, around 70 percent of all societies allowed a man to have two or more wives. Today, polygyny is allowed in many nations in the Middle East, and it also exists among *some* indigenous peoples of Africa, Southeast Asia, Melanesia, and Amazonia. American news stories give the impression that many Mormons still practice polygyny, but in fact the church outlawed it in the nineteenth century,

---

monogamy Each individual is allowed to have only one spouse at a time.

polygyny One man is allowed to have multiple wives.

polyandry One woman is allowed to have multiple husbands.

group marriage Several women and several men are married to one another simultaneously.

polygamy Multiple spouses.

and the vast majority of Mormon faithful disavow the practice.

Polyandry is rare. It is documented in fewer than a dozen societies—less than 1 percent of the world's cultures. Group marriage, so far as we know, has never been a characteristic form of marriage in a whole human society. Indeed, most anthropologists believe that group marriage, where it has occurred, has been a short-lived phenomenon brought about by highly unusual circumstances.

Many Westerners misunderstand the nature of polygamous marriages. We fail to recognize the social and economic conditions that make these forms of marriage advantageous. We now look at these conditions for polygynous and polyandrous societies.

Polygyny

Many people who view their nations as modernized believe that polygyny is an outmoded form of marriage. Commonly polygyny is interpreted as a manifestation of patriarchy (men force women into the relationship); as reducing female marital happiness (what woman wants to be part of a "harem"?); as harmful to children (wouldn't the kids of each wife be better off if each has their *own* father?); and as a way to provide men with additional sexual partners (at the expense of each wife). There is some truth to each of these opinions, but they do not tell the whole story of polygyny.

Because so many societies known to anthropology formerly allowed polygyny, many explanations have been offered. Many polygynous peoples practice sexual abstinence for several years after marriage, a custom called the *postpartum sex taboo*. The taboo commonly lasts two to four years. If it is followed, this reduces the birthrate, which might be beneficial, and also allows each newborn to nurse longer, leading to better child nutrition and health. Because of the taboo, polygyny allows husbands a legitimate sexual outlet, protecting new mothers and their children from having children too close together.

Some suggest that polygyny is a response to a shortage of adult males, because of hazardous male activities like warfare and hunting. If there regularly are more adult females than males, then polygyny increases the chances that all women will find husbands and therefore helps provide her and her children with resources and an inheritance.

Disparity in the age of marriage might contribute to the frequency of polygyny. Typically, males are quite older than their wives, partly because they need time to accumulate resources for bridewealth, as discussed later. So, the number of women of marriageable age increases relative to the number of men, allowing some men to have more than one wife and all women to have husbands. Polygyny, then, would solve a social problem caused by a discrepancy in marriage ages for women and men.

In each of these three explanations, it is difficult to disentangle effects and causes. For example, does the postpartum sex taboo help cause polygyny? Or do polygynous men not demand sex from their wives with young children because they have other wives, making the taboo more likely to develop as a means of increasing childhood survival and health? Does the fact that men marry later in life than women make polygyny more likely? Or do men marry later because they need resources to acquire a wife, *because* of the fact that polygyny makes wives in such short supply that women's fathers demand resources for them? Whether these sorts of factors, or other sets, account for polygyny is debatable, especially to humanistically inclined anthropologists.

However, it is generally agreed that men acquire many benefits from plural wives. Men themselves generally recognize the benefits. In societies that allow it, polygyny ordinarily is the preferred form of marriage for most men. Generally, men of high rank and status or wealthy men are the ones who have plural wives, although there are exceptions.

Men usually have both social and economic incentives for marrying several women. Socially, a man's status commonly is related to the size of his family and, hence, to the number of his wives and children. Also, when a man marries more than one woman, he acquires a new set of in-laws—fathers- and brothers-in-law whom he can call on for support, reciprocal relationships, and/or political alliances.

There are also short- and long-term economic benefits, especially in horticultural and pastoral adaptations, where a woman's labor is important in providing food and wealth to her family. The more wives and children a man has, the larger the workforce available to his household. In pastoral societies in Africa and elsewhere, polygyny enables a man to increase the size of his herds because he has more herders (wives and children) to tend livestock. Similarly, in those farming societies in which female labor is important, a polygynous man has more family members to tend fields and harvest crops. As he grows older, he will have more children and grandchildren to look after his herds or work his fields and care for him. Thus, as long as he has the resources to support them, a man usually tries to acquire additional wives.

GLOBAL CHALLENGES AND OPPORTUNITIES

Marriage and Family in Global Society: The Case of Japan

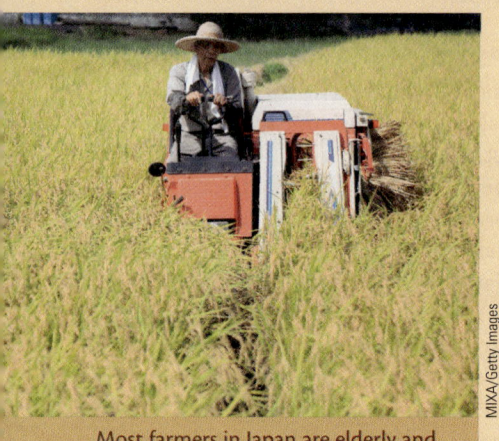

Most farmers in Japan are elderly and many men are bachelors. For two or three decades, Japanese farmers have found it difficult to find wives, due to the perceived hard conditions on farms compared to city life.

As interactions between people of diverse nationalities and cultural traditions increase, people from different regions have more chances to get to know one another. Students cross national boundaries in search of better educations or new cultural experiences. Employees of multinational companies fly all over the world buying and selling. Migrants settle in new homelands. Tourists go abroad to see the world or just to increase their stock of travel stories and photos to show and tell their friends. Sometimes intimate relationships develop from these and other kinds of contacts.

In the old days, when discussing international, intercultural, or interracial relationships, many people talked about the importance of "sticking to your own kind." More polite people discussed all the "problems" such marriages would have because of "society's attitudes." Such attitudes are still around, of course, but such marriages are becoming so common that soon almost everyone will know someone who has married inter-someplace or inter-someone. Perhaps we will someday live in a world where most people consider everyone their "own kind."

Some effects of globalization on marriage and family are more indirect and subtle than people having more chances to meet and fall in love with those of different backgrounds. Take Japan, for example. Japan has been buying from and, especially, selling to the global marketplace since the late nineteenth century, when the nation was "opened up" by the Americans under threat of force. After losing World War II and having two cities destroyed by the only nuclear weapons ever detonated against civilian targets, Japan recovered within two decades. It already had many advantages over countries that Westerners then called *underdeveloped*. It was predominantly urban. Most of its citizens were well educated. It had been industrialized for decades and was reindustrialized in the 1950s and 1960s. It was comparatively homogeneous linguistically and culturally as well as "racially," so most Japanese agreed on their values and goals. It was politically stable with little crime.

After World War II, Japan was the first non-Euro-American nation to develop its economy from global trade. By the 1970s, Japan was such an economic powerhouse that American car makers and electronics manufacturers justifiably felt threatened. As it grew wealthy by exporting its autos, motorcycles, consumer electronics, and other high-tech products, more and more of Japan's rural people left the family farm in search of a better life in the city. This is a common, predictable effect of development: people migrate from farms to cities because of job opportunities and other attractions of city life. Urban households buy their food from farms, theoretically increasing the income of rural people with their purchases.

But marriage and family problems developed in the Japanese countryside. There was an ancient custom known as *primogeniture*, in which the eldest son inherited the family farm, including the farmhouse, equipment, any livestock, and the land. Younger sons made their own ways, perhaps working for their eldest brother on the family estate, joining a Buddhist monastery, or moving to another region. As for women, if a woman's parents were able to arrange her marriage to an eldest son, she moved in with her husband's family, to live with her father- and mother-in-law. Usually, marrying an eldest son was a desirable match for a woman with rural parentage. Although she would have to work hard serving her husband's parents as well as working on the land of her husband, she had considerable economic security for herself and her children, and eventually *she* expected to become the mother-in-law of her eldest son's wife. Then she could take life a bit easier.

As Japan's economy grew after the war and rural-to-urban migration picked up, younger sons from farms migrated. There was still considerable family pressure on eldest sons to remain behind on the family farm. Many Japanese value what's left of their countryside and rural life. Parents, grandparents, and other relatives did not want land that had been in their family to be sold off. Japanese people love rice for its symbolic value as well as for its bodily nourishment. The dominant political party did not want to see the country become even more dependent on imported foods, so it limited rice imports by various means and heavily subsidized Japan's remaining rice farmers. It might appear that the eldest sons were doing well.

Unfortunately, few Japanese women were interested in marrying an eldest son. Farm work is hard, and small farm towns are boring. Many Japanese city women have never been to a farm, and most who have would never dream of moving there. A farm wife probably will live with her husband's parents, with little privacy, and will have to care for them when they grow old. Throughout the countryside, new marriage norms eroded the ability of parents to control the marriages of their daughters, so even most young, rural women were unwilling to marry a farm boy. Better to marry a *salaryman*—a professional man with a reliable and well-paying job in Tokyo or Kyoto or Osaka or another city where work is easier and payoffs higher. In cities, salarymen work long hours and might not come home until midnight, but until recently Japanese wives expected much less socially and romantically from their husbands than Western wives. Odds are, a Japanese husband will turn control over his salary to his wife, who can use it for household expenses and save for their children's education.

The shortage of wives for farmers became a rural crisis. In one village in the late 1980s, of unmarried persons between ages 25 and 39, 120 were men and only 31 were women, a ratio of 4:1. Some Japanese villages organized to find wives for their bachelors. One mountain village placed newspaper ads, promising free winter skiing vacations to all young women who visited and agreed to meet its men. Over a five-year period, 300 women responded, but none became wives of a village man. In another mountain village of 7,000, there were three bachelors for every unmarried woman, so the local government became a marriage agent. It brought in 22 women from the Philippines, South Korea, Thailand, and other Asian countries to marry its men, many in their 40s and 50s. Some marriages endured, but others ended in divorce because of the labor demands of farm life, the burden wives bore in caring for their husband's elderly parents, and cultural differences. Small businesses developed that offered counseling services for bicultural couples and served as marriage brokers to match Japanese men with foreign women.

Even today, many Japanese farm men remain bachelors. Farming in Japan is now primarily a part-time occupation—farmers find off-season jobs in construction or other tasks, unable to make an acceptable living even with government subsidies. And farming is now largely performed by older persons. For example, in one important rice-growing area, between 1980 and 2003, the number of people making most of their money from farming fell by 56 percent, and the number of people between ages 15 and 59 fell by 83 percent. There was one increase, though: there were 600 more farmers older than 70 in 2003 than in 1980.

In the 1990s, many Japanese began to worry about another marriage and family problem: more and more women are postponing marriage into their 30s or choosing not to marry at all. Many continue to live with their parents long past the age when formerly they would have married and had children. Some Japanese refer to these women as *parasaito* ("parasite singles"), because they reside with parents even though many have well-paying jobs. Stereotypically, parasaito are first-class consumers of luxury goods, buying such expensive purses, shoes, and clothing that they seem overly self-indulgent in a culture that still values humility and submission to authority.

However, the choices these young women make are understandable, given their circumstances. Rents in Japanese cities are among the world's highest. Companies have a tendency to get rid of women once they have children. Women know that once they have children much of their time will be spent seeing that the kids get the high grades and test scores that are so important for their future careers. Many Japanese women have good reason to believe that their future husbands will be inattentive because of job pressures.

Still, such choices will worsen one of Japan's problems. For three decades, Japan's birthrate has been falling. In 2010, an average Japanese woman had only 1.2 children over the span of her life. A mean fertility rate of about 2.1 children is required just to replace the population. As a consequence, since 2007 Japan's population has actually been declining. While a fourth of Japan's people are over the age of 65, only 13 percent are under 15. Japanese have the highest mean life spans in the world: 81 years for men, 88 years for women. After leaving the labor force, Japanese live two or three decades. How will the country support so many aged persons in the future?

Polygyny is allowed as a form of marriage in many of the world's cultures. This is a Maasai man with his wives and children. Maasai are a cattle-herding people of Kenya and Tanzania.

What determines whether a particular man is *able* to acquire more than one wife? The answer is usually wealth: only well-to-do men are able to afford more than one wife. "Afford," however, does not mean what Westerners might think; it is often more a matter of being able to *acquire* additional wives than of being able to *support* them. Most polygynous peoples have the custom of bridewealth (discussed later), which requires a prospective groom and his relatives to give livestock, money, or other wealth objects to the kin of the bride. Although fathers and other relatives are typically obliged to help a young man raise bridewealth for one wife, only a minority of men can get together sufficient resources to provide bridewealth for additional wives.

From the female perspective, in many societies polygyny has the beneficial effect of ensuring that virtually all women find husbands. Becoming married is often important for a woman's welfare because marriage legitimizes her children, and in many cultures children are her main or only source of social security—they are the people she depends on to support her in old age. There is another reason a woman wants to marry: to ensure that her children are well provided for. In the majority of polygynous societies, inheritance of land, livestock, and other wealth and productive property passes from fathers to sons. A woman need not marry to bear children, but she does want a husband to ensure that her sons have an adequate inheritance (her married daughters usually acquire their resources from their own husbands). Thus, in societies in which for some reason there are more adult women than men, polygyny provides a means for almost all women to gain the benefits of husbands for both themselves and their children.

There often are social and economic advantages for the co-wives of a polygynous man. Contrary to the view that no woman would want to share a husband with another woman, in many cases wives don't mind having co-wives. Often the most beneficial marriage for a woman is to a man of wealth and status—the type of man most likely to have married other women. Not only will the woman herself be better provided for, but her children may also receive larger inheritances of land, livestock, wealth, or other property. In addition, co-wives may lighten a woman's workload. Co-wives usually work together and cooperate on chores such as producing, processing, and preparing food, tending livestock, and caring for children. Thus, in many societies, it is not unusual for a wife to encourage her husband to take additional wives to assist her in her chores.

However, polygynous marriages have inherent problems. A common problem is rivalry between co-wives and favoritism by husbands. Several strategies are used in polygynous societies to minimize friction. One way is for a man to marry women who are sisters, a widespread practice known as *sororal polygyny*. The rationale for sororal polygyny is that sisters are raised together, are used to working together, have preexisting emotional bonds, and are likely to be less jealous of one another. Sisters are, therefore, likely to be more cooperative than wives who are not related to one another—a point consistent with evolutionary psychology (see Chapter 5).

In most cultures in which a man marries a number of women who are unrelated, each wife usually has her own separate dwelling, which helps to minimize conflict among the co-wives. Also, co-wives are usually allocated different livestock to care for, and they may have separate gardens to tend and harvest. The effect of such practices is that each wife, together with her children, is semi-independent from the other wives. Despite such practices, rivalry and jealousy among co-wives are problems in many polygynous marriages.

Polyandry

Polyandry, the simultaneous marriage of one woman to two or more men, is a documented practice in only about a dozen societies. Much has been written about this unusual form of marriage, but we have not yet satisfactorily explained it. In the past some argued that female infanticide is partly responsible, reasoning that the death of large numbers of girls would produce a shortage of adult women, which would lead some men to be willing to share a wife. All else being equal, female infanticide does indeed have the effect of decreasing the number of marriageable women, but far more human groups allow many of their female infants to die than practice polyandry. Female infanticide is not a *general* explanation for polyandry.

Rather than discussing general explanations, we note that wherever polyandry exists, it does so as an alternative form of marriage. Like polygyny, polyandry is culturally *allowed*, but it is not the *predominant* form of marriage; most couples are monogamous even where polyandry is allowed. Therefore, to understand the reasons for polyandry, we indicate some of the special conditions that lead some people (namely, husbands and their joint wife) to choose to join in a polyandrous marriage.

The insufficiency of a family's land to support all its heirs is one such condition. Many families in farming communities have faced the following dilemma: our land is barely adequate, and all available farmland is already owned by another family or by a landlord, so we cannot provide all our children with enough land to support them and their families. In Ireland and some other parts of Europe and in Japan, one solution was *primogeniture*, or inheritance by the eldest: the oldest son inherited the farm and most of its property, and the younger sons had to find other ways of supporting themselves. Younger sons served in the army or became priests or found some other occupation. Daughters who did not marry usually either remained at home or joined a nunnery.

Some peoples of the Himalayas developed another solution—polyandry. The rugged topography and high altitude of Tibet and Nepal sharply limit the supply of farmland. A farm may be adequate to support only a single family, but many couples have three or more sons. If the sons divide their inheritance by each marrying a wife, over time the land would become so fragmented that the brothers' families would be impoverished. To solve this problem, sometimes all the sons marry one woman. This form of polyandry, called *fraternal polyandry*, helps to keep the farm and family intact and limits the number of children in the family. Although the oldest son usually assumes primary responsibility for the wife and children, the joint wife is not supposed to favor him or his brothers sexually. When children are born, ideally each brother treats them as if they were his own, even if he knows that a particular child was fathered by one of his brothers.

What are the benefits of fraternal polyandry? For the brothers, sharing a wife preserves the family property, keeping the land, the livestock, the house, and other wealth together. Also, one brother can stay in the village and work the family land during the summer, while another brother takes the livestock to high mountain pastures and a third brother (if present) visits towns in the lowlands to sell the family's products. This system also has advantages for the wife, who has multiple husbands to work for her and help support her and her children. Her life is usually less physically strenuous, and she usually has a higher standard of living than a woman married to only one man.

Although Himalayan polyandry has economic advantages, problems can arise. A younger brother can decide at any time to end the arrangement, claim his portion of the family property, marry another woman, and establish his own family. The oldest brother does not have this option because, as head of the family, he bears primary responsibility for supporting the wife and children.

Marriage Alliances

Cultures vary in the importance they attach to the tie between wives and husbands. In some cultures, there is no formal wedding ceremony. Instead, a couple is socially recognized as "married" when they regularly live together and as "divorced" when one of them moves out. Each partner retains her or his own separate property, so the separation or divorce is not very "messy." In the contemporary United States, the wedding ceremony is often an expensive affair; marriages are supposed to endure; and couples usually own houses, furniture, and other property jointly. Yet about half of all new American marriages will end in divorce, many quite messy because of conflicts over property and custody of the children. For many Americans, monogamy turns out to be *serial monogamy,* meaning only one legal spouse at a time.

Many cultures consider the marital relationship to be far more serious. In some, marriage establishes lasting social relationships and bonds not just between the couple but also between their families and other relatives. The relationships between kin groups created by intermarriage are frequently important not only socially but also economically, politically, and often ritually. Marriage establishes an *alliance* between the members of two kin groups, and in many cultures **marriage alliances** are critical for the well-being and even survival of the intermarried groups. This appears to have been the case among the ancient Israelites. As Moses says in Genesis (34:16): "Then we will give our daughters unto you, and we will take your daughters to us, and we will dwell with you, and we will become one people."

The Yanomamö are a horticultural and hunting tribe of the Amazon rain forest. Most Yanomamö villages justifiably feared attacks by enemies, so a village had to be prepared to defend itself. Also, men of each village periodically went on raids intended to capture the women and resources of their enemies. Villages therefore needed to establish and maintain military alliances for mutual defense and offense, because the more men a village could mobilize as warriors, the more likely it was to be successful in conflicts. Having allies was also helpful in case of military defeat: a defeated group could take refuge with an allied village, whose members would feed and protect the refugees until they could establish productive gardens in a new location. Intermarriage was a key strategy in creating and maintaining these alliances. If two or more villages had intermarried, their alliance was as strong as a Yanomamö alliance could be.

The Yanomamö illustrate how intermarriage creates and helps maintain important political relationships between villages. Among many peoples, these relationships are important to families or entire communities. If marriages are a means of establishing ties that are critical to a group's material well-being or survival, then the choice of which group to marry into may be too important to be left entirely up to the younger woman and man whose marriage creates the relationship. Older, wiser, and more responsible people should be making such critical decisions.

Understanding that who marries whom is so important to families and even larger groups helps to explain one widespread custom—*arranged marriages*—that many Westerners view as an infringement on a person's freedom to choose. Try looking at it from a different perspective: Under certain conditions, a young couple's freedom to choose their own spouse is an infringement on the freedom of their parents and other relatives to form advantageous relationships with other families. How serious this infringement is, and whether the "freedom" of one party or another takes precedence, is not absolute but depends on circumstances. Perhaps some of our readers will find arranged marriages less offensive when they realize that in many societies a poor marriage choice puts more people at risk than just the couple themselves.

The importance of the intergroup ties created by intermarriage is also revealed by two other widespread customs. In one, called the **levirate**, if a woman's husband dies, she marries one of his close kinsmen (usually a brother). The relationships between the intermarried kin groups are too valuable for a woman to be returned to her own family because then she might marry into another kin group. Therefore, a male relative of her deceased husband takes his place. Notice also that the levirate provides most widows with a new husband, which generally enhances her life. The levirate was known to the ancient Semitic peoples (see Deuteronomy 25: 5–10).

The converse custom, the **sororate**, also preserves the affinal ties between kin groups. If a woman dies, her kin group is obliged to replace her with another woman from the group, and no additional bridewealth is transferred. The Zulu of southern Africa, as well as

---

marriage alliances Relationships created between families or kin groups by virtue of intermarriage between them.

levirate Custom whereby a widow marries a male relative (usually a brother) of her deceased husband.

sororate Custom whereby a widower marries a female relative of his deceased wife.

many other African peoples, practiced both the levirate and the sororate. In societies with these customs, marriages—and the relationships they create—endure even beyond death.

Marital Exchanges

In most cultures, the marriage of a man and a woman is accompanied by some kind of transfer of goods or services. These *marital exchanges* take numerous forms, including the North American custom of wedding showers and wedding gifts. In these, the presents given by relatives and friends supposedly help the newlyweds establish an independent household. We give things that are useful to the couple jointly, with food preparation and other household utensils the most common type of gift. Most couples today even register at stores so that their relatives and friends will provide the items they want.

Comparatively speaking, the most unusual feature of North American marital exchange is that practically nothing is transferred between the relatives of the groom and bride: the couple treats the gifts as their private property. Like most of our other customs, this seems natural to us. Of course, the gifts go to the couple—what else could happen to them?

Lots of things. For now, notice that the pattern of couples receiving gifts fits with several other features of Euro-American marriage. First, each marriage creates a new nuclear family, which usually results in the establishment of a new independent household. The couple need their own stuff. In contrast, if the newlyweds moved in with one of their relatives, they would not have as great a need for their own pots and pans, wine glasses, silver candlesticks, dishes, and other household items.

Second, North American marriage-gift customs fit with cultural values about the privacy of the marital relationship: it is largely a personal matter between the husband and wife, and their relatives should keep their noses out. If the in-laws get along and socialize, that's great, but our marriages generally do not create strong bonds between the families of the bride and groom. (In fact, the two families often compete for the visits and attention of the couple and their offspring.) As we saw in Chapter 8, gifts make friends, and vice versa. The fact that the in-laws do not exchange gifts with each other is a manifestation of the absence of a necessary relationship between them after the wedding. If, in contrast, the marriage created an alliance between the two sets of relatives, then some kind of an exchange would probably occur between them to symbolize and cement their new relationship.

Third, wedding gifts are presented to the couple, not to the husband or wife as individuals, and are considered to belong equally and jointly to both partners. But there are marriage systems in which the property of the wife is separate from that of her husband; if divorce should occur, there is no squabbling over who gets what and no need for prenuptial legal contracts. Among some Western Pueblo Native Americans of the Southwest, men usually went to live with their wives, meaning that sisters stayed together. A woman might let her husband know he was no longer welcome by placing his personal belongings outside the door. Children stayed with their mothers, of course.

With this background in mind, what kinds of marital exchanges occur in other cultures?

Bridewealth

Bridewealth is the widespread custom that requires a man and/or his relatives to transfer wealth to the relatives of his bride. It is easily the most common of all marital exchanges, found in more than half the world's cultures. The term *bridewealth* is well chosen because the goods transferred are usually among the most valuable symbols of wealth in the local culture. In sub-Saharan Africa, cattle and sometimes other livestock are the most common goods used for bridewealth. Peoples of the Pacific islands and Southeast Asia usually give their bridewealth in pigs or shell money and ornaments.

Bridewealth is mentioned in the Old Testament. In Genesis, a man named Shechem defiled a young woman and then asked her fathers and brothers to give her to him: "Ask me for as great a bride price and gift as you will, and I will give whatever you say to me. Only give me the young woman to be my wife" (Genesis 34:12, English Standard Version).

One of the most common rights a man and his relatives acquire when they transfer bridewealth to his wife's family is rights over the woman's children. Reciprocally, one of a wife's most important obligations is to bear children for her husband. This is well exemplified by the Swazi, a traditional kingdom of southern Africa. A Swazi marriage is a union between two families as well as between the bride and groom. The payment of bridewealth—in cattle and other valuables—to a woman's relatives establishes the husband's rights over his wife. A woman's main duty to her husband is to provide

---

bridewealth Custom in which a prospective groom and his relatives are required to transfer goods to the relatives of the bride to create or validate the marriage.

him with children. If she is unable to do so, her relatives must either return the bridewealth they received for her or provide a second wife to the husband, for which he need pay no extra bridewealth. Reciprocally, a man must pay bridewealth to gain rights of fatherhood over the child of a woman, even though everyone knows he is the child's biological father. If he does not do so, the woman's relatives will keep the child; if the woman herself later marries another man, her new husband will not receive rights over the child unless he pays bridewealth.

Brideservice

Brideservice is the custom in which a husband is required to spend a period of time working for the family of his bride. A Yanomamö son-in-law is expected to live with his wife's parents, hunting and gardening for them until they finally release control over their daughter. Among some Ju/'hoansi bands (see Chapters 7 and 8), a man proves he can provide by living with and hunting for his wife's parents for 3 to 10 years, after which the couple is free to camp elsewhere.

Like bridewealth, the brideservice custom was known to ancient Israelites. In Genesis 29, Jacob agreed to work for seven years for the foreign father of Rachel in return for her. But by the custom of the foreigners, Jacob first had to marry Leah, the eldest daughter, before her father would give him Rachel. So, Jacob worked 14 years for both his brides. You will also realize Jacob practiced sororal polygyny (Genesis 29: 1–30).

Brideservice is the second-most common form of marital exchange; it is the usual compensation given to the family of a bride in roughly one-eighth of the world's cultures. Sometimes it occurs in addition to other forms of marital exchange, however, and occasionally it can be used to reduce the amount of bridewealth owed.

Dowry

Marital exchange is called **dowry** when the family of a woman transfers a portion of its own wealth or property to the woman (their daughter) and/or to her husband and his family. The main thing to understand about dowry is that it is *not* simply the opposite of bridewealth; that is, it is not "groomwealth." The woman and her family do not acquire marital rights over her husband when they provide dowry, as they would if dowry were the opposite of bridewealth; rather, the bride and her husband receive property when they marry, rather than when the bride's parents die. By providing dowry, parents give their female children extra years of use of the property and publicly demonstrate their wealth.

Often dowry is the share of a woman's inheritance that she takes into her marriage for the use of her new family. Dowry may represent an occasion for a family to display their wealth publicly by ostentatiously moving furniture and clothing from their house to that of their daughter's husband. Among other peoples, the family of a man will not allow him to marry a woman unless she and her family are able to make a dowry payment. A common cultural rationale for dowry is that women do not contribute as much to a family as do men, so a family must be compensated for admitting a new female member. (Interestingly, this rationale is usually found among societies in which the domestic labor of the female is both onerous and valuable.)

Historically, dowry transfers were common in Eurasian (Europe, southern Asia, and the Middle East) cultures. Most peoples who practiced it were intensive agriculturalists and had significant inequalities in wealth. It is a relatively rare form of marital exchange, occurring in only about 5 percent of the societies recorded by anthropology.

Although a minority of societies practice dowry, some of these societies are quite populous. Dowry is common today in parts of southern Asia (India, Bangladesh, and Pakistan), where dowry includes jewelry, household utensils, women's clothing, and money. Much of the dowry is presented to the bride on her wedding day, but her parents and maternal uncle often provide gifts periodically throughout the marriage.

In recent decades, the demands of Indian families for dowry have led to thousands of tragic deaths. Rather than a one-time marital exchange, some Indian families demand additional, continual payments from the parents of a woman who has married one of their sons. They ask for large sums of cash, household appliances like refrigerators and televisions, motorbikes, and other consumer goods. If the wife's family refuses, their daughter may be severely injured or even killed by burning (in "accidental kitchen fires"), beatings, withholding food, falls, or other retaliations. About 7,000 Indian women suffered "dowry deaths" in 2003, according to official figures, but the actual number is likely much higher. If these numbers sound large, be aware that India has more than a billion people, so dowry deaths are not common statistically.

---

brideservice Custom in which a man spends a period of time working for the family of his wife.

dowry Custom in which the family of a woman transfers property or wealth to her and/or her husband's family upon her marriage.

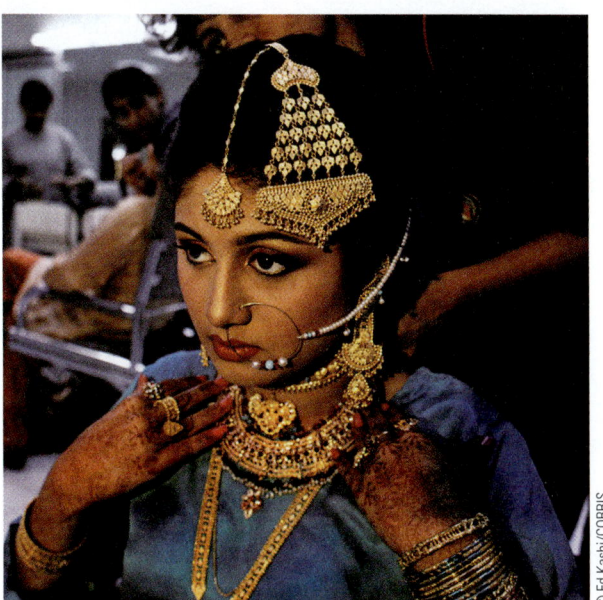

In most societies that have the dowry custom, a woman takes wealth from her family into her marriage. This jewelry-bedecked Pakistani bride is waiting for her wedding.

There are other forms of marital exchanges, including some in which both sets of relatives exchange gifts as a material symbol of the new basis of their relationship. And the three forms just discussed are not mutually exclusive. For example, in most of traditional China, both bridewealth and dowry occurred at most marriages between well-off families. The groom's family would make a payment to the bride's, and the bride's family would purchase some furniture and other household goods for their daughter to take with her when she moved into her husband's household. For wealthier families, dowry was usually displayed as it was transported ostentatiously through the streets between the houses of the bride and groom. Dowry thus became a Chinese status symbol. Sometimes, if the bride's family was substantially poorer than the groom's, part of the bridewealth payment would be spent on purchasing goods for the woman's dowry. This was legal and common until after the Communist Revolution in 1949, when Communist Party leaders outlawed both bridewealth and dowry, with only partial success.

Although the preceding information about marriage rules, forms, alliances, and exchanges has barely introduced these complicated topics, enough has been presented to glimpse both the cross-cultural diversity of marriage customs and the societal importance of marriage. Marriage is tied up with economics, politics, and religion. Similar interrelationships among marriage, politics, and religion are seen in the contemporary United States, as the recent culture wars over gay marriage illustrate.

Same-Sex Marriage and the Culture Wars

In the early 1990s, some Americans became concerned that love relationships between gay and lesbian persons might be formally recognized by laws allowing same-sex marriage. A 1993 court case in Hawaii ruled that the state had to show a compelling reason to prohibit same-sex marriage. This raised the possibility that Hawaii would allow marriage between same-sex couples and then other states would be legally obliged to recognize same-sex couples who married in Hawaii. In response to this threat to traditional marriage norms and values, the United States Congress passed the Defense of Marriage Act (DOMA), and President Bill Clinton signed the act into law in September 1996. Section 2 of DOMA provides that no state or territory is required to recognize marriages between same-sex partners made in another state. Section 3 states "the word 'marriage' means only a legal union between one man and one woman as husband and wife, and the word 'spouse' refers only to a person of the opposite sex who is a husband or a wife." The law therefore defines marriage as opposite-sex monogamy.

Despite DOMA, same-sex marriages are not illegal in the United States as a whole. The main provision of DOMA is that no state is compelled to recognize a same-sex marriage that is legal under the laws of another state. If a couple received a marriage license in Massachusetts or California, for example, no other state had to honor their spousal rights, such as freedom from inheritance taxes, Social Security or veterans survivor's benefits, or health care benefits given to spouses.

DOMA did not go far enough in the view of many Americans and their political representatives. In early 2004, the newly elected mayor of San Francisco issued marriage licenses to gay and lesbian couples. In May of the same year, Massachusetts became the first state to legalize same-sex marriages. Alarmed at the prospect of other states passing similar legislation, President George W. Bush and conservatives in the U.S. Congress pressed for an amendment to the U.S. Constitution. After several rewrites, when brought to a vote on July 14, 2004, the amendment read:

> Marriage in the United States shall consist only of the union of a man and a woman. Neither this Constitution, nor the constitution of any state, shall be construed to require that marriage or the legal incidents thereof be conferred upon any union other than the union of a man and a woman.

In the vote, the proposal failed to gain even a majority in the U.S. Senate, where a two-thirds vote is required for passage of a constitutional amendment. Leftists, liberals, and most moderates opposed it. Liberals saw it as the latest attempt at gay bashing or another symbol of cultural intolerance. Some viewed it as an effort by neoconservatives and religious fundamentalists to gain political support in the November 2004 elections by forcing their opponents (mainly Democrats) to vote yes or no. This then would allow them to claim that the "no" Congress people were antifamily and didn't share mainstream values. However, some conservatives opposed it because they believed it infringed on states' rights.

Same-sex marriage became so politicized mainly because it is a skirmish in the American "culture wars." Among other battles are whether there are absolute standards of right and wrong; the role that Judeo-Christian teachings should have in schools, courtrooms, and other public institutions; whether various behaviors and attitudes are symptoms of moral decline; too much tolerance of pornography and sexual permissiveness; and how much multicultural diversity "one nation under God" can absorb without tearing itself apart from within.

Same-sex marriage and gay and lesbian sexual desires provide ammunition for culture warriors: Are they "immoral" or just another "alternative lifestyle"? Are homosexual desires, like heterosexual desires, rooted in genes and hereditary, or is being gay a "choice"? Is being lesbian or gay a "mental disorder," and, if so, can it be "cured"? Would gay marriage have undesirable consequences for the family, children, and the nation as a whole? If so, what, exactly? Would same-sex marriage be a slippery slope, leading to other forms of marriage, like polygamy?

Polls reveal a large shift in American public opinion about same-sex marriage since the 1990s. An April 2013 article in *Time* reviewed opinion polls that showed 27 percent support in 1996, 37 percent in 2005, and a fairly steady 2 percent yearly increase of support since then. Polls showed the first (slim) majority support for same-sex marriage in 2011. In eight polls conducted in 2013, an average of 51 percent supported marriage rights for gays and lesbians, whereas 43 percent were opposed. As you might expect, there is an enormous difference in support between older and younger people: 73 percent of people 18 to 29 years old support same-sex marriage, but only 39 percent of those over 65. Such statistics suggest that same-sex marriage has gained remarkable support in less than 20 years and that support will increase as older people pass away (however, many elderly have changed their views in the last several years.) Thus, on the cover of its April 8, 2013, issue *Time* had a photo of two men kissing with the words "Gay Marriage Already Won."

There are many reasons for any large-scale change in popular opinion. In this case, one reason is that some national figures who ordinarily fight on only one side of the culture wars defected when their children came out, such as Dick Cheney (secretary of defense under George Bush) and Rob Portman (an Ohio senator). Another is that most people have realized that preferences for same-sex is neither a choice nor a disease but largely genetically based. Third, medical technology has provided new ways of making babies, leading to gay nuclear families: about 115,000 children were living in same-sex households in 2010. Finally—and probably most importantly—most people now know someone who is gay or lesbian, and they seem pretty normal rather than posing some kind of problem or threat to society. If a preference or behavior once rare or hidden becomes more common or open, norms, values, and worldviews generally alter to accommodate it.

By mid-2013, 12 states and the District of Columbia legally recognized marriages between gays and lesbians. All New England states now issue marriage licenses to same-sex couples. Supporting laws in three states went into effect in the summer of 2013. Also, by 2013 another 10 states had passed laws giving gay and lesbian domestic partners all or nearly all the rights of heterosexual married couples, such as joint property, inheritance, and shared parenthood.

In 2013, the U.S. Supreme Court issued rulings that were applauded by those who support same-sex marriage. Back in 2008, the California State Supreme Court had ruled that same-sex couples have the right to marry. But the very next November, voters passed a ballot initiative that amended the state constitution to recognize only heterosexual marriages. The California initiative was challenged in court by a gay couple, and the court decided in favor of the couple. On June, 26, 2013, the U.S. Supreme Court allowed the lower court's decision to stand. In effect, this decision allowed same-sex marriage in California, making it the thirteenth state to give gay couples the legal rights of marriage.

In that same ruling, the Supreme Court struck down the 1996 Defense of Marriage Act, the federal legislation providing that U.S. law considers only opposite-gender monogamy to be legal marriage. The Court did not "legalize" same-sex marriage, as is sometimes said—whether same-sex marriage is legal is a state issue. The immediate impact of the decision is that it mandates the awarding of federal benefits to same-sex couples who have marriage licenses in the 13 states that issue them. So the rights of same-sex couples continue to vary from state to state.

These recent developments make it appear that popular support for same-sex marriage will lead to a national acceptance in a decade or two. However, majority popular support at the national level may not translate into federal legislation. Most poll respondents believe that the issue is more a matter for states to decide rather than the federal government, suggesting many people are uncertain that their private opinions should become national policy. It is noteworthy also that only four states have legalized same-sex marriage by means of a popular vote. All four of those votes were in 2012.

Indeed, most states explicitly prohibit same-sex marriage. Thirty states forbid it in constitutionally, most using language similar to that in the original DOMA, and constitutions can be difficult to amend. Another seven have laws against it. In most of these states, legislatures do not seem likely to change their statutes anytime soon. The chances that their citizens will elect enough representatives and senators to pass federal laws allowing federal recognition of same-sex marriage in the next 20 years are slim.

Many who object to same-sex marriage hold that the major function of marriage is nurturing and successfully enculturating children. They insist that children need both a mother and a father, and no substitutes will do just as well. Strong opponents of same-sex marriage also hold that marriage between one woman and one man is the bedrock of human society, so changing it is likely to endanger social order in lots of unpredictable ways. The Catholic Church and conservative Protestants remain opposed to adoption by lesbians and gays, with one Protestant leader saying it harms kids "because it intentionally creates motherless or fatherless families." In July 2004, in a Saturday radio address, former American president Bush said, "The union of a man and a woman in marriage is the most enduring and important human institution."

Supporters of legal recognition of same-sex marriage make several arguments. One is that such recognition is a legitimate human right, which makes continued legal opposition a form of discrimination. Another is that there is no evidence that same-sex parenting harms children, whether they be adopted or born to female partners. There also is no reason to think that same-sex marriage will harm traditional marriage institutions, thus creating a slippery slope that will lead to who-knows-what. Finally, many believe that same-sex marriage is the most recent battle for equal rights under the law: the 1960s had the civil rights movement, the 1970s and 1980s the women's movement, and in the early 2000s the comparable issue is same-sex marriage.

No matter how fiercely culture wars are fought to preserve the normative marriage practices of the moment, we can be sure that these practices will change and then change again. Aside from the cultural diversity in marriage norms and practices already covered, consider American history. Whether people can marry outside their race or ethnicity, what goes on during courtship, how people choose their spouse, what they expect from marriage, what obligations wives have toward husbands, how enduring marriages will be, how the children resulting from the "union" of a man and a woman are raised—all these and most other features of marriage as we know it today would be viewed with consternation and even horror by North Americans of a century ago. Just a few decades ago, some people would have foretold the horrific effects on society if blacks and whites were ever allowed to marry, if premarital sex were to become common, if many women were the main family breadwinners, if half of all marriages ended with divorce, and if large numbers of couples entrusted their preschool-aged children to something called "day care centers" for 40 hours a week. National legalization of same-sex marriage faces enormous political hurdles. Perhaps a greater realization of the diversity of marriage and family in space and time will help convince some culture warriors that their cause is not as important as they have come to believe.

Postmarital Residence Patterns

In modern Euro-American societies, most newly married couples establish a new domestic group (household) in their own apartment, condo, or house. Elsewhere, couples do not set up a new household but more often move into an existing household—that of either the husband or the wife. Where most newly married couples in a society establish their residence is known as the **postmarital residence pattern**. Comparative work shows that the Western pattern, in which couples form new households separate from their parents, is uncommon.

> **postmarital residence pattern** Household in which the majority of newly married couples establish their residence.

What are the common patterns? By splitting enough hairs, it is possible to identify a dozen patterns, but here we present only six (in order from most to least frequent):

1. **Patrilocal**—Couples live with or near the parents of the husband.
2. **Matrilocal**—Couples live with or near the wife's parents.
3. **Ambilocal**—Couples may choose to live with either the wife's or the husband's kin; roughly half of all couples choose each.
4. **Bilocal**—Couples move back and forth between the households of both sets of parents according to preferences and circumstances.
5. **Neolocal**—Couples live apart from both parents, establishing a separate dwelling and independent household.
6. **Avunculocal**—Couples live with the maternal uncle of the husband.

If this seems like a lot of terms, that's because there are a lot of residence patterns! About 70 percent of all societies have patrilocal residence as the predominant pattern. Thirteen percent have matrilocal residence. Bilocality, ambilocality, neolocality, and avunculocality together account for the remaining 17 percent.

Influences on Residence Patterns

What sorts of factors affect postmarital residence patterns, including whether newly married couples live separately or move in with some other relatives? And, in societies in which most couples co-reside with some relatives, what affects which set of relatives?

> **patrilocal residence** Residence form in which couples live with or near the husband's parents.
>
> **matrilocal residence** Residence form in which couples live with or near the wife's parents.
>
> **ambilocal residence** Residence form in which couples choose whether to live with the wife's or the husband's family.
>
> **bilocal residence** Residence form in which couples move between the households of both sets of parents.
>
> **neolocal residence** Residence form in which a couple establishes a separate household apart from both the husband's and the wife's parents.
>
> **avunculocal residence** Residence form in which couples live with or near the mother's brother of the husband.

Although there is no simple answer, property rights and inheritance forms are important influences on postmarital residence. In societies in which men own the most important productive property and inheritance passes from fathers to sons, brothers have good reasons to join their fathers (and each other) in a common household to cooperate and protect their interests in land, livestock, or other wealth. When the sons of most families in a community bring their wives and children into their father's household, this behavior leads to the residence pattern anthropologists call *patrilocal*. Where important resources are controlled or owned by women, and especially if female labor is important in supplying food for their families, then sisters tend to live and work together. *Matrilocal* residences develop as the sisters bring their husbands to live with them.

Ambilocal and bilocal patterns are most common in societies in which inheritance of important resources passes through both sexes and the labor of both women and men is important to household subsistence. Most hunter-gatherers have one of these two patterns. As explained in Chapter 7, most families in a foraging band need or want to maintain access to several territories, so the rights to gather and hunt in a particular area are flexible. Nuclear families may live off and on with the husband's and wife's bands, depending on sentimental ties or short- or long-term availability of resources. If all or most couples do this, the result is bilocal residence. Or, the couple may settle with whichever parental family has the most resources or with whichever they have good relations, leading to ambilocality.

Industrialized nations are usually neolocal for two major reasons. First, job availability forces many couples to move away from the place where they were born and raised. This is especially true for "upwardly mobile" couples seeking higher incomes, better opportunities, and the more materially rewarding lifestyle valued by many. Second, in capitalistic industrialized countries, most workers do not rely on their family connections for access to their livelihood but instead sell their labor on an impersonal market to an employer they have never met. In other words, most ordinary citizens do not inherit *productive* property from their parents and do not rely on their parents for their livelihood. This leads most couples to establish independent domiciles free from parental control and interference. The result is neolocal residence and a cultural emphasis on nuclear family ties, making some citizens wonder what is causing all those other weird residence patterns—once they know of their existence.

Although control over resources and form of inheritance are important overall influences, no single factor "determines" postmarital residence. For instance, if most couples rely on the wife's family for access to the resources they need to survive and raise children, then most couples will live with the wife's family and matrilocal residence will be the pattern. But a multitude of other factors also affect residence choices. In fact, in some societies, even though women have much control over land, residence is not matrilocal because these other factors are locally more important than keeping sisters together in a common household. Similar complexities apply to the other residence patterns, so there is no single explanation.

Other complications also make generalizations difficult. For one thing, a great many peoples do not have a single residence pattern; rather, where people live varies over time. Among some Inuit (Eskimo) peoples, often couples lived neolocally in the summer and patrilocally in the winter. For another, even within a single society, different families make different choices. For example, China's industrial economy is growing at a staggering rate, and its residence is transforming from the pre-twentieth-century patrilocal pattern to a neolocal pattern. Yet many rural couples live with the husband's family, and even many young urban couples live with relatives because of housing shortages and the (ever-weakening) obligation to support one's elderly parents.

Lest the subject of postmarital residence seem trivial, notice that patrilocal residence has the effect of isolating an inmarried wife and daughter-in-law in the household that includes a set of brothers and their wives. Conversely, notice that matrilocal keeps sisters together. What effects might these two patterns have on women's abilities to control their own lives and make their own choices?

Residence and Households

Other reasons exist for our interest in residence patterns. One is that they affect the kinds of family relationships that are most important in a human community.

Both matrilocal and patrilocal residences place a new nuclear family (usually created by a new marriage) with one set of relatives, either that of the husband or wife. In turn, who a newly married couple lives with influences who they will cooperate with, share property with, feel close to, and so forth. If postmarital residence is patrilocal, for instance, then the husband lives with and works with his own blood relatives (his father and brothers, paternal uncles and cousins *through his father*). The wife is likely to cooperate in household chores, gathering, gardening, and doing other tasks with members of her husband's family, more than with her own.

Postmarital residence also affects the relatives with whom children are most likely to develop strong emotional bonds. For example, if residence is matrilocal the children of sisters (who are cousins *through their mothers*) live together in a single household, much like biological sisters and brothers. They are likely to have similar relationships with their cousins through their mothers as with their real siblings. The children of brothers, on the other hand, will live in different households and are less likely to play together and develop strong emotional attachments.

Most important, the prevailing pattern of residence affects the kinds of household and family units that exist among a people. Consider neolocal residence, for example. If all or most newlyweds set up their own households, distinct from and independent of that of either of their parents, then a new household and family unit is established with each new marriage. This pattern emphasizes the social and economic importance and independence of nuclear families because mothers and fathers—and not more distant relatives—are most likely to be the main teachers of their children and breadwinners for the household. Of course, most couples maintain ties with their parents, siblings, and other relatives, but neolocal residence tends to lead to an emphasis on nuclear families as the most culturally important and stable family unit.

In the United States, neolocal residence has economic consequences, although few people would think of them. Most young couples aspire to live in a "single family dwelling," preferably sooner rather than later. In the last half of 2007, falling real estate prices and homeowner defaults on their mortgage payments contributed to a severe recession. Many homeowners fretted that they would not make as much money when they sold their houses as they had anticipated from past experience or expert forecasts. This was the "housing crisis," which also affected the construction industry. Now, think of what would happen to the construction industry and homeowner property values if large numbers of newly married Americans began practicing a postmarital residence other than the neolocal one by moving in with one of their parents.

Kinship Diagrams

Some notational symbols are needed in the remainder of this chapter and the next. They allow us to show diagrammatically how any two persons are (or

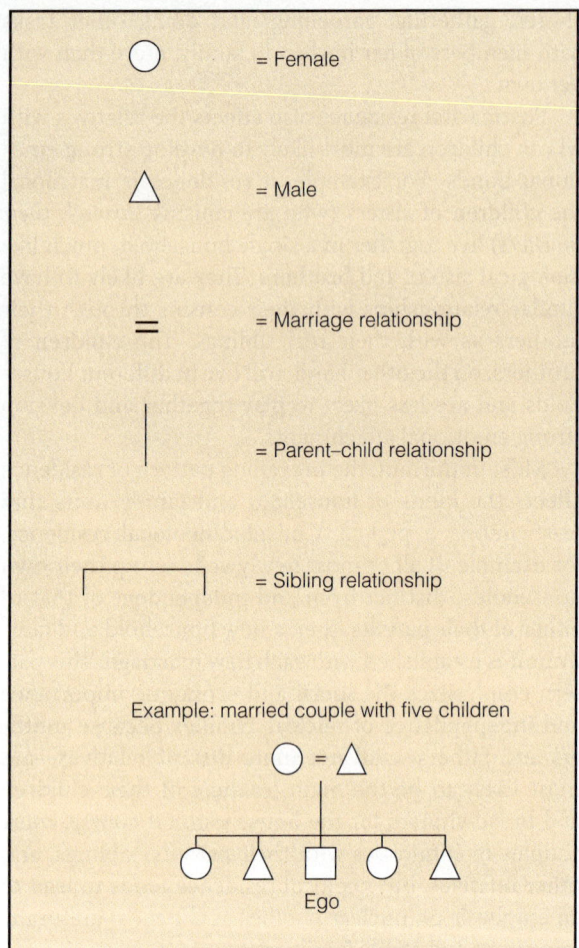

Figure 9.1 Symbols Used on Kinship Diagrams.

believe themselves to be) related by bonds of kinship. The symbols are shown in Figure 9.1, along with how they are used to show a married couple with five children. By stringing a number of symbols together, we can make a complete chart—called a *genealogy*—that shows all the relatives of a given individual and how they are related to that individual. In these charts, or kinship diagrams, it is useful to have a reference individual, or a person to whom everyone on the chart is related. It is customary to call this reference individual "Ego." In Figure 9.1, Ego is symbolized by a square to show that his or her gender is irrelevant for the purposes of the genealogy. (If Ego's gender mattered, we would symbolize him or her with either a triangle or a circle.)

Family and Household Forms

People use relationships created by marriage and family ties to create different kinds of households, some as small as a mother and her children, others composed many dozen members.

Matrifocal Households

Some people believe that the nuclear family is the basic unit of kinship. (Notice that "individuals" cannot be the basic unit of kinship because kinship is inherently about *relationships* among individuals.) Possibly, though, those who think the nuclear family is somehow "basic" believe this only because they live in a society in which a couple and their offspring are the most visible family form.

There is another view: that the "basic unit" of kinship is a woman and her offspring. People who believe this point out that fathers are more frequently separated from their children than mothers. Fathers may separate temporarily or permanently for many reasons. In subsistence economies, men may be absent for long periods hunting, herding, trading, raiding, or carrying out other duties. In communities and modern countries where most families depend on wage labor, husbands/fathers may take jobs in distant cities or countries for many months or even years, sending money back to their home villages or towns.

Historically, male absence for extended periods was especially common in regions that were colonies of a major world power. In sub-Saharan Africa, especially, European colonial powers imposed taxes on men or introduced new commodities that soon became virtual necessities, such as kerosene lanterns, nails, metal tools, and cooking utensils. In order to earn money to meet expenses, married men went to work for foreign companies on distant diamond or gold mines or left their families to work on plantations owned by Europeans. This pattern continues in much of Africa and other regions even today. For the families left behind, the result is the **matrifocal family**, where a mother (with or without a husband) bears most of the burden of supporting her children economically and nurturing them emotionally and intellectually.

Matrifocal families occur in modern industrial societies as well, whenever households are "female-headed,"

---

matrifocal family Family group consisting of a mother and her children, with a male only loosely attached or not present at all.

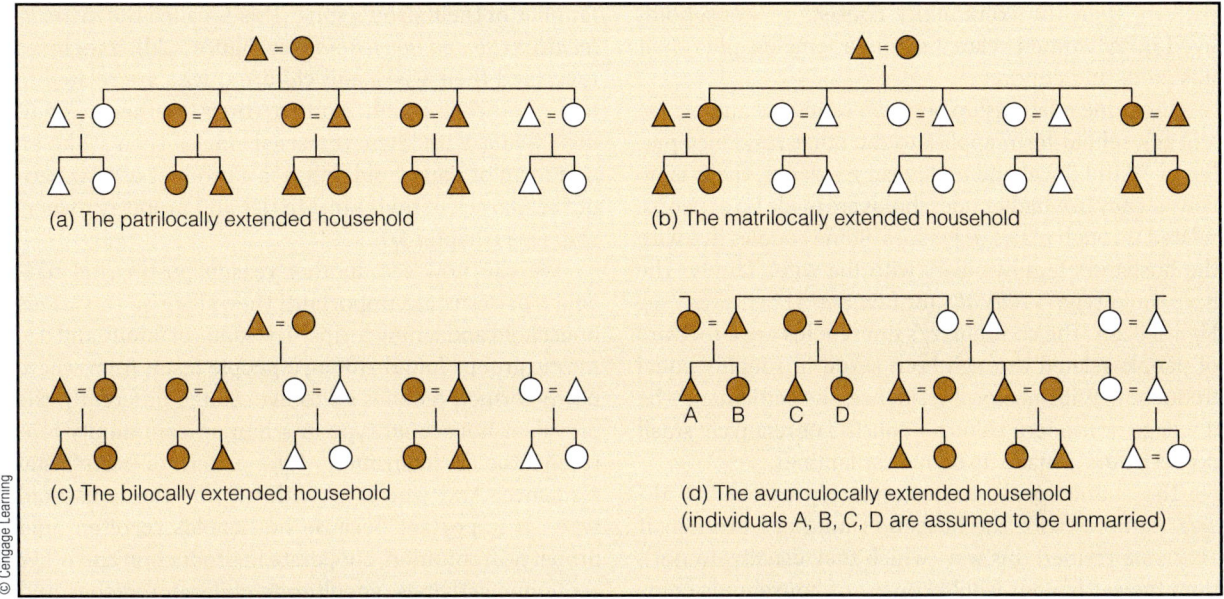

Figure 9.2 Household Forms. The shaded individuals are members of a single household.

as the U.S. Census Bureau calls them. Some say that matrifocal families are an important cause of poverty, crime, and other social problems today. Adult men would act more responsibly if they had jobs that supported their nuclear families, they say. Sons need male role models and supposedly find them elsewhere if their fathers are not around. Mothers would be much better mothers if they didn't have to struggle so hard to pay the bills.

In modern nations, it is true that poor families are more likely to be headed by a female than affluent families are. But this does not mean that matrifocal households are a significant cause of poverty and other social ills. Matrifocal families are also a consequence of poverty: lack of job skills and a multitude of social factors lead to high unemployment among men, causing many women to decide that having a permanent male presence is too costly. Female-headed households in the United States and elsewhere are not necessarily the result of men's refusal to act responsibly or of women's moral choices: they also are adaptations that people make to their economic and social environment.

Extended Households

Extended families are made up of related nuclear families. Because the related nuclear families usually live in a single household, here we use *extended family* and *extended household* as synonyms. Extended households typically include three and sometimes four generations of family members.

Many anthropologists think that the form of family (household) that is prevalent in a society depends on its postmarital residence pattern. For example, with patrilocal residence, the married sons of an older couple remain in the household of their parents. Sometimes, each son builds his own house on his parents' land, near their dwelling, but they cooperate with one another and pool or share resources. As they grow up and marry, the daughters leave to live with their husbands' parents. If all the sons and daughters of a couple do this, the resulting household type is called *patrilocally extended*—brothers live in a single household with their own nuclear families and parents (see Figure 9.2a). If all families in the village, town, or other settlement follow this pattern, then the settlement consists of patrilocally extended households. Notice that the residents of each household are related to one another through males. The married women of the community live scattered in the households of their husbands. Perhaps many of them have married out of the community altogether.

The converse occurs with matrilocal residence. The mature sons leave as they marry, and the daughters bring their husbands to live with them in or near their parents' households. The household type formed by the co-residence of daughters and sisters with their parents is called the *matrilocally extended household* (see Figure 9.2b). The sons of an elderly couple are scattered in the households of the women they have married, either in their own home community or in another community. If most people follow this residence

CHAPTER 9 Marriages and Families 215

pattern, then the community consists of households lived in by women related through females, plus their husbands and children.

The same relationship between residence and prevalent household form applies to the other residence patterns. With bilocal and ambilocal residence, there is no consistency in whether households are made up of people related through males or females. Some couples live with the husband's family, others with the wife's family. The household type is *bilocally* (or *bilaterally*) *extended* (see Figure 9.2c). The community's households are a mixture of people related through both sexes, in roughly equal frequency. With neolocal residence, the settlement—be it village or modern suburb—consists of relatively small domestic units made up of nuclear families.

The avunculocal residence pattern associates nuclear families with the husband's mother's brother. If everyone resided this way (which they usually do not), then the settlement would consist of households composed of older men (the household heads) and the families of their sister's sons. This is called the *avunculocally extended household* (see Figure 9.2d). It includes men (and their wives and children) who are related to one another through women (their mothers). Adult men living with their maternal uncles seems like an odd form of household, but it is a product of how people keep track of their kinship ties and property ownership (see Chapter 10).

We can now see another reason postmarital residence patterns are important: they give rise to various household and family forms. The kinds of family and domestic groups found among a people result from where newly formed families go to live. Stated differently, the prevalent household type in a human community represents the crystallization of the pattern of postmarital residence. And who lives with whom—the household type—is important because households so often hold property in common, cooperate in production and other economic activities, enculturate children together, and sometimes even worship the same ancestral spirits.

SUMMARY

1. **Discuss the main theories of the culturally universal incest taboo.** Incest taboos are rules that regulate who may have sex with whom. The taboo is more puzzling than it seems, and four main hypotheses try to account for it: "Marry Out or Die Out," "Peace in the Family," "Inbreeding Avoidance," and "Familiarity Breeds Disinterest."

2. **Analyze why marriage is difficult to define cross-culturally.** The wide diversity in marriage customs and beliefs makes marriage difficult to define, but there is some agreement on its major functions for both individuals and societies. Some form of marriage is nearly universal, although the particular form of marriage, the kinds of rights and duties it establishes, and many other aspects of the marital relationship vary. The Nayar and Tiwi illustrate unusual forms of marriage, and the Musuo of southern China seem to have no marriage at all.

3. **Describe the forms of marriage and some of the ways cultures use marriage relationships for wider purposes.** Marriage systems are commonly classified by the number of spouses an individual is allowed: polygyny, monogamy, polyandry, and group marriage, although the last is very rare. No single explanation of marriage forms seems sufficient. Marriage is often the cornerstone of alliances between families or larger kin groups, as illustrated by the Yanomamö. The levirate and sororate are customs that preserve relationships between intermarried kin groups even after the death of a spouse.

4. **Describe the main patterns of marriage exchanges and the cultural rationales behind them.** New marriages are usually accompanied by the exchange of goods or services between the spouses and the families of the bride and groom. The most common forms of marital exchange are bridewealth, brideservice, and dowry. These exchanges are used to create affinal relationships, compensate a family or larger kin group for the loss of one of its members, provide for the new couple's support, or provide a daughter with an inheritance that helps her attract a desirable husband.

5. **Evaluate changes in attitudes toward same-sex marriage and why the issue is so controversial.** In the United States, polls reveal that the percentage of people expressing support for laws allowing same-sex marriage has increased since the 1990s. Despite increases in support, the issue is a major battle in the culture wars, or what kind of nation is most moral, prosperous, and stable.

6. **Discuss patterns of postmarital residence and some major influences on them.** From most common to least common, postmarital residence patterns are patrilocal, matrilocal, ambilocal, bilocal, neolocal, and avunculocal. There are many influences on which of these forms will be most prevalent in a given community, including economic forces and inheritance patterns. But no single factor is adequate to explain the cross-cultural variation in residence patterns.

7. **Explain why household forms are important in a human community.** Generally, the prevalent forms of family and domestic groups in a community arise out of many couples living with one or another set of relatives. Patrilocally, matrilocally, bilocally, and avunculocally extended families are often interpreted as the crystallization of postmarital residence patterns. Household forms influence which kinship relationships are most emphasized among a people.

10 Kinship and Descent

All peoples recognize and keep track of relationships between family members, but they do so in several ways. This is an extended family in Mumbai (formerly "Bombay"), India.

William Albert Allard/ National Geographic

Introducing Kinship
  Why Study Kinship?
  Cultural Variations in Kinship

Unilineal Descent
  Unilineal Descent Groups
  Descent Groups in Action
  Avunculocality Revisited

Nonunilineal Descent
  Bilateral
  Cognatic

Influences on Kinship Systems

Cultural Construction of Kinship
  Logic of Cultural Constructions
  Varieties of Kinship Terminology
  Why Do Terminologies Differ?

Where's Our Backbone?

LEARNING OBJECTIVES

After reading this chapter, you should be able to:

1 DISCUSS why kinship is important in creating relationships, forming groups, and organizing activities in preindustrial cultures.

2 DESCRIBE the two main forms of unilineal descent and the kinship groups that result from them.

3 DESCRIBE the two main forms of nonunilineal descent, bilateral and cognatic.

4 ELABORATE on the cultural construction of kinship, and explain the wider associations of four of the major terminological systems.

Humans are among the most social mammals. We are born into, live with, and die among other people. Young children rely on parents and other adults for the food, shelter, protection, and socialization needed to raise them to social maturity. Even as adults, we rely on cooperation with others for survival, economic well-being, and emotional gratification. When we die, relatives, friends, and coworkers mourn our passing.

Social groups based on kinship are those whose members recognize themselves as biologically related according to some culturally diverse principles. In this chapter, we cover how kinship relationships are used in a variety of ways by different peoples to organize relationships and create cooperative groupings. We also describe some of the main ways that members of different societies culturally construct their kinship systems and kinship terminologies.

Introducing Kinship

Like relationships established by marriage and family/household forms, relationships and groups defined by kinship organize a variety of tasks and activities. The kind of tasks and activities, and the kinds of relationships and groups, vary from people to people, as by now you have come to expect.

Why Study Kinship?

Why are anthropologists interested kinship? In Western society and that of developed nations, kinship relationships certainly are important in individuals' lives. But, compared to many other peoples that anthropologists work among, kinship is not an important *organizing principle* of society as a whole. Instead, different kinds of specialized groups organize different kinds of activities. For example there are economic groups (small businesses, corporations), religious groups (churches, synagogues, mosques, temples), and educational groups (schools, colleges). Each of these groups organizes different realms of our lives, and individuals belong to several such groups and associations. Some groups are *formal,* meaning their members are organized as a group, with officers, membership criteria, explicit goals, rules, and so forth. You might belong to formal groups such as a university, conservation organization, church, political party, and company.

At the same time, you are active in informal *networks* made up of fellow students, neighbors, friends, and coworkers if you socialize with them after work. The members of your social network do not necessarily have any relationship to one another, but you have personal relationships with each of them as individuals.

Notice two important characteristics of these groups and networks. First, they are *voluntary:* if your interests change, or if you find another group or network that satisfies you, you are free to change jobs, churches, neighborhoods, and friends. Second, for the most part, the groups have *nonoverlapping membership:* each typically consists of a different collection of people. We cooperate and interact with different individuals in the various groups to which we belong. Members of each group have varying and sometimes contradictory expectations about how we should behave because we perform different roles in each. Our behavior differs according to the identity and expectations of the particular persons (the *social context*) we are associating with at the moment—we act one way at home, another at religious services, and yet another at work. People at our place of worship seldom observe how we act on the job, which often is lucky for us.

In contrast, among many indigenous peoples, one lives with, works with, socializes with, and often worships with the same people, most of whom are relatives.

Kin groups and kin relationships are *multifunctional*, meaning that the same groups organize many aspects of people's lives, such as who cooperates in work, who owns which lands, who carries out rituals together, and who quarrels with whom. We could not understand modernized nations without knowing about businesses, schools, churches, governments, and laws. Similarly, we cannot understand kinship-based societies without understanding their kinship groups and relationships.

Cultural Variations in Kinship

In over a century of studying kinship systems and analyzing their role in cultures, anthropologists have discovered surprising variations. Here are three of the most important variations.

Ways of Tracing Kinship Relationships

In most of North America and Europe, people believe they are related equally and in the same way to the families of both their mother and father. Particular persons develop closer ties with one or another side of their family according to circumstances and personal preferences, such as whether only one set of grandparents live nearby. But there is no systematic *cultural pattern* of feeling closer to or socializing with relatives according to whether they are paternal or maternal kin.

In many other parts of the world, people place primary importance on one side of the family—either the paternal or the maternal side—in preference to the other. For example, in many cultures, individuals become members of only their father's kin group. In such systems, relatives through one's mother are considered relatives, but of a different and less important kind than paternal relatives. There are also systems in which kin groups are organized around maternal relationships, and paternal kin are culturally deemphasized.

Normative Expectations of Kin Relationships

The kinds of social relationships a people believe they should have with various kinds of relatives are part of the norms of kinship. Kinship norms are surprisingly variable from people to people. There are societies in which brothers and sisters must strictly avoid one another after puberty; in which sons-in-law are not supposed to speak directly to their mother-in-law; in which a boy is allowed to joke around with his maternal uncle but must show utmost respect toward his paternal uncle; and in which people are expected to marry one kind of cousin but are absolutely forbidden to marry another kind of cousin. In brief, many social behaviors

One way kinship systems vary is in whether the most important relationships are traced through males, females, or both sexes. On this Micronesian woman's home island, relationships through females are emphasized.

toward relatives that members of one culture regard as normal are different in other cultures.

Cultural Construction of Relatives

Except for fictive kinship (see Chapter 9), all biological kinship relationships are created through reproduction. When a woman gives birth, her relatives and those of her mate become the biological relatives of the child. The kinship relationship between any two people appears to depend on how these individuals are related biologically.

Yet anthropologists claim that kinship is a culturally constructed—as opposed to a biologically determined—phenomenon. Peoples differ in how they use the biological facts of kinship to create groups, allocate roles, and classify relatives into various kinds. In North America, whether a woman is our maternal or paternal aunt makes no difference: we still call her *aunt* and think of both our maternal and paternal aunts as the same kind of relative. But the side of the family makes a difference in some other kinship systems, where the father's sisters and mother's sisters are considered different kinds of relatives and are called by different terms.

Keeping this overview of kinship diversity in mind, let's look at kinship in more detail.

Unilineal Descent

Consider what it means if people are biological ("blood") relatives. Defining kinship in strictly biological terms, someone is your relative because you and that person share a common ancestor in an earlier generation. Thus, your sister is the female child of your parents, your aunts and uncles are the children of your grandparents, your first cousins are the grandchildren of your grandparents, and your second cousins have the same great-grandparents as you. Stated differently, people are biological relatives if they are *descended* from a common ancestor who lived some number of generations ago.

Notice that you are descended from 4 grandparents, 8 great-grandparents, 16 great-great-grandparents, and 32 great-great-great-grandparents. Everyone alive today who is descended from these 32 people is related to you to some degree. Going back in time, the number of your ancestors doubles every generation. So, even if you count back only four or five generations, you have an enormous number of living *biological* relatives descended from those ancestors. This is why it's not very unusual if you are descended from George Washington or another founding father or mother.

Obviously, no society keeps track of all biological kin. From the total range of potential relatives, all cultures consider some as more important than others. The number of relatives is reduced in two main ways: (1) by forgetting or ignoring more remote kinship relationships, and (2) by emphasizing some kinds of kinship relationships and deemphasizing others. All peoples use the first method, or they would recognize tens of thousands of relatives. In the West, most people have little reason to keep track of relatives more distant than second cousins because they have little interaction with them. (As an exercise, try to name all of your second cousins.)

Many peoples also use the second method: they place more importance on some relatives than on others. The most common way to do this uses the sex of connecting relatives as the basis for defining which kin are close or most socially important. For example, if a given culture places more importance on relatives traced through males, then individuals will think that their father's relatives are more important than their mother's relatives—for some purposes, at least. Relationships through females will be deemphasized and perhaps forgotten after two or three generations. If you lived in such a culture, your second cousins on your father's side might be quite important relatives, but you might barely know your second cousins through your mother.

Culturally speaking, then, kinship relationships are defined by how people trace (keep track of) their descent from previous generations. How people in a given culture trace their descent is called their **form of descent**. Descent can be traced through males, females, or both sexes.

Cultures that trace relationships through only one sex have **unilineal descent**: people place importance on either their mother's ancestral line or their father's ancestral line, but not both. The two main categories of unilineal descent are these:

▎ **Patrilineal descent**—People trace their primary kinship connections to the ancestors and living relatives of their father. In cultures with patrilineal descent, a person's father's relatives are likely to be most important in his or her life. Individuals are likely to live among their father's kin, and most property is inherited by sons from fathers.

▎ **Matrilineal descent**—People trace their most important kinship relationships to the ancestors and living relatives of their mother. In matrilineal descent, it is the mother's relatives who are most important in a person's life. People are most likely to live with or near their mother's relatives and usually inherit property from their mother or mother's brothers.

Of these two forms of unilineal descent, patrilineal is the most common. In the most common way of calculating frequencies, 41 percent of societies are patrilineal, 17 percent are matrilineal. The remaining 42 percent combine relationships through females and males in tracing their familial connections.

Let's look at each form of unilineal descent more closely to see which relatives are considered most important for an individual. In Figure 10.1, the patrilineal

---

form of descent Principle through which people trace their descent from previous generations.

unilineal descent Descent through "one line," including patrilineal and matrilineal descent.

patrilineal descent Form of descent in which individuals trace their most important kinship relationships through their fathers.

matrilineal descent Form of descent in which individuals trace their primary kinship relationships through their mothers.

Figure 10.1 Patrilineal Descent.

relatives of the person labeled *Ego* are shaded. The kinship diagram shows that Ego's patrilineal kin include only those relatives related to Ego through males. For instance, Ego's father's brother's children are related to Ego through males, whereas Ego's other first cousins (through Ego's mother or father's sister) are not.

Looking at patrilineal descent another way, we see that Ego's patrilineal kin include all the people descended *through males* from the man labeled *Founder* in Figure 10.1. In fact, any two individuals shaded in the diagram are related to each other through males. Women as well as men are patrilineal kin. However, because incest and exogamy rules usually prohibit sex and marriage between patrilineal relatives, the children of two sisters are never patrilineal kin: their "patrikin" are their father's relatives.

How does patrilineal descent affect behavior between different relatives? In all sorts of culturally variable ways, but the most widespread and important effects are the inheritance of property and obligations to relatives. In patrilineal societies, property is passed down through the male line or, in other words, from fathers to sons. We can see the significance of this effect by contrasting it with inheritance in North American society. You think of yourself as related in the same way to both your grandfathers. But if you lived in a patrilineal society, your father's father would play a far more significant role in your life, and it would be from him and your father that you would expect to inherit wealth or receive land rights. Your mother's father would pass his property on to his sons and sons' sons—not to you because you are related to him through his daughter,

not his son. A similar distinction would exist between paternal and maternal uncles: paternal uncles would be far more important.

In patrilineal kinship systems, individuals have greater obligations to patrilineal relatives. People know their mother's family, of course, and often have close emotional ties with them, depending on residence and individual circumstances. But one's primary duties are to relatives through the father, not through the mother. For example, if you are a man, you mainly work the land or care for the livestock of your father's family, you remain with or near your father's household through most of your life, you are obliged to care for your parents in their older years, and so forth. Because most patrilineal peoples are also patrilocal, most often a woman leaves her own family when she marries to join her husband's family. In regions like East Asia and most of South Asia, families with daughters brought them up only to have them leave upon marriage, so a great many families preferred male children to female children. The Globalization Challenges and Opportunities box discusses some consequences of the preference for sons in China's recent history.

In contrast, if you lived in a matrilineal society, your most important relatives would be your mother, mother's mother, mother's mother's mother, plus the daughters of all these women and their children. In Figure 10.2, Ego's matrilineal relatives are shaded. Note that only one set of cousins—Ego's mother's sisters' children—is shaded in the diagram. They are all related to Ego through female links, and therefore Ego is likely to have closer relationships with them than with other

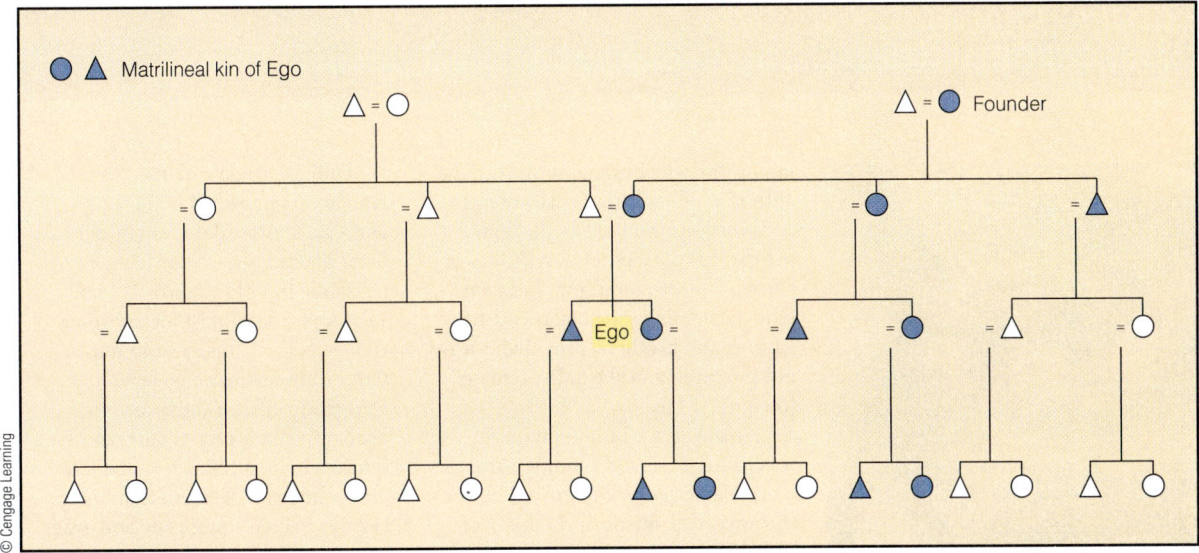

Figure 10.2 Matrilineal Descent.

cousins. Property is most likely to be inherited from one's mother and maternal grandmother and from the brothers of these women. In matrilineal societies, men usually leave most of their property not to their own children but to their sister's children. As a result, maternal uncles (mother's brothers) are important figures in one's life, and in some respects they assume the role with its rights and duties that we usually associate with fathers.

In unilineal descent systems, relationships such as aunt, uncle, and cousin differ from those to which most of our readers are accustomed. Some cousins, in particular, are more important relatives than other cousins: father's brothers' children in patrilineal systems, mother's sisters' children in matrilineal systems. Not all cousins are culturally perceived as the same kinds of relatives in unilineal societies. This fact leads anthropologists to distinguish between *parallel cousins* and *cross cousins*. Two sets of cousins are parallel cousins if their parents are siblings of the same sex, so your parallel cousins are your mother's sisters' children and your father's brothers' children. People are cross cousins if their parents are siblings of the opposite sex, so your cross cousins are your father's sisters' children and your mother's brothers' children. The significance of this distinction is that in unilineal descent systems, one set of parallel cousins always belongs to the same kin group as Ego, as you can see by contrasting the cousins shaded in Figures 10.1 and 10.2. On the other hand, no cross cousin is ever in Ego's kin group in a society with a unilineal descent form.

Unilineal Descent Groups

In Chapter 9, we saw how various peoples form extended households by associating nuclear families together in patterned ways. Much larger groups of people—also known as **descent groups**—can be established on the basis of kinship ties.

Take matrilineal descent, for example. A matrilineal descent group exists when people who are descended from the same woman through females recognize their group identity and cooperate for some purposes. When a matrilineal rule of descent establishes a group of people all related to one another through females, we say that the group is created using the *matrilineal principle*. We can state the matrilineal principle as "Everyone joins the descent group of his or her mother." Alternatively, we can say, "Only children of the female members of a group become members." Looking back to Figure 10.2, we see that all the individuals in the diagram are members of a single descent group. The children of the group's men join the descent groups of their own mothers because of incest and exogamy rules.

Conversely, groups can develop by repeated application of the *patrilineal principle:* in any given generation, only males transmit their membership in the group to their offspring. The result of applying this

descent group Group whose members believe themselves to be descended from a common ancestor.

GLOBAL CHALLENGES AND OPPORTUNITIES

Patrilineality and Globalization in China

After the one-child policy and economic growth since 1980, Chinese parents make great efforts and incur high expenses to educate their child through college. These parents celebrate their daughter's graduation.

China has one of the world's oldest civilizations, going back at least to the Shang dynasty of about 3,500 years ago. For most of this history, the Han Chinese, the most numerous cultural/ethnic and linguistic group, were rather rigidly patrilineal and patrilocal. Property inheritance, family names, responsibilities to honor ancestors, obligations to others—all these and more passed from fathers to sons. When a man and woman married, the woman usually left her own home and family to live patrilocally. When a couple moved in with the husband's family, the wife became subject to the authority of his parents (as was he) and worked hard to keep the family prosperous (as did he). A wife was not completely alienated from her own biological family. She could visit her parents and brothers, provided it was not too often and she didn't remain too long.

However, a woman's main duty was to her husband's family. After a couple married a wife bowed before the ancestral shrine and tablets of her husband's family, symbolizing the transfer of duties to her in-laws. If a man was wealthy enough to support them, he could take concubines, even moving them into his household. His wife was not supposed to object provided he lived up to his obligations to support her and her children. All these practices and beliefs were reinforced by the philosophical tradition called Confucianism. Some scholars even call the above characteristics the "Confucian family."

Going along with the patrilineal and patrilocal system was a strong cultural preference for sons. Girls were expensive to raise and could not carry on the family name. The resources and time expended on a girl's childhood usually brought little return when she married out. Chinese strongly desired male children. In fact, one reason for taking a concubine was if the wife did not produce a son. The failure to bear a son was one of the seven reasons a man could divorce his wife, if he so desired.

Chinese trade with the West and Japan intensified in the 1800s and 1900s. After decades of political disorder and poverty for Chinese peasants, in 1949 Chairman Mao Zedong's Communist forces won a civil war. The Chinese Communist Party soon instituted government ownership of land and most other productive property. Chairman Mao's reforms helped China become more independent of Western dominance. He also helped restore law and order and undertook specific policies to improve the lives of women. To aid the goal of socialist development, the Chinese government placed great emphasis on public education for both sexes.

In the last half of the twentieth century, the lives of women (relative to those of men, at least) improved substantially. This happened even in rural areas, according to anthropologist Yun-xiang Yan. Young women have a stronger voice in choosing their husbands and now usually make the final decision about whom to marry, if only by vetoing her parents' selections. Couples can go out together, which means that marriages are more likely to be based on romantic love rather than formally arranged. Women's education exposes them to new ideas and gives many of them new economic opportunities by helping to level the playing field in the job search.

After Mao's death in 1976, his successor, Deng Xiaoping, began the economic reforms that led to China's phenomenal growth by exporting factory goods to the global economy. China's leaders had long realized that they had to do something to reduce the rate at which the nation's population was growing if China was to avoid a food crisis and develop its economy. In 1979, they instituted a law that became known as the "one-child policy." Under it, couples who lived in cities could have only one child. Generally, in rural areas, couples were allowed two children. The law was further relaxed for China's 56 minority peoples. Knowing the continued cultural preference for sons, in practice officials in rural regions allowed a couple to try again for a boy if the first child was female. But there were penalties for having extra children: employers penalized people in pay and promotions, extra fees were imposed for health care and education, fines could be imposed, and extreme social pressure was applied to encourage conformity.

Still, the old preference for sons remained. In the 1980s and 1990s, many couples found ways of eliminating unwanted female pregnancies and children. These included abortions, hiding second pregnancies from officials, and leaving one's community during late pregnancy to have a secret baby that, if female, was often placed in an orphanage. In the 1980s and 1990s, significantly more boys than girls were born. As a consequence, projections suggest that by about 2020, China will have approximately 30 million more males than females. Where these men will find their spouses is a problem that receives little Western media coverage, but it is potentially important to China's future stability.

The one-child policy helped lower China's population growth, although other factors also contributed heavily to couples' choice to have fewer children. The policy also resulted in tens of millions of Chinese who have no sisters or brothers. The publicity (some say "propaganda") campaign that accompanied the policy, along with a multitude of other factors, significantly raised the status of females in China. Today, whether a Chinese couple has a boy or girl matters much less than it used to—what matters most now is that their only child receives the education that will allow her or him to get ahead in their careers. Many parents, along with grandparents, are quite attentive to their only son or daughter. Only children are sometimes called "little emperors," especially if they are boys, because of what some people view as extreme parental indulgence.

Unlike real emperors, children are under a lot of pressure to succeed in school and to pass the national exams that lead to placement in Chinese colleges. Obligations to live up to parental expectations generally are greater among Chinese than among North Americans, and this extends to parents' wishes about colleges and careers. Some Chinese call the result of the one-child policy "4-2-1": one child is the center of attention of two parents and four grandparents. But 4-2-1 cuts both ways: the same six adults have such high expectations for success that many children who don't measure up feel terrible about disappointing their older relatives. Parents care about their children's success because they love their little emperors, of course, but also because they expect that their children will become their main source of support in their elder years. As Vanessa Fong discusses in her 2004 book *Only Hope,* rising expectations for upward mobility by both parents and children results in intense competition in schools, but also in new frustrations when rising hopes are not realized.

As is also true in Japan and South Korea, Chinese parents make large sacrifices to improve the life chances of their children. Some spend many hours a week going over lessons. They try to get their 6-year-olds into the best elementary schools so they will have a head start. They pay big bucks to send their children to cram schools, which offer extra lessons after the regular school day that will give a leg up on the intense competition over the college entrance exams. Private companies, both Chinese and foreign, specialize in selling educational materials to Chinese families. Learning English is viewed as one key to a successful future. In 2003, Disney was marketing packages titled "Magic English" and "Baby Einstein," and Time-Warner was market-testing a 40-CD interactive set of English lessons in Shanghai that sold for around $3,300.

principle for several generations is a group of people related to one another through males, as you can see in Figure 10.1. Assuming the patrilineal kin group is exogamous, the children of the group's women become members of their father's patrilineal group.

A **unilineal descent group** is a group of relatives all of whom are related through only one sex. A *matrilineal descent group* is a group whose members are (or believe themselves to be) related through females. Stated in another way, members are people who trace their descent through female links from their common female ancestor. A *patrilineal descent group* comprises people who trace their descent through males from a common male ancestor.

Unilineal descent groups can be small or enormous, depending mainly on the genealogical depth of the group—that is, on how far back in generational time any two members of the group must go to trace their relationships to each other. A small matrilineal group with a few dozen members might consist of people descended matrilineally from a woman who lived four or five generations ago. A large matrilineal group with many hundreds of members might consist of people who trace their ancestry back to a woman who lived 9 or 10 generations ago. Anthropologists often use genealogical depth as a way to define different kinds of unilineal groups. From "shallowest" to "deepest," these groups are called unilineally extended families, lineages, and clans. (There are other types not discussed here.)

Unilineally extended families consist of people who cooperate and have mutual obligations based on common descent from an ancestor who lived three or four generations ago. Extended families may be defined either patrilineally or matrilineally. Such families may or may not live in the same household (see Chapter 9), but they recognize their close ties, may hold common property, may cooperate in work, and may have shared ritual responsibilities.

Lineages are unilineal groups composed of several unilineally extended families whose members are able to trace their descent through males or females from a common ancestor who typically lived four or five or more generations in the past. By the conventional definition, the extended families that make up the group must be able to state how they are related to one another for anthropologists to call the group a lineage. Lineages may be either patrilineal (*patrilineages*) or matrilineal (*matrilineages*).

Clans are unilineal descent groups whose members believe they are descended from a common ancestor through either the male line (*patriclans*) or the female line (*matriclans*). The major difference between a clan and a lineage is generational depth. With clans, the common ancestor lived so far in the past that not all the members of the clan are able to state precisely how they are related to one another. Like lineages, clans are usually exogamous. Members of the clan think of themselves as relatives and frequently refer to one another as "clan brother" or "clan sister." In many societies, clans own or control land and other forms of property. Generally, each clan is further subdivided into several lineages.

Among many peoples, clans are *totemic,* meaning that their members are symbolically identified with certain supernatural powers associated with particular animals, plants, and natural forces such as lightning, the sun, and the moon. Clans commonly take the name of their primary totemic symbol, and often have names such as bear clan, sun clan, reed clan, water clan, and eagle clan. Commonly the association with particular supernatural powers entitles specific clans to organize particular religious rituals. Although the functions of clans vary from people to people, they are usually among the most significant economic, social, and political units in the society.

Often people need to call upon different numbers of relatives for different purposes. A woman may need help with her gardening chores and will ask her extended family members for help. Or a group may need to defend itself against enemies, for which purpose they need to mobilize dozens or even hundreds of men to serve as warriors, so they call upon their lineage-mates or clan-mates for aid. Unilineal descent is a useful organization for these and many other purposes because it allows people to mobilize varying numbers of their relatives when they need assistance. Using one of the unilineal descent principles, smaller kin groups can be nested inside larger ones.

---

unilineal descent group Group of relatives formed by tracing kinship relationships through only one sex, either female or male, but not both.

unilineally extended families Group of nuclear families formed by tracing kinship relationships through only one sex.

lineage Unilineal descent group larger than an extended family whose members can actually trace how they are related.

clan Named unilineal descent group, some of whose members are unable to trace how they are related, but who still believe themselves to be kinfolk.

In patrilineal societies, kinship relationships through males are emphasized. These Indian men are celebrating a holiday.

For example, in a patrilineal society, a nuclear family is a part—a "segment"—of a patrilineally extended family. In turn, the extended family is a segment of a larger group (a small patrilineage), while the small patrilineage is a segment of a larger patrilineage, which in turn is a segment of a patrician. Using this *segmentary organization,* dozens, hundreds, or even thousands of relatives can be mobilized, depending on the circumstances. The flexibility of segmentary systems makes them useful for many political purposes (see Chapter 12).

Descent Groups in Action

To introduce general principles of kinship, the preceding description is abstract. However, like families, descent groups are made up of living people who work in gardens, own common property, conduct rituals, teach their children, construct their dwellings, and carry out innumerable other activities together. When people work together for common purposes, they have ways of ensuring the continuity of social relationships over time, assigning members to roles and allocating duties and rights to them, making decisions that affect the members, and expressing their group's identity. In a word, they are *organized.* In many regions even today, descent groups and kinship relationships provide and organize a variety of cooperative activities.

Two examples illustrate this. One is a patrilineal people of a Pacific island who call themselves the Tikopia. The other is the Hopi, a matrilineal Native American people of the Southwest.

Tikopia: A Patrilineal Society

Tikopia is a western Pacific island with only 2 square miles of land. In the late 1920s, when Raymond Firth studied it, about 1,200 people lived on the island. Tikopians viewed their people as belong to one of four patriclans, each with its own name. Each patriclan is subdivided into several patrilineages, averaging 30 to 40 members. The members of each patrilineage trace their descent back to a common ancestor—the founder of the patrilineage—who lived four to six generations ago. The oldest male member of a patrilineage is usually

CHAPTER 10 Kinship and Descent 227

its head. Lineages are exogamous, so the children of a lineage's women are not members of it.

Tikopian lineages control rights to land and certain other kinds of property. Each lineage owns house sites and several parcels of land planted in the four major crops, including yams, taro, coconut, and breadfruit. The families of the lineage have the right to plant and harvest crops on lineage land. They cannot, however, sell, trade, or give it away to members of other lineages. Thus, patrilineages own land and allocate use rights to parcels among their members, and each family acquires most of its food through farming the land of their lineage.

Ordinarily each nuclear family cultivates mainly the lineage land of its husband-father. Female members of a patrilineage retain their use rights to their own lineage's land even after they marry. Usually the head of her lineage will allow her to use a particular piece of land for her family. A woman may not, however, pass any rights to this land along to her children, for it belongs to her patrilineage as a whole not to her as an individual.

The social rank of individuals is also determined largely by their lineage membership and their status within their patrilineage. One lineage of each clan is considered the senior lineage, which makes it also the highest ranking. Because of its superior rank, the senior lineage also has the right to select one of its male members to serve as the chief for the whole clan. Tikopian kinship thus has a political dimension because authority over others is gained largely through lineage membership and rank.

Tikopia beliefs about supernatural powers also are tied into the kinship system. Each clan has specific ritual duties to perform. Each of the four clan chiefs serves as the clan's religious leader and organizer of important religious ceremonies. Each clan has its own ancestral spirits, who were the deceased chiefs of the clan. Each clan also has its own deities, with whom its chief acts as intermediary.

One religious duty of clan chiefs is to carry out rituals that ensure the availability of food for the whole island. Tikopians believe that each of the four major subsistence crops is mystically associated with a particular clan, and so the gods of this clan control the crop. The chief of that clan performs the rituals that ensure the continued supply and fertility of whichever crop "listened to" (as the Tikopia phrase it) the gods of his clan. Thus, each clan—in the person of its chief—has ritual responsibilities toward the other three clans. A patrilineage, too, has an ancestral home with sacred shrines where its members gather to honor their deceased ancestors.

Tikopia exemplifies the diverse functions that commonly assigned to descent groups. Patrilineages control use rights to land and some other kinds of property. Lineage membership influences an individual's social rank and privileges. Patriclans have political functions and their chiefs carry out rituals that Tikopians believe are essential for the well-being of all islanders.

Hopi: A Matrilineal Society

The Hopi of northeastern Arizona traditionally had about 50 exogamous matriclans, some of which are now extinct. Hopi clans are not residential groups; rather, most clans have members who live in more than one of the Hopi's nine villages, or *pueblos*. Each clan is subdivided into several matrilineages. A Hopi pueblo often is a single large apartment-like building divided into many rooms in which families reside. The female members of a Hopi matrilineage usually live in adjoining rooms within a single pueblo.

Traditionally the Hopi are matrilocal, so after marriage a man usually joins the extended household of his wife. Most matrilocally extended households consist of one or more older women, their daughters together with their husbands, and sometimes even their granddaughters and their husbands. Because of lineage and clan exogamy and matrilocal residence, husbands are "outsiders" to their wives' families, and—as the Hopi say—their real home is with their mother's extended family.

The women of a matrilineage usually live close to one another throughout most of their lives, whereas the married men of the matrilineage live scattered among the households of their wives. Even while living with the families of their wives, Hopi men remain members of their mother's lineage and frequently return to their matrilineal home for rituals and other responsibilities or in case of divorce.

Most property, including ceremonial objects, is inherited matrilineally. Living space in a pueblo, for instance, passes from mothers to daughters. Traditionally, the Hopi were a horticultural people, skillfully working the arid land to produce corn and other crops. Each lineage has use rights over particular parcels at any one time. When a husband moves in with his wife and her relatives after marriage, he brings little property other than his clothing and a few personal items. The house, its furnishings, the food stored there, and other goods remain the property of his wife's family. A man provides food for himself and his family by working in the fields of his wife, but the products of his farm labor belong to his wife.

Membership in a matriclan also establishes one's relationships with the supernatural world. Each clan is mystically associated with a number of supernatural powers called *wuya*. Clans usually take their name from their principal wuya, such as bear, rabbit, corn, badger, snake, cloud, sun, and reed. In prayers to their wuya, members of a matriclan ask for protection and for bountiful harvests.

Hopi religion features a ritual calendar that includes a large number of annually required ceremonies. In most cases, each ceremony is "owned" by the members of a certain clan, meaning in Hopi culture that this clan has primary responsibility to see that the ceremony is performed on time and in the proper manner. Every clan represented in a particular village has a clanhouse, in which the masks, fetishes, and other sacred items used in the ceremonies it owns are kept when not in use. The clanhouse usually consists of a room adjoining the dwelling of the senior female member of the clan. This woman, the *clan mother*, is in charge of storing ritual objects and seeing to it that they are treated with the proper respect.

There is also a male head of each clan with religious duties. He is in charge of organizing the men of the clan to perform the clan ceremonies. The male head of a clan teaches his younger brothers or sister's son the ritual knowledge they will need to know to perform the ceremonies properly. In this way, culturally important ritual knowledge is kept within the matriclan.

Finally, the combination of matrilineal descent and matrilocal residence affects relationships between fathers and children. A child's relationship with her or his father is usually close and tolerant. A father seldom punishes his own children. Culturally, this is not considered his appropriate role because, after all, children and fathers belong to different matrilineages and matriclans. The father's sisters and brothers likewise exhibit warm feelings for their nieces and nephews, often providing them with gifts and affection. The main disciplinarians of children are their mother's brother and other members of their mother's kin group. This is partly because a child's behavior reflects well or poorly on the kin group of the mother, so members of this group have the primary duty of monitoring and correcting children.

Hopi illustrate how the matrilineal principle recruits people into kin groups in which they perform various economic, political, and religious roles. They also show how the form of descent found among a people influences interpersonal relationships, including between fathers and children and maternal uncles and their nieces and nephews.

Neither the Tikopia nor the Hopi "typify" patrilineal and matrilineal kinship. A wide range of diversity occurs in patrilineal and matrilineal systems. The two peoples do illustrate some of the main differences between patrilineal and matrilineal peoples with respect to recruitment into groups, allocation of roles, nature of emotional attachments, and organization of important activities.

They also illustrate than kinship is more than a biological relationship. For example, both Tikopia and Hopi—and everyone else—is related to their mother's sister's children in the same biological way. But the nature and importance of this biological relationship varies between the two people. Some of the biological facts of kinship are downplayed or ignored in tracing how people are related, while others are socially emphasized and carry a lot of weight in the lives of people. This is why anthropologists commonly say that kinship is *culturally constructed*, not biologically determined.

Avunculocality Revisited

Hopi women have a great deal of influence on domestic life and control over property—land in particular (more on this in Chapter 11). Because Hopi are matrilocal, sisters live together and their husbands live apart from their matrilineal relatives for as long as their marriage lasts.

Like Hopi, most matrilineal people are matrilocal. However, more than one-third of all matrilineal societies have avunculocal residence, in which married couples live with or near the husband's mother's brother (see Chapter 9). Now that we are aware of matrilineal descent and know that matrilineages and matriclans often control property, we can understand this unfamiliar residence pattern.

The mere fact that a people are matrilineal does not necessarily mean that women control property and politics. That is, *matrilineality*—descent through females—should not be confused with *matriarchy*—rule by women or dominance by women. In many matrilineal societies, elder men own or control the use and allocation of land and other forms of wealth and have more of a say than women in public affairs. (Among Hopi, for example, men have most of the responsibility for organizing and performing rituals involving ceremonial masks, costumes, and dancing.) Of course, in contrast to patrilineal peoples, in a matrilineal society, a lineage elder has authority over his *sister's* children more than his *own* children.

Among matrilineal peoples in which adult men control most property (usually land), how can a male lineage elder exercise control over the sons of his

The unmarried status of these young Hopi women is shown by their hairstyle. In Hopi villages, traditionally the husbands of women worked the land of their wives' families and moved into their wives' households. Hopi matrilineages and matriclans also organize many other economic and ceremonial activities.

sisters and get them to help him with everyday tasks? Conversely, how can married brothers look after their interest in land and other property that they expect to inherit from their matrilineage? The answer is avunculocal residence (see Figure 9.2d in Chapter 9). If an older man's sister's sons bring their wives to live with them in a common residence, then the elder and younger male members of a single matrilineage live in a single place. Once they marry, women of the matrilineage live scattered among the households of their own husband's mother's brothers, as do their children. If a people have matrilineal descent, then avunculocal residence tends to localize related males in about the same place, whereas matrilocal residence scatters male matrilineage mates among the households of their wives.

Perhaps you find this confusing, which is one of our points: the kinship systems of preindustrial peoples are often very complicated. Cutting through the complexities, avunculocal residence localizes male matrilineal relatives who have a common interest in land, wealth, or other material property. In matrilineal societies in which men have most control over wealth, avunculocal residence makes perfect sense.

Nonunilineal Descent

Once you understand how people become members of various kinds of unilineal groups, they seem simple enough. If your society is matrilineal, for instance, you and everyone else joins their mother's kin groups and, as a consequence, everyone in your lineage or clan is related through females.

Actual social life is rarely so rule-governed. In real societies where either unilineal principle is the norm, the actual membership of lineages and clans is not as well defined as the principles make them appear. For instance, in matrilineal systems, circumstances vary and change: adoptions, childless women, inability to get along with one's matrikin, insufficiency of land owned by the matrigroup, and other factors make it likely that some individuals will join a group other than that of their mother. More generally, even in unilineal systems, there is some degree of choice about which group to join, depending on personal preferences and circumstances. Still, there is a norm or rule about what "should" happen.

In societies with **nonunilineal descent**, individuals do not regularly associate with either matrilineal or patrilineal relatives, but they make choices about whom to live with, whose land to use, and so forth. There are different forms of nonunilineal descent, two of which are most common: bilateral and cognatic.

Bilateral

In **bilateral** (two-sided) **descent**, kinship relationships are traced through both genders, and relatives through both parents are about equal in importance. As you recognize, bilateral kinship exists in most contemporary Western countries, but it is also common in other parts of the world. In contrast to unilineal descent, bilateral peoples have no large property-holding kin groups like lineages. Rather, tracing kinship relationships bilaterally produces associations of relatives anthropologists call kindreds. A **kindred** consists of all the people that a specific person recognizes as related to himself or herself.

To understand bilateral kinship and kindreds, imagine a Canadian woman named Liz. Liz recognizes her relatives through her father and mother as pretty much equal and interacts with them in much the same way (unless she has established strong bonds with some people because they live close by or for some other personal reason). The more distant the relationship, the less likely Liz is to interact with or even know who her relatives are. She is likely to see many of her kindred in the same place only at such events as weddings, funerals, and occasional family reunions. Many of Liz's relatives do not know one another (e.g., her cousins on her mother's side are unlikely to know her cousins through her father). All the members of her kindred do not consider themselves relatives, and they certainly do not own any common property. How could they? Their common connection to Liz is what defines them, not their relationships to one another.

As this hypothetical example shows, a kindred is *ego focused*; each individual is the center of his or her own set of relatives. Only you and your siblings share the same kindred; your mother has a different kindred, as do your father and all your cousins. In contrast, unilineal descent groups are *ancestor focused*; people are members of a descent group because they recognize descent from a common ancestor.

Cognatic

In societies with **cognatic descent** (also called *ambilineal descent*), people are members of several kin groups simultaneously and have options about which of their kin relationships to activate. Cognatic descent has elements of both unilineal and bilateral systems. Individuals are potentially members of both their mother's and their father's kin groups, so they make choices about which of several kin groups they can potentially associate with. Choices are commonly based on factors such as chances of inheriting rights to land use or other forms of property or wealth, the desire to associate with a relative of high status or rank, childhood residence, and emotional ties. For example, you might decide to reside and cooperate with your mother's relatives if her kin group has a lot more land available for you to cultivate than does your father's group. Or if a coveted political office or honorific title is about to become vacant in your father's group, you might decide to try to acquire it by moving in and working with his relatives.

A cognatic descent group consists of all people who can trace their descent back to the common ancestor (founder) of the group through either male or female links. Thus, some people are members because of a female ancestor, others because of a male ancestor. The existence of organized groups is a main difference between cognatic descent and bilateral kinship: you and all members of your kindred could never hold property or wealth in common, because the social boundaries of your kindred are too indefinite.

Cognatic descent is found in all world regions, but it is especially prevalent among Polynesians, such as the Samoans, Hawaiians, Tahitians, and the Maori of New Zealand. Details vary from island to island, but generally speaking, people can join any cognatic group or groups to which they can trace ancestry. Membership

---

nonunilineal descent Form of descent in which individuals do not regularly associate with either matrilineal or patrilineal relatives, but make choices about whom to live with, whose land to use, and so forth.

bilateral kinship Kinship system in which individuals trace their kinship relationships equally through both parents.

kindred All bilateral relatives recognized by an individual.

cognatic descent Form of descent in which relationships may be traced through both females and males.

in the group bestows rights to agricultural land, house sites, and some other kinds of property.

In cognatic societies, most people retain membership in several groups simultaneously. However, they only activate some options by, for example, contributing labor and foods to feasts sponsored by the groups to demonstrate their interest in and commitment to the groups. The islands of Samoa provide an example. Each Samoan village has a council that plans communal activities, levies fines, and performs other functions for the whole community. Each village includes several cognatic kin groups known as *'aiga*. Although each 'aiga has branches represented in several villages, every 'aiga has an ancestral village that its members consider their homeland. In its homeland village, each 'aiga has the right to select one or more of its men to hold important titles. These title holders serve as the 'aiga's representatives to the village council. Acquisition of a title carries great honor as well as authority to regulate use of the 'aiga's land, resolve disputes among the 'aiga's members, organize feasts and ceremonial gifts, and assess the members for contributions to marriages, funerals, and other events.

When a title becomes vacant because of death or some other reason, all members of the entire 'aiga have a voice in choosing the new holder of the title, whether they live in the homeland village or not. Because people belong to several 'aiga at the same time, they have a say in choosing the new title holder for several groups, although they do not necessarily exercise their rights in every 'aiga to which they belong. Because men belong to several groups, they have the right to compete for and gain a title in these groups. A young man might anticipate a future title vacancy in one of his 'aiga and decide to move to the village where that 'aiga is represented on the council to concentrate his energies on acquiring that particular title. This general kinship and village-level political organization persists in much of rural Samoa to this day.

The Samoan 'aiga illustrates some common functions of cognatic kin groups: They can hold property and regulate access to land, organize cooperative activities, and serve as the basis for acquiring honored and authoritative political roles. But in cognatic systems, the range of individual choice about group membership

In bilateral societies, kindred are ego focused and usually come together only on special occasions, such as weddings, funerals, and, as here in Maine, family reunions.

CONCEPT REVIEW: Forms of Descent and Kinship

Forms	Defining Characteristics	Associated Kin Groups
Unilineal		
(a) Patrilineal	Through male line	(Patri)lineages and (patri)clans
(b) Matrilineal	Through female line	(Matri)lineages and (matri)clans
Nonunilineal		
(a) Cognatic	Through either male or female line	Cognatic descent groups
(b) Bilateral	Equally through both parents of Ego	None: members of Ego's kindred associate only temporarily

is much wider than in unilineal descent. Individuals have several options to form strong relationships, only some of which they activate.

The Concept Review will help you keep track of the various forms of descent and the kinds of groups associated with each form.

Influences on Kinship Systems

Anthropologists have wondered for decades why cultures have the form of kinship they do. Why are the Tikopia patrilineal, the Hopi matrilineal, the English bilateral? Are there any general explanations? So far no one has identified a single factor or even a small number of factors that account for why different cultures develop different kinship systems. A number of factors, however, *influence* (as opposed to *cause*) which form of kinship a people will have.

One influence is how people relate to their environment. For example, about 60 percent of foraging peoples are nonunilineal, mostly bilateral. Why? Nonunilineal kinship gives individuals and nuclear families a lot of choice about which of their many kin relationships to activate at any given time. The Ju/'hoansi (see Chapter 7) and most other foragers must adapt to seasonal, annual, and spatial fluctuations in wild food availability. This makes it beneficial to keep your options open by maximizing the number and range of people to whom you can trace kinship connections, which is facilitated by nonunilineal kinship. This influence is consistent with materialist approaches (see Chapter 5).

Relationships with the environment affect other descent forms, too. About three-fourths of pastoral societies are patrilineal. According to one hypothesis, nomadic herding is associated with patrilineal descent because livestock are most commonly owned by men, although among many people wives and daughters actually care for the herds or flock day by day. To conserve labor in protecting and moving animals to seasonally available pastures, brothers often combine their animals into a single herd. This is one reason ownership of animals typically passes from fathers to sons. Brothers tend to stay together to cooperate in herd management and look after their common inheritance. Therefore, brothers live together along with their father, which anthropologists call the "patrilocal residence pattern."

Patrilineal descent has also been viewed as a way to improve success in intergroup warfare. Examples include the Maring of New Guinea (see Chapter 8) and the Yanomamö of the Amazon (see Chapter 9). Patrilineal descent encourages male solidarity (bonding) and thereby increases male willingness to cooperate in battles, as well as decreases the chances of male relatives becoming antagonists. Evolutionary psychology (see Chapter 5) might explain patrilineal descent in these terms. Several cross-cultural studies have found an association between patrilineal descent and warfare frequency. But exactly why this correlation exists is a subject of much dispute, especially because war also is important among many matrilineal peoples.

A comparative study of central and southern African societies presented evidence that many societies that were formerly matrilineal became patrilineal after people adopted cattle herding. The argument is that owning cattle tends to benefit sons over daughters, because cattle are so often used to pay bridewealth. Sons, not daughters, therefore inherit cattle, which potentially they use to acquire more wives, which in turn gives them advantages over other men. Also, many African herders must defend their livestock against raids by neighboring pastoralists. This makes it advantageous to keep related men together, encouraging patrilocal residence and dispersing female relatives. Over generations, patrilineal descent develops as a consequence because men who stay together through most of their lives tend to form close relationships and to pass ownership along to sons.

What sorts of factors influence the formation of matrilineal descent? Many anthropologists think it is connected to how people acquire food. Matrilineal descent is more likely to be found among horticultural peoples than among foragers or intensive agriculturalists (see Chapter 7); 56 percent of matrilineal cultures are horticultural, but only 8 percent are pastoral or combine herding with farming. This association is probably related to the fact that women perform so much of the daily subsistence work in most horticultural populations, as we discuss in Chapter 11.

For evolutionary psychology (sociobiology), the most puzzling aspect of matrilineal descent is that most men give more material support to their sister's children than to their own children. This is "puzzling" because ordinarily men are more closely related to their own children than to the children of their sisters, and evolutionary psychology predicts that people are more likely to help closer genetic relatives than more distant ones. Back in 1974, Richard Alexander suggested that matrilineal descent can be explained in terms of genetic relatedness. Under some conditions, a male is more likely to be more closely related to the children of his sister than to the children of his wife.

When will an average man be more closely related genetically to his sister's children than to his own? The answer: when the "probability of paternity" falls below about 0.25—that is, when an average man is only about 25 percent sure that the children of his wife are, in fact, his children. The mathematics of this response are outside our scope. But the idea is that a man and his sister are pretty certain they have the same mother, so they automatically have some genetic relatedness even though there is good chance they have different fathers. Therefore, a man knows that his sister's children are related to him. But if there is about a 75 percent chance that he is not the father of his wife's children, then few of his own children are genetic relatives. Therefore, it pays off genetically to support his sister's children rather than those of his wife.

Around one-sixth of human societies are matrilineal. Is it likely that there are this many societies with a paternity probability lower than 0.25? No, because this assumes that in the matrilineal one-sixth of all societies, a woman is roughly three times more likely to be impregnated by a man other than her husband. Although sexual behavior, and especially extramarital sexual behavior, is difficult to research, this number is unrealistic.

However, evolutionary psychology can *potentially* help us understand why there are so many societies whose social organization is based on kinship. Groups that own resources, cooperate in labor, raise children together, go to war together, and the like are most often relatives in preindustrial societies. Generally, this is consistent with evolutionary psychology because relatives should be more altruistic towards one another than nonrelatives. Critics of the approach argue against this idea in several ways, most notably that humans are more likely to cooperate with people they trust. We tend to trust people we know well, and whom do we know better than those we were raised with, regardless of whether they are our biological relatives?

To conclude, a lot of controversy surrounds the causes of kinship systems, and probably most anthropologists doubt that any universal explanation exists. It may be that cross-cultural variations in kinship systems are influenced by so many kinds of factors that no generalized explanation is possible. As a simple example, *all else equal,* chronic warfare might tend to favor patrilineality; horticulture might tend to favor matrilineality. However, many horticultural societies also have serious warfare, and other factors certainly influence the form of descent. Therefore, the processes that "influence" will be complicated and outcomes variable.

Cultural Construction of Kinship

In Chapter 2, we noted that a major component of cultural knowledge is the way a people construct the real world, both natural and social. Kinship relationships and groups are an important part of social reality in all human cultures. Just as cultures differ in the ways they trace their descent and form social groupings of relatives, so do they differ in how they identify kinds of relatives, with labeled categories. The labeled categories are called **kin terms**, and the way a people

---

kin terms Labels that individual use to refer to his or her relatives of various kinds.

classify their relatives into these categories is called their *kinship terminology*.

You might think that kin terms reflect the way those relatives are related to biologically (genetically). In English, this is true for *some* terms: *mother, father, sister, brother, son,* and *daughter* all define individuals related to you in distinct (unique) biological ways. For example, no other female relative other than your *sister* shares your parentage (setting aside considerations of fictive kinship, such as adoption, foster parenting, and step relatives).

However, other English kin terms do not faithfully reflect genetic relatedness. Consider *uncle* and *aunt*. They refer to siblings of your parents, distinguished only by their gender. But the individuals you call *aunt* and *uncle* are related to you in four different ways: your father's siblings, your mother's siblings, your father's siblings' spouses, and your mother's siblings' spouses. The same idea applies to some other terms: a particular term may group together several individuals related to you in different ways. Thus, *grandfather* and *grandmother* includes both your mother's and your father's father. *First cousin* refers to a wide range of people connected to you biologically in different ways.

Even terms with seemingly unambiguous biological referents like *sister* and *brother* are treated in varying ways. In old China and Korea and many other places, terms for siblings were modified by birth order, producing distinctions like *first brother, fourth brother,* and *second sister*. The Chinese and Koreans applied the Confucian respect for elders to sibling terminology: the fact that elder brothers outranked younger ones was reflected in how they addressed one another.

Thus, a people's kinship terminology reflects biological relationships only imperfectly. More fundamentally, kin terms reflect the norms, rights and duties, and behavioral patterns that characterize social relationships among kinfolk. Speaking broadly, collapsing relatives with different biological relationships into a single term reflects the cultural fact that people think of them as the same kind of relative. In turn, people conceive of them as the same kind of relative because they have similar kinds of relationships with them.

As already described, peoples vary in the ways they trace their main kin ties, in the kinds of relationships and groups created by those ties, and in how they classify relatives into labeled categories. These variations do not perfectly reflect the degree of genetic relatedness between relatives, so anthropologists commonly say that kinship is *culturally constructed*. The **cultural construction of kinship** implies two things: (1) as children grow up in a certain community, they socially learn the logic by which their culture classifies "relatives" into categories, and (2) those categories do not simply reflect biological/ genetic relationships. (If they did, we might be justified in saying that kinship is *biologically determined*.) In fact, as we'll see in a moment, the labeled categories of kinship sometimes hardly match up at all with biological relationships.

Logic of Cultural Constructions

Before we can discuss particular kinship terminologies, we need to understand the logic by which they are culturally constructed. By "logic," we mean the principles that people use to distinguish one kind of relative from others. There are many principles, but only five are relevant for our purposes.

First, every kin term has a reciprocal term. For example, the reciprocal term for *grandfather* is either *granddaughter* or *grandson*. If you call a woman *mother*, she will call you *son* or *daughter*. (In English, the reciprocal term for *cousin* is *cousin*.)

Second, for some terms, the gender of the individuals to whom the term applies makes a difference. In English, gender matters for terms like *brother* and *sister, uncle* and *aunt,* and *grandfather* and *grandmother*. Indeed, gender is the only criterion that distinguishes the relatives just mentioned from one another. Gender is irrelevant, however, for *cousin*.

Third, kinship terms usually reflect whether the individual referred to is of the same or a different generation than Ego's. In English, specific terms are used for relatives in Ego's own generation (like *cousin*), in Ego's parents' generation (*aunt*), and in Ego's children's generation (*niece*). In describing kinship terminologies, we call Ego's parents' generation *the first ascending generation* and Ego's children's generation the *first descending generation*. Although the terms used in most kinship terminologies reflect generational differences, some systems use terms that transcend generations.

Fourth, the sex of the relative who connects Ego to another relative often matters. The distinction between cross and parallel cousins illustrates this logical principle: among many peoples, mother's brother's

---

kinship terminology Logically consistent system by which people classify their relatives into labeled categories ("kinds of relatives").

cultural construction of kinship Idea that the kinship relationships a given people recognize do not perfectly reflect biological relationships; reflected in the kinship terminology.

daughter is called by a different term than mother's sister's daughter. Often, too, father's sister and mother's sister have different labels.

Side of the family is a fifth criterion by which kin terminologies are constructed. In English, side of the family is irrelevant: your relatives through your mother receive the same terms as relatives through your father. As we know, many other cultures place special emphasis on relationships through females (mothers—matrilineal) or males (fathers—patrilineal). As you suspect, this emphasis is reflected in terminological systems.

These five principles are among the ones that various peoples use to culturally construct kinship. The most general point is that different peoples combine these logical principles—as you can see, they are logical *possibilities*—in various ways to form categories or kinds of relatives.

Varieties of Kinship Terminology

The world's diverse peoples have developed many ways of classifying relatives into labeled categories. The classification systems have names like Eskimo, Hawaiian, Sudanese, Iroquois, Omaha, and Crow. (Don't be misled by the names of these systems. The American anthropologist Lewis Henry Morgan developed the classification system for kinship terminology in 1871. He named each system after the first people among whom he encountered it. In fact, all the systems are found on many continents, although four of them were named after the Native American peoples that Morgan learned about.)

Here we cover only four systems: Eskimo, Hawaiian, Iroquois, and Omaha. We further simplify things by considering only terms used for relatives in Ego's generation and in Ego's first ascending (parental) generation. To make these systems easier to understand, we translate the terms into their closest English equivalents. Keep in mind that these translations are only rough approximations and that some terms have no exact English equivalents.

Eskimo

Eskimo terminology is the easiest for English speakers to understand because this is the system most of us are familiar with (see Figure 10.3). In this system, Ego's biological mother is called *mother,* and Ego's biological father is called *father.* These are the only two persons to whom these terms apply. The term *aunt* is used for both Ego's father's sister and Ego's mother's sister, and the term *uncle* is used for Ego's father's brother and mother's brother. The terms *brother* and *sister* are used for only the children of Ego's mother and father. The term *cousin* is used for all children of Ego's uncles and aunts.

Hawaiian

Hawaiian terminology uses the fewest terms (see Figure 10.4). All of Ego's relatives in the first ascending generation are called either *mother* or *father.* Mother

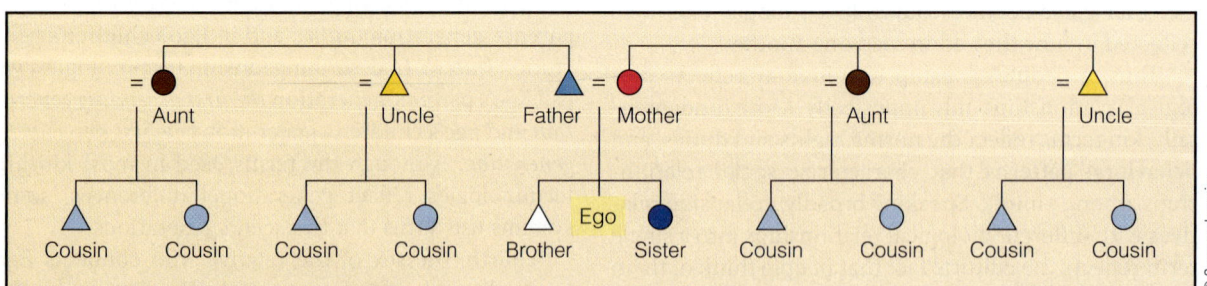

Figure 10.3 Eskimo Kinship Terminology.

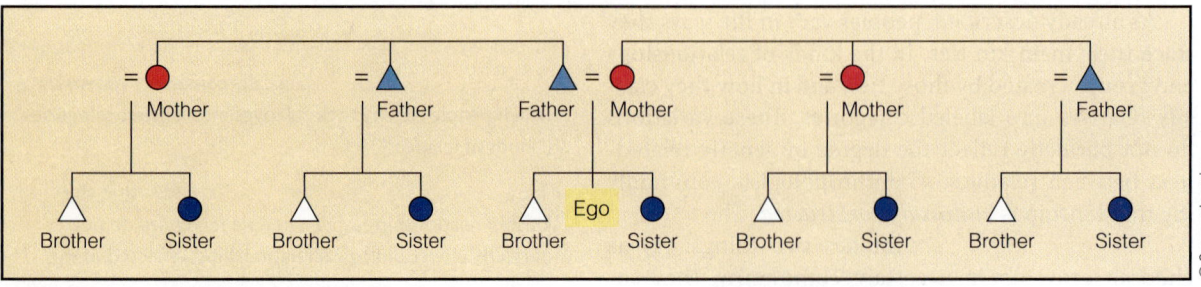

Figure 10.4 Hawaiian Kinship Terminology.

is extended to include Ego's mother's sister and Ego's father's sister, and *father* is extended to include father's brother and mother's brother. In Ego's own generation, all relatives are called either *brother* or *sister*. Thus, Hawaiian terminology includes no terms equivalent to the English terms *uncle, aunt,* and *cousin*. Although the Hawaiian system extends the terms *mother* and *father,* this does not mean that individuals are unable to distinguish their biological parents from their other relatives of the parental generation.

Iroquois

People who use the Iroquois terminology categorize relatives very differently than the Hawaiian and Eskimo systems (see Figure 10.5). The term *father* includes the father's brother but not the mother's brother. *Mother* includes the mother's sister but not the father's sister. The mother's brother and father's sister have their own unique terms. Looking at Ego's own generation, we also see a difference. The children of the father's brother and mother's sister are called *brother* and *sister*. The children of the mother's brother and father's sister are called by a term that might be translated as *cousin*. This is how we label it on the diagram, because of its familiarity, but it could also be labeled *child of father's sister* or *child of mother's brother*.

Although these distinctions may seem unusual to us, it also exists in the Omaha system, so we need to understand the logic behind it. Peoples who use the Iroquois system distinguish between parallel and cross cousins. They give their parallel cousins the same terms they use for their own brothers and sisters. They distinguish cross cousins from parallel cousins, calling cross cousins by a unique term (here we translate the term as *cousin,* although obviously it has no exact English equivalent).

To understand the logic behind calling parallel cousins *brother* and *sister* and cross cousins by a different term, go back to the terms used for Ego's parents' siblings. Ego's father's brother and mother's sister are called *father* and *mother,* respectively. Thus, it is logical to call their children *brother* and *sister*. (What do you call the children of the people you call *mother* and *father*?) Ego calls his father's sister by a term that might be translated as *aunt,* although the indigenous term is sometimes close to "female father." Ego's mother's brother is *uncle* (or "male mother"). So, it is logical to call their children (Ego's cross cousins) by another term we might translate as *cousin*.

Omaha

Omaha terminology is difficult for English speakers to grasp (see Figure 10.6). The terms used in the first

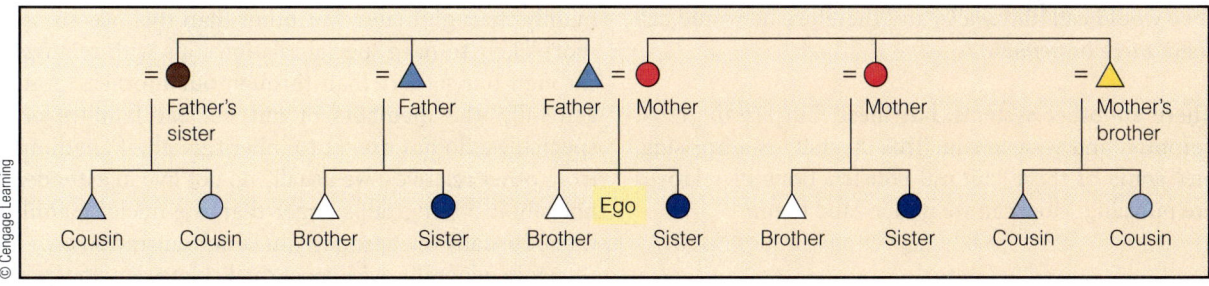

Figure 10.5 Iroquois Kinship Terminology.

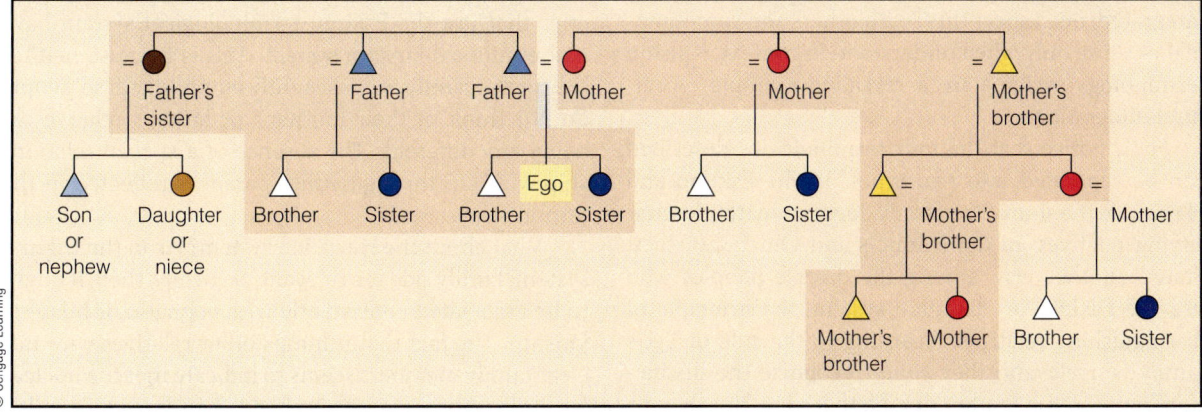

Figure 10.6 Omaha Kinship Terminology.

ascending generation are identical to the terms in the Iroquois system, and parallel cousins are called *brother* and *sister*. The difference between Iroquois and Omaha is how cross cousins are treated. Omaha terminology has no term similar to English *cousin*. In addition, in Omaha terminology, a distinction is made between cross cousins on the mother's side (the children of mother's brother) and cross cousins on the father's side (the children of father's sister). The mother's brothers' daughters are called *mother,* and the mother's brothers' sons are called *mother's brother*. Thus, Ego's maternal cross cousins are grouped with individuals in Ego's parents' generation. For Ego's paternal cross cousins, the term depends on Ego's sex. If Ego is a male, he calls his father's sisters' children *niece* and *nephew*. If Ego is a female, she calls her father's sisters' children *son* and *daughter*.

Why are there two separate terms for father's sisters' children, depending on the sex of Ego? This distinction is perfectly logical. Remember that kinship terms are reciprocal and that Figure 10.6 shows only the terms used by Ego. To understand why the sex of Ego is important in this relationship, ask: What would father's sisters' children call Ego? In Figure 10.6, you see that Ego is their mother's brother's child. Thus, if Ego is female, they would call her *mother,* and she would reciprocate by calling them *son* or *daughter*. If Ego is male, they would call him *uncle,* and therefore he would call them *niece* or *nephew*.

There are other systems, but these four are the most common and widespread. This diversity is surprising, and some of these cultural constructions of relatives are puzzling. How can we understand them?

Why Do Terminologies Differ?

In previous chapters, we emphasized that cultures are integrated: one aspect "fits" with others and sometimes makes sense only when understood in context. Kinship terminology systems are a revealing example of cultural integration.

First, notice that the four terminologies described can be separated into two types. In the Eskimo and Hawaiian, the side of the family does not matter in classifying relatives; in the Iroquois and Omaha, it does. Stated another way, among the diverse peoples who use the Eskimo or Hawaiian system, the principle of distinguishing relatives according to the side of Ego's family is irrelevant; they *could* recognize the distinction between the mother's and father's kin, but they do not. Among the many cultures who use the Iroquois or Omaha system, the principle of distinguishing relatives according to family side *is* relevant. Why should the side of the family matter in some terminological systems but not in others?

As you've guessed, the side of the family matters in some terminologies because some people trace their descent through only one of their parents. The side of the family makes no difference in other systems because these populations trace their kin connections equally through both parents. *In general*—there are exceptions—the way a people trace their descent affects the relationships between kin, which affects the terms used to refer to various kin.

Consider the Eskimo classification. Contrasting to other terminologies, it differs in two main ways: (1) it makes no distinctions between Ego's father's and mother's relatives, and (2) no other relatives of any kind are lumped together with nuclear family relatives. Assume that these two features mirror people's ideas about how various kin are related. We might conclude that people think (1) that both sides of the family are equally important to an individual (more accurately, there is no systematic *social pattern* of importance through one side over the other) and (2) that nuclear family relatives are somehow special and thought of differently than are other kinds of relatives. In the case of North America, traditionally our surnames are inherited mainly through males, but other than this, we are no more likely to have special relationships with relatives through our fathers than through our mothers. And, generally, the members of our nuclear families *are* special: we do not expect to inherit much, if anything, from other relatives; we usually do not live in extended households; kin groups larger than the nuclear family do not usually own property in common; and so on.

More generally, we expect the Eskimo classification of relatives to be associated with cognatic or bilateral kinship. And usually it is: about 80 percent of all societies that use the Eskimo terminological system have a nonunilineal kinship system. This is because neither side of the family is consistently emphasized, so people do not think of their mother's or father's relatives as being any different. The absence of a special relationship with kin through either parent is reflected in the terminology.

What about the Hawaiian system? As in the Eskimo system, family side is irrelevant. Logically, then, it ought to be associated consistently with cognatic or bilateral kinship. The fact that it lumps other relatives with nuclear family members seems to indicate that the nuclear family is submerged or embedded in larger extended households. Ego should have important relationships with the siblings of his or her parents and with their children. Despite this logic, the Hawaiian terminology is not as consistently associated with cognatic or bilateral kinship as is the Eskimo terminology; in fact, about 40 percent of societies with the Hawaiian classification are unilineal. The Hawaiian system is apparently also compatible with unilineal descent.

And the Iroquois? Ego's father and father's brother are assigned a single term, which is different from mother's brother. The mother and the mother's sister are given the same term, which is not the same term that Ego uses for the father's sister. Thus, Ego distinguishes between maternal and paternal aunts and uncles in the first ascending generation. The fact that the side of the family matters in this generation seems to imply unilineal descent. And, the Iroquois system is usually found among peoples who trace their descent unilineally: about 80 percent of all Iroquois terminologies occur in unilineal descent forms. If you look back at Figure 10.5, you will see that Ego uses *brother* and *sister* to refer to relatives he calls *mother* and *father*. This certainly makes logical sense—if you call someone *mother*, it follows that you will call her son *brother*. The cross cousins have a separate term because ego does not call their *mother* and *father*.

The Omaha system carries the distinctions between the mother's and father's side "down" into Ego's own generation. If you compare Figures 10.5 and 10.6, you will see that the Omaha differs from the Iroquois by distinguishing cross cousins according to whether they are related to Ego through Ego's mother or father. The mother, mother's sister, and mother's brother's daughter are lumped together, although they are members of different generations. The mother's brother and mother's brother's son likewise are lumped together under a single term.

What can explain this way of classifying relatives? The fact that these relatives are all related to Ego through Ego's mother must mean something, and the fact that they are classified together and distinguished only by their gender must be significant. Indeed, both these features are clues to the logic behind the Omaha terminology. It is found among peoples who use the patrilineal principle to form kin groups.

How does patrilineal descent make sense of the Omaha system? In Figure 10.6, we have lightened the background around those relatives in the diagram who belong to Ego's own patrilineal group. Notice that the cousins in Ego's group are called *brother* and *sister*, which reflects the social fact that they are in Ego's own lineage. We have also lightened the background of those relatives who are members of Ego's mother's patrilineal group. Notice that all the members of this latter group are assigned only two terms—one for the male members of the group and one for the female members of the group. The two terms have no English translation, but they mean roughly "female member of my mother's group" and "male member of my mother's group." Their common *social identity* as members of Ego's mother's kin group overrides the *biological fact* that they are members of three generations. If you have followed the argument, you will agree that the Omaha system makes perfect sense, provided it is associated with patrilineal descent forms. And, indeed, more than 90 percent of all cultures that use the Omaha terminological system are patrilineal.

Another system, the Crow, is essentially the mirror image of the Omaha. You will not be surprised to learn that the Crow system is strongly associated with societies that have the matrilineal form of descent.

Thus, kin terminologies make sense once we understand that they reflect the prevalent relationships and groupings produced by various ways of tracing kinship connections. The ways people culturally construct and label their relatives reflect the social realities of their kinship system, though not perfectly. These ways look mysterious until we understand these classifications and labels in the context of the kinship systems that give rise to them. The Eskimo terminology used by Americans would probably look strange to people who use, say, the Omaha terminology. Our failure to distinguish between relatives through one's mother and father would be strange because to them these relatives are clearly differentiated, given the way their kinship systems place people in different kin groups.

The various peoples who use one or another of these kinship classification systems cannot state the logic of their classifications in the same way we just did. For instance, people who use the Omaha terminology cannot tell you why they label their relatives as they do because they lack a comparative perspective of their own kinship system. Presumably, to them, their mother, mother's sister, and mother's brother's daughter are called by the same term because all these women are the same kind of relative, just as *aunts* and *cousins* are all the same kind of relative in some other cultures. They do not realize that in "Eskimo" systems these females all have separate terms, nor do they know that their terminology reflects the groupings and relationships of their kinship system.

Then again, people who use the Eskimo system cannot account for their kin terms, either, until, of course, they become aware of the diversity in human kinship systems discovered in the past century by anthropologists. The way we classify kinfolk seems quite natural—biologically based—until we learn that other people do it differently.

Where's Our Backbone?

In the last two chapters, we described four forms of marriage: monogamy, polygyny, polyandry, and group marriage. We've also seen that there are a few peoples who might not have any marriage system at all, depending on how *marriage* is defined. We've outlined four ways in which married couples arrange their residence after they marry: patrilocal, matrilocal, neolocal, and ambilocal. There also are other, rarer forms of postmarital residence not considered here. We've seen how nuclear families are commonly embedded in extended families of several types: sisters stay together and bring their husbands in among one people; several brothers bring their sisters in among another people. We've seen that diverse peoples around the world have traced kinship relationships through their fathers, their mothers, through both parents, and through either parent according to choice and circumstances. We've shown that various peoples culturally construct their kinship categories in ways that look mysterious—even incomprehensible—to people who construct their kinship systems in some other way.

Piercing through all the key terms and complexities, this knowledge has two wider lessons for people living in the twenty-first century. The first is that diverse human groups have developed a wide range of ways of marrying, forming families, living together, and keeping track of their relatives. There is no single right way to run a marriage system, to organize family life, or to reckon which distant relatives are most important. There is variability. Anthropologists have not—and perhaps never will—explain this variability in the scientific meaning of *explain*. But consider how many ways human beings have organized marriage and kinships relationships—relationships that many modern people think are "only natural" or "based on biology" or "morally correct" or are their nation's "backbone."

The second lesson is also a simple one: change. Marriage and sexual and family practices have changed throughout humankind's history, and we can be certain that they will change more as circumstances continue to evolve. It might be unlikely that other ways of thinking about and organizing marriage, family, and kinship will emerge in the future. However, it is good to keep in mind that in the 1970s the idea that people could acquire cash from a machine called an ATM by inserting piece of plastic called a debit card seemed far-fetched, as did personal computers, mobile phones, large numbers of unmarrieds living together, and females outnumbering males in higher education.

SUMMARY

1. **Discuss why kinship is important in creating relationships, forming groups, and organizing activities in so many preindustrial cultures.** Many of the functions and activities organized by specialized groups in modernized, urbanized societies are organized by kinship groups in many premodern cultures. Kinship groups often organize economic, political, military, ritual, and other activities. Kinship ties also help form a person's social identity and often determine one's social rank.

2. **Describe the two main forms of unilineal descent and the kinship groups that result from them.** Although kinship derives from biological relatedness, societies vary in their kinship systems. One variation is how people trace their relationships back to previous generations—in how they trace their *descent*. Peoples with unilineal descent emphasize relationships traced only through one sex. The matrilineal or patrilineal principle forms descent groups composed of people related through females and males, respectively. In order of increasing inclusiveness and genealogical depth, the main kinds of descent groups are extended families, lineages, and clans. The island people of Tikopia exemplify patrilineal descent, and the Native American Hopi exemplify matrilineal descent.

3. **Describe the two main forms of nonunilineal descent, bilateral and cognatic.** People who trace

their kinship relationships bilaterally have no kin groups larger than extended families because the kindreds of different individuals overlap so much. Unlike unilineal descent, kindreds are Ego focused, and large numbers of Ego's relatives are likely to congregate only on certain occasions, such as weddings, funerals, and family reunions. In cognatic descent, people have options to trace their ancestry through both males and females. Individuals are able to join any of the groups to which they can trace ancestry and can choose those groups with which they want to associate closely, as illustrated by the Samoan 'aiga.

4. **Elaborate on the cultural construction of kinship, and explain the wider associations of four of the major terminological systems.** A people culturally construct their kinship systems by applying logical principles in diverse ways. This application produces several systems of kin terminology, of which we discuss four: Eskimo, Hawaiian, Iroquois, and Omaha. Generally speaking, the ideas people have about how they are related to one another are strongly influenced by how the descent form of their society sorts people into groups and establishes relationships of certain kinds between kinfolk.

11 Gender in Comparative Perspective

STAN HONDA/AFP/Getty Images

Cultures differ greatly in the degree to which women participate in culturally valued roles and receive rewards proportionate to their contributions to families, economic activities, and to society at large.

Sex and Gender

Cultural Construction of Gender
  The Hua of Papua New Guinea
  North American Constructions

Multiple-Gender Identities
  Native American Two Spirits
  Hijra of Hindu India

The Gendered Division of Labor
  Understanding Major Patterns
  Fertility Maintenance
  Reproductive Roles
  Relative Strength
  Compatibility with Child Care
  Understanding Variability

Gender Stratification
  Is Gender Stratification Universal?
  Influences on Gender Stratification
  Descent and Postmarital Residence
  Gender Stratification in Industrial Societies

LEARNING OBJECTIVES

After reading this chapter, you should be able to:

1. **DESCRIBE** how male-female physical differences affect gender roles and relationships.
2. **EXPLAIN** the phrase "cultural construction of gender" and its importance.
3. **ANALYZE** the relevance of the acceptance of multiple-gender identities for the understanding of gender.
4. **DISCUSS** the factors that influence the widespread patterns and the cross-cultural diversity in the gendered division of labor.
5. **ANALYZE** why it is so difficult to determine whether any societies have complete gender equality.
6. **DESCRIBE** the three most important influences on gender stratification from a comparative perspective.

Human beings feel, think, and act within a cultural framework that affects our private lives, interests, attitudes, worldviews, social behavior, and other aspects of how we define themselves. Beginning around 1970, the feminist movement is one of the most powerful social and political forces of recent times. It resulted in increased anthropological interest in the role of gender in human relationships and in society generally. In the early twenty-first century, issues connected to gender are one of the most popular research and teaching specializations. Even anthropologists who do not conduct research in gender as such now take gender into account in our research on other subjects. We recognize that many human relationships are permeated by people's cultural knowledge about gender.

Like kinship and age, gender is a universal basis for organizing group activities and allocating roles to individuals. Your identity as a male or female or as a member of an alternative gender makes a difference in who you are, what you have, how you interact, and what you can become. Anthropological research shows that in different cultures, gender matters to different degrees and in different ways. These cultural variations and the factors that affect them are the subjects of this chapter.

Research in gender is so vast that we must focus on only four of the main issues to which anthropologists have made important contributions: (1) the cultural construction of gender, (2) multiple (as opposed to dual) genders, (3) the gendered division of labor, and (4) gender stratification. Where relevant, we suggest ways in which anthropological findings and perspectives help understand gender (sex) roles and beliefs about gender in contemporary societies.

In any society, gender is a key dimension of a person's *social identity:* how other people perceive you, feel about you, and relate to you is influenced by the gender to which they assign you and by how your culture defines gender differences. Less obviously, an individual's *self-identity* is affected by cultural beliefs and ideas: your conception of yourself depends partly on how your culture distinguishes masculinity and femininity, allocates roles to one or the other sex, and uses symbols (such as dress, behavior, speech style, and sexual preferences and practices) to help define differences between females and males. Even when interacting with someone of your own sex, your social behavior is affected by your culture's norms, categories, worldviews, symbols, and other ideas and beliefs that influence your group's conceptions about gender. Many males are careful not to assume "feminine" poses or speech styles, for example. Finally, just as gender identity affects interactions between individuals, so do beliefs about gender affect behavior in a variety of social settings and contexts: in the workplace, home, school, church, and political arenas, to name a few.

Sex and Gender

The world's peoples vary in the significance they attach to whether a person is female or male and in what specific behaviors they expect from females and males. To emphasize such cultural variations, we make a conceptual distinction between *sex* and *gender*. Most people think that visible sexual features are determined by the X and Y "sex chromosomes." In reality, the visible and behavioral expression of sex chromosomes are influenced by embryonic development, how physiology transmits hormones to cells and tissues, and other biological processes. A person's genetic makeup and physiology—in interaction with other factors in the environment—forms physical characteristics like genitals, hormones, and secondary sexual characteristics (breasts, pelvis, body size, musculature, and the like). Of course, not all individuals can be identified as a member of a *dichotomous* (female-male) category on the basis of their genes. Various peoples treat this ambiguity in different ways, as we shall see.

Females and males differ genetically in many ways. However, a couple of biologically based ("sexual") differences that have special importance in comparative studies of various cultures.

First is **sexual dimorphism**: at maturity, *most* males are physically larger and stronger than *most* females. Sexual dimorphism is a product of our evolutionary past and is a trait we share with our evolutionary cousins—gorillas and chimpanzees. This difference in size and strength has many implications, two of which are that men are more likely than women to win physical fights, and are better able to handle tasks that involve a lot of strength. Sexual dimorphism is often considered to be a "given" condition, determined by humanity's evolutionary past. Indeed, all human populations exhibit dimorphism, but comparative research suggests the sex-based differences in size are less in societies in which females contribute most to food production.

Second are differences in reproductive physiology: only women become pregnant, carry children until birth, and produce the milk that their newborns and infants require. Men do contribute sperm in one way or—with modern in vitro technology—another. *Biological* fatherhood may end there, but almost all peoples assign the role of *social* father to the biological father or another man. *Social* fathers support their partners before, during, and after pregnancy. In most cultures, fathers and other men help to greater or lesser degrees with the care of infants and children, although this varies a lot from people to people.

For anthropological interests, sexual dimorphism and reproductive physiology are the two most important ways the sexes differ biologically. We do not agree on the overall significance of such differences for human cultures. We do agree, though, that various cultures also construct differences and similarities between males and females other than those based on biological differences.

Cultural Construction of Gender

The phrase **cultural construction of gender** means that different cultures have distinctive ideas about males and females and use these ideas to define manhood/masculinity and womanhood/femininity. The word *construction* evokes the act of "building"—from the raw materials provided by sexual differences, different cultures build up their ideas and beliefs about how the sexes differ and what these differences mean. How males and females perceive and define themselves and each other, what it means to be a woman or a man, what roles are appropriate for men and women—these and many other dimensions of femaleness and maleness are culturally variable, not universal to the human species or constant across all cultures.

The notion that gender is culturally constructed is too easily and often misunderstood. Some scholars (especially those in the biological sciences) mistakenly believe that anthropologists claim that genetic (physical) differences between the sexes do not matter. They think we claim that differences in male and female behaviors are determined by culture, not genes.

A few anthropologists do make this claim, of course, especially those whose theoretical orientation is more humanistic than scientific (see Chapter 5). But most accept that biological differences between females and males "matter"—are relevant for both ideas and behaviors—in all cultures. However, anthropology's focus on cultural diversity makes us aware that human groups define and make use of these differences in a multitude of ways. In *symbols*, various peoples attach cultural meanings to female-male differences that go well beyond biological/anatomical distinctions. In constructing *social reality*, male-female differences are minimized in some cultures, maximized in others. In *values*, "patriarchy" crudely describes some groups, "sexual equality" others. In *behavior patterns*, some groups fairly rigidly differentiate between female and male activities and roles, whereas others allow both sexes to participate in similar kinds of activities according to individual preferences and circumstances. Our fascination with such variations does not imply that we deny biological realities.

One implication of the cultural construction of gender is that there are no cultures that are "natural" with

---

sexual dimorphism Physical differences based on genetic differences between females and males.

cultural construction of gender Idea that the characteristics a people attribute to males and females are culturally, not biologically, determined.

respect to their beliefs about gender. (This includes your own culture, by the way.) This fact makes it very difficult to determine the impact of biological (sexual) differences on the behaviors of females or males because everywhere cultural (gender) constructions obscure and complicate the impacts of genes. Notice, though, that this does not mean that genetic differences are not important. It means only that their effects are difficult to determine.

The Hua of Papua New Guinea

The Hua of Papua New Guinea are a people whose cultural construction of gender differs markedly from that familiar to most of our readers. Studied by Anna Meigs in the 1970s, the Hua are a patrilineal, horticultural people who live in mountain villages of 100 to 300. As we shall see, Hua culture constructs gender on the basis of female-male differences that most other people do not recognize. Because of this cultural construction, Hua believe that later in life a woman can become like a man and a man can become like a woman.

How do Hua culturally construct gender? They believe that bodies contain a life-giving substance (like a vital essence) that they call *nu*. They think of nu as a real, physical substance—not a mystical or magical power—that can be transferred from one person to another and gained and lost in various ways. Symbolically, nu is associated with growth and maturity. Female bodies contain lots of nu, which in Hua belief makes women grow faster and age more slowly than men but also makes them moist. On the other hand, males naturally contain a smaller amount of growth-inducing nu, so they need extra to help them grow up. Hua explain many of the differences between men and women by the amount of nu: men are stronger and fiercer because they are drier, for example.

Nu is both gaseous (breath) and liquid (blood, sweat, semen, female sexual secretions). A transfer of nu between individuals is either harmful or helpful, depending on the nature of the relationship between the giver and the recipient. Transfer of nu may occur during eating, sexual intercourse, and other kinds of direct and indirect contact. For example, a woman can transfer her nu to people when she serves food to them. Nu from her bodily secretions and under her fingernails adheres to the food and gets ingested by her children or her husband.

A woman also transfers nu to a man when she has intercourse with him. Giving nu to a man in the act of intercourse is harmful to the man because it pollutes and debilitates him. Intercourse is also damaging to a man because he contributes his own scarce nu (in the form of breath and semen) to a woman during sex. She gains strength and vitality at his expense.

The amount of nu can be regulated by the kinds of food eaten. Various events in people's lives require an increase or decrease of nu. Women need extra nu during pregnancy, so they eat lots of foods considered rich in nu. (Broadly speaking, these are fast-growing foods with high moisture content.) During menstruation, though, women have too much nu, so they avoid the same kinds of food.

Young males do not have enough nu for full growth and maturation, so during certain periods of boyhood, they are encouraged to eat foods with lots of nu. At other times, when they are undergoing the initiation ceremonies that make them into strong men able to fight to defend the village, they are supposed to avoid nu-rich foods because such foods will weaken and sicken them. In fact, during male initiation ceremonies, there are strict taboos against eating not only these foods but also foods from gardens tended by women or foods prepared by women. These taboos keep the boys free of the pollution caused by contact with women.

Nu makes women polluting to males. The greater the difference in nu between a woman and a man, the more dangerous that woman is to that man. But both men and women can and do lose or gain nu, depending on their activities, their diet, and their age. After decades of engaging in sexual intercourse with women and eating foods touched by their wives and other women, middle-aged and elderly men have taken lots of nu into their bodies. They become invulnerable to further contamination by contact with females and therefore may eat nu-rich foods and participate in sexual intercourse with less anxiety than younger men. Gaining nu over the years makes them become "like women." Hua call them *figapa*, which Meigs interprets as a third gender category. Figapa are "like women" because their bodies contain lots of substances that the Hua symbolically consider feminine.

For their part, women lose nu whenever they menstruate, handle and prepare food, and have babies. Over their life course, nu leaves a woman's body. Therefore, Hua believe, women become less and less dangerous to males as they grow older. Women who have given birth to more than two children have lost enough nu that they are no longer polluting. They therefore become "like men." Hua say they are *kakora*, which is a fourth gender category. People who are kakora are eligible to live in the men's house, partly because they are no longer hazardous to men.

Thus, Hua culture recognizes two bases for gender distinctions. One is a person's genitals, which make one either male or female. The other is the quantity of nu in the body, which is affected by a person's stage of life and previous life events and activities. The latter criterion gives rise to the two additional nondiscrete (more or less) gender categories of figapa and kakora. Although the figapa-kakora distinction is relevant in only certain ritual contexts, it is significant that people who are genitally male or female are classified with the opposite gender for certain purposes.

Hua clearly illustrate the cultural construction of gender. The objective physical distinctions between the sexes—genitals, beards, breasts, and so on—are recognized and relevant in all known cultures, as we shall see. But, as Meigs shows for the Hua, cultures use the (metaphorically) raw material of these differences to construct varying beliefs about the ways in which females and males differ. To Hua, men and women differ not only in the usual physical ways but also in the quantity of nu each has. These beliefs in turn affect the attitudes each sex holds about the other and the behavior each sex adopts toward the other. Hua men fear the possibility of feminine pollution and therefore try to minimize their contact with women, their intake of food prepared by women, and their sexual relations with women.

North American Constructions

The more different some culture's beliefs are from your own, the more obvious it is that those beliefs are a cultural construction rather than biologically determined. Because Hua beliefs pertaining to male-female relationships seem exotic to most Westerners, the fact that gender is culturally constructed among these people is readily apparent. All people's ideas about gender are culturally constructed, however, including yours and mine. To stimulate thought, we briefly present some ideas on the construction of gender in Euro-American culture.

Speaking generally, many North Americans see females as compassionate, emotional, socially skilled, physically fragile, and family oriented. Males are taken to be more selfish, rational, tolerant of physical discomfort ("tough"), coordinated, and individualistic. Of course, these dichotomous characteristics were always simplistic, and increasingly people no longer hold these opinions at all.

Consider the possible effects of these cultural conceptions on the uneven distribution of occupational roles between women and men in the modern American economy. The predominant pattern is for members of each sex to move into jobs for which they are believed to be best suited, given cultural conceptions of gender. This happens for several reasons. First, individual men and women more often seek those jobs that they find appropriate for their sex or that they think they have the best chance of getting or succeeding in; people apply for certain kinds of jobs according to their desirability, based in part on their beliefs about "sex roles." Second, employers tend to hire people according to their own cultural conceptions of which sex is likely to do well in a particular job; the employment market (the market for labor) itself allocates men and women into certain kinds of jobs. And, third, everyone has a tendency to stereotype other people's constructions: even if *you* don't think you are best suited for a traditional female role, you may think that other people think you are. Your perceptions of other people's constructions might encourage you to limit your options to what you think their constructions are. Thus, the market for labor responds to job seekers' constructions, employers' constructions, and everyone's perceptions about other people's constructions.

Constructions of gender-connected occupations are changing rapidly, yet many jobs remain disproportionately female or male. Thus, women predominate in jobs that involve nurturing (e.g., nursing, day care, elementary school teaching, social work, pediatric medicine), routine interactions with the public (e.g., receptionists, clerks, restaurant waiters, tellers), repetitive use of fine motor skills (word processing, sewing and stitching), and cleaning and housekeeping. A few of the jobs in which men predominate are those involving outdoor activity (equipment operation, driving, carpentry and construction), high-level decision making (management, administration), and knowledge of mathematical principles (science, engineering, computer programming).

Perhaps these and other patterns are what you'd expect. Your expectations grow out of who you actually see working at what jobs and your ideas about which gender is best suited for what jobs. True, some of these differences might have a loose biological basis. However, how much of these occupational differences result from the American cultural construction of gender, which defines females as having certain inherent characteristics and males as having a contrasting set? How much do the educational system, popular media, parental voices, peer opinions, and other social forces affect occupational choices?

Today, most of us recognize that "a woman can be tough" and that "men have a feminine side." We accept that women make fine CEOs and governors and that men can perform well as nurses. There are lots of stay-at-home dads and breadwinner moms. Indeed, an

Although constructions of gender are different now than they were even a decade ago, women still hold far more jobs as receptionists, secretaries, and file clerks than men do.

increasing number of women in two-earner households make more money than their husbands. More men are teaching elementary and middle school, although many parents of their female students still keep an eye on them. In the political arena, in 2008 Sarah Palin was a candidate for vice president of the United States. Hillary Clinton was nearly the Democratic nominee for president and went on to become secretary of state. Both Palin and Clinton often acted "tough" and were "fighters" in their campaigns, which helped convince voters they could be competent as commander in chief. Is it possible that someday our cultural knowledge will be that, although the sexes *on average* differ in size and strength and that women are the ones to bear and nurse the next generation, few other biological differences matter much for career choices?

Multiple-Gender Identities

When your authors (and your grandparents) were in high school, few if any of us had heard of multiple-gender identities. There were males, females, and others, although few of us were aware of the meaning of "others." We knew vaguely of cross dressing ("transvestites"), but transsexual was not a gender category. If any of our male friends were gay or any of our female friends were lesbian, certainly we would have recognized them as such. Their sexuality would have been apparent in other dimensions of their lives and we would have recognized them. Of course, these ideas were mistaken.

Native American Two Spirits

Many peoples tolerate and even institutionalize diversity in gender roles and sexual orientation. Biologically male or female individuals who, for one reason or another, wish to adopt aspects of the role or behavior of the other sex are allowed to do so with little or no social stigma or formal punishment. In such cultures, a boy who cannot or does not wish to conform to male roles is not forced to follow norms nor is he socially ostracized. He is allowed to act like a woman in certain respects or contexts. Conversely, a girl who shows an affinity for activities culturally defined as male is allowed to participate in manly roles when she becomes an adult. In short, in many cultures, people can adopt the behaviors and roles typical of the other sex in features such as clothing, work, and sexual preference, with little or no social stigma or legal punishment from other members of their communities.

These practices or customs are often called *gender crossing* or *transsexualism*. In many cultures, it is expected that a certain number of people are born who, when they mature into adulthood, will become like the other sex in some ways. Rather than stigmatizing such persons or trying to force them to live up to the group's standards of femininity or masculinity, they are accommodated and integrated into social life. Their alternative sexual identity is *institutionalized*.

Most North Americans will interpret "institutionalized gender crossing" as a way that cultures accommodate lesbians, gays, and bisexuals. This interpretation is generally correct; however, there is much more to gender crossing than sexual orientation, as we shall see. First, let's consider briefly how anthropological thinking about gender crossing has changed recently.

Until the 1970s or 1980s, most of us viewed gender crossing in the following way. In any society, some individuals are born who do not fit into existing sexual identities of "male" or "female." There are some boys who do not want to go to war, hunt, or compete in politics, but instead prefer to hang out with girls, do domestic work, tan skins, or otherwise act in ways culturally considered feminine. Likewise, some girls display an affinity for actions culturally associated with masculinity, preferring to play boy games, use weapons, dress like males, and so on. In many human societies, such persons eventually learn to outwardly conform to the normal sex roles. If they do not conform, they are considered deviant and punished or stigmatized throughout their lives. In some societies, though, a legitimate role exists that allows them to satisfy their inclinations while serving the group in various ways. Institutionalized gender crossing is a cultural mechanism that provides a legitimate outlet for people who otherwise might be unhappy or cause problems in the social life of the community.

Comparatively speaking, this is a favorable image of cultures that allow gender crossing. Anthropologists often view the institutionalization of gender crossing as a lesson "we" can learn from "Others." Some human groups do not insist on rigid conformity to their sexual stereotypes, but allow diversity, in contrast to chauvinistic cultures like the anthropologists' own. Unlike "us," "they" normalize individual variation in aspects such as dress style, sexual orientation, work activities, mannerisms, and the like, rather than rigidly insisting on uniformity. And unlike many of "us"—who view men who act like women and women who act like men as morally degenerate, dangerous to society, or genetically abnormal—"they" do not despise or ostracize such individuals, but provide them with legitimate roles in the community's social life. The usual lessons were (1) "we" ought to be more like those Others by tolerating variation and accepting people as individuals whom we value and who can contribute in various ways, and (2) not all peoples in the world require conformity to their society's normal sex roles, so there is no reason to think our intolerance is universal and, therefore, inevitable. These two lessons are well worth pondering.

Still, some anthropologists today think this view somewhat disparages gender-crossed individuals because it assumes they cannot live up to the expectations of their "real sex," so they are allowed to "alter their sex." Furthermore, the view assumes that, in all cultures, people classify individuals as belonging to one of only two genders (female and male), so that a woman who doesn't want to be completely a woman must become partly like a man, and vice versa.

multiple-gender identities Definitions of sexual identities beyond the female and male duality, including third and fourth genders such as man-woman or woman-man.

Many peoples recognize more than two gender identities by culturally constructing **multiple-gender identities**. If gender can be culturally constructed, then there is no necessary reason to assume that all peoples will construct only two genders. Some peoples define a third or even a fourth gender of "man-woman" or "woman-man" (or "not woman-not man," or "half man-half woman," as some indigenous terms often translate). These third- or fourth-gender identities go beyond Euro-American definitions of homoeroticism, transvestism, transgendered, or other concepts familiar in the Western cultural tradition.

Multiple-gender identities are well documented for many Native American peoples. In his 1998 book *Changing Ones,* Will Roscoe reports that more than 150 Native American cultures had institutionalized multiple-gender identities for males, or females, or both sexes. Males adopted the dress, tasks, family roles, or other aspects of womanhood. Females took on activities usually associated with manhood such as warfare or hunting. By doing so, they took on alternative third or fourth gender identities. Far from being ridiculed, ostracized, despised, or otherwise socially stigmatized, such individuals in most cases were treated with respect and valued for their contributions to their families or group.

Native American tribes all had their own word for such roles in their language, but gender identities varied so much from people to people that applying a single English word is problematic. The preferred modern term is *Two Spirits,* derived from a Siouxan phrase referring to persons who had both female and male spirits. We use Two Spirits here, along with *man-woman, woman-man,* or *third-* or *fourth-gender identity,* depending on context.

Among the Navajo of the Southwest, for example, families and local communities generally welcomed third-gender persons. An anthropologist in the 1930s quoted a Navajo elder:

> If there were no *nadle* [men-women], the country would change. They are responsible for all the wealth in the country. If there were no more left, the horses, sheep, and Navaho would all go. They are leaders just like President Roosevelt.
>
> (Quoted in Roscoe 1998, 43)

The elder surely exaggerated, but his statement indicates the Navajo's recognition of the contributions of men-women. They often managed their family's property, supervised work, and became medicine men or took on other ritual responsibilities. On the other hand, we should assume that Navajo (like other people) vary in their opinions, so there was unlikely to have been unanimous approval or tolerance of nadle.

People with female genitals could adopt alternative roles as well, which also were valued in many Native communities. A girl who came to be known as Woman Chief was adopted by a Crow family during the nineteenth century. Like boys, she hunted deer and bighorn sheep while growing up. When the man who raised her was killed, she took responsibility for the family, acting as both father and mother. Later in life, she helped save her camp from an attack by the Blackfoot and went on horse-raiding parties. Eventually, Woman Chief took four wives and participated in council deliberations in her band, a role usually reserved for men.

As you might expect, most early Anglo observers of Two Spirits misunderstood these individuals and their roles in society. They overemphasized the sexual orientation of the person, whereas in fact their sexual behavior varied from tribe to tribe and from individual to individual within the same tribe. In most cases, even when Two Spirits were homosexual, sexual behavior was not the aspect of the role that was considered the most important element by the people themselves. Furthermore, Two Spirits rarely engaged in homosexual activity with *one another*. Where homosexuality was an aspect of the role, the people with whom relations occurred were not considered homosexuals at all.

A more accurate portrayal of third and fourth genders defines the roles as multidimensional, thus recognizing that practices varied not only from tribe to tribe, but also from individual to individual within the same tribe. Nonetheless, certain patterns are apparent. Serena Nanda identifies several features of gender variants that were widespread (not universal) among Native American peoples. Here are four of the main characteristics:

- Cross-gender occupation or work activities: a preference for the work of the opposite sex and/or for work set aside for their third- or fourth-gender identity
- Transvestism: in most cultures, a dress style different from the style of men and women—most commonly cross-dressing but sometimes a combination of female and male garments
- Associations with spiritual power or a spiritual sanction: possession of special powers derived from spiritual forces, often combined with a personal experience interpreted by the group as a calling
- Same-sex relationships: the formation of sexual and emotional bonds with members of the same sex, who were not themselves men-women or women-men

These four widespread characteristics of third- and fourth-gender identities provide a convenient way to organize our discussion, but the variability of the role must always be kept in mind. No single dimension is "typical."

Cross-Gender Occupation or Work Roles

Adopting the work roles of the opposite sex was a widespread feature of Two Spirits. This aspect often received special attention in various Native communities. Probably more than any other single dimension, occupation/work best defines the role. A famous Navajo *nadleehi* who died in the 1930s was unusually skilled in weaving blankets, a typically female task. In many tribes, individuals who performed the tasks of the opposite sex often excelled at the work, in the opinions of their communities. Sioux Two Spirits (called *winkte*) dressed like women and lived in their own tepees at the edges of camps. The quill and beadworks of a winkte were often highly valued because of their fine quality. Among the matrilineal, matrilocal Zuni of the American Southwest, a *lhamana* (man-woman) was looked upon favorably by the women of his family because he stayed with the household of his birth rather than leave upon marriage. Matilda Cox Stevenson, a nineteenth-century ethnographer, wrote that Zuni lhamana would do almost double the work of a woman because they were not burdened by childbirth or the heaviest duties of child care. In spite of such examples, to say that all gender variants exhibited "sex role reversal" in work performance is simplistic; the most famous Zuni man-woman was We'wha, who participated in both female and male tasks.

Commonly, a child who showed an inclination for the work of the opposite sex was considered by others to be suited for an alternative gender role. For example, girls who acted as though they wanted to go hunting or use weapons were seen as potential women-men. A Mohave adult told a 1930s ethnographer that adults "may insist on giving the child the toys and garments of its true sex, but the child will throw them away" (Roscoe 1998, 139). A child could not control such behavior, in the Mohave view, for the kinds of dreams a child had affected whether the child would become a man, a woman, a man-woman, or a woman-man. Among the Zuni, as children grow up, they experience several rites of passage that initiate them into ceremonial groups and instruct them in the ceremonial and work duties appropriate for their sex. While a child, one Zuni man-woman underwent the first male initiation ceremony but not the second, making him an "unfinished male" (Roscoe 1991, 144), who could participate in some male activities but not others, such as warfare and hunting.

Transvestism

Wearing the clothing of the opposite sex was especially common and culturally significant among the tribes of the Great Plains, including the Arapaho, Ankara, Blackfoot, Cheyenne, Crow, Gros Ventre, Hidatsa, Iowa, Kansa, Mandan, Omaha, Osage, Oto, Pawnee, Ponca, and speakers of the Siouan language. Although common, transvestism was not found in all cultures with gender crossing. Sometimes men-women dressed like men, sometimes like women, and sometimes their choice of clothing depended on the situation. Among the Navajo, some nadleehi (men-women) wore women's clothing; others did not or only sometimes did so. Woman Chief, the adopted Crow woman, did not wear men's clothes, although she adopted many other aspects of the male role.

After whites began settling the West, most regarded men-women (whom many simplistically categorized as "sodomites") as disgusting or sinful. Because it was a visible manifestation of the Two Spirit role, transvestism was especially abhorrent to Anglo government officials, missionaries, educators, and settlers. Due to formal punishments and white ridicule, this symbol of alternative gender identity had largely disappeared by the early twentieth century.

Associations with Spiritual Powers

Usually, communities perceived Two Spirits as having some sort of unusual powers or abilities derived from spiritual sources. The Cheyenne of the Great Plains used a term that translates "half man-half woman." These people served as masters of ceremony for the important Scalp Dance that followed a successful raid by a war party. They also possessed powerful love medicines, so their services were sought by young men and women who wanted to attract heterosexual partners. Lakota believed that winkte could predict future events and could bestow lucky names on children. Osh-Tisch (whose name translates as "Finds Them and Kills Them"), of the Crow tribe, had a vision as a youth and became a powerful medicine person. One Navajo man-woman memorized numerous curing chants and learned to construct dozens of the intricate sand paintings used in curing rituals (see Chapter 14). He was widely credited with near-miraculous healing powers.

"Same-Sex" Relationships

The sexual orientation of Two Spirits varied from people to people, as well as from person to person within a single tribe. Understandably, reliable information on the sexual orientation of third- and fourth-gendered persons is rare. Some seem to have refrained from sex altogether. But the most common pattern was for men-women to be sexually active with men and sometimes women, but not with other men-women. These relations (most Anglo-Americans or Canadians would culturally categorize them as "homosexual relations") in most cases were an expected aspect of the role. Thus, a (genitally) male Two Spirits would engage in sex with men of his group, without stigma or punishment for either party. The man would not be considered homosexual because he had not had relations with *another man* but with a *man-woman*. In some tribes, a man would take a man-woman as a second "wife"—again apparently without stigma.

Even less is known about the sexual practices of women-men, and often early observers just stated that they were women who avoided marriage, or refused to marry. It appears, though, that they most commonly had relations with females. The complications of characterizing a person's sexual orientation are shown by a Mohave woman-man who had three wives (sequentially). All three eventually left her, and later in life, the woman-man became very active sexually with men.

This old photo of the Zuni Two Spirit named We-wha shows him dressed as a woman, although he altered both his attire and work roles.

After contact with Euro-Americans, Two Spirit identities were suppressed in most regions where Native Americans still lived, especially after the confinement of so many Natives to reservations in the 1800s. The majority of whites—settlers, traders, government agents, missionaries, and others—found the existence of a *legitimate* role such as man-woman or woman-man abhorrent. Because most viewed the custom as sinful, as harmful to Indian character, or as an obstacle to Native assimilation into Anglo society, they often imposed legal or social punishments for third and fourth genders. For example, in the 1920s, large numbers of Indian children were taken away from their families and communities—by force, when necessary—and placed in on- or off-reservation government-run boarding schools. In these Indian Schools (as they are known today), the explicit goal was to socialize and educate Indian children into Anglo culture. By separating Native children from their families and traditions, the theory was, they could be more quickly and thoroughly assimilated into white society. Of course, young people who showed signs of assuming alternative gender identities were punished.

Through such educational and legal mechanisms, multiple-gender identities were suppressed. Even some tribes that had once accepted third and fourth genders came to reject such persons. For instance, in the 1940s, some Winnebago told an ethnographer that "the [Two Spirit] was at one time a highly honored and respected person, but that the Winnebago had become ashamed of the custom because the white people thought it was amusing or evil" (quoted in Roscoe 1991, 201).

Hijra of Hindu India

With 1.2 billion people and dozens of languages and ethnicities, India is one of the world's most diverse countries. Hinduism, the predominant religion, believes in the existence of multiple gods, many of whom are androgynous (having both female and male characteristics). Many Hindu sects are devoted to the worship of specific deities, such as Rama, Vishnu, and Shiva.

In Hindu parts of India, there is a category of persons called *hijra*. Most are people born with male genitals who have chosen to undergo an operation that removes their testicles and penises. The operation is a rite of passage that transforms them into "neither man nor woman," in the phrase of ethnographer Serena Nanda. Hijra thus are members of a culturally constructed third gender.

Hijra form communities in urban areas of India, especially in the north. In part, these are religious communities, for they worship Bahuchara Mata, one of the avatars of the Hindu Mother Goddess. Hijra also identify with Krishna and Shiva, two other deities with anomalous genders. Because of their status as a third gender and their identification with these gods, other Hindus view hijra as spiritually powerful, able to bless people and events.

In the neighborhoods where they live, these spiritual powers lead Hindu families to call on hijra to perform various services. They dance at temple festivals and perform at life crisis ceremonies, such as childbirth and weddings. After a child is born, hijra dance and sing to bless the baby. After a wedding ceremony, hijra are called in to pray, sing, and dance to ensure that the couple will be prosperous and bear sons. The families pay them for these ritual services. Hijra also are potentially dangerous because of their ability to issue powerful curses. Hijra do not discourage this belief, for it helps them if they have problems collecting their fees.

The majority of hijra are born with male genitals. The rite of passage that emasculates them is translated as "rebirth," for it is viewed as transforming the person from an "ordinary, impotent male" (Nanda 1999, 26) into the hijra identity. Emasculation is culturally interpreted as a religious obligation of a would-be hijra, for sacrificing one's genitals shows dedication and sincerity of intent. It is witnessed by other hijra and makes it difficult for "fake hijras" (Nanda 1999, 37) to join the community just so they can take advantage of the opportunity to receive payment for ritual services.

After the surgery, which is surrounded by lengthy ceremonies and taboos, feminine pronouns (*she, her*) are usually applied to the person. Most of the time, hijra dress as females and assume female gestures, postures, gaits, and hairstyles, even when not working in ceremonies.

Becoming a hijra provides security—both social and economic—for persons whose lives might otherwise be difficult. Hijra residents of a town or city form households with people like themselves, although many maintain relationships with the families they were born into. Many people refer to one another using fictive kinship terms (Chapter 9) like "sister" and "granny." There is a well-developed social system, including a hierarchy, but most hijra eventually rise to the top of the hierarchy. The health and old-age needs generally are managed.

Economically, hijra occupy a legitimate niche in Hindu society, which provides them with some economic security. The leaders of a hijra community that lives in a particular neighborhood constantly investigate whether Hindu families are about to give birth or have a wedding. When a family is identified, the group marks their distinctive sign on the house with chalk as a signal that no other hijra house should show up for the birth or wedding ceremony. Hijra perform in groups of three to five or more persons—singing, dancing, drumming, and clowning, often with sexually suggestive themes and movements. Payment is in money and items like rice, candy, and clothing. Typically, hijra are dissatisfied with the amounts and may threaten to curse or shame the families. In addition to ritual performances, some hijra make their living by acting as prostitutes and live in "houses" of a different kind. Others go out begging for alms.

It is uncertain whether most male and female Hindus accept hijra as a legitimate and nonstigmatized third-gender category. Serena Nanda, who worked extensively with hijra, seems to think their gender identity is viewed with ambivalence by other Hindus. Certainly, Hindus hold diverse opinions about them. Nonetheless, the wider society allows them to live in their midst and provides payment for their ceremonial performances.

Native American Two Spirits and Indian hijra show that attitudes of intolerance, fear, and hatred of transsexuals and homosexuals are not universal among humanity. The knowledge that lots of cultures accept alternative gender roles is relevant for attitudes in twenty-first-century societies. Indeed, in many modern nations, acceptance of alternative sexualities and gender is increasingly common, especially among young people. However, anthropology offers no hard and fast lessons on this or most other issues: just because a behavior pattern is common, widespread, or even universal among humanity does not mean that all humans should accept it. And there are many peoples whose attitudes toward homoeroticism and alternative genders are highly negative.

The Gendered Division of Labor

The **gendered** (or **sexual**) **division of labor** refers to the patterned ways productive and other economic tasks are divided between women and men. Each gender has access to the products and/or services produced by the other, making the tasks of males and females, to some extent, complementary. This is one aspect of a people's gender (or sex) roles—the rights, duties, and expectations one acquires by virtue of one's membership in a gender category.

We must correct one misconception about this topic immediately: that it is only natural for men to be the breadwinners for their family. Hundreds of field studies provide all the data needed to discredit this idea. Breadwinning—that is, producing the supply of food and other material needs and wants of domestic groups—is definitely not an activity of men exclusively, or even largely. As discussed in Chapter 7, in many societies, men produce most of the food, but in others women's contribution to daily subsistence equals or exceeds that of men.

This finding contradicts the opinion of those who think that patriarchy is rooted in the "fact" that men's work is more important to physical survival and material well-being than women's work. Those who hold this view argue that women are usually economically dependent on men, which in turn makes women socially subordinate to men. But where patriarchy exists, it is not because the tasks men do are somehow more important to family and group survival than women's tasks. This ethnocentric idea probably comes from the way most modern industrial economies worked in the mid–twentieth century: by and large, men earned the money that allowed their families to purchase the goods they needed to survive. It is falsely concluded that the same economic dependence of wives on husbands characterized other peoples.

Besides, it is impossible to say whether male or female activities, taken in their totality, are more or less important. Bearing and nursing children seem pretty significant. Often, if a task is performed by males, it is *symbolically* considered more important, but whether it is *objectively* more important is ambiguous.

These are the anthropologist's usual warnings about confusing the beliefs and practices of one's own experience with those of all humans. Most people's ideas about what is and is not "natural" for humans to think and do are products of a specific culture at a particular time. Unless we become educated about the cultural diversity of humanity, we consistently—and usually mistakenly—conclude that the ideas and practices of our own society are universal or just "human nature."

So, Man the Breadwinner and Woman the Homemaker do not accurately describe the sexual division of labor in other cultures. Humankind is too diverse for that. Despite cultural variation, however, there are cross-cultural regularities and patterns in the sexual division of labor. What are the main patterns, and can they be explained?

---

gendered (sexual) division of labor Kinds of productive activities (tasks) assigned to women versus men in a culture.

Understanding Major Patterns

Table 11.1 summarizes a vast amount of comparative work on the gendered division of labor. The specific tasks toward the left of the table are more likely to be performed by males; those to the right are more likely to be done by females. The nearer a task is to the left, the more likely it is to be performed by males and vice versa.

A few comments are needed to clarify the table. First, it does not portray the division of labor in any specific society. Rather, it represents a composite of information drawn from hundreds of societies in various parts of the world. For example, the tasks listed as "Predominantly Females" should be interpreted as those done by women in most societies; however, among a particular people, men perform one or another of these tasks. Tasks listed as "Exclusively Males" are those carried out by men in all or nearly all societies, with few exceptions.

Also, the table includes only those activities that produce some kind of material product. Omitted from the table are other activities that are predominantly or exclusively male, such as holding political office and fighting in wars. Also absent are some activities, such as caring for infants, that are predominantly or exclusively women's work in all cultures. Our discussion is limited to activities usually considered "economic tasks."

Table 11.1 reveals two patterns. First, all human groups divide *some* kinds of labor by gender in similar ways. That is, some tasks are done mainly or nearly exclusively by one gender in most societies. For instance, hunting, clearing land, preparing the soil, working with hard materials, and cutting wood are exclusively or predominantly men's work in the great majority of societies. Gathering wild plants, processing plant foods, and cooking are mainly the work of females in most cultures. In short, although the table shows that groups vary in the kinds of tasks allocated to women and men, there are *widespread* (although not *universal*) patterns; consistently, some tasks are more likely to be done by men, others by women. The first question is, Why are some tasks done mostly by women, whereas others are done mainly or entirely by men?

The second pattern concerns the tasks in the column headed "Either or Both Sexes." These tasks are about equally likely to be performed by men or women,

TABLE 11-1 Patterns in the Gendered Division of Labor

General Category of Activity	TASKS THAT ARE PERFORMED BY				
	Exclusively Males	Predominantly Males	Either or Both Genders	Predominantly Females	
Extracting Food and Other Products	Hunting Trapping	Fishing	Gathering small land animals	Gathering shellfish, mollusks	Gathering wild plant foods
		Clearing land Preparing soil	Planting crops Tending crops Harvesting crops		
		Tending large animals	Milking animals	Caring for small animals	
	Woodworking Mining Lumbering			Gathering fuel	Fetching water
Manufacturing Processing, and Preparing Goods for Consumption	Butchering				Processing, preparing plant foods Cooking
	Boat building Working with stone, horn, bone, shell Smelting ore Metalworking	House building Making rope, cordage, nets	Preparing skins Making leather products	Making clothing Matmaking Loom weaving Making pottery	

Source: Adapted from Murdock and Provost (1973).

depending on the particular society. Members of either gender may do them, or both may work cooperatively on them. For example, whether men or women plant, tend and harvest crops, milk animals, or work with skins or leather varies from people to people, with no clear pattern apparent. These tasks are so variable from people to people that we cannot make generalizations; whether they are done by women, men, or both depends largely on local circumstances. Our second question is, What determines the cross-cultural variability in the sexual division of labor? Why are women more heavily involved in agriculture (planting, tending, and harvesting crops) in some societies than in others, for example?

This section focuses on hypotheses that deal with the first question. We put off discussion of the second question until the next section.

Why are some tasks nearly always done by men, whereas others are performed by women in most cultures? Biological/physical differences between the sexes—such as sexual dimorphism—provide one possible explanation. Perhaps tasks are assigned in such a way that the members of each sex do what they are physically able to do best.

This possibility seems like biological determinism. If understood properly, though, it is not. Physical differences between men and women are only *relevant* in explaining the sexual division, not *determinative*. To say that physical differences are relevant is to say the following: because of biological differences, men can perform certain kinds of tasks more effectively than women, and vice versa, and these differences are reflected in the widespread cross-cultural similarities in the sexual division of labor.

Consider an example. Anthropologists used to say that one task was everywhere done by men: hunting. Hunting seems to require certain biological capabilities—such as speed, strength, and endurance—that give men an advantage over women. Hunting also was thought to be incompatible with certain responsibilities universally borne by women for biological reasons: pregnancy, lactation (breastfeeding), and child care. Pregnant women would have a hard time chasing game. Lactating mothers would have to quit the hunt several times a day to nurse their infants. Because men could hunt more effectively than women, in foraging populations men hunted. In contrast, gathering required less strength and endurance. Because men had to spend so much of their time hunting, which women couldn't do as efficiently, gathering is largely women's work.

These arguments are partly valid, but female and male biological differences do not make it physically mandatory that males are the hunters and females are the gatherers in foraging populations. For one thing, not all kinds of hunting—and not all tasks connected to hunting—require superior strength, speed, and endurance. For another, there are questions about whether males typically have more "endurance" than females. Finally, there is no necessary biological reason a woman could not give up hunting only during her pregnancy and lactation and leave her older children in camp under the care of someone else.

At any rate, it is just not true that hunting is *universally* a male activity. When BaMbuti Pygmies of the Zaire rain forest hunt animals with nets, the women help by driving game into the nets held by men. In another part of the world, Agnes Estioko-Griffin describes hunting by women among the Agta, a mountain tribe of the Philippines who live on the island of Luzon. Agta men do most of the hunting, but women often accompany them in teamwork efforts, and women frequently hunt together without the company of men. Interestingly, sometimes women take their infants with them on the hunt, carrying the children on their backs. People like the Agta and BaMbuti show that the "man the hunter" image is oversimplified.

But such cases do not make the image entirely wrong. The great majority of peoples in which hunting is a significant means of acquiring food are foragers or horticulturalists. In most foraging cultures, women do most wild plant gathering. Men also contribute plant foods among most foragers, which makes images of "woman the gatherer" also oversimplified. As for horticultural peoples, the *pattern* is for women to do most of the planting, weeding, and harvesting of cultivated plants, whereas men hunt to provide meat. These patterns are not *universal* but are *widespread* enough that many anthropologists believe there must be some physical differences between men and women that are relevant in explaining them.

What specific female-male biological differences are likely to be most relevant in explaining the similarities in the sexual division of labor? Four main arguments have been proposed, briefly summarized in the Concept Review: (1) the possibility that regular heavy exercise depresses female fertility, (2) the fact that women and men have different roles in reproducing the population, (3) the relative overall strength of the two sexes, and (4) the biological fact that only women give birth to and nurse infants and young children. We discuss each factor, although the first two do not seem very plausible in our view.

Fertility Maintenance

One potentially relevant physical characteristic is that heavy exercise can reduce a woman's fertility. Modern female athletes—especially long-distance runners—often

CONCEPT REVIEW

Female/Male Differences Affecting Major Patterns in the Gendered Division of Labor

Fertility Maintenance Strenuous, prolonged physical exercise by women leads to lowered body fat and hormonal changes that reduce female fertility, so most strenuous tasks are done by males.

Reproductive Roles Populations need relatively few adult males to sustain numbers, so societies protect females by assigning hazardous tasks to males.

Physical Strength Most men are stronger than most women, so tasks requiring greater strength generally are performed by males.

Child Care Compatibility Women are universally bearers and primary caregivers of young children, so females tend to perform those tasks that can be combined most effectively with child care.

do not menstruate or ovulate monthly. This is because of a combination of a low body fat ratio and hormonal changes in women who engage in prolonged physical exercise. Some anthropologists suggest that work activities requiring heavy exertion would reduce women's fertility. For example, hunting often requires wielding weapons such as bows and spears that are powered by muscles alone, locating and tracking prey, and running down animals once they are shot. Lumbering and clearing land for planting also involve physical exertion such as swinging heavy axes for hours at a time. Conceivably, female fertility would be so decreased by such strenuous activities that the population would not be sustained over the course of many generations.

These Tuareg women from Niger are processing millet, an African grain. Processing and preparing plant foods after the harvest are mainly women's work in the majority of cultures.

CHAPTER 11 Gender in Comparative Perspective 255

However, hunting among most foragers and horticulturalists is not as strenuous as portrayed, nor are many other activities that are exclusively or largely done by males. In fact, women commonly do many tasks as physically demanding as those done by men, such as hauling water, gathering firewood for fuel, and planting and harvesting crops. Although fertility maintenance could be relevant among a few peoples, it is unlikely to be a widespread factor and certainly does not account for the widespread patterns in the sexual division of labor.

Reproductive Roles

Another possibility arises from the fact that fewer men than women are biologically necessary to maintain population size. A man produces enough sperm to father many thousands of children (theoretically), whereas a woman can bear a child only every year or so. Because only a few sexually active men can impregnate a large number of women, the size of the population seemingly depends more on the number of women than the number of men. Also, in all known societies, women are far more involved than men in the care of infants and young children. For these reasons, fewer males than females are needed to sustain a population. For the sexual division of labor, this difference in reproductive roles might imply that males are more expendable, which helps explain why so many hazardous roles (like hunting and fighting battles) are male roles: the group can afford to sacrifice some of its males but must protect its females as much as possible. If men "have" to perform such dangerous roles, then many other tasks are left to women by default.

Males are expendable only "theoretically," however, and if "all else is equal." In those societies—and there are a great many of them—in which warfare is a serious threat, large numbers of males are needed to protect the entire group. In fact, among many peoples, group survival itself depends on the ability to mobilize many warriors and to make political/military alliances with friendly neighbors. Only in their reproductive role are males "expendable"; in other respects, large numbers of males are essential for group survival. *If* there is a biological explanation for males performing more hazardous activities, it is not because a group finds many of its males to be expendable.

Relative Strength

Another biological factor is the average difference in physical strength between men and women, which allows men to perform tasks requiring great strength more efficiently. In Table 11.1, superior average male strength is *relevant*—once again, no anthropologist claims it is all-important—in many tasks under the heading "Exclusively Males" and in some of the tasks labeled "Predominantly Males," such as clearing land and preparing soil. On the other hand, strength has no obvious relationship to other "Exclusively" or "Predominantly" male tasks, such as trapping, butchering, and working with fibers. Note again that some female tasks also require significant strength, like gathering fuel, fetching water, and even processing food with pounders. Relative strength does influence patterns in the sexual division of labor, but other factors also matter.

Compatibility with Child Care

A fourth biologically based difference is that women are the bearers, nursers, and primary caregivers of infants and young children. This reproductive fact means that women are most likely to perform those tasks that can be combined with pregnancy and child care. Back in 1970, Judith Brown argued that such tasks have four characteristics:

- They are fairly routine and repetitive and do not require much concentration.
- They can be interrupted and resumed without significantly lowering their efficient performance.
- They do not place the children who accompany their mothers to the site of the task in potential danger.
- They do not require women and children to travel very far away from home.

The gathering of various products and the domestic work listed in Table 11.1 are highly compatible with child care. In addition, among horticultural peoples, garden tasks such as planting, weeding, and tending crops, and harvesting usually are done by women; these activities, too, generally seem highly compatible with caring for children. Notice that child care compatibility is most likely an important factor among peoples with high fertility. Where most couples have few children, this factor becomes less relevant as a basis for allocating productive work.

In sum, biological factors do help explain cross-cultural patterns in the division of labor by gender. Female-male differences in strength and child care roles have the most widespread relevance, although the other two factors might matter among specific peoples. Notice, though, that even if all four factors in combination totally

Despite cultural diversity in the gendered division of labor, widespread patterns exist. For example, men are more likely to construct substantial buildings than women. These Micronesian men are installing the roof on a structure to be used as a cookhouse.

explained the widespread patterns shown in Table 11.1 (which they do not), none of them can explain the *differences*. In fact, no biological difference between males and females alone can explain the cross-cultural diversity in the sexual division of labor. Biological differences in strength, reproductive physiology, and ability to care for infants are roughly constant in all human populations. But a condition that is constant in all groups cannot, by itself, account for things that vary between the groups. Constants cannot explain variability and diversity. We need other hypotheses to account for the cross-cultural variability in the gendered division of labor.

Understanding Variability

Here we discuss only one of the most important variations. There is a fairly consistent pattern in the degree of women's versus men's involvement in certain agricultural tasks, specifically in those tasks labeled "Either or Both Sexes" in the middle column of Table 11.1. Recall the distinction between horticulture and intensive agriculture (Chapter 7). In most horticultural groups, much—and in some societies nearly all—of the everyday garden work is done by women. For example, in traditional cultures in parts of the Pacific, the Amazon basin, and tropical Africa, women do most of the planting, weeding, tending, and harvesting of crops. Men participate in farming by clearing new land and preparing the plots or fields for planting. In contrast, among peoples who rely more heavily on intensive agriculture, women's actual work in the fields and direct contribution to the food supply are less important. To phrase the relationship in a few words: women are more likely to be involved *directly* in food production in horticultural than in intensive agricultural communities.

There are several reasons for this general pattern. First, in the New World, horticultural Native Americans had few or no domesticated animals (Chapter 7), so men's contribution to the food supply focused on hunting. Most routine garden work fell to women because such work is generally compatible with pregnancy and child care. In contrast, most intensive agriculturalists relied on livestock for meat, dairy products, hides, wool, and other products derived from animals. Men spent relatively little time hunting and so had more time for farming.

Also, prior to the twentieth century, in Europe and Asia nearly all intensive agriculturalists used the animal-powered plow to turn the earth prior to planting. Some researchers have suggested that most women are not strong enough to perform the heavy work of plowing efficiently. (You might remember, though, that draft animals provide most of the muscle power

Whether or not a task is compatible with caring for young children seems to be an important influence on the sexual division of labor. This woman from the Malagasy Republic is looking after her baby and harvesting rice at the same time.

for plow agriculture, which makes this suggestion difficult to evaluate. Also note that men are stronger than women only "on average.")

There is another reason women are less involved in direct cultivation in intensive agricultural societies. In Europe and Asia ("Eurasia"), the horticultural and intensive agricultural adaptations tend to involve the farming of different kinds of crops. Roughly half of horticultural societies grow *root crops* like yams, sweet potatoes, manioc (cassava), or taro. In contrast, about 90 percent of intensive agriculturalists rely on *cereal crops* like rice, wheat, corn, barley, and millet.

This difference affects women's involvement in actual farm work. Root crops can be stored in the ground for variable periods after they first become ready to eat, so they typically are harvested continuously during the growing season (think of familiar root crops like carrots or potatoes, which gardeners pull or dig up as needed). Either daily or a few times weekly, a woman goes to the garden and returns with root crops for herself, her children, and her husband. In contrast, cereals (which are the seeds of annual plants) tend to ripen at about the same time each year, usually near the end of the growing season. They have to be harvested in a short period of time, dried and processed, and stored for the rest of the year.

How does crop type affect the work of men and women? Cereal crops generally require a lot of labor to process (e.g., drying and grinding) before cooking. Plant processing is women's work in most cultures (Table 11.1). Also, people who rely on wheat, rice, barley, or other cereal grains usually face periods of intense labor requirements. At the beginning of the growing season and at harvest time, there is a need for laborers who can do a lot of hot, heavy work in a short period that is best not interrupted by other tasks. Such work is generally done by men (see the preceding section). In contrast, root-growing horticultural peoples tend to spread cultivation tasks out more evenly over the entire year, making gardening a day-in, day-out, repetitive task that requires less strength and that is more compatible with child care.

A third reason is warfare. Where war was frequent and serious, men in horticultural communities defended the local village, neighborhood, or kin group from enemies. In regions such as highland New Guinea and parts of the Amazon, group survival depended on the ability to defend land and resources from attack. Community welfare often was improved by taking over the land of enemy neighbors, so offensive as well as defensive warfare was common. Men were not actually fighting their enemies most of the time, of course, but maintaining community defenses and guarding against surprise raids did require significant amounts of (predominantly male) time.

For most peoples, making alliances with other groups improved the odds of success in warfare. Forming and maintaining alliances required a lot of politicking, mutual visiting, and exchanges, requiring substantial male time and energy. Also, male solidarity ("male bonding") was advantageous, so in many groups where warfare was prevalent, there were elaborate male-only rituals or social events that strengthened ties between men and helped socialize boys into manhood and the warrior role (mentioned in Chapter 14). All these pressures related to defensive and offensive warfare led men to concentrate much of their time and resources in fighting, preparing to fight, or maintaining the political relationships needed for success in organized fights. Routine garden tasks were left to women, partly by default.

In sum, comparative field research shows that women are less involved in direct food production among intensive agricultural than among horticultural peoples. Three of the most important factors that influence female involvement in cultivation tasks are as follows:

- Among horticultural peoples, men spend more time hunting than they do in intensive agricultural adaptations, so men have less time for cultivating crops.
- Compared to horticultural communities, intensive agriculturalists tend to grow cereal crops, making it more likely that men concentrate more on farm work and women more on domestic work, including processing foods before cooking.
- Horticultural peoples tend to be subjected to pressure from hostile neighbors, so men are busier fighting, guarding, politicking, exchanging, and creating bonds and relationships among themselves.

In brief, as agricultural systems become more intensive, other factors change that usually lead to reduced women's involvement in direct food production.

It is important to emphasize that these relationships are *generalized*, meaning that they may not hold for any particular people. Horticultural peoples "tend to" be more affected by warfare pressures, intensive agriculturalists are "more likely to" grow cereals than roots, and so forth. Obviously, there are many exceptions to the general patterns.

Consider the Kofyar of Nigeria, for example. They construct terraces, spread goat manure over their fields, use compost, and practice other methods of increasing yields that lead anthropologists who observe them to call their farming "intensive." Yet quantitative studies in the 1990s reveal that Kofyar women work about as much as men in agriculture. The Kofyar and many other peoples do not have the relationship between cultivation intensity and male labor that comparative research says they "ought to have" or "predicts they will have."

The Kofyar and other exceptions to the general pattern illustrate two other points. First, the existence of a general relationship established by comparative research does not tell us what any particular group of people are doing or thinking. The culture of any people is a product of a complex interaction among their history, adaptation, beliefs, and other factors. In any particular group, factors *unique* to that group may be more important than factors that are *generally* important. So, the fact that Kofyar women work the land about as much as men does not "disprove" the general point that women's labor becomes less important as agriculture becomes more intensive.

Second, just because there are exceptions does not invalidate a generalization provided, of course, that the general pattern is well established. If we are interested in the factors that influence the cultural variations in the sexual division of labor, then we must do comparative work to look for general patterns. The fact that particular cultures do not fit the pattern does not invalidate the generalization—at least not until the number of exceptions becomes large enough to make us suspicious of the existence of the general pattern.

As you realize by now, the preceding discussion is an example of the materialist theoretical approach discussed in Chapter 5. How a people acquire food (by horticulture or more intensive methods) influences the kinds of tasks women and men do (given differences in physical strength and reproductive roles). So, the material conditions of life interact with biological differences between women and men to produce the overall pattern of the division of labor along gender lines. That, at least, is the materialist argument.

Gender Stratification

A fourth main issue in the anthropological study of gender is **gender stratification**, or the degree to which human groups allocate material and social rewards to

> **gender stratification** Degree to which males and females are unequal in dimensions such as status, power or influence, access to valued resources, eligibility for social positions, and ability to make decisions about their own lives.

TABLE 11-2 Important Components of Gender Stratification

Dimension of Gender Stratification	Specific Questions for Societies
Kinds of social roles men and women perform	Are some roles limited to males and females? If so, which roles and how are they rewarded?
Value placed on contributions to groups	Are men's contributions viewed as more important—symbolically and/or practically?
Female deference to males	Do women defer socially to husbands or male relatives? How much, and in what contexts?
Access to positions of power and influence	Do women hold offices in the political arena? Who controls household and domestic tasks?
Control over personal lives	Do women make marital, sexual, childbearing, work, and other important decisions for themselves?
General beliefs about the sexes	Are men and women viewed as equally capable intellectually and psychologically?

© Cengage Learning

women and men *based on their gender.* Other sources of unequal rewards include class, caste, family origins, and race (covered in other chapters). Here, we discuss only rewards based on whether one is a male or a female. We ignore such complications as third- or fourth-gender identities.

Gender stratification is sometimes referred to as "the status of women," which can be high, low, or intermediate. Whatever we call it, gender stratification is difficult to define because it includes many components that interact in complex ways. Some dimensions that are useful indicators for comparing the degree of gender stratification cross-culturally are listed in Table 11.2.

Of course, gender stratification is more complicated than this (or any) table can summarize. But the table does show some of the main features that constitute the overall pattern of gender stratification in particular cultures. It also is helpful in comparing the degree of gender stratification across cultures. Obviously, gender stratification is *multidimensional,* which makes it difficult to categorize gender stratification among any particular people as "high," "moderate," "low," or "nonexistent." Why is it so difficult?

For one thing, some components are not consistent with other components. Studies of family life often report that women have a great deal of control in making decisions about child rearing and about the allocation of domestic resources, even though they have little independence outside the domestic context. For instance, in two Andalusian towns of southern Spain, David Gilmore's fieldwork showed that wives have great autonomy in managing household affairs. He believes this is because many women are able to live near their own mothers, so that wives and their mothers frequently "gang up" on a husband. Even in male-privileged societies like traditional Korea, Japan, and China, the eldest female in a household usually managed household affairs with a fair degree of autonomy. Yet in these countries, and in many other societies, women hardly participated in public affairs, had barely any property of their own, had little voice about their marriages, and were clearly subordinate to their fathers, husbands, and husband's fathers—socially and even legally.

Another factor complicating gender stratification is that, in most cultures, a woman's status changes over the course of her life. For example, in traditional East Asia and South Asia, most families were patrilocally extended (see Chapter 9), so when women married, they left their own family and moved into or near the house of her husband's parents. A young wife was subjected to the authority of her husband's mother and was duty-bound to work extremely hard. But, as a woman settled into the household, had a son, and aged, her status improved and she gradually took over control of the household from her mother-in-law. Eventually, she became the everyday manager of the household and was an authority figure over her own daughters-in-law after her sons married. The same pattern of women's status improving with age appears in numerous other cultures.

Finally, in more complex societies like modern nations, distinctions of rank or class (considered in Chapter 13) or of ethnic affiliation (see Chapter 16) often outweigh male-female distinctions. That is, wealth or perceived membership in a racial or ethnic category are other bases of inequality that may be difficult to disentangle from gender stratification.

So, gender stratification is not a unitary phenomenon—not a single thing. Like other social relationships, male-female relationships are complex. This is not surprising. Concepts like "gender stratification" are used by contemporary social scientists. The people whose lives anthropologists study may not have this cultural concept at all. Nor are women's and men's lives in any community so simple that anthropologists (or anyone else) can categorize them unambiguously by statements like "Women have low status in culture X," although many people continue to do so.

Is Gender Stratification Universal?

In spite of complexities, there are significant cultural variations in gender stratification. Even humanistic anthropologists who usually mistrust comparisons and objective measurements recognize that there is much less gender stratification among the Native American Hopi, Zuni, and Iroquois than among the Yanomamö or Tukano of the Amazon basin. Gender stratification is a meaningful concept to use for answering certain questions, such as these: Are there societies in which women and men are equal? Are there matriarchical societies?

The answer to the second question is a qualified no. The qualification is due to disagreement over the meaning of the term *matriarchy*. Logically, matriarchy could be defined as the mirror image of patriarchy: for a people to be matriarchical, women should enjoy all the unequal rights and receive the same kinds of rewards that men have among peoples most would agree are *patriarchical*.

However, the term is not always used this way. Anthropologist Peggy Reeves Sanday worked among an Indonesian people, the Minangkabau, who by her definition are matriarchical. She writes, "Defining a female-oriented social order as the mirror image of a male form is like saying that women's contribution to society and culture deserves a special label only if women rule and act like men" (Sanday 2002, xi). Sanday argues that this outmoded definition led early twentieth-century anthropologists to search the world for "primitive matriarchies," without success. Their failure to discover matriarchy resulted from the fact that one cannot "find something that has been defined out of existence from the start" (xi). She prefers a conception of matriarchy that emphasizes maternal meanings where "maternal symbols are linked to social practices influencing the lives of both sexes and where women play a central role in these practices" (xxi).

So, the popular definition of *matriarchy* ("female dominance") is not the only way to conceptualize the term. If we choose to think of matriarchy as rule by females, then despite the fictional stories and the occasional old adventure movie in which the hero gets captured by "amazons," not a single instance of clear female domination over men has ever been found by ethnographers. Clearly, there have been and are individual women who hold great power, control great wealth, and are held in high esteem. Certainly, there are queens, female chiefs, and individual matriarchs of families and kin groups. But if we define matriarchy as a social system in which women have the rights and receive the material, social, and symbolic rewards that only men receive in a host of societies, then such a social system has not been documented.

The first question—whether there are cultures in which men and women are equal—has a more uncertain and complex answer. Some scholars believe that women are never considered fully equal to men. They interpret the ethnographic record as showing that gender hierarchy—inequalities based on gender—exists among all peoples.

Those who believe that male dominance/female subordination is universal point to two fairly well-established generalizations. One applies to the realm of political institutions. In political life, gender hierarchy always exists. In no known society are the primary political authority roles restricted to females. But, in many societies, all women are denied the right to succeed to political offices, making office holding a male prerogative. Among most peoples, even kin-group leadership roles are monopolized by men. Male elders of a lineage or clan decide how the group's land and other resources are to be used and allocated, how the group's wealth objects are to be disposed of, whether the group is to engage in a battle to avenge a wrong, and so on. (As we shall soon see, however, women often do have significant influence over these matters, especially in matrilineal societies.)

The other realm of life with gender hierarchy is religion. In many societies, women are excluded from holding major religious leadership roles. To be sure, there are societies—lots of them, in fact—in which *particular rituals* are performed by and for women, as in female initiations. But there are many societies in which females are forbidden to participate in the most important *public* rituals. Even among matrilineal peoples like the Hopi and Zuni of the American Southwest, it is men who wear the costumes in public dances that benefit the whole community.

According to some scholars, then, the activities of males are universally regarded as more important than those of females. Women as a social category are everywhere culturally devalued relative to men as a social category. Complete gender equality does not exist.

However, there is another way to interpret the ethnographic record. Many scholars note that most fieldworkers—and hence most of the ethnographic information available to shed light on the issue of gender hierarchy—have been biased in two ways. The first is the *androcentric* (male) bias. Most fieldworkers were males until 1970s, and most of them were not very interested in local women's lives. Also, simply because they were themselves men, fieldworkers had little access to women's points of view, so they often unwittingly took local men's values, attitudes, and opinions as representative of the entire group. Female points of view were largely unreported, so reports were not objective and/or incomplete.

The second possible source of fieldwork bias is the tendency to *essentialize* other peoples. Basically this means that, first, we simplify the complexities of their lives in our own minds and writings, and, second, we have an ethnocentric tendency to impose outside concepts and standards (e.g., "inequality") on Others. For example, look again at the list of "important components" of gender inequality in Table 11.2. Whose list is this? "Ours," of course. If we claim that some people have gender stratification based on Our criteria, then we are deemphasizing Their criteria. In fact, we might come to one conclusion using Ours, but this conclusion might vary from Theirs. As you realize, this objection is especially likely among humanistically inclined anthropologists, who tend to emphasize "the Native's point of view."

In short, some scholars—especially humanistic ones—think that many fieldworkers have been biased. Because of this bias, the ethnographic record is not objective. Those ethnographers and comparative researchers who say that there are no societies with total gender equality or even matriarchy have been misled. Or perhaps they are misleading themselves.

In contrast, some anthropologists have found cases of what they consider sexual equality. Those who believe that female-male equality exists in some cultures can point to particular people who they think document their belief. Here we consider two such peoples.

The Iroquois, a matrilineal and matrilocal people of northeastern North America, are the most famous

Iroquois women's control over cultivated foods and their distribution gave them relatively high status.

case of women achieving equality (or only "near equality?") with men. Iroquois women produced the corn and other cultivated foods, put foods in storage in the residential longhouses, and largely controlled how they were distributed from the storehouses. Iroquois men were away from their apartments in the longhouse much of the time, engaged in warfare or cooperative hunting expeditions. After the introduction of the fur trade into northeastern North America in the seventeenth century, men often were away searching for beaver pelts or raiding their neighbors for pelts. The matrilineally related women of a longhouse influenced their inmarried husbands' behavior by withholding provisions from their hunting trips and war parties. Only men had the right to hold the most powerful political offices because only males could be elected to the great council of chiefs. But it was the older women of the various matrilineages who selected their groups' representatives to the council. These women also had the right to remove and replace men who did not adequately represent the group's interests. Also, women had a voice in the deliberations of the council itself. They could veto declarations of war and introduce peacemaking resolutions.

Across the Pacific from the Iroquois are a people called the Vanatinai. Living in a small island off the southeast coast of Papua New Guinea, the Vanatinai are a matrilineal people. Maria Lepowsky, who worked among Vanatinai in the late 1970s, reports considerable gender equality among them. Women own and inherit gardens and other property, including wealth in pigs and valuables made of shell. Women choose whom they will marry and their husbands render brideservice, but divorce is easy and many people marry several times. Polygyny is possible, but the consent of the first wife is required. There is much overlap in the division of labor: both men and women garden, fish, and care for pigs. Men do a lot of child care also and gender distinctions are not symbolically marked by initiation rituals (Chapter 14) as in many cultures. Symbolically, Vanatinai view men as "life takers" (although warfare is not very intense), and women as "life givers." Warfare earns men some prestige, but women also are seen as dangerous and powerful from their knowledge of witchcraft. Women play important roles in most public rituals, know spells, and can communicate with the ancestors and other spirits. Perhaps most indicative of equality is the possibility that a woman can achieve the status of *gia* ("giver"), the most prestigious and influential position. They do so by actively engaging in reciprocal exchanges, both among their own people and on overseas trading expeditions in which they give and receive shell valuables. Women may even organize these expeditions. Lepowsky, unfortunately, does not provide relative numbers of female and male *gia*.

So, is gender hierarchy in favor of males a cultural universal or not? Certainly, some ethnographers have been and are biased—but does this bias account for all reports of female subordination? Certainly, the Iroquois, the Hopi (see Chapter 10), Vanatinai, Minangkabau, and many other peoples demonstrate that women in some cultures have achieved considerable control over their own lives and over public decision making—but do such cases represent full *equality* of males and females? Indeed, would we know "total equality" if we saw it in a society? What would it look like? Would men and women have to carry out the same kinds of economic tasks before we can legitimately claim they are completely equal? Is monogamy necessary, or can a society be polygynous and still qualify? How should family life be organized before we can say that husbands in culture X do not dominate their wives? Shall we require that women occupy 50 percent of all leadership roles before we say they have equal rights? (If so, neither Iroquois nor Vanatinai would have gender equality.)

Many questions must be answered before we can say whether gender hierarchy is universal—the most important of which is whether we would know complete gender equality if we were to encounter it!

Why is the question important? Many anthropologists think that the more cultures we encounter with gender equality, the greater the chances that modern societies can achieve equality. At the very least, lots of examples of equality would show that patriarchy is not inevitable because so many peoples are not patriarchical. Feminist psychologists, sociologists, historians, biologists, and other scholars have examined ethnographic descriptions of various Other Cultures, looking for equality or even matriarchy. Their reasoning also is that, if anthropologists have discovered numerous cultures in which women have achieved equality, then women will be more likely to achieve equality in the future. Their hope is that there are many such cultures. Their worry is that there are few or none.

Although not silent, the ethnographic record on gender equality is filled with ambiguity and uncertainty. It is ambiguous both because gender stratification is so multidimensional, making "total" equality difficult to recognize, and because of the problem of whose standards and criteria should be applied to actual cultures.

At any rate, how much does it matter for the cause of sexual equality *today* if women are "universally" or "nearly universally" subordinate? What matters most is that women and men are a good deal more equal in some societies than in others, which allows us to study the conditions under which future equality is likely to be possible. To argue that because women have always or usually been subordinate, they will forever be subordinate is analogous to assumptions 40 years ago that computers will never be mass-marketed. Thirty years ago mobile phones like those we have today were unknown. Ten years ago the United States had never elected an African American president. Just because no human group has achieved some state in the past does not mean that none will achieve it in the future. It does not mean that we should give up trying to achieve it today and for the future. And it certainly does not mean that twenty-first-century women have achieved about all the equality they are likely to achieve.

Here is a more answerable question: what influences the degree of gender stratification in a society?

Influences on Gender Stratification

As the preceding discussion implies, no one has shown that a small number of factors are the primary determinants of gender stratification. Here, we discuss only a few generalizations that point to the kinds of influences that are most widespread and important.

Women's Contributions to Material Welfare

Some materialists argue that women's role in production strongly influences their property rights, their role in public affairs, their degree of personal freedom, and other dimensions of their overall status. One idea is that, where women produce a high proportion of the food, shelter, clothing, and other necessities of existence, men will recognize their contributions and reward women with influence, property, prestige, dignity, and other benefits. In other words, the gendered division of labor and the proportion of valued goods women produce are strong influences on gender stratification.

Such ideas seem to apply to some foraging and horticultural peoples, among whom women's gathering or gardening contributes much of the food consumed by their households. Women's productive labor gives them a status closer to equality with men than they have among peoples in which women's subsistence contributions are not as great. For example, among the BaMbuti and Aka, two foraging Pygmy groups of the central African rain forest, women's labor is critical for success in net hunting, and ethnographic studies on both these Pygmy peoples report male-female equality or near equality. Among the Ju/'hoansi, too, considerable equality exists between women and men. Both the Iroquois and Vanatinai are horticulturalists, which fits, yet numerous other peoples of the Amazon basin and Melanesia also practice horticulture, and women there are quite subordinate.

But everyone's status is "closer to equality" in most hunter-gatherer and many horticultural populations (see Chapters 7 and 13). So, perhaps the relative lack of gender stratification in these adaptations results not from women's importance as food providers but from some other factor or influence that reduces inequalities of all kinds.

Women's Control over Key Resources

A more complex materialist proposal is that women's contribution to production, by itself, is not enough to "earn" them relative equality. It is *necessary* for women to contribute heavily to material welfare to gain resources, rights, and respect, but this alone is not *sufficient*. (Analogously, consider enslaved persons.) One specific hypothesis is that women must also own productive resources (land, tools) or have considerable control over the distribution of the products of their labor, or both. If women own productive resources and have a great deal of say over what happens to the goods they produce, then they can have some influence on the activities of men. Overall, this gives them more equality. Peggy Reeves Sanday found some support for this hypothesis in a cross-cultural study done in the 1970s.

This hypothesis seems to account reasonably well for some specific cases. For instance, Iroquois women controlled the production and distribution of important resources. They used this control to nominate their kinsmen to chiefly positions and to influence the public decision making from which they were formally excluded. Likewise, Hopi women (Chapter 10) owned land and had considerable control over the distribution of its products. Women had relatively high status in both these societies, as they did among many other Native American peoples.

Along the same lines, in many West African and Caribbean societies, women are more active than men in market trade in foodstuffs, handicrafts, textiles, and other goods produced by themselves. Sometimes market-trading women are able to transform their independent control over exchangeable resources into more equitable relationships with men. Wives commonly maintain a separate income from that of their husbands, which they are free to spend on themselves and their children. Among the Yoruba of Nigeria, women are active in market trade and in craft production, which gives them access to income and economic security independent of their husbands and other men. Many women purchase houses in urban areas and use the rent to improve their own and their children's economic well-being and social autonomy. According to Sandra Barnes (1990, 275):

> Property frees the owner from subordinating herself to the authority of another person in domestic matters. It places her in a position of authority over others and in a position to form social relationships in the wider community that are politically significant. Property owning legitimates her entry into the public domain.

The economic independence that some Yoruba women are able to acquire translates into increased participation in neighborhood associations and other public affairs and allows them much freedom from male authority. A wider generalization would be that control over resources increases women's independence from men and allows women to form associations with other women that act like mutual support networks.

Thus, many ethnographic and comparative studies suggest that controlling resources is one way for women to get respect and independence from husbands, brothers, and other men. This ability to acquire some measure of control over family resources helps to account for why so many North American wives have demanded and received more help from their husbands in housework and child care. In recent decades, married women in increasing numbers have acquired wage- and salary-earning jobs. Between 1970 and 2011, in the United States, the percentage of all married women who were employed doubled. Even the presence of young children does not keep most American women from entering the workforce: between 1975 and 2011, the percentage of married women with children under age 6 who were working for a wage rose from 39 percent to 64 percent. Among the reasons for increases in married women's employment are the inadequacy of one person's (formerly, the husband's) income to support the family at an acceptable living standard, structural changes to a more service-oriented economy (less goods producing, with a decline in factory employment), the increasing value women place on personal fulfillment through career advancement (partly because of the feminist movement), and dramatic increases in the numbers of women who have college degrees.

As a result of entering the workforce as wage and salary earners, many married American women have gained considerable economic independence from their husbands. Women also are earning higher percentages of household income: between 1970 and 2010, women's contribution to household income rose from 26 percent to 38 percent. Between 1987 and 2010, among two-earner households the percentage of wives who earned more than their husbands rose from 18 percent to 29 percent. Husbands have, therefore, lost economic leverage in the household relative to their wives. Increasingly, wives have psychological

Where women commonly earn income for themselves by marketing products, as in Jamaica, their overall status tends to be relatively high.

GLOBAL CHALLENGES AND OPPORTUNITIES

Bridal Photos in Taiwan: Globalization and Localization

Outwardly, most contemporary weddings in Taiwan seem to mimic those in the United States and most of Europe. However, Taiwanese attach meanings to wedding photos that most Westerners do not.

Taiwan, South Korea, Singapore, and Hong Kong are sometimes called East Asia's "Four Little Dragons." (The big dragon, of course, is China.) In the 1970s, the Little Dragons developed rapidly by exporting clothing, consumer electronics, toys, and automotive accessories to North America and Europe. Hong Kong and Singapore have been financial centers for decades. South Korea is now the ninth-largest economy in the world, producing ships, motor vehicles, TVs, DVDs, and other high-tech equipment for the global marketplace.

Like the other Little Dragons, Taiwan is about as modern as any place on our planet. Its employment structure is about the same as North America and Europe: only 5 percent of its people work in agriculture, 37 percent are employed in industry, and 58 percent make a living in services. Taiwan has three cities with populations greater than 1 million; the largest is the capital, Taipei, with nearly 3 million people. Annual income per person in Taiwan is over $30,000. Of its 23 million people, 96 percent can read and write. Its people are mostly healthy and long-lived. There are around 30 million cell phones. Taiwan, and especially Taipei, is developed, urban, connected, cosmopolitan—global.

Its weddings look global, too. Or, rather, they look global if by *global* you mean "modeled after those of the West," which is exactly what *global* means to many people. Taiwanese young people meet and date, and if they fall in love and marry, their wedding ceremonies are familiar to the eyes of Westerners—at least, to Western secularists. Most weddings include white gowns, tuxedos, flowers, and lots of photos.

What is not familiar is that most couples go to an expensive photo salon *before* their wedding banquet and before the ceremony itself to have pictures taken. Ordinarily, these pictures are displayed at the wedding ceremony itself. And, according to Bonnie Adrian, who studied weddings in Taiwan in the 1990s, in the photos the bride is hardly recognizable as herself. At great expense, she visits a professional makeover stylist in a salon. The stylist shapes the bride's eyebrows with a razor, often removing them entirely only to reapply new ones later with an eyebrow pencil. Next she applies foundation makeup to cover any blemishes; usually this is a light color because fair skin is desirable. Then the stylist attacks the eyes, applying shadow, liner, and false lashes. The goal is to produce a round-eyed look. The lips are next. The foundation makeup has already made the facial features indistinct, so the bride's natural lip color and shape are barely visible. New lip shapes are applied with a brush, depending on the look the stylist wishes to impart, and the lipstick color is added. Finally, the nails are fixed and the hair styled. Typically, all this takes three hours or longer.

ammunition against their husbands' domestic incompetence or laziness—they've put in a full day's work on the job just like their husbands. The legal system has also helped by increasingly considering family violence more than just a private family matter as well as by prosecuting or garnishing the wages of "deadbeat dads." Unhappy wives are more able to support themselves economically after divorce or separation, reducing the need for a husband to support them and their children. Although wage and salary equality are improving, in the aggregate women still receive only 82 percent of men's compensation (an increase from 62 percent in 1979).

In the twenty-first century, increasing numbers of North American couples are "role reversed." Husbands-fathers stay at home with young children while wives-mothers are the breadwinners. Some believe this pattern reverses the natural order of

What about the groom? He will have his hair cut and styled so that nothing looks out of place, and he may wear a bit of makeup to ensure that his facial features show up properly under the photographic lights. But overall, he is recognizably himself. In the wedding and photos, at least, his appearance is secondary.

Next, the couple visits a photographer who specializes in prewedding photos and takes hundreds or thousands of pictures. By the time the photographer has finished, usually a whole day has passed—and several thousand dollars have changed hands. The prints are huge, and on the day of the wedding banquet, they are prominently displayed so that all can admire the beauty of the bride.

One interpretation of all this "framing the bride" (as Adrian titles her 2003 book) is that Taiwanese wedding customs have taken on a Western flavor. Consciously or not, it looks like Taiwanese couples have chosen the Western model. Is this yet another example of "cultural imperialism"—the makeover of indigenous customs based on the foundation of the West?

Adrian believes this interpretation is simplistic. In old Taiwan, women viewed marriage not as the fulfillment of romantic dreams, but as the beginning of a life of hard work for her husband's family and for the welfare of the children she would soon bear. This attitude carries over into contemporary Taiwan. Today women and men in love have plenty of opportunities to be intimate before they marry. So, they often postpone marriage until they feel ready to have children and undertake the responsibilities of parenthood. When a modern Taiwanese woman marries, she feels she is sacrificing a lot of freedom in the interest of her husband and their offspring. The photo, usually hung in the bedroom, will remind her and him of how beautiful and free she was before the trials of family responsibility wore her down.

Weddings, banquets, and photographs also reflect implicit competition—what Americans used to call "keeping up with the Joneses." The more photographs and the more work the photographer must do to make them perfect, the greater the expense, and most of this expense is paid for by the groom and his family. The groom would be embarrassed if the photos were not up to standards, and his wife might remind him of his failure to live up to cultural expectations in future quarrels. At the obligatory wedding banquet, the amount and quality of food must also be up to normative expectations—and so must the quality of the wedding photos. The groom's family would suffer a humiliating loss of face if they did not honor their son's marriage and welcome their new daughter-in-law with an ostentatious banquet and expensive photographs.

These kinds of photographs made before the wedding itself in Taiwan do not primarily document the events of the marriage. They are not records of the ceremony. Rather, they are commemorations of the bride; Adrian (2003, 235) says, "they construct brides," meaning that they build an image of the woman before her marriage so that, after the marriage, her new family can see an idealized depiction of the woman she once was.

What are the wider lessons of bridal photos in contemporary Taiwan? Consciously or not, Taiwanese take something from the realm of global culture and use it for their own culturally meaningful purposes. To say it differently, they *localize the global* by shaping the photos to fit their own traditions and reconfiguring what comes in from the outside world to mesh with their own cultural attitudes and beliefs and social practices. Korea, Japan, and many other nations have accepted many ideas and practices from the outside, remaking them to fit their own traditions. Humanity does not need to become all alike just because we interact with one another in new global settings.

male-female family roles and thus is ultimately harmful to children, who look up to their parents as role models. Others hold that the feminist movement has helped liberate men as well as women from old cultural attitudes: as economic or familial circumstances warrant, or as couples prefer, parents can reverse, switch, or alternate caretaking and breadwinning roles. Has feminism given both sexes more freedom of choice?

With most women now out in the world of work, and with the families of so many married women now virtually dependent on their income to pay the bills, more women are demanding equal pay for equal work, equal treatment and opportunity in the workplace, equal legal rights, and equal respect. As in other societies, in North America, women's success in obtaining control over important resources empowers them relative to men.

Descent and Postmarital Residence

The form of descent and postmarital residence also influences the degree of gender stratification. Women in matrilineal and matrilocal societies have greater equality in many areas of life. What is it, specifically, about matrilineality and matrilocality that gives relatively high status to females? It is not usually that "women rule" in these societies, in a political or legal sense.

As the matrilineal peoples discussed earlier illustrate, one reason there tends to be a high degree of gender equality is that women have a lot of control over life-sustaining resources. Where land, wealth, and other property passes mainly from mothers to daughters, wives have more independence from husbands and some matrilocal peoples view husbands as working for their wives and their wives' families. Commonly—but not universally—in matrilineal, matrilocal societies, husbands are rather loosely attached to their wives' households, and divorce and remarriage rates are relatively high. It may be easier for dissatisfied husbands to leave and remarry than to deal with lots of conflicts with their wives and her relatives (including her brothers).

Other elements of matrilineality and matrilocality also benefit women. Two factors contribute to their equality. First, because husbands live with the families of their wives, sisters remain with or close to one another throughout their lives. A typical wife thus has her mother, sisters, and other female relatives around to support her in domestic quarrels. Second, in many matrilineal and matrilocal societies, domestic authority over a married woman is divided between her husband and her brother. Alice Schlegel suggests that this arrangement increases her freedom because each man acts as a check on the other's attempts to dominate her.

This situation contrasts markedly with patrilineal and patrilocal societies, such as old China, Korea, Japan, the Middle East, and most of India and Pakistan. In these societies, when a woman married into a family, she was given household tasks to perform for most of her waking hours. Only when she herself bore sons and heirs to her husband's family did her status improve, and only after she herself became a mother-in-law to her sons' wives could she relax a bit. In East Asia, the Confucian social and moral philosophy, which held that women must be submissive to men, affected the way wives and daughters-in-law were treated. Even in modern times, many women feel that marriage results in a loss of freedom and that the heavy duties of family life are burdensome, which in Taiwan affects even wedding practices (see the Globalization box). In the Islamic parts of southern Asia and in the Middle East, the teachings of the Koran generally supported a woman's subordinate status in the home as well as in public. But also important were the social facts that wives became members of the households of their husbands' parents, and the lines of authority over them were clearly and legally redrawn upon their marriage. Socially, a wife had few viable alternatives to submitting to her husband's family and relatively few sources of support when she was treated poorly. In contrast, in most matrilocal and matrilineal cultures, women do have alternatives to suffering the dominance of their husbands, and they are more likely to receive support from their own birth families.

Gender Stratification in Industrial Societies

We conclude by bringing together some of the information and ideas covered in this chapter and briefly suggesting how they might be relevant to women living in modernized or modernizing nations.

Anthropological research on gender stratification reveals that women's roles and rights, and the restrictions placed on them, vary from place to place and from time to time. Although it is probably impossible to decide whether gender stratification is totally absent in some culture somewhere, we certainly know that sexual equality varies—and varies significantly. So, there is reason to think that modern societies can move further toward eliminating barriers to female opportunity and achievement. Patriarchy does not seem to be part of the human genome.

Some of our discussion of gender stratification suggests that any change that improves women's independent access to material resources and to social support will have positive impacts on their status in other realms of life. If married women have their own source of income independent of their husbands, then they are better able to become empowered within their families and to escape relationships with men who are physically or psychologically abusive. If, as in matrilineal and matrilocal societies, women are able to maintain relationships of "sisterhood" (i.e., support from other women) and/or of extended family ties (i.e., aid from their own relatives), then they can mobilize these supportive relationships in times of hardship. If women have legal recourse to sue discriminating employers and would-be employers, then their opportunities and compensation on the job will be improved by the threat of monetary damages.

Going back to the very first point in this chapter: the knowledge that ideas and beliefs about gender are culturally constructed rather than biologically given should—*if taken seriously and understood properly*—lead women and men alike to realize that at least some of the sexual differences they believe exist are differences of our own culture's making. It is a biological *reality* (with some qualifications) that women have the physical tools to bear and nurse children and that men on average are larger and stronger than women. But the level of importance of these biological realities varies from people to people. As technology powered by fossil fuels replaces tools powered by human muscles, differences in size and strength need not and do not matter as much as they used to for the division of labor or for gender role in other contexts.

SUMMARY

1. **Describe how male-female physical differences affect gender roles and relationships.** Physical differences between females and males are recognized and relevant to social behavior in all known cultures, but these differences matter in different ways and to different degrees. For anthropological interests, the two most important genetically based differences are sexual dimorphism and reproductive physiology, which affect who performs economic tasks and childcare responsibilities. In modern times, such physical differences are less relevant than in preindustrial eras.

2. **Explain the phrase "cultural construction of gender" and its importance.** A person's sex is determined biologically (by genes), but gender is a cultural construction. The cultural construction of gender means that cultures vary in how they perceive the physical differences between the sexes, in the significance they attribute to those differences, and in the way those differences are made relevant for self-identity, task and role allocation, access to property and power, and so forth. The Hua of Papua New Guinea illustrate the cultural construction of gender.

3. **Analyze the relevance of the acceptance of multiple-gender identities for the understanding of gender.** Human groups differ in their tolerance of individual variations in gender identities. Many peoples allow gender crossing, in which males are allowed to enact female roles, and vice versa. Others recognize multiple sexual identities, in which there are not only two, but three or four genders, roughly corresponding to man-woman or woman-man. With their acceptance of Two Spirits, Native American peoples seem especially tolerant of gender crossing and to allow for multiple-gender identities. The hijra are a socially recognized third gender in India, which further suggests that alternative genders are legitimate roles in many human societies.

4. **Discuss the factors that influence the widespread patterns and the cross-cultural diversity in the gendered division of labor.** Despite cultural variations, widespread patterns exist in the gendered division of labor. Four biological factors that influence the broad cross-cultural similarities are (1) the depression of fertility that seems to occur when a woman engages in heavy exercise, (2) the possibility that women are more necessary than men to maintain population size, (3) superior male strength, and (4) the degree of compatibility of a particular task with the care of infants and young children. No female/male biological difference can account for cultural diversity in the gendered division of labor. Generally, female labor is more important in subsistence tasks in horticultural populations than among intensive agriculturalists. The reasons for this difference are the types of crops grown (root crops versus cereal grains), the amount of time needed for food processing, and the greater prevalence of warfare in horticultural groups.

5. **Analyze why it is so difficult to determine whether any societies have complete gender equality.** The nature of gender stratification and the reasons why it varies are controversial, due to problems of definition and the possible biases outsiders bring to their work. Anthropologists have yet to discover any peoples who are matriarchical, as the term is commonly used. People like the Iroquois and Vanatinai have been viewed as examples of equality between the genders. But even specialists in gender studies cannot agree whether gender hierarchy is universal or whether there are societies with complete equality between men and women. This is mainly because gender stratification is multidimensional and because "complete equality" is so difficult to define.

6. **Describe the three most important influences on gender stratification from a comparative perspective.** Many forces affect gender stratification in human societies. Among some of the most important widespread influences are women's relative contributions to subsistence, women's ability to control key resources, and the pattern of descent and postmarital residence. These influences are relevant for gender equality in the twenty-first century.

12 The Organization of Political Life

In many state-level societies, political authority is vested in formally elected bodies, such as the parliament of the United Kingdom.

Forms of Political Organization
  Bands
  Tribes
  Chiefdoms
  States
  Inca Empire

Social Control and Law
  Social Control
  Law

Legal Systems
  Self-Help Systems
  Court Systems
  Incipient Court Systems
  Courts of Mediation
  Courts of Regulation

LEARNING OBJECTIVES

After reading this chapter, you should be able to

1. **EXPLAIN** what is meant by political organization.
2. **LIST** the four main types of political organization and how they structurally differ from one another.
3. **EXPLAIN** what is meant by social control.
4. **DISCUSS** legal systems and how they differ from other forms of social control.
5. **DISCUSS** the two major forms of legal systems and the variants within the two forms.
6. **EXPLAIN** the relationship between the legal system found in a society and the political organization of that society.

Every society has some form of political system—those institutions that organize and direct the collective behavior of the population. In the preceding chapters, we discussed the diversity in family and kinships organization. Among other things, these systems serve to define the economic and social obligations and privileges of the members of the society relative to one another. The political organization of the society, on the other hand, is the overarching institution that directs the collective economic activities and relations to other societies. In the smallest and earliest societies, this distinction between individual and group behavior is virtually imperceptible. In these societies, political leadership and organization is informal and even ad hoc. Only when a specific need for leadership arises does some individual assume an overt leadership role. However, in larger and more complex societies, this distinction is readily apparent. In general, the larger the population, the more formalized the leadership and the more complex the political organization.

Likewise, as mentioned in Chapter 2, all societies define certain behavioral patterns that are approved or acceptable and patterns that are disapproved or unacceptable. There are always some individuals who will not conform. Therefore, all societies develop mechanisms of social control by which the behaviors of individuals are constrained and directed into acceptable channels. By means of social control, a society encourages normatively proper behavior and discourages unacceptable actions; the objective is to maintain harmony and cooperation. The most serious deviations from acceptable behavior, which threaten the cohesiveness of the group, fall under that aspect of social control known as law, also discussed in this chapter. In the least organized societies, law and political organizations exist independently. As political organization becomes increasingly formalized and structured, governmental institutions take over legal institutions, until legal institutions become part of the formal political structure.

Forms of Political Organization

When we speak of the political organization of a particular society, we frequently are left with the impression that political boundaries and cultural boundaries are the same. But the boundaries of a *polity*, or a politically organized group, may or may not correspond with the boundaries of a particular way of life. For example, the Comanche of the Great Plains, who we will discuss later, shared a common language, customs, and ethnic identity, yet politically, they were never organized above the local group. Thus, the term *Comanche* refers to a people with a common language and culture who never united to carry out common political objectives.

At the other extreme, we find highly centralized polities that incorporate several culturally and socially distinct peoples. The United States is unusual in this regard only in the degree of cultural heterogeneity in the population. France, though predominantly "French," also includes Bretons and Basques as well as numerous recent immigrants from Africa, Asia, and elsewhere. India has several hundred different ethnic groups. Russia, China, Indonesia, and the Philippines also integrate highly diversified populations into a single polity. In fact, every large and most small country in the world today politically encompasses several ethnic groups.

In this discussion of political organization, we are taking an evolutionary perspective. By this, we mean that the known political systems of the world are going to be grouped based on the degree of increasing organizational complexity. On this basis, political systems may be divided into four basic forms: bands (simple and composite), tribes, chiefdoms, and states. However, it is important to note that political systems actually exist along a continuum of increasing complexity. As a result, the political systems of many societies do not clearly fall into one category or another.

Bands

As the least complex form, **bands** were the earliest human political structure. As more complex political systems developed, band-level societies were unable to compete for resources. Thus, bands survived until the modern period only in regions of the world with limited natural resources. Most known band-level societies were found in the deserts and grasslands of Australia, Africa, and the Americas. A few others live or lived in the tropical forests of Africa, Asia, and South America and in the boreal forest and tundra regions of North America and Asia.

Bands consist of a number of families living together and cooperating in economic activities throughout the year. Band-level organization most frequently was found among peoples with foraging economies, which usually dictated low population densities and seasonal mobility. As a result, only a relatively small number of people could stay together throughout the year. Bands ranged in size from only a dozen to several hundred individuals. The adaptive significance of the band's size and seasonal mobility is described in Chapter 7. In this chapter, we are concerned with leadership statuses and the political organization of bands.

The smallest bands, called **simple bands**, were actually extended families. Leadership was informal, with the oldest or one of the older male or female members of the family serving as the de facto leader. Decision making was usually reached through consensus and involved both adult males and adult females. Because all members of the band were related either through descent or by marriage, they were exogamous units, and members of the band had to seek spouses from other bands. Thus, although an autonomous economic and political unit, every simple band was, by social necessity, allied through intermarriage with other bands, usually territorially adjacent ones. Simple bands usually had names, although the names may have been informal and may have simply referred to some prominent geographic feature associated with the band's usual territory.

Resource availability influenced the formation of such small groups. Simple bands often were associated with the hunting of nonmigratory game animals, such as deer, guanaco, moose, or small mammals, which occupy a limited territory on a year-round basis and are found either singly or in small herds. The foraging activities of simple bands usually did not generate any significant surpluses of food, which necessitated the year-round hunting of game animals. Effective hunting required only a few male hunters who had intimate knowledge of the seasonal shifts in range of these animals within their territory while effective gathering of wild plants required only a few females who had intimate knowledge of local plant resources. The natural resources of such areas could be exploited most effectively by a small and highly mobile population.

Composite bands consisted of a larger aggregation of families, sometimes numbering in the hundreds. In contrast to simple bands, composite bands encompassed unrelated extended families. Although leadership in composite bands was still informal, it had to be more defined since the leader was not related to all of the members of the group. Such leaders frequently have been called **big men**. Big men did not hold formal offices, and leadership was based on influence rather than authority over band members. **Influence** is merely the ability to convince people that they should act as you suggest. **Authority** is the recognized right of an individual to command another person to act in a particular way. Thus, a big-man leader could not, by virtue of his position, make demands or impose rules

---

band Small foraging group with flexible composition that migrates seasonally.

simple bands Autonomous or independent political units, often consisting of little more than an extended family, with informal leadership vested in one of the older family members.

composite bands Autonomous (independent) political units consisting of several extended families that live together for most or all of the year.

big men Political leaders who do not occupy formal offices and whose leadership is based on influence, not authority.

influence Ability to convince people they should act as you suggest.

authority Recognized right of an individual to command another to act in a particular way; legitimate power.

CONCEPT REVIEW: Political Organization

Form	Characteristics	Associated Equalities and Inequalities
Bands		
(a) Simple	Local, economically self-sufficient residence group Single extended family, usually numbering 25 to 50 people Family head with leadership based on influence	Egalitarian
(b) Composite	Local, economically self-sufficient residence group Several extended families, usually numbering from 50 to several hundred individuals Big-man leadership based on influence	Egalitarian
Tribes	Several economically self-sufficient residence groups Usually numbering between 1,000 and 20,000 people A few formal leadership positions with limited authority, with access based on inheritance and/or achievements Group cohesion maintained by sodalities	Primarily egalitarian with some societies showing the traits of ranking
Chiefdoms	Several economically interdependent residence groups Usually numbering from a few thousand up to about 30,000 Centralized leadership, with a hereditary chief, with full formal authority	Ranked societies
States	Usually numbering from the tens of thousands up to several million Centralized leadership, with formal full authority, supported by a bureaucracy	Stratified societies

on the members of the band, and his decisions were not binding on others. Because big-man status did not involve a formal office, no prescribed process existed for attaining leadership status. A man might emerge as the leader through a variety of personal accomplishments or qualities such as his proven ability in hunting or warfare, the supernatural powers he possessed, or merely his charisma. There was no set tenure in the position, which was filled by a man until he was informally replaced by some other leader.

Like simple bands, many composite bands were nomadic groups that moved within a relatively well-defined range. Because of their greater size, composite bands were not as cohesive as simple bands and were politically more volatile. Disputes between families could result in some members joining another band or even the band splitting into two or more bands.

Composite bands formed because economic pressures facilitated or necessitated the cooperation of a larger number of individuals than found in a single extended family. As in the case of simple bands, the behavior of the principal game animals was an important influence. Composite bands were associated with the seasonal hunting of migratory animals that form large herds, such as bison and caribou. Migratory herd animals usually appeared only seasonally in the range of a particular composite band as the herd moved between its summer and winter ranges. Because bison and caribou migrated in herds that sometimes numbered in the tens of thousands, there was no difficulty in locating the herds on the open grasslands and tundra. Unlike the hunters of nonmigratory animals, who secured game steadily throughout the year, hunters of migratory animals frequently took most of their game only twice a year, as the herds passed through their territories during seasonal migrations.

Successful hunting of large herds of animals requires maneuvering the herd into situations where large numbers could be slaughtered. Herds might be run over a cliff, into a holding pen, or into a lake where hunters in boats could kill them. Regardless of the method used, all these strategies required a larger group of hunters than was available in a simple band. Thus, composite bands were formed to bring together a sufficiently large number of hunters to control the movements of large herds of animals.

The Comanche of the southern Great Plains of the United States illustrate the nature of composite bands. These horse-raising, bison-hunting people were politically autonomous until the Red River War of 1875. During the early and middle years of the nineteenth century, the Comanche numbered about 6,000 to

7,000, divided between 5 and 13 residence groups, each of which was a composite band. Comanche bands had only vaguely defined territories, and two or more composite bands frequently occupied the same general area or had overlapping ranges. Membership in Comanche bands was fluid: both individuals and families could and did shift from one band to another, or a number of families might join together to establish a new band. Some anthropologists have theorized that only five major bands existed, with a varying number of secondary bands appearing and disappearing from time to time.

A band consisted of a number of families, each headed by an older male member who was "peace chief" or "headman." One of these family heads also served as the peace chief for the entire band. There was no formalized method of selecting either the family heads or the head of the band. As the Comanche say, "No one made him such; he just got that way." A Comanche peace chief usually was a man known for his kindness, wisdom, and ability to lead by influencing other men. Although a war record was important, peace chiefs were not chosen from among the most aggressive or ambitious men. Such men usually remained war chiefs—great warriors who periodically recruited men to raid neighbors—but frequently had little influence outside war and raiding.

A band peace chief was responsible for the well-being of the band. Through a consensus of the family heads, he directed the seasonal movement of the band and the bison hunts. He did have men who voluntarily assisted him. In the morning, the peace chief usually sent out two men to scout the area around the camp for the presence of enemy raiding parties. He also sent a crier through the camp periodically to announce plans for the movement of the camp, an upcoming hunt, or some other cooperative activities. During the bison hunts, the peace chief called on a number of men from the camp to police the hunt and restrain overly eager hunters from scattering the herd and thus spoiling the hunt for others.

In an extraordinarily individualistic and egalitarian society, Comanche band leaders had to strive for and maintain consensus. If a dispute arose and a consensus could not be reached, individuals and families were free either to shift residence to another band or even to form a new band under another leader.

Comanche composite bands were economically and politically autonomous residence units. Only seldom did two or more bands come together for any unified action, and never did leaders of the bands come together to discuss issues. At the same time, there was a strong consciousness of common identity—of being Comanche. Comanche's freely traveled between bands to visit, marry, and even shift residence. There was an informally reached general consensus on whether relations with a particular neighboring group were friendly or hostile. Thus, on the band level of political organization, populations are fragmented into numerous independent political resident units that operate only at the local-group level. These various residence groups share a common cultural identity and usually attempt to maintain harmonious relations with one another, but they lack any political structure capable of organizing all the various residence groups into a single unit for collective actions.

Tribes

Tribes differ from bands in that they have formally organized institutions that unite the geographically scattered residence groups, give the society greater cohesiveness, and make possible a more united response to external threats. These institutions are called **sodalities**. Sodalities take various forms: they may be based on large kin groups, such as clans and lineages; on nonkinship units, such as age sets; or on voluntary associations, such as male and female societies. Regardless of their exact nature, sodalities unify geographically dispersed communities into political units. Although tribal-level societies usually are egalitarian, with leadership dependent in part on the persuasive abilities of individuals, there are formalized political offices with institutionalized authority. Although tribes vary greatly in structure, here we examine only one tribal-level society.

The Cheyenne of the Great Plains numbered between 3,000 and 3,500 during the early 1800s. The Cheyenne, like the neighboring Comanche, were horse-mounted bison hunters. They were divided into 10 main nomadic local groups or villages, which averaged between 300 and 350 persons. Village membership was not based on kinship, although the members of a particular village usually were related either by blood or by marriage. Village membership was relatively stable, and marriages between villagers were common. Although

---

tribe Autonomous political unit encompassing a number of distinct, geographically dispersed communities held together by sodalities.

sodalities Formal institutions that cut across communities and serve to unite geographically scattered groups; may be based on kin groups (clans or lineages) or on non-kin-based groups (age grades or warrior societies).

a particular village usually frequented a certain range, there was no sense of village territoriality. Periodically and seasonally, family camps and subvillage camps broke off from the main village.

The only time the entire tribe came together was in early summer, when all the widely scattered villages gathered into a single camp at a predetermined location. This crescent-shaped encampment stretched for several miles from end to end, with the open portion facing east. Within the tribal encampment, every village had a designated location; while camped together, they performed the great tribal ceremonies (e.g., the Arrow Renewal, the Sun Dance, and the Animal Dance). At least one and possibly two of these rituals were performed, depending on the particular ritual needs of the tribe at that time. After the performance of the ritual, the tribe as a unit staged the great summer bison hunt. After the hunt, the tribe again scattered into smaller village camps.

Politically, the tribe was controlled by the Council of Forty-Four and the warrior societies. The Council of Forty-Four, which had both political and religious duties, was headed by the Sweet Medicine chief, who was the keeper of the most sacred of the Cheyenne religious bundles. Second to him in importance were four other sacred chiefs, each representing specific supernatural beings. Under these five sacred chiefs were 39 ordinary chiefs.

Chiefs served in their positions for 10 years and could not be removed for any reason. Serving as a chief placed a burden on the individuals. Chiefs usually were selected from among the older men, all of whom had war records. When an individual was chosen as a chief, he was to act like a chief, not an aggressive warrior. A chief was to be generous, kindly, even tempered, and aloof from everyday disputes. In short, he was expected to display ideal human behavior at all times. He was to take care of the poor, settle disputes between individuals, and be responsible for the ritual performances that protected the tribe.

The major sodalities were the warrior societies, of which there were five. These were formal voluntary associations of men, each with its own style of dress, dances, songs, and set of four leaders. As young warriors, men were recruited by the different societies until all had joined one or another. The phrase *warrior societies* is slightly misleading. The heads of the various societies were what some call the *tribal war chiefs*. Although this group planned and led attacks on their enemies, the different societies did not fight or operate as military units in battles. In battles, men fought as individuals, and members of several societies may have been present in a particular raiding party.

Subordinate to the council of chiefs, the warrior societies cooperated as a group only in policing the camps. During the summer tribal encampment, the Council of Forty-Four appointed one of the societies as camp police. Later, when the village scattered into separate camps, the members of the council who lived in the village appointed one of the warrior societies to police the camp. After being appointed, the warrior society usually carried out its function with little direction from the chiefs. Its members scouted the area around the camp to check for the presence of any enemy raiding parties and intervened in any serious disputes between village members.

There are two points to be emphasized about the political organization of tribal societies in contrast to those of simple and composite bands. First, there were now some formalized political and religious offices that bequeathed some limited authority and prerogatives. However on the whole, tribal societies were still basically egalitarian (see Chapter 13). Few positions were hereditary, and most leaders were selected on the basis of personal qualities and individual merit.

Second, like bands, little economic specialization existed; except for cooperation in communal hunts, families produced their own food and manufactured their own clothes and other material goods. From an economic perspective, each of the scattered residential groups or villages was capable of sustaining itself without support from other; therefore, it was not economic necessity, convenience, or efficiency that led to this higher level of tribal political organization. Although sodalities unite tribes at a higher level of cohesiveness than bands, the mere existence of sodalities is not sufficient to generate or maintain the cohesiveness of a tribe. It is likely that external threats, either real or perceived, necessitated the cooperation in warfare of a large group of people and were the major factor that united geographically dispersed groups. Thus, warfare—the existence and activities of hostile human neighbors—was an important force in creating the political integration of separate communities. The conflict over hunting territories between Cheyenne and Comanche during the early nineteenth century illustrates the advantage of tribal over band organization in competition over resources. The Cheyenne and Comanche were equally well armed and adept at warfare. However, although numerically smaller, the Cheyenne were able to militarily force the Comanche southward out of the central portion of the Great Plains. The difference was that the tribally organized Cheyenne were able to mobilize greater manpower for conflicts than the politically fragmented bands of the Comanche.

Chiefdoms

Like tribes, **chiefdoms** also consisted of multiple residential groups or villages. However, unlike tribes, chiefdoms had a highly formalized and centralized political system. A chiefdom was governed by a single chief, who usually served as both political and religious head of the polity. The chief had authority over members of the chiefdom, and the position often was hereditary within a single kin group, which based its rights chiefly on supernatural powers. Thus, a chiefdom was not an egalitarian society but a ranked or stratified society (see Chapter 13) with access to resources based on inherited status. With authority and power conferred by supernatural beings, governing was not by consensus but by decree.

Most chiefdoms were associated with horticultural societies in which craft or regional specialization in production had emerged. There was a need for regularized exchanges of goods either between geographically dispersed communities or, at times, within a single community. This economic exchange was managed through redistribution, with the chief occupying the central position in the flow of goods (see Chapter 8).

In earlier historic periods, chiefdoms probably were found throughout much of the Old World. During more recent periods, such political systems were primarily concentrated in Oceania (Polynesia, Micronesia, and Melanesia) and in the Americas (the circum-Caribbean and coastal portions of South America and the northwestern coast of North America).

The Polynesian-speaking people of Tahiti, an island in the southeastern Pacific, illustrate many characteristics typical of a chiefdom. This relatively large, mountainous, volcanic island had a population of about 100,000 at the time of European discovery. Tahiti was divided among about 20 rival chiefs. Although most of these chiefdoms were about the size of the average tribe and significantly smaller than the largest tribes, their political organization differed significantly.

The economy of Tahiti was based largely on farming, with taro, breadfruit, coconuts, and yams being the main crops. Pigs and chickens were also raised, and fish and other seafood supplemented the food supply. Food production was sufficient not only to meet the needs of the population but also to produce surpluses for export to other islands. Although sufficient food was produced in all regions, there were significant regional differences in the types of food produced because Tahiti varied ecologically.

Tahitian society had at least three and possibly four distinct classes, depending on how finely one wants to divide the units. *Arii*, or chiefs, and their close relatives

A Samoan chief is pictured here in traditional dress.

formed the ruling elite. The arii were divided into two groups: the *arii rahi*, or sacred chiefs, and the *arii rii*, or small chiefs. Under these chiefs were the *raatira*, or subchiefs, and the *manahune*, or commoners. The sacred chiefs were viewed as descended from the gods, whereas the commoners were merely created by the gods for their use. The subchiefs were the offspring of intermarriage between the sacred chiefs and commoners, whereas the small chiefs were the products of still later intermarriages between sacred chiefs and subchiefs. Once these four classes were established, class endogamy became the rule.

The sacred chiefs, viewed as gods on Earth, evoked both reverence and fear. Whatever the highest-ranking sacred chiefs touched became *tabu*, or sacred, and could not be used for fear of supernatural punishment. Such a chief had to be carried on the back of a servant, lest the

> **chiefdoms** Centralized political systems with authority vested in formal, usually hereditary, offices or titles.

ground touched by his feet became tabu. He could not enter the house of another individual for the same reason. The lifestyle of the chief's family differed from that of others: they had larger and more elaborate houses, the largest canoes, insignia of their rank, and particular clothing.

Unlike in band and tribal societies, resources in chiefdoms were individually owned. Land was owned mainly by the chiefs and subchiefs, but ultimate authority rested with the sacred chiefs within the polity. Although sacred chiefs could not withhold the title to lands from the families of subchiefs, they could banish an individual subchief. Crafts were specialized, and craftspeople were attached to particular sacred chiefs and produced goods for them. Thus, the sacred chiefs directly controlled craft production and communal fishing. The chiefs could make demands on the property of the subchiefs and commoners. If someone refused, the chief could have the recalcitrant banished or make him or her a sacrificial victim. Theoretically, the sacred chief was the head judicial figure in the polity, but some believe that the chief seldom intervened in disputes between individuals; the chief usually used these powers only against people who challenged his authority.

The sacred chief in each polity was the focal point for redistributive exchanges (discussed in Chapter 8). The chief periodically demanded surplus production from all his subjects for a public redistribution. Such events were associated with a number of occasions: a rite of passage for a member of the chief's family, the organizing of a military attack, religious ceremonies, or the start of the breadfruit harvest. During such ceremonies, the chief distributed the goods collected to all his subjects.

States

Although they had a centralized political system, chiefdoms were still kinship-based structures. Even in Tahiti, the sacred chiefs authority rested in large part on his control over families of subchiefs, each of whom had his own inalienable rights to lands—and thus families—of commoners. As a result, the number of people who could be effectively integrated into a chiefdom was limited. In Polynesia, most chiefdoms ranged from only a few thousand to 30,000 persons. Polities with larger populations require a political structure based on institutions other than kinship.

> **state** Centralized, multilevel political unit characterized by the presence of a bureaucracy that acts on behalf of the ruling elite.

States, like chiefdoms, have a centralized political structure. States are distinguished from chiefdoms by the presence of a bureaucracy. A chiefdom is basically a two-level system: (1) the chiefs (which in Tahiti included the subchiefs), who have varying levels of authority and power, and (2) the commoners, or the great mass of the populace. A state has three levels: (1) the ruling elite, (2) a bureaucracy, and (3) the populace.

In states, as in chiefdoms, highest authority and power reside in the ruling elite, the formal political head or heads of the polity. States vary greatly in the types of political leaders present and in the basis for the leaders' authority and power. Leaders in the earliest states frequently were considered to be the descendants of gods, and thus themselves gods on Earth. The Inca of Peru and the pharaohs of Egypt were leaders who ruled as gods. Other political leaders, although not claiming to be gods, have legitimated their positions with claims of having been chosen by God. Early European kings legitimated their claims to leadership on such a basis; and as English coins still proclaim, the queen rules *Dei gratia*—by the "grace of God." Other states have evolved political leadership that uses strictly secular ideas to justify its authority. In countries where leaders are elected by a vote of the populace, rule is legitimized by the internalized acceptance of such ascendance to office. Even leaders of strictly secular kingdoms, dictatorships, and oligarchies can, if in power for a sufficient time, have their rule accepted by the populace as "legitimate." We have more to say about legitimization in Chapter 13.

Although they differ greatly in political leadership, states all share one characteristic: a bureaucracy that carries out the day-to-day governing of the polity. In simple terms, a *bureaucrat* is a person to whom a political leader delegates certain authority and powers. The bureaucrat thus acts on behalf of the political leader. Lacking any inherent authority or powers personally, bureaucrats depend on the continued support of political leaders. Using bureaucrats as intermediaries, political leaders could expand the size of their polities both geographically and demographically, while strengthening their political control over the population. Bureaucrats could engineer such expansion without threat of revolution and political fragmentation because they lacked any personal claims to independent political legitimacy.

In addition to differences in their political structure, state-level polities differ from bands, tribes, and chiefdoms in two other important ways. First, they can and usually do have multiethnic populations, including members of a number of ethnic groups who not only have distinct cultural traditions but frequently speak different languages as well. One of these ethnic groups is usually the politically dominant group. Second, with few exceptions, states have market economies (see Chapter 8) and depend in varying degrees on external trade with neighboring groups.

Inca Empire

The Inca Empire of ancient Peru was typical of a state-level organization. From the capital of Cuzco, the ruler, or *Sapa Inca*, controlled a multiethnic empire of between 6 and 12 million subjects who spoke dozens of different languages and extended over 2,500 miles from modern-day Ecuador to central Chile. Dissected by some of the highest mountain ranges and most inhospitable deserts in the world, the Inca Empire existed without a writing system for communication, a monetary system for exchange, or wheeled vehicles for transporting goods. In spite of this limited technology and hostile terrain, the central government was able to organize human labor for massive public works projects, ranging from buildings and terraced fields to a 9,500-mile highway network that stretched the length and breadth of the country.

The Sapa Inca was also able to mobilize and supply armies numbering in the tens of thousands for extended periods of time. The Inca Empire was a state created through the military conquest and incorporation of smaller neighboring states. However, it was the administrative abilities of its leaders—more than their military might—that gave the empire its political cohesiveness.

The Sapa Inca was believed to be the direct descendant of the Sun God. Thus, the Sapa Inca was a divine being, with absolute authority and control over all the people and resources of the empire. Succession was not clearly defined. Any son of the Sapa Inca had a legitimate claim to his father's position. To avoid conflict, the Sapa Inca usually chose one of his sons as his successor before his death, but the death of the Sapa Inca usually resulted in conflicts between potential heirs.

The empire was administratively divided into four geographic regions, each with its own head. The regions were divided into provinces with governors and regional capitals. The provinces were, in turn, organized on the basis of what some have called a "decimal administration" of hierarchically nested administrative units based on population size. The largest, with a population of 10,000 households, was called a *huno*, which was divided into units of 5,000, 1,000, 500, 100, 50, and, finally, 10 households. Each unit had an official head responsible to the person above him. Periodically, a census was conducted and adjustments made. This was the ideal administrative model; the actual structure varied somewhat from province to province due to local demographic and ethnic factors.

Regional heads were members of the Incan royal family. In some provinces, relatives of the Sapa Inca also filled the position of governor. However, in most cases provincial governors and other provincial officials were drawn from local elite families, and these families even held hereditary rights to these offices. Beneath these officials and their families was the great mass of people, the commoners.

Land was divided into plots used by individual families and households, and land used for the support of public functions. Every household in the empire was given sufficient land to meet its economic needs. Households and local communities were basically self-sufficient. Food and other goods produced on their land and within the family belonged to the family.

The government of the empire was supported by a labor tax, not a tax on production. Every household was required to supply labor for state purposes. Some assignments were for a number of days per year, others were yearlong, and still others lifelong. The major function of provincial officials was to assign tasks, organize work parties, and oversee the work.

The majority of commoners paid their labor tax by working part of the year farming public fields, tending herds of state-owned animals, weaving cloth, making pottery, repairing public buildings, working on public roads, or performing some other local task. In every province, food, clothes, and other utilitarian goods produced by state tax labor were stored in public buildings. State-owned food, clothes, and other goods were used to support the army, visiting government officials, and commoners who had been assigned long-term labor tasks that made it impossible for them to be self-supporting. In return for their services, all provincial officials in charge of 100 households or more were allowed to use tax laborers to farm their fields, tend their herds, build their houses, and make their clothes and other goods.

In the 1530s, the Spanish conquered the Inca Empire and murdered the last Sapa Inca. However, the provincial governmental structure and the "decimal administrative" system were incorporated into the government of colonial Peru.

The emergence of states increased the complexity of political units. Bureaucracies not only allowed for specialization in governmental functions but also made possible the effective integration of large land areas and populations into political units. For example, chiefdoms seldom exceeded 30,000 persons, whereas modern states have populations in the millions.

The Inca were able to construct cities such as Machu Picchu despite mountainous terrain.

Social Control and Law

All societies have clearly defined rules that govern the relationships between members. Not all individuals in any society will conform to these rules. There will always be some who behave in a socially unacceptable manner. Thus, among all peoples, there are formal and informal ways to correct the behavior of individuals. In general, we call these mechanisms *social control*. One form of social control is the law.

Social Control

Social control refers to the diverse ways in which the behaviors of the members of a society are constrained into socially approved channels. All cultures have certain behavioral norms that most people learn and begin to conform to during enculturation. But all societies have individuals who, to one degree or another, deviate from those norms. Violations of norms usually result in sanctions or punishments for the offender, which serve both to correct the behavior of particular people and to show others the penalties for such deviance. The severity of sanctions and the process by which sanctions are imposed differ greatly, depending on the seriousness culturally attached to the violated norm, the perceived severity of the violation, and the overall political and legal system of the people.

Children who get into mischief usually are corrected by their parents. In our U.S. society, parents may impose sanctions ranging from scolding to spanking to withdrawing privileges. Correcting children trains individuals in proper behavior at an early age.

The community also applies informal sanctions against children and adults who are not behaving properly. Gossip, or fear of gossip, serves as an important method of social control in most societies. Most people fear the contempt or ridicule of their peers, so they try to conform to acceptable behavioral norms. People attempt to hide behavior that would be the subject of gossip, scandal, and ridicule. Individuals whose known behavior consistently violates social norms may even find themselves ostracized by friends and relatives (the severest of informal punishments). Informal economic penalties also may be imposed. A family may withdraw economic support in attempts to modify the errant behavior of a member.

A wide variety of supernatural sanctions may assist in controlling individual behavior; in some cases, these

> **social control** Mechanisms by which behavior is constrained and directed into acceptable channels, thus maintaining conformity.

supernatural sanctions are automatically imposed on particular types of behavior. Whether the commission of these acts becomes public knowledge or not, and thus regardless of whether other punishments are inflicted on the individual, the commission still endangers one's immortal soul. Supernatural sanctions can be more specifically directed. In many societies, including some Christian ones, an individual may place a curse on another person by calling on a supernatural being. Fear of sorcery or witchcraft (see Chapter 14) frequently serves as another important form of social control. Most victims are people who offended a witch or sorcerer in some way, often through a breach of social norms.

Law

Law is the highest level of social control, and legal punishments usually are reserved for the most serious breaches of norms. The question of how law can be distinguished from other forms of social control is not easy to answer. In societies that have court systems, the distinction is formalized, but in societies with no such formalized legal systems, the distinction is not so clear-cut. E. Adamson Hoebel (1954, 28) defined law in the following way: "A social norm is legal if its neglect or infraction is regularly met, in threat or in fact, by the application of physical force by an individual or group possessing the socially recognized privilege of so acting." Law so defined was and is present in virtually every society.

In a legal action, some individual or group must have publicly recognized authority to settle a case or punish a violation. In societies with courts, the authority is obvious; however, in societies that lack courts, the authority becomes less clear. What emerges frequently is an ad hoc authority; that is, because of the peculiarities of the case, a particular individual or group becomes recognized by the community as the authority responsible for its resolution. In some cases, the victim may be the recognized authority. In the victim's absence (as in the case of murder), the victim's family, clan, or kin group may be placed in the role of authority. Such ad hoc authority is discussed later in some of the examples.

Implicit in all legal actions is the intention of universal application, which means that in identical cases, the sanction imposed is the same. Although one might argue that no two legal cases have been or will ever be identical, the notion of universal application requires that the law be consistent and thus predictable; the arbitrary imposition of sanctions is not law.

Hoebel limited legal sanctions to physical sanctions; however, other scholars have argued that this definition is too narrow. A legal sanction does not have to be some form of corporal punishment, nor does it have to involve the loss of property. Based on his work with the Kapauku of New Guinea, Leopold Pospíšil contended that the impact of psychological sanctions can be more severe than that of actual physical punishment. For this reason, he stated, "We can define a legal sanction as either the negative behavior of withdrawing some rewards or favors that otherwise (if the law had not been violated) would have been granted, or the positive behavior of inflicting some painful experience, be it physical or psychological" (Pospíšil 1958, 268).

Legal Systems

On the basis of procedural characteristics, two main levels of complexity and formality can be defined: self-help legal systems and court legal systems.

Self-Help Systems

Self-help legal systems, also called *ad hoc systems*, are informal and exist in the absence of any centralized or formalized legal institutions capable of settling disputes. Such systems are associated with band-level societies and most tribal-level societies. In such systems, there is only civil law. All legal actions concern only the principal parties and/or their families. The reason for terming the legal procedure in these societies *self-help* will become clear.

Self-help legal systems may be divided into two main forms: familial and mediator. In *familial* systems, all actions and decisions are initiated and executed by the families or larger kin groups involved. *Mediator* systems add the formal presence of a neutral third party—the mediator—who attempts to negotiate and resolve the dispute peacefully.

In familial systems, legal actions are handled by the families involved. A legal offense only indirectly concerns the community as a whole. When an individual or a family determines that its rights have been violated, the imposition of the proper sanction falls to the plaintiffs; in other words, the offended party assumes the role

---

law Kind of social control characterized by the presence of authority, intention of universal application, obligation, and sanction.

self-help legal systems Informal legal systems in societies without centralized political systems, in which authorities who settle disputes are defined by the circumstances of the case.

GLOBAL CHALLENGES AND OPPORTUNITIES

Multinational Corporations Versus the Nation-State

If the annual revenue of corporations is equated to the gross domestic product of countries, the United States would rank 1st, but Walmart would rank as the 23d largest economy in the world.

Over the past decade or so, scholars have increasingly noted how the global economy and the development of multinational corporations are eroding the authority and sovereignty of the governments of nation-states of the world. In fact, many have come to question the continued viability of the present political systems. Here we are not going address all of the issues but focus on the growing economic power of multinational corporations versus existing national governments.

In 2010, the 1,000 largest corporations had revenues total $32 trillion, an amount equal to almost half of the gross world product of $70 trillion. In addition, they directly employed 67 million people. However, some of these corporations are far larger than others. If one compares annual corporate sales revenues of particular corporations to the gross domestic product (GDP) of individual countries, one would find that of the world largest "economies," 58 are countries and 42 are corporations. In 2010, the global sales of Walmart would rank it as the 23th largest economy in the world—slightly behind Sweden. Royal Dutch Shell, the world's largest oil company, would rank 27th. Remember, we are speaking of total sales, not profits.

In the last few years we have become increasingly aware of the fact that the United States, as well as all of the developed countries in the world, is in debt. Who directly or indirectly controls most of this debt? In 2010, the 25 largest multinational banks controlled over $40 trillion in assets, in the form of loans to countries, corporations, and individuals throughout the world. These banks control the flow and allocation of capital necessary to maintain the global economy. Never before in human history have nongovernmental institutions had such economic power.

It is important to understand the fundamental differences between corporations and national governments. The most basic function of a government is to promote and protect the collective well-being and economic interest of its citizens. The interest of a corporation, in contrast, is far more limited. Corporations exist only to produce profits for their owner, usually an ever-changing, anonymous group of stockholders or investors. To encourage corporate leadership to produce ever-greater profits, performance bonuses are frequently given to corporate executives. Thus, both owners as well as management have direct, vested interest in corporate profits.

Friction has always existed between governments and corporations. Ideally, governments attempt to regulate corporate activities so as to increase the economic and social benefits to their citizens. Corporations, on the other hand, attempt to minimize governmental constraints or regulations on their activities so as to maximize profits. As long as corporations were basically domestic corporations, companies whose operations were confined to a single country, there was no question as to the ultimate power of the government to regulate their behavior. The United States and most other countries have a large body of corporate regulatory laws: minimum wage laws, worker safety laws, environmental laws, and product safety laws, to name only some. In addition, governments usually have a large body of tax laws that serve to encourage or discourage certain economic behaviors, both individual and corporate, while raising revenue to support the necessary infrastructure to serve and protect both individual and corporate economic and social interests.

The major factor that has allowed for the change in the relative power of nation-states and corporations is "free trade," which has led to the development of multinational corporations. The Internet has played a role, too, by creating the instantaneous flow of information, but here we will explore free trade in more detail.

Free trade began to emerge in 1948, when the General Agreement on Tariffs and Trade (GATT) talks were established. These talks are concerned with negotiating reductions in tariffs, with the eventual objective of achieving "free trade." A central element in global economy, free trade means that goods, commodities, and services may be moved and marketed across international borders without regulations or restraints.

In 1995, the World Trade Organization (WTO) became the successor to GATT. Headquartered in Geneva, Switzerland, the WTO monitors and enforces existing binding agreements between the 142 member countries, and it is working to develop still other agreements. WTO has the same legal status as the United Nations and serves as a global commerce agency. The stated objective of the

WTO is to ultimately create a fully integrated global economic system in which all goods, commodities, and services flow without any interference or control by local national governments.

To this end, once the government of a country adopts one of these agreements, the WTO has the power to enforce the agreement. Any existing law in any of the member countries may potentially be considered an obstacle to free trade, and thus illegal. The authority to determine whether the law of a particular country is "protectionist" rests solely with panels of appointed bureaucrats of the WTO. If the WTO finds against a country, that country has one of only three options: (1) change the law, (2) pay compensation, or (3) have trade sanctions imposed. There is no appeal of a WTO decision.

In essence, member countries have surrendered an important part of their political sovereignty to the WTO. For example, the European Union (EU), for public health concerns, banned the sale of beef containing artificial hormones. The United States challenged this ban, and the WTO ruled against the EU, saying that a country cannot ban the import of a food as a precautionary health measure. The EU has to present scientific proof that artificial hormones are unsafe. What this means is that while EU farmers cannot raise or sell beef containing artificial hormones, they have to compete with such beef imported from the United States. Countries have the right to regulate their production of goods, commodities, and services within their borders but cannot impose these regulatory standards on goods imported from other countries, since to do so would be a restraint on trade.

Free trade has allowed for the development of multinational corporations that produce goods or provide services, and market them globally free from tariffs and quotas. The regulatory laws of a country apply only to those goods, commodities, and services produced within its own borders. If other countries have less demanding regulations, and thus lower costs, then a corporation can outsource portions of its operations there without incurring any penalty. Competing domestic corporations are at a decided economic disadvantage. Another consequence of the global economy is the ability of multinational corporations to shift profits from high-tax countries to countries with lower tax rates, thus increasing their profits.

Apple Inc. is a good example of how a multinational corporation can shift production of goods to countries with less stringent environmental and labor laws to lower production costs, while shifting profits to low-tax countries to shield those profits. In this regard, Apple does not differ from other multinational corporations. Apple is one of the largest information technology companies in the world, producing and marketing Mac computers, iPods, iPhones, and iPads, among other things. Headquartered in Cupertino, California, the firm had a total revenue in 2012 of $156 billion and a profit of $68 billion. Although Apple is a U.S. company, most of the products it makes and most of its sales are outside the United States. Apple products are designed, tested, and marketed in California. However, most of the materials and components come from foreign countries, and the assembly of Apple products is done elsewhere, usually in Asia. In fact, over 150 other companies are involved in the production of Apple products. These products are sold either via the Internet or at one of the 406 Apple Stores in 39 countries (as of May 2013).

Originally, Apple produced products in California but quickly began outsourcing production to companies overseas, particularly China. Why? There were two main reasons: labor laws and environmental regulations. Most of the work on the production of Apple products does not require a particularly skilled labor force, and labor costs in the United States are high, particularly in comparison to China and other Asian countries. The United States also has labor safety laws and even child labor laws. In addition, many components in Apple products require the use of some toxic substances that are potentially hazardous. Not only is it far cheaper to contract the actual production out to suppliers located in countries where these laws are less stringent, but potential regulatory problems are the suppliers', not Apple's.

Actual cost of production is only one cost; corporate taxes are still another. With import and export taxes no longer an issue, corporate taxes become the concern. In regard to avoiding corporate taxes, Apple has also proven innovative. Apple sells its products directly to consumers through its worldwide network of Apple Stores. Profits from sales within the United States are subject to corporate taxes. However, to protect profits from Apple Stores' sales in Europe, Africa, and Asia from U.S. corporate taxes, Apple created a subsidiary in Ireland and another "Irish" subsidiary in the West Indies. This practice is known as the "Double Irish."

U.S. tax law allows for transfer pricing, meaning that a U.S. company can avoid paying taxes on profits earned overseas by selling or leasing intellectual property rights to a wholly owned "foreign" subsidiary. This "foreign" subsidiary then leases rights to a

continues on next page

second "foreign" subsidiary, which is also wholly owned by the U.S. corporation. Ireland is ideal because its corporate laws allow for the legal shifting of profits between Irish subsidiaries. The first "Irish" subsidiary is actually registered in a country without any corporate taxes, usually in the West Indies—in this case, Baldwin Holding Unlimited in the British Virgin Islands. The other "Irish" subsidiaries, Apple Operations International and Apple Sales International, are located in Ireland, whose corporate tax rates are extremely low—12.5 percent compared to 35 percent in the United States. The U.S. corporation then assigns partial ownership of rights to its "Irish" subsidiary in the West Indies. Apple profits from the sales of its products in Europe, Asia, and Africa go to the Apple international subsidiary in Ireland. The vast majority of these profits are then paid as "royalties" to the subsidiary in the West Indies, which in turn pays small royalties to the corporation in the United States, banking the rest of the profits. Apple's international office in Ireland has over 3,000 employees who actually manage the company's international operations and sales. However, Baldwin Holdings has no listed office phone number or address in the British Virgin Islands, and its only listed director is also Apple's chief financial officer, who lives in California. Actually, there is no need for Apple to have a physical presence in the Virgin Islands since these transfers are handled electronically. Through these and other subsidiaries throughout the world, Apple minimizes the corporate taxes it pays, not just to the U.S. and other foreign governments, but to local governments as well. In 2011, Apple earned $34.2 billion and paid a total $3.3 billion in corporate taxes, or 9.8 percent.

Apple is not alone; virtually all multinational companies play a similar tax game. Pfizer, with 172 subsidiaries, is the largest and most profitable drug company in the world. Although about 40 percent of its sales are in the United States, it has paid no corporate taxes in the United States for 5 years. Microsoft, Citigroup, Google, Facebook, and hundreds, if not thousands, of multinational U.S. and foreign corporations have done likewise. The problem is that these corporations cannot bring these profits back into the United States without paying taxes. As a result, over the years the amount of profits held in these tax-free overseas accounts has, as of 2012, accumulated to an estimated total of $1.7 trillion.

The CEOs and boards of directors of the world's largest corporations now have more economic power than the political leaders and governments of all but a minority of the world's countries. Multinational corporations operate in what has become a regulatory vacuum, resulting in the diminished ability of national governments to regulate their own domestic economies. The economic power and importance of a few of the multinational banks became evident in the economic crisis that started in 2007 when the United States had to pour hundreds of billions of dollars into banks and investment houses that were "too big to fail."

In effect, what these multinational corporations are collectively doing is imposing sanctions—punishments—on the citizens and governments of the developed countries. They are punishing the citizens of these countries for their high wages and safety and environmental concerns by outsourcing their jobs to cheaper, less developed countries with less stringent labor and environmental laws. They are punishing the governments of these countries by denying them the revenue—tax income—critical to maintaining the infrastructure of these countries.

It is not just that some of these multinational corporations have become economically powerful; it is that they are becoming increasingly powerful. They are absorbing smaller domestic companies, while at the same time multinational corporations are increasingly merging with other multinational corporations. The big are getting bigger. In the United States, this pattern is most readily evident in the airline industry. What happened to Northwest, Continental, TWA, and Pan Am, to mention only some of the once-prosperous airlines that no longer exist? Increasingly important decisions that both directly and indirectly dramatically affect the daily lives and well-being of billions of people in the world are being made by a decreasing number of corporate executives and boards, and not by their governmental bodies.

of authority. Such a system has some problems in implementation, but not as many as one might anticipate. This is not a system of "might makes right." Certainly cases arise in such societies in which the weak are victimized by the strong. In cases of legal redress, however, there is a community consensus in support of the victim and usually a recognized means by which even the weakest members of the community can gather support adequate to impose appropriate sanctions on the strongest.

The Comanche exemplify how a familial legal system operated and how victims weaker than their opponents could nonetheless obtain redress. One of the most frequent Comanche offenses was "wife stealing." Most older Comanche men were polygynous, and some of their wives were significantly younger than their husbands. Among young Comanche men, it was considered prestigious, though illegal, to steal the wife of another man. Under Comanche law, the injured husband could demand either his wife back or some property, usually horses, in compensation. The husband had the responsibility of imposing these sanctions. In such actions, the community played no direct role, but a husband could not ignore the loss of a wife. If he did ignore it, the community would ridicule him, and his prestige would decline. Thus, not only did the community support the husband in pressing his claim, but they informally pressured him to act.

In imposing these sanctions, the husband was allowed to use whatever physical force was needed, short of killing the offender. In cases in which the men involved were physically about equal, the two met to negotiate and discuss the husband's demands. Behind these negotiations was the potential threat that the husband might physically assault the defendant.

In cases where the husband presented little or no physical threat to the defendant, institutionalized means existed whereby the husband could gain physical backing. Although it lowered his prestige in the community, he could call on his relatives for support; with his male relatives present and prepared to support his demands physically, the husband could then negotiate with the defendant. The defendant always had to stand alone. Even if he had asked his kinsmen for support, they would not have responded for fear of community ridicule.

In cases where the husband was an orphan or lacked kinsmen, he could call on any other man he wanted to prosecute his case. He usually asked for the assistance of one of the powerful war leaders in the band. Such a request was so prestigious that a war leader could not refuse. At the same time, such a request was demeaning to the man asking for help and greatly lowered his prestige. As a result, it usually required a great deal of social pressure to force a man to ask for assistance. Once the request was made, the issue was between the defendant and the war leader alone. On approaching the defendant, the war leader would call out, "You have stolen my wife," and then proceed to exact whatever demands the husband had requested. For his action, the war leader received nothing in payment other than the admiration of the community; the husband received the settlement. Although this process was used most commonly in wife-stealing cases, it could be used for other issues as well. Thus, Comanche legal institutions gave any individual the means to marshal overwhelming physical force to protect his rights.

A more formalized type of legal procedure is found in the mediator system. In this system, disputes are still between individuals and families, and the offended party or the person's family has the position of authority. However, a third party is called on, usually by the offending individual or his or her family, to attempt to negotiate a mutually agreeable solution. The mediator has no authority to impose a settlement. The aggrieved party and/or family must agree to accept the compensation negotiated.

The Nuer, a pastoral society of Sudan, provide an example of how mediator systems operate. The Nuer live in small villages of related families. Although villages are tied together through lineages and clans, there is no effective leadership above the village level. The only formalized leaders who transcend the local units are *leopard-skin chiefs*, who wear a leopard-skin cloak to indicate their positions. These men have no secular authority to enforce their judgments but only limited ritual powers to bless and curse.

The most important function of leopard-skin chiefs is mediating feuds between local groups. The Nuer are an egalitarian, warrior-oriented people. Disputes between individuals frequently result in physical violence, and men occasionally are killed. The killing requires that the kinsmen exact retribution. Any close patrilineal kinsman of the murderer may be killed in retaliation, but at least initially the kinsmen of the victim attempt to kill the murderer himself. Immediately after committing a murder, the killer flees to the house of a leopard-skin chief. This dwelling is a sanctuary, and as long as the man stays in the chief's house, he is safe. The victim's kinsmen usually keep the house under surveillance to try to kill the murderer if he ventures out.

The leopard-skin chief keeps the murderer in his house until a settlement is arranged. The chief will wait until tempers have cooled, which usually requires several weeks, before he begins to negotiate the case. First, he goes to the family of the murderer to see if they are willing to pay cattle to the victim's family in compensation. Seldom do they refuse because one of them might be killed in retaliation. After the murderer's family has agreed to pay, the chief proceeds to the family of the victim, offering so many cattle in compensation. Initially, the victim's family invariably refuses, saying that they want blood, that cattle cannot compensate them for the death of their beloved kinsman. The leopard-skin chief persists, usually gaining the support of more distant relatives of the victim, who also pressure the family to settle. The leopard-skin chief may even threaten to place a curse on the family if they continue to refuse to settle for a payment rather than blood. The family finally agrees and accepts cattle, usually about 40, as compensation. Even though the matter is formally settled, the killer and his close patrilineal kinsmen will avoid the family of the victim for some years so as not to provoke spontaneous retaliation.

Up to this point, we have examined legal systems that operate without a formalized or centralized political structure capable of resolving disputes. In many of these societies, law, not subordination to a common set of formal political institutions, defines boundaries. To see what we mean, consider the Nuer. The Nuer distinguish among a *ter*, a feud within a local Nuer groups that is a legal action subject to arbitration; a *kur*, a fight between members of two distant Nuer groups that cannot be arbitrated; and a *pec*, a war with non-Nuer people. Nuer believe that disputes within a localized group should be resolved by legal means (i.e., peacefully), whereas disputes between individuals who are not members of the same local group should be resolved by extralegal means, including organized warfare. Legal processes serve to repair and maintain social relations between families; thus, law serves both to maintain the cohesiveness and to define the boundaries of the society.

The Jivaro, a horticultural and foraging people of eastern Ecuador, also illustrate how law defines social boundaries. By the 1950s, the Jivaro had been reduced to slightly more than 2,000 persons settled in more than 200 scattered family households. Such households usually consist of a husband, his wife or wives, their children, and possibly a son-in-law or other relatives. Households are grouped into "neighborhoods," which consist of a number of households living within a few miles of one another; the membership of a neighborhood is fluid. Poor hunting, a dispute with other households, or other factors might result in a family's moving away. Neither corporate kin groups nor formalized leadership positions exist. Except for household heads, only a few men are called *unta*, or "big," but their informal leadership role is limited and transitory.

Politically, the Jivaro are organized at a band level. Although they have only limited political institutions, the Jivaro have a strong sense of common cultural identity and territorial boundaries. Living in adjacent or nearby territories are four other "Jivaroan" groups, who speak mutually intelligible dialects, share the same basic customs, and at times trade with Jivaro households. Despite their minimal political integration, there is no question about which households are Jivaro and which belong to the other four groups.

With this political organization, the methods used to settle disputes define the effective boundaries of the society. Disputes between Jivaros are resolved by legal means, whereas disputes with members of other societies are resolved through extralegal means. Like the Nuer, the Jivaro make a sharp distinction between a feud and a war. A **feud** is the legal means by which a sanction is imposed on another family for the murder of a kinsman. As a legal procedure, a feud proceeds in a manner quite different from a war.

As in most societies, murder is the most serious offense. According to Jivaro beliefs, few deaths are attributable to natural causes; most are the result of physical violence, sorcery, or avenging spirits. Deaths caused by physical violence and witchcraft are considered murders, which have to be avenged by the kinsmen of the deceased. In most cases of physical violence, the murderer is readily identifiable. In cases of poisoning and witchcraft, divination is used to determine the guilty party.

Determination of the guilty party and whether they are Jivaro or non-Jivaro affect how the victim's kinfolk avenge the death. If the guilty party is Jivaro, the kinsmen of the victim attack the household of the murderer with the goal of killing the man himself. If they are not successful in finding him, they may kill a male relative of his, even a young boy. They normally will not harm women or little children, except when the victim was a woman or a child. Even if they have the opportunity to kill more, only one individual will

---

feud Method of dispute settlement in self-help legal systems involving multiple but balanced killings between members of two or more kin groups.

be killed. This is a legal action, and Jivaro law allows only a life for a life.

If the guilty party is determined to be a non-Jivaro, the relatives of the murdered person attack the household of the guilty party, trying to kill as many people as possible. They attempt to massacre the entire family, with no regard for either sex or age. In some cases, they attack nearby households as well, attempting to kill even more members of the group. This is a war, not a legal action.

The Jivaro, the Nuer, and other peoples who lack a centralized and formal political structure nonetheless have definite means of maintaining social control. To those of us who have formal governmental institutions that are supposed to handle our grievances and right the wrongs done to us, self-help systems look rather anarchic. However, rules govern such systems.

Court Systems

A number of factors distinguish a **court legal system** from a self-help legal system. First, authority resides not with the victim and his or her family but with a formalized institution, the court. The court has the authority and the power to hear disputes and to unilaterally decide cases and impose sanctions. Authority in legal matters is a component of political authority; thus, fully developed court systems can exist only in societies that have centralized formal political leadership—that is, chiefdoms or states. Second, most court systems operate with formal public hearings, presided over by a judge or judges, with formally defined defendants and plaintiffs. Grievances are stated; evidence is collected and analyzed; and, in cases of conflicting evidence, oaths or ordeals may be used to determine truthfulness. Finally, only in court systems does one find substantive law clearly divided into criminal law and civil law.

Court systems in turn may be divided into three categories: (1) **incipient courts**, (2) **courts of mediation**, and (3) **courts of regulation**. All court systems mediate disputes as well as regulate behavior; however, as societies become increasingly complex, the primary focus of the court shifts from mediating disputes to regulating behavior. This shift results in a qualitative difference not only in courts but in the nature of the law itself. Associated with this shift is an increasing codification of the laws. Laws and their associated sanctions become standardized and rigid, and civil laws are steadily transformed into criminal laws. Court systems begin to emerge with the concept of "crime against society"—the need to control individual acts that might endanger the society as a whole, as opposed to acts that threaten only individuals. Herein lies the distinction between criminal law and civil law.

Incipient Court Systems

True court systems can be found only in societies that have centralized political systems—chiefdoms or states. However, some tribal societies have what might best be termed *incipient courts*. Although a tribal-level society, the Cheyenne, as described earlier in this chapter, demonstrate the development of an incipient court system. At times, both the Council of Forty-Four and the warrior societies assumed the role of de facto judges and courts. The Cheyenne recognized that certain individual actions threatened the well-being of the group and thus had to be controlled. Some of these actions were purely secular, whereas others were religious. Designated warrior societies were formally empowered by the council to enforce secular laws and regulations. For example, in preparation for a communal bison hunt, camp members would be told to refrain from independent hunting. A single hunter could disturb the herd; thus spoiling the hunt for the group. To prevent this one of the warrior societies was designated by the council to police the area around the village. If the warrior society discovered someone hunting illegally, they became the de facto judges and court and immediately imposed sanctions on the offender, often beating him with whips, shooting his horses, and slashing his tepee with knives.

court legal systems Systems in which authority for settling disputes and punishing crimes is formally vested in a single individual or group.

incipient courts Court systems in which judicial authorities meet, frequently informally, in private to discuss issues and determine solutions to be imposed. Evidence is not formally collected, and the parties involved in these cases are not formally consulted.

courts of mediation Court systems in which the judges attempt to reach compromise solutions, based on the cultural norms and values of the parties involved, that will restore the social cohesion of the community.

courts of regulation Court systems that use codified laws, with formally prescribed rights, duties, and sanctions.

Other secular criminal violations were handled just as swiftly. The Council of Forty-Four was responsible for the religious, or sacred, well-being of the tribe; thus, any action that endangered the supernatural well-being of the Cheyenne was their concern. The murder of a Cheyenne by another Cheyenne was the most heinous of crimes. Such a crime was said to bloody the sacred arrows, the most sacred of Cheyenne tribal medicine bundles. The arrows were symbolic of Cheyenne success in hunting (their main economic activity) and warfare. Murder within the tribe polluted the arrows and thus made the Cheyenne vulnerable to their enemies and less successful in their hunting. When a Cheyenne died at the hands of another Cheyenne, the Council of Forty-Four became a de facto court. Although there was no formal hearing, the council met and discussed the case by themselves. In small societies like the Cheyenne, there was no need for a formal hearing with witnesses—the members of the council knew all of the relevant facts concerning the events. There were two issues they had to decide. First, they needed to determine whether the act was a murder. If so, then the sacred arrows had to be "renewed," or ritually purified. Second, they had to decide on the sanction to be imposed—usually exile for a period of years. For the Cheyenne, there could be no capital punishment without again polluting the sacred arrows.

Another matter the Cheyenne also had to deal with was determining when a suicide was a "murder." There were several cases of Cheyenne women committing suicide for what the council determined to be trivial reasons. These were not considered murder, and so the arrows were not renewed. In other instances, however, suicide was treated as murder. In one case, for example, a mother became infuriated when her daughter eloped with a young man of whom she did not approve. The mother found the girl and beat her with a whip while dragging her home. Once inside the tepee, the girl seized a gun and shot herself. In another case a young girl divorced her husband and returned to her parents' home. Sometime later, the mother found the girl participating in a young person's dance and beat her; the girl hanged herself. The council decided in these cases that these girls' deaths were murder on the basis that they had been driven to suicide by their mother. In both cases, the sacred arrows were renewed and the mothers banished from the tribe.

In other cases, the council had to determine when the murder of a Cheyenne was justified. In one case, a man attempted to rape his daughter, who resisted and picking up a knife killed him. While the council had the sacred arrows renewed, the girl was not banished, and the girl was not treated as a murderer by the people. In still another case, a man named Winnebago took the wife of another man, who retaliated by taking one of Winnebago's other wives. Enraged Winnebago killed the man and was banished by the council. After returning from his banishment, which lasted 5 years, Winnebago argued with and killed another man. Again the council banished Winnebago, who took up residence with the Arapaho tribe. Later a Cheyenne named Rising Fire became involved in a dispute with Winnebago. Knowing Winnebago's reputation, Rising Fire shot and killed him. The council took no action.

Courts of Mediation

The key difference between court systems is not how the legal hearings are conducted but the manner in which breaches of the law are determined and suitable sanctions imposed. In courts of mediation, few laws are codified, and the judges follow few formalized guidelines as to what constitutes a legal violation or the sanction that should be imposed. This is not to say that judges act arbitrarily in these matters, but that they have tremendous latitude in their actions. What they apply is a **reasonable-person model**. Using prevalent norms and values, they ask the question, How should a reasonable individual have acted under these circumstances? To determine the answer, they must examine an individual's actions within the social context in which the dispute occurred: What were the past and present relationships between the parties involved? What circumstances led up to the event? Thus, judges attempt to examine each case as a unique occurrence. Although some sanctions are imposed as punishments, other sanctions are designed to restore as fully as possible a working, if not harmonious, relationship between the parties involved.

One difficulty in attempting to describe courts of mediation is our limited knowledge of such systems. Polities that had courts of this nature were some time ago brought under European colonial rule. Their courts were soon modified by and subordinated to European colonial courts, which were more regulatory in nature. The example we use is the Barotse judicial system, as described by Max Gluckman. The Barotse made up a multiethnic state in southern Africa that at the time of Gluckman's study in the 1940s had

---

reasonable-person model Model used in legal reasoning that basically asks how a reasonable individual should have acted under these circumstances.

been under British rule for 40 years. The British had removed more serious offenses from the jurisdiction of this court. Despite these factors, the basic Barotse legal concepts aptly illustrate a mediation type of court system.

The Barotse state had two capitals: a northern capital, where the king resided; and a subordinate southern capital, ruled by a princess. All villages in the state were attached to one or the other of these capitals. The capitals were identical in structure; each had a palace and a council house. Courts of law were held in the council house.

The titular head of the court was the ruler; in practice, the ruler seldom was present at trials. In the center at the back of the house was the dais, or raised platform, where the ruler was seated if present. There were three ranked groupings of judges. The highest-ranking group of judges was the *indunas*, or councilors, who sat to the right of the dais. The second-highest-ranking group was the *likombwa*, or stewards, who sat to the left. These two groups were divided into senior members, who sat in the front, and junior members, who sat behind. The third group consisted of princes and the husbands of the princesses, who represented their wives. This group sat at a right angle to the likombwa.

A case was introduced by a plaintiff, who was allowed to state his or her grievance at length with no interruption; the defendant was then allowed the same privilege. The statements of witnesses for both sides followed. There were no attorneys for either side; the judges questioned and cross-examined the witnesses. After all the testimony had been heard, the judges began to give their opinions, starting with the most junior indunas, followed by the others in order of increasing seniority. The last judge to speak was the senior induna, who passed judgment on the case, subject to the ruler's approval.

In judging a case, the Barotse judges used a reasonable-person model. The reasonableness of behavior was related to the social and kinship relationships of the individuals involved. Also, a breach of the law usually did not happen in isolation, and many individuals could be at fault; so one case frequently led to a number of related cases. In passing judgment and imposing sanctions, the judges considered numerous factors. One of the most important was the kinship relationship between the parties. The judges attempted to restore the relationship and reconcile the parties—but not without blaming those who had committed wrongs and not without imposing sanctions. The judges' opinions frequently took the form of sermons on proper behavior. As Gluckman (1973, 22) notes:

> Implicit in the reasonable man is the upright man, and moral issues in these relationships are barely differentiated from legal issues. This is so even though ... [they] distinguish "legal" rules, which the ... [court] has power to enforce or protect, from "moral" rules which it has not power to enforce or protect. But the judges are reluctant to support the person who is right in law, but wrong in justice, and may seek to achieve justice by indirect ... action.

Courts of mediation have great potential for meeting the basic social purpose of the law, which is the maintenance of group cohesiveness. There is one serious drawback: such a system is workable only in a culturally homogeneous political unit, that is, it works only if the judges and the parties involved share the same basic norms and values.

Courts of Regulation

In the second millennium B.P., the Code of Hammurabi, the earliest-known set of written laws, was created in Babylon. The code covered a variety of laws. One section dealt with physicians. It set the prices to be charged for various types of operations, based on the ability of individuals to pay. It also decreed, among other things, that if a surgeon operated on an individual using a bronze knife and the patient died or lost his eyesight, the surgeon's hand was to be cut off. The laws defined in the Code of Hammurabi reflect the emergence of regulatory laws. The role of the court was no longer to merely arbitrate disputes and strive for reconciliation but to define the rights and duties of members of an increasingly heterogeneous community.

Courts of regulation were a natural outgrowth of state-level polities, which evolved socially and economically distinct classes and encompassed numerous culturally distinct peoples. As relationships between individuals in the population became depersonalized, the law, too, became increasingly depersonalized. This change in the nature of law was compounded by the political incorporation of diverse peoples who frequently had conflicting cultural norms and values. The use of a reasonable-person model is workable only as long as there is a general consensus on what is "reasonable." In increasingly complex and stratified societies, the possibility of such consensus declined. Mediation of disputes works well in small, kinship-based societies, where all parties recognize the need for reconciliation

CONCEPT REVIEW: Legal Systems

Form	Characteristics	Associated Political System(s)
Self-Help		
(a) Familial	Legal concepts based on accepted social norms and behaviors of the society Ad hoc sanctioning authority limited to victim and/or victim's family, with implicit support of other community members	Band
(b) Mediator	Legal concepts based on accepted social norms and behaviors of the society Ad hoc sanctioning authority limited to victim and/or victim's family, with implicit support of other community members Use of a third-party mediator, with limited if any authority, to negotiate a settlement	Composite bands and most tribal peoples
Courts		
(a) Mediation	Legal concepts based on the reasonable-person model Formal judges who have the authority to hear cases and impose sanctions	Some tribal peoples have rudimentary court systems; however, true court systems appear with chiefdoms and smaller states.
(b) Regulation	Laws and sanctions are formally codified Formal judges who have the authority to hear cases and impose sanctions	States

In courts of regulation, the authority of judges is usually limited.

through compromise. In sharply divided societies, the need for mediation is not as great because reconciliation in itself is not seen as a gain. Compromise is viewed only in terms of what is lost. Laws were thus created to bring order and stability to the interactions between individuals who were not social equals. With law divorced from social norms and values, justice was no longer simply a moral or ethical issue, but came to be viewed in terms of consistency, or precedent.

The separation of law from social norms and values also opened the door for the "politicization" of the laws. Laws were created to serve political ends, as various groups vied with one another for the creation of laws that would protect, express, or further their own goals, interests, and values. This situation is particularly evident in multiethnic and religiously and economically diverse state-level systems such as that of the United States. Given the cultural pluralism, religious diversity, and economic inequality of the United States, it would be impossible to create a code of laws that could equally protect the interests of all classes and that would be consistent with the norms and values of all groups. As a result, many people find themselves subject to laws and sanctions, some of which they judge either immoral or unethical; at times, people find that laws violate their own cultural values. We see this with groups who think that abortion is murder and thus should be made illegal, and with groups who oppose capital punishment on the grounds that the state does not have the right to kill individuals. During the Vietnam War, we saw it with draft resisters who argued that the state did not have the right to order men to fight in a war they considered immoral. Less obvious is the manner in which numerous ethnic minorities, notably Native Americans, subordinate their cultural norms and values to comply with the legal system. With the emergence of states and courts of regulation, law ceased to be an expression of the social norms and values of the society and frequently impose on the population new standards of behavior that many people feel are unjust, if not immoral.

SUMMARY

1. **Explain what is meant by political organization.** Collective action—in economic and social activities as well as relations with other groups of people—is a prerequisite for the survival of a group of people. To be effective, group activities must have leadership and organization, which are the basis for political structure. All societies have some form of political organization.

2. **List the four main types of political organization and how they structurally differ from one another.** The four major categories of political organization are bands, tribes, chiefdoms, and states. Found among foraging societies, the band is the simplest and least formal level of political organization. The two forms of band organization are simple bands and composite bands. In simple bands, the highest level of political organization is the extended family, with the highest level of political leadership being the heads of the various families. These simple bands are economically self-sufficient and politically autonomous. Because a simple band has as its core a group of related individuals, band members are forced to seek spouses from outside the band; they are exogamous units. Thus, kinship ties through marriage serve as the primary link between bands. Composite bands are larger than simple bands and include a number of unrelated families. Leadership in composite bands is vested in "big men," or informal leaders, who have influence but not authority. The key element in tribal societies is the sodality, which transcend local residence groups and bind the geographically scattered members of the society into a cohesive unit. Sodalities may be either kinship based, as in the case of clans, or nonkinship based, as in the case of warrior societies or age grades. Leadership in such groups is more structured, with formal political offices. Chiefdoms have formal, hereditary leadership with centralized political control and authority. The associated redistributive economic exchange system focused on the chief economically integrates the various communities within the political unit. The state is the most complex level of political organization. States have centralized power and control, but the key characteristic of a state is a bureaucracy—individuals acting on behalf of the political elite, thus enabling the centralized power figures to maintain control of a greater number of individuals.

3. **Explain what is meant by social control.** Individual differences, conflict, and competition within the group must be controlled and channeled in such a manner that the internal cohesiveness and cooperation of the individual members of the group are maintained—thus the need for social control. Social control consists of the various formal and informal methods used to control and channel the behavior of individual members of a society into approved behavior.

4. **Discuss legal systems and how they differ from other forms of social control.** Law and legal systems

are merely the highest level of social control. Law is defined as having three attributes: (1) authority, (2) intention of universal application, and (3) sanction. By this definition, all societies have law.

5. **Discuss the two major forms of legal systems and the variants within the two forms.** There are two major forms of legal systems: self-help systems and court systems. In self-help systems, the responsibility and authority for determining a breach of the law and imposing the proper sanction fall to the victim or victim's family (or both). In court systems, formal judges determine where a law has been violated and impose sanctions against the violator.

6. **Explain the relationship between the legal system found in a society and the political organization of that society.** In societies with no centralized political systems, bands, and some tribes, legal systems are self-help. As discussed, this system is not as arbitrary as we might think. In the case of murder or killing, the result may be a feud between families, but a feud—sharply distinguished from a war—is part of the legal process. In societies with centralized political systems, chiefdoms, states, and some tribes, violations of the law are handled by courts. Court systems usually can be categorized as either courts of mediation or courts of regulation. In relatively homogeneous societies, most court systems take as their primary objective the mediation of disputes between individuals and the restoration of harmonious social relationships. In more heterogeneous groups, courts usually become more regulatory in nature, with formally defined laws and sanctions.

13 Social Inequality and Stratification

Enormously wealthy and desperately poor people coexist in nearly all contemporary nations. This photo illustrates living conditions in a neighborhood in Freetown, Sierra Leone.

Equalities and Inequalities

Equalities and Inequalities: Three Systems
 Egalitarian Societies
 Ranked Societies
 Stratified Societies

Castes in Traditional India

Classes in Industrial Societies: The United States

Maintaining Inequality
 Ideologies
 American Secular Ideologies

Theories of Inequality
 Functionalist Theory
 Conflict Theory
 Who Benefits?

LEARNING OBJECTIVES

After reading this chapter, you should be able to:

1 **EXPLAIN** *egalitarian*, *ranked*, and *stratified*.

2 **DISCUSS** the primary differences between castes and classes.

3 **DESCRIBE** how ideologies are important in maintaining inequalities in stratified societies.

4 **EVALUATE** the functional and conflict theories of stratification.

"We hold these truths to be self-evident, that all men are created equal, that they are endowed by their Creator with certain unalienable Rights." As you know by now, whether in fact all "men" are believed to have been created equal depends on which society you happened to be born into. Whether you have certain "unalienable rights," and the nature of these rights, also varies from people to people. In this chapter, we consider another dimension of cultural diversity—the allocation of culturally valued rewards. The essence of this topic is "who gets what and why?" Gender, race, and ethnicity are two other bases for allocating rewards and are covered in other chapters (Chapters 2 and 11).

Equalities and Inequalities

Inequality refers to the degree to which culturally valued material and social rewards are received disproportionately by individuals, families, and other kinds of groups. To the extent that inequality exists in a group or whole society, its members receive varying levels of benefits. Although specific rewards vary by culture, in comparing societies, anthropologists commonly distinguish three reward categories.

The most tangible is *wealth*—ownership of or access to valued material goods and to the natural and human resources needed to produce those goods. The national economies of modern nations measure wealth in money (total GDP or GDP per capita). Preindustrial peoples who do not use money may value consumables like shelter and beads and resources that can be used to produce the consumables.

The second kind of reward is *power*—the ability to make others do what you want based on coercion or legitimate authority (see Chapter 12). Wealth and power go together among some peoples, each mutually reinforcing the other. But not always: esoteric (secret) knowledge often enhances the power of men and women who have little wealth. On the Micronesian island of Pohnpei, people believe that many elderly people possess secret knowledge that they often do not disclose until just before their death, if at all. Sorcery and witchcraft also can make people powerful (Chapter 14).

The final type of reward is *prestige*—the respect, admiration, and overt approval other group members grant to individuals they consider meritorious. Prestige (*honor*, *status*) is a social reward, based on judgments about an individual's personal worthiness or the contributions the individual makes to others in the group. Norms, values, worldviews, and other cultural knowledge affect prestige. For instance, many North Americans admire "self-made" persons who have succeeded in life by their own talents and efforts. However, such individuals would be looked down on as self-centered and ungenerous in many other cultures.

The distribution of each kind of reward varies among societies. Some societies allow ambitious individuals to acquire wealth, power, and prestige; whereas others make it difficult for anyone to accumulate possessions, gain power over others, or put themselves above their peers socially. It is important to understand that what people think about the distribution of rewards does not necessarily correlate with the actual distribution, especially with wealth. In modern capitalist nations, people's beliefs about wealth distribution are commonly mistaken.

Equalities and Inequalities: Three Systems

To introduce the ways societies differ in inequality, anthropologists often use an influential classification developed by Morton Fried way back in 1967. Fried

---

inequality Degree to which individuals, groups, and categories differ in their access to culturally valued rewards.

CONCEPT REVIEW: Systems of Equality and Inequality

Form	Main Characteristics
Egalitarian	Rough equality between families in access to necessities, possessions and wealth objects; wide access to and sharing of productive resources; influence and prestige based on age and personal qualities and achievements
Ranked	Limited number of formal social roles or positions (offices, titles) that confer some authority; access to prestigious titles and offices determined largely by hereditary, family/kinship ties; rights to resources allocated by those of higher rank
Stratified	Sharply unequal distribution of material resources and wealth; large inequalities in access to power and social rewards (prestige)
Caste	Named, endogamous, ranked groups with membership normatively based on birth; occupation and activities constrained by caste membership; interaction between members of different castes governed by social rules (segregation, pollution)
Class	Vague definition and imprecise membership determined by a combination of birth and achievement; class membership broadly determined by occupation and wealth level, variably affected by inheritance

identified three basic types of societies based on their level and kinds of inequality: **egalitarian**, **ranked**, and **stratified**. (The Concept Review provides a quick look at the major differences between the three systems.) We need to clarify four points about Fried's classification.

First, the categories do not refer to access to rewards based on gender or age. When we call a society *egalitarian*, for example, we do not mean that females and males receive equal or nearly equal rewards, that elderly people and young people are socially equal, or that unskilled and lazy people are valued just as much as skilled and diligent people. Even in egalitarian societies, social distinctions are based on gender, age, and personal qualities. Essentially, *egalitarian* means there are few differences in the rewards received by families or other kinds of kin groups within a society. *Egalitarian* especially refers to peoples among whom wealth, power, and prestige are not inherited along family lines. At the other end of the continuum, in *stratified* societies, there are major differences in rewards between families or kin groups, in addition to other distinctions such as gender, age, and personal qualities.

Second, Fried's three categories are merely points along a continuum of inequality. It is impossible to pigeonhole all human societies into one of these types because most fit somewhere in between the three categories. The terms *egalitarian*, *ranked*, and *stratified* are mainly short descriptions of the kinds and range of variation in inequality found among the world's peoples.

Third, egalitarian-ranked-stratified is the temporal order in which the three forms developed. Until about 10,000 years ago, nearly all humans lived in egalitarian societies. Ranked societies developed in a few areas about then, and a few thousand years later, stratification developed in some early chiefdoms and in the great civilizations (see Chapters 7 and 12). After that, over the next 4,000 to 5,000 years, stratified societies spread throughout much of the world, as some peoples and nations conquered and ruled over others.

Fourth, it is important to distinguish two bases for equality and inequality. For clarity, we simplistically refer only to the far ends of the equality–inequality continuum. Equality may exist because people culturally *value* life in that kind of society: people strive to maintain equality among themselves. Alternatively, it

---

egalitarian society Form of society in which there is little inequality in access to culturally valued rewards.

ranked society Society with a limited number of high-ranking, privileged social positions; groups are ranked relative to one another.

stratified society Society with marked and variably heritable differences in access to wealth, power, and prestige; inequality is based mainly on unequal access to productive and valued resources.

may exist because it is a regular *outcome* of how their system works: people are not actually striving to all be equal, but the way their economy and society works lead to equality. That is, equality is *generated*, regardless of whether people desire it.

Similarly, for inequality people (some or most people, at least) may positively value a high degree of inequality, believing it is necessary for the welfare of all or is supernaturally ordained. Alternatively, inequality may exist because it is regular outcome of how a particular economic and political system works. That is, people (some or most people, at least) may desire more equality, but their efforts to produce it fail, because the economic or social system continually generates it.

Egalitarian Societies

In egalitarian societies, aside from distinctions based on sex and age, minor differences exist among individuals and families in rewards. People who work hard, who have attractive personalities, or who possess valuable skills may be rewarded with respect and prestige from other members of their group. Egalitarian groups have various cultural mechanisms to prevent any individual from becoming too "big." And, even respected people have few, if any, more possessions or power than others.

Mobile hunting and gathering peoples, such as the Inuit, Ju/'hoansi, Hadza, and BaMbuti are egalitarian. James Woodburn identified three reasons rewards are comparatively evenly distributed among such foragers.

1. Most obviously, the band or camp must move frequently for effective adaptation (see Chapter 7). Mobility makes it difficult to transport possessions and hence to accumulate possessions or other forms of wealth.

2. The cultural value foragers place on reciprocal sharing (see Chapter 8) prevents individual persons or family groups from becoming wealthier than their bandmates. Because sharing food and most durable possessions is normatively expected, hoarding and accumulation are negatively valued. Therefore, even if someone tried to accumulate, he or she would find it difficult to do so because other people demand their share, and failure to adhere to the norms of sharing and to live up to egalitarian values is socially punished by public ridicule or worse.

3. Mobile foraging families are not tied to specific territories but have the right to visit and exploit the resources of many areas, often due to extended family ties (see Chapters 9 and 10). If anyone tries to be the boss or exercise control over behavior, other people have the option to leave and live elsewhere.

Like most mobile hunter-gatherers, the Ju/'hoansi are an egalitarian people.

In sum, if people move around in their environments a lot, are required to share food and other possessions, and have a range of options about where to live and whom to live with, then inequality in wealth and power does not have much chance of developing. If inequality should develop, it does not have much chance of persisting for very long.

Not all foragers are or were egalitarian, however. As discussed in Chapter 7, the Native Americans of the Northwest Coast lived in ranked societies because, in their rich environment, the three conditions just listed did not exist. Northwest Coast people were more sedentary, accumulated wealth for redistribution to validate and acquire rank, and formed kin groups that were associated with particular territories.

Most traditional horticultural peoples also are egalitarian, although others are ranked. In most of the hundreds of occupied islands of Melanesia there are tribal peoples (Chapter 12) who live from growing tree and root crops, keeping pigs, and fishing if they lived along coasts. In most Melanesian societies, men compete for prestige by organizing large feasts on special occasions such as weddings, funerals, or just to distribute foods and valuables to draw people into debt. If a man is unusually successful in organizing large feasts, he rises up to become a *big man*—someone whose name is widely known, to whom many men owe goods or favors, and who usually has several wives to help with gardening and pig keeping. Melanesian peoples vary in the degree to which big men have more wealth than other men. In some, there are noticeable differences in possessions, but in others, big men distribute so much of their wealth to others that they live pretty much like everyone else.

Melanesian peoples with big men are considered egalitarian societies by most anthropologists, despite the fact that some men were notably "bigger" than others. They illustrate the cautions we discussed earlier: typologies anthropologists use to depict human cultural variability must be applied carefully so that they enlighten rather than obscure the lives of actual peoples.

Ranked Societies

Any particular Melanesian tribe or even village may have many big men, some "bigger" than others. And the number of big men varies over time, depending on how many men have done well in any decade or generation. This is because *big man* is not an office into which someone is recruited, but an informal status that some men achieve based on their ambitions and accomplishments.

In contrast, in ranked societies, there are a limited number of high-ranking social positions, usually titles or some kind of formal offices that grant authority. People who hold the title can issue commands and expect to have them obeyed. The titles also confer high honor on the people who hold them. In most cases, the privilege of holding a title or occupying an office is largely or entirely hereditary within certain families, lineages, clans, or other kin groups. If you are born into a group that does not have the hereditary right to the title or office, normatively (but not always in fact) you cannot succeed to the office regardless of your talents or ambitions.

An excellent example of a ranked society is Tikopia, the small Polynesian island whose kinship system we described in Chapter 10. Tikopia's 1,200 persons were divided into four patricians, each with its own chief who exercised authority over his clanmates. Each clan in turn was divided into several patrilineages. Every patrilineage had a head, believed to be the oldest living male descendant of the man who founded the lineage about four to six generations ago. Alongside this ranking of individuals within a single lineage, the various lineages of a single clan were ranked relative to one another. One lineage of each clan, supposedly the original, "senior" lineage from which the "junior" lineages had budded off generations ago, was considered the noble lineage. Members of other lineages of the clan deferred socially to members of the noble lineage, according to Tikopian standards of etiquette. In addition, the noble lineage of each clan selected one of its members as chief of the whole clan. Clan chiefs had authority to punish troublemakers and the duty to perform rituals connected to agriculture and other common concerns.

Chiefs and other members of the noble Tikopia lineages had little more wealth than anyone else, however. The nobility received tribute from other lineages of their clan, but they gave away most of it in the many public activities they organized and financed through redistribution (see Chapter 8). The chief and nobility of each clan could not deny access to land and ocean resources to members of other lineages because each lineage was considered to have inalienable rights to certain pieces of land. High-ranking Tikopians, then, received high esteem and token tribute from other islanders, but they did not use this tribute to make themselves notably wealthier than lower-ranking people. They were honored and could issue commands in certain contexts, but their wealth was not great. It is mainly in this respect that ranked societies contrast with stratified societies.

Stratified Societies

Within a society or nation, a *social stratum* consists of families who have roughly the same access to rewards. Stratified societies have two distinguishing characteristics:

- There are marked and enduring inequalities between strata in access to all three kinds of rewards: wealth, power, and prestige. The inequality may last through generations because the positions that bring rewards are themselves hereditary or because being born into a certain stratum gives individuals better or worse opportunities. Birth into a certain class affects whether a person has a head start in life, thus enhancing her or his competitiveness relative to others.

- Inequalities are based primarily on unequal access to productive resources such as the land and tools people need to make their living or the education and training needed to succeed. In stratified societies, a minority of people control access to the resources other people need to survive at culturally acceptable levels.

Stratified societies vary in their cultural beliefs about the possibilities of social mobility—that is, about movement up and down the social ladder. In some, such as North America, Europe, New Zealand, Australia and other contemporary democracies, upward or downward mobility is possible through education, special skills, hard work, good luck, or other circumstances. In East Asia, educational performance is so important for a child's success that most parents expend enormous resources in schooling, including even preschool. In other stratified societies as in traditional India or in Europe before the Industrial Revolution, one's position is considered fixed, often because of beliefs that existing inequalities are hereditary and/or ordained by supernatural beings.

Social scientists distinguish two major kinds of strata: **classes** and **castes**. Two general differences between class and caste systems stand out. First, by definition, castes are *endogamous* groups: they have cultural norms or laws that require individuals to marry within their caste. As discussed in Chapter 9, rules that mandate marriage within one's own group have the effect of maintaining the distinctiveness of the group relative to other groups. This is because normatively there is no possibility of upward mobility through inter-caste marriage. One's caste membership is theoretically hereditary: One is born into the caste of one's parents, one marries someone in the same caste, and one's children are likewise born into and remain members of one's own caste. In contrast, most class societies allow people to marry someone of a different class; in fact, intermarriage between classes is a common avenue of social mobility.

Second, caste systems have enforced norms or laws regulating social relationships among members of different castes. For example, norms or laws may prohibit direct physical contact between castes or may forbid members of different castes from eating from the same bowl or drinking from the same wells. In some societies, high-caste members believe they will be spiritually polluted if they touch members of other castes. Indeed, they often must perform rituals to cleanse themselves after accidental contacts.

Both of these general differences mean that castes have more permanent membership and more rigid social boundaries than classes. This does not mean that it is easy to tell whether some particular stratified society "has" castes or classes. Some societies have elements of both. For instance, some scholars have suggested that black–white relations in the American South were more castelike than classlike until the mid–twentieth century. There was no possibility of upward mobility into the white "caste" for blacks because no one could overcome the cultural stigma of dark skin color. Interracial marriage was legally prohibited or culturally taboo, so that the two races were virtually endogamous. Explicit laws against certain kinds of "intercaste" contacts and interactions—known as *segregation laws*—forced blacks to live apart from whites, forbade them to enter certain white business establishments and public restrooms, prohibited drinking from the same water fountains, made them send their children to all-black schools, and so forth. Most whites did not believe blacks were "polluting" in the spiritual sense of the word, but many whites did believe blacks were "unclean" in another sense and tried to minimize contact with them.

Usually the term *stratification* refers to differences in wealth, influence, and status within a single society. There are great inequalities among societies also, such

---

class System of stratification in which membership in a stratum can theoretically be altered and intermarriage between strata is allowed.

caste Stratification system in which membership in a stratum is in theory hereditary, strata are endogamous, and contact or relationships among members of different strata are governed by explicit laws, norms, or prohibitions.

as between nations and even between whole continents in the modern world. Whether future globalization will reduce economic inequalities among nations—and, if so, whether it will be sooner rather than later—is hotly debated. The effect of globalization on inequality *within* nations is also unclear. Many believe inequality is increasing in both the "developed" and the "developing" worlds. In the former, many working-class people are losing unionized, factory jobs, while the owners of the factories (including stockholders) make higher profits and grow wealthier by relocating their operations overseas. In the latter, some people are better able to obtain new jobs in globalized factories and leap ahead of other citizens who are unable to take advantage of the new opportunities. (Globalization Challenges and Opportunities discusses this issue.)

Castes in Traditional India

India's traditional caste system is the most famous and best known. It is complex and highly variable from region to region, so we present only a general picture. Traditionally, the people of India recognized five main social categories, four of which are *varnas*. (A varna is not itself a caste.) Each category is ranked relative to the others in honor and degree of ritual purity, and each is broadly associated with certain kinds of occupations.

The highest varna is the Brahmins, or priests and scholars; next is the varna of nobles and warriors, the Kshatriyas; third are the Vaishas, or merchants and artisans; and ranked lowest are the Shudras, or farmers, craftspeople, and certain other laborers. Although the varna are associated with certain occupations, not everyone in a given varna follows that occupation. A fifth category—outside and ranked below the four varnas—is the untouchables, to whom falls work considered polluting to the varna.

The varnas arose in the second millennium B.C.E. when the Aryans invaded and conquered what is now northern India, incorporating most of the smaller states that already were in the region. Over centuries, they became large, inclusive categories into which specific castes are placed. The villages in which most Indians formerly lived are divided into much smaller and specific groupings called *jati* (castes, as the term is usually used). For example, in a particular village, the Shudra varna might be represented by several jati with names such as weaver, potter, and tailor. There are thousands of such castes in India, distributed among the many thousands of villages, with each village containing a variable number of castes.

India's traditional caste hierarchy is so intimately tied up with the ceremonies and worldview of Hinduism that the two are almost inseparable. (Hinduism is incredibly diverse, so here we present only a simplified depiction of it.) Hindu religion holds that spiritual souls are reborn into different physical bodies at various stages of their existence—this is the doctrine of *reincarnation*. Souls seek an end to the cycle of earthly birth, death, and rebirth, but to achieve this end, each soul must be reborn many times in many bodies, both animal and human. Souls attempt to move from lower forms of life to higher ones: from animals to humans (of various ranked castes) to gods.

The body into which a soul is born depends on how closely that soul adhered to proper standards of behavior in previous lifetimes. For souls that were placed in human forms in their previous incarnation, standards include avoidance of activities that Hindus believe are polluting. Among the most polluting activities are handling and working with animal carcasses or human corpses, touching excrement and other waste materials, dealing with childbirth, and eating meat. Not only are people who regularly perform these activities polluted themselves, but any members of a higher caste who come into physical contact with them likewise become polluted and must bathe ritually to cleanse themselves. One's present place in society—one's "station in life"—varies with the degree to which one is associated with pure or impure activities. In turn, whether one is associated with pure or impure activities depends on one's behavior in previous lives, including the degree to which one has allowed oneself to become polluted or failed to cleanse oneself in previous incarnations.

The caste of a person depends—not perfectly, of course—on actions in previous lives. People are born into a low caste either because their soul has not yet been through enough lifetimes to have reached a higher form, or because their misdeeds in a previous lifetime merit reincarnation into a low caste. Thus, all "men" were not created equal in the Hindu worldview; it is legitimate that some castes have more power and privilege and more status and wealth than others.

Each caste (jati) is broadly associated with certain occupations. Each village contains a number of castes, most of which are named according to the occupation traditionally performed by their members. Thus, a village might include castes of priests, merchants, blacksmiths, potters, tailors, farmers, weavers, carpenters, washers, barbers, leather workers, and "sweepers" (the last refers to those who remove human waste matter from people's houses). Just as activities are ranked in Hindu beliefs according to their degree of purity and

GLOBAL CHALLENGES AND OPPORTUNITIES
Globalization and Inequality in China

Globalization leads to new kinds and degrees of economic inequalities both between and within nations. This Hong Kong man stands in front of his holdings in Shanghai, People's Republic of China.

Inequalities at the global level began centuries ago. As early as the 1500s, the products of the two American continents were shipped to Europe. Mesoamerica and the Andes were the homelands of the two great New World civilizations: the Aztec and the Inca, respectively. Like the upper classes in Europe, the Aztec and Inca elite surrounded themselves with treasures, many in gold and silver. The trade (and plunder) of these precious metals produced huge fortunes for some Europeans and affected balances of military power.

By the 1700s and 1800s, products were pouring out of the conquered regions of the Americas and Asia. In the islands of the Caribbean, northern Brazil, and the American South, enslaved Africans produced the cotton, tobacco, sugar, and cacao that were worn, smoked, eaten, and drunk by western Europeans. In Asia, spices, tea, porcelain ("china"), hardwoods, and other products produced by peasants and craftsmen were shipped over land or, later, over sea to satisfy European appetites and tastes. Britain's colony in India, for example, provided early English textile factories with cotton and other fibers. In the process, India's own highly skilled textile weavers suffered. Although the costs of transporting goods from Asian, African, and American colonies were high, Europe's climate did not allow the production of tropical crops, and the labor costs of both African American slaves and Asian peasants were a fraction of the costs of production.

As these brief examples show, the effects of globalization on inequalities are several centuries old, at least. During the nineteenth and twentieth centuries, the growth of economies in the richer regions of North America, Europe, New Zealand, and Australia dramatically outpaced growth in Africa, Latin America, South Asia, and East Asia (except in Japan). Whether continued globalization in the twenty-first century will increase or decrease the economic gap between poor and rich nations is hotly disputed. (See Chapters 7 and 8 for more on the benefits and costs of globalization.)

A revealing example is China, which has experienced the world's fastest growth since the 1980s. China's economic growth rate has hovered between 7 and 12 percent for nearly three decades because of its plentiful labor, its central government that seemingly values growth above other goals, the work ethic of its citizens, and the loosening of restrictions on internal migration and foreign investment. Hundreds of millions of Chinese have experienced increases in their living standards by moving from rural villages to work in factories in Shanghai, Guangzhou, Shenzhen, Beijing, and dozens of other cities along the eastern and southern coasts.

Hundreds of thousands of Chinese factory owners, real estate investors, and market entrepreneurs have

---

impurity, so occupations and those who perform them are ranked. Working with animal carcasses is defiling, so leather working is a defiling occupation, and leather workers are so polluting as to be untouchable. The same applies to sweeping: people who remove human wastes from houses or spread excrement over village fields are polluted, and their touch pollutes those of higher castes. Therefore, members of the leather working, sweeping, and other castes associated with defiling occupations were traditionally untouchable. (Discrimination against people of untouchable ancestry is now illegal in modern India, although it still occurs in many rural regions.) Untouchables usually live in their own special section of the village, separate from members of higher castes. Because they contaminate temples by their entry, they cannot go inside a temple. Their touch contaminates water, so they must use separate wells. These and other restrictions on their behavior are sometimes extreme.

Members of high-ranking castes, however, such as priests, landowners, warriors, and merchants, need the services of low-ranking castes. Again, this is because Hinduism defines some essential activities as polluting, so members of castes who would be defiled by these activities need lower castes to perform these services for them. The bullocks needed for farming die, become fabulously wealthy. However, hundreds of millions in rural areas have yet to participate significantly in the economic boom. Untold thousands lost their livelihood when local officials did not compensate them when a new factory took over the land they were farming. Hundreds of coal miners have died from mine collapses, and tens of millions of Chinese experience some of the planet's worse air pollution from coal-fired power plants (see Chapter 7). (As you can see, China is a country with lots of large numbers.)

Lately, many migrants (precise numbers are unknown) have returned to their roots in the countryside, setting up businesses or finding employment in emerging interior industries. For many, city life and factory work have not been as rewarding as they had hoped. Most young workers eat at factory dining rooms and live in factory dormitories with numerous roommates sleeping on bunk beds. As the Chinese economy developed, younger workers expect a better life and grow dissatisfied with low wages and poor work conditions that the first generation of factory workers found acceptable. This has happened repeatedly in the historical spread of industrialism, so China is not unique.

Since the 1980s, China's government has funded education generously. Its colleges and universities turn out more graduates than any other country. In the 2000s, the number of college and university students quadrupled. In 2013, 7 million students graduated. They are not particularly interested in factory work, yet there are not nearly enough professional and service jobs to employ them: in the winter of 2012–2013, the unemployment rate of Chinese college graduates between 21 and 25 was 16 percent. In contrast, only 4 percent of people with an elementary school education were jobless, due to the high demand for factory labor producing for the global market. Like their counterparts in other parts of the world, China's well educated have high expectations that are likely to be frustrated. And the government has plans for 250 million of its citizens to migrate to cities in the next 20 years and has begun constructing their living spaces.

With a land area almost equal to that of the United States, China's population is four times larger than that of the United States. Its economy is the world's second largest. It faces serious problems of energy supply and resource depletion. Demonstrations and other forms of social unrest are increasing due to factors like working conditions in factories, widespread corruption, increasing economic inequalities, censorship of information on the internet and other media, treatment of dissidents, and conflict between the Han majority and several ethnic minorities.

In a nation of nearly 1.4 billion, including 56 minorities, Chinese leaders might be correct in believing that effective governing requires measures and policies that citizens of nations with a different past and a vastly contrasting present find abhorrent. Leaders often speak of maintaining a "harmonious society" and keeping China "stable." Many scholars of China write about an implicit bargain that the government has made with citizens: "we will help keep your living standards rising if you don't threaten China's stability." Not a desirable bargain by standards of nations that developed over a century ago, but perhaps a necessary, given China's circumstances.

Source: Chang (2009); *New York Times* online editions of June 2, 6, 9, 13, and 22, 2010 (retrieved June 22, 2010); *Columbus Dispatch*, June 16, 2010, pp. A6, A7.

---

so someone has to remove dead cattle from the village. Brahmin women give birth just as other women do, so the women of some low-ranking caste have to serve as midwives because handling blood and placentas would pollute Brahmin women. Everyone passes bodily wastes, so someone must remove these wastes from the houses of high-caste members, lest these substances pollute their occupants. Accordingly, each caste has its proper role and function in the economic, social, and religious life of the village.

In Hindu beliefs, one's soul is reincarnated into a higher or lower form partly according to how well one fulfills the obligations of one's caste in the present life. Leather workers, for instance, cannot do much to improve their lot in this life, but by faithfully fulfilling their obligations to members of higher castes, their souls will attain higher reincarnations in future bodies.

Although the castes are interdependent in that each "needs" the products and services made by the others, one should not conclude that intercaste relations are harmonious, or that the complementary tasks associated with each caste are entirely mutually beneficial. A great deal of friction and outright conflict exist between individual members of different castes. In fact, local castes as a whole group sometimes

Hinduism regards certain substances and activities as spiritually defiling or polluting. Ritual bathing—here in the Ganges River—removes the pollution.

organize themselves with a council to pursue their common interests.

Although most castes had names that referred to occupations, in fact, members of a single caste made their living in diverse ways. Most members of lower castes were farmers, regardless of their caste name, and many higher-caste persons engaged in farming as well. Also, there was no simple relationship between caste membership and access to resources or wealth; some Brahmins were poor, some smiths wealthy.

Many people think caste hierarchies and restrictions are no longer important in India. Indeed, given the anonymity of city life, restrictions on behavior clearly are hard to maintain, and many lower-caste urbanites are well-educated, middle-class people. So, caste distinctions have withered (but not died) in urban areas. In parts of the countryside, however, where most people are still farmers, caste distinctions remain, although in weakened form. For decades, the government of India has given preferential treatment in hiring to members of lower castes, so having a lower caste identity may bring some benefits.

Classes in Industrial Societies: The United States

In class societies, individuals and families have different levels of ownership of productive property and material goods, have varying degrees of influence over public decisions made by a government, and differ in the respect or esteem accorded their position in the traditional society or contemporary nation.

An important point to make about classes is that they are seldom organized *as classes*. There are no occasions on which the members of a given class come together for discussion or common action (unlike, say, an extended family or lineage). Indeed, members of a single class do not necessarily believe they have much in common with one another (unlike the members of a labor union). Many people cannot precisely identify the class to which they belong (unlike Indian jati or varna). Thus, about four-fifths of Americans refer to themselves as "middle class." People cannot say how many classes exist in their societies, but use phrases like *working class* and *upper class*. In fact, there is considerable debate within the social sciences over what the term *class* means, or whether it has any other than the vaguest meaning.

The concept of class might be vague, but no one can deny the enormous differences in wealth, power, and prestige that exist in class societies. The term *class* refers to all the people in a given stratified society who receive comparable levels of rewards. Members of different classes have different access to the material resources (income, property, wealth), influential relationships (social networks, political contacts), and "sophisticated" cultural knowledge (formal education, "social graces") that are positively valued. Unlike caste membership, people are potentially able to move up or down in a class system during their lifetime. Interclass marriage, personal talent, hard work and effort, and good luck can allow upward mobility. More commonly, being born into a given class puts one so far ahead of or behind others that few people rise or fall very far in the class structure during their lifetime.

In this section, we concentrate on the class structure of one industrialized society—the United States. In this country, the kind of work one does (occupation) is often assumed to be the best single overall indication of class membership. ("What kind of work do you do?" or "Where do you work?" is one of the first questions American adults ask of new acquaintances, and the answer gives a lot of information about a person very quickly.) Occupation is generally a good indication of income, and one's income influences so much else: overall lifestyle, access of one's children to education, the kinds of people with whom one associates socially, the kind of church or club to which one belongs, and so on.

Unfortunately for our desire to make societies neat and orderly, the different criteria used to define class membership are not always mutually consistent. For instance, people disagree on the prestige of many occupations—attorneys, physicians, and academicians are despised by some but granted high prestige by others, for example. For some occupations, there is a disjunction between income and prestige—nurses and teachers are held in higher regard than plumbers and assembly-line workers, but often they do not earn as much.

So, it may be difficult to decide to which class some individual belongs. One way around this ambiguity, favored by some sociologists, is to separate the three kinds of rewards from one another and define a separate class ranking for each reward. We can distinguish classes defined on the basis of prestige (*status groups*, as some call them) and on the basis of income or wealth (*economic classes*), for instance. The definitions and methods used for ranking the classes depend partly on our interests.

In the United States, the most widely accepted approach to stratification uses the concept of economic class, in which class membership depends largely on individual and family wealth. Using wealth as the primary basis for assigning class ranking has four major advantages.

1. Wealth is more measurable than other indications of class membership (although cash income alone does not measure it adequately).

2. Wealth is the best single indication of the overall benefits individuals and families are receiving from their citizenship in the nation. Money cannot buy you love, happiness, brains, or many other things, but it can buy you much of what Americans value (including education and consumer goods and, nowadays, better looks and tighter bodies).

3. Extremely high wealth is generally correlated with ownership of productive resources such as factories, financial assets, stocks, and income-producing real estate. Many wealthy people own the nation's large businesses or made their money in finance. Either they built their companies themselves, or their ancestors made fortunes through business activity and passed their ownership along to the current generation. Many of the wealthiest persons gain most of their income from the stock market, which means either they earn large annual dividends or they get their earnings by buying low and selling high. However, notice that many persons become wealthy by selling their skills on the market, in industries like entertainment media, medicine, law, and sports.

4. Wealth levels broadly determine people's access to political power. Through political contributions, the wealthy have a greater say in who gets nominated and elected to important offices, which is why many Americans push for campaign finance reform. Through lobbying efforts, the rich enjoy greater influence on the laws and policies of the nation than their numbers warrant. By providing much of the funding for think tanks and other public advisory groups, the wealthy subsidize the expertise of many economists and other social scientists who advise government. People who serve in the government as elected or appointed officials may later work in the private sector, which covets both their expertise and their political connections.

TABLE 13-1 Distribution of Household Income in the United States, 2011

Quintile	Percentage of Income Earned
Poorest fifth	3.8
Second fifth	9.3
Third fifth	15.1
Fourth fifth	23.0
Richest fifth	48.9
Richest 5 percent	21.3

Source: United States Census Bureau (2013), Table F.2, "Share of Aggregate Income Received by Each Fifth and Top 5 Percent of Families," www.census.gov/hhes/www/income /data/historical/families/ (retrieved June 15, 2013).

For these and other reasons, we can learn the most about class inequalities in the United States by focusing on the distribution of wealth.

Income inequality is one measure of the distribution of wealth. Table 13.1 summarizes income inequality for 2011, the latest year for which the U.S. Census Bureau has published information. In the table, American households are divided into fifths (quintiles) based on their 2011 cash income. For example, the poorest one-fifth of households earned only 3.8 percent of all income, whereas the richest quintile earned 48.9 percent of the total income earned by all households. The table also shows that the richest 5 percent of American households earned 21.3 percent of the total family income in 2011.

U.S. Census Bureau data over the past 30 years reveals that income inequality has increased. Between 1960 and 1980, the relative shares of income received by each quintile remained nearly constant. During those 20 years, the bottom three-fifths (the "poorest" 60 percent) of American households earned about one-third of all cash income. The richest quintile earned a bit over 40 percent. However, by 2010, the share of the poorest 60 percent had fallen to 28 percent—a *loss* of about 5 percent. In 2010, the richest one-fifth earned 48 percent of all cash income, a *gain* of about 7 percent from 1980.

To make much the same point, between 1960 and 1980, the ratio of the incomes of the most affluent fifth to the poorest fifth was about 8.0, whereas in 2011 the ratio was 12.9. Considering the ratio of the richest 5 percent to the poorest 20 percent, inequality has increased even more, from 2.8 in 1980 to 5.6 in 2011.

The relative benefits of economic growth since around 1990 have been distributed unequally, going far more to the affluent than to the poor and even to those who view themselves as middle class.

However, the distribution of income alone does not tell the complete story of inequality in the United States, because figures on annual *income* do not show how much *wealth* is owned by families of different classes. Yearly income figures such as those in Table 13.1 greatly underestimate the economic inequality in the United States. For example, in 2010 the bottom 90 percent of Americans had 56 percent of the yearly income but held only 23 percent of the wealth held by families. People's standards of living are not determined directly by their annual income, nor is their influence on government policies at the local, state, and national levels. If we consider the distribution of wealth, we see that middle-income families, and even families generally considered affluent, own little in comparison with the truly wealthy.

Surveys funded by the federal government provide estimates of the net worth (wealth) of American families. *Net worth* includes all family assets (property) owned minus debts. Debts include mortgages, credit card balances, student loans, and other money owed by a family. *Tangible assets* include property such as residential homes, farms, and other real estate, plus motor vehicles, household possessions, and the like. Tangible assets directly affect standards of living. Added to tangible assets are the money value of *financial assets*, such as savings in banks and retirement accounts and money invested in bonds, and stocks. Financial assets vastly increase a family's economic security, for they can be withdrawn from banks or sold on the stock market to increase wealth or keep material assets from falling during recessions. Savings and, especially, investments also earn additional future income and wealth, although not without risk.

The Federal Reserve Board (the "Fed") is the semigovernmental institution that tries to regulate the economy by affecting interest rates. Every three years, the Fed publishes a *Survey of Consumer Finances* that estimates the wealth held by American families.

The Economic Policy Institute, a private, nonprofit institution, uses Federal Reserve surveys and other data to estimate the concentration of wealth in the United States. For 2010, the Economic Policy Institute concluded that the richest 20 percent of families held 89 percent of the wealth, the middle quintile held 2.6 percent, and the poorest quintile had negative net worth (they owed more than they owned). Comparing the 1 percent of rich families to everyone else, the wealthiest 1 percent owned 35.4 percent of the wealth, whereas the bottom 95 percent owned 36.9 percent of the wealth. That is, in 2010 the wealthiest 1 percent had about the same amount of wealth as the bottom 95 percent put together.

Another way to illustrate how wealth inequality has risen over the last few decades is to compare the *wealth ratio* for various years: the ratio of the wealth owned by the very richest Americans to the median wealth. In 1983, the wealthiest 1 percent of Americans owned 131 times the wealth of the median American. In 1998, the wealth ratio grew to 168. In 2010, the ratio was 288.

Maintaining Inequality

One issue in studying stratification is understanding how such large inequalities first developed millennia ago, in prehistory. This issue cannot be addressed here, other than noting that inequalities between people usually originated out of a complex combination of intensive agriculture, control over scarce resources, large-scale cooperation, and conquest warfare. Most archaeologists who study stratification in prehistory agree that significant inequalities (deserving of the term *class*) did not exist until after the evolution of civilization (see Chapter 7).

Furthermore, we know that in most stratified societies, a conquering militaristic group imposed its rule over the indigenous population of a region. This was true in African states such as Bunyoro and Zulu and in the ancient civilizations of the Americas such as the Aztec and Inca. Conquest of the weaker by the militarily stronger was also important in forming the ancient Old World civilizations of East Asia, Mesopotamia, and India.

Knowing the conditions that led to the *origin* of inequalities in the past may not be very relevant to another issue in contemporary societies: how do such high degrees of inequality in stratified societies *persist?* As the United States illustrates, a small percentage of the population typically control most of the wealth and wield a great deal of influence over public affairs. Why does the relatively underprivileged majority allow them this power and privilege? Why doesn't inequality produce more conflict and even revolts and revolutions?

In fact, class conflict has surfaced historically in a wide range of stratified societies. Resentment, rebellion, and occasional attempts at revolution occur in stratified societies in all parts of the world (which is not to say that they are universally present). Human lifetimes are so short that most of us live through only a few such events, and most of them are far away. In the long term of history, though, a great many powerless and poor people did not simply accept their place in the hierarchy.

One possible explanation of how stratification persists is that members of the highest stratum (hereafter called the *elite*) use their wealth and power to organize an armed force stronger than that of their opposition. If the elite somehow monopolize control over weapons or organize a loyal army, then they can use coercion and threats to maintain their access to rewards and resources. Elites do sometimes use armed force to put down rebellions, and certainly the ever-present threat of coercion and fear of punishment deters resistance to the elite's wealth, prestige, and power.

Yet in most stratified societies, with some exceptions elites prefer not to actually use force. Use of military might is costly to them. Suppose the elite wait for rebellions to occur and then use police or armies to put them down. Even if rebellions fail, suppression by police and armies produces more hatred and resentment and more awareness of the relative wealth and power of the elite. Repression increases fear, as intended by elites, but it also can backfire and lead to a greater probability of future rebellion. Notice also that the elite's reliance on brute force and oppression to maintain their wealth and power potentially reduces or eliminates their honor and esteem, one of the three major rewards of stratification, and one that some members of the elite class presumably covet. Furthermore, those who supply the military might—armies, guards, thugs, or police—must be paid or otherwise provided for by the elite. Payment requires resources. Either the elite can take these resources from their own wealth, thus reducing it, or they can increase their exploitation of the majority population, thus breeding still more hatred and resentment toward themselves. Finally, relying entirely on the loyalty of an army is risky because this allegiance may change, as many dictators know or fear. In sum, reliance on threat and armed force alone is both costly and risky.

None of these points deny that armed force is an important way to sustain the powers and privileges of upper class people. Probably few elites have remained in power for many generations without using force and periodically suppressing rebellions

The difference between the net worth of the very rich and everyone else is much larger than the gap in annual incomes. This couple seems to have the status that used to be called "jet set."

and dissent. Nonetheless, stratification systems that rely entirely or largely on force seem to be short-lived and unstable and have been replaced by those that use other mechanisms. What other mechanisms are available?

Ideologies

We address this question by noting yet another reason coercive force alone is seldom solely responsible for maintaining inequality. A single rebellion can have many causes, but a persistent *pattern* of rebellion is caused mainly by the lower strata's perception that they are exploited or not receiving their fair share of rewards. Seeking out and eliminating rebels does little to change the reasons people rebel. The instigators may be sanctioned or eliminated, but the underlying discontent that causes persistent conflict remains. Imprisoning or killing instigators removes them from rebellions, but sometimes removing one instigator creates several more instigators (think of modern terrorism). Sooner or later, there will be new instigators who organize new rebellions and attacks. Furthermore, while armies or police eliminate rebels, innocents are usually killed, injured, or harmed economically. This can alienate those who otherwise would be more passive about their place in the world. For these and other reasons, armed force alone is unlikely to eliminate the perceptions of unfairness, injustice, cultural domination, or other attitudes that cause rebellions and violence.

It helps elites maintain their privileges if they can influence the perceptions of the underprivileged about why they are underprivileged. For example, if poor people think it is God's will that they are poor, they are less likely to rebel than if they believe they are poor because of exploitation. Or, if they think the elite use their property and power to benefit everyone in the society, they are less likely to challenge the elite. Or, if they think that a concentration of property and power is inevitable because that's just the way human life is, they will be less likely to resist. Or, if they think that they, too, can acquire property, power, and prestige through their own achievements, they are more likely to put their effort into improving their own position rather than taking the risk of being punished or killed. Finally, if "the masses" are divided internally on the basis of values, ethnic identities, real threats from enemies, perceived threats from Others, religious attachments, regional loyalties, and so forth, then they are less likely to unite in the political arena.

To state the general point, if members of the lower strata adopt a set of beliefs that justifies and legitimizes the rewards received by the higher strata, then they are more likely to try to join the system rather than to beat it. In such beliefs, the elite have a powerful and relatively cheap tool with which to dampen opposition to their power and privileges. Moreover, these ideas increase the prestige of the elite. If people believe that inequality is the will of the gods, or that the activities of the elite benefit all, or that the elite became elite through intelligence and hard work, then the elite deserve the honor and respect of everyone else. (Not surprisingly, elites find it easy to believe such things about themselves.)

We call those ideas and beliefs that explain inequality as desirable or legitimate **ideologies**. The term *ideology* also has a broader meaning, often referring to any set of ideas held by a group—as in the phrases *leftist political ideology* and *feminist ideology*. Here we use the term in the narrow sense, to refer only to ideas that justify the status quo of inequality. Ideologies often are part of a people's world view (Chapter 2).

In many stratified societies, ideologies are based on religious world views. We are familiar with the notion of the "divine right of kings" from feudal Europe—certainly a handy supernatural mandate for kings and aristocracies! Similar notions are common in non-Western stratified societies. For instance, in Bunyoro, a kingdom in East Africa, the health and welfare of the ruler were mystically associated with the fertility and prosperity of the whole kingdom. Anything that threatened his life was believed to be a threat to everyone. In many ancient civilizations, such as the Aztec, the Inca, the Japanese, and the Egyptian, the ruler himself was believed to be a divine or semidivine being. In pre-twentieth-century China, the emperor had the "Mandate of Heaven," meaning that Heaven itself had granted him secular authority over the vast Chinese Empire for as long as he ruled it wisely and humanely. In traditional India, as we have seen, Hindu beliefs about reincarnation and pollution were so intertwined with the caste system that they both explained and legitimized its inequities.

The preceding examples illustrate a few ways religion serves ideological functions. In stratified societies, religion commonly gives the elite a supernatural mandate, provides them with the supernatural means to punish people, and gives them ritual functions to perform that are believed to benefit the whole population.

American Secular Ideologies

Do similar kinds of religious ideologies exist in modern industrial societies, some of which are as highly stratified as any preindustrial society?

Some people who are critical of the impacts of the Judeo-Christian heritage of the West believe this religious tradition supports greed and accumulation. In fact, however, many New Testament passages warn Christians about the accumulation of wealth. The best known are the story of the rich man and Lazarus (Luke 16:19–31) and the passages about the rich man who came to Jesus seeking salvation (told in Matthew 19:21–24, Mark 10:21–25, and Luke 18:22–25). Lesser-known scriptures say the poor are blessed and the rich are oppressors (Luke 6:20–24, James 2:2–6, and James 5:1–6). Two passages in Acts (2:44–45 and 4:32–37) seem to instruct Christians to hold their possessions in common, which not only does not support wealth accumulation but is a rather anticapitalist teaching.

Furthermore, most citizens do not believe that the richest Americans have a supernatural mandate for their wealth. The wealthiest families do not justify their income and ownership of property and financial assets by invoking religious authority or divine will. Religion is not generally used to justify the wealth and power of particular individuals and families. At most, some wealthy claim to be "blessed," but most take credit for their own success or admit that they are "lucky."

Finally, Judeo-Christian teachings historically have been and still are used to support social and political movements that seek to correct inequalities that are believed to be unjust. The nineteenth-century antislavery movement is one example. More recent examples include the civil rights and liberation theology movements. A variety of churches and denominations are resolutely against the Establishment in their beliefs. In the political realm, certainly many officeholders attend church and find ways to work their religious faith into their speeches to certain audiences. But few gain politically by claiming they are God's chosen officials. Even

---

ideologies Ideas and beliefs that legitimize and reinforce inequalities in stratified societies.

suspicion that a politician thinks he or she is carrying out divine will is a political liability (although some citizens will believe it, depending on whether they agree with his or her policies).

In brief, with regard to the issue of who has what and why, most Americans, and Westerners generally, are *secularists:* they explain the unequal distribution of rewards by events here on earth, not by the will of heaven.

Ideologies do not have to be based on religion, however. There are only two essential features of ideologies:

1. They justify (legitimize) inequality by affecting people's consciousness, not by threatening or using physical coercion.
2. They are believable to large numbers of people, based on existing cultural knowledge.

In the first condition, *consciousness* refers to cultural attitudes, values, worldviews, and so forth. In the second condition, *believable* means that effective ideologies match people's general ideas about how their society works. Ideologies must make sense in terms of existing cultural knowledge, or they will be ineffective. **Secular ideologies** as well as religious ideologies can have both features.

Many social scientists argue that secular ideologies take two forms in the modern United States. One is that the whole nation benefits from inequality. Because a few people are very wealthy, many citizens believe that the middle and lower classes are better off than they would be if wealth were distributed more equally. After all, the chance to get rich motivates people to do their best, and we all win when our fellow citizens perform up to their potential. Besides, the accumulation and investment of wealth are necessary to create jobs from which poor and middle-class people benefit. The most familiar recent example of this notion are justifications for tax cuts for wealthy people (note that a tax cut has the same effect as increasing income). If wealthier people are made even wealthier, the argument (or ideology?) goes, they will invest their extra income in expanding businesses, thus creating jobs that eventually trickle down to everyone. Putting more resources into the hands of the rich will "grow the economy," thus benefiting everyone, according to this economic theory (or ideology?).

A second secular ideology is that the elite earn their rewards through their own merit and efforts. They are smarter, more ambitious, hardworking, willing to take risks, and so forth. In short, the elite have personal qualities that account for their success. This is, of course, accurate for some members of the elite. Those who inherited their wealth or were lucky enough to buy the right stock at the right time or get into (and/or out of) the right housing market early enough, however, receive the same rewards as those who earned their rewards by performing actual work.

To the extent that they are widely believed, these two ideas fit with Americans' other beliefs about the way people are and how their society works. They are compatible with widespread beliefs about human motivation—people are basically selfish and need strong incentives before they will make the effort to get a good education and have a responsible career. Such ideologies also fit with many American values such as individual freedom, progress, the work ethic, and private ownership of property.

Of course, many Americans do not believe these two ideas. (If you do not believe them, then they are not effective ideologies for you.) Others believe these ideas are an accurate portrayal of how the whole nation benefits from economic inequality. (If you fall into this camp, you will think these ideas are objectively true, rather than merely ideologies.) Your personal opinion depends on your class, upbringing, ideas about human nature, political views, and so forth. Can a comparative perspective shed any light on the issue of whether stratification benefits society at large, or mainly members of the elite class themselves? To answer this question, we look at the major theories of inequality.

Theories of Inequality

Sociologists and anthropologists distinguish two theories to analyze stratification. One holds that a high degree of inequality in the distribution of rewards is necessary, morally justified, and beneficial to all members of society. This view is called the **functional theory of inequality**.

A contrary view holds that a high degree of inequality not only is unjust or even immoral but also robs the whole society of the benefits of much of its potential talent, which lies undeveloped in many of those at the bottom of the socioeconomic ladder. This view is

---

secular ideology Ideologies that justify inequality on the basis of its society-wide benefits rather than religious teachings, beliefs, and values.

functional theory of inequality Theory holding that stratification is a way to reward individuals who contribute most to society's well-being.

American candidates for high office must profess their religious faith to go far, as Rick Santorum, Mitt Romney, and Newt Gingrich did in the 2012 Republican primary elections. However, candidates who claim to be divinely chosen usually lose also.

known as the **conflict theory of inequality**. It holds that a high level of inequality offers few benefits to anyone except the elite and, indeed, is harmful to the whole society because of the conflicts it creates and the lack of equal opportunities it entails.

Functionalist Theory

The functionalist theory holds that inequality is necessary for a stratified society to motivate its most talented and hard-working members to perform the most important roles. Some roles (including jobs) require more skill and training than others. In most cases, the more skill and training required for a job, the fewer the number of people qualified to do the job and the more valuable their abilities are to the whole group. Functionalists argue that unequal rewards are effective ways to recruit the most able individuals into the most socially valuable roles. Unless there are rewards for those with the talents most of us lack, they will have no incentive to put those talents to work in activities that benefit all of us.

Also, in the functionalist view, inequality is not only socially useful but also morally justified. If society as a whole is to enjoy the fruits of the labor of its small number of well-trained, talented, and hardworking individuals, it is only fair and right that it reward these individuals with material goods, respect, and control over public decision making.

The functionalist analysis of inequality makes sense. People who do the most valuable things often get great rewards. However, it is difficult to measure the *social* "value" of various activities, as the 2007 global financial crisis so clearly shows—from whatever value was added by the financial sector should be subtracted the

conflict theory of inequality Theory holding that stratification benefits mainly the upper stratum and is the cause of most social unrest and other conflicts in human societies.

CHAPTER 13   Social Inequality and Stratification

lost value of those who suffered from it. It is reasonable that rewards be proportionate to personal qualities like effort and skill, but the two are not always correlated nor can they be measured objectively.

Two other objections are possible within the framework of the functionalist theory itself. First, there is no reason to believe that the high degree of inequality that *actually exists* in stratified societies is necessary to ensure that those with the scarcest talents fill the most valuable roles. In industrialized nations, for example, how many dollars does it take to motivate a qualified individual to manage a major company? In the United States, chief executive officers (CEOs) of large corporations have enjoyed enormous increases in compensation packages: between 1978 and 2011, CEO compensation increased 725 percent, whereas the compensation of workers increased 5.7 percent (both figures are adjusted for inflation). In 2012, American CEOs earned 273 times the compensation paid to workers. This is part of a 40-year upward trend from the 1965 earnings ratio (20), the 1978 ratio (29), and the 1995 ratio (123). The highest CEO/worker income ratio was in 2000, at 383!

CEOs in 2011 earned over 7 times more than CEOs earned in 1978. Were the top executives of American companies responsible for a sevenfold increase in productivity and profits between 1978 and 2011? How did they get so much better in 33 years? In 2011, an average worker worked 231 days to earn what a CEO earned in one day. On any given day, is a CEO 231 times more valuable to the company than an ordinary worker? Would companies be managed just as well if their CEOs made only 50 times what their workers made?

Speaking more generally of elites, is there an actual relationship between the compensation (rewards) of elites and their contributions to their groups or to the nation as a whole? Obviously, there is no way to measure this relationship. Compensation is mostly set by markets, but markets respond to supply and demand, not to the "value" that some activity or role has for society at large.

For these reasons, one objection to the functionalist theory is that no one knows how much inequality is needed to motivate people. Nor does anyone know how to calculate the benefits that elites actually offer to their group or to society at large. In brief, there is no reason to think that the *high degree* of inequality that actually exists in some stratified society is necessary for the nation to enjoy the benefits of *some degree* of inequality. Is there any reason to think that the United States as a nation would be worse off if the wealthiest 20 percent owned only 49 percent of the wealth rather than 89 percent?

Second, functionalists assume the system of stratification *effectively* places qualified individuals in important roles. It is a large assumption, however, that those who are best able to perform the most important roles are those who are usually recruited for them. In all systems of stratification, there is a powerful element of inheritance of wealth, prestige, and power. Even assuming that most members of elite classes of the present day actually earned their rewards, many will pass their resources along to their heirs. Sons and daughters, nieces and nephews, and the like may or may not be talented, hardworking, and meritorious. Even if elite families do not transmit wealth to their children, the latter still have a head start in life from the extra help they get in education, job prospects, contacts through social networks, and other privileges. Certainly, children born to poor families can and do succeed, but they must overcome more obstacles than those born to privilege. If every generation were born with nearly equal access to the means to succeed in life, we could be more confident that those who occupy the most important roles are those who are best qualified to fill them. What have the children of the wealthiest Americans done to earn their inheritance? The functionalist theory that those who receive the highest rewards are most deserving would be more plausible if the (metaphorical) playing field in which people compete were leveled.

Suppose there were some way to calculate the amount of inequality that is optimal for a given society. Suppose further that the society could devise some way of beginning each generation with everyone on an equal footing, with truly equal opportunities to compete. (This could be partly accomplished by steep inheritance taxes, which are often opposed by those who in other contexts—such as those who oppose the continuation of racial preferences in hiring—say they believe in equal opportunity for all.) Then the functionalist theory of inequality might apply. But no stratified society has ever achieved this condition, partly because these questions are unanswerable and partly because the wealthy and powerful would have to consent to such a change, and they have no incentive to do so.

Conflict Theory

The conflict theory agrees with the objections to functionalism just given. But it goes much further. Conflict theorists claim that stratification is based ultimately on control over productive resources, such as land, technology, information, and labor. Once elites gain control over these resources—by whatever means—they get other people to do work that benefits themselves. How this is organized varies among different kinds of economic systems. In ancient preindustrial states and some chiefdoms, the noble class controlled the land and other productive resources and the commoners had to provide tribute and labor to the nobility in return for the privilege of using it. In parts of feudal Europe, serfs were tied to their estate and ordinarily had strong rights over the land they worked, but each year they still had to contribute a certain number of days of work or a certain proportion of their harvest to their lord.

As for the capitalist economic system, Karl Marx—the nineteenth-century "father" of conflict theory—argued that capitalist societies include only two fundamental classes. Members of the capitalist class (or *bourgeoisie*) own the factories and tools. Members of the working class (or *proletariat*) have only one thing to sell on the market: their labor. To earn their living, workers must sell their labor to some capitalist. This seems like an equitable arrangement. The capitalists buy the labor they need to operate their factories, mines, and fields to sell goods and make profit. The workers get the jobs they need to support their families by selling their time and skills for a wage set by the market for labor (Chapter 8).

But, Marx noted, the goods the workers produce must be worth more on the market than the workers themselves receive in wages, or there would be no profit for the capitalists. The difference between the amount capitalists receive for the goods they sell and their costs (including the amount they pay their workers) is *profit.* In Marx's controversial view, profit is based on the exploitation of workers. The belief that workers receive a fair day's wage for a fair day's work is merely an ideology.

Critics of conflict theory say that conflict theorists are ideologues themselves, though of a different political persuasion. If one looks for "exploitation" in an economic relationship, one can usually find it. Critics of conflict theory claim that the value-laden term *exploitation* does not adequately characterize relationships between chiefs or kings and commoners, between lords and serfs, or between capitalists and workers. Conflict theorists play down the valuable services that elite classes perform, such as maintaining social control, organizing the society for the provision of public goods, and accumulating productive resources (capital) put aside to increase future production.

Conflict theorists are criticized for being ideologues themselves, though of a different political persuasion than functionalists. If one wants to find exploitation in Conflict theorists hold that stratification exists and persists because elite classes are able to exploit others. This woman is boxing up clothing for shipment. Is her employer therefore exploiting her, as Karl Marx claimed?

Many conflict theorists assume it is possible to organize a complex society without rewards as unequal as those that exist in real stratified societies. This is an unrealistic view of human nature, according to some critics of the approach. They say this is one reason "communism" has collapsed almost everywhere. Complex societies are always hierarchically organized, with centralized leadership. Many critics believe the functions of leaders, controllers, and organizers are so valuable to society at large that they deserve the rewards they receive. And who is to say what/how much/what kinds of rewards elites deserve?

Who Benefits?

Contrasting the two theories, we see that functionalism emphasizes the positive aspects of stratification, whereas conflict theory emphasizes the negative side. Functionalists say the class structure benefits society at large, including the less well-off, who would be even less well-off without inequality. Conflict theory points to the costs of stratification not just to those on the bottom of the social ladder but also to society at large. A country or other form of society loses the undeveloped potential of its underprivileged members. Societies also suffer the periodic violent conflicts (rebellions, revolutions) or the ongoing disorder (crimes, labor strikes, political dissent) that result from a high degree of inequality and inherited privilege.

Conflict theorists argue that many of the problems that have afflicted modern North America in the last couple of decades are caused (or at least made worse) by increasing inequality. Much resentment toward "the system" comes from people's sense that their lives will not get better or are getting worse. Unable to identify the causes of their frustrations, some white conservative groups find scapegoats in African Americans and Jews, immigrants, the United Nations, and all those South Asian, South American, and Chinese laborers who work for "peanuts." Unable to make a personally acceptable living in a socially acceptable manner, inner-city youths turn to drug dealing and other kinds of crime. Economic hardship contributes to family breakups. Poorer people need more social programs, funded by taxpayers, who watch stories in the media about people cheating the government and so elect representatives who provide *fewer* services—for the poor, at least. More generally, the sense of national unity and social responsibility is undermined by worsening inequality, according to conflict theorists.

Does anthropology's comparative perspective have anything to say about who benefits from inequality? In premodern stratified societies, elites did indeed perform some vital roles for the whole population, just as functionalists claim. For example, elites organized labor to construct and maintain public works projects, provided relief to regions struck by famine or hardship, promoted large-scale foreign trade, and raised a military force to provide for the defense of the political unit (see Chapter 12). Some kind of central authority is useful and may be necessary for such tasks to be coordinated effectively. Cooperation on a large scale, involving hundreds or thousands of people, requires organization. Organizing hundreds or thousands of people requires leaders and decision makers. Provided they make decisions they believe are in the public interest, decision makers deserve rewards.

On the other hand, elites took on some roles that probably were created to maintain their positions at the top of society. Ordinary people regarded the religious functions of elites or of the priests they supported as indispensable to the general welfare, but in fact the rituals did not bring rain, sustain the fertility of land and females, or assuage the anger of the gods. That elite classes in ancient civilizations regulated access to land, irrigation water, and other resources seems socially useful and even necessary, but it was partly because elites themselves controlled so many resources that other people's access to them had to be "regulated." Governmental elites provided some law and order that benefited everyone, but the elite's power, wealth, and internal political rivalries produced crimes and violent conflicts that otherwise would not have occurred.

From this comparative perspective, we can question whether some of the benefits provided by elites in industrialized nations mean they deserve the rewards they receive. Perhaps some of the benefits provided by elite classes exist only because society's institutions are organized in such a way that elites can be well compensated. (If there were no role called "attorney," how often would you need to pay for one?)

Who benefits from the inequality in stratified societies? Functionalists are probably correct in assuming that some degree of inequality is needed for motivation. Most people also agree that unequal rewards for unequal efforts and talents is a fair standard. However, we do not know how much inequality is necessary to provide incentives, much less whether some particular stratified society—including whichever one you are a citizen of—has approximately the right amount. We do know that power and privilege are partly or largely inherited, and, therefore, the current members of the upper class are not automatically more talented and diligent than everyone else. Looking at other stratified societies, we see that elites do provide some useful services for the population at large. But we also see that many widespread ideas about their functions are "just ideologies." It is easy to imagine that many of their "essential roles" are useful only under circumstances that previous elite classes had a hand in creating and that present elites use their privilege and power to perpetuate.

Most citizens in stratified societies would benefit from inequality, if only there were some way to find out what the optimum amount of inequality is for a particular society, if only there were some way to achieve this optimum initially, and if only there were some way to ensure that opportunities to succeed and achieve are equal for children born in varying circumstances. But, so far, no known human society has ever achieved this Utopia.

SUMMARY

1. **Explain *egalitarian, ranked, and stratified*.** The terms *egalitarian*, *ranked*, and *stratified* refer to societal differences in inequality in wealth, power, and prestige. Forager egalitarianism is explained by the frequent movements of camps, the ability of individuals to choose their band affiliation, the cultural value placed on sharing and the social pressure against making oneself stand out, and the difficulties of maintaining exclusive access to a territory. Many horticulturalists also are relatively egalitarian, as illustrated by the "big men" of Melanesia. In ranked societies such as Tikopia of Polynesia, there are a set number of honored positions (chiefs, titles) to which only a small number of people are eligible to succeed. Stratified societies, found in all ancient civilizations and states and all modern nations, have marked and enduring inequalities in access to all three kinds of rewards.

2. **Discuss the primary differences between castes and classes.** In caste systems, there is little or no mobility between castes, the castes are legally or normatively endogamous, and higher-caste persons consider those of the lowest castes to be unclean or polluting. Castes are best known from India, where they were intimately associated with the Hindu doctrines of reincarnation and pollution. Classes exist in all modern countries. In the United States, the best criterion of class membership is wealth. Studies conducted by scholars and by the federal government reveal differences in income and enormous disparities in the distribution of wealth.

3. **Describe how ideologies are important in maintaining inequalities in stratified societies.** How do the highly unequal distribution of rewards persist? Mobilization of armed force by the elite is an insufficient explanation. Cultural beliefs that inequality is inevitable, divinely ordained, or beneficial to society as a whole provide ideologies that justify and reinforce the power and privilege of elite classes. Among many peoples of the past and present, religious beliefs provided ideologies, as exemplified by most ancient civilizations and states. In modern countries, ideologies tend to be more secular, mainly because effective ideologies must be compatible with people's overall cultural ideas about how their society works. In the United States, secular ideologies include prevalent ideas about the society-wide benefits of inequality, about the fairness of unequal rewards for unequal talents and efforts, and about how the well-to-do achieved their wealth.

4. **Evaluate the functional and conflict theories of stratification.** Functionalist and conflict theories offer sharply contrasting ideas about

stratification. Functionalists hold that societies offer unequal rewards to those individuals who use their talents to perform the most socially valuable roles. Conflict theorists claim that inequality is based ultimately on control over productive resources. Comparisons suggest that although elites often do perform valuable services for society at large, many of their "functions" are illusory. Also, many benefits of stratification exist only because past elites have set up the structure of society so that elite "services" are necessary. Functionalists are correct that some degree of inequality in rewards is necessary to motivate individuals. However, there is no way of knowing whether a given society has the optimal amount. No society ever succeeded in establishing the equal opportunity required for the functionalist theory to be correct.

14 Religion and Worldview

The religion of a people includes their traditional ways of communicating and interacting with supernatural powers. These Buddhist monks are praying at a temple in Thailand.

Defining Religion
  Beliefs About Supernatural Powers
  Myths and Worldviews
  Rituals and Symbols

Theories of Religion
  Intellectual/Cognitive Approaches
  Psychological Approaches
  Sociological Approaches

Supernatural Explanations of Misfortune
  Sorcery
  Witchcraft
  Interpretations of Sorcery and Witchcraft

Varieties of Religious Organization
  Individualistic Organizations
  Shamanistic Organizations
  Communal Organizations
  Ecclesiastical Organizations

Revitalization Movements
  Melanesian Cargo Cults
  Native American Movements
  Fate of Revitalization Movements

LEARNING OBJECTIVES

After reading this chapter, you should be able to

1. **DESCRIBE** how anthropologists define and think about cultural diversity in religion and worldview.
2. **ANALYZE** the strengths and weaknesses of the three main anthropological theories of religion and worldview.
3. **ANALYZE** how witchcraft and sorcery might benefit individuals and groups.
4. **DISCUSS** how anthropologists classify the diversity of religions and worldviews into four major categories, and analyze the relationships between these categories and social life.
5. **DESCRIBE** revitalization movements, the conditions under which they are most likely to occur, and their fate.

All peoples have some form of religion. Religion is related to worldview (Chapter 2)—conceptions of reality that affect interpretations and perceptions of things and events and, therefore, how individuals act in patterned ways. Like other dimensions of culture, religion and worldview vary remarkably among the world's diverse peoples. In this chapter, we introduce this diversity. We begin with a description of some of the most important aspects of religion from a comparative perspective, using examples. Then we cover some of the main theories social scientists employ to understand religion. Next, we look at some of the major forms of religion that have most interested anthropologists. We conclude by discussing religious movements, which often occur when a people are undergoing rapid change and foreign domination.

Defining Religion

For anthropologists the major difficulty in defining religion is encompassing all the diverse religions of humanity. We cannot define religion simply as "belief in a god" or even as belief in "gods." Some peoples do not have any "deities" at all, but rather believe in other kinds of spiritual beings and powers that are not gods in the common sense of the word. A nineteenth-century definition that many scholars still use is E. B. Tylor's **animism**, or "belief in spiritual beings." Most modern conceptions follow Tylor's lead: all religions include beliefs that some kind of spiritual or supernatural powers exist. In expanding on Tylor's definition, we also present an overview of religious diversity.

Beliefs About Supernatural Powers

In Chapter 4, we described how nineteenth-century anthropologists proposed that religion had passed through evolutionary stages. Early, rudimentary forms of religion evolved into more complex forms. For Tylor, the three stages of religion were animism, polytheism, and monotheism. Monotheism occurs, he argued, in complex ("advanced," "evolved") societies. But, in fact, elements of animism exist even within religious traditions commonly considered monotheistic. Christianity, for example, has many kinds of spiritual beings such as saints, angels, Satan, and the souls of deceased and living humans.

Spiritual *beings* usually have qualities such as the ability to assume a bodily form, a personality with emotions, and a consciousness and will. Usually spiritual beings respond to human actions in some way: If you communicate with them (by chanting, music, prayer, and other ways of sending messages), they will listen. If your actions displease them, they will react negatively, later if not sooner. Some beings have human origins or are associated with living or deceased persons such as souls, ancestral ghosts, and important people who did such notable things that they became gods. There are numerous other kinds of beings: spirit helpers, nature spirits, demons, zoomorphic spirits, forest spirits, and so on. The characteristics people attribute to supernatural beings vary enormously: they can be unpredictable or consistent, irrational or reasonable, vengeful or forgiving, amoral or just.

In the religious traditions of Western civilization—Judaism, Christianity, and Islam—the supreme being is all-knowing and all-powerful, expects sacrifices or

---

animism Belief in spiritual beings.

worship, and pays attention to human behavior and morality. The gods that many other peoples believe in have none of these characteristics, however. They can be tricked and manipulated. Often, they are commanded more than worshipped. Sometimes people do not believe gods are concerned about the morality of human actions: They do not punish wrongdoing, in either this life or the next. There is no belief that *sin* (violation of a commandment or divine moral precept) even exists.

"Beings" are not the only kind of supernatural powers. The worldview of various peoples includes beliefs in powers that are more like mystical substances or forces than beings. For example, before becoming predominantly Christian, Polynesians believed in *mana*, a diffuse, incorporeal power that permeated certain people and things. Mana lent supernatural potency to objects, which explained unusual qualities such as why some fishing lures worked so well. The gods gave mana to certain people, which explained extraordinary success or why chiefs had the right to receive privileges and issue commands. Specific pieces of land were infused with mana, which explained why they produced such bountiful harvests.

In contrast to beings such as gods, supernatural *forces* or *substances* generally cannot take on a physical appearance and have no will of their own. Rather, they are known mainly by their effects: mana makes a chief successful; pollution sickens a woman or man. In many cultures, the beliefs about how powers work are indefinite: one performs a ritual and utters an incantation (spell), and the effect that the rite and spell are intended to cause simply happens. This is generally known as *magic*, discussed later in this chapter.

Myths and Worldviews

Beliefs about supernatural powers are not the only dimension of religion. Religion also includes **myths**—oral or written stories (narratives) about the actions and deeds of supernatural powers and cultural heroes. Sometimes, myths explain how the entire universe was created. They may recount how and why people, animals, plants, and natural features originated. Myths may explain how a people acquired their tools and customs and how they came to live where they do. They often tell why people should or should not act in certain ways, and what happened to someone in the past who did something people are forbidden to do. A people's mythology is often their major *teachings*—they learn their group's beliefs about creation, natural phenomena, customs, moral standards, social distinctions, and many other things.

North Americans mostly learn their mythology in formal settings: Myths are taught at church and, to a

In this depiction of a biblical myth, Eve offers forbidden fruit to Adam. Their original sin explains the origin of evil in the Judeo-Christian worldview.

lesser extent, at home. (Here we need to emphasize that calling the Bible, Koran, Torah, and other religious texts *myths* is not intended to imply that they are false.) In many societies, however, there are no formal worship services. Elders recount myths informally, sometimes in moments of leisure. Myths are repeated regularly on days set aside for religious performances. They are sung or chanted while one is doing daily tasks. The fact that myths sometimes are recounted rather casually does not mean that their importance in a people's way of life is negligible. A people's worldview—and therefore their behavior—is affected by their myths.

A people's myths are more than stories they tell after dark, recite on appropriate occasions, or instruct and perhaps scare children. Mythologies do more than satisfy curiosity and help pass the time. They help to form a people's worldview—their conceptions of reality and

myths Stories that recount the deeds of supernatural powers and cultural heroes in the past.

CHAPTER 14 Religion and Worldview 317

In Japan, *torii* mark off shrines used for Shinto religious ceremonies like offerings and prayers from ordinary, secular spaces. This huge torii rests in the bay at Miyajima and is now a favorite tourist destination.

the interpretations of events that happen in society and the natural world. Worldview and myths affect people's beliefs about how they ought to relate to the world and to one another (see Chapter 2), and therefore they affect how people behave in their everyday lives.

Rituals and Symbols

People everywhere believe that gods, ghosts, demons, ancestral spirits, and other supernatural beings take an active interest in worldly affairs, particularly in the lives of human beings. You can ask them for blessings or aid through prayer. Sometimes you can command them to do things for you or for other people. Human behavior can control or influence powers. In the context of religion, the organized performance of behaviors intended to influence spiritual powers is **ritual**. By definition, rituals have certain properties.

> **ritual** Organized, stereotyped, symbolic behaviors intended to influence supernatural powers.

Rituals are *stereotyped:* definite patterns of speech or movement, or definite sequences of events, occur in much the same way in performance after performance. In general, people performing rituals want supernatural powers to do things on their behalf. For example, some central Canadian Inuit believe that their hunts for sea mammals fail because an undersea goddess is angry about the people's misconduct. They persuade the goddess to release the game by performing a ritual in which camp members publicly confess their violations.

Rituals the world over have *symbolic* aspects. These symbolic aspects are so important that some anthropologists define ritual itself as *symbolic behavior.* For example, rituals often occur in *places* that have symbolic significance to the performers. They may be held where some mythological event occurred or where the women who founded a matrilineage were born. Muslims are supposed to make pilgrimages to the holy city of Mecca at least once in their lifetime. Millions of Hindus journey to the city of Varanasi to pray and bathe in Ganga Ma (Mother Ganges). To die and be cremated in Varanasi and have your ashes mix with the river can help you achieve *moksa*, spiritual liberation. Buddhists may go to the site of the Bodhi Tree, where 2,500 years ago Siddhartha's meditation led to his enlightenment and transformation into the Buddha. In Shinto, the ancient indigenous religion of Japan, shrines at which people pray to spirits and to their ancestors are set apart from other spaces by a torii, an arch supported by two pillars.

There are other ritual symbols. Rituals often involve the display, touching, and manipulation of *objects* that symbolize an event (e.g., the cross), a holy person (statues of Jesus and Mary), a relationship (wedding rings, the symbol of holy matrimony), and a variety of other things. Water among many peoples serves as more than drink: bathing in certain rivers or purifying oneself by ritual washing is common among the world's peoples. Buddhist and Hindu temples are filled with statues and relics. The *language* and *behavior* of ritual carry deep symbolic meanings, as in the Christian rituals of worship, hymn singing, prayer, baptism, and communion.

Anthropologists often classify rituals on two bases. The first basis is their *conscious purposes*—the reasons people themselves give for performing rituals. For example, some people believe that divination rituals allow them to acquire information from a supernatural power about some past event, such as illness, or to foretell the future. Familiar examples include tarot cards, crystal balls, and palm reading. There are curing, sorcery, sacrificial, and exorcism rituals. There are rituals to renew the world, to make a man out of a boy and a woman out of a girl, to make people and nature fertile, to bring blessings from deceased ancestors, and to free the soul from a dead person's body.

Many peoples use rituals to control the weather. The Hopi (discussed in Chapter 9) believe the rainfall that replenishes springs and streams and nourishes crops is brought by supernatural beings. These beings, called *kachinas*, live in the peaks of mountains to the west of Hopi villages. They bring life-giving rain to the Hopi cornfields when they come in the form of clouds. In the spring and summer, the Hopi believe, kachinas dwell in the villages. During this period, men wearing masks of the kachinas perform ritual dances, impersonating and honoring the spirits. The spirit enters the body of the dancer, who thus becomes the kachina. The dances bring rain to the Hopi cornfields.

The second basis of classifying rituals is their *timing*—on a regular schedule (like weekly worship services or annual religious holidays) or simply whenever some individual or group wants or needs them (like funerals or prayers for a sick person). If rituals are held regularly (seasonally, annually, daily, monthly), they are called *calendrical rituals*. The Hopi, Zuni, and other Pueblo peoples follow a

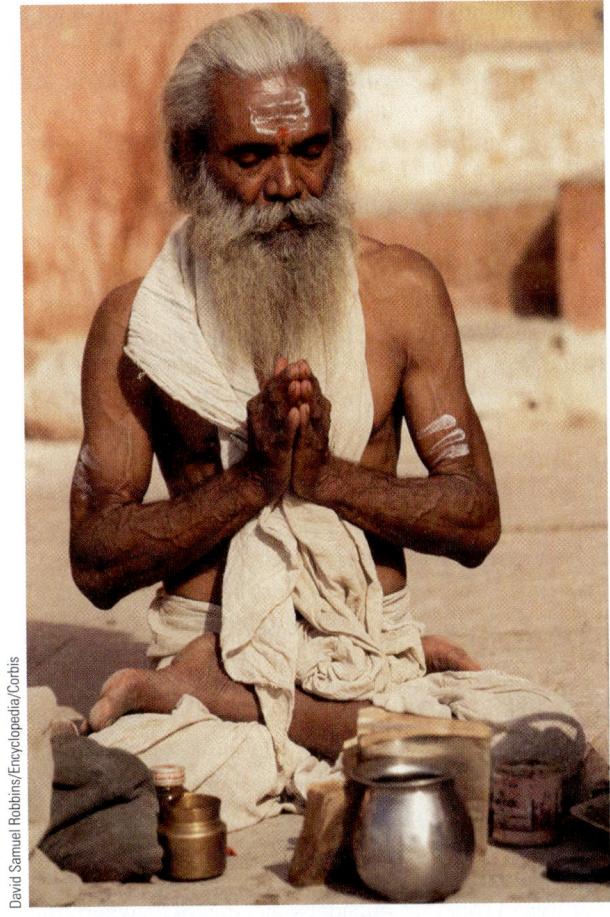

As this Hindu religious pilgrim praying in Varanasi, India, illustrates, rituals include symbolic behavior and objects.

ritual calendar in which certain rituals are performed by certain groups at the same time every year, in the same sequence. The same cycle is repeated the following year.

In contrast, *crisis rituals* are performed whenever some individual or group needs, wants, or asks for them—for purposes of curing, ensuring good hunting or fishing, burying or honoring the dead, or accompanying other events that happen sporadically or unpredictably. The supernatural curing practiced by shamans, described later, is the most widespread type of crisis ritual.

With this brief and broad overview of religion in mind, we consider some of the major theoretical orientations offered to understand or explain religion.

Theories of Religion

Why do all cultures have religious beliefs, myths, and rituals? With regard to beliefs, people cannot actually prove the existence of supernatural powers such as ghosts, gods, demons, angels, souls, mana, and so forth. Although people who follow a particular religion may believe that traditional accounts of their past reflect historical events, outsiders to the religion are more likely to consider at least parts of them entirely mythical. Indeed, some people who do not share the beliefs of a given culture think such beliefs result from ignorance or superstition.

As for rituals, people who are outsiders to a religion and worldview are unlikely to believe that rituals are effective. To nonbelievers, most rituals seem like a waste of time and resources. For example, when a Trobriand Islander plants a yam garden, he does some things that "work" in the way he thinks they do: He clears the land, removes the weeds, and so forth, just as anyone should for success. But a Trobriander also does other things to grow yams and other crops—things that outsiders consider unnecessary and perhaps even wasteful. He hires a magician to perform rites and spells to improve his yam harvest. Outsiders (nonbelievers) to Trobriand beliefs understand what the gardener gets out of the first kind of activity: a yam harvest, if nature cooperates. But what does he get out of the magic rites and spells? How did Trobrianders come to believe that magical rites are needed? And why continue to practice them, even when actual experience must often demonstrate that the magic doesn't work.

We can look at this behavior in another way to see a main problem in understanding the rituals of Other cultures. From an outsider's perspective, when the Trobriander plants a crop and weeds his garden, his actions are effective in attaining the goal he has in mind—they work in more or less the way he thinks they do. But when the garden magician performs rites and spells, his actions do not achieve the result he has in mind. The magic does not "really work." How, then, did the Trobrianders get the idea that they do and why keep doing the magic? (Of course, we could answer,: "Because that is all they know," but that implies they are bound by their beliefs, in which case nothing would ever change.)

Speaking broadly, to those who do not share the particular religion's beliefs, rituals do not have the effects performers intend. The crazy woman is not "truly" restored to sanity by exorcizing the demon; no spirits "really" enter the body of the medicine man; there were no "genuine" witches in Salem, Massachusetts, in 1692. Why, then, do so many people believe in the power of ritual?

intellectual (or **cognitive**) **approach** Notion that religious beliefs provide explanations for puzzling things and events.

Some people who consider themselves sophisticated say that religious beliefs and rituals are rooted in ignorance and superstition. All anthropologists reject (or should reject) this nonanswer to the question, Why religion? Its ethnocentrism is apparent: Superstition is something that someone else believes in but you do not. Many of our own beliefs seem superstitious to others, and undoubtedly many of the accepted truths of the twenty-first century will be considered superstitions by the twenty-second century. Even if we think such beliefs and practices are superstitious, we still have not explained them. Why does one form of superstition develop in one place and another form in another place?

You already have thought of possible answers. If rituals do not have the effects people intend—if weather magic does not affect the real weather, for example—they may have other effects that people find useful or satisfying. If the conscious reasons people give for performing rituals seem inadequate, perhaps their meaning is entirely symbolic: they convey and reinforce deep meanings and values that help people cope with life or that tie people together. As for myths, if they are not accurate historical accounts, perhaps they are symbolic statements that help people make sense of reality and give meaning to real-world things and events. Maybe religious truths are a different kind of truth than scientific truths: They cannot be subjected to tests and experiments to see whether they work the way people think they do, but they nonetheless work on another level.

Social scientists have proposed many theories for why religion exists. Some theories hold that beliefs, myths, and rituals provide benefits that people want or need but cannot acquire without religion. Broadly, social scientists have proposed three types of theories: the intellectual (or cognitive), the psychological, and the sociological.

Intellectual/Cognitive Approaches

Those who posit the **intellectual** (or **cognitive**) **approach** assume that humans seek explanations for the world around them. Religious beliefs help satisfy the human desire to understand and explain things and events. Without religion, much of the world would be incomprehensible and inexplicable, which (these scholars argue) would be intolerable to the mind of a conscious, reasoning, problem-solving species like *Homo sapiens*. For example, religion satisfies the human demand for understanding by providing explanations for the movements of the sun, moon, and stars. *Origin myths* explain things like the creation of the sky, land, and water; where animals and plants come from; and where people got their language, tools, rituals, and other customs and beliefs. The essential purpose of religion, in the intellectual view, is to provide people with explanations.

Sir James Frazer was an influential scholar who championed the intellectual approach. His most famous work was *The Golden Bough,* published in 12 volumes at around the turn of the twentieth century. One of Frazer's main interests was the development of rational thought. He argued that human thinking progressed through three stages that he called magic, religion, and science. The earliest cultures practiced *magic;* they attempted to control the world by performing rites and spells. Later cultures came to believe in the existence of supernatural beings, who demanded that people worship them or make sacrifices to them, giving birth to *religion.* Finally, people realized that neither magical techniques nor worship of imaginary beings enabled them to explain or control events. With the advent of *science,* the errors of magic and religion were replaced with knowledge of true cause-and-effect relationships. In Frazer's view, magic, religion, and science are alternative worldviews: Each provides people with an intellectual model of the way the world works and a means to manipulate events and people. Because science is a superior system of knowledge, Frazer thought it was replacing magical and religious beliefs.

The idea of Frazer and others that religious beliefs provide people with explanations for things and events is correct, as far as it goes, but it surely is an incomplete explanation for religion. Religion does satisfy curiosity about the world, but this is not its only function. The people whom Frazer called "savages" possess and use practical knowledge just as "civilized" peoples do—a Trobriander knows that he must care for his yams as well as perform garden magic. Conversely, many "scientific" people believe in and practice religion—including many persons who make their living practicing the science for which religion supposedly substitutes! Those scientists who go to church apparently find little or no contradiction between their religious beliefs and worship and their scientific knowledge and practice. Religious beliefs do not simply substitute for objective knowledge. People don't "have" religion because they "lack" science. Somehow, the two are complementary.

Although few scholars today hold that religion exists solely or even mainly to provide "prescientific" people with explanations their culture would otherwise lack, the intellectual approach is by no means passé. Clifford Geertz, a leading humanistic theorist (see Chapter 5), argued that religion provides its believers with the assurance that the world is *meaningful*—that events have a place in the grand scheme of things, natural phenomena have understandable causes, suffering and evil happen to good people for some good reason, wrongs will be righted and injustices corrected. Cultural beings (i.e., humans) cannot tolerate events that contradict the basic premises, categories, and worldview of their cultural tradition. Yet such events do occur periodically. Because of religion, people are able to maintain their worldview in spite of events that seem to contradict it. Religion, Geertz believed, reassures believers that the world is orderly rather than chaotic, all within the framework of their existing cultural knowledge.

Stewart Guthrie also views religion in cognitive terms. Guthrie thinks the essence of religion is the belief that natural phenomena have humanlike properties. He points out that people tend to see the world *anthropomorphically:* We tend to attribute human motives, purposes, feelings, senses, and other characteristics to living and nonliving things that are not human. For example, thunder is the voice of the gods, clouds are the spirits of our ancestors, the sun is our life-giving father, Mother Earth is alive, the wind is the breath of a god. Anthropomorphism is natural to human thought, and most of us regularly think or react in this way, as when you think your computer hates you, you swear at your car, or you interact with your pet as if it were a person.

When we see the world as "peopled" with spirits (as in animism), or think that different gods control various aspects of nature (as in polytheism), or believe that one god created and controls everything (as in monotheism), we are attributing human characteristics to the natural world. In Guthrie's view, this actually is a smart thing to do. If you think there are no humanlike beings making things happen and you are wrong, then the consequences are costly. If the earth is in fact our mother, but we mistreat her and her children, then she might punish us. But if we think anthropomorphically about the earth and take steps to worship and protect her, then no harm is done. If there is a war god, and our enemy sacrifices to him but we do not, we may all be killed, so why take the chance? As Guthrie phrases it, religion is then a "good bet."

However, not all rituals that result from beliefs that humanlike beings control natural processes are "harmless." In fact, many rituals are quite costly. They require sacrifices to deities or ancestors, and they consume time and energy that could be used in other ways. In some societies, religious beliefs are costly indeed. In some ancient Mesoamerican civilizations, priests pierced their bodies with thorns to make themselves bleed because they believed the gods demanded blood sacrifices. Humans were also sacrificed. Attributing human properties to nonhuman entities is not always harmless: religion often helps motivate individuals and groups of individuals to do horrific things to others—and sometimes to themselves.

Psychological approaches hold that religion helps individuals and groups cope with crisis, uncertainty, grief, stress, trauma, and other emotional distress. This Iraqi woman cries at a funeral.

Psychological Approaches

The notion that religion helps people cope with times of trouble, stress, and anxiety is a common one. Sicknesses, accidents, misfortunes, injustices, deaths, and other trials and tribulations of life can be better handled emotionally if one believes there is a reason and meaning to them or that one's troubles can be controlled or alleviated by means of ritual. Scholars who make such arguments follow the **psychological approach**.

In anthropology, a well-known psychological theory of religion was proposed by Bronislaw Malinowski, whom we introduced in Chapter 5. Malinowski thought that religion (including magic) serves the valuable function of giving people confidence when they are likely to be unsuccessful despite their best efforts. There are always natural phenomena that people cannot control and that constantly threaten to ruin their plans and efforts. Belief in the power of ritual to control these (otherwise uncontrollable) elements instills confidence and removes some of the anxiety that results from the uncertainties of life. Not only do rituals relieve our worries, but they may also help us be more successful in activities by making us more confident of success.

People grow frustrated—and occasionally violent—when they cannot control what happens to them or those they care about. Our lives are filled with uncertainties and unknowable futures. Our families and friends don't always do what we want or what we think is right for them. Accidents happen. Stock markets fall. Housing prices collapse. Our relatives pass away. Bosses fire us. Crops fail. Professors fail us. We fail ourselves. Religion (and in this context, especially "faith" in a power with more knowledge and power than humans have) is there to offer hope and comfort. Often, it helps us cope with frustrated hopes by telling us what we can do to make things better. For example, during

> **psychological approach** Idea that the emotional or affective satisfactions people gain from religion are primary in interpreting religion.

a 2007 drought in Georgia, people got together to pray for rain. It did rain later.

Another specific psychological theory of religion holds that, as self-conscious beings, we humans are aware of our own mortality. Knowing that we will eventually die causes us great anxiety and leads us to worry about our own death. Experiencing the serious illness or death of a parent or other relative likewise produces grief and psychological stress for most people. We must have some way of coping emotionally with the grief over the death of our loved ones, and with the anxiety caused by the knowledge of our own mortality. Religion helps us cope by denying the finality of death and by leading us to believe in a pleasant afterlife, in which our souls are immortal.

The notion that belief in life after death helps to calm our fears and alleviate our anxieties seems reasonable. This theory is tainted by an ethnocentric assumption, however: although nearly all religions include beliefs about some kind of afterlife, in a great many cultures, that afterlife is far from pleasant. The Dobu people of Melanesia believe that human bodies also have a ghostly form, experienced in the real world as a shadow or a reflection. During life, the ghostly self goes out at night and appears in the dreams of other people. Once the corpse rots after death, the ghosts of people go to a place called the Hill of the Dead, where they have a "thin and shadowy" existence and mourn for their homeland. How are such beliefs about the afterlife "comforting"?

Certainly, religion is psychologically useful. For some people some of the time, it relieves anxieties, calms fears, and helps them cope emotionally with life's uncertainties and hardships. That religion often serves such functions is indisputable. Yet, sometimes religious beliefs actually increase our anxieties, fears, and stress levels. Consider the Kwaio, a people of the Solomon Islands. Kwaio believe that women are polluting to men, so Kwaio wives are expected to take elaborate precautions to avoid polluting their husbands when preparing food for them. If a man dies of an illness, his wife may be blamed, and perhaps killed, for her "offense." Just whose anxieties and fears are relieved by this belief?

The general point of the Dobu and Kwaio examples is that, from a psychological perspective, religion has two faces. On the one hand, it does—for some people, some of the time, in some respects—help us cope emotionally with times of trouble and hardships. On the other hand, beliefs about supernatural powers and what they do often create fears and anxieties that would not otherwise exist. Pleasant afterlives ("Heaven") offer us comfort and hope. But what *psychological* benefit does the threat of eternal damnation ("Hell") offer? This question leads logically to the sociological approach.

Sociological Approaches

"Societies need religion to keep people in line," you may have heard people say. The idea of this **sociological approach** is that religion instills and maintains common values, leads to increased conformity to cultural norms, promotes cohesion and cooperation, promises eternal rewards for good deeds and eternal damnation for evil acts, and so forth. Those who champion the sociological approach hold that religion exists because of the useful effects it has on human societies—because of its *social functions*. Religion helps societies maintain harmonious social relationships between individuals and groups. It encourages people to respect the rights of others and to perform their proper duties. It is part of the socialization process that instills deeply held values in children.

Consider the Ten Commandments, for example, which serve as a moral code for the three major religions of the West. Two prescribe how people ought to feel and act toward God and other people, and eight give rules for actions, including the five "thou shalt nots" (see Exodus 20:3–17). Note that five of the divinely ordered prohibitions are against the commission of acts that could result in harm to others, such as killing and stealing. God gave us commandments that will, if obeyed, lead to good relationships with others and therefore promote earthly social order. More general Judeo-Christian moral guidelines are the Golden Rule ("Do unto others as you would have them do unto you") and love of one's neighbor (Matthew 19:19); both are useful prescriptions for harmonious social life.

Religion also enhances the cohesion of society by making people sense their interdependence on one another and on their traditions. Emile Durkheim, a French sociologist of the early twentieth century, was influential in formulating this perspective. Durkheim's view was that the main function of religion in human society is to promote *social solidarity,* meaning that religion has the effect of bringing people together and enhancing their sense of unity, cohesion, and reliance on their society's customs. Groups of people who share the same beliefs and who gather periodically to perform common rituals experience a feeling of oneness and harmony.

sociological approach Emphasizes effects of religion on maintaining the institutions of society as a whole by instilling common values, creating solidarity, controlling behavior, and so forth.

This crowd is gathered for a ritual in Irian Jaya, Indonesia. French sociologist Emile Durkheim proposed that rituals involve gatherings and common activities that enhance social solidarity among a group of people.

The most important social function of religion, Durkheim believed, is to strengthen social solidarity. There also are other versions of the sociological approach. One is that religion helps to maintain social order (that is, religion serves as a social control mechanism—see Chapters 12 and 13) by increasing conformity to norms, inculcating shared values in children, reminding people to act responsibly, teaching moral lessons through myths and doctrines, legitimizing the existing social structure, and so forth.

One mechanism by which religion maintains social control is by offering rewards for good behavior and punishments for antisocial behavior. When people have an accident or get sick, they may think they are being punished for some crime or deviant action, for example. This deters the individual from future deviance and also serves as an example to others, teaching them to act properly in the future. In the afterlife, gods may reward virtue and punish sinful behavior. Such socially useful effects of religion are widespread.

Not all peoples have such beliefs, however. In some worldviews, gods and other kinds of spiritual beings have little or no interest in the morality or immorality of human actions. There is no concept of "sin" as behavior that violates a doctrine or divine will, and the fate of a person in this life or in the afterlife is not related to her or his moral character or conduct.

Like the cognitive and psychological approaches, the sociological theory applies in some cases but not in others. At some times, in some places, and in some contexts, religion teaches the difference between right and wrong and thus encourages social harmony. It strengthens solidarity by bringing people together. It inculcates the belief that good behavior is rewarded and bad behavior is punished eventually, if not immediately.

But also, sometimes religion has effects that few people believe are socially useful. It has contributed to wars and led to persecutions. It can help unite the members of one country, or of one faith, yet promote wars between them and other countries or other faiths. It is a source of disunity as well as unity within many societies, in the past as well as present. It often contributes to ethnocentrism, racism, intolerance of people who believe differently, gender discrimination, and other socially harmful attitudes and practices. In stratified societies, its beliefs have supported vast social differences in powers and privileges (Chapter 13). Occasionally, as among the ancient Mayans and Aztecs, it has led people to sacrifice blood from their own bodies by piercing with thorns and has led priests to drag war captives to temples where their hearts are offered as sacrifices to the gods. When used as ideologies, religious beliefs may support all kinds of inequalities and injustices. There may be some respects in which such impacts are "socially useful," but clearly they are not useful to *everyone*.

Supernatural Explanations of Misfortune

One occurrence that many peoples attribute to the action of spiritual powers is personal misfortune, including death, illness, and events that many Westerners consider accidents. Many beliefs and rituals of various societies are concerned with explaining, preventing, and curing illness and disease.

Cross-culturally, two major complexes of beliefs about misfortune are common. First, many peoples believe that sickness or other unfortunate occurrences are caused by the action of spiritual powers. The violation of a taboo can lead to sickness. The ancestral spirits of kin groups cause their members to become ill because of conflict or bad feelings within the group. Similar beliefs often apply to accidents that many Westerners attribute to bad luck or carelessness. Drownings, falls, snakebites, prolonged failure to succeed at some activity—such events are evidence of unfavorable supernatural intervention. The victim has offended a god or spirit, who brings an "accident" as punishment.

Second, many people think illnesses or other misfortunes are caused by the action of some evil human using special supernatural powers against the afflicted person. The belief that certain people, called *sorcerers* and *witches*, have powers to harm others by mystical means is enormously widespread among humanity. Sometimes, witches and sorcerers are thought to strike randomly and maliciously against people who are innocent of any wrongdoing. More commonly, they direct their evil magic or thoughts toward those against whom they have a grudge. Because they are so puzzling and common among humanity, sorcery and witchcraft are worth considering in more detail.

Sorcery

Sorcery is the performance of rites and spells intended to cause supernatural harm to others; that is, sorcery is a form of evil magic. In some cultures, almost everyone learns to harm their enemies by sorcery techniques. Among such peoples knowledge of sorcery rites and spells is widespread. In other cultures, sorcery is a more specialized practice; only certain people inherit or acquire the knowledge of how to recite spells and perform the rites correctly.

In 1890, Sir James Frazer proposed that magic (including sorcery) is based on two kinds of logical principles or assumptions. Both involve a symbolic identification of something (e.g., an object or action) with something else (e.g., an event or a person).

The *imitative principle* is often stated as "Like produces like." That is, if an object resembles a person and the sorcerer mutilates the object, then the same thing will happen to the person. The so-called voodoo doll is a familiar example. In another kind of imitative magic, the magician or sorcerer mimics the effects she or he wants to produce. For example, sorcerers among the Dobu of Melanesia cast spells by imitating the symptoms of the disease they want their victims to suffer.

The second logical premise underlying magic and sorcery is the *contagious principle,* stated as "Power comes from contact." That is, things once in contact with someone can be used in rites and spells to make things happen to that person. By performing sorcery rites and spells on such objects as hair clippings, bodily excretions, nail parings, umbilical cords, or jewelry and clothing, one can cause harm to one's enemies. In societies in which sorcery rests on the contagious principle, people must dispose of objects they have been in contact with, including things have come out of or off of their bodies, lest one of their enemies use them for sorcery.

Sorcery practices are related to the social life of a people. For example, who accuses whom of sorcery reflects how individuals and groups relate to one another. In any society, certain kinds of social relationships are especially likely to be beset by conflict. Co-wives of a polygynous man may be jealous over their husband's favors or may compete for an inheritance for their children. People who have married into a kin group or village may be viewed as outsiders who are still loyal to their own natal families. Two men who want the same woman, or two women who want the same man, have reasons to dislike each other. Men who are rivals for a political office have conflicts of interest.

These and other kinds of relationships are sources of tension and conflict within a human group. Which relationships are likely to cause tensions and conflicts depend on the way the society is organized: brothers-in-law are allies in one society, but their interests regularly conflict in another society, for instance. The relationships most

sorcery Performance of rites and spells for the purpose of causing harm to others by supernatural means.

likely to be tense are *patterned*, meaning that individuals who have these relationships with one another are most likely to experience conflicts.

Suppose you were brought up among a people who explained illness or accident by sorcery. If you became ill or suffered misfortune, you would not suspect just anyone of causing harm. You would ask, Who has a motive to perform evil magic against me? Who envies me? Who would profit from my sickness or death? With whom have I recently quarreled? These people are your prime suspects, and they are the ones you or your family is most likely to accuse.

Members of most cultures reason in much the same way. They believe sorcerers do not strike randomly but harm only their enemies or the people toward whom they feel anger, envy, or ill will. Accusations of sorcery, therefore, usually follow the prevalent lines of social tensions and conflicts: individuals who have similar kinds of relationships are most likely to suspect and accuse one another, so sorcery accusations usually reflect social tensions and conflicts.

Witchcraft

Witchcraft is another explanation that people in many societies give for personal misfortune. There is no universally applicable distinction between sorcery and witchcraft. Whereas sorcery usually involves the use of rites and spells to commit a foul deed, anthropologists usually define **witchcraft** as the use of psychic power alone to cause harm to others. Sorcerers manipulate objects; witches need only think malevolent thoughts to turn their anger, envy, or hatred into evil deeds. (The English language's main distinction between the two—witches are female, sorcerers usually male—is not useful cross-culturally.) Many cultures believe in the existence of both kinds of malevolent power, so sorcery and witchcraft are often found among the same people. Like sorcery accusations, accusations of witchcraft are likely to be patterned because people most often believe that both witches and sorcerers harm only people they dislike, hate, envy, or have a conflict with.

Cultures vary in the characteristics they attribute to witches and in how witches cause harm. The following examples illustrate the diversity.

- The Navajo of the American Southwest associate witches with the worst imaginable sins. Witches commit incest, bestiality (sex with animals), and necrophilia (sex with corpses); they change themselves into animals; they cannibalize infants; and so on.

- The Nyakyusa of Tanzania hold that witches are motivated mainly by their lust for food; accordingly, they suck dry the udders of people's cattle and devour the internal organs of their human neighbors while they sleep.

- The Azande of southern Sudan believe witches possess an inherited substance that leaves their bodies at night and gradually eats away at the flesh and internal organs of their victims. Witches, as well as their victims, are considered unfortunate because the Azande believe a person can be a witch without even knowing it. Witches can do nothing to rid themselves permanently of their power, although they can be forced to stop bewitching some particular individual by overcoming their bad feelings against their victim.

- The Ibibio of Nigeria believe witches operate by removing the spiritual essence (soul) of their enemies and placing it in an animal. This makes the victim sick, and he dies when the witches slaughter and consume the animal. Sometimes Ibibio witches decide to torture, rather than kill, a person. In that case, they remove the victim's soul and put it in water or hang it over a fireplace or flog it in the evenings. The afflicted person will remain sick until the witches get what they want out of him or her.

- The Lugbara, a people of Uganda, claim that witches—who are always men—walk around at night disguised as rats or other nocturnal animals. Sometimes they defecate blood around the household of their victims, who wake up sick the next morning.

- The Gebusi of Papua New Guinea blame all illnesses on witchcraft. They attacked and killed so many persons whom they identified as witches that nearly one-third of all deaths among them resulted from revenge against witches.

Someone who does not share these beliefs probably thinks they are logically outrageous. No one's soul leaves his or her body at night to cavort with other witches, for example. It might seem that these beliefs are socially harmful as well, as the Gebusi illustrate. Beliefs about witchcraft, fear of witchcraft, and accusations of witchcraft engender conflict and aggression among a people. Finally, the punishments that many suspected and "proven" witches receive offend

witchcraft Use of psychic powers alone to harm others by supernatural means.

our notions of social justice. As we know from the witch hunts of European and American history, the truly innocent victims of witchcraft are often the accused witches, who sometimes are cruelly executed for crimes they could not have committed.

Interpretations of Sorcery and Witchcraft

Given the seemingly harmful effects and the injustices that frequently result from imagined sorcerers and witches, why do so many of the world's peoples think that some or all of their misfortunes are caused by the supernatural powers of their enemies? Many answers have been offered to such questions. In line with the overall theoretical approaches discussed earlier, the answers fall into two categories: cognitive and sociological. (In the following discussion, for simplicity, we use the term *witchcraft* to refer to both witchcraft and sorcery because the ideas presented have been applied to both kinds of beliefs.)

Cognitive Interpretations

The most influential cognitive interpretation is that witchcraft explains unfortunate events. Most people find the idea of coincidence or accident intellectually unsatisfying when some misfortune happens to them or their loved ones, so they search for other causes. Their logic is something like this: I have enemies who wish me harm, and harm just came to me, so my enemies are responsible.

The best-known example of how people account for misfortune by witchcraft are the Azande of Africa. Azande attribute prolonged serious illnesses and many other personal misfortunes to witchcraft. Ethnographer E. E. Evans-Pritchard (1976, 18) describes their beliefs:

> Witchcraft is ubiquitous.... There is no niche or corner of Zande culture into which it does not twist itself. If blight seizes the groundnut crop it is witchcraft; if the bush is vainly scoured for game it is witchcraft; if women laboriously bail water out of a pool and are rewarded by but a few small fish it is witchcraft; ... if a wife is sulky and unresponsive to her husband it is witchcraft; if a prince is cold and distant with his subject it is witchcraft; if a magical rite fails to achieve its purpose it is witchcraft; if, in fact, any failure or misfortune falls upon any one at any time and in relation to any of the manifold activities of his life it may be due to witchcraft.

This does not mean that Azande are ignorant of cause and effect and therefore attribute every misfortune to some witch who is out to get them. When a man seeks shelter in a granary and its roof falls and injures him, he blames witchcraft. But the Azande know very well that granary roofs collapse because termites eat the wood that supports them. They do not attribute the collapse of granaries in general to witchcraft. It is the collapse of this particular granary at this particular time with this particular person inside that is caused by witchcraft. Don't granaries sometimes fall when no one is sitting inside them? And don't people often relax in granaries without the roof falling? It is the coincidence between the collapse and the presence of a particular person—a coincidence that many other peoples consider bad luck—that Azande witchcraft explains.

Another cognitive benefit is that witches serve as scapegoats. When things are going poorly, people do not always know why. Witchcraft provides an explanation. It also provides people with a means to do something about the situation: identify, accuse, and punish the witch responsible. If, as is often the case, things still do not improve, there are always other yet to-be-identified witches. People can blame many of their troubles on witches—evil enemies conspiring against them—rather than on their personal inadequacies, bad luck, or wider economic or social conditions in their societies.

Sociological Interpretations

One sociological interpretation is that witchcraft reinforces the norms and values that help individuals live harmoniously with one another. Every culture has notions of how individuals ideally ought to act toward others. Witches typically are the antithesis of these cultural ideals. They act like animals or actually change themselves into animals. They mate with relatives. They often put on a false front, pretending to be your friend by day while they eat your liver by night. They have no respect for age or authority. They are in league with the forces of evil (in the Judeo-Christian tradition, witches made compacts with the Devil, agreeing to be his servant in return for worldly pleasures). All the most despicable personal characteristics of people are wrapped up in the personality of witches, whom everyone is supposed to hate. So, witches symbolize all that is undesirable, wicked, and hateful. Just as one should despise witches, so should one hate all that they stand for. In short, by providing a hated symbol of the abnormal and the antisocial, the witch strengthens cultural conceptions of normatively approved social behavior.

Another argument is that witches provide an outlet for repressed aggression, and thus beliefs about witches lower the overall amount of conflict in a society. Writing about the Navajo in 1944, Clyde Kluckhohn argued that Navajo culture emphasizes cooperation and good relationships between members of the same extended household. When bad feelings do develop within the household, Navajo culture encourages people to suppress them. But, pent-up hostilities have an outlet in the form of witches, whom people are allowed to hate and gossip about. Because most of the persons the Navajo believe to be witches are members of distant groups, usually little action is taken against them. Solidarity between relatives of the in-group is preserved by displacing hostility to people of the out-group.

Another sociological interpretation is that witchcraft beliefs serve as a mechanism of social control. This might work in two ways. First, many people believe in the existence of witchcraft but do not know which specific members of their community are witches. This leads individuals to be careful not to make anyone angry; after all the offended party might be a witch. Second, individuals who fail to conform to local norms of behavior are most likely to be suspected and accused of being witches. People who are always mad at somebody, who carry grudges for prolonged periods, who always seem envious and resentful of the success of others, who have achieved wealth but selfishly refuse to share it in the culturally accepted manner—such violators of these and other normative standards frequently are believed to be the likely perpetrators of witchcraft. Fear of being accused and punished presumably increases adherence to the norms and ideals of behavior.

Most of our readers probably deny that they believe in sorcery and witchcraft. Those who do believe probably have *wicca* (which some call *paganism*) in mind, which obviously is different from the way we have used witchcraft and sorcery to refer to supernatural powers employed for harmful, antisocial purposes. Of course, we could broaden our definitions of sorcery and witchcraft to include paganism by removing the "antisocial" elements. Then wicca becomes almost the same as *magic*, as anthropologists usually use the term.

Or we could change the definition in another way. We could remove the part of the definition that refers to "supernatural powers." Then sorcery and witchcraft would include beliefs that unknown persons harm others using techniques that cannot be demonstrated to be real or that are not observable. In the United States, Senator Joseph McCarthy played on people's fears in the 1950s by claiming that the government and Hollywood were filled with Communists dedicated to overturning all that Americans hold dear. In the 1980s and 1990s, various supremacists blamed certain political factions and minorities for social problems and what they believed to be the degeneration of their nation's values. Will there be other *witch hunts* in the twenty-first century?

Varieties of Religious Organization

As we know from earlier chapters, in comparing cultures, anthropologists develop classifications based on differences and similarities. By their very nature, classifications are simplifications of the real world. Those that anthropologists use to describe and understand religious diversity are no exceptions. Classifications must be broad to show contrasts, but that same broadness necessarily obscures most details. As humanistic anthropologists remind us, by categorizing diverse human religions into only few forms or types, we oversimplify and distort. In previous chapters, we defined categories like nomadic pastoralism, balanced reciprocity, chiefdoms, and ranked societies, and then used particular peoples and cultures as examples of the "type" or "form." In other words, often we described particular cultures to illustrate or exemplify some general category.

We mention this because some humanistically inclined anthropologists (Chapter 5) are critical of classifications in general. They tend to believe that each culture has so many unique particularities that shoving it into any general comparative framework disserves its members and distorts their culture. As we've seen when researching and discussing Other cultures, anthropologists study cultural constructions about "race," "kinship," "gender" and the like. But anthropologists ourselves use constructions also when we make comparisons and contrasts; that is, we develop the "cultural constructions" that we use to understand Other cultures. On what basis, then, do comparative anthropologists construct their classifications of Other cultures? Humanistic scholars tend to think the basis is not objective—not based on the reality of actual peoples and cultures, but constructed in the minds of certain (mostly scientifically inclined) anthropologists.

This issue is especially notable for religion and worldview because it so easy to judge the beliefs, myths, and rituals of Others in a negative way. At one extreme, agnostics and atheists may think all things religious are "superstitious" and that beliefs about ancestral spirits and gods and witches need to be corrected by "education." At the other extreme, in considering the religions of Others, devout believers of certain faiths may view them as the hand of Satan at work producing pagan rituals, heathenish beliefs, idolatry, and the like.

With such objections in mind, developing contrasts between forms of religion (classifications) does provide a general picture of religious diversity among humanity. To avoid misunderstandings, it is important to be aware that there are many differences between religions and world views we place in the same category. A classification also allows an understanding of the cultural contexts of religious beliefs and practices.

Long ago, Anthony Wallace proposed an influential classification of religions. Wallace originally used the word *cult*, a term that calls to mind exotic and usually short-lived sets of beliefs and practices that revolve around a "cult leader." To avoid such negative connotations, here we use the phrase *religious organization*. The word *organization* emphasizes the social groups and relationships that coordinate activities to control or worship specific supernatural powers for various purposes. *Religious organization* does not mean the "entire religion" of a people. Rather, a people's total religion includes many different kinds of organizations devoted to different purposes, like curing illness, controlling weather, worshipping gods, hunting animals, divining the future, renewing nature, protecting people from enemies, saving souls, and keeping ancestral spirits happy.

Wallace originally distinguished four types of religious organizations:

1. **Individualistic**. Each individual has a personal relationship with one or more supernatural powers, who serve as the person's guardians and protectors. The aid of the powers is solicited when needed for personal goals.
2. **Shamanistic**. Some individuals—shamans—have relationships with supernatural powers that ordinary people lack. They use these powers primarily for socially valuable purposes, to help (especially cure) others in need. They may also act on behalf of their band or village to cause supernatural harm to the group's enemies. Usually shamans organize and direct crisis rituals.
3. **Communal**. The members of a particular group gather periodically to perform rituals that benefit the group as a whole. There are no full-time religious specialists, as is also true of individualistic and shamanistic cults. Usually, leaders who control and direct the rituals are elders or respected members of the group on whose behalf the rituals are performed.
4. **Ecclesiastical**. Some societies have full-time religious practitioners who form a religious bureaucracy. The actual practice of religion is managed or carried out by formal, specialized officials—priests—who perform mainly calendrical rituals. The priesthood is usually materially supported by institutionalized governmental authorities through taxation or redistributive tribute (see Chapters 8 and 12).

The Concept Review provides a quick overview of these four forms of religious organization.

So defined, these religious organizations are not randomly distributed among the world's peoples. Rather, they occur in a rough evolutionary sequence. Most notably, in many foraging bands and horticultural tribes—such as the Inuit, Ju/'hoansi, and Yanomamö—shamanistic rituals are common, whereas ecclesiastical rituals occur mainly in stratified chiefdoms and states. Be aware, though, that the evolutionary matching of kinds of religions with kinds of economic and political organizations is rough and general.

Despite complications, there is a general pattern. The religions of hunter-gatherer bands differ generally and significantly from those of complex chiefdoms and states. Because one of our major points is that religious beliefs, myths, and rituals are embedded in the context of a people's entire cultural system, we discuss how they relate to economic and political organization.

Individualistic Organizations

The defining characteristic of individualistic organizations is that individuals intentionally seek out particular spirits or other supernatural powers to protect and help them. As their name suggests, they emphasize

---

individualistic organizations Religious organizations based on personal relationships between specific individuals and specific supernatural powers.

shamanistic organizations Religious organizations in which certain individuals (shamans) have relationships with supernatural powers that ordinary people lack.

communal organizations Religious organizations in which the members of a group cooperate to perform rituals intended to benefit all.

ecclesiastical organizations Religious organizations in which a full-time priests perform rituals believed to benefit believers or the whole society, usually in large buildings dedicated to religious purposes or deities; found in complex societies.

> **CONCEPT REVIEW** Varieties of Religious Organization
>
> | Form of Organization | Major Characteristics |
> |---|---|
> | Individualistic | Each individual has a special relationship with one or more supernatural powers who serve as personal guardians and protectors. Individuals seek assistance from their guardian spirits when needed. |
> | Shamanistic | Some persons—shamans—have power to contact supernatural beings at times of crisis to help (especially cure) individuals. Shamans may also act on behalf of their band or village to harm enemies. |
> | Communal | Members of a well-defined group gather periodically for collective rituals that generally benefit the group as a whole. "Elders" often have special roles in rituals. |
> | Ecclesiastical | Societies or their divisions have full-time religious officials—priests—organized into a religious bureaucracy supported by tribute or tax. Priests officiate at calendrical rituals that benefit the whole society or political unit, making people dependent on priests and rituals for their spiritual and material welfare. |

direct, personalized interactions between individual persons and supernatural powers.

The best-known examples are **vision quests**. Vision quests are widespread among Native American peoples but are especially important for the Great Plains tribes. To Plains peoples, the world is charged with spiritual energy and power, which exists in inanimate objects, such as rocks or mountains and earth and sky, as well as in living animals and plants. Humans require the aid of supernatural powers and beings in many activities—in hunting, warfare, and times of sickness or other troubles.

Spiritual power most often comes to individuals in visions. Visions play an important role in religious life because through them people achieve the personal contact with the supernatural that is essential in various endeavors. Spiritual powers occasionally make contact with individuals for no apparent reason, coming to them as they sleep or even as they are walking or riding alone.

More often, humans—especially young men—seek out these powers through an active search, or quest, whose purpose is to acquire a vision. There are places that supernatural powers are believed to frequent: certain hills, mountains, or bluffs. A young man goes to such a location alone. There he smokes and fasts, appealing to a power to take pity on him. Among one Native American people, the Crow, sometimes a man will amputate part of a finger or cut his body to arouse pity. The vision commonly appears on the fourth day because four is a sacred number to the Crow.

The way the power manifests itself varies. Sometimes the man hears the spirit speak to him. Sometimes the spirit comes in the form of a dreamlike story. In other instances, it simply materializes before his eyes, taking the form of a bear, bison, eagle, or some other large animal. Sometimes small animals like rabbits, field mice, and dogs also appear. The power tells the man how it will help him. It might give him the ability to predict the future, locate enemies, find game, become a powerful warrior, or cure illness. It tells him the things he will have to do to keep his power—what songs to sing, how to paint his war shield, how to wear his hair, and so forth. It also tells the man some things he cannot do; for example, if the power comes from an eagle, the man might be prohibited from killing "his brother," the eagle. As long as the man continues to behave in the prescribed manner, the power will be his supernatural protector, or *guardian spirit.* Through the spirit, the man acquires special powers other men do not have.

There is no known culture in which individualistic organizations make up the entire religion. Even among the Native Americans of the Great Plains, among whom the vision quest is unusually well developed, shamanistic and communal organizations also exist.

> **vision quest** Attempt to enlist the aid of supernatural powers by intentionally seeking a dream or vision; example of individualistic religious organizations.

Religious healing aids people in societies at all levels of complexity and development. This South Korean woman is leading a *kut*, a ritual that helps her clients with physical, psychological, and family problems.

Shamanistic Organizations

A **shaman** is a person publicly recognized as having a special relationship to supernatural powers, which he or she frequently uses to cure sickness. In many societies (especially among foraging peoples), shamans are the only kind of religious practitioner; that is, they possess the only kinds of abilities not available to ordinary people. Usually, shamans are not full-time specialists. Rather, they carry out their tasks whenever their services are needed, usually in return for a gift or fee. Otherwise, they live much like everyone else.

People believe shamans possess several qualities. They have access to the power of spiritual beings, which anthropologists usually call *spirit helpers*. The effectiveness of shamans to cure or to cause harm comes from their ability to contact their spirit helpers. Shamans commonly communicate with spirit helpers by achieving an altered state of consciousness, referred to as a *trance*. They reach trance in various ways: through the intake of drugs, ritual chanting, or participation in percussive or rhythmic music. The Tungus, the northeast Asian people from whom English acquired the word *shaman*, use tambourines and drums to achieve the trance in which they journey to the spirit world to discover the cause of illness.

Peoples who practice shamanism interpret trance as a sign that some spirit, usually one of a shaman's spirit helpers, has physically entered the shaman's body. The spirit takes over (possesses) the shaman's body and speaks to the assembled audience through his or her mouth. When possessed, the shaman becomes a *medium*, or mouthpiece, for the spirits. Shamans may lose control over their actions and their voices may change quality because a spirit is speaking through them.

> **shaman** Part-time religious specialist who uses his special relationship to supernatural powers for curing members of his group and harming members of other groups.

People culturally interpret the unusual behavior and strange voice as evidence of genuine possession and is a sign of a shaman's power.

The way a person becomes a shaman varies from people to people, for the details of the role are defined by local cultures. Many scholars argue that shamans are individuals who are unusual in some way: they hear voices, parts of their bodies tremble uncontrollably, they dress or act in strange ways, and so forth. Members of their community interpret their "difference" as a sign that they have been chosen by a spirit to become a healer. However, just as often shamans are normal people who act like everyone else when not in the role of shaman. Ju/'hoansi healers use dance and percussive hand clapping to achieve the trance state that makes them powerful and able to diagnose and cure illness. When not in the role of healer, however, they are indistinguishable from other people. Thus, whether shamans are believed to be "different" from other people varies cross-culturally.

Shamans are usually considered to have knowledge and powers that others lack. They acquire these in three major ways. Sometimes they undergo a period of special training as an apprentice to an experienced shaman, who teaches the novice chants and songs and how to achieve the trance state. Among other peoples, shamans must endure difficult deprivations, such as prolonged fasting, the consumption of foods culturally considered disgusting, or years of sexual abstinence. In still other cultures, shamans are individuals who have experienced some unusual event. For example, they may have miraculously recovered from a serious illness or injury, or they claim to have had an unusual dream or vision in which some spirit called them to be its mouthpiece.

In some cultures, shamans, the healing experts, work alone during the actual cures, although many other people may be physically present. Sometimes, though, shamans have helpers in the curing tasks. Among the Navajo of the American Southwest, shamans (called "singers") have assistants who fetch objects, help construct the elaborate sand paintings used in curing, supply food and drink for all-night cures, and perform other duties. Navajo singers truly need the help of assistants: in olden times, some of the curing ceremonials lasted nine nights.

Some people say that the shaman "is the world's oldest profession," by which they mean that shamanism predominates among the "simplest" known peoples. Perhaps this is true, but shamanism also can be complexly organized. Among the Zuni, who now live on a reservation in western New Mexico, 12 special groups

As these Jamaicans illustrate, healing physical and psychological ailments are important activities and functions of religions.

of people (sometimes translated into English as "medicine societies") are recognized as knowledgeable about curing. Different medicine societies know the secret techniques for curing various illnesses. If a Zuni becomes ill with specific symptoms, he or she goes to the appropriate society to be healed. Once healed, the person has learned the secrets of the society and so is usually then initiated into it.

Communal Organizations

Like shamanism, communally organized religions have no full-time specialists who make their living as religious practitioners. They do have leaders—often elderly persons or individuals with a special interest in the results of a ritual—who manipulate the symbolic objects or address the supernatural. Communal rituals are held to intercede with the supernatural on behalf of some group of people, such as a kin group, an age group, a village, or a caste. To illustrate, we consider two widespread kinds of communal rituals organized by descent groups: ancestral rituals and rites of passage.

Ancestral Rituals

Most worldviews hold that people have a spiritual dimension—a *soul*—that lives on after the physical body has perished. Beliefs about the fate of the soul after death vary widely. Some peoples—such as Hindus and Buddhists—believe the soul is reincarnated into another person or animal. Others hold that the soul passes into a spiritual plane, where it exists eternally with a community of other souls and has no further effects on the living. Still others believe souls become malevolent after death, turning into ghosts that cause accidents or sickness or terrify the living, so have to be appeased in some way.

Another common belief about the fate of souls after death is that they interact with and affect the living, especially their descendants. The many peoples who hold such beliefs perform rituals to induce the spirits of their deceased ancestors to do favors for them or simply to leave them alone. Beliefs and rituals surrounding the interactions between the living and their departed relatives are called **ancestral rituals**, or *ancestor veneration.*

China and other parts of East Asia are famous for ancestor veneration. In the past, and among many families today, patrilineally extended families in China kept tablets and shrines in a prominent place in the house. Printed or engraved on the tablets were the names of the deceased males of the family or lineage, providing a kind of reminder of their existence in the afterlife. Periodically—often even daily—the males of the house and their wives and children gathered and prayed at the shrine. Offerings would be made to ensure the contentment of ancestral spirits in the afterlife, including food, clothing, and ghost money—purchased pieces of paper that were ritually burned so that the ancestors would receive and use them in the afterlife.

The Lugbara of Uganda provide another example. The patrilineage is an important social group to the Lugbara. As the most important members of the lineage, lineage elders oversee the interests and harmony of the entire group. They serve as the guardians of the lineage's morality, although they have no power to punish violations physically. The Lugbara believe the spirit of a deceased person may become an ancestral spirit of her or his lineage. The spirit punishes living descendants who violate Lugbara ideals of behavior toward lineage mates. People who fight with their kinsmen (especially their older relatives), who deceive or steal from their lineage mates, or who fail to carry out their duties toward others are liable to be punished by a spirit. Sometimes this happens because the spirit sees an offense committed and makes the offender ill. More commonly, spirits do not act on their own initiative to make someone sick. Rather, they act on the thoughts of an elder who is indignant because of the actions of some lineage-mate. John Middleton (1965, 76) describes Lugbara beliefs about the power of lineage elders to cause illness by invoking ancestral spirits:

> [The elder] sits near his shrines in his compound and thinks about the sinner's behavior. His thoughts are known by the [spirits] and they then send sickness to the offender. He "thinks these words in his heart"; he does not threaten or curse the offender. For a senior man to do this is part of his expected role. It is part of his "work," to "cleanse the lineage home." Indeed, an elder who does not do so when justified would be lacking in sense of duty toward his lineage.

In Lugbara, we see how elders maintain harmony and cooperation in the lineage by invoking the power of deceased members. This is a common feature of ancestral rituals.

Matrilineal peoples have similar ways of recognizing and appeasing ancestors. Consider the Ndembu of Zambia. When an Ndembu woman experiences fertility problems, people often say that she is forgetting her ancestress or doing something disapproved by an ancestress. The cure consists of a lengthy ritual in which many members of the matrilineage make the victim "remember" her relative.

Why do some societies have rituals devoted to spirits of deceased ancestors? Like other "why" questions, this one is controversial. Many anthropologists agree, however, that such beliefs are related to the degree of importance of large, distinctive kin groups in a society. The greater the importance of kin groups such as lineages and clans in making public decisions, regulating access to resources, allocating roles, controlling behavior, and so on, the more likely a society is to develop rituals that control or worship ancestors. This is consistent with sociological interpretations of religion and worldview.

Rites of Passage

Rites of passage of some kind are universal in human cultures (Chapter 2). Every people celebrate or

---

ancestral rituals Rituals intended to worship, honor, or beseech the deceased ancestors of a kin group.

rites of passage Rituals celebrating, causing, and/or symbolically marking the stages of life as defined by their culture.

symbolically mark the stages of life as defined by their culture. Birth and death—the beginning and end of life—are nearly everywhere marked by some kind of ritual process. Most peoples also celebrate transitions between life stages such as puberty, marriage, childbirth, and entry into some new role or position. Rites of passage have long been a major area of field research in anthropology.

One variety of rites of passage is **initiation rituals**, those that incorporate males and/or females into new roles or into new social groups. They are especially well studied, partly because "strange" and sometimes "painful" things occur during them. Initiation rituals ceremonially *recognize* or, often, culturally are believed to *cause* bodily changes between childhood and adulthood, often around the time of sexual maturation—which is why they are popularly called *puberty rites*.

Male initiation rituals are common on all continents. However, in some societies in the interior mountains of New Guinea they often involve psychological trauma and considerable physical pain. Among some New Guinea tribes, the process of making a man out of a boy takes many years. A group of boys nearing puberty go through the initiation ritual sequence together, as a cohort. Typically, they are removed from their mothers and contact with all females is severely restricted. They go to reside with adult men in the communal *men's house* of the village, where they will sleep for most of the rest of their lives and into which they must be "initiated." Usually the rituals occur in several stages, with different events happening to the boys at each stage.

At different stages, the boys are initiated into manhood by undergoing trauma and pain. Commonly adult men berate them for their misdeeds or weakness, make them go without water for long periods, force them to eat unpalatable foods, beat them with switches, place sticks in their noses to induce bleeding, and make cuts in their penises. The various stages frequently take 10 or more years before the boys are "completed" men, ready for marriage and fatherhood, hard physical labor, war, and politicking.

Fewer societies make the attainment of adulthood for girls into an initiation ritual. Some say this is because the physical signs of maturity are more obvious in the female body, so it is less essential for them to be socially recognized and proclaimed. Whatever the reason, where they occur, initiation rites for females most often emphasize attainment of physical maturity, instruction in sexual matters and childbearing, and reminders of adult duties as wives and mothers.

Mescalero Apache are one people who have ceremonies that recognize and celebrate girls' attainment of puberty. Each year, around the Fourth of July, the people celebrate the attainment of womanhood in a ceremony that lasts four days and four nights. Apache girls in the region who have had their first menses in the last year go to a place where a large tepee is erected. During the ceremony, the girls are regarded as reincarnations of White Painted Woman, a spiritual being who gave many good things to the people. The girls are blessed by singers (specialists who have gone through lengthy training to learn the stories and chants) and by their relatives and friends. Those attending participate in traditional songs and dances dedicated to the four directions and the spirits associated with them.

The Apache ceremony places a lot of emphasis on the girls becoming the "Mothers of the Tribe," perhaps because the Apache are a matrilineal people. On the fourth day, singers recount the history of the Apache and the girls are reminded of their ancestry and obligations. The ceremony honors the girls as individuals, reaffirms their commitment to the community and vice versa, urges them to act responsibly, and upholds and re-creates Apache traditions annually. According to ethnographer Claire Farrer (1996, 89), "almost invariably, the girls report having been changed, not only into social women but also at a very basic level. They are ready to put aside their childhoods and become full members of their tribe and community." The ceremony thus helps the girls make the social transition to adulthood, with all its rights and responsibilities.

Like ancestor veneration, rites of passage are "communal rituals" because they require cooperation by the members of a group to achieve socially valuable goals.

Other Communally Organized Rituals

Two kinds of communal religious organizations are widespread and deserve brief description.

Totemism is the cultural belief that human groups have a special mystical relationship with natural objects such as animals, plants, and, sometimes, nonliving things. The object (or objects) with which a group is associated is known as its *totem*. The group most often is a unilineal kin group, such as a clan. The totem frequently serves as a name of the group—for example, the bear clan, the eagle clan, the sun clan.

---

initiation rituals Rites of passage whose purpose is to incorporate males and/or females into new roles or into new social groups.

totemism Form of communal religious organization in which all members of a kin group have mystical relationships with one or more natural objects.

The nature of the relationship between the members of the group and its totem varies widely. Sometimes the totem is used simply to identify the group and its members, much like our surnames. Often, a mystical association exists between the group and its totem object. People believe they are like their totem in some respects. Or, the totem may be used as a symbol of differences between clans. In many populations—most notably some of the aboriginal peoples of Australia—the members of a clan treat their totem like a clanmate, believing that the totem gave birth to their ancestors in a mythical period. The welfare of the clan is mystically associated with the welfare of the totem, so periodically the clan gathers for rituals that ensure the reproduction of its totem.

Seasonal rituals that control natural processes and seasonal rhythms often are communally organized. Eastern Pueblo peoples who have lived along the Rio Grande of New Mexico for hundreds of years organize agricultural, hunting, fertility, and other rituals by season. As among Zuni and Hopi, the same rituals occurred in the same sequence year after year. The same ceremonial groups are responsible for organizing and staging them. They require large-scale cooperation by the entire community, bringing people together several times a year for a common purpose believed to benefit all.

These examples show why many kinds of communally organized religions are called *rites of solidarity*. The rituals have conscious purposes—respecting ancestors, marking and/or causing transitions from one stage of life to the next, controlling nature. In addition, they provide a ritual means to strengthen and maintain good relationships among the group's members. Also, in most cases, those who lead them are supposed to have good character and to remain pure around the days of the performance, thus upholding values, norms, and other kinds of cultural standards.

Ecclesiastical Organizations

In Chapter 7, we showed that occupational specialization accompanied the development of civilization and states. Civilizations and states developed among New World peoples, such as the ancient Incas, Aztecs, and Mayans. They also evolved in the Old World cities of ancient Mesopotamia, Egypt, East Asia, and India. In these regions, and later in most other world regions, specialization extended into the religious dimension of cultural systems. Rather than organizing rituals on a communal basis—in which a wide range of people controlled and participated in the performance—a formal bureaucracy of religious specialists controlled many public rituals. The religious bureaucracy probably also had a large voice in formulating the religious laws, which prescribed certain kinds of punishments for those who violated them.

These religious specialists are known as **priests**. It is instructive to compare priests with shamans. In addition to their more specialized status, priests differ from shamans in several respects. First, with the exception of people like the Zuni, shamans are not organized as a group and cooperation between them is minimal. Indeed, many peoples believe that enemy shamans engage in supernatural battles with one another, with the stronger shaman winning the battle, which leads to the recovery or death of the sick person. In contrast, priests are hierarchically organized and are usually subsidized and supported by a formal government, either by the high-ranking chiefs of a large chiefdom or by the state (see Chapter 12). Second, priests undergo a lengthy period of formal training because they must master the complex rituals needed to perform their role. Third, the priests were at or near the top of the social ladder in ancient civilizations, so individual priests lived much better than the population at large. Fourth, shamans typically perform mainly crisis rituals, whenever some person requires their services. The rituals at which priests officiate tend to be calendrical—they occur at regular intervals because the powerful gods that the rituals appease demand regular praise or sacrifice.

A final difference is especially revealing. With the development of a *priesthood* comes a strong distinction between priest and layperson. The layperson has little control over the timing of religious performances. The population at large relies on the priesthood to keep it in the proper relationship to supernatural powers. This creates a sense of spiritual dependence on the priesthood and on the state apparatus that so often sponsors it, a dependence that reinforces the high degree of stratification found in states.

These state-sponsored rituals are called *ecclesiastical* (meaning "of or pertaining to the church") because their priesthood was highly organized and their rituals were usually held in grand buildings that served as

---

seasonal rituals Form of communal religious organization in which group cooperation is required to ensure the seasonal changes that restore or maintain life.

priest Kind of religious specialist, usually full-time, who officiates at large-scale, bureaucratically organized rituals that keep the population in proper relationship to deities or cosmic forces.

temples. The organization of ecclesiastical religions was largely under the control of the government. Officials exacted tribute or taxes to finance the construction of temples, the livelihood of the priesthood, the sacrifices that often accompanied state rituals, and other expenses needed to support and organize religious activities on a fantastically large scale.

There is little question that ecclesiastical organizations provided rituals, myths, and beliefs that supported the domination of the ruling family or dynasty. (See Chapter 13 for more on ideologies.) The content of the beliefs, myths, and rituals almost invariably expressed the dependence of the entire population on the ruler's well-being and on the periodic performance of rituals. A common belief of official state religions is that the ruler is a god-king: he not only rules by divine mandate but is himself a god or somehow has divine qualities. This was true of most of the ancient civilizations and of the states that developed in sub-Saharan Africa. The complex chiefdoms of Polynesia and the Americas had comparable ideas (see Chapter 12).

The ancient complex chiefdoms of Hawaii had marked social distinctions between the noble and commoner classes. The nobility was viewed as endowed with a supernatural power called *mana*. Mana was partly hereditary, and within a single family the eldest child inherited the most mana from his or her parents. The highest-ranking noble, the paramount chief, was believed to be descended from one of the gods of the islands. This descent gave him the right to rule because he had more mana than anyone in the chiefdom. Other nobles (lesser chiefs and their families) were relatives of the paramount chief and thus also were endowed with mana. Mana gave chiefs the power to curse those who were disloyal or disobedient or who violated some taboo, which further reinforced their authority. Hawaiians believed the prosperity of a chiefdom and everyone in it depended on the performance of certain religious rituals held in grand temples. Because commoners did not have enough mana to enter a temple, only priests and nobles could perform the rituals needed to ensure prosperity. Everyone in the chiefdom thus relied on the social (and religious) elite for their well-being.

In ecclesiastical organizations, many rituals are held to keep the entire polity in a beneficial

One hallmark of ecclesiastical religious organizations is enormous structures like this Buddhist temple called Daibutsu-den, the world's largest wooden building. Originally built in the 700s in Nara, Japan's earliest capital, Daibutsu-den is part of a larger temple complex called Todai-ji.

relationship with supernatural beings. For example, in the state religion of the ancient Aztecs, the gods had to be periodically appeased or they would cause the world to end in a cataclysm. To keep the gods' goodwill, the priesthood periodically performed human sacrifice at temples, offering the heart of the victim (usually a war captive) to the deities. Aztec priests also stuck sharp thorns into their tongues, earlobes, and even genitals as blood offerings to the gods. The ancient Egyptians believed their pharaoh would rule in the afterlife—just as in the present world—so when he died, he took much of his wealth, his wives, and his servants into the next world with him. Japanese believed the emperors of their nation were descended through males from the sun goddess. In later Japanese history, the emperors were so set apart from the mundane world that political affairs were handled by the shogun, who ruled in the name of the emperor. The emperor of old China—who was at various times in the history of Chinese civilization the most powerful man on the planet—ruled so long as he had the mandate of heaven.

Organizing ecclesiastical rituals on a grand scale consumed enormous resources, but they did not necessarily wipe out other kinds of local-level rituals. Common people usually continued to rely on local shamans to cure them, to practice magic, to believe in witches and sorcerers, and to worship their ancestors. In ancient China, Korea, and Japan, for example, each household and lineage continued to revere its own ancestors through communal rituals and to make offerings to them at family shrines. In Korea, female shamans help families cope with anxieties and stresses even today, and even among families that are devout Christians.

In medieval Europe, Catholicism was ecclesiastical. The authority of the Church was tightly interwoven with the exercise of secular power, although conflict often arose between popes and various kings. Only in the past few centuries has the formal alliance between the power of government and the will of the gods been broken for any length of time. We should not assume that even this official separation between church and state will necessarily be permanent. As the recent history of Iran and Afghanistan suggests, the intermingling of political and ecclesiastical authorities can be reborn in the modern world. This may even happen in democratic nations.

Revitalization Movements

So far, we have discussed religion in cultures that are changing slowly. When a people's way of life or physical survival is threatened by contact with powerful outsiders, often they seek the aid and protection of the supernatural. They may form and join social movements, often called **revitalization movements**.

Revitalization movements are most likely to occur when three conditions coalesce: (1) rapid change, usually caused by sudden exposure to unfamiliar people, customs, and objects; (2) foreign domination—or even widespread fear of foreign domination—which leads to a sense of social, ethnic, or even racial inferiority; and (3) the perception of relative deprivation, meaning that people sense they lack wealth, power, and esteem relative to those who dominate them. Historically, revitalization movements were especially common during colonialism, in which a foreign power subjugated an indigenous people. (Colonialism did not always lead to revitalization movements, however.)

Revitalization movements usually originate with an individual (a *prophet*) who claims to have had a dream or vision. Sometimes the prophet claims to be a savior (a *messiah*) sent by a spiritual being to save the world from destruction. In the dream or vision, the prophet received a message (a *revelation*) from a god, an ancestor, or another spiritual power.

Revelations typically include two kinds of information given by the spirit or spirits and taught by the prophet. The first is a statement about what is wrong with the present-day world, about why people's lives have changed for the worse. Prophets and followers commonly blame the introduction of corrupting foreign objects and habits—such as tobacco, alcohol, money, new religions, formal schooling, the relaxation of old moral standards—for the troubles of today.

Second, revelations usually include a vision of a new world and a prescription for how to bring it about. In some cases, the message is vague and secular, with the prophet claiming that earthly lives will improve if people do (or stop doing) certain things. However, the message is often *apocalyptic:* the prophet says the present world will end at a certain time, and only those who heed his message will be saved. The expulsion or death of foreigners is a frequent theme of apocalyptic visions: foreigners will be drowned in a flood, burned in a fire, swallowed up by an earthquake, or killed by deities or ancestors. Another common theme is the reversal of existing political and economic dominance relations: foreigners will work for us, we will have the wealth instead

revitalization movement Religious movements that create a new way of life for a society or group.

of them, and we will tax them and make laws that they must obey. Nearly always, the prophets' revelations are *syncretic*; that is, they combine elements of traditional myths, beliefs, and rituals with introduced elements.

The following examples from two regions illustrate revitalization movements.

Melanesian Cargo Cults

The area called Melanesia in the southwest Pacific experienced numerous revitalization movements in the early to mid–twentieth century. Melanesians placed great cultural value on wealth and its distribution as the means to become a big man or powerful leader (Chapter 13). The value they placed on wealth led them to be most interested in the material possessions of German, English, French, and Australian colonial powers. Because European wealth was brought to the islands by ship or plane, it became known as *cargo*, and the various movements that sprang up with the aim of acquiring it through ritual means became known as **cargo cults**.

To Melanesians, all Europeans were fantastically wealthy, yet the Melanesians seldom saw them do any work to earn their possessions. Europeans who lived in the islands certainly did not know how to make trucks, canned foods, radios, kerosene lanterns, stoves, and so forth. In many traditional Melanesian religions, technology was believed to have been given to people by deities or spirits. It followed that European objects came from their God. Furthermore, when the Europeans who lived in Melanesia wanted some new object, they simply made marks on papers and placed them in an envelope or asked for the object by speaking into metal things. Some weeks later, the object was delivered in ships or airplanes. Surely, the cargo was made by spirits, and the acts Westerners did to get their spirits to send cargo were rituals. Melanesians therefore believed that they, too, could acquire this wealth through the correct ritual procedure, which they frequently believed Europeans were selfishly withholding from them.

Numerous prophets sprang up among diverse Melanesian peoples, each with his own vision or dream, each with his own story to explain why the Europeans had cargo and the Melanesians had none, and each claiming to know the secret ritual that would deliver the goods. The prophet often claimed to have received a visit from one of his ancestors or a native deity, who told him that the whites had been lying to people about how to get cargo.

The Garia of the north coast of Papua New Guinea illustrate common themes of cargo cults. Like most other indigenous peoples, missionaries came to the Garia. Also, like many other peoples, the Garia initially adopted Christianity for reasons other than those the missionaries had in mind. They assumed missionaries knew the ritual secrets that were the "road to cargo." The missionaries would give it to the Garia if only they practiced what the missionaries preached: church attendance, monogamy, worship of the true God, and cessation of pagan practices such as sorcery and dancing. Based on their belief that the missionary lifestyle and Christian rituals held the secret of cargo, many Garia converted to Christianity early in the twentieth century.

But the cargo did not arrive. The Garia grew angry as they concluded that the missionaries and other Europeans were withholding the true ritual secret of how to get cargo to keep all the wealth for themselves. In the 1930s and 1940s, two Garia prophets arose. They told the people that the missionaries had been telling them to worship the wrong gods. God and Jesus were both really deities of the Garia, not of whites. The Europeans knew the secret names of God and Jesus and asked them for the cargo with secret prayers. All along, Jesus had been trying to deliver the goods to the Garia, but the Jews were holding him captive in heaven. To free him, the Garia had to perform sacrificial rituals. To show him how poor they were and to make him feel sorry for them, they had to destroy all their native wealth objects. If they did these things, Jesus would give the cargo to the ancestral spirits of the Garia, who would in turn deliver it to the living.

Native American Movements

Revitalization movements also occurred among Native Americans, whose sufferings at the hands of white traders, settlers, armies, and administrators are well documented. Two movements were especially important, both precipitated by a deterioration of tribal economic, social, and religious life.

Handsome Lake

In the 1600s and 1700s, the Seneca of New York and Pennsylvania were one of the members of the League of the Iroquois (Chapter 11), a loose confederation of different tribes who agreed to live in peace and come to one another's aid in case of attack by surrounding tribes. Like other members of the League, the Seneca traditionally were matrilineal horticulturalists. Men hunted, traded

> **cargo cults** Melanesian revitalization movements in which prophets claim to know secret rituals that will bring wealth (cargo).

for furs, and went on raids against neighboring tribes, while women owned most of the farmland and did most of the planting and harvesting of corn and other crops.

By 1800, the Seneca had lost most of their land to the new state of New York, Anglo settlers, and land speculators. Whites committed many atrocities against them in the 1780s and 1790s, partly because most Seneca supported the British during the American Revolutionary War. Devastating diseases—such as smallpox and measles, which wiped out millions of Native Americans all over the continent—reduced the tribe to a fraction of its former numbers. Seneca men had been proud warriors and hunters, but these activities became more difficult because of the loss of land and the presence of whites. The American government waged psychological warfare against them, intentionally corrupting their leaders with bribes and liquor and generally attempting to dehumanize and demoralize them.

Seneca men turned to alcohol and drank away most of what little money they could still earn from the fur trade. Neighboring peoples, who once feared the Seneca and other members of the League of the Iroquois, ridiculed them. Witchcraft accusations increased internal conflicts and divisions within their communities. Many women lost their desire for children and took medicines that caused them to abort or become sterile altogether. A way of life—and perhaps an entire people—was dying.

In 1799, a Seneca man named Handsome Lake lay sick. Three angels cured him and gave him a revelation from the Creator. Handsome Lake reported that the Creator was saddened by the life of the people and angry because of their drunkenness, witchcraft, and use of abortion medicines. The Seneca must repent such deeds. Handsome Lake had two more visions during the next year. He prophesized an apocalypse in which the world would be destroyed by great drops of fire, consuming those who did not heed his teachings. People could save themselves and delay the apocalypse by publicly confessing their wrongs, giving up sins such as witchcraft and drinking, and performing certain traditional rituals.

The apocalypse did not occur, but Handsome Lake was able to give his teachings a new, more secular twist between 1803 and his death in 1815. He continued to preach temperance because, he said, the Creator had never intended whiskey to be used by Indians. He encouraged peaceful relations with both whites and other Indians. He urged that the scattered reservations of the Seneca be consolidated, so that the people could live together as one community. Family morality must be impeccable: sons were to obey their fathers, divorce (commonplace among the matrilineal Seneca in aboriginal times) was no longer to be allowed, and adultery and domestic quarreling were to cease. Handsome Lake also succeeded in changing the traditional division of labor, in which women cultivated the crops and men who worked in the garden were considered effeminate. Seneca men took up farming and animal husbandry and even fenced their fields and added new crops to their inventory.

Peyote Religion

Peyote is a small cactus that grows in the Rio Grande valley of Texas and northern Mexico. When eaten, it produces a mild narcotic effect. The ritual use of peyote among northwestern Mexican Indians predated European conquest. However, its consumption as the central element in a revitalization movement dates only from the last two decades of the nineteenth century.

In 1875, two southern Plains tribes, the Kiowa and Comanche, lost their land after military defeats. During their confinement to reservations in southwestern Oklahoma, the Lipan-Apache introduced them to peyote. By the 1880s, a revitalization movement began after the two tribes began consuming peyote at religious services. Like many movements, peyotism subsequently spread, reaching about 19 Indian groups in Oklahoma by 1899. During the early twentieth century, the church spread rapidly to other Indian communities throughout the western United States and Canada. Peyotism was and is syncretic, adopting many elements of Christian theology and worship along with the consumption of peyote as a sacrament.

The peyote movement had no single prophet or leader. Local churches developed their own versions of services and rituals. One early leader was John Wilson, a Caddo/Delaware from western Oklahoma who had learned to ingest peyote from the Comanche. While eating dinner in the early 1890s, Wilson collapsed. Thinking him dead, his family began preparations for the burial. But a Caddoan named Enoch Parker told the family that he had learned in a vision that Wilson was not dead. Indeed, Wilson revived three days later. He reported that a great Water Bird had sucked the breath and sin out of his body, causing his collapse. Jesus brought him back to life after three days, telling him that his sins had been removed and that he was to teach the Indian people to believe in God and to use peyote to communicate with him.

Until his death in 1901, Wilson proselytized the peyote religion among the Osage, Delaware, Quapaw, and other groups. He preached that they needed to believe in God and Jesus, work hard, act morally, and stop drinking alcohol. They were to abandon their traditional religious practices because the spirits that formerly had aided them could be used for evil as well

GLOBAL CHALLENGES AND OPPORTUNITIES
Religious Diversity in the United States

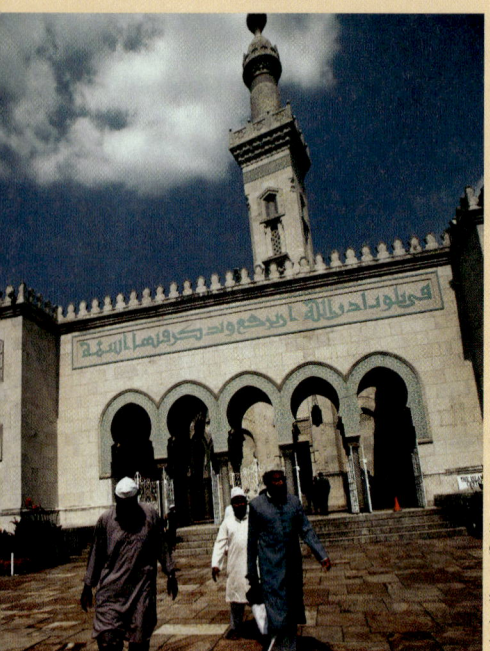

Global migration and other kinds of contacts increasingly bring people of different religious faiths together spatially, leading to new challenges for religious accommodation. This mosque is located in Washington, D.C.

Most modern nations have *religious pluralism*, meaning that followers of many different religions live inside their boundaries. For centuries, India has been home to Hindus, Muslims, Sikhs, Christians, and Jains. Since 1949, China has been officially atheistic according to its ruling Communist Party, but in fact China has Confucians, Daoists, and Buddhists—and 20 million Muslims. Muslims are concentrated in China's western provinces, where the ethnic group called Uyghur live. Violent clashes between Uyghur and Han occurred in the spring of 2010, and relations remain uneasy. Most countries in sub-Saharan Africa are pluralistic, partly because of the way colonial powers established their boundaries and partly because of the spread of Islam and, later, Christianity.

In recent decades, international migration and global contacts have increased religious pluralism. The United Kingdom has hundreds of thousands of Hindus and Muslims, most from its former colonies in South Asia. Turks migrated to Germany and other countries for work and many remained there. European nations like France, the Netherlands, Denmark, and Belgium have large numbers of Muslims from the Middle East.

Most North Americans think of Europe as religiously tolerant ("too tolerant," some say), but in recent years several European countries have debated passing regulations and even laws about Muslim dress and mosques. In early 2010, a parliamentary committee in France recommended a ban on Muslim women wearing face veils in hospitals, schools, public transportation, and government offices. The ban is now enacted. In 2012 in France, the public learned that many butchers were following Islamic practices (*halal*) in which butchers kill animals by slitting their throat rather than stunning them to minimize the pain of slaughter. Not surprisingly, much of the non-Muslim public was outraged by what they interpreted as cruelty, but butchers claimed it was too expensive to keep up two slaughter methods. In April 2010, the Belgian parliament prohibited women from wearing clothing that partly or fully covers their faces. Violators could be fined or even jailed up to week. The citizens of Switzerland voted in a law forbidding the construction of any more minarets, the tall towers in mosques at which Muslims are called to prayer five times each day.

as good purposes. Wilson attracted a large number of adherents among the Osage, who combined the use of peyote in worship services with the Christian teachings they had learned in mission schools.

Many Western Natives provided meaning and moral direction to tribal life during a period of rapid and harmful change. The peyote religion continues today on many reservations, especially in the central and western United States. It was legally incorporated as an official church—now known as the Native American Church—in 1918. Those who follow the Peyote Road eat pieces of the cactus during services, treating it as a deeply meaningful sacrament. Many members of the Native American Church say that the Creator intended peyote to be used by Indians. Periodically, the legislatures of some states have tried to outlaw the use of peyote because the cactus is a legally banned substance defined by the wider society as a "dangerous drug." So far, the courts have upheld the right of church members to consume peyote as a part of their religious sacraments.

Fate of Revitalization Movements

What ultimately happens to revitalization movements? Many with apocalyptic messages simply disappear when the end of the world does not occur. Other movements have been remarkably tenacious. In Melanesia, certain areas saw the rise and fall of

The United States remains predominantly (75 to 80 percent) professed Christian, although there are large differences in doctrines and lifestyles between denominations such as Episcopalians and Southern Baptists. Today students from around the world acquire visas to study in American and Canadian universities. Employers are looking for people who have high-tech professional job skills, for which American workers are either numerically insufficient or overpaid (in the rationales given by labor or management). Except for the Jewish faith (6 million, or about 2 percent), it is difficult to know the numbers of non-Christian religions represented in the United States. The United States has about 4.7 million Muslims (most of them native-born Americans), 2.7 million Buddhists, 1.1 million Hindus, and 1 million Baha'is. There are also the indigenous religions of Native Americans and beliefs like Wicca.

The United States faces the problem of accommodating religious diversity. In 2007, the issue arose in an American university. About 10 percent of the students at the University of Michigan, Dearborn, are Muslims. Muslims should pray five times a day and, as part of their preparation, they should wash their feet. To accommodate the students, the university installed foot-washing stations in some restrooms. Other students objected to what they claimed was special treatment for members of one religious faith. An outside organization, Americans United for Separation of Church and State, got involved because a public university built a facility to accommodate the followers of a particular religious doctrine, which they held to be a violation of the U.S. Constitution. Supporters of the footbaths responded by saying that the footbaths could also be used by other students, such as athletes, and that many of the university's holidays and the calendar itself accommodate the beliefs of Christians and Jews.

Similar issues have arisen in other universities, including whether cafeterias should be required to prepare special foods (without beef) for Hindus and whether exams should be rescheduled for a particular religious holiday for a religious minority. Some issues have been around for a long time, but their relevance is magnified by religious pluralism. Should Christian prayers be offered at meetings of city councils? Should Christian crèches be displayed on public properties? In the name of equal time, should intelligent design be taught as an alternative to evolution in the classrooms of public schools? (If the answer is yes, then should public schools also include the origin beliefs of Native Americans such as Navajos and Lakotas, of Hindus, and of numerous other religions?)

Increased religious diversity scares some Americans, including many who do not view themselves as religious. Until after 9/11, the religious affiliation of immigrants was not much of an issue in whether their numbers should be controlled. It is worth recalling, however, that the Catholicism of Irish and Italian immigrants was an issue when large numbers of those immigrants arrived. After 9/11 and other events, Americans are more likely to worry about allowing Muslims to enter, legally as well as illegally. Today, hardly anyone publicly questions the concept of religious freedom as a basic American value, but many feel that this value does not mean that members of all religions should be allowed to immigrate.

numerous prophets, each claiming to have the cargo secret. People followed again and again because they had no other acceptable explanation for cargo, for why whites had it and they lacked it, or for how they could acquire it. Certainly, their own worldly efforts—working for Europeans in mines and plantations, growing and selling coffee, copra, cocoa, and so forth—did not reward them with the fantastic wealth that whites enjoyed with virtually no effort. In some regions, cargo cults became political movements or parties. This was the fate of cargo cults among the Garia, Manus, Tannese, and some Malaitans.

Other movements do not end suddenly, wither away, or transform into a more secular, political movement. They retain their religious character, frequently teaching that contentment is to be found within oneself rather than in worldly material things. After his death in 1815, Handsome Lake's teachings became codified as the Code of Handsome Lake and is influential even today. Peyotism also became formally organized. Like many other revitalization movements that give birth to new religions, the adherents of peyotism are thus far largely confined to a single ethnic category: Native Americans.

Other movements grow over the centuries. From humble beginnings, they eventually attract millions of believers. They develop a formal organization, and the religious specialists called priests (including ministers, pastors, and the like) replace the prophets. The ancient prophets and disciples become the founders of the religion, their lives take on mythical proportions, and their revelations become texts that are considered sacred by believers. Followers become organized into an institutionalized church, which formalizes and codifies the texts so that they become official doctrines and creeds. The teachings and rituals cross national and ethnic boundaries. Beliefs and rituals go from being "local" to becoming "national" and sometimes "global."

Most of the major religions of the modern world began as revitalization movements, including Judaism, Christianity, Islam, and Buddhism. These religions are sometimes called *world religions* because they have spread outside their original homelands. Today, more and more people are becoming familiar with world religions, not just through books and TV documentaries, but also through firsthand experience. Globalization brings old religions to new places, raising issues of how to accommodate religious pluralism (see the Global Challenges and Opportunities feature).

SUMMARY

1. **Describe how anthropologists define and think about cultural diversity in religion and worldview.** Defining religion is difficult because a definition should encompass all the diversity of religions found among humanity. Broadly, religion includes three components: beliefs about the nature of supernatural powers, myths about the historical actions of such powers and culture heroes, and symbolic rituals intended to influence them. These components affect a people's worldview and, hence, behavior in the secular world.

2. **Analyze the strengths and weaknesses of the three main anthropological theories of religion and worldview.** Most theories fall into three basic categories. Intellectual/cognitive approaches hold that the most important purpose of religion and worldview is explaining things, events, and actions that are otherwise inexplicable. Psychological theories claim that myths, beliefs, and rituals function to help individuals cope with stresses, fears, uncertainties, grief, and other aspects of their lives. Sociological theorists argue that religion helps hold societies together by imparting common values and norms, punishing and rewarding people according to their behavior, and providing ritualized occasions in which people gather and thus increasing social solidarity. Among one or another people, religion is probably helpful in all these ways. Not only is each theory incomplete, but for each there are many instances in which religion actually has opposite effects to the theory's principles. It is likely that no single theory can explain religion itself or the great diversity of human religions.

3. **Analyze how witchcraft and sorcery might actually benefit individuals and groups.** Many peoples believe that supernatural beings or forces cause group or personal misfortune, such as deaths, illnesses, and "accidents." The malevolent powers of sorcerers and witches are blamed for misfortune in the world view of a great many societies. Accusations of sorcery and witchcraft tend to be patterned and to reflect prevalent conflicts and tensions in the organization of society. Although beliefs in sorcery and witchcraft at first glance seem harmful, anthropologists have argued that they have useful functions. They might provide emotionally useful explanations for why bad things happen to good people. They also might reinforce right behavior by providing hated symbols of wrong behavior and serve as a social control mechanism.

4. **Discuss how anthropologists classify the diversity of human religions and worldviews into four major categories, and analyze the relationships between these categories and social life.** Religions and worldviews may be classified according to the ways rituals are organized, although any such classification is necessarily a simplification of the diversity of the world's religions. Four organizational modes are individualistic, shamanistic, communal,

and ecclesiastical. In a generalized way, there is an evolutionary sequence to these organizations: they tend to be associated with different levels of cultural complexity. Ecclesiastical forms are regularly found in complex chiefdoms and states, where they legitimize and rationalize the powers and privileges of ruling families and elite classes.

5. **Describe revitalization movements, the conditions under which they are most likely to occur, and their fate.** Revitalization movements originate with prophets who claim to have received a revelation, which usually is syncretic and often apocalyptic. Most often, they are indigenous reactions to cope with current conditions, such as colonial domination, that are oppressive. Examples include Melanesian cargo cults, Handsome Lake movement among the Seneca of New York, and the peyote religion in many North American peoples. Most revitalization movements disappear, but some are transformed and develop into formal churches that evolve into world religions if they eventually attract tens of millions of members.

15 Art and the Aesthetic

Kevin R. Morris/Encyclopedia/Corbis

The Pervasiveness of Art

Forms of Artistic Expression
  Body Arts
  Visual Arts
  Performance Arts

Art and Culture
  Secular and Religious Art
  Art and Gender
  Social Functions of Art

The Shakers of the nineteenth century emphasized simplicity and utility, not ornamentation and aesthetics, in the objects they manufactured. Yet today many of their products are considered works of art. Shaker chairs such as those hanging from the walls of this house are highly prized by collectors.

LEARNING OBJECTIVES

After reading this chapter, you should be able to:

1. **DISCUSS** the disagreement over whether art is or is not a cultural universal.
2. **LIST** the various forms of body arts.
3. **DISCUSS** the different forms of visual arts.
4. **DISCUSS** the different forms of performance arts.
5. **EXPLAIN** how art is integrated into our religious lives.
6. **EXPLAIN** how gender, identity, and social status are reflected in art.

Art is one of those elusive terms we all know and use, and think we understand, but it is difficult to define. Anthropologists are far from agreement on what constitutes art or even if it is a cultural universal. Many agree with Toni Fratto that "there is no such thing as art. . . . Art in itself is not a universal human phenomenon but a synthetic Western (cultural) category." Other anthropologists have defined *art* by saying it is not utilitarian. The difficulty is, When does something stop being utilitarian and become art? Richard Anderson uses a Tikopean wooden headrest as an example. Any block of wood, even a log of the proper size, might serve as a headrest. A person might go farther by cutting away portions of the block or log to form legs, which Anderson argues still serve the utilitarian purpose of lessening the weight of the block. If, however, the person carves designs on the headrest, this carving becomes its artistic component, and the object becomes art. According to Anderson, it is this artistic component, the design, that transforms the object from the realm of the utilitarian to the realm of art. Thus, it is ornamentation placed on the object—not its functional design—that defines it as art. In this chapter, we take a very different perspective, arguing that art is a universal that permeates every aspect of human life.

There is much more to human life than acquiring necessities like food, clothing, and shelter. There is also more to living than producing and using things for their utilitarian value. All peoples have both a sense of and a desire for the aesthetic: those things that appeal to the eye, the ear, the taste, the touch, the emotions, and the imagination. Such sensory experiences are important not only for their functional value but also because their color, form, design, sound, taste, and feel are pleasurable in their own right. Commonly, these experiences are sought after to stimulate our imaginations and emotions by creating feelings of happiness, fear, and even anger. These expressions of the aesthetic are what we generally call art—the subject of this chapter.

At what point is a piece of wood, stone, or ivory transformed into a work of art? When does noise become music? When do body movements become dance, and words become poetry, literature, or song lyrics? When does a shelter become architecture? Are there any limitations on what can be considered art? Can the preparation and serving of food be considered art? Is the painting or alteration of the human body art?

Something becomes **art** when its purely utilitarian or functional nature is modified for the purpose of enhancing its **aesthetic** qualities and thus making it more pleasurable to our senses. Artists can produce art objects that only they themselves will see or hear, but most of the time art is displayed publicly or used in social events such as gatherings or ceremonies. In such contexts, art objects sometimes take on an additional function: they become a means of communication. Thus, Western artists often claim they are trying to "make a statement" through their artwork, although we all recognize that the artistic message is in the eye of the beholder. In other cultures, too, artistic creations communicate messages that can have both religious and secular meanings.

art Any human action that modifies the utilitarian nature of something for the primary purpose of enhancing its aesthetic qualities; or actions, objects, or words valued largely for their aesthetic pleasure or symbolic communication.

aesthetic Qualities that make objects, actions, or language more beautiful or pleasurable, according to culturally relative and variable standards.

Obviously, art is inseparable from the aesthetic, and the aesthetic is an elusive quality because it is subjective. Anthropologists since Franz Boas have argued that there are no universal standards for art. Something one society might find beautiful or pleasing, others might consider ugly, disgusting, or even repulsive. As we frequently hear, "There is no accounting for taste."

Aesthetics cannot be separated from culture. Just as we learn other aspects of our culture, so we learn what is beautiful. Beauty is culturally determined. Aesthetics is unrelated to complexity, difficulty, or skill in creation or performance. Although we might appreciate the craftsmanship that went into making a piece of pottery or the difficulty in performing a particular piece of music, we may or may not find the end product aesthetically pleasing. During a visit to Scotland, the English writer Samuel Johnson complained about bagpipe music. On being informed that bagpipes were an extremely difficult instrument to play, Johnson replied, "I wish it was impossible."

Not only does every culture, as well as every individual, have its own ideas about what is aesthetically pleasing, but aesthetics change within a culture over time. For example, examining European or Chinese art over the past 2,000 years, one finds dramatic changes in both the nature and the complexity of designs. Thus, the idea of what is beautiful is not only subjective but also volatile and ever changing.

The Pervasiveness of Art

In the urban, industrial world, we usually think of artistic creation as a separate and distinct kind of activity, and artistic objects as a special set of things. We also commonly think of art only in terms of "fine art": painting, sculpture, music, and dance. If pressed, we might add great architecture, literature, and even poetry. We tend to categorize as art only those things whose sole or basic value is aesthetic. Artists, in turn, are those painters, sculptors, composers, writers, architects, performers, and others who produce these things of aesthetic value. Individuals not directly involved in the production of "art" are commonly seen as merely the audience or consumers—people who buy, see, and hear art.

The notion that art is a conceptually separate realm of social and cultural existence is not found among all peoples. As anthropologists have long noted, Native American peoples had no word for art in their languages. Similarly, other traditional peoples in other parts of the world frequently lack words for art. The basic reason for this is that art is integrated into virtually every aspect of their lives and is so pervasive that they do not think of it as something separate and distinct. The idea of "art for art's sake" is a recent Western cultural phenomenon that in some ways both distracts and diminishes the reality of human creative expressions. If we define art broadly, then it permeates virtually every aspect of our lives. All of us search for and attempt to create that which is aesthetically pleasing; thus, we are all "artists." Creative artistic expressions are found in even the most mundane and commonplace acts of the daily lives of all peoples. Consider, for example, three behaviors that most of us think of as "mundane" rather than "artistic": dressing for the day, residing in a particular place, and eating.

We begin the day by ornamenting our bodies. From among our clothes, we make choices about what to wear based on colors and styles appropriate for the day's events. We make choices on how to wear our hair and even the color of our hair. We may paint our faces and further adorn our bodies with jewelry of varying kinds, worn on our fingers and arms, around our necks, in our ears, noses, and—in recent years—other parts of our bodies. Some of us have our bodies permanently decorated with tattoos. By these everyday acts, we are artists, attempting to enhance the aesthetic qualities of our persons by making ourselves a work of art. Through these acts, we are also adept communicators of messages about ourselves; through hair, makeup, dress, jewelry, and other ways of adorning our bodies, we present to the public certain images of ourselves.

Consider your home. In finding or building a place to live, we don't just look for something that will meet our physical needs; aesthetic appeal also plays an important role. We alter our homes by changing walls, adding rooms, remodeling the bathroom or the kitchen, and repainting everything in different colors inside and outside. We decorate the inside with furniture, rugs, paintings, posters, mirrors, and a host of knickknacks and smaller things. If we have a yard, we may remove or add trees, shrubs, flower beds, and fences. Even temporary apartment and college dormitory dwellers try to make a place their own. Although some of these additions and changes may be of utilitarian value or need, most serve to enhance the aesthetic appeal of the place where we live.

Finally, think about mealtimes. Whether we eat food raw or cooked, boiled, baked, fried, hot, or cold, and whether we season it with salt, pepper, garlic, or other herbs and spices, we are attempting to create something pleasing to our sense of taste. Our quest for new and exciting ways of preparing food seems endless, giving rise to the steady flow of new cookbooks from publishers. Nor is eating food a purely utilitarian act. We set the table and arrange the repast in bowls and on plates, which

These men in Morocco are producing traditional pottery.

have usually been purchased for their aesthetic appeal. In our food preparation and serving, we attempt to create something that is appealing to both the palate and the eye. (Chinese, incidentally, are far more conscious of this artistic quality of food than are most North Americans.)

Even in our daily lives, then, we attempt to immerse ourselves in the aesthetic. The search for the aesthetic is reflected in the appearance of our persons, our homes, and our meals, as well as in our places of worship, recreation, and work. Much of our day is filled with music, song, dance, drama, comedy, literature, and sports, which we listen to, participate in, and sometimes create. Art is a cultural universal. But beyond this, the artistic impulse is seen in the everyday lives of individual human beings, for we are all both producers and consumers of art.

Forms of Artistic Expression

Although art permeates all aspects of human activity, from clothing and furniture to music and theater, space constraints do not permit us to discuss all these diverse forms of artistic expression. For this reason, we limit our discussion to certain categories: body arts, visual arts, and performance arts.

Body Arts

People around the world are highly creative in altering their physical appearance. Almost anything that can be done to the human body is probably being done or has been done in the past. **Body arts**, or the temporary or permanent enhancements or beautification of the human body, are found in all societies. For convenience, we focus on the body arts of physical alterations, body painting, and tattooing and scarification.

Physical Alterations

In most societies, people attempt to physically alter their bodies. Head and body hair is treated in many different ways. In Western societies, hair is styled and often artificially colored. Some people shave their head, their beard, and even their legs and armpits. Others let their beard and mustache grow and style them in various ways. Still

---

body arts Artificial artistic enhancement or beautification of the human body by painting, tattooing, scarification, or other means.

others, particularly middle-aged men, attempt vainly to have replacement hair grow on the top of their head. In most Western societies, these actions are mainly a matter of fashion or personal taste; in other societies, such actions may have deeper cultural meanings.

In parts of Africa, a woman's status—for example, whether she is unmarried or married, or is a mother or a widow—is indicated by her hairstyle. Among the Hopis, adolescent girls of marriageable age wear their hair in a large whorl on each side of the head, creating the so-called butterfly hairstyle. After marriage, they wear their hair long and parted in the middle. Children among the Osage had their hair cut in patterns indicating their clan membership.

Wearing beards is not always a matter of personal taste and fashion. In many societies, such as Hasidic Jews, Mennonites, Amish, some Muslim sects, and Sikhs, wearing a beard is an act of religious belief. In the ancient world, social status was frequently associated with beards. In Egypt, only the nobility were allowed to wear beards. Not only did noblemen wear beards, but women of the nobility frequently wore artificial beards as well to indicate their social rank. In contrast, in ancient Greece, only the nobility were allowed to be clean shaven; men of commoner status had to let their beards grow.

Hair alterations are usually reversible because hair will grow back. Other parts of the body are altered permanently. Cranial deformation or head shaping has been and is still widely practiced among the peoples of the world. The skull of a baby is soft and, if the baby's head is bound, the shape of the skull can be permanently changed, flattening the back and the forehead or lengthening the head. In parts of France, cranial deformation was virtually universal until the eighteenth century. A baby's face was tightly wrapped in linen, resulting in a flattened skull and ears. In the Netherlands, babies once wore tight-fitting caps that depressed the front portion of the skull. The elite classes of the ancient Andean civilizations elongated the skull, as did the ancient Egyptians. Some peoples of central Africa bound the heads of female babies to create elongated skulls that came to a point in the back.

Some peoples permanently altered other parts of the body as well. In China, the feet of female children of high-status families were bound at the age of 5 or 6 to deform the feet and keep them small. Not only were small feet considered attractive, but foot binding was practiced as a visible indication that the family was sufficiently wealthy that its women did not have to engage in physical labor. At the age of 5 or 6, girls among the Karen Padaung of Myamar (Burma) have brass rings placed around their necks. As they grow older, more rings are added so that by the time they reach adulthood, their shoulders have been pressed down making their necks appear longer. In Western societies, plastic surgeons alter physical appearance by changing the shapes of the eyes, nose, mouth, and jowls or by increasing or decreasing the size of breasts, lips, thighs, hips, and waistlines.

The most widespread form of physical alterations to the body is the piercing of some part of the body for the attachment of ornaments. Ear piercing is probably the most common and widespread. One or more small holes are pierced in one or both ears for the attachment of metal ornaments or feathers. However, some groups—such as the Maya, Aztecs, and many other Native American societies—cut open and stretch their ear lobes so they could insert decorated clay, wood, stone, or metal ear spools up to 2 or more inches in diameter.

In parts of Africa and among many Native American peoples, holes were cut in either the lower and upper lips or both and were expanded so that large lip plugs, up to 3 inches in diameter, could be inserted. Sometimes, only women wore these disks, other times only men, and in some cases both. Among the Eskimo and Aleut both men and women wore one or two labrets in their lower lips. Only high-status women among the Northwest Coast societies wore labrets in their lips. Among groups such as the Suya and Kayapo of the Amazon basin, only men wore discs, in their lower lips. In Africa, only women wore discs, and usually only in their lower lip. Some groups, however, like the Sara in Chad, wore discs in both their upper and lower lips, while the Malonde women of East Africa wore them only in their upper lip.

Nose piercing takes two forms: nostril piercing and nasal septum piercing. With nostril piercing, one or more holes are made in the nostril. In South Asia and the Middle East, many women wear a gold ring or jewel in their right nostril. In other parts of the world, men and women place feathers or other decorative items in their nostril piercing. More extreme are nasal septum piercing found in Native America, Africa, and Oceania. In some cases, people insert nose rings in gold or brass through the opening; others insert bone, tusk, or shell ornaments or feathers.

Today, the widest range of body piercings is found in North America and Europe. Not only do many individuals have ear, nose, and lip piercings; some have piercings in their tongues, eyebrows, nose bridges, breasts, and pubic areas as well.

Body Painting

Painting is a less drastic and a temporary way of changing an individual's appearance. Some peoples paint only their faces, while others paint almost their entire bodies.

In some cases, body painting has religious significance and meaning; in other cases, it is purely secular, designed to enhance the person's physical appearance. Many peoples in Papua New Guinea cover their faces and limbs with white clay when a relative or important person dies, as a sign of mourning and respect for the deceased. The aboriginal peoples of Australia painted their bodies with red and yellow ocher, white clay, charcoal, and other pigments. During rituals, individuals were painted with elaborate designs covering most of the body. The colors and designs were standardized and had symbolic meaning. Ritual specialists who knew these designs did the painting for religious ceremonies. Outside of ritual contexts, for many Australian peoples, body painting was a secular and daily activity, performed by family members on one another. Individuals were free to use whatever colors and designs pleased them, so long as they were not ritual designs.

Among the most famous body painters are Nuba of the Sudan. Nuba body painting serves to note the individual's age, kin group, and ritual status as well as enhancing their appearance by emphasizing their physical strength and health. Starting at about age 5, girls paint their bodies completely in either red or yellow ochre. They continue painting until the beginning of their first pregnancy. Although some men just paint their bodies in black, others paint their bodies in elaborate designs using a range of contrastive colors. While all men paint their bodies, young men between the ages of about 14 and 25 are the most active. Unless they are involved in some seasonal agricultural task, they paint a new design on their body every day or two. This painting frequently requires an hour or two of work. To prepare their bodies, they shave off all of their body hair, including the eyebrows and pubic hair, since virtually all parts of their bodies maybe be painted. Some designs are nonrepresentational bars and bands; others are representational, usually of animals. New designs may also be incorporated. In their body painting, Nuba men attempt to achieve both balance and symmetry.

Tattooing and Scarification

Tattooing and the related practice of scarification are widespread. Tattoo designs, achieved by etching and

Notice the ways the clothing and jewelry of these Maasai women serve to enhance their appearance.

placing a colored pigment under the skin, have been practiced by diverse peoples. When the skin is too dark for tattooing designs to be seen, people may use scarification, the deliberate scarring of the skin to produce designs on the body.

Tattooing has a long history as an art form. It was practiced by the ancient Egyptians as well as by the ancient Scythians, Thracians, and Romans in Europe. The ancient Bretons, at the time of the Roman conquest, were reported to have had their bodies elaborately tattooed with the images of animals. In the fourth century C.E., when Christianity became the official religion of the Roman Empire, tattooing was forbidden on religious grounds—it was an affront to god. Tattooing virtually disappeared among European peoples until the eighteenth century, when it was discovered in the Pacific and Asia by sailors and reintroduced to Europe as a purely secular art.

Robert Brain noted an important difference between body painting and tattooing and scarification: paint is removable, whereas tattooing and scarification are indelible and permanent. As a result, tattooing and scarification are usually associated with societies in which there are permanent differences in social status.

In complexity of designs and parts of the body tattooed, peoples differed. Among some people, tattooing was limited to a few lines on the face, chest, or arms. For others, complex designs covered most of the body from the face to the legs. In some cases, every adult had some tattoos; in other societies, only certain individuals had tattoos. The significance and meaning of tattoos varied, but most had socioreligious significance. The more fully tattooed an individual was, the higher the social status.

The adornment of the body by tattoos is most elaborate in the scattered islands of Polynesia. In fact, the word *tattoo* itself is Polynesian. The word, like the practice of tattooing sailors, came into use as a result of the voyages of Western explorers and whalers in the seventeenth and later centuries. Tongans, Samoans, Marquesans, Tahitians, the Maori of New Zealand, and most other Polynesian peoples practiced tattooing, which everywhere was connected to social distinctions such as class or rank, sex, religious roles, and specialization. Polynesian peoples are all historically related, so it is not surprising that marking the body with tattoos is found on almost all islands, albeit to different degrees and with somewhat different styles.

The Nuba men of Sudan are widely known for their elaborated body painting.

Many Maori had large areas of their bodies covered with tattoos, which could be on the torso, thighs, buttocks, calves, and, most notably, the face. Skilled tattoo artists used several instruments to incise the curvilinear patterns characteristic of most Maori tattoos. One was a small chisel made of bone and etched into the skin with a hammer. Apparently, no anesthetic was used to relieve the pain; and, in fact, tolerating the pain of the procedure may have been part of its cultural significance. To make pigment, several kinds of wood were burned for their ashes. After the artist made the cuts, pigment was rubbed into the wounds to leave permanent markings. The most skilled tattoo artists were rewarded with high prestige and chiefly patronage, and their craft was in such high demand that they traveled widely over New Zealand's two huge islands.

Both Maori men and women wore tattoos, although men's bodies were more thoroughly covered. For both sexes, tattoos were seen not merely as body ornamentation or expression of one's personal identity. Having tattoos brought certain privileges. Men who did not undergo tattooing could not build canoe houses, carve wood, make weapons, or weave nets. Untattooed women could not help in the gardens with sweet potatoes, the Maori staple vegetable crop.

Maori facial tattoos, called *moko*, have special importance. Women were tattooed on the lips and chin, often near the time of their marriage. Male facial tattoos were designed by splitting the face into four fields—left versus right of the nose, and upper versus lower at roughly eye level. Moko were basically symmetrical on the vertical axis, with curvilinear designs on the forehead and eyebrows, cheeks, and mouth regions. In many cases, virtually the whole male face was tattooed. Not just any moko design could be worn by just any male; designs were related to factors such as hereditary status, place of birth, and achievement in battle. Social restrictions thus were placed on the wearing of facial tattoos, suggesting they were important symbols of group identity and personal achievement. North Americans might see echoes of their own styles of clothing, jewelry, hairstyle, and other personal ornamentations in Maori and other Polynesian tattoos.

On other Polynesian islands, tattooing was similar to the Maori in broad pattern but varied in detail. In Samoa, for instance, a group of boys was tattooed together on the hips and thighs in their early teens, accompanied by much ceremony. The primary recipient of the tattoo was the son of a high-ranking chief, and other boys participated to share his pain and, therefore, publicly show their respect and loyalty. Supposedly, Samoan women disdained men as sexual partners if they did not have tattoos. Traditionally, Samoan girls received tattoos only on the backs of their knees, which they were not supposed to reveal to others. It is interesting that in Samoa, greater and more elaborate male tattoos were connected to different sexually based biological functions. There was a saying:

The man grows up and is tattooed.
The woman grows up and she gives birth.

(Milner 1969, 20)

According to one interpretation, voluntary tattooing gives pain to men just as childbirth causes pain to women. Perhaps the male experience of pain by tattooing is connected to Samoan women's contempt for tattooless men.

In all of Polynesia, it was the people of the Marquesas whose bodies were most covered by tattoos. The highest-ranking chiefs had tattoos on even the soles of their feet. Alfred Gell argues that this relatively thorough covering of the body in the Marquesas wrapped the body in images in order to protect it from spiritual dangers. Gods and spirits were not tattooed; tattoo images protected the human body from spiritual harm.

Decorating the body by cutting and creating scars, or scarification, is more limited than tattooing among the world's peoples. Like tattooing, scarification is practiced for numerous reasons. Depending on the culture, both men and women may be scarred. Sometimes the scarred design is on the face; in other cases, the chest, breast, back, and even the legs and arms may be elaborately covered with such designs. Sometimes scarification forms part of the puberty rite or some other initiation rite. Among the Nuer of South Sudan, a series of horizontal cuts is made on the foreheads of men who have completed male initiation rituals. These cuts symbolically mark and communicate a young man's maturity and courage. After the cuts scarify, the scars become permanent symbols of Nuer manhood.

Visual Arts

Visual arts are produced from material, tangible objects, so they are part of the material culture of a people. They may be religious or secular in meaning and use. Usually, they are permanent in that they are meant for long-term use, but sometimes they are created for

> **visual arts** Arts produced in a material or tangible form, including basketry, pottery, textiles, paintings, drawings, sculptures, masks, carvings, and the like.

CHAPTER 15 Art and the Aesthetic   351

one-time use only and then destroyed. Visual arts encompass a wide range of basketry, ceramics, textiles, clothing, jewelry, tools, paintings, masks, and sculpture, to name only a few examples. Metal, wood, stone, leather, feather, shell, paper made of fibers, pigments, and other materials are used in their creation. The two main factors that transform a material item into a visual art are form and ornamentation.

Form

The physical form or shape of an object is a reflection of its utilitarian function, the materials available, the technical knowledge and skill of the person producing it, and the general lifestyle of the society. Nomadic or seminomadic foraging and pastoral people often produce items that are lightweight and easily transportable. One might think the visual arts of nomadic or seminomadic people are "less refined" than those of more settled peoples. But Inuit peoples of the arctic precisely carved small art objects out of soft soapstone and decorated many of their portable tools with figures of animals. Shields and hides were elaborately painted among many nomadic peoples of the American plains. Plains Indians heavily decorated their clothing and moccasins with paint, quill and beadwork, thus allowing people to carry their art along with them. Native Americans of the western United States, especially the Southwest, used pigment to paint or hard stones to etch images of animals, celestial objects, people, mythological beings, and other things on rocks. The prehistoric people who created these images might have moved according to the season, but their art was stationary and long lasting. Today, we know these images as pictographs and petroglyphs, also called rock art.

Rock seems like a difficult object to use as a canvas, but the world's peoples have used other unusual materials as well, including sand (as we shall see later). Of course, the availability of wood, stone, clay, hides, and other natural materials does influence what people can create and how. The kinds of tools the artist uses to paint, etch, or sculpt are also important influences on the final artwork. Metal tools have advantages over stone tools in giving artistic form to a raw material. Peoples also differ in their technical knowledge of how to work stone or wood, and how to model clay or metals.

Within these natural and technical limitations, the form of an object is the result of the interplay of utilitarian function and aesthetic style. The function/style debate has long interested archaeologists. Prehistoric stone tools display a bewildering variety of forms. In North American archaeology, extensive typologies have been created to classify projectile point types, which differ in size, relative length and width, and shape (straight, concave, convex, or even serrated). Some are unnotched; others are notched on the bases or sides. Many of these differences are undoubtedly related to function, but others seem to be purely stylistic. Great variability is also present in the vessel shapes and decorations of another archaeological favorite, pottery. Pottery vessels vary tremendously from one group to another, as well as within the same group of people over time.

One does not have to look at peoples remote in time or space to see that the form of an object that has utilitarian purposes is part of the artistic expression of a people. Look at something as mundane and "functional" as the legs of tables and chairs in our own culture. The legs can be straight or tapered, or round, square, or rectangular. The table may have a pedestal base. All are equally functional; they keep the seat or the top off the floor. The differences are a question of aesthetics, not of function. Thus, the physical form of an object may be part of its aesthetic appeal; however, it is sometimes difficult to determine where function ends and the aesthetic begins.

Ornamentation

Ornamentation is design added to the physical form of an object. Humans are highly creative in developing ways of adding ornamentation to material items. Ornamental designs may be woven or carved into an object. They may be painted, incised, molded, or sewn onto an object. Or a combination of these techniques may be used to decorate an object.

In basketry and textiles, designs are commonly woven onto the item during its construction. For baskets, different colors of plant fibers, either natural or artificially dyed, are used for the designs. The same is true in the weaving of textiles, for which different-colored yarns are used. Not all textile designs are created using fibers of contrasting colors. By using a variety of waving techniques, weavers may create different designs within a fabric using only a single color.

Carving refers to creating a design by removing parts of the original form. Wood, stone, clay, ivory, shell, and bone may have carved designs. An object may be carved in three dimensions so that the form itself becomes the design, as in a piece of sculpture. Or the form of the object will remain the same, with only shallow relief carving of a design on the surface.

Painting is certainly one of the easiest and most versatile methods of ornamenting an object. It is possibly the oldest method of ornamentation; European cave paintings are at least 20,000 years old. All one needs to paint is a range of colors. To make colored pigments, a variety of different materials may be mixed with water, oil, or fat, such as charcoal, plant materials, and natural mineral pigments. Paintings can be applied to wood, stone, clay, textiles, paper, or leather. Paintings can be applied to flat surfaces, such as cave walls, exposed rocks or cliff walls, wooden furniture, or canvas. They may be made on round or irregular surfaces, such as pottery, masks, and sculpture.

Incising consists of decorating an object by scratching lines into the surface. Like painting, incising appears to be one of the earliest ways of adding designs to an item. Incising is most commonly used on ivory, bone, and shell. In these cases, the scratched lines are frequently accentuated by adding some type of colored pigment, usually black or a dark color, so one can more readily see the design itself. Incised designs are also occasionally used for decorating clay pots and leather.

Designs on ceramics and metal are commonly modeled by raising certain areas above the surface. There are two ways in which this form of ornamentation can be accomplished. One is by making additions to the object after the surface area is finished. In pottery, for example, designs may be formed by placing little balls or coils of clay on the surface after the body of the pot has been formed. A similar technique is sometimes used in adding designs to metal items, as when metal wires shaped into designs are welded to the surface. More commonly, though, molds are created with designs carved into the surface area. Clay can be forced into these molds, or metal poured into them. After the object is removed from the mold, the design areas stand out as raised areas on the object surface.

Sewing is often used to add ornamentation to cloth or leather. Glass, bone, or shell beads may be sewn onto an item, forming designs, as on moccasins or clothing. Designs may be created by sewing with various colored threads of hair, plant fiber, quills, or metal, or by sewing different colors of fabrics together, as in a patchwork quilt.

Although meaningful cross-cultural studies of visual arts are difficult, comparative studies have been made of stylistic elements found in ornamental designs. Working with the idea that art reflects the creator's view of society, John Fischer studied the use of stylistic elements in 28 different societies around the world. He divided the societies on the basis of their degrees of social equality and inequality (see Chapter 13), thinking that the artistic expressions of egalitarian (primarily foraging) societies would differ from those of socially stratified (primarily intensive agricultural) societies. He examined the stylistic elements in terms of their relative complexity, use of space, symmetry, and boundedness. Fischer found that in egalitarian societies, designs tended to repeat similar, symmetrical elements, with large areas of empty space without enclosures. In more stratified societies, ornamentation was characterized by asymmetrical designs that integrated unlike elements and more fully filled enclosed areas. Fischer interpreted these differences as symbolically reflecting the differing social realities of egalitarian and stratified peoples. Egalitarian peoples tend to live in small, scattered isolated groups, whereas in stratified societies, people live in crowded communities.

This discussion has only touched upon some of the ways in which peoples add ornamentation to and create design on objects. When it comes to ornamenting objects, humans are highly creative. When most people think of artistic creativity, they think of the artist as creating a novel object (e.g., a unique drawing or sculpture) using some medium (e.g., paper or wood). Looking in broad cross-cultural perspective, we see that humanity as a whole has also been enormously creative not only in its styles but also in its techniques of ornamentation and in some of the surprising materials used.

Art of the Northwest Coast: An Example of Style

In visual arts, some two-dimensional image (e.g., a painting or drawing) or three-dimensional form (e.g., a sculpture or mask) is created. Cultures vary in many ways in their visual arts: the themes or subjects portrayed, the purposes of the artwork, the relationship between the artist and the public, and so forth.

Stylistic conventions are an important variation. In visual arts, stylistic symbolism may be especially important because artists in many cultures are not especially concerned with realistic portrayals of people or nature, but use conventional representations understood by themselves and the public. But, even when the intention is a realistic portrayal, symbolic representation may be necessary. In a painting or drawing, for example, three-dimensional reality is portrayed on a two-dimensional surface, and the stylistic conventions of different cultures may handle this problem of representation in various ways.

The art of some of the Native Americans of the Northwest Coast, from southern Alaska to Oregon, is one example of stylistic variation in imagery and two-dimensional representation. Although they were hunters, gatherers, and fishers—rather than cultivators— Northwest Coast peoples were largely sedentary villagers, which was made possible by the abundance and reliability of coastal and riverine food resources, especially fish (see Chapter 7). Their social and political organization included large descent groups, chiefly roles, and hierarchical ranking (see Chapter 13). Sponsoring the creation of art objects, displaying them, and/or using them in ceremonies were the ways groups and high-ranking people proclaimed their wealth and social position.

Northwest Coast art is famous for its sheer quantity, quality, and style. Many major Canadian and American museums contain substantial collections of masks, wooden sculptures, incised silver jewelry, carved boxes, finely woven blankets, and sometimes larger objects such as "totem poles" and painted house fronts. Animals, humans, and spirits are the most common subjects of the art of these peoples, although many creations represent animal-human-spirit at the same time. Because of the unique style used to represent these subjects, most Northwest Coast art is easily recognizable.

Animals such as beavers, ravens, hawks, frogs, bears, and killer whales were common subjects of the art, but their depiction was not intended to be realistic. Artists created animals by combining design elements representing what was culturally considered their most distinctive body parts. For example, beavers have two large incisors, a scaly (often hatched) tail, a rounded nose, and forepaws (often holding a stick). Hawks are portrayed by emphasizing their distinctive beak, which is turned backward and often touches the face. Frogs are suggested by wide and toothless mouths. Bears usually are identified by paws with claws and a large and heavily toothed mouth. Images of killer whales have a large toothed mouth, a blowhole, and an exaggerated dorsal fin. Using such conventional design elements, Northwest Coast artists carved animals onto boxes, masks used in a multitude of ceremonies, huge cedar tree trunks representing a group's or individual's ancestry (commonly mislabeled "totem poles"), and other three-dimensional objects.

Painters are familiar with the problem of representing the world on flat surfaces. In the Western and many other artistic traditions, three dimensions are represented on two-dimensional surfaces (canvas or paper) by such techniques as relative sizes of images, perspective, and coloration, all intended to create the visual illusion of depth. Northwest Coast artists painted on many two-dimensional surfaces, including the flat sides of boxes and communal house fronts. They also wove representations of animals into blankets and incised lines into bracelets and other metal jewelry. Most often, their work on flat surfaces tried to retain as many as possible of the design elements characteristic of each animal, so that each animal representation would be readily identifiable. A common technique was to split the animal down the middle and paint profiles on each half of the surface. The result was a representation that distorted the actual shapes of the body and its characteristic parts, but retained the elements that conventionally identified the animal.

Yet another stylistic characteristic of Northwest Coast art is the artists' apparent intolerance of empty spaces. The subject's body, limbs, and even hands and feet were generally filled in by design elements. Most commonly, curvilinear patterns, stylized eyes, or faces were painted or carved inside body parts. Thus, one frequently observes a face on an animal's torso or an eye pattern on a leg joint.

Performance Arts

Performance arts encompass music, song, and dance, which use voice, instruments, and movement to delight the senses and communicate. (Theater/drama is also a performance art, but we do not cover it here.) Music, song, and dance are closely interrelated. Dancing is

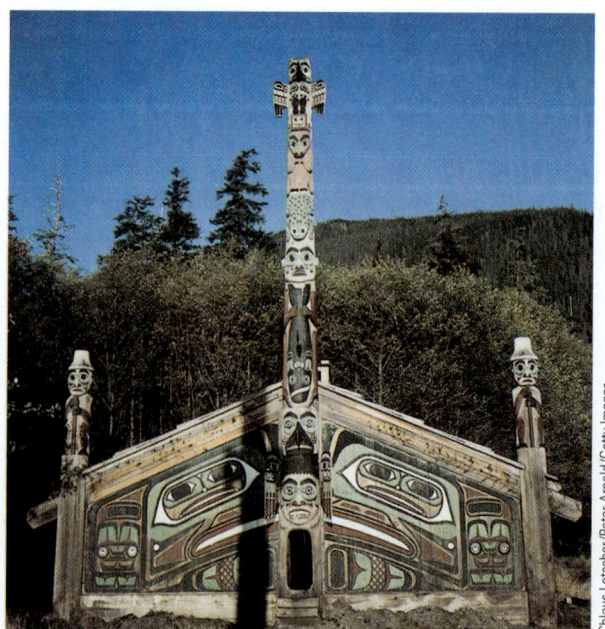

Along the Northwest Coast, houses were elaborately decorated with designs that were symbolic of the family and its heritage. This Tlingit house is in Ketchikan, Alaska.

---

performance arts Forms of art such as music, percussion, song, dance, and theater/drama that involve sound and/or stylized body movements.

usually to the accompaniment of music, especially rhythms created partly by drumming, clapping, or other kinds of percussion. Singing is often accompanied by instrumental music. Traditional religious ceremonies and pageants commonly integrate music, song, and dance.

An interesting aspect of performance arts is that not only do we watch or listen to such formal performances, but we also frequently perform them ourselves, in many cases for pure pleasure. We play our own pianos or guitars, we sing in the shower or as we drive, and we take part in social dances. The dual dimension of these art forms has been questioned by some anthropologists. Speaking only of dance, Adrienne Kaeppler has asked, "Is participation in rock and roll in any way comparable to watching ballet? Indeed, should 'dances of participation' and 'dances of presentation' be classified as the same phenomenon either in our own or other cultures, let alone cross-culturally?" She further questions whether dance performances for the gods should be categorized with social dancing, since their purposes are so different. Similar questions may be asked of music and song, which so often are part of religious rituals. For example, Osage rituals integrated music, song, dance and theatrical performances to communicate ideas that could not be expressed by words alone. Francis LaFlesche argued that these rituals were not merely prayers for supernatural assistance but were educational as well. They were a manner of recording and transmitting the collective knowledge of the society, communicating social messages to the assembled participants. Thus, even within a society, the purposes of performance arts may differ significantly, depending on whether they are religious or secular in nature.

People raised in the Judeo-Christian religious tradition are quite familiar with the many functions of music in religious services. The lyrics of familiar hymns sung to praise God are an integral part of worship rituals. Music also helps to create the mood and sense of reverence for the service and is capable of altering the emotional state of the participants. The shared experience of singing in unison may help draw the congregation together, enhancing what many Christian denominations call their fellowship. In these and other ways, music is important in making the congregation receptive to the messages delivered by the sermon and prayers.

Music and other forms of performance arts are essential to the religious experience for diverse peoples in all parts of the world. The *voudon* (voodoo) religion of the Caribbean heavily incorporates performance arts into religious ceremonies. Followers of voudon consider themselves people who "serve the spirits" (*loa*). Many loa originated and now live in West Africa, where the ancestors of modern Afro-Caribbean peoples were enslaved during the era of the slave trade beginning in about 1500. Voudon temples are elaborately decorated with sacred objects, paintings, and symbolic representations of various loa, which show the devotion of the worshippers and make the temple attractive to the spirits. Through drumming, music, and energetic dancing, voudon worshippers induce the loa to leave their spiritual homes and take over the bodies of those who worship them. When the loa possess their human servants, the latter speak with the voices of the loa, wear the loa's favorite clothing, eat their foods, drink their beverages, and generally assume their identity. Visiting petitioners with problems can ask questions of the worshipper/loa, who may answer with directions about what course of action to take. Voudon drumming, music, and dancing are so totally integrated into temple rituals that the religion is unimaginable without it.

Among many peoples, music, dance, and other forms of performance arts are essential elements of curing ceremonials. !Kung shamans use percussion, song, and dance to induce the trance state they believe is necessary for curing sick people. The power to heal, !Kung believe, comes from a substance called *nlum*, which, when heated up by dancing and trance, allows shamans to draw sickness out of people. While women produce a definite rhythm by clapping and singing, the curers circle the fire in short, synchronous dance steps. The experience of music and dance causes the nlum inside their bodies to boil up into their heads, inducing trance. In this spiritually powerful state, shamans heal by placing hands on the sick, shrieking at the same time to drive out the affliction.

Music is essential to the healing process among many other African peoples. The Tumbuka-speaking peoples of northern Malawi combine singing, drumming, and dancing in all-night curing sessions. Some kinds of illness are caused by a category of spirits called *vimbuza*. Vimbuza are the powerful spiritual energy of foreign peoples and wild animals (especially lions). Vimbuza cause various kinds of illness and even death when they possess someone. Tumbuka believe that health requires a balance between bodily cold and hot forces (similar to the bodily "humours" of old Europe). When vimbuza enter the body, they create an imbalance between hot and cold forces, leading to the buildup of heat that is culturally interpreted as sickness.

Tumbuka diviner-healers (curers) both diagnose illnesses and direct elaborate healing ceremonies that include drumming, music, and dance. The most essential part of the curing ritual is a shared musical experience in the context of a group gathering, with every individual present expected to contribute to the music

CONCEPT REVIEW: Forms of Artistic Expression

Body Arts	Alterations to the physical appearance of the body, including, but not limited to, physical alterations, painting, tattooing, and scarification
Visual Arts	Material, tangible objects that are part of the material culture of a people, including—but not limited to—basketry, pottery, textiles, clothing, jewelry, tools, furniture, painting, masks, and sculpture
Performance Arts	Arts meant to be heard, seen, or personally performed, including music, song, dance, and theater

making. Even patients themselves participate in the total experience by singing, clapping, and dancing. As the sick person dances to the accompanying rhythm of drums and music, the heat inside the person's body increases. This leads the possessing spirit to expend excess energy and cool off. By thus restoring the balance between hot and cold, the individual is cured, at least temporarily. Steven Friedson, who worked among the Tumbuka, briefly summarizes the importance of music and performance to healing among just a few African cultures:

> Africans approach healing through music and dance. Azande "witch doctors" eat special divinatory medicines, activated by drumming, singing, and dancing. In northern Nigeria among the Hausa, the sounds of the *garaya* (two-stringed plucked lute) and *buta* (gourd rattle) call the divine horsemen of the sacred city of Jangare to descend into the heads of *boorii* adepts, thus healing the people they have made sick. Similarly, the various *orisha* and *voudon* spirits of the Guinea Coast, called by their drum motto, mount their horses (possess their devotees). The resultant spirit-possession dance, though religious in nature, is in the first instance often a therapy for those afflicted by the same spirits. Spirit affliction is healed through music and dance in Ethiopia and Sudan, wherever *zar* cults occur.... Central, southern, and parts of Equatorial Africa have examples of the *ng'oma* type of healing complex, whose name... points to the centrality of music in curative rites.
>
> (Friedson 1998, 273–274, references in the original deleted)

In the early 1980s, the authors of this book first heard about a medical practice that involves integrating music into the treatment of both biomedical and psychological disorders. At the time, we thought the field now called *music therapy* was a new mode of treatment and a new occupation. As the preceding examples illustrate, many other cultures have long recognized the connection between music and healing and have integrated the performance arts into their treatments.

Like other forms of aesthetic expression, comparative studies of performance arts are difficult and few. Alan Lomax's comparative studies of dance and song rank with the most ambitious. Lomax and his collaborators analyzed film footage of peoples from around the world, comparing their body movements in everyday activities with their dance movements. They found that dance movements were formalized repetitions of the movements found in daily life. Lomax further argued that the form of dance was correlated with the relative complexity of the society.

In his comparative study of songs, Lomax found that differences in song styles were also correlated with societal complexity. The songs of less complex peoples, such as egalitarian foragers, included more vocables (sounds, not words). Words were not enunciated as clearly in their songs, and there was more repetition of vocables and words. The songs of the most complex peoples included fewer vocables, less repetition, and more words, which were more clearly enunciated. Although Lomax's conclusions concerning the correlation between dance and song and relative cultural complexity have been questioned, there are some interesting parallels between his findings and those of Fischer on stylistic elements in ornamental designs.

Art and Culture

Anthropologists are not interested in art simply for art's sake. As we have already seen with the examples of body, visual, and performance arts, art is embedded in a cultural context. Three of many features of this context are religion, gender, and identity.

Secular and Religious Art

In our discussions of the various forms of art, we mentioned that certain artistic products are sacred and others are not. There are both sacred and secular designs, forms, dances, songs, music, and literature. This division between secular and sacred cuts across many forms of art and across most cultures.

In contemporary industrial society, the greatest artistic energies are expended in the creation of secular art, although such art may at times include religious themes. If, for example, you examine the works of the greatest Western painters, architects, and composers of the last century, you will find that most of their work is secular. This was not always true. The great art of earlier periods was for the most part concerned with religion, partly because religious and political authorities so often sponsored artists and their creations. The pyramids and great temples of ancient Egypt were related to conceptions of the afterlife and other dimensions of the supernatural world. While visiting pyramids and great statues of the pharaohs, one must remember that the pharaohs were gods on Earth.

In classical Greece, the cradle of Western European artistic traditions, religion was a central focus for most of the greatest artistic accomplishments. The Parthenon in Athens was the temple of Athena. Most of the greatest Greek public statuary depicted gods such as Poseidon, Zeus, Apollo, and Aphrodite. Much Greek drama had strong religious overtones and was associated with the god Dionysus. In Rome, secular art became more prominent. The great buildings were usually palaces and theaters, while public monuments honoring the triumphs of living or recently dead heroes filled Roman cities. In the Middle Ages, religion regained preeminence. The great buildings of the medieval and Renaissance periods were cathedrals, while the greatest artists of the time labored to fill these buildings with frescoes, mosaics, paintings, statuary, and other artistic works as well as music, song, and pageantry dedicated to the worship of God.

The 1700s saw an emphasis on reason and science, the Industrial Revolution, the rise of capitalism, and the beginnings of modern political democracy. Ever since, Western art has become increasingly secular. The largest buildings in our cities are no longer dedicated to religion, but to government, commerce, or athletics. Contemporary painters choose secular subjects, from realistic landscapes and buildings to abstract designs and cans of Campbell's soup. The most illustrious composers and performers today seldom produce or perform religious music, but focus on secular and, at times, even irreligious themes. For those of us who learned our culture in a society dominated by secular art, it is important to remember that for most peoples and for most of human history, religion and religious art have been preeminent. The most elaborate artistic achievements of a great many peoples are associated with religious ceremonies: visual arts, music, dances, ornamentations, architecture, and their associated mythologies.

We have already discussed examples of the integration of performance arts like music and dance into African healing practices. Another people for whom art—both visual and verbal arts in this case—is part of curing rituals is the Navajo of the American Southwest. In Navajo belief, the most common cause of illness is the loss of harmony with the environment, often because of the person's violation of a taboo or other transgression. When illness strikes and a diagnosis is made, a Navajo "singer" (curer or shaman) is called on to organize a complex curing ceremony.

In curing ceremonies (and there were traditionally dozens of such ceremonies), the singer addresses and calls on the Holy People, who are spiritual beings believed by Navajo to have the power to restore sick people to harmony and beauty. Ceremonies usually occur in a hogan (house) at night, and in theory the procedures must be executed perfectly for the cure to work.

For the ceremony, the singer creates images of the Holy People out of various colored sand, called sand paintings. Navajo sand paintings are visual representations of the Holy People that are created, used in a single ceremony, and then destroyed. Most sand paintings are stylized scenes of events involving various Holy People that occurred in the mythological past. Each sand painting is part of a ceremony that also includes other sacred objects (such as rattles and prayer sticks) and lengthy songs or chants recited by the singer. The songs/chants that are recited over the sand painting and the patient may last for hours. Most songs/chants tell of the myths depicted in the specific sand painting.

In their years of learning to become singers, Navajo singers must memorize the lengthy songs and chants they recite over sick people to restore their harmony with the world. Singers also learn to make sand paintings that represent specific mythical scenes and events. To make the images, a singer, usually with the help of his family members and/or apprentices, collects, grinds and mixes sand and other materials of various colors, including white, red, yellow, black, and blue, with charcoal, corn pollen, and various plant materials. Pictures are created by carefully dribbling fine grains of sand through the fingers onto the prepared floor of the hogan.

There are literally hundreds of sand paintings. Most ceremonies involve a combination of many sand paintings used in association with particular chants. Because some are quite large and enormously detailed, they often take hours to create. But all must be exact representations of the ideal model of the mythical scene or event depicted. The images are stylized drawings of the Holy People, many of whom are depicted with weapons and armor. Most scenes represented in the sand paintings are from particular myths familiar to the patient and audience.

Sand paintings are made for the express purpose of inducing the Holy People to come to the hogan where the ceremony is held. The Holy People are attracted by their images in the sand painting; and, once consecrated with pollen, the sand images and the Holy People become one and the same and thus holy. This process of transforming the sand figures into actual spiritual beings is termed *transubstantiation* and is a commonly occurring feature of religious art. The very same idea is found in the Eucharist of the Roman Catholic Church, with the conversion of wine and bread into the "blood and body of Christ." During the ceremony, the patient is seated on the sand painting itself, which is now imbued with the presence of the Holy People. The singer completes the transfer of power to the patient when he rubs the patient's body with the sand of the images of the Holy People. After each phase of the ceremony is finished, the sand painting is destroyed and the sand carefully removed from the Hogan.

Navajo sand paintings certainly are works of art. Some non-Navajos who have seen them think it is a shame to destroy such beautiful images that the singers and their helpers have worked so hard to create. But in the context of Navajo beliefs, sand paintings are made for specific curing ceremonials held for particular patients. That is their purpose—not expressing the singer's creativity, making an artistic statement, celebrating Navajo culture, or publicly displaying the singer's talents. For Navajo, fulfilling that purpose requires that the paintings not be permanent.

Navajo sand paintings and the singing of curers are clearly religious, but the division between their secular and religious purposes is not always clear, particular to nonmembers of the society. If you travel in the Southwest, you will see Navajo "sand paintings" for sale. Many of these have depictions of the Holy People. However, they have not been consecrated with pollen. They are nothing but sand glued on a board. Perhaps not surprisingly, some traditional Navajo object to this use. Somewhat different are the so-called kachina dolls of the neighboring Hopi. Kachinas are the supernatural spirits of the Hopi, and the kachina ceremonies or dances are among their most important religious activities. When a man puts on a sacred kachina mask, that spirit becomes embodied in him. During certain of these ceremonies, the kachinas (the men wearing the masks) will give the girls figures carved out of cottonwood and painted in the image of kachinas. Although called "dolls," they are neither toys nor sacred items. They are mnemonic devices to help the children learn about, and recognize, the 500 or so different kachina spirits. As secular objects, kachina "dolls" are sold to visitors.

Religious symbolism is often used to decorate clothing and other secular objects; but it does not necessarily make them sacred or imbue them with power. Religious considerations have other effects on secular art as well, frequently placing limits on secular artistic expressions. The use of certain types of motifs or themes may be religiously forbidden. The Koran prohibits the use of human images, which are viewed as idolatry. Thus, many Islamic peoples extended this ban to include any pictorial representation of humans or animals. As a result, much of the art of Islamic peoples is devoid of naturalistic representations, focusing instead on elaborate geometric or curvilinear designs. The Shakers emphasized singing and dancing as important parts of their religious services but prohibited the use of musical instruments.

Art and Gender

Gender differences are often reflected in body, visual, performance, and verbal arts. Colors and designs are sometimes considered male or female, most familiarly reflected in clothing and body decoration. Gender also influences who creates and performs certain types of visual, performance, and verbal arts. The BaMbuti Pygmies of the African rain forest have a ritual performance involving dance and music they call *molimo*. They view the forest as like their parent and, like any parent, the forest looks after its children—themselves. Therefore, when misfortune strikes, it must be because the forest is asleep. To wake up the forest, at night the women and children retire to their huts while the men make molimo music outside. Women are not supposed to know that the molimo is just a long, flutelike instrument stored in a local stream, but instead believe it to be some kind of forest animal. (In fact, women seem to know all about the molimo.)

As discussed in Chapter 11, men and women are usually involved in the production of different types of material items, and usually the individuals involved in production decorate the items as well. In many cases, the aesthetic qualities of the items are an integral part of the production process itself, as with the shape of a pottery vessel or metal tool, or the design in a blanket or a basket. In other instances, however, decorative arts are separate and distinct from the production of the basic item, and decorative artists may be defined by gender.

Among the Plains Indians, beadwork and quillwork were produced by women. The only men who produced beadwork and quillwork were *berdaches,* men who dressed and acted as women (see Chapter 11). Although both women and men painted hides, there were distinct differences in subject matter. Women painted only geometric designs. The hide containers called *parfleches* used for the storage of food and clothing were made by women and were painted only in geometric designs. Representational designs of people, horses, and other animals and supernatural beings were painted only by men. Tepees and buffalo robes, though made by women, were painted by either men or women, depending on whether the design was to be geometric (by women) or representational (by men).

Some visual art objects are made for specific rituals or ceremonies. Initiation rites are usually held for only one sex (see Chapter 14). The art produced for them, therefore, is sometimes "sex-specific." In many cultures of the highlands of Papua New Guinea, long bamboo flutes are played at male initiation ceremonies. Women are not supposed to know about the existence of the flutes. Many initiation ceremonies also include carved and painted masks, supposedly kept secret from women and uninitiated boys.

Performance arts are often carried out during religious ceremonies. Men have historically played the dominant role in most religions. Not surprisingly, in most societies, men dominate the performance arts associated with religion. For example, even though many of the Hopi kachinas (spirits) are female, in kachina dances all dancers, even those impersonating female spirits, are men. In ancient Greek drama, the roles of women were played by men. In Western Europe, women were not allowed to participate in certain performance arts long after they had become secularized. The role of Juliet, in the original productions of Shakespeare's play, was performed by a young boy because women could not be actors in Shakespeare's time. It was not until the late seventeenth century that women could perform in the English theater.

Social Functions of Art

Does art exist solely to satisfy the human desire for the aesthetic? Perhaps, but if so, why have humans expended such incredible energy in its creation? Perhaps art also has a critical role in human social life and cultural existence. Through the use of art, people can express their identities as members of particular groups, while at the same time demonstrating their individuality. Through the production, consumption, and use of art, we can express our personal individuality, our group identities (including ethnic affiliation), and even our social status.

Individuality

Many of us attempt to express our individuality by creating or displaying art, as shown by the widespread appeal of handmade goods produced by skilled craftspeople. Since the advent of the Industrial Revolution, the attraction of handmade over machine made goods has been their individuality. This individuality is not solely the result of the differing technical skill of the makers; also, the makers have consciously tried to make every item unique by varying colors and designs. Thus, if one looks at Oriental rugs, Native American jewelry, pottery and baskets, Maya textiles from Guatemala, or wood carvings from New Guinea, rarely does one find two identical items. If they are identical, it is probably because they were produced for the commercial market.

Similarly, our clothing and houses express our individuality. Even though we usually conform to the norms of our society in clothing styles, most of us abhor uniforms, and thus we enhance our clothes in some manner to make them uniquely ours. In their dwellings, people also attempt to express their individuality. Although all Maori dwellings were carved and painted, different designs and images were used. Today in suburban North America, builders of subdivisions usually vary the houses by using a range of floor plans, building materials, and colors. Many residents of older neighborhoods, though, still think the new subdivisions lack character, style, and individuality.

Social Identity

As well as displaying our individuality, art is a means of expressing social identity, publicly displaying what kind of person you are or which group of people you identify with. In the 1960s and early 1970s, many young people wore long hair, beads, and baggy clothes decorated with peace signs and upside-down flags. Some traveled the country in old Volkswagen minibuses or school buses

GLOBAL CHALLENGES AND OPPORTUNITIES: The Market Economy and Traditional Visual Arts

Every summer since 1922 the "Indian Market" has been held in Santa Fe, New Mexico. More than any other event this market has helped elevate the status of Pueblo pottery from curio to art form.

Globalization and, more recently, the global economy are influencing all forms of artistic expression—body arts, visual arts, and performance arts. Increasingly, traditional art forms are being commoditized and marketed in competition with other art forms. Since this is a highly complex topic, this discussion is limited to something manageable: how integration into the market economy is affecting the traditional visual arts.

As we discussed at the beginning of this chapter, members of more developed societies commonly believe that for an object to be considered "art," it can have no function other than being a decorative, aesthetically pleasing, object—a painting, a sculpture, a vase, and so forth. Thus, art is sharply distinguished from that which has a utilitarian use. In contrast, in traditional societies, there are no "decorative objects": virtually every material object has some utilitarian function, secular or religious. Thus, by necessity, their artistic expressions have to be incorporated into their utilitarian objects—the form of and ornamentation on clothing, pottery, basketry, household items, sacred objects, tools, and weapons. However, people differ on which types of these utilitarian objects are most suitable for this artistic expression. Since religion is by nature highly conservative and less subject to change, we are going to focus on secular art. The traditional secular arts of the native peoples of the United State are an ideal example for two reasons. First, over a century ago, these peoples became economic integrated in to an industrialized market economy. Thus, these societies have already experienced the changes that other traditional peoples in the world are only now confronting. Second, anthropologists and other scholars have studied the arts of Native American people to a greater extent than any comparable population in the world. Yet there is such complexity in the changes in Native American art that we are limiting this discussion to the changes in only two of these artistic traditions: Plain beadwork and Pueblo pottery.

Until the last decades of the nineteenth century, most Native Americans produced their own clothing and domestic goods. These items were produced by hand and usually for other family members; trade in these items was limited. The category of utilitarian goods in which their artistic traditions found their greatest expression varied regionally. Among the nomadic groups on the Great Plains, it was usually in leather goods; clothing, footwear, cradle boards, and storage and personal bags. Initially, these items were decorated with either painted designs or designs made of sewn and dyed porcupine quills. Later they acquired European glass trade beads, and beadwork became the primary means of decorating these items. Every Plains society developed its own preferences in designs and colors. Although some were more talented and creative than others, virtually every woman, and a few men, produced beadwork. Although beaded clothing and footwear were worn daily, particularly fine items were put back to be worn only for special occasions.

Among the Pueblo peoples of the Southwest, their greatest secular artistic expressions were found in their pottery. Settled, farming peoples, these tribes regarded pottery as extremely important in their daily lives, and they made a wide variety of different utilitarian pots: mixing bowls, serving bowls, storage jars, water ollas, water canteens, and many others. These pots were usually decorated with painted designs. Like the peoples of the Plains, every Pueblo developed its own distinctive style of pottery, and every potter attempted to develop her own. Rarely were two pots identical in their painted designs. This same basic characteristic of secular art finding its greatest expressions in only certain aspects of the utilitarian material culture is generally true for traditional, preindustrial, peoples throughout the world.

The Industrial Revolution, which we discussed in Chapter 4, dramatically reduced the production of individually crafted handmade domestic items in the United States and Western Europe. Mills and factories mass-produced cloth, clothing, pots, pans, dishes, tools, furniture, and similar utilitarian goods. In many cases, these items were finer and more durable that handcrafted items; but in all cases, they were far less labor intensive and thus less costly. Very quickly manufactured goods replaced traditional handmade goods among the peoples of Western Europe and the dominant society in the Americas. While the middle and lower classes could purchase mass-produced manufactured utilitarian goods from the local stores or the Sears-Roebuck catalog, the wealthier wanted something finer, something unique, something handmade. This resulted in the so-called Arts and Crafts movement, which emerged in the United States and Western Europe during the late nineteenth producing handcrafted furniture, pottery, metal work, and other domestic goods for the home. In other words, finely crafted, unique, handmade domestic objects, although still utilitarian, were being transformed, if not into "art," then at least into something different, more desirable, and certainly more expensive.

During this same period, the Native American peoples of the Plains and Pueblos saw their economies greatly altered as they became integrated into the local U.S. market economy. Machine-made mass-produced clothing, ceramic and metal pots, pans, dishes, and other household items started quickly replacing handmade pottery among the Pueblos and beaded clothing among the Plains peoples in their daily lives. Their utilitarian value greatly diminished, these items were now produced in far lower quantities—in some cases precipitously. Initially, it appeared that beadwork and pottery production among some of these societies might actually cease and the art traditions associated with them vanish. However, they were saved in part by commoditizing their art for a newly emerging market in souvenir or curios.

The last decades of the nineteenth century witnessed the convergent of western tourism and an increasing nostalgia for the American past. These factors, together with the prevalent belief in the "vanishing Indian," made Indian items an ideal souvenir for travelers or mementos of the vanishing past of others. In this new market, Native Americans items were not being sold for utilitarian use or for their aesthetic appeal, but rather as something strange, exotic, or nostalgic. Pueblo pottery was ideally suited for this new market since pottery could be readily displayed as decorative objects on shelves or tables. Plains beadwork was more problematic in that it could not be readily displayed or adapted for display; moreover, with few exceptions, tourists did not wish to dress like an "Indian." A tourist might buy a pair of beaded moccasins and wear them a few times before putting them a way, but other beaded items had little appeal. A beaded cradleboard or beaded dress might have exotic appeal, but few people wanted to hang one on their wall. Plains peoples did develop a few specialty items for the non-Indian trade, such as beaded watch pockets, gauntlets, women's purses, and valises for men. However, the market for such items was small relative to the Plains population. Another factor affected an item's marketability as a souvenir or curio: it had to be relatively inexpensive.

Thus, the market economy had different effects on these two artistic traditions. Plains beadwork became more limited as the members of these societies made a distinction between their "daily clothes," which were mass-produced machine goods, and their beaded "Indian clothes," which were now only worn on special occasions. Production of other beaded items, such as storage bags and cradleboard, also declined or disappeared. As a result, fewer and fewer women became active bead workers, and bead working became a specialized occupation within the native communities, with a few individuals making and selling items to other members of the native community. Thus, the primary market for beaded items remained other natives.

In contrast, although less pottery was being used within the Pueblos, the demand for Pueblo pottery by nonnatives was dramatically increasing and changing the Pueblo pottery tradition. Pueblo potters began producing new inexpensive items for tourists. Pots became smaller, and wide variety of new forms appeared, such as pitchers, teapots, candlesticks, ash trays, animal and human figures, cups, plates, and handled baskets. By the 1920s, a few potters, such as Maria Martinez, were beginning to be recognized for their outstanding work and signing their names to their pottery. However, these individuals were the exception. The primarily market until well after World War II was still for inexpensive curio or souvenir pots made by anonymous potters.

In the 1960s and 1970s, Native American traditional arts were redefined by the dominant society as "ethnic art." Now defined as "art," prices for Native American items escalated, and "Indian curio stores" became "Indian art galleries." So lucrative did the making of Indian art become that non-Indians started producing "Indian art." In 1990. Congress passed the Indian Arts and Craft Act, stating that only objects made by an enrolled member of a federally recognized tribe could be sold as "Indian made." The escalating value of "Indian art" has had minimal effect on Plains bead work, as the market for bead workers remained primarily other Indians for their personal use. In contrast, Pueblo pottery has been dramatically affected. Not only can an individual earn a relatively good living, but a well-known potter can become prosperous. Now marketed to nonnatives as art, all pieces are now signed by the potter. In attempts to gain ever higher prices for work, in an increasingly competitive market, potters have and are creating innovative forms and decorating techniques to readily distinguish their work from that of others.

continues on next page

In summary, plain bead work and Pueblo pottery represent the two extremes in the effects of the market economy on the traditional secular art of Native American peoples. Today, most bead work and most pottery are no longer produced by family members for family members, but by artisans for sale to others. However, these two markets are very different. Bead work has remained an artistic tradition associated with utilitarian goods that are marketed to other members of the native community. Its daily utilitarian function has disappeared, replaced by its social function of maintaining the social identity of group. Pueblo pottery is now produced primarily as decorative art objects for sale to nonnatives. Its daily utilitarian function has disappeared, superseded by its economic role as an important source of cash income. While some pottery still strongly reflects the Pueblo artistic tradition, increasing the pottery produced by Pueblo artisans, reflects the aesthetic tastes of the nonnative buyers. As a result, unlike beadwork, much of it has lost its "ethnic identity"; it is just "art."

The traditional visual arts of the Plains and Pueblo peoples have survived because they have become commoditized. Plains bead workers have found a highly specialized local market; other members of their community. Pueblo potters have established a national/global market for their pottery as either "art" or "ethnic art." As other traditional peoples throughout the world are increasingly integrated into the global market economy, their art traditions are going to confront similar challenges.

that were handpainted in strange colors and designs. The minute you saw them, you knew they were "hippies." Clothing styles, hairstyles, and other art forms are commonly used to indicate social group identity, from the black leather jackets painted with club emblems of motorcycle gangs to the shepherd crook spears and red sashes of the Cheyenne Dog Soldier society.

A widespread use of art to express social membership has to do with ethnic affiliation. In Chapter 16, we discuss ethnic boundary markers in more detail, but here it is important to note that art is one of the common expressions of ethnic identity. Clothing styles and decoration are important visual markers of ethnic identity. Plaid kilts are markers of Scots as much as beaded clothing and feather headdresses are of Native Americans. A woman in Guatemala wearing a *huipuli* is a Maya. If you see a man wearing a cowboy hat and boots in Europe, you can guess that he is probably an American tourist.

Ethnicity is expressed in more than clothing. The full range of artistic forms—body, visual, performance, and verbal arts—is employed to display one's ethnic identity. Thus, we speak of ethnic art, ethnic dance, ethnic music, ethnic songs, ethnic literature, and ethnic foods. Despite our use of the word *ethnic* in such contexts, ultimately, of course, all art is ethnic art because it is associated with a specific ethnic group and everyone is a part of some ethnic group. For various reasons, people value and pay premium prices for the art produced by ethnic groups other than their own.

From an anthropological perspective, much of the multicultural movement in contemporary North America—and particularly in colleges and universities—is really about understanding and appreciating "ethnic" forms of artistic expression. When Anglo-Americans talk about "other cultures," often they are referring to African, Hispanic, Asian, and other "non-Anglo" Americans. When they "celebrate diversity," often they are celebrating differences in literature and other forms of verbal art, interpreting graffiti as a legitimate art form, listening to African or Mexican music, eating South Asian or Vietnamese foods, and so forth. Overall, the multicultural movement has had a positive influence on intercultural tolerance and understanding. In fact, multiculturalism is part of what anthropologists have been trying to get across to their students for nearly a century. But perhaps more people ought to realize that appreciating multicultural diversity should mean far more than celebrating diversity in forms of artistic expression.

Social Status

Finally, relative social status within societies is reflected in the use of art. As discussed earlier, body arts are frequently an indicator of social status. Other art forms also indicate status. In many ranked and stratified societies, the rights to use certain art forms may be the property of families or status groups. Only certain individuals have the right to wear or use particular colors or designs, sing particular songs, dance particular dances, and even tell particular stories. This control over the use or performance of particular artistic expression is a symbolic indicator of individual social position within the society.

Similarly, in contemporary Western society, we use art to demonstrate our relative status. We display our status in our homes, automobiles, furnishings, and clothing, communicating to the world, "Look what we can afford to buy." We also demonstrate our status in what we hang on our walls, read, listen to, and watch. In our consumption of visual, performance, and verbal arts, the evaluation, of course, is more subjective and difficult to measure. But for many people, opera, ballet, and classical music have higher status than comedy, square dancing, and country and western or rap music. Classical literature has higher status than romance novels, science fiction, and comic books.

SUMMARY

1. **Discuss the disagreement over whether art is or is not a cultural universal.** All cultures have artistic objects, designs, songs, dances, and other ways of expressing their appreciation of the aesthetic. The aesthetic impulse is universal, although cultures vary in their ways of expressing it and in the social functions and cultural meanings they attach to it. However, people raised in the Western tradition are inclined to think of art as something set apart from everyday life—as when we use the phrase "fine arts"—yet we all express ourselves aesthetically in many ways, including how we dress, decorate our houses, and eat our meals.

2. **List the various forms of body arts.** People around the world change their bodily appearance by such means as physical alterations, application of body paints, tattoos, and scarification. These decorations of the body are used for a variety of purposes, including beautification, expression of individual or group identity, display of privilege or social position, and symbolic indication of social maturity.

3. **Discuss the different forms of visual arts.** In the visual arts, humankind as a whole has shown enormous creativity in form, style, design, techniques, materials, and many other features. Ornamentation of tools, clothing, basketry, houses, and practically all other material objects is a universal practice.

4. **Discuss the different forms of performance arts.** Performance arts include the use of sound and movement for both aesthetic and communicative purposes. In pre-industrial cultures, performances of music (including song and percussion), dance, and theater often involve audience participation, as they often do in the everyday lives of people everywhere. Often, performance art is tightly integrated into a people's spiritual and religious life.

5. **Explain how art is integrated into our religious lives.** Perhaps many forms of art began as "sacred" in that they were connected to the appeal to or worship of spiritual beings. Certainly, the religious elements of artistic expression are important not only in the history of Western art but also in the

artistic traditions of people the world over. In their complex curing ceremonies, Navajo singers used both visual arts (sand paintings) and performance arts (chants/songs) in appealing to the Holy People. Distinguishing "sacred" and "secular" art seems like a simple thing, but objects with religious significance are often used for practical purposes.

6. **Explain how gender, identity, and social status are reflected in art.** Art is connected to other social and cultural elements such as gender, identity, and status. In many societies, certain arts and art forms are associated with women and others with men. Ethnic identity is commonly expressed in art and serves as ethnic boundary markers. Finally, within societies, relative social status is frequently expressed in the consumption of art.

16 Ethnicity and Ethnic Conflict

A city sacred to Jews, Muslims, and Christians, Jerusalem has been and is a major source of ethnic/religious conflict in the world.

Ethnic Groups
  Situational Nature of Ethnic Identity
  Attributes of Ethnic Groups
  Fluidity of Ethnic Groups
  Types of Ethnic Groups

Civilizations

The Problem of Stateless Nationalities

Responses to Ethnic Conflict
  Homogenization
  Segregation
  Accommodation
  Results

LEARNING OBJECTIVES

After reading this chapter, you should be able to:

1. **DEFINE** ethnic group.
2. **EXPLAIN** what we mean when we say ethnic identity is situational.
3. **EXPLAIN** the attributes of ethnic groups.
4. **DESCRIBE** the different levels of ethnic identity.
5. **EXPLAIN** why ethnic conflict is so prevalent in the world today, and describe an "artificial county."
6. **EXPLAIN** ethnic homogenization.
7. **ELABORATE** on the meanings of ethnic segregation and ethnic accommodation.

With the collapse of the Soviet Union and the end of the Cold War in the 1990s, many people thought we had entered a new, safer, and more peaceful era. But instead of peace, we are now faced with growing conflicts that are becoming ever more violent and destructive. In the past decade or so, several million people have fallen victim to wars, while tens of millions more have joined the ranks of refugees. Central governments exist in name only in parts of Africa and Asia. Large regions of some of these countries are under the control of rebel armies or outlaw groups. Concerns increase about nuclear proliferation and biological warfare. Concerns are also rising about terrorist groups and their expanding capabilities for destruction. It is not just that conflict is a problem—it is a growing problem. Most, but not all, of these conflicts are basically ethnic conflicts.

Globalization has changed the nature of ethnic conflict. In the not too distant past, ethnic conflicts were limited to particular geographic regions or countries. With vastly improved transportation and communications systems, however, together with increasing international migrations of peoples and the emergence of ethnically mixed urban populations, conflicts are no longer geographically localized. Ethnic groups may strike their enemy anywhere in the world. Associated with this increased capability, the tactics of ethnic guerilla warfare also changed—from targeting primarily opposing armies and paramilitary groups to the increased targeting of civilian populations. The first evidence of this change came in 1972, when the Irish Republican Army began bombings in London. The following year, the Black September Organization, a Palestinian militant group, killed 11 Israeli athletes competing in the Olympic Games in Munich, Germany. Since the 1970s, many other groups have become involved in such attacks. In 1985, Sikh separatists allegedly bombed an Air India flight between Montreal and London. In 1995, Basque separatists began attacking targets throughout Spain. In 2002 and again in 2010, Chechen rebels attacked civilian targets in Moscow, almost 1,000 miles from Chechnya.

Globalization has also resulted in the emergence of higher and a more ominous level of ethnic identity and conflict, which Samuel Huntington calls *civilizations*. A civilization consists of a large number of otherwise linguistically and socially distinct ethnic groups who share a common, usually religious, cultural tradition that unites them in opposition to members of ethnic groups from other civilizations. By the beginning of the twenty-first century, an Islamic identity in opposition to a Western (Judeo-Christian) identity has begun to emerge. Al Qaeda, with members drawn from a wide variety of Islamic ethnic groups and countries, sees Islamic peoples collectively involved in a struggle with Western peoples in general—thus their terrorist attacks on New York City, Washington, London, and Madrid. The U.S.-led invasions of Afghanistan and Iraq, with the military support of other, primarily Western countries, have served to validate Al Qaeda's assertions in the minds of many Islamic peoples. The 2013 bombing in Boston, though an independent action of two individuals, was a product of this broader conflict.

Ethnic Groups

Over the past few decades, the terms *ethnic* and *ethnicity* have become part of our everyday vocabulary, as have the terms *ethnic food, ethnic vote, ethnic conflict, ethnic clothes, ethnic neighborhood,* and *ethnic studies.* In the 1960s, anthropologists began studying ethnicity as a distinct social phenomenon, and since that time literature on ethnicity has proliferated. Part of the increased scholarly interest in ethnic groups came as a result of Nathan Glazer and Daniel Moynihan's study of ethnic groups in New York City. They found that "in the third generation, the descendants of the immigrants confronted each other, and knew they were both Americans, in the same dress, with the same language, using the same artifacts, troubled by the same thing, but they voted differently, had different ideas about education and sex, and were still, in many essential ways, as different from one another as their grandfathers had been" (1963, 13). Thus, while a population may develop a new ethnic identity, in this case American, they will retain many of their earlier cultural believes and practices.

What is an ethnic group? First, it is necessary to realize that all peoples, not just minority populations, have an ethnic group identity. In essence, an **ethnic group** is a named social category of people based on perceptions of shared social experience or ancestry. Members of the ethnic group see themselves as sharing cultural traditions and history that distinguish them from other groups. Ethnic group identity has a strong psychological or emotional component that divides the people of the world into opposing categories of "us" and "them." In contrast to social stratification (discussed in Chapter 13), which divides and unifies people along a series of horizontal axes on the basis of socioeconomic factors, ethnic identities divide and unify people along a series of vertical axes. Thus, ethnic groups, at least theoretically, cut across socioeconomic class differences, drawing members from all strata of the population.

Before discussing the significance of ethnic differences and conflicts in the modern world, we need to examine the varying dimensions of ethnic group identity, including (1) the situational nature of ethnic group identity, (2) the attributes of ethnic groups, (3) the fluidity of ethnic group identity, and (4) the types of ethnic groups.

Situational Nature of Ethnic Identity

One of the more complicated aspects of ethnicity is that an individual's ethnic group identity is seldom absolute. A person may assume a number of different ethnic identities, depending on the social situation. For example, in the United States, an individual may simultaneously be an American, a Euro-American, an Italian American, and a Sicilian American. The particular ethnic identity chosen varies with the social context.

When in Europe or among Europeans, the person would assume the identity of American, in contrast to German, French, or Italian. In the United States, the same individual might assume the identity of Euro-American, as opposed to African American or Native American. Among Euro-Americans, the person might take the ethnic identity of Italian American, as opposed to Irish American or Polish American. When among Italian Americans, the individual might be identified as Sicilian American, as opposed to an Italian American whose family came from Rome, Naples, or some other region of Italy.

The situational nature of ethnic identity demonstrates what some have called the **hierarchical nesting** of identity. A particular ethnic group forms part of a larger collection of ethnic groups of like social magnitude. In turn, these ethnic groups may collectively form still another higher level of ethnic identity, which may be nested in yet another higher level. Thus, ethnic identity does not simply divide the world into categories of "us" and "them" but into varying, hierarchically ranked categories of "us" and "them."

Attributes of Ethnic Groups

Two main attributes help to define and identify an ethnic group: an origin myth or history and ethnic boundary markers.

Origin Myth

Each ethnic group is the product of a unique set of social and historical events. The common or shared historical experiences that serve to unite and distinguish the group from other groups and give it a distinct social identity constitute the group's **origin myth**. By *myth,* we do not mean to imply that the historical events did not really happen or that the group is not what it claims to be. We mean only that these particular experiences serve as the ideological charter for the group's common

---

ethnic group Named social group based on perceptions of shared ancestry, cultural traditions, and common history that culturally distinguish that group from other groups.

hierarchical nesting Occurs when an ethnic group is part of a larger collection of ethnic groups, which together constitute a higher level of ethnic identity.

origin myth Collective history of an ethnic group that defines which subgroups are part of it and its relationship to other ethnic groups.

identity and provide the members with a sense of being different from other people. Origin myths play an integral part in creating and maintaining ethnic group identity: they define and describe the origin and collective cultural historical experiences of the group.

Not all historical events are equally important; origin myths make selective references. Wars and conflicts are frequently emphasized because they clearly distinguish "us" from "them." The origin myth imbues the group's members with feelings of distinctiveness and, often, superiority in relation to other groups. What makes an origin myth so powerful is that mythic themes and concepts are embedded in virtually every aspect of the people's popular culture: stories (written and oral), songs, dances, games, music, theater, film, and art. So pervasive are these mythic images in everyday life that members of the group learn them passively rather than consciously. Thus, all members of the group are well versed in the basic tenets of the group myth, and in the minds of most, these ideas become an unquestioned "truth." In larger, more sophisticated groups, the origin myth also takes the form of a written, purportedly objective history formally taught in schools. American history as taught in elementary and high school is not merely the objective, political history of a particular nation-state; it is also the story of the American people. Thus, it serves as the officially sanctioned origin myth of the American ethnic group. Similarly, English, French, Japanese, and Russian history as taught in their schools is the "authorized" origin myth of those groups.

When you realize that history as taught in schools is, in fact, the collective origin myth of the group, you realize the significance of including or excluding a particular subgroup of the population. Using American history as an example, we can see how historical events play a critical role in the emergence and definition of a distinctively American ethnic identity. Among these events are the landing of the *Mayflower*, the American Revolution, the Civil War, the westward expansion, and the world wars. Certain historical groups, such as cowboys and cavalry, are used as embodiments of American ideals and identity. Americans are the descendants of the various peoples who collectively participated in these and other group-defining events. Thus, it is not surprising that every American subgroup is sensitive to its portrayal in these events. To African Americans, it is important that American history acknowledges that the first man to die in the American Revolution was an African American, that African Americans fought as soldiers in the Revolutionary War and Civil War, that a high percentage of cowboys were African Americans, and that African American cavalrymen played an important part in winning the West. Similarly, public acknowledgment and recognition that their groups were active participants in some, if not all, of the major defining events of American history are equally important for American populations. Although Christopher Columbus never actually saw what is today the United States, we celebrate Columbus Day, in recognition of the contributions of Italian Americans. We have monuments and parks recognizing the contribution of General Tadeusz Kosciuszko, the Polish volunteer who fought in the American Revolution, which serves to honor not only him but Polish Americans. The public honoring of the Japanese American volunteers, who fought in World War II is to recognize not just their individual patriotism but the patriotism of the Japanese American community in general. It is inclusion in the collective origin myth that legitimizes a people's status as members of the group.

Ethnic Boundary Markers

Every ethnic group has a way of determining or expressing membership. Overt factors used to demonstrate or denote group membership are called *ethnic boundary markers*. Ethnic boundary markers are important not only to identify group members to one another but also to demonstrate identity to and distinctiveness from nonmembers. Because these markers distinguish members from all other groups, a single boundary marker is seldom sufficient. A marker that might distinguish one ethnic group from a second group may not distinguish it from a third group. Thus, combinations of markers are commonly used. Differences in language, religion, physical appearance, or particular cultural traits serve as ethnic boundary markers.

As we discussed in Chapter 3, speech style and language are symbols of personal identity: we send covert messages about the kind of person we are by how we speak. Language, therefore, frequently serves as an ethnic boundary marker. A person's native language is the primary indicator of ethnic group identity in many areas of the world. In the southwestern United States, Hopi and Navajo members are readily distinguished by their language alone. However, just because two populations share a common language does not mean they share a common identity, any more than the fact that two populations speak different languages means they

---

ethnic boundary markers Any overt characteristics that can be used to indicate ethnic group membership.

have two distinct identities. For example, the Serbs, Croats, and Bosniaks of what was Yugoslavia speak dialects of Serbo-Croatian. They are, however, distinct and historically antagonistic ethnic groups. Conversely, a person may be Irish and speak either Gaelic or English as a native language. At one time the German government granted automatic citizenship to ethnic German refugees from Eastern Europe, but a difficulty in assimilating these refugees was that many spoke only Polish or Russian. Thus, one does not have to speak German to be an ethnic German.

While the spoken language may not clearly distinguish two groups, the orthography, or written forms of the language may. Serbo-Croatian is written using three different alphabets. The Serbs use Cyrillic, the Croatians Roman, and the Bosniaks Arabic characters. Yiddish spoken by the Ashkenazi Jews is basically a dialect of German. However, German is written in Roman script, while Yiddish uses the Hebrew alphabet. Urdu and Hindi are the same language, but Urdu is written in Perso-Arabic script, while Hindi is written using Nagari script.

Like language, religion may serve as an ethnic boundary marker. The major world religions, such as Christianity, Islam, and Buddhism, encompass numerous distinct groups, so that religious affiliation does not always indicate ethnic affiliation. But, in many cases, religion and ethnic group more or less correspond. The Jews may be categorized as either a religious or an ethnic group. Similarly, the Sikhs in India constitute both a religious and an ethnic group. In still other situations, religious differences may be the most important marker of ethnic identity. As we mentioned earlier, the Serbs, Croats, and Bosniaks speak the same language; the most important distinction between these three groups is that the Serbs are Eastern Orthodox, the Croats are Catholic, and the Bosniaks are Muslim. Conversely, the Chinese ethnic identity transcends religious differences. A person is still Chinese, or Han, whether he or she is a Christian, Taoist, Buddhist, or Marxist atheist. However, Chinese Muslims, called Hui, are one of the officially recognized 56 ethnic groups of China.

Physical characteristics, or phenotypes, can sometimes indicate ethnic identity. It is impossible to identify Germans, Dutch, Danes, and other northern European ethnic groups by their physical characteristics. A similar situation is found in those regions of the world in which populations have been in long association with one another. Thus, physical characteristics do not distinguish a Zulu from a Swazi, a Chinese from a Korean, or a Choctaw from a Chickasaw. However, with the massive movements of people, particularly over the past few hundred years, physical characteristics have increasingly emerged as a marker of ethnic identity. Members of the three major ethnic groups in Malaysia—Malays, East Indians, and Chinese—are readily distinguishable by their physical appearance. The significance or lack of significance of physical characteristics in ethnic identity may also vary with the level of ethnic identity we are considering. The American identity includes almost the full range of human physical types. However, at a lower level of identity—Euro-American, African American, and Native American—physical characteristics do serve as one marker of ethnic identity. Yet within these groups, physical characteristics alone cannot be the only marker. Some Native Americans physically look like Euro-Americans or African Americans, while some African Americans might be identified as Euro-Americans or Native Americans on the basis of their physical appearance alone.

A wide variety of cultural traits, clothing, house types, personal adornment, food, technology, economic activities, or general lifestyle may also serve as ethnic boundary markers. Over the past 100 years, a rapid homogenization of world material culture, food habits, and technology has erased many of the more overt cultural markers. Today, you do not have to be Mexican to enjoy tacos, Italian to eat pizza, or Japanese to have sushi for lunch. Similarly, you can dine on hamburgers, the all-American food, in Japan, Oman, Russia, Mexico, and most other countries. Cultural traits remain, however, the most important, diverse, and complex category of ethnic boundary markers. For the sake of brevity, we limit our discussion to one trait—clothing (see also Chapter 15).

Clothing styles have historically been the most overt single indicator of ethnic identity. In the not too distant past, almost every ethnic group had its own unique style of dress. Even today, a Scottish American who wants to publically indicate his ethnic identity can wear a kilt, and a German American may wear his *lederhosen*. Similarly, on certain occasions, Native Americans wear "Indian clothes" decorated with beadwork. These are not everyday garments and are worn only in social situations in which people want to emphasize their ethnic identity. In many regions of the world, however, people still wear "ethnic" clothes every day. In highland Guatemala, clothing, particularly women's clothing, readily identifies the ethnic affiliation of the wearer. Guatemalan clothing styles actually indicate two levels of ethnic identity. If a woman wears a *huipil*, a loose-fitting blouse that slips over the head, she is a Native American. Non–Native American women, called *Ladinas*, dress in Western-style clothes. The

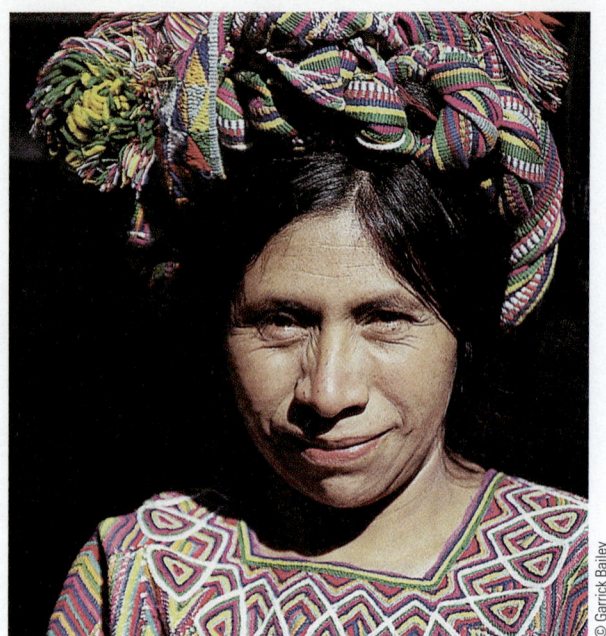

The dress of this woman not only identifies her as a Maya Indian but also indicates that she is from the town of Nabaj in Guatemala.

style, colors, and designs on the huipil further identify where a particular woman is from: Nahuala, Chichicastenango, Solola, or one of the other hundred or so Native American communities in highland Guatemala.

Fluidity of Ethnic Groups

Ethnic groups are not stable groupings. Ethnic groups vanish, individuals and even communities change ethnic identities, and new ethnic groups come into existence.

During the past 500 years, numerous ethnic groups have vanished. Massachusetts, Erie, and Susquehannock were not originally place names but the names of now vanished Native American ethnic groups. Still other ethnic groups in Asia, Africa, Oceania, Europe, and the Americas have vanished as well. Extinction of an ethnic group seldom means biological extinction, though. In most cases, the members of one group are absorbed into the population of a larger group. The Tasmanians of Australia are typical of what happened to many smaller ethnic groups. Numbering at most 5,000 when the British began colonizing the island of Tasmania in 1802, the population was so ravaged by wars and massacres that only a handful survived by 1850; the Tasmanians as a viable ethnic group had ceased to exist. In 1869, the last full-blooded Tasmanian man died, and in 1888, the last full-blooded Tasmanian woman died. Even today, however, mixed-blood descendants of the Tasmanians can be found among the Australian population.

Both individuals and communities can move between ethnic groups. During the sixteenth and seventeenth centuries, French Protestants, called *Huguenots*, fled persecution in France and settled in large numbers in England and the English colonies in North America. These people quickly became absorbed into the English population. Over the past 200 years, Americans have absorbed numerous immigrant populations.

Ethnogenesis is the emergence of a new ethnic group. Ethnogenesis usually occurs in one of two ways: (1) a portion of an existing ethnic group splits away and forms a new ethnic group, or (2) members of two or more existing ethnic groups fuse to form a new ethnic group.

Probably the most common cause of ethnogenesis is the division of an existing ethnic group. At one time, the Osage, Kansa, Omaha, Ponca, and Quapaw Indians of the central United States were a single ethnic group. The origin myths of these peoples tell how at different times portions broke away, until there were five distinct groups. In the 1700s, small groups of Muskogee/Creek Indians began moving south into Florida, where they eventually developed a distinct identity as the Seminole. Similarly, as Bantu-speaking peoples spread throughout central and southern Africa, they became separated, and new ethnic groups formed. As the Spanish Empire in the Americas disintegrated during the early 1800s, new regional ethnic identities (such as Mexican, Guatemalan, Peruvian, and Chilean) began to emerge among the Spanish-speaking peoples in that region. In 1652, the Dutch began settling near the Cape of Good Hope in southern Africa. These people eventually developed their own distinctive dialect of Dutch, called *Afrikaans*, and their own ethnic identity: Boers.

In other cases, members of two or more ethnic groups fuse and a new ethnic identity emerges. In England, the Angles, the Saxons, and the Jutes fused and became known as the English. The original Euro-American ethnic group was not the result of a split among the English people but rather a fusion of English, Dutch, German, Scots, Irish, French Huguenots, Scotch-Irish, and other European settlers residing on the coast of North America. Most African American groups in the Americas are the result of the fusion of

ethnogenesis Creation of a new ethnic group.

CONCEPT REVIEW: Levels of Ethnic Identity

Civilizations — Groupings of nationalities on the basis of a shared or common cultural historical tradition. In most cases, this shared cultural tradition takes the form of religion.

Nationalities — Ethnic groups who collectively own, or feel that they own, a specific geographic region, or homeland, in which they have exclusive rights.

Subnationalities — Ethnic groups whose identities are nested within that of a larger national identity.

---

numerous distinct African groups. Intermarriage between French traders and Native Americans in Canada resulted in the emergence of the Metis; a socially and culturally distinct population. Similarly, in South Africa, the Cape Coloured, people of mixed Dutch and Khoikhoi ancestry, are socially and politically distinct from both whites and Africans.

Types of Ethnic Groups

From our discussion and examples so far, it should be apparent that the term *ethnic group* covers a range of social groupings. In general, ethnic groups fall into two main categories: national and subnational.

A **nationality** is an ethnic group that has a feeling of **homeland**, a geographic region over which they collectively have exclusive rights. Implicit in this concept is the assumption of an inherent right to political autonomy and self-determination. In contrast, **subnationalities** lack the concept of a distinct and separate homeland and the associated rights to separate political sovereignty and self-determination. A subnational group sees itself as a dependent and politically subordinate subset of a nationality.

Although it is easy to define the difference between ethnic nationalities and subnationalities, sometimes it is far more difficult to classify particular groups. The ethnic groups in the United States demonstrate some of the difficulties in classification. With some ethnic groups, there is no doubt: Italian Americans, German Americans, Polish Americans, Scottish Americans, and Irish Americans are all subnational groups. At another level of identity, the same is true for African Americans. None of these groups has a concept of a distinct and separate geographic homeland within the United States. Hence, they are subnational groups that, together with many other groups, collectively constitute the American ethnic nationality.

For other ethnic groups within the United States, their status is not as clear. What is the status of Native American groups such as the Navajo, the Hopi, the Cheyenne, and the Cherokee? These groups have historic homelands within the United States. They also have histories quite distinct from those of other Americans. In recent years, they have been asserting increased political autonomy and self-determination within their reservations or what were their reservations. Although there is disagreement, many Native American individuals and groups still consider themselves distinct nationalities. For example, many Iroquois in the United States and Canada still see themselves as members of a distinct and sovereign nation, even issuing their own passports. The U.S. government recognizes most American Indian groups as distinct groups with collective legal and political rights. No other ethnic groups in the United States have officially recognized governments and limited rights of self-determination. There are also some differences of opinion concerning their ethnic status among the Spanish-speaking people in the southwestern United States. Until the mid–nineteenth century, Texas, New Mexico, Arizona, and California were part of Mexico, when the United States acquired this region through military conquest. Most of the native Spanish-speaking

---

nationality Ethnic group that claims a right to a discrete homeland and to political autonomy and self-determination.

homeland Geographic region over which a particular ethnic group feels it has exclusive rights.

subnationalities Dependent subgroups within a larger nationality that lack the concept of a separate homeland and make no claim to any inherent right to political autonomy and self-determination.

people in this region think of themselves as Mexican American or Spanish American, a subnational group. There is, however, a group who sees themselves as "Mexicans" living in a land that is rightfully part of Mexico, a region they call Atzlan.

The distinction between nationality and subnational ethnic group is important because of their different political implications. As we shall see, the demands of subnational groups for equal rights and treatment have long been a source of conflict in countries such as the United States. However, these groups compete within the existing political framework. In contrast, the demands of nationalities for independence and sovereignty create major political problems.

Civilizations

There are higher levels of identity than ethnic nationalities. There are identities which create aggregates of ethnic groups for joint action. Just like with ethnic groups, these identities divide the world into larger groupings of "us" and "them." Frequently these identities are based on speaking a common language, which is the result of a partially shared history. English-speaking peoples can act together in relations with other non-English-speaking groups. Not surprisingly, when in conflict with other peoples, the Americans, Canadians, English, Australians, New Zealanders, and other English-speaking peoples are usually supportive of each other. The reason is not just that these groups share a common language but that they also share basically common cultural values, norms, and worldview as well. Thus, they understand each other better that they understand other people. The same is true of Spanish-speaking peoples in Latin America, Arabic-speaking peoples in North Africa and the Middle East, and Turkic-speaking peoples in the Middle East and Central Asia, to note only some.

There is, however, still a higher level that Samuel P. Huntington, one of America's foremost political scientists, noted in 1996 in his widely read book, *The Clash of Civilizations and the Remaking of World Order*. He sees the world coalescing into seven or eight "**civilizations**," which he identifies as Western (Protestant-Catholic), Slavic-Orthodox (Christians), Confucian, Japanese, Islamic, Hindu, Latin American, and possibly African. Huntington argues that increasing contact between peoples is not serving to lessen cultural differences, but rather to make people more acutely aware of those cultural factors that divide them. People are increasingly identifying with others of like cultural heritage. The result will be a "political" realignment based on cultural heritage, or "civilizations." To Huntington, religious traditions indicate fundamental cultural differences between peoples, and religion forms the cultural core of what he terms "civilizations." Huntington does not see the coalescence of civilizations as replacing existing ethnic identities or ending internal conflicts. He does, however, see these various civilizations increasingly competing with one another, and the boundaries separating these civilizations becoming the "fault lines" along which future conflicts will occur. Ethnic and ideological wars will be superseded by wars between civilizations; the most imminent of these clashes is between Western and Islamic civilizations.

Most anthropologists see problems with Huntington's concept. One of the main problems is with the "seven or eight" civilizations he defines. Should Japanese be considered a separate civilization, or is it a part of a larger East Asian civilization? Should Western and Slavic-Orthodox be two separate civilizations or one Christian civilization? Should Latin American be separate from Western? On the other hand, he seems to be correct in his assertion that increased contact is resulting in a heightened awareness of cultural similarities and differences between peoples. All other things being equal, ethnic groups have a tendency to identify with groups most like themselves. For lack of a better term, we can apply *civilization* to the larger aggregates of ethnic nationalities. However, how many such civilizations exist, and which ethnic nationalities belong to these aggregates are not clearly evident.

The Problem of Stateless Nationalities

It is difficult for most Americans to understand the causes and bitterness of ethnic conflict in other parts of the world. We think of *nationality* and *nation* as one and the same. An American is any person who is a citizen of the United States. Most of us think of ourselves primarily as Americans and only secondarily as Irish, Italian, or Japanese Americans. This mindset about the meaning and significance of ethnicity is due mainly to our history as a nation of immigrants—with the exception of Native Americans, most immigrants renounced their claims to their national homelands when they came to the New World. For the most part, the ethnic

> **civilization** Form of complex society in which many people live in cities.

groups in the United States are subnationalities, not nationalities. Thus, from our common perception, a Russian is a person from Russia, a Nigerian is a citizen from Nigeria, and so forth. Equating country of origin with ethnic nationality, we view ethnic conflicts in other regions of the world as comparable to conflicts between subnational groups within the United States. We think ethnic problems within a country are the result of some combination of social, political, and/or economic discrimination—resolvable and reparable by political reforms—and we minimize their political significance. However, armed ethnic conflicts are not between subnational groups but between distinct nationalities.

The ethnic conflicts in Northern Ireland and in Israel and Palestine have proved particularly bitter. In 1922, after several centuries of British colonial domination and periodic rebellions by the native Irish, the Irish Free State (now the Republic of Ireland) was established. Not all of Ireland was given independence, however. In the seventeenth century, to control the Irish, the British evicted Irish farmers from the northernmost portion of the island and colonized the region with Scottish Presbyterians, who became known as the Ulster-Scots, or *Scotch-Irish* in the United States. The Ulster-Scots did not identify themselves as Irish and had no desire to become part of an independent Ireland. Recognizing the wishes of the Ulster-Scots, at independence the British partitioned the island. The northern six counties became Northern Ireland and remained part of the United Kingdom. Many Irish did not and do not accept the legality of this partitioning of Ireland. To them, Northern Ireland is part of the Irish homeland and thus should be part of the Republic of Ireland. In 1968, the Irish Republican Army (IRA), a secretive guerrilla army that is illegal in the Republic of Ireland, began waging a guerilla war with the objective of reuniting Northern Ireland with the Republic of Ireland. Bombings, ambushes, and assassinations claimed more than 2,200 lives before the IRA announced in 2005 that it would end its military operations. Several splinter groups have still not agreed, and sporadic bombings and shootings still occur. The news media frequently report the problems in Northern Ireland as conflict between the British and the Irish or between Catholics and Protestants; in reality, it is neither. The root of the problem is the conflicting claims of two rival and hostile ethnic groups: the Irish and the Ulster-Scots. The Ulster-Scots have emerged over the past 400 years as a distinct nationality who claim the northern part of Ireland as their homeland. In contrast, the Irish see the area as an integral and inalienable part of the Irish homeland.

After an absence of almost 2,000 years, the Jews began returning to their historic homeland in Palestine in 1882. During the early twentieth century, Jewish settlements in Palestine grew, and in 1948, the Jewish settlers proclaimed the state of Israel. In the war that followed, the Arab League, Jordan, Egypt, Syria, and Iraq were defeated, and the Israelis gained control over most of the area west of the Jordan River and the Sinai. Periodic fighting continued, however. The 1967 Six-Day War resulted in the Israeli occupation of the Palestinian areas of the West Bank and the Gaza Strip, but it did not bring an end to the fighting. For the past 75 years, conflict between Israelis and Palestinians has been constant, varying only in the intensity and the nature of violence. The problem is similar to the problem in Northern Ireland: two nationalities—Israelis and Palestinians—claim the same geographic region as their legitimate homeland. Although some progress has been made recently toward peaceful settlements of the conflicts in Northern Ireland and between Israelis and Palestinians, such agreements are tenuous. These situations remain volatile. In Israel and Northern Ireland, it is impossible to resolve the conflict to the total satisfaction of both nationalities.

These two conflicts vividly illustrate the strength of nationalist sentiments. In both cases, we see groups of educated, rational human beings willing to sacrifice their lives and economic well-being in unending conflicts for what they consider their nationality's legitimate political rights.

Such conflicts are more common in the modern world than most of us realize. The world is divided into about 200 countries, but there are 3,000 to 5,000 distinct ethnic nationalities. As a result, the populations of most countries encompass many distinct nationalities. China officially recognizes 56 distinct nationalities. Some estimates are as high as 300 ethnic nationalities in Indonesia. Ethiopia has at least 70 nationalities. Only a handful of countries are peopled by members of a single nationality and are thus ethnically homogeneous.

The ethnic nationality problem is further complicated because current political boundaries frequently divide members of a nationality and their historic homelands. For example, Hungarians are found not only in Hungary but also in the adjacent portions of Romania and Serbia. Somalis live not only in Somalia but also in the adjacent Ogaden portion of Ethiopia. The world is filled with ethnic groups who do not fully recognize the legitimacy of "their" central government and who aspire or may potentially aspire to political sovereignty or unification with another country.

GLOBAL CHALLENGES AND OPPORTUNITIES

The Global Economy, Migration, and Transnational Communities

Although one might think this picture is of someplace in south Asia, this Hindu temple is in Middlesex County, New Jersey.

Today over 215 million people, or 3 percent of the world population, live in countries other than the one in which they were born—a much higher percentage than at any other time in human history. The global economy has changed the patterns of migration. Between 1500 and World War II, most migration was from Europe and Africa to the Americas. While the Americas, particularly the United States, is still a major destination for migrants, most of the migrants to the United States are now from Asia and Latin America. For the first time Europe has become a major destination for migrants from Asia and Africa. Within Asia, the Persian Gulf States have become a destination for migrants from South and Southeast Asia. Not only has the magnitude and direction of human migration changed and increased, but the nature of the new overseas ethnic communities formed by these migrants has changed as well. We have seen the increasing development of what some are calling **transnational** ethnic communities. However, it is important to note than not all immigrants form transnational communities, and such communities have existed throughout history. It is the number and importance of these communities that have increased significantly in recent decades.

Transnational ethnic communities are communities of a particular ethnic group that are geographically scattered. Some members of the group remain within the home country; others live in ethnic enclaves in other countries and frequently on other continents. Unlike earlier immigrant groups to the Americas and even most immigrants today, members of these ethnic enclaves maintain their social boundaries, their languages, and their religious and cultural traditions. They are not attempting to assimilate into the new neighboring populations. Neither their ethnic nor their political identities are being subordinated to that of the dominant ethnic group among whom they live or to their country of residence. They have a tendency to either directly or indirectly be involved in the politics of their homeland. Economically, they are only partially integrated in the economy where they live, frequently sending money to relatives who remain at "home" and even owning homes and even business in their home country. This feeling of primary identity with their ancestral homeland and ethnic group persists even among their descendants who were born overseas. Why is this phenomenon more prevalent today than in the past?

First, it is natural for an individual to be proud of his or her ethnic group. It is also natural for individuals to feel more social cohesion with other individuals whose cultural behaviors and practices they understand and whose basic beliefs they agree with. It is an unusual individual who totally rejects his or her native ethnic community and joins another. Thus, not surprisingly, immigrant ethnic groups tend to settle together and form enclaves.

Contemporary immigrant groups fall into two major categories: economic immigrants and political refugees. Political refugees are not voluntary immigrants. They have relocated from their home country for only one reason—they had to. Few political refugees move to another country with the idea that they are going to remain there permanently; their intention is to eventually return. Thus, they create transnational communities. However, only a small portion of immigrants are political refugees. The vast majority are economic immigrants.

Americans have a tendency to misjudge the motives of economic immigrants. In our folk mythology, we commonly see these people as coming to America in search of "a new life" and not just economic opportunity. The myth is correct, but only partially. Many of the European immigrants during the late nineteenth and early twentieth centuries did reject their homeland. Many would not even have their children learn their ancestral language. They wanted them to be "Americans." However the myth is based on those immigrants who stayed. Although there are no official records, it appears that perhaps one-third of the European immigrants

---

transnationals Members of an ethnic community living outside their country of origin.

returned to Europe and that during the Great Depression of the 1930s, more immigrants returned to Europe than came from Europe. A high percentage of economic immigrants have always come for economic opportunity, with the ultimate objective of eventually returning to their home.

There are political as well as social and cultural reasons that transnational communities have proliferated during the last 50 or so years. It is important to remember that the Canada and the United States are the most predisposed of developed countries to attempt to socially and politically integrate immigrants. Although most European countries have naturalization programs for immigrants, they are more stringent, and in most cases, the children of noncitizens born within their borders are not given automatic citizenship. For the millions of residents from South and Southeast Asia living in the Gulf States, there is no choice—they are never going to be socially or politically integrated into the local Arab population. They are guest and foreign worker and will always remain such. It is expected that they will eventually return home.

The main barrier to the integration of recent immigrants to the United States and Canada is the degree of social and culture differences. In the century prior to World War II, the greatest immigration to these countries was from Europe. These immigrants were overwhelmingly Christians and Jews, just like the dominant populations of their home countries. In addition, although unlike the dominant population, most were from Eastern and Southern Europe, and they still shared the same basic Western cultural beliefs and values. In contrast, many of the more recent immigrants to Europe and the United States and Canada are from very different cultural traditions and religions. Many are Muslims, Buddhists, and Hindus. Religion and culture tend to more sharply socially segregate and distinguish them from the members of the dominant society, making assimilation more difficult.

Finally, earlier immigrants had difficulty maintaining social and economic contact with their family and friends in their homelands. The postal service and trans-Atlantic or -Pacific telephone service were slow and expensive; even if family members or friends back home had access to telephone service. Travel home by boat was slow and expensive (if they could afford it). Thus, once in the Americas, contact with their native communities was limited and over time eroded.

Recent advances in communications and transportation technology have changed this scenario dramatically. Today, thanks to e-mail, Facebook, Twitter, Skype, iPhones, and cell phones, communication with distant family and friends is quick and inexpensive. Money transfers can be made electronically, while legal documents can be faxed or scanned. In addition, thanks to the Internet, one can be well informed about news and events at home, while air travel is quick and relatively inexpensive if one needs to travel home.

There has been still another important change in the immigrant population. Before World War II, most immigrants were poor unskilled or semiskilled laborers or farmers. Today a growing portion of this population consist of highly educated and technologically skilled individuals: MDs, PhDs, teachers, engineers, accountants, health professionals, and even business and financial managers and executives.

What is happening is that ethnic groups are being geographically dispersed. Most will remain in the home community, while others will live in scattered enclaves in different countries throughout the world. Thanks to modern information technology, they can remain in constant social contact, not only with family and friends in their home community, but with family and friends in other scattered enclaves as well. Individuals can readily travel between these communities for business, weddings, funerals, and other events. Among many of these groups, marriages are arranged with individuals back home or in other enclaves. Money also readily flows between members these dispersed communities for economic support and business investments.

In spite of being geographically separated, the members of the group thus maintain their collective social and economic cohesiveness and solidarity. Unlike in the past, ethnic identity is not being changed or eroded by immigration. Many ethnic nationalities are become globalized. This globalization has many consequences. Nonresident members of these groups are an important source of the capital and technical expertise needed for the economic development of the home community, which is usually less developed. At the same time, nonresident members of some stateless ethnic groups are frequently the source of money and material support for secessionist movements in their homelands. Involvement of nonresident immigrants in the politics of their homeland is not new or unexpected. In the early twentieth century, for example, Irish immigrants and their children in the United States were an important source of money, guns, and men for the Irish Republican Army in their revolt against British rule; and the first president of the new Republic of Ireland was Éamon de Valera, who was born in New York City.

For the most part, nationality problems were not created by the nationalities themselves. As we discussed in Chapter 4, the current political boundaries for most of the world are legacies of European colonialism and expansion, drawn by Europeans for their own interests, with little regard for the interests of any indigenous peoples or the boundaries of the ethnic groups affected. As a result, most European colonial possessions were a polyglot of ethnic groups, many of whom had long histories of hostilities toward one another. Sometimes the land and people of an ethnic group were divided between two or more European colonies. To make matters worse, colonial powers frequently moved people from one colony to another to supply labor. For example, the British settled Indian laborers in Burma (Myanmar), Malaya (Malaysia), Fiji, Ceylon (Sri Lanka), Kenya, Uganda, South Africa, Trinidad, and British Guiana (Guyana).

The end of the colonial period did not end the ethnic conflicts in the world. As European powers granted independence to their colonies, they made little attempt to redefine political boundaries. In most cases, these newly independent countries had the same boundaries and ethnic composition as the former colonies. Because these political divisions were imposed from the outside by European military power, some scholars have termed the former colonies "**artificial countries**," countries with no historic political cohesion. For many ethnic groups, independence only meant that their European colonial rulers were replaced by a new set of rulers who in many case belonged to ethnic groups with whom they were historical hostile.

The only attempt by a colonial power to redefine the political boundaries of a colony in an attempt to avoid internal conflicts occurred with the partitioning of India by the British in 1947. British India consisted of several hundred distinct ethnic groups as well as two major religious divisions. India did not exist—and had never existed—as a unified country before British domination. As independence approached in the 1940s, hostilities between rival Muslim and Hindu factions became so intense that British officials decided that a unified, independent India was impossible. They decided that India had to be divided into two countries: India (predominantly Hindu) and Pakistan (predominantly Muslim). The problem was the lack of clear geographic boundaries separating these groups; in many regions, the populations were mixed Hindu and Muslim. An East Pakistan and a West Pakistan were carved out on either side, separated by 1,000 miles of what was to be India. However, the Princely State of Kashmir was not partitioned because while the vast majority of the population was Muslim, most of the land was owned by wealthy Hindu, and the ruler was a Sikh. Thus, the future status of Kashmir was left undetermined. After the official announcement of the boundaries, massive migrations began as millions of Muslims and Hindus found themselves on the wrong sides of the borders. These migrations were stimulated by extremists on both sides, who massacred Muslims living in what was to become India and Hindus in what was to be Pakistan. Some estimate that as many as 1 million people were killed in these riots. The granting of actual independence to the two countries in 1947 made the situation worse because of the Kashmir question. The new Indian army quickly occupied Kashmir, and the first India-Pakistan war broke out. This war formally ended in 1949, with most of Kashmir occupied by India. However, the Kashmir issue is far from settled as a militant Muslim activist movement still exists, and Pakistani and Indian troops still occasionally exchange gunfire.

The creation of two separate states out of British India addressed—but did not solve—only one of the region's ethnic/religious problems. The day before independence, the Naga people in India's easternmost Assam province declared an independent Nagaland. In 1963, the Indian government, in an attempt to pacify the Naga secessionists, created the new state of Nagaland with limited autonomy. However, periodic armed clashes still occurred between Naga nationalists and Indian authorities. More recently, a Sikh separatist movement emerged, demanding an independent Kalistan in Punjab. The violent tactics of the Sikh nationalists resulted in the Indian army attacking the holiest Sikh religious shrine, the Golden Temple in Amritsar, in 1984. Later that year, two Sikhs assassinated Indira Gandhi, the prime minister of India, causing more violence between Sikhs and Hindus. In 1985, Sikh militants bombed an Air India flight en route between Montreal and London. A militant Sikh separatist movement continues today although most of its active members live in communities outside India. In addition, there are active separatist movements among the Bodo, Gorkha, Tripari, and Tamil. As if India's problems with its religious/ethnic minorities were not sufficient, the Hindu extremist are becoming increasingly hostile to non-Hindu minorities.

---

artificial countries Multinationality countries created by external powers; usually applied to former colonies.

Pakistan has also experienced internal ethnic difficulties. Both parts of Pakistan were Muslim, but there were major ethnic differences between the two. East Pakistanis were predominantly Bengalis; West Pakistan was more heterogeneous ethnically but dominated by the Punjabi. Although West Pakistan had a smaller population, the capital was located there after independence, and the Punjabi gained dominance in the government and the military. In West Pakistan, a separatist movement was started by the Balochi, who sought an independent Baluchistan, soon after independence. However, the first major conflict emerged with the Bengalis in East Pakistan. Although the Bengalis were economically exploited and discriminated against, it was not until the government attempted to impose the Urdu language in the schools of East Pakistan that the situation came to a head. In 1971, the East Pakistanis revolted and, after a short but bloody war aided by India, succeeded in establishing the state of Bangladesh.

The independence of Bangladesh did not totally solve its ethnic problems for its Bengali majority. The tribal peoples of the Chittagong Hill now have a militant separatist movement. Nor did the separation of Bangladesh did end the ethnic problems of present-day Pakistan. The government and the military are still controlled by Punjabi, who constitute about 45 percent of the population. There are active nationalism movements among both the Balochi and the Sindhi peoples. However, the greatest potential internal ethnic threat in Pakistan is with the Pushtun, who constitute over 15 percent of the population concentrated along the border with Afghanistan. Since the mid–eighteenth century, the Pushtun have politically dominated Afghanistan, which is a de facto Pushtun state. The present border was created by the British in 1893 and inherited by Pakistan in 1947. The border politically divides the Pushtun peoples, about one-third of whom live in Afghanistan and two-thirds in Pakistan. Neither the Pushtun nor the government of Afghanistan fully acknowledges this border. The Pushtun are a tribal people known for their military prowess, and neither the British nor the Pakistani governments have ever attempted to bring them under their direct political control. Nor has Pakistan, like the British before them, attempted to fully control the border. Following the British pattern, the Pushtun tribal areas in Pakistan along the border are designated as either Federally Administered Tribal Territories or Provincially Administered Tribal Areas. These areas are and have been politically autonomous.

During the period of Soviet military occupation of Afghanistan from 1979 to 1989, many Afghan Pushtuns took refuge among the Pushtuns in Pakistan. From bases in these areas, Pushtun leaders organized and equipped the Pushtun mujahedeen militias to fight the Soviets. In the civil wars that followed the Soviet withdrawal, the Taliban, an ethnically Pushtun religious political movement, gained control of most of Afghanistan and gave sanctuary to Al Qaeda, a pan-Islamic group who had supported them in their war with the Soviets. On September 11, 2001, Al Qaeda staged their attack on the World Trade Center and the Pentagon. In response, the United States attacked Afghanistan. Defeated, the Taliban and Al Qaeda took refuge in the Pushtun tribal areas of Pakistan. It is from these bases in the Tribal Areas that the Taliban are now staging their attacks on NATO and government forces in Afghanistan. As long as the Taliban are able to operate with impunity from their bases in Pakistan, the conflict in Afghanistan can continue indefinitely. Under pressure from the United States the Pakistani army is staging limited attacks on Taliban bases, and the Taliban are responding with terrorist attacks in Pakistan. The vast majority of Pushtun tribal groups appear either neutral or anti-Taliban. The fear is that if the Pakistani Army invades the tribal areas, it would result in the Taliban becoming a Pushtun nationalist movement, which would greatly increase the scope and complexity of the present conflict.

British India was by far the largest and most ethnically complex of the former European colonial possessions. Similar secessionist movements have taken place and are still occurring throughout the old colonial world—the Muslim ethnic groups on Mindanao in the Philippines, the Aceh and Papuan peoples in Indonesia, the Karen and Kachin peoples in Myanmar (Burma), the Bakongo peoples in the Cabinda portion of Angola, the Tuaregs in Mali and Niger, and the Lozi in Namibia, to name only some. Two secessionist movements have been crushed in bloody wars: the Tamils in Sri Lanka and the Igbo in Nigeria. In addition to the Bengalis in Bangladesh, two separatist movements have been successful in gaining independence: South Sudan and Eritrea. In other places, such as Rwanda and Burundi, conflict between rival ethnic groups has resulted in massive genocide. Certainly, it is facile to lay all the blame on colonialism for these and other conflicts in the postcolonial era. But it is undeniable that violence between ethnic nationalities, each believing its political and territorial claims are legitimate, is one of colonialism's most unfortunate and long-lasting legacies.

Not all ethnic conflicts are confined to the old colonial world, however. For example, the Kurds (who live in the mountainous regions of Turkey, Iraq, Iran, and Syria) have had an active separatist movement since the 1960s. At different times, they have fought the Turks, the Iraqis, and the Iranians. In 1950, China invaded and occupied Tibet, a region that the Chinese consider part of China. A Tibetan revolt in 1959 was crushed, but Tibetans still seek political autonomy under the Dalai Lama, their spiritual leader.

Recently, some of the most violent ethnic conflicts have been in Europe and the former Soviet Union. In the early 1990s, Yugoslavia disintegrated as the republics of Slovenia, Croatia, Bosnia, and Macedonia proclaimed their independence. Yugoslavia was reduced to only two of the former six republics: Serbia and Montenegro. Hundreds of thousands of ethnic Serbs found themselves living in Croatia and Bosnia. Supported by the Serb-controlled Yugoslavian army, Serb nationalists in Croatia and Bosnia rebelled, took control of regions in both republics, and demanded unification with Serbia. With more than 100,000 dead and more than 1 million homeless, the war in Bosnia has been the bloodiest and most destructive war in Europe since World War II. In 1995, the Bosniaks, Croats, and Serbs reached an agreement. Fighting stopped, and NATO troops occupied zones between the warring factions.

Ethnic conflict spread to the Kosovo province of Serbia in 1998, when the Albanian majority in the province organized the Albanian Liberation Army and called for an independent Kosovo. Attempts by the Serbs to crush the rebellion resulted in armed intervention by NATO forces in 1999 and the military occupation of the province. In 2000, ethnic conflict spread to Macedonia as Albanian nationalists rebelled against Macedonian control of their regions of the country. NATO peacekeepers are today in Macedonia. The question remains whether long term workable political solutions can be found for the ethnic problems in Bosnia, Kosovo, and Macedonia.

This is only a sampling of armed nationalist conflicts. Nationalist movements are difficult to defuse. In most cases, the recognized national governments lack the military resources to fully defeat them. Even when a government has overwhelming resources, such as the British in Northern Ireland, guerrilla wars are difficult to win decisively. As a result, few separatist movements have been extinguished. In some cases, the central governments have either disintegrated or lost control over most of the country. In other cases, the central governments have adopted policies of geographical containment and lessening of direct conflict. A graphic example of this approach is in Western Sahara, formerly Spanish Sahara. In the early 1970s, Spain committed itself to a policy of independence and self-determination for its colony. However, in 1976, before independence was achieved, Morocco occupied the northern portion of the region, claiming it was historically part of Morocco. In 1979, Morocco occupied the southern portion of the region. The Spanish did not resist the Moroccan occupation. But the local Sahrawi population rejected Moroccan domination, formed the Polisaria Front, and started a guerrilla war. Unable to defeat the guerrillas but unwilling to withdraw, the Moroccan government partitioned the region with a 2,500-kilometer-long sand "wall" equipped with electronic devices to detect movements; the purpose of the wall was to separate the portion Morocco controlled from the area it did not control. In 1989, the Moroccan government agreed to a referendum sponsored by the United Nations, but as of today, the future of Western Sahara has yet to be resolved.

Almost yearly the number of unresolved ethnic conflicts increases and the number of peoples and regions affected widens. There are about 150 ongoing armed conflicts in the world today, and the majority of these conflicts may be classified as nationalist movements. Central governments as a whole have been unsuccessful in achieving complete military victories over separatist groups, but nationalist separatist groups themselves seldom have been successful in achieving political victories.

Bangladesh was recognized by the United Nations only because it was a *fait accompli,* backed by the overwhelming military support of India. In contrast, the United Nations was extremely slow to extend recognition to Slovenia and Croatia. Only when it appeared that Yugoslavia might militarily intervene did the United Nations act, and then only in hopes of preventing a war. The recent problems of chaos and starvation in Somalia have been limited to the southern portion of the country. When the central government of Somalia disintegrated in 1991, the leaders in the north declared their independence and established their state of Somaliland. Although Somaliland is politically stable, it has yet to be granted recognition by any country. The United Nations and the Organization of African Unity have taken the position that northern and southern Somalia will "remain" united, and they act as if no government exists in the north.

One may well ask why separatist movements are seldom extended official recognition. In Chapter 1, Article 1, of the Charter of the United Nations, the right of a people to self-determination is recognized. The United Nations, however, also recognizes the sovereignty and territorial integrity of existing states. Thus, recognition of a secessionist group would be considered intervention in the affairs of a sovereign member state. Other governments have also pledged not to recognize separatist states. In 1964, the Organization of African Unity adopted the policy that "the borders of African States on the day of independence constitute a tangible reality," and this organization thus firmly opposes any changes in the political boundaries of Africa. The real, unstated reason is that almost every country in the world has one or more minority nationalities that either have or potentially may develop an independence movement. Therefore, existing countries make both formal and informal agreements to maintain the current political status quo.

Responses to Ethnic Conflict

How do countries respond to internal ethnic conflicts? The most obvious solution is to divide the country, giving the members of each dissatisfied nationality their own land and independence and allowing them to establish their own country or merge with another country. Peaceful solutions to ethnic questions are rare, however. Most governments would rather fight a long, destructive, and inclusive war than officially recognize the independence of a rebellious nationality. Governments take this stance partly because they fear setting a precedent. As a result, most ethnic conflicts have been resolved—and future solutions will probably have to be sought—within the existing political structure. Historically, such internal responses to ethnic issues have taken three forms: (1) ethnic homogenization of the population through the elimination of rival ethnic groups, (2) segregation of ethnic groups, and (3) political accommodation of ethnic groups.

Homogenization

Ethnic homogenization is the process by which one ethnic group attempts to eliminate rival ethnic groups within a particular region or country. Historically, ethnic homogenization has taken one of two main forms: ethnic cleansing or assimilation. The term *ethnic cleansing* entered our vocabulary in reference to the warfare in the republics of what was formerly Yugoslavia. *Ethnic cleansing* is the physical elimination of an unwanted ethnic group or groups from particular geographic areas. It involves genocide and/or relocation.

Genocide is the deliberate and systematic attempt to physically destroy the members of the rival population. The objective may be the total destruction of the group, the reduction of their numbers, or a stimulus for the surviving members of the group to migrate. The process is the same: the indiscriminate slaughter of men, women, and children of the targeted ethnic group. Today, when we think of genocide, we think of the recent events in Sudan, Bosnia, or Rwanda or the killing of millions of Jews and Gypsies by the Germans during World War II, but genocide has been a recurrent event in human history. Only the magnitude of the killing has varied. In the late 1970s and early 1980s, thousands of Native Americans were massacred by the Guatemalan army. The Turks instituted a policy of systematic killing of Armenians during the early years of the last century. During the colonial period, the English, Dutch, French, Spanish, Portuguese, Belgians, and Germans were periodically guilty of genocide. Incidents of genocide are found even in American history, beginning with the slaughter of the Pequots in Connecticut in 1637 and ending with the massacre of more than 150 Sioux at Wounded Knee, South Dakota, in 1890. Genocide has been and still is a far too common response to ethnic conflict and rivalry.

Relocation is the forced resettlement of an unwanted ethnic group in a new geographic location. The forced relocation of the target population may be either in conjunction with genocide, as in the Darfur region of Sudan, or separate from it. Sometimes the unwanted group is forced outside the boundaries of the country, becoming what today we term *refugees*. In other cases, an ethnic group is forcibly moved to a new area within the boundaries of the existing state, where it is assumed that they will pose less of a problem.

At the outbreak of World War II, the Soviet Union was home to several million ethnic Germans who had settled in Russia during the eighteenth century. In 1924, a separate German autonomous republic within Russia was established along the Volga River for the so-called Volga Germans. When Germany attacked the Soviet Union in 1941, Stalin, fearing that the ethnic Germans might join the invaders, ordered them moved from Russia and Ukraine to Kazakhstan, Siberia, and other remote areas.

---

ethnic homogenization Attempt to create a single ethnic group in a particular geographic region.

ethnic cleansing Elimination or removal of an unwanted ethnic group or groups from a country or a particular geographic region; usually involves genocide and/or relocation of the population.

genocide Deliberate attempt to eliminate the members of an ethnic category or cultural tradition.

relocation Forced removal of the members of a particular ethnic group from one geographic region to another.

Genocide is a frequent consequence of ethnic conflict. Forensic experts uncover the bodies of Bosniak men murdered by Serbs after the capture of Srebrenica in 1995.

After World War II, the boundaries of much of Eastern Europe were redrawn. That portion of Germany located east of the Oder River was given to Poland, and 7 million German residents were forcibly evicted. At the same time, Czechoslovakia evicted almost 3 million resident Germans from their homes. After independence, many East African countries expelled many East Indians who had settled there during the colonial period. In American history, Native Americans were regularly relocated as the frontier moved west. The largest and best known of these relocations occurred in the 1830s, when the Five Civilized Tribes were forced to move (along the so-called Trail of Tears) from their homes in the southeastern states to what is today Oklahoma. Most indigenous tribes of the United States experienced similar resettlement programs. In Bosnia and Croatia, the main objective of all the combatants had been the relocation of the other ethnic populations. The killings, rapes, and destruction were the tactics used to encourage them to abandon their homes.

Assimilation is the social absorption of one ethnic group by another dominant one. Assimilation may be total, in which the ethnic identity of one group is lost, or partial, in which one ethnic group assumes a subordinate identity. Assimilation may be either forced or passive. In **forced assimilation**, the government adopts policies designed to deliberately and systematically destroy or change the ethnic identity of a particular group. The ultimate objective is the absorption of the group into the dominant ethnic group. A key target of a forced assimilation policy is the elimination of ethnic boundary markers: language, religion, modes of dress, and any cultural institution that readily distinguishes the population. If these boundary markers are destroyed, the group loses much of its social cohesiveness. For example, until recently, the Bulgarian

assimilation Merging of the members of one ethnic group into another, with the consequent abandonment of the former group's identity.

forced assimilation Social absorption of one ethnic group by another ethnic group through the use of force.

380 PART IV Anthropology in the Global Community

government pursued a policy designed to assimilate its Turkish population. Turks were not free to practice their Islamic religion, and they were forced to speak Bulgarian in public and adopt Bulgarian names.

One of the best examples of forced assimilation was the Indian policy of the United States in the latter part of the nineteenth and early twentieth centuries. Federal policy attacked Native American ethnic identity from several directions. Reservation lands, which were owned communally, were broken up, and the land was allotted (deeded) to individual members of the tribe in order to destroy community or village life. Many ceremonies such as the Sun Dance and the peyote religion were made illegal. Traditional or hereditary tribal leaders were not recognized, and tribal governments were either dissolved or reorganized along an American political model. People who worked for the government were commonly forced to cut their hair and wear "citizen's" (Western-style) clothes. Native American children were taken from their families and placed in boarding schools, where they were forbidden to speak their native language, had their hair cut, were made to dress in citizen's clothes, were taught Euro-American technical skills, and were indoctrinated with Euro-American Christian values and attitudes. As the head of the Carlisle Indian School said, "You have to destroy the Indian to save the man." Canada and Australia established similar policies for the assimilation of aboriginal peoples.

Assimilation need not be the result of a conscious official policy to solve an "ethnic problem" by incorporating the population into the cultural mainstream. Another form, called **passive assimilation**, occurs without any formal planning or political coercion. Unless strong social barriers prevent assimilation, social and economic forces frequently result in more dominant ethnic groups absorbing members of less powerful groups with who they are in contact. The dominant ethnic group does not necessarily have to be the largest, but it must be the most socially prestigious and economically powerful group. Many of the governments in Latin America have historically followed a laissez-faire policy toward Native American groups. Guatemala has not had a policy of forced assimilation. In Guatemala, the primary differences between Ladinos and Native Americans are not biological but social and cultural, and people who are identified as Native Americans are informally socially and economically discriminated against. As a result, more ambitious and educated Native Americans frequently have abandoned their native languages, dress, and lifestyles (ethnic boundary markers) and re-identified themselves as Ladinos. During the past 100 years, the Native American population in Guatemala has decreased from about 75 percent of the total population to less than 50 percent; passive assimilation is the primary cause of this decrease.

History shows that there are other ways of managing ethnic differences. People do not have to resort to ethnic homogenization; they can either segregate or accommodate other ethnic groups.

Segregation

The political, social, and economic **segregation** of different ethnic groups has a long history in human society. In these situations, the dominant ethnic group does not attempt to eliminate the group, but rather places legal restrictions on the actions of the members of the group. In most cases, they have no political rights. They may not be permitted to own land, or they may own land in only certain restricted areas. Marriage between them and members of the dominant group may be prohibited. They may also be restricted to certain economic occupations. Not only is there no attempt to assimilate them into the dominant ethnic groups, but legal restrictions maintain their ethnic identities.

There are two major reasons such ethnic relationships develop: (1) the dependent ethnic group performs a needed economic role, or (2) the dependent ethnic group is so powerless that it presents no threat, economic or political, to the dominant society. The Jews and Gypsies in Europe are examples of groups that survived as segregated ethnic groups. Jews were merchants and craftspeople at a time when most Christian Europeans were farmers. Thus, the dominant society was economically dependent on them. Gypsies, on the other hand, were a small, powerless group that presented no threat to the dominant society.

African Americans performed critical agricultural labor in the American South. After the Civil War and the end of slavery, the southern states passed so-called Jim Crow laws, which placed political, social, and economic restraints on African Americans. These new laws kept African Americans from threatening

passive assimilation Voluntary social absorption of one ethnic group by another ethnic group.

segregation Enforced separation of ethnic groups, in which the dominant ethnic group places legal restrictions on the actions of the members of the other group.

> **CONCEPT REVIEW**   **Responses to Ethnic Differences**
>
> | | |
> |---:|:---|
> | **Ethnic homogenization** | The elimination of ethnic difference within a region or country |
> | **Ethnic cleansing** | The physical elimination of an unwanted ethnic group or groups |
> | **Genocide** | The elimination of an unwanted ethnic group or groups by killing the members of the group or groups |
> | **Relocation** | The elimination of an unwanted ethnic group or groups by physically moving them outside the boundaries of the region or country |
> | **Assimilation** | The elimination of an unwanted ethnic group or groups through the process of destroying their social identity |
> | **Forced** | The process of destroying the social identity of an ethnic group by eliminating their ethnic boundary markers |
> | **Passive** | The process of destroying the social identity of an ethnic group through conscious or unconscious social and economic discrimination and "voluntary" elimination of ethnic boundary markers |
> | **Segregation** | The physical separation of an ethnic group and the imposition of social and economic restraints that limit their contact with other ethnic groups |
> | **Accommodation** | The creation of a balanced political relationship between two or more ethnic groups, with each allowed to maintain its own social identity and cultural traditions with some degree of local autonomy |

the continued political and economic dominance of Euro-Americans, while allowing Euro-American farmers and landowners the continued use of their labor. In contrast, government officials segregated Native Americans from the general population by placing them on reservations where their actions could be controlled. It was not until 1924 that U.S. citizenship was extended to all Native Americans, and not until 1948 that Native Americans living on reservations were allowed to vote in state and local elections in Arizona and New Mexico.

Accommodation

An alternative to ethnic homogenization or segregation is some form of political **accommodation** that formally recognizes and supports the ethnic and cultural differences of the population and gives them some degree of localized autonomy. Accommodation takes many forms. One form is to adopt a strategy of official recognized ethnic pluralism. For instance, Canada has two main nationalities: Anglo-Canadians (English speaking) and French Canadians (French speaking). Both English and French are formally acknowledged as official languages. Although Quebec is the only province in which French Canadians are the majority, French speakers are found throughout other provinces. Within Quebec, French is the official language. Belgium also has two major national groups: the Flemish (Dutch speakers) and the Walloons (French speakers). Both Flemish and Walloon are the official languages of Belgium, although internal political divisions are officially either Flemish or Walloon. The capital, Brussels, is officially bilingual. Czechoslovakia was also officially bilingual—Czech and Slovak.

However, many countries are home to more than two main nationalities, none of which are dominant. Yugoslavia had eight major nationalities: Serbs, Croats, Bosniaks, Slovenes, Montenegrins, Macedonians, Hungarians, and Albanians. The largest of these groups,

accommodation Creation of social and political systems that provide for and support ethnic group differences together with local autonomy.

the Serbs, constituted only about one-third of the population. Recognizing the long history of hostility and conflict between these groups, after World War II, Marshall Josip Tito, the head of their liberation army and prime minister, adopted an ambitious scheme to try and give each group its own region of political control and autonomy. Separate republics were established for the Serbs, Croats, Slovenians, Montenegrins, and Macedonians. Although no separate republic was created for the Bosniaks (Muslims), they were the largest group in the ethnically mixed republic of Bosnia. The Albanians and Hungarians were given autonomous provinces within the republic of Serbia. Yugoslavia was organized as a confederacy, with a relatively limited central government and with a great deal of local autonomy given to each of the republics.

However, in most countries, one nationality constitutes the majority of the population and politically and economically dominates the smaller nationalities within its borders. For various reasons, some countries have created a limited number of regional enclaves and given these minorities some degree of political autonomy within this enclave. In the 1920s, the Soviet Union created a large number of internal "autonomous" ethnic political units called *republics, okrugs,* and *oblasts.* The degree of internal autonomy varied with category. Republics had the most autonomy and could have their own official language. With the collapse of the Soviet Union, many of the republics became independent countries; however, many of the smaller ones were incorporated into modern Russia. China also has "autonomous" ethnic areas; the five largest—Tibet, Guangxi, Ningxia, Inner Mongolia, and Xinjiang—are "autonomous regions." In addition, there are more than 100 smaller "autonomous prefectures" with some ethnic groups occupying several geographically scattered prefectures. As we have discussed, along its border with Afghanistan, Pakistan has what it terms Tribal Areas for the Pushtun. In these tribal areas, the Pushtun are governed by their traditional institutions with virtually no interference from the central government. In 1998 and 1999, the United Kingdom allowed for the creation of regional parliaments for Scotland, Wales, and Northern Ireland. With a predominantly Inuit population, Denmark made Greenland an autonomous region in 1979. In 2009, Greenland adopted Kalaalligut (an Inuit language) as its official language. Canada established Nunavut, a separate territory for the Inuit, in 1999. In addition to French and English, Inuktiut and Inuinnagtun, two Inuit languages, are the official languages of the territory. The Philippines established an autonomous region in 1989 for the Muslims on Mindanao. Indonesia established Aceh as an autonomous area in 1999. Panama has a number of autonomous areas for Native American groups. In 1952, the United States granted "commonwealth" status to Puerto Rico and in the 1970s, following a policy of self-determination, began extending increased autonomy to the over 350 federally recognized native tribes. These are just some of the ethnic autonomous areas of the world. However, it is important to note that the degree of "autonomy" differs greatly from one to another.

Results

Having looked at the various means by which people have responded to ethnic differences, we can now examine the results. What are the results of ethnic cleansing? No American can deny that ethnic cleansing does not work. In most regions of the United States, one need only look about them. How many Native American faces do you see? Yet America was once entirely Native American. American Indian peoples were massacred and the defeated survivors driven steadily westward to lands considered less desirable. Today, most Native Americans live in the western states.

Setting aside the moral issues, ethnic cleansing is seldom a permanent solution. Except for very small groups, rarely has one ethnic nationality been successful in destroying another. Even though it may be greatly reduced in number, the targeted group usually survives. The history of genocidal attacks by the other group becomes an integral part of the origin myth of the victimized group and thus serves to strengthen—not weaken—their identity. Genocide also creates hatred and distrust between groups that can persist for centuries after the actual event and make future political cooperation difficult, if not impossible.

Relocation also produces mixed results. As in the case of genocide, the forced removal of a people becomes part of their origin myth and strengthens their cohesion and identity. Among the Cherokee of both North Carolina and Oklahoma, the Indian Removal of the 1830s has become a defining element of their ethnic identity. Removal of a people from their homeland in no way negates their claims to the lands they lost. Four hundred years after the Irish were evicted from Northern Ireland, the Irish Republican Army is fighting to reclaim this portion of the lost Irish homeland. The Jews were expelled from Jerusalem in the first century C.E. and dispersed over Europe, North Africa, and the Middle East. Yet, in the past century, the Jews have returned to Israel to reclaim their homeland. The collective memory of a nationality is long. Old wrongs are seldom forgotten, and lost homelands are never truly relinquished.

Assimilation—whether passive or forced—is not always effective, either. There is no question that throughout history, smaller groups have been absorbed by larger groups, but assimilation is usually a slow and uncertain process. As we discussed, over the past 100 years in Guatemala, Native Americans have slowly declined as a percentage of the total population. We might therefore assume that passive assimilation has proved effective in this case. However, considering absolute rather than relative population, we find that the Native American population actually increased from 1 million to about 4 million during the same period. The main problem with passive assimilation, then, is that population growth often creates new members as fast as or faster than members become assimilated.

Another problem is that people are not willing give up their ethnic identity; if they did, forced assimilation would not be necessary. The forced assimilation policies in the United States were unsuccessful in regard to Native Americans. Loss of language, material culture, and other cultural institutions that functioned as ethnic boundary markers did not destroy ethnic identity or group cohesiveness because new cultural institutions and ethnic boundary markers emerged to replace the old. From a population of only about 250,000 in 1890, the Native American population of the United States has risen to more than 2 million today, and their major political demands are for greater tribal self-determination. So genocide, relocation, and forced or passive assimilation may be effective to a greater or lesser degree, but none of these practices, under most circumstances, truly resolves ethnic problems. More often, they postpone the formulation of workable policies and are even counterproductive—they worsen rather than alleviate conflicts. Besides these "pragmatic" considerations, genocide and forced assimilation are so morally abhorrent that few modern governments would publically admit to pursuing such policies. Relocation, likewise, poses ethical dilemmas; most groups are moved against their will, and some other nationality must be relocated to make room for the migrants. In the modern world, there is nowhere to relocate to without violating some other group's territorial rights. Finally, as we have seen, passive assimilation is usually slow and its result uncertain.

Political accommodation and local autonomy is the only practical and morally acceptable solution. But how well does it work, and what are the problems in maintaining a multinational state? First, we will look at the countries that have adopted the strategy of recognized ethnic pluralism. In January 1993, by mutual agreement, Czechoslovakia peacefully split into the Czech Republic and the Republic of Slovakia. In Canada in the 1960s, a separatist movement emerged among the French Canadians in Quebec; and in the 1976 elections, the Parti Québécois, the separatist party, won control of the government of Quebec. Although in a 1980 referendum in Quebec voters rejected separation from Canada, the issue was not resolved; and in 1995, a second referendum was held on Quebec separation and failed by less than 1 percent. There are still many people in Quebec who support separation from Canada. At some time in the future, there may be a third referendum. Belgium has an active Flemish nationalist movement. In every case many, if not the majority, of the members the smaller of the two national ethnic groups, wants independence. This is not because their individual rights or liberties are threatened; rather, they feel their collective ethnic identity is being eroded or diminished. As for Yugoslavia, after Tito's death in 1980, the presidency of Yugoslavia revolved among the presidents of six republics. In 1991, Slovenia declared its independence. As discussed earlier in this chapter, many of the other republics quickly followed suit, and a series of extremely bloody multisided wars frequently broke out, resulting in the disintegration of Yugoslavia.

The creation of political autonomous regions for ethnic minorities within countries with a numerically dominant ethnic nationality has also had mixed results. Russia and China have both have problems with secessionist movements within some their autonomous regions. In 1994–1995 and again in 1999–2000, Chechen secessionists in the Autonomous Republic of Chechnya were involved in extremely bloody and destructive rebellions. Even today, Chechen separatists stage terrorist attacks in Russia itself. There are active secessions movements among the Tibetans and Uyghurs in the autonomous regions of Tibet and Xinjiang in China. Indonesia and the Philippines created autonomous areas as a response to successions movements; however, succession movements among the Aceh in Indonesia and the Muslim groups in the southern Philippines continue. The United States created the special political status for Puerto Rico in response to an increasingly militant independence movement. There was even an attempt to assassinate President Harry Truman in 1950. This strategy was successful only in that the Puerto Rican separatists today are attempting to achieve independence through political means.

Figure 16.1 Nationalist organizations use various means to communicate their message of separation. These cartoon panels showing the Basque flag are from a booklet distributed by Basque separatists in northern Spain.

The creation of separate parliaments for Scotland and Wales has not been sufficient for many Scot and Welsh nationalists—they want total independence within the European Union.

There are two problems with addressing nationality differences through the creating of "autonomous regions." One, is how much autonomy does the particular ethnic group actually have? In most cases, the group has only limited internal control over their population and their resources. The second is that autonomy is not the same as sovereignty, and many groups aspire for total independence.

Finally, it is important to note that countries that are home to multiple ethnic nationalities are inherently unstable unless one ethnic group's dominance over the others is so great as to be indisputable. Otherwise, there has to be an excepted and stable social, political, and economic balance between the resident ethnic nationalities. The two factors that most seriously threaten the political stability of such countries are differential rates of population growth and relative differences in economic development. If the population of one group grows more rapidly than that of another, it threatens the existing social and political balance of the country. Differences in economic growth may result in changes in the relative economic well-being of the different nationalities and the feeling of exploitation by some.

The evolving global economy requires close cooperation between countries and nationalities. Rising nationalism directly threatens the global economy. Although we cannot change our basic human feelings, we can more clearly understand those factors that unleash ethnic emotions and attempt to minimize them.

SUMMARY

1. **Define ethnic group.** An ethnic group is a named social grouping of people based on what is perceived as shared ancestry, cultural traditions, and history. Ethnic group identity divides the world into categories of "us" and "them."

2. **Explain what we mean when we say ethnic identity is situational.** An individual's ethnic group identity is seldom absolute but changes with the social context. An individual may assume various hierarchically ranked identities. This characteristic is called the hierarchical nesting quality of identity.

3. **Explain the attributes of ethnic groups.** The two main attributes of an ethnic group are origin myths and ethnic boundary markers. The origin myth or history describes the common or shared historical experiences that define the social boundaries of

the group. Ethnic boundary markers are those overt characteristics that make its members identifiable. Ethnic boundary markers may include language, religion, physical characteristics, and other cultural traits such as clothing, house types, personal adornment, food, and so on.

4. **Describe the different levels of ethnic identity.** There are three categories of ethnic identity: nationality, subnationality, and civilizations. An ethnic nationality is an ethnic group that shares a feeling of homeland and the inherent right to political sovereignty. A subnational group is an identity nested in a larger national identity. A subnationality claims neither a separate homeland nor rights to political sovereignty. Recently, some scholars have argued that another important level of ethnic identity is emerging: civilizations. A civilization is a grouping of a number of distinct nationalities on the basis of a shared or common cultural historical tradition, generally religion.

5. **Explain why ethnic conflict is so prevalent in the world today, and describe an "artificial country."** Much of the conflict in the world today is between ethnic nationalities. There are 3,000 to 5,000 ethnic nationalities in the world, but only about 200 separate countries. Most countries are "artificial countries" whose boundaries and thus ethnic compositions was a product of European imperialism. Ethnic conflict is the result of stateless nationalities wanting to establish their own independent countries.

6. **Explain ethnic homogenization.** Frequently, more powerful groups have attempted to resolve ethnic differences by the elimination rival ethnic groups. In some cases, the men, women, and children of the rival group are killed—this is known as genocide. In other cases, the members of the rival ethnic group are physically removed from a geographic area—this is known as relocation. Finally, in still other cases, the dominant group attempts to assimilate the other group or groups by eliminating their ethnic boundary markers in hopes of destroying their identity.

7. **Elaborate on the meanings of ethnic segregation and ethnic accommodation.** If the dominant group does not wish to destroy a rival group, it may adopt either policies of segregation or accommodation. Segregation consists of legally limiting the rights and movements of the members of the group. Accommodation consists of formally recognizing and supporting the cultural differences that define the group and in many cases designating a particular geographic region in which members of the group have some degree of collective group autonomy.

17 World Problems and the Practice of Anthropology

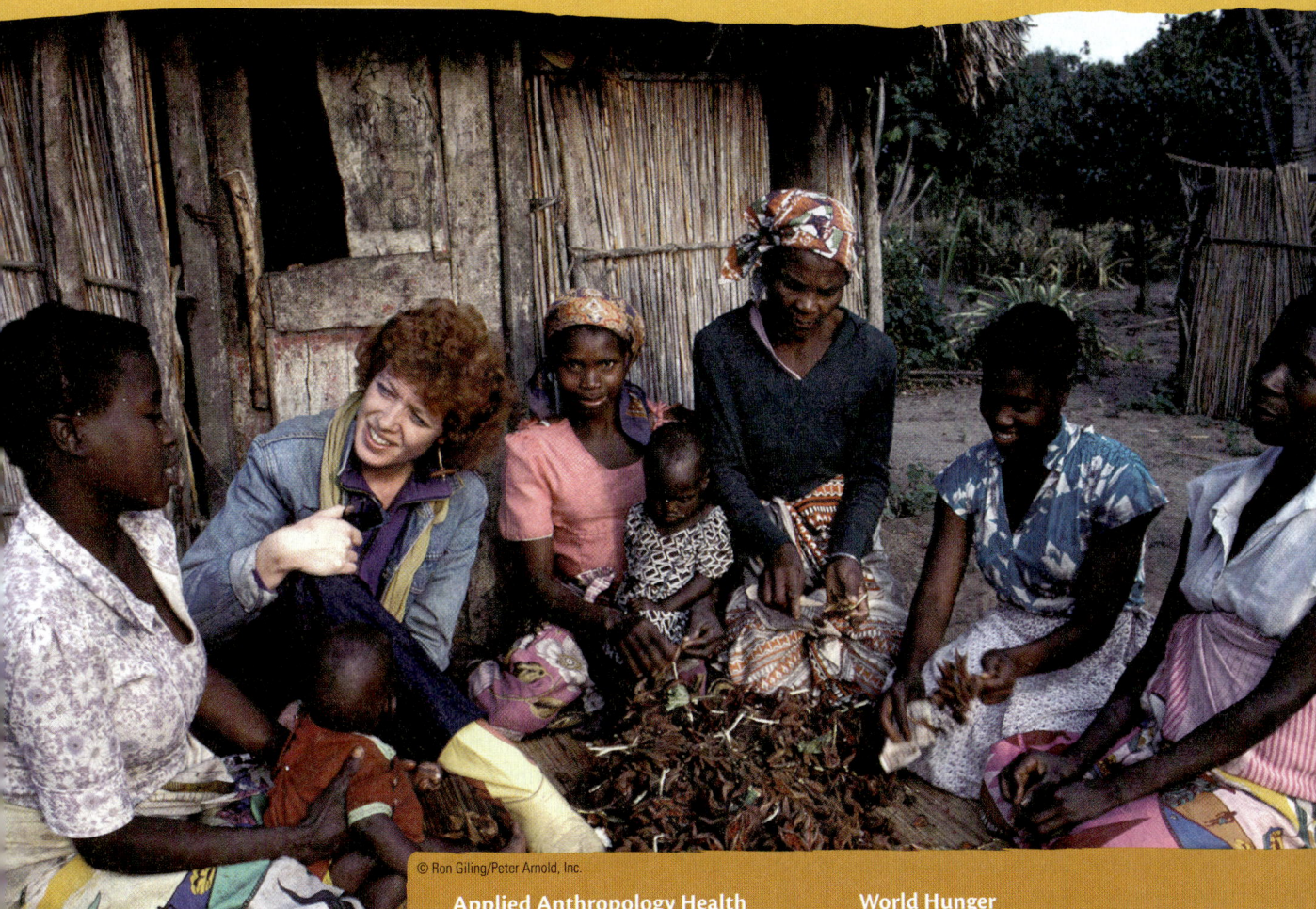

© Ron Giling/Peter Arnold, Inc.

Applied Anthropology Health and Health Care
  Medical Anthropology
  Scientific Medicine and Traditional Healing

Population Growth
  Anthropological Perspectives on Population Growth
  Costs and Benefits of Children in the LDCs

World Hunger
  Scarcity or Inequality?
  Is Technology Transfer the Answer?
  Agricultural Alternatives

Anthropologists as Advocates
  Indigenous Peoples Today
  Vanishing Knowledge
  Medicines We Have Learned
  Adaptive Wisdom
  Cultural Alternatives

Because of anthropology's emphasis on fieldwork, ethnographers often become intimately involved with the people they work among, which makes them more likely than most outsiders to listen to local voices.

LEARNING OBJECTIVES

After reading this chapter, you should be able to:

1. **DEFINE** applied anthropology and discuss its importance today in understanding the cultures of other peoples.
2. **DEFINE** medical anthropology.
3. **COMPARE** the differences between Western or scientific medicine and most traditional systems of healing.
4. **IDENTIFY** the unfavorable consequences of rapid population growth.
5. **EXPLAIN** why the population growth rates are high in the poorer regions of the world.
6. **DESCRIBE** the two explanations for world hunger.
7. **IDENTIFY** some of the possible solutions for hunger.
8. **DISCUSS** how globalization is changing the lives of indigenous peoples and destroying the cultural traditions of these peoples.
9. **ANALYZE** the potential importance of the cultural knowledge of indigenous peoples.

Increasing numbers of anthropologists today are using their training to help solve human problems. In the private sector, for example, anthropologists work in a variety of roles—from training international businesspeople to become culturally sensitive when dealing with people from other countries, to observing how humans interact with machines. Governmental agencies and international organizations employ anthropological expertise to address problems connected to development, health, education, social services, and ethnic relations. In the first part of this chapter, we show some of the specific contributions anthropologists have made to understanding the problems of population growth and hunger. In the second part, we discuss the anthropologist as advocate.

Applied Anthropology

Applied anthropology is most simply defined as the application of anthropological perspectives, theory, empirical knowledge of cultures, and methods to help assess and solve human problems. The subfield has grown dramatically since the early 1970s, partly because the number of people earning PhD degrees in anthropology has outstripped the number of academic jobs available and partly because larger numbers of anthropologists want to use their expertise to help people and organizations.

What special talents or insights do applied anthropologists bring to problem solving? What unique contributions can anthropologists make to programs and agencies? The simple answer is that anthropologies do not think like other people. In studying and explaining the issues, applied anthropologists combine the holistic and relativistic perspectives, which we discussed in Chapter 2. We think you will see that it makes a major difference in more fully understanding some the cultural issues involved in health, population growth, and world hunger. Finally, we will discuss the role of anthropologists as advocates for smaller indigenous peoples of the world.

Quite often, applied anthropologists work in the lesser developed countries (LDCs), which are often collectively known as the Third World. Terms such as *developed, less developed, First World,* and *Third World* convey a certain prejudice resulting from a Western view (e.g., Third World to whom?). Because they are familiar terms, however, we continue to use them as shorthand descriptions of major world regions.

> **applied anthropology** Subfield whose practitioners use anthropological methods, theories, and concepts to solve practical, real-world problems; practitioners are often employed by a governmental agency or private organization.

Health and Health Care

Medical Anthropology

The study of health and health care falls under the heading of medical anthropology, the largest and most rapidly growing specialty in applied anthropology. While most medical anthropologists are cultural anthropologists, physical anthropologists, linguists, and sometimes even archaeologists are involved in the study of health issues. Here, we are just going to treat medical anthropology as an aspect of cultural anthropology.

First, it is important to note that health is a critical issue in every society, and every culture has a manner of dealing with disease and illness. Second, it is important to note that cultural behaviors, and changes in these behaviors, can have health related consequence for a community. Cultural anthropologists study a wide range of health and health-related topics. Here, we are going to discuss only two broad overlapping categories: (1) the study of what can be called traditional or folk medicine and (2) programs by which "Western" or "scientific medical" practices can be made compatible with traditional medical beliefs and practices.

Scientific Medicine and Traditional Healing

Traditional medical beliefs and practices differ greatly not only from "scientific medicine" but from each other as well. Thus, there is tremendous cultural diversity in health and health care. Without understanding these differences, it is impossible to adequately address the health concerns of a particular community. These differences fall into interrelated areas: the causes of particular illnesses and the treatment of these illnesses.

In his cross-cultural study of illness, G. P. Murdock found that explanations of illness fell into one of two categories: natural causation and supernatural causation. Natural causation "accounts for the impairment of health as a physiological consequence of some experience of the victim in a manner that would appear reasonable to modern medical science" (1980, 9), such as infection, stress, organic deterioration, or an accident. Supernatural causation account for the health impairment as the consequence of something "supernatural," such as fate, contagion, sorcery, soul loss, spirit aggression, and so forth. Western or

Western medical professionals, such as this doctor working in Kenya, frequently confront cultural barriers in treating traditional peoples. One role of medical anthropologists is to study traditional health beliefs and practices to improve the delivery of health services for traditional peoples.

"scientific" medicine explains all illness as the result of natural causes. Non-Western or traditional medicine most frequently uses some combination of natural and supernatural causes to explain illnesses. How a society explains the causes of illness in turn affects the curing practices used by their medical practitioners.

Scientific medicine views illness as a solely a physical problem, the result of natural causes, thus its treatment focuses on the physical elimination, alteration, or containment of the illness to either correct, cure, or give some degree of physical relief to the patient. To achieve these objectives, scientific medicine relies heavily on the use of surgical techniques and/or various drugs. Traditional medicine usually takes what is sometimes called a "holistic" approach to treatment: treating the mental, physical, and spiritual aspects of the illness. Thus, treatment usually involves, in part, religious healing rituals.

Numbering over 300,000, the Navajo are not only the largest native group in the United States but also the most studied of any tribal group in the world. The Navajo make a distinction between what might be termed "commonplace" and "serious" illnesses. Commonplace illnesses are treated by bonesetters and herbalists. Serious illnesses result "from the disturbance of the normal order, harmony, or balance among the elements of the universe" (Wyman 1983, 536). To cure the individual, this order, harmony, or balance has to be restored. Since the cause is supernatural, both the diagnosis and the cure take the form of religious rituals. Health and healing are a central focus of Navajo life, as virtually all Navajo religious ceremonies are healing rituals with a patient. Making a distinction between symptoms and causes, the individual first sees a diagnostician, usually a "hand trembler"—an individual with an inherent ability to determine the cause of the illness. By passing his hand over the body of the individual, he determines the cause and which ritual the individual needs to restore their harmony or balance. The actual ritual is performed by a highly trained specialist called a "singer." Since the learning of a ritual or "sing" usually requires several years of study as an apprentice to an established singer, each singer is a specialist in only a limited number of rituals of the several dozen possible rituals used. Varying in length from an hour to 9 days, the rituals involve songs, memorized prescribed prayers, sand paintings, the taking of various herbs, ritual bathing with yucca, and/or offerings of corn pollen.

There are two important limitations on traditional Navajo healing. First, these rituals can only be performed within a specific geographical region, the traditional Navajo area defined by their four sacred mountains. Second, they require a trained singer who knows the needed ritual. The number of singers has declined relative to the total population during the twentieth century. Some of the rituals have become extinct or known only by very few individuals. As a result of these and other factors, the Navajo have added two new religious healing traditions: the Native American Church and Pentecostal Christianity.

A Pan-Indian religion, the Native American Church (NAC), involving the use of the peyote cactus, first became popular among the Navajo in the 1930s (see discussion in Chapter 13). Health and the curing of illness are the primary reasons for meetings among the Navajo. Held from sundown to sunrise and presided over by a "roadman," NAC meetings involve spontaneous prayers and the ingestion of peyote to restore the health. Because only limited ritual knowledge is required to conduct a meeting, it is far easier to become a roadman than a traditional singer. Also, because they last only one night, peyote meetings are far less time-consuming and costly for the patient and their family than most traditional Navajo healing rituals. Another advantage of the NAC is that its meetings are not geographically restricted to the land between the four sacred mountains and can be used by Navajo living well removed from the reservation.

Euro-American Christian missionaries began working among the Navajo in the nineteenth century, and many of the early clinics, hospitals, and schools on the reservation were operated by missionaries who were openly hostile to traditional Navajo religious practices. As a result, relatively few Navajo actually converted to Christianity. This started to change in the 1950s when traveling Protestant evangelical ministers began holding tent revivals on reservations that emphasized spiritual healing. Because of the lack of a formal organizational structure, any individual so motivated could become a minister and establish his or her own church. As a result, independent Pentecostal churches with Navajo ministers quickly appeared and spread throughout the reservation. Although some prayer and healing meetings are held for individuals in homes, most are held in churches or large tent camp meetings. These larger meetings usually involve sermons and Bible readings, hymn singing, the giving of testimony, and prayers for healing. For individuals, healing may involve lying on the hands, the use of oils, Bible readings, and healing prayers by the entire congregation. Pentecostal meetings, like NAC meetings, are not restricted by geography. However, they also have an advantage over NAC in that an ill individual does not have to schedule a special meeting but may attend any of the regularly scheduled Pentecostal meetings or revivals.

There is and has been antagonism between many of the traditional religious leaders and the leaders of the Native American Church and the Pentecostal churches. However, for the most part, individual Navajos appear to move among the three groups, depending on the particular circumstances.

The traditional Navajo do not see any basic conflict between their ideas and religious practices and "scientific" medicine as provided by the Indian Health Service and/or the Navajo tribe. As noted, they make a distinction between the symptoms and the cure. Thus, when Western medical care can prove effective treatment, as in the case of surgical procedures or medicines such as antibiotics, they have no difficulty in accepting this care. Western medicine is seen as only addressing the symptoms.

Perhaps not surprising, Western trained physicians are at times equated with traditional herbalists and bonesetters, not singers. The causes of illness are supernatural, and the actual cure thus requires a religious healing ceremony to restore harmony and balance. The main problem has not been the Navajo rejection of "scientific medicine" but rather the reverse—the Western-trained health professionals and their hostility and rejection of traditional Navajo healing practices. Some physicians would even reject patients who had undergone a traditional healing ritual.

In what may have been the earliest example of applied medical anthropology, in 1944, Alexander and Dorothea Leighton wrote *The Navajo Door*. This "introduction to the health beliefs and practices of the Navajos [was] written . . . for Indian Bureau employees providing medical care. The message in part was that Navajo ceremonials, while not adequate therapy for appendicitis or tuberculosis, did have great psychotherapeutic and social value; traditional healers were to be respected as potentially valuable allies" (Kunitz 1983, 149). In his 1983 study of the changes in morbidity patterns among the Navajo, Kunitz found that while death rates from infectious diseases, particular tuberculosis, had declined dramatically, death rates from alcohol-related accidents, alcoholic cirrhosis, homicide, and suicide, particularly among young adults in their 20s and 30s, had dramatically increased. In the last few decades, drug abuse could also be added to these health problems. Kunitz argues that the increased social conflict within families and communities, which are the underlying causes of these health problems, are in large part the result of stress brought on by increasing relative poverty on the reservation. Poverty is a health issue that cannot be addressed by scientific medicine. However, one can also argue that while the three healing traditions now utilized by the Navajo cannot alleviate the poverty on the reservation, by stressing the spiritual harmony and balance within the family and the community, they can alleviate some of the social problems and conflict that result in many of the health problems.

Population Growth

One of the consequences of globalization has been the phenomenal increase in Earth's population. In the last 50 years, world population has more than doubled, jumping from 2.5 billion to more than 7 billion. Most of this growth is occurring in the poorer countries of the world, which creates a wide range of problems. Whereas the standard of living in the developed countries of North America, Europe, and Japan is increasing, the standard of living for most of the rest of the world's people is declining, and differences in population growth rates are the primary reason. In addition, overpopulation in Latin America, Africa, and parts of Asia is resulting in increasing ethnic and social conflict, environmental degradation, and massive migrations of people from the underdeveloped to the more developed countries of the world. Why are the poorest peoples of the world continuing to have large families, while the wealthier peoples are having fewer and fewer children? What is the reason for this inverse correlation?

Anthropological Perspectives on Population Growth

Anthropological insight on this issue is twofold. First, anthropologists study human reproductive behavior—including the choices couples make about how many children to have—holistically, meaning in terms of the total system in which people live their everyday lives. By understanding the overall context of behavior, we can understand how the birthrates of a region result from local conditions—especially economic conditions faced by many rural poor. Second, anthropologists have conducted detailed fieldwork in local communities to uncover the major causes of high birthrates in Third World settings.

There is an apparent paradox about the comparatively high birthrates of many underdeveloped countries. An average North American family is able to afford more children than an average Nigerian family. Canadians and Americans have more money to house, feed, clothe, educate, and otherwise provide for their children. Yet they have only two or three children, whereas the Nigerian family averages six or seven. And this is the most puzzling thing about high fertility: it continues despite its adverse consequences for those very nations that experience it and whose citizens cause it—the LDCs.

Why do these people continue to have so many children? Are Asian, Africans, and Latin Americans too ignorant to realize they cannot afford to support so many children? Can't they see the strain that all these children put on their nations' educational, health, and agricultural systems? Isn't the refusal of couples in these countries to practice birth control even when condoms and pills are available a perfect example of their backwardness and ignorance?

Not at all.

Costs and Benefits of Children in the LDCs

Too often, when we learn that rural people in parts of the Third World average six, seven, or more children per couple, we think this is economically irrational. They must be having large families for other noneconomic reasons. Probably "children are highly valued in their traditional culture." Or maybe "men have higher prestige if they have lots of children." Perhaps "they are not educated enough to recognize the effects of having such large families." It could be that "they don't know how to prevent pregnancy."

Part of our error comes from our failure to grasp the conditions of their lives that lead them to bear more children than we do. Just because children are an economic liability in a highly mobile, industrialized, urbanized, market economy society does not mean they are a liability everywhere. Many demographers argue that rural people in the LDCs have high fertility not simply because of cultural preferences but because children are economically useful. Village-level ethnographic studies suggest that children do indeed offer a variety of material benefits to their parents in the LDCs.

One such study was done in the Punjab region of northern India by anthropologist Mahmood Mamdani. He researched a family planning project that aimed to reduce the birthrate in seven villages. Mamdani found that in the village of Manupur, people accepted the birth control pills and condoms offered by the staff of the program, but most refused to use them. The reaction of the project's administrators was like that of many outsiders when local people do not behave in ways they seemingly ought to behave: they blamed the "ignorance" and "conservatism" of the villagers. To the staff, the benefits of having fewer children seemed obvious. The amount of land available to most people was barely adequate, so by reducing family size, people could stop the fragmentation of land that was contributing to their poverty.

However, the village's parents interpreted their economic circumstances differently. They believed that children—especially sons—were economically beneficial, not harmful. Villagers of all castes and all economic levels reported that children were helpful to a household in many ways. They helped with everyday tasks such as washing, gathering animal dung to use as fertilizer, weeding fields, collecting firewood, and caring for livestock. Even young children supplemented family income by doing small jobs for neighbors. When they grew up, sons were the major source of support for their elderly parents because one or more of them usually continued to live with their parents and farm the land or work in other occupations. Adult sons often went to cities, where part of the money they earned from their jobs was sent back to help their parents and siblings.

In short, Mamdani argued, the residents of Manupur recognized that the benefits of children exceeded their costs to the parents. Outsiders did not recognize this fact because they did not fully grasp the economic circumstances under which people were actually living.

Like people everywhere, however, the people of this region of India proved capable of altering their behavior as their circumstances changed. In 1982, 10 years after Mamdani's study, Moni Nag and Neeraj Kak restudied the village of Manupur. They found that couples had changed their attitudes about desirable family size: about half of all couples were now using contraception or had accepted sterilization after they had two sons. The reason was that changing economic conditions in the region had made children less valuable to families. Parents did not need as much children's labor as before. The introduction of new crops and farming methods had almost eliminated grazing land in the region, so boys were no longer useful for tending cattle. Increasing reliance on purchased chemical fertilizers reduced the value of children's labor in collecting cattle dung to spread on fields. Chemical weed killers reduced the amount of hand work necessary for weeding. A new crop, rice, did not take as much work to grow as the old staples.

The increased value of formal education also led people to have fewer children. Because more outside skilled jobs were available, parents became more interested in providing a secondary education that would increase their children's ability to acquire high-paying jobs. Opportunities for women increased, and secondary school enrollment rates for girls more than doubled between 1970 and 1982. Sending more children to secondary school raised the costs of child rearing. Parents had to pay for clothing and textbooks for their children who attended school, which was a significant expense for poorer families. Accordingly, they wanted and had fewer children.

Finally, most couples believed that having lots of sons was not as necessary as it had been 10 years earlier. People still desired sons for old-age support, but many believed sons were not as dependable as they used to be. Many sons no longer brought their wives with them to live on the family land, but instead left the village to live on their own. One elderly man said:

> Children are of no use any more in old age of parents. They also do not do any work while going to school. My son in the military does not keep any connection with me. My son living with me has two sons and one daughter. I have advised him to get a vasectomy.
>
> (Nag and Kak 1984, 666)

All these and other changes increased the economic costs and decreased the benefits of having large families, and couples reacted to these changes by having fewer children. In this region of northern India, then, ideas and attitudes about desirable family sizes were not fixed by tradition but changed as people adapted their family sizes to changing circumstances.

Researchers in other parts of the world also report that children offer many economic benefits to their parents, explaining why high fertility persists in most LDCs. On the densely populated Indonesian island of Java, rural parents do not have to wait for their children to grow up to acquire the benefits of their labor. Children ages 6 to 8 spend 3 to 4 hours daily tending livestock, gathering firewood, and caring for their younger siblings. By the time they are 14, girls work almost 9 hours a day in child care, food preparation, household chores, handicrafts, and other activities. Most of the labor of children does not contribute directly to their family's cash income or food supply, so it is easy to see how outsiders might conclude that children are unproductive. However, children accomplish many household maintenance tasks that require little experience and skill, which frees the labor of adult family members for activities that do bring in money or food. Ethnographer Benjamin White suggests that large families are more successful economically than small families in Java.

Similar findings have been reported by ethnographers working in rural Nepal, Bangladesh, Samoa, and the Philippines. Unlike suburban and urban North Americans, farming families in the LDCs use much of the time of even young children productively. As children grow older, they are used to diversify the economic activities of a household, earning cash themselves or performing subsistence work that frees their parents for wage labor.

In many countries, the grown children of rural people migrate to a city in their own country or to a developed country. They acquire jobs—which are well paid relative to what they could earn in their own villages—and send much of the cash back to their families. Such remittances contribute half or more of the family income in Western Samoa, Tonga, and some other small nations of the Pacific, both because migrants feel a continuing sense of obligation to their parents and siblings back home and because many of them hope to return to their islands someday. Remittances are also a major source of family income (and, as a by-product, of national income) in countries like Nigeria, Ghana, Pakistan, India, Mexico, Central America, and parts of the Middle East.

In most parts of the world, children are also the major source of economic support in their parents' old age because rural villagers lack pension plans and Social Security. As Stanley Freed and Ruth Freed have pointed out, in many parts of India parents prefer to bear two or three sons to ensure themselves of having one adult son to live with them, in case one son dies or moves elsewhere.

Such factors mean that children are perceived (in most cases, correctly) as both more valuable and less costly than most citizens of the developed world perceive them. We should not assume that couples in the LDCs are too ignorant to understand the costs of having many children or to appreciate the benefits of small families. Nor should we think they are prisoners of their "traditional cultural values," which have not changed fast enough to keep up with changing conditions. Instead, we should assume that they make reproductive decisions just as we do. Then we can begin to understand the economic and other conditions of their lives that often lead them to want more children than affluent couples in urbanized, industrialized countries want. We can also see why birthrates are falling in so many LDCs today. It is not simply the increased family planning education and the recent availability of contraceptive devices. Lowered fertility is also a response to the increased urbanization of most nations, to the growth in wage employment over subsistence farming, to the rising emphasis placed on education for both girls and boys, and to other factors that have changed the circumstances of family lives.

As we have seen, rising human numbers contribute to the resource shortages faced by LDCs today. One of the resources in shortest supply is one of the things people cannot do without: food. Most North Americans see malnutrition and overpopulation as two sides of the same coin. In the popular view, the "fact" that there are "too many people" in the world is the major reason there is "too little food to go around." And the solution to world hunger is "more food"—that is, increased production by the application of modern agricultural technologies. In the next section, we try to convince you that neither the problem (too many people) nor the solution (more production through better technology) is this simple.

World Hunger

Hunger is endemic in much of the world today. The World Food Programme of the United Nations recently estimated that 800 million people go to bed hungry every night and that 24,000 people die of hunger or hunger-related causes every day. Hunger afflicts poor people in parts of southern Sudan, Mozambique, Ethiopia, Chad, Bolivia, Peru, Bangladesh, Pakistan, and India. Even in countries considered "moderately developed" or "rapidly developing," there are regions of extreme poverty and hunger, as in Indonesia, Egypt, Brazil, and Mexico. Women and children constitute the vast majority of the malnourished. Children are especially at risk; if malnutrition does not kill them, it frequently causes lifelong mental and physical disabilities. In this section, we discuss the conditions that contribute to hunger in the Third World. Our focus is on chronic malnutrition or undernutrition on a worldwide scale, not on short-term famine in particular countries or regions. (The reason we focus on *chronic* hunger is that the immediate causes of famine are more likely to be political upheavals and conflicts that disrupt food production or distribution than economic or demographic forces.) First, we discuss two alternative explanations for hunger. Then we describe attempts to increase the food supply by modern technological methods, showing why such attempts are so often unsuccessful and counterproductive. Throughout, we suggest anthropological insights into the problem.

Scarcity or Inequality?

What causes hunger? In any given region, people are hungry for a variety of reasons. On a worldwide basis, however, two explanations for hunger are most commonly offered. The first, which we call the **scarcity explanation of hunger**, is that the major cause of widespread hunger in the LDCs is *overpopulation*: in the twentieth century, populations have grown so large that available land and technology cannot produce enough food to feed them. The second, which we call the **inequality explanation of hunger**, holds that the *unequal distribution of resources* is largely responsible for chronic hunger on a worldwide basis: so many people are hungry today because they lack access to the resources (especially land) needed to produce food.

The scarcity explanation holds that not enough food-producing resources exist to provide the poor with adequate nutrition. In countries like India, Bangladesh, El Salvador, Kenya, and Ethiopia, populations have grown so large in the last century or two that there is not enough land to feed everyone. This argument holds that food-producing resources like land, water, fertilizers, and technology are absolutely scarce, that is, there are not enough resources for the size of the population. In brief, the scarcity explanation holds that hunger is caused by too many people.

Although not our focus here, the scarcity explanation accounts for starvation by saying that chronic hunger turns into outright famine when some sort of disaster strikes. With so many people chronically undernourished, anything that disrupts food production (e.g., droughts, floods, plant diseases, insect infestations, or political disturbances) will reduce food supplies enough to turn hungry people into starving people.

The inequality explanation arose, in part, as a reaction to the excesses of the scarcity explanation, which (some believe) blames the victims of hunger by saying that their own (reproductive) behavior causes their hunger. The inequality explanation holds that resources are not absolutely scarce. In fact, there is enough productive capacity in the land of practically every nation to feed its people an adequate diet, if only this productive capacity were used to meet the needs of the poor.

---

scarcity explanation of hunger Holds that there are not enough land, water, and other resources to feed all the people of a country or region an adequate diet, given current technology.

inequality explanation of hunger Notion that hunger is not caused by absolute scarcity but by the unequal distribution of resources and how these resources are used.

Instead, too many productive resources are used to increase the profits of wealthy landowners and to fulfill the wants of the more affluent citizens of the world.

The inequality explanation says that poor people are hungry because of the way both the international economy and their own national economies allocate productive resources. The international (global) economy allocates resources on the basis of ability to pay, not on need. For example, if affluent North American consumers want coffee and sugar, wealthy and politically powerful landowners in Central America will devote their land to coffee and sugar plantations for export, because this is how they can make the most money. If North Americans want tomatoes and other vegetables during the winter, large landowners in northwest Mexico will produce them, rather than the beans and corn that are major staples for Mexican peasants. The national economies of countries with hungry people work in a similar way. Urban elites have the money to buy luxuries, and urban middle- and working-class families pressure governments to keep food prices low. As a result, too much land is used to produce crops sold to city dwellers at prices made so low by government policy that the rural poor cannot feed themselves. In brief, according to the inequality explanation, hunger is caused mainly by the use of and unequal access to resources.

Which explanation is correct? As is often the case, the two are not mutually exclusive. Both are correct to a certain degree, depending on time and place. The scarcity explanation is correct: All else being equal, the amount of land available per person has been and is being reduced by population growth. Moreover, as the population grows, land of increasingly poorer quality has to be cultivated, reducing its productivity. And as families grow poorer, they have less money to acquire new land or to buy fertilizer or other products that will increase the productivity of their land. These arguments are the kind we encounter regularly in the popular news media. It is hard to see how such conclusions can be wrong.

But these conclusions could be right and still tell only part of the story. The explanation for hunger is more complex than "too many people" combined with "low farm productivity." Hunger is created by human institutions as much as by population increase and unproductive technologies and farming methods. For example, at a growth rate of 3 percent a year, a population will double in less than 25 years. Does this mean that in 25 years everybody will have only half the amount of food? Of course not. Land that formerly was underused will be brought into fuller production, more labor-intensive methods of cultivation can bring higher yields per acre, people can change their diets and eat less meat, and so on. People will adjust their cultivation methods, work patterns, eating habits, and other behaviors to the new conditions rather than tolerate hunger.

Or, rather, they will adjust if they have access to the resources they need to do so. And this is a large part of the problem in many LDCs: it is not just that there are too few resources, but that too few people own or control the resources available. In their books *Food First* and *World Hunger: Twelve Myths,* Frances Moore Lappé and Joseph Collins question what they call "the myth of scarcity." They claim that every nation could provide an adequate diet for its citizens if its productive resources were more equitably distributed.

We do not attempt to present a complete discussion of the evidence to show that inequality is as important as scarcity in explaining hunger around the world. There are several excellent contemporary studies by anthropologists of the relationships among population, resource distribution, and hunger. Here, we discuss a well-known historical example, the Irish potato famine of 1845–1850, because it personally affected the ancestors of so many North Americans and because it illustrates the changes that are occurring in agricultural production in the world today.

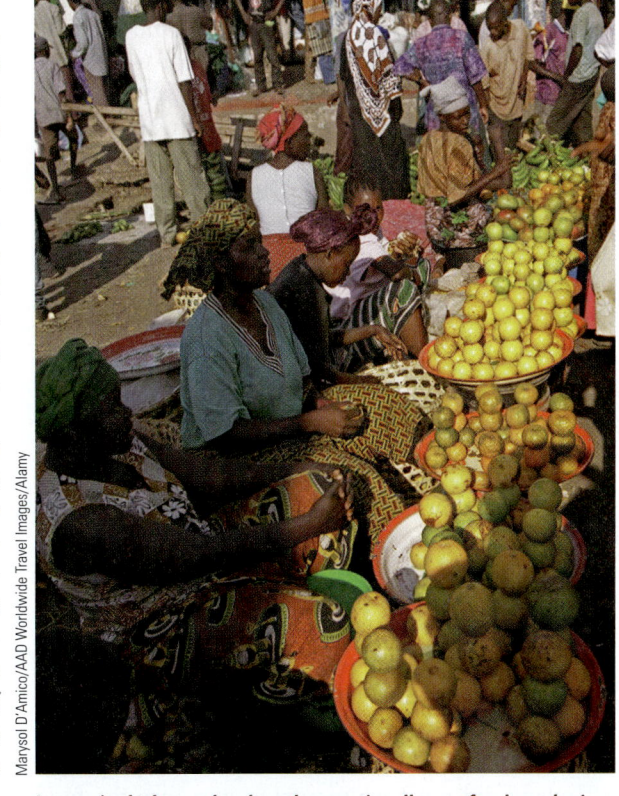

Increasingly, lesser developed countries allocate food producing resources for the production of export cash crops.

In the early nineteenth century, Ireland was an agriculturally diverse country in which large landowners controlled most of the land. Politically and economically, the island was controlled by England. Starting in the last decades of the eighteenth century, large landowners had begun increasingly allotting their land to the production of cash crops for export to England, where the Industrial Revolution was transforming the economy. English mills needed Irish wool and flax in their production of textiles, and England needed Irish wheat, meat, butter, and other food products to help feed the increasing numbers of factory workers. The export of wool, in particular, had resulted in a significant reduction of land available for farming as many wealthy landowners evicted their tenant farmers to turn their land into sheep pastures. Still other large landowners focused on raising wheat, flax, and other exportable grains. Only a small portion of the population of Ireland worked on the large estates or in the towns or cities. The vast majority of the population survived as small subsistence farmers. Their landholdings, either owned or rented, were so small—usually less than 5 acres—that they had to plant a crop that yielded the most in terms of subsistence value. Thus, they planted potatoes, which, in a normal year, would yield sufficient food to feed their family, with a small surplus they could sell. The sale of a few potatoes and some irregular wage work produced the only cash income most families had. Malnutrition was common in rural Ireland during the early nineteenth century.

In 1845, the potato blight struck, destroying between a third and half of the potato crop. The severity of the blight varied from one part of the country to another. However, in every region, small farmers quickly found themselves short of food, with little if any cash, little in the way of property to sell, and little chance of finding wage labor. Many families were quickly reduced to starvation. As the blight continued in 1846 and 1847, conditions became increasingly difficult. Several million starving people began wandering the countryside in a desperate search for food or jobs or anything to keep them alive. Many simply abandoned their farms, while others were evicted for nonpayment of rent. Hundreds of thousands gathered in the port cities, where, ironically, a few found work loading ships with wool, flax, wheat, meat, butter, and other agricultural products for shipment to England. Starvation in Ireland was not the result of a lack of agricultural resources, but rather the people of Ireland did not have money to purchase the food that was grown and exported. One estimate found that, during the famine, Ireland was exporting to England food sufficient to support 18 million people. In 1845, the population of Ireland had been about 8.5 million. When the famine ended in 1850, only about 6.5 million remained. An estimated 1 million people had died of starvation or related causes, while another 1 million had emigrated to North America, England, or Australia.

The economic relationship between agricultural Ireland and industrialized England that existed during the early nineteenth century is seen on a global scale today. Poorer, primarily agricultural, countries are increasingly allocating their resources to the production of exports to wealthier, more developed countries, while at the same time their populations are growing rapidly.

There is no denying that population growth contributes to hunger and poverty. But we should not conclude that "too many people" is *the* problem, or that the scarcity explanation is sufficient. Population growth always occurs within a political and economic context, and this context greatly influences the degree to which poor people can adjust to it. In a similar vein, it is fascinating that many economists recognize that famines do not result mainly from an absolute scarcity of food, but rather from the inability of some groups—usually the poorest groups—to gain access to food. There is also increasing recognition that development ought to be measured by more than "income" and ought to mean more than material affluence.

The combination of population growth and increasing land concentration is doubly devastating. Even if they manage to hang on to their land, the poor will get poorer if their numbers grow. If their increased poverty makes it necessary for them to borrow from the wealthy, to sell part of their land to raise cash, or to work for low wages to make ends meet, they are likely to grow poorer still. This "double crunch" is precisely the experience of the rural poor in many LDCs.

Is Technology Transfer the Answer?

One commonly proposed solution for world hunger is to apply modern scientific know-how and technology to areas in which agriculture is still technologically underdeveloped. This solution seems simple: Thanks to agricultural machinery, plant breeding, modern fertilizers, pest control methods, advances in irrigation technology, genetic engineering, and so on, the developed countries have solved the nutrition problem for most of their people. We have developed science and technology and applied it to agriculture. The LDCs need only adopt our know-how and technology to solve their hunger problems. In this view, the main thing hungry countries need is a transfer of our food production technology.

There are many problems with the **technology-transfer solution**. We can touch on only a few. First, many of the methods developed for application in temperate climates fail miserably when transported to the tropics, where most hungry people live. This is largely because of the profound differences between tropical and temperate soils and climates.

Second, many experts doubt that so-called high-tech solutions to food problems are appropriate to economic conditions in the LDCs. Labor is much more available than capital in these nations, so to substitute technology (machinery, herbicides, artificial fertilizers, etc.) for labor is to waste a plentiful factor of production in favor of a scarce one. Besides, those who need to increase production the most—the poorest farmers—are those who can least afford new technology. And borrowing money for new investments involves risks because many small farmers who borrow from rich landowners lose their land if they default.

Third, new technologies often come as a package deal. For instance, new crop varieties usually require large amounts of water, pesticides, and fertilizers to do well. Small farmers must adopt the whole expensive package for success. The expense, combined with the logistics of long-term supply of each element of the package in countries with uncertain transportation and political regimes, makes many farmers wary of innovations. Further, many new high-yielding varieties of crops are hybrids, which means that farmers cannot select next year's seeds from this year's harvest. Rather, they must purchase their seeds every year from large companies, many of which operate internationally. Is it a good idea to make the world's farmers dependent on a few suppliers of genetic material for their crops?

Fourth, agricultural experts from the developed world often report problems of "resistance" by peasant farmers. Sometimes, peasants cling tenaciously to their traditional crops, varieties, and methods of cultivation even when genuine improvements are made available to them. This famed cultural conservatism of peasants seems downright irrational to many technical experts.

But some anthropologists who have conducted village-level fieldwork offer an alternative interpretation of peasant resistance to change. Living in intimate contact with local people, fieldworkers are sometimes able to perceive problems the way peasants do. Subsistence farmers who are barely feeding their families cannot afford to drop below the minimum level of food production it takes to survive. Traditional crops and varieties give some yield even when uncontrollable environmental forces are unfavorable because over the generations they have adapted to local fluctuations of climate, disease, and pests. The new varieties might not fare as well. Because the consequences of crop failure are more severe for poor subsistence farmers than for well-off commercial farmers, the poor farmers minimize their risks by using tried and true crop varieties and methods. Peasant cultural conservatism thus may be a sound strategy, given the conditions of peasant lives.

Finally, the technology that some believe is wise to transfer to other parts of the world may not be as effective or as efficient as they think. Modern mechanized agriculture requires a large amount of energy to produce its high yields. Studies done in the 1970s suggest that on modern commercial farms in the United States, on average about 1 calorie of energy is required to produce about 2 calories of food. The "energy subsidy" to agriculture goes into producing and running tractors, harvesters, irrigation facilities, chemical fertilizers, herbicides, pesticides, and other inputs. The payoff for this energy subsidy is enormously high yields, in terms of both yields per acre and yields per farm worker. In traditional agricultural systems, however, for every 1 calorie of energy expended in agricultural production, 15–50 calories of food energy are returned (the amount depends, of course, on local conditions, cultivation methods, crop type, and a multitude of other factors). The main reason traditional agriculture is so much more energy efficient is that human labor energy, supplemented by the muscle energy of draft animals, is the major energy input.

Many questions follow from this difference in energy subsidy. Is there enough energy for modern mechanized agricultural methods to be widely adopted around the world? If there is, can the rural poor of the Third World afford them? What will happen if the rural poor have to compete on a local level with the well-off farmers who can afford to purchase and

---

technology-transfer solution The notion that developing nations can best solve their hunger problems by adopting the technology and production methods of modern mechanized agriculture.

maintain the new technologies? What will be the local and global environmental consequences of agricultural mechanization on such a large scale? The worldwide price of oil was high in 2012, but what will happen to it if tens or hundreds of millions of additional farmers mechanize their operations? Can such methods be used indefinitely—are they ecologically sustainable?

We raise such questions not because the answers are obvious. Some experts—mainly economists—believe that the new problems new technologies create will be solved by even newer technologies. Others say it is too risky to count on a future of uncertain technological salvation, and the consequences of being wrong are too severe to do so. Some believe that whatever future scarcities of energy or other resources occur will stimulate the search for alternative sources, so that the free market will save us. Others claim we are near the limits of our planet's ability to produce affordable food and other products.

To point out that technology transfers are not economically or ecologically feasible for many regions is not to say that modern food-producing methods are always harmful or should not even be considered as solutions for world hunger. It merely points out that mechanized technologies have problems of their own and that "experts" do not have all the answers. Are there other solutions that avoid or minimize some of the problems with transfers of technology? Some agricultural scientists, anthropologists, and other scholars are researching alternative methods of boosting food production—methods that are productive and sustainable, yet avoid some of the high energy requirements and the problems associated with mechanized agriculture.

Agricultural Alternatives

Since the early 1980s, increasing numbers of agricultural scientists have been taking another look at traditional farming practices, that is, methods of cultivating the soil that have been used for decades or centuries by the people living in a particular region. In the past, technical experts in agricultural development often scorned traditional farming methods, which they viewed as inefficient and overly labor intensive. But today, there is increasing awareness of the benefits of traditional methods.

This awareness stems partly from the failure of so many agricultural development programs for the Third World. It also stems from the environmental movement that began in the developed countries in the 1970s, which called attention to the negative environmental impacts of mechanized agriculture. In addition to the high energy requirements of mechanized agriculture previously discussed, some farming practices commonly used in the developed countries cause environmental problems. Such problems include water pollution from fertilizer runoff, poisoning of farm workers and wildlife from agricultural chemicals, soil erosion from failure to rotate crops, and increasing resistance of insects because of exclusive reliance on pesticides.

In addition to negative environmental impacts, technologies such as machinery, pesticides, herbicides, and fungicides are too expensive for many traditional farmers. Sometimes they are inappropriate or uneconomical to use on the small plots that are characteristic of farms in many parts of the world. They may be unfamiliar to local people, who understandably are reluctant to abandon proven cultivation methods for alternatives they perceive to be riskier.

Considerations such as these led some agricultural scientists to ask: Are there *viable* alternatives to mechanized agricultural technologies and practices? Some experts believe there are. The main goals of such alternatives are minimization of negative environmental impacts, affordability to small farmers, reliance on technologies and locally available resources, adaptation to local environmental conditions, and long-term sustainability.

Over the centuries, traditional farming systems have evolved that meet many of these goals. Increasingly, agricultural scientists and development agencies look at traditional agriculture not as a system that should be replaced but as a set of farming techniques they can learn from. Much research on this topic is ongoing; here, we present brief descriptions of only two traditional methods: intercropping and resource management.

Intercropping

One method used by traditional farmers in many parts of the world (in the tropics, especially) is intercropping, also known as multiple cropping or polyculture. In contrast to monoculture, intercropping involves the intermingling of numerous crops in a single plot or field. It has been practiced for centuries by shifting cultivators, whose plots usually contain dozens of crops and varieties.

Although intercropped fields look untidy, this method offers several benefits, stemming from the diversity of crops growing together in a relatively small space. Many plant diseases and pests attack only one or a few crops, so if there are several different crops, yields may still be good despite an outbreak. In regions where water supply is a problem and rainfall is erratic, some crops suffer during droughts but others will still produce a harvest. The varying growth patterns and root structures of diverse crops have useful ecological benefits: erosion is reduced because more of the soil is covered, and sun-loving weeds are suppressed by the shade of the crops themselves.

Traditional farmers in some parts of the world have learned over the centuries that many crops grow better when planted together. Leguminous crops, such as beans, peas, and peanuts, take nitrogen (a necessary plant nutrient) from the air and store it in their roots. Intercropping legumes with crops that need lots of nitrogen can increase yields. This is done in Mexico and Central America, where traditional farmers have long intercropped corn, beans, and squash. The stout corn plants provide support for the bean vines to climb, and the ground-hugging squash plants keep the soil covered. African farmers intercrop sorghum with peanuts and millet with cowpea with similar benefits.

Traditional Resource Management Practices

In many parts of the world, traditional farmers actively take steps to control the plant species growing in areas that, to outsiders, look "wild" or "abandoned." They are, in other words, managing their resources so they can continue to use them indefinitely. Two brief examples illustrate these management practices.

The Kayapo of the Xingu River basin of Brazil farm in the forest by shifting cultivation. According to anthropologist Darrell Posey, who has worked among the Kayapo for years, the Kayapo manage the forest carefully. One of their traditional practices is the creation of "islands" of forest in deforested areas. They move composted soil made from termite and ant nests and vegetation into open areas and transplant crops and other useful plants. The created and managed environment provides plant foods, medicines, and building materials and attracts some of the animals hunted by the Kayapo.

The Lacandon Maya of the state of Chiapas in southern Mexico practice slash-and-burn agriculture. Although the staple crop is corn, they plant many other crops in the cleared fields, including several tree species that yield fruits. Lacandon farmers clear and plant new plots frequently, but they do not simply abandon a plot once its main crops are harvested. Rather, they return to it for many years to harvest the long-lived fruit trees and other species they planted. Even while the natural forest is regrowing, the Lacandon continue to use the land. They manage their fallowing fields and thus integrate their exploitation of the land with the natural process of forest regeneration.

We have presented some of the reasons many scientists and others concerned with agricultural development are reconsidering traditional agriculture. It is all too easy to romanticize traditional farmers, to think that they really have had the answers all along and that only recently have so-called experts been forced to pay attention. This view, too, is simplistic. In all likelihood, solutions to the food crisis will require a mixture of traditional and modern technologies. It is, however, encouraging that the knowledge and methods embedded in traditional agricultural adaptations are taken seriously by the World Bank and other institutions in a position to make critical decisions.

Anthropologists as Advocates

Anthropologists do not merely define problems. From the earliest origins of the discipline, anthropologists as individuals have been politically active, using the information and incites gained from their research to voice their concerns about a wide range of public policy issues. Franz Boas (see Chapter 5) took an active role in attacking racist stereotypes during the first decades of the twentieth century and publicly opposed U.S. immigration laws based on racist ideas. Margaret Mead (see Chapter 5) was certainly the best-known advocate for women's rights in the United States during the mid–twentieth century. As individuals, anthropologists have been and still are activists concerned with a wide range of particular and global issues. However, no single issue has concerned anthropologists as a group more than the rights of indigenous peoples.

This should not be surprising. Much of anthropological research has focused on the study of these peoples, and field research is a highly personal experience. As a result, anthropologists as a group more clearly understand the problems of these peoples than other outsiders, and collectively we know them and value them not just as individuals but also as friends. In the late nineteenth century, American anthropologists were engaged in advocating the rights of American Indian peoples. As members of the Lake Mohonk Conference, the Association on American Indian Affairs and other Indian rights organizations, lobbied Congress for changes in the laws concerning American Indian tribes. In 1972, David Mayberry-Lewis, a Harvard anthropologist, and his wife Pia, cofounded Cultural Survival, the largest U.S.-based organization advocating the rights of the indigenous peoples. The director of Survival International, the major London-based indigenous rights organization, is British anthropologist Stephen Corry. Throughout the twentieth century and today, anthropologists continue to fight for the rights of indigenous peoples. Thus, it is fitting that we end this book by advocating the rights of indigenous peoples to preserve their cultural systems.

Indigenous Peoples Today

The vast majority of stateless ethnic nationalities are those commonly referred to as indigenous peoples. Unfortunately, the term indigenous is somewhat ambiguous in it that it refers to anything "native." *Indigenous peoples* as we use the term refers to "culturally distinct groups that have occupied a region longer than other immigrant or colonist groups" (*Cultural Survival Quarterly,* Spring 1992, 73). Generally, these indigenous peoples are small-scale societies whose population numbers in the hundreds or thousands and who make their living by foraging, farming, and/or herding. Sometimes, they are termed *tribal peoples* or, more recently, *Fourth World peoples.*

Indigenous peoples survive as ethnic enclaves within larger nation=states. The governments, controlled by the dominant ethnic group or groups of these countries, usually claim ultimate control over the land, resources, and lives of the indigenous people who live within their officially recognized national borders. For indigenous peoples, the colonial world still exists. The Human Rights Council of the United Nations estimates that there are 370 million indigenous peoples in the modern world. Among them are the Native peoples of the Americas; the aboriginal peoples of Australia and other islands of the Pacific; the Sami (formerly known as the Lapps) and other reindeer-herding peoples of northern Europe and Asia; hundreds of "tribal" cultures of eastern Asia, Southeast Asia, and southern Asia; and numerous smaller ethnic groups of Africa. Estimates can and do vary greatly due to a lack of agreement on which particular groups should or should not be counted as "indigenous."

These small, culturally distinct societies have survived up to the present day in the remote jungles, swamps, mountains, deserts, tundra, and other "undeveloped" regions of the world for only one reason: they did not have anything their larger and far more powerful neighbors wanted. Global economy is rapidly changing their relationship with the outside world. The growth of industrialization together with a global population explosion is creating ever-increasing demands for food, timber, minerals, energy, and water. The lands presently occupied by these indigenous peoples constitute the last "undeveloped" or "underdeveloped" lands in the world.

> **indigenous peoples** Culturally distinct peoples who have occupied a region longer than peoples who have colonized or immigrated to the region.

The lands of the indigenous peoples are the last "frontier." The remaining jungles and woodlands of the world are rapidly being cleared for timber and/or for new farm and ranch lands. Vast river valleys are being damned and flooded for hydroelectric power. No region is too remote or isolated to be safe from "development" if rich deposits of oil, natural gas, iron, copper, nickel, bauxite (aluminum ore), gold, or valuable minerals are discovered.

The rights of indigenous peoples became an issue at the time of Columbus's landing in the Americas. Questions of whether the native peoples of the Americas—or, for that matter, any indigenous people—had any inherent rights to their land, resources, or political sovereignty were debated in Spain. Although legal particulars differed from one colonial power to another as well as over time, a basic consensus was reached early in the colonial period: indigenous people did have some rights based on prior occupancy. However, more "civilized" peoples could unilaterally claim dominion over them and make use of any land and resources that were either not utilized or "underutilized." "Civilized" peoples had both a right and an obligation to uplift indigenous peoples and to act in their "best interest." "Civilized" peoples also had the right to travel and trade wherever they wanted without interference from indigenous peoples. Finally, if an indigenous people resisted, then the "civilized" peoples had the right to use military force against them. Racism, ethnocentrism, and social Darwinist ideas about the inevitability and desirability of progress provided the moral justification for the treatment of indigenous peoples.

Such attitudes and policies affected the governing of most indigenous peoples in the colonial possession of European nations. With the collapse of these colonial empires, the leaders of the new independent countries adopted the same basic attitudes and policies toward the resources of "their" indigenous minority communities. Here, we are going to discuss only three groups in three different regions of the world to show some of the ways in which globalization is destroying the lives of indigenous peoples.

The San

Within the southern African nation of Botswana lies the Central Kalahari Game Reserve (CKGR), larger in land area than Switzerland, it is the second largest game reserve in all Africa. The CKGR was established in 1961, partly to provide the indigenous hunter-gatherers of the region—the San—with adequate resources for their subsistence needs. In the 1960s and 1970s, local groups of San used the territory as they always had for subsistence foraging, hunting and gathering of food plants. In the 1980s, European environmentalists began pressuring Botswana officials to remove the people from the CKGR and declared the area solely a game reserve, with no hunting allowed. By the 1990s, the San were "encouraged" to move outside the reserve by various methods, including failure to repair a needed well, intimidation by selective enforcement of game laws, and (allegedly) severe physical punishments of accused "poachers."

By 2002, the government had resettled nearly all of the resident San, about 1,000 individuals, in two settlements outside the boundaries of the reserve, where having no jobs, no wild plant foods to gather and animals to hunt, they live primarily off of government issued rations. This action was taken partly in the name of conservation. However, the government also argued that it was for the "good" of the San, so "that they may be provided with modern facilities, schools, clinics, etc. and to integrate them into modern society." According to Robert Hitchcock (1999, 54) the San "expressed that the reason they were being removed was so that well-to-do private citizens could set up lucrative safari camps in the reserve." In 2002, the San filed a legal case in the High Court of Botswana. In 2006, the court finally ruled that their eviction was "unlawful and unconstitutional," they had a right to live on the reserve, and the government had to issue them hunting permits. Justice Phumaphi of the Botswana High Court, stated that forbidding them to hunt was "tantamount to condemning [them] to death."

In spite of the court ruling, the government still attempted to keep the San from returning to the reserve by capping their only water well and by refusing to issue hunting permits for San hunters and arresting hunters. Recently, the government began issuing armbands to San which they have to wear if they are on the reserve. Meanwhile, a new tourist lodge complete with a swimming pool has been established. However, the San cannot take water from the lodge swimming pool or any of the water wells on the reserve, which are for animals. In responding to criticism, the Bushman welfare minister stated, "To those who think for some reason that opening lodges for tourists in the Kalahari while we are banning the Bushmen from accessing their water borehole [well] is immoral, I say, 'would you prefer your tourists sweaty?'" He added, "They should have realized by now, it will be much better for them to go back to the relocation camps, where there is no shortage of home-brew and other alcoholic beverages to quench their thirst, rather than persisting in living on their 'ancestral land' in the Kalahari."

Arguing that their right to hunt was irrelevant, if they did not have access to water, the San took their case to court asking for the water well to be opened. In February 2011, Botswana's Court of Appeals ruled in favor of the San, stating that their treatment was "degrading." The San now have the right to open one or more water wells; however, they have to do this at their own expense. As one relocated San stated, "We thought the government would help us. . . . But I think the government is killing us."

In 2013, acting on a proposal by Conservation International, an American organization, plans have been made for the creation of a "wildlife corridor" connecting the Central Kalahari Game Reserve and Kagalagadi Transfrontier Park. In spite of earlier court rulings, this plan calls for the removal of several hundred resident San.

Dongria Kondh

Numbering only about 8,000, the Dongria Kondh are a small tribal people in India. Living in the jungle-covered Niyamgiri hills in Orissa state, the Dongria Kondh support themselves by growing small crops of millet, peas, and beans and by collecting fruits, plants, and palm oil in the jungle, some of which they sell in the towns at the foot of the hills. As one young tribal member stated, "We get everything from the jungle like the fruits we take to the market. This is . . . our source of life." Speaking their own distinct language, Kui, they are neither Hindu nor Muslim. They have their own native religion, the mountains being their "temples," the homes of their gods and the places they pray and make sacrifices. The region is so remote that their villages lack schools, electricity, television, and telephones. Only a few have had any formal education.

Their isolation is rapidly ending, however. Vendanta Resources, a London-based but Indian-controlled multinational corporation, has constructed a $1 billion aluminum refinery at the base of the Niyamgiri hills. The government of Orissa, one of the poorest states in India, has agreed to allow Vendanta to strip-mine the Niyamgiri hill for bauxite ore, from which aluminum is made. This open pit mine will necessitate not only the clearing of much of the jungle, but the destruction of most of the hills as well. For the Dongria Kondh, the strip mining will destroy not just their economy and religion, but their whole way of life. Local environmentalists attempted to legally stop the development in court, arguing that the mining violates the Indian Forest Conservation Act. In July 2009, activists in London demonstrated at the annual meeting of Ventanta.

The physical and cultural survival of the Yanomamö and other Amazonian peoples is threatened by opening up their traditional lands to mining, logging, ranching, and other extractive industries.

In October 2009, after a 9-month investigation, the British government found, among other things, that Vandata "did not respect the rights of the Dongria Kondh" and "did not consider the impact of the construction of the mine on . . . [their] rights." The government further stated that "a change in the company's behaviour is essential." Although legally a British company, Vendata ignored the government's rulings, saying in effect that it was really an Indian company. In spite of national and international outcry, Vendata still proceeded with the project, while the issue remained unresolved in the Indian court system.

In December 2012, the Dongria Kondh, together with thousands of other tribal people, demonstrated to voice their opposition to the mine before India's Supreme Court announced it final decision. Finally, in April 2013, the Supreme Court ruled, stating, "If the project, affects their [tribal] religious rights, especially their right to worship their deity known as Niyam Raja, in the hill tops of the Niyamgiri range of hills, that right has to be preserved and protected. We find that this aspect of the matter has not been placed before the Gram Sabha [local self-governments] for their active consideration." The court then requested that the Gram Sabha of the two local districts inform the union Environment Ministry of their decision within 3 months. Thus, the issue is still not fully resolved.

Kayapo

Brazil began planning for a massive development of hydroelectric dams in the Amazon basin in the mid-1970s; however, it was not until the late 1980s with funding from the World Bank that planning began in earnest. The plan called for a major hydroelectric dam to be built on the lower Xingu River. With a relatively small reservoir covering only about 150 square miles of jungle, this dam would be capable of producing 11,000 megawatts of electricity, making it potentially one of the world's three largest producers. However, for the 3 to 5 months during the dry season, lower Xingu dam would be able to produce little if any electricity. Thus, the construction of lower Xingu dam would necessitate the construction of five other dams on the upper Xingu. While these new dams would not produce as much electricity as the dam on the lower Xingu, controlled water releases into the river from the larger upstream reservoirs would allow the main dam to generate the maximum amount of electricity throughout the year. The largest of these upstream reservoirs would flood over 2,500 square miles of forest, while the reservoirs of the other four would cover several thousand additional square miles. The result would be a massive flooding of the valley of the Xingu and its tributaries, affecting the lands of 37 different native tribes numbering 25,000 people and result in the relocation of many of them.

Realizing that these reservoirs would flood their lands and those of their neighbors, leaders of the Kayapo contacted other indigenous leaders to protest. In early 1988, two Kayapo leaders traveled to Washington with anthropologist Darrell Posey to speak against the project to officials of the World Bank and U.S. congressional officials. In February 1989, a large multitribal meeting, the Altamira Gathering, was held to show their opposition. With international news coverage and support from international organizations, the World Bank deferred action on the loan.

In July 2005, without any consultations with the indigenous groups, the Brazilian National Congress approved the construction of what is now called the Belo Monte dam on the lower Xingu. There appears to be two reasons why the Brazilian government changed its position: a Chinese-Brazilian company is planning to build the world's largest aluminum refinery in the region, and the financial support from China means Brazil no longer needs a loan from the World Bank.

In spite of renewed protest by the Kayapo and other tribes and legal delays in local courts, in April 2010, the Brazilian government awarded the contract for the construction of the Belo Monte dam pending approval from the Brazilian Institute of Environment and Renewable Natural Resources. The institute gave full approval in June 2011. In May 2013, 22,000 construction workers were on were on site starting to build the dam when 200 native people from 8 indigenous groups occupied part of the site stopping construction. The government responded by saying that they will not negotiate with native people. As one Kayapo leader stated earlier, "There will be bloodshed."

Before Americans become too judgmental about the actions of other governments, we have to remember our own not too distant past. In 1882 the federal government acknowledged that 518 acres of farmland in Cataract Canyon belonged to the Havasupai. However, all of their land outside the canyon belonged to the federal government. In 1919, Grand Canyon National Park was created on the lands surrounding Cataract Canyon. At different times, park officials have attempted to stop the Havasupai people's seasonal hunting and gathering activities in the park as well as attempting to relocate them to another more distant reservation. In the 1930s, the Havasupai camp near the park visitor center was burned by rangers on the basis that it was an "eyesore" and they had no right to be there. It was not until 1975 that the Havasupai Reservation was official expanded to include land outside their small canyon.

In the mid-1940s, the Mandan, Hidatsa and Arikara peoples of the Fort Berthold Reservation in North Dakota were as they had always been: farmers cultivating the rich farmlands along the Missouri River. In 1947, the U.S. government forced the sale of over 150,000 acres of their best land and built the Garrison Dam, flooding the richest portion of the reservation.

Fishing for salmon at Celilo Falls on the Columbia River was the main economic activity of the Wishram and Wasco peoples. In 1952, construction began on the Dallas Dam, which flooded the falls and destroyed their fishing economy.

In 1960, the U.S. government built the Kinzua Dam, flooding 10,000 acres of the Alleghany Reservation in New York, forcing the relocation of 600 Seneca Indians.

The rich coal deposits on Black Mesa in northern Arizona had been known since the nineteenth century. In the 1960s, Peabody Coal wanted to develop these coal deposits to supply nearby coal-powered electrical generators. However, the title to the land was in dispute. Although the mine area was fully occupied, as it had been for 150 years or more, by scattered pastoral families of Navajos, the Hopi, whose farming villages were located about 25 miles to the southwest, also had a claim. While a 50-50 split in the mineral royalties was readily negotiated, the problem of surface ownership remained. In 1963, federal courts decided the Hopi and Navajo had an equal land title, and the U.S. Congress ordered the land divided in 1974. In 1977, the courts drew the boundary, giving much of the surface in the mine area to the Hopi and ordering between 10,000 and 13,000 Navajos to relocate. Deborah Lacevenza (1988) summarizes what happened: "The idea that this relocation was caused by a land dispute between the Navajo and Hopi is a distortion . . . a diversion created by business interest in order to gain access to the land and its energy resources."

Do indigenous people have the right to control the use of their own lands? Do indigenous peoples have the right to live the way they wish? Do indigenous people have the right to determine their own futures? What is the difference between the San and the Germans, the Dongria Kondh and the Japanese, the Kayapo and the Russians? All six groups have their own distinct histories, homelands, languages, cultural traditions, and political institutions. The only difference is that unlike the Germans, Japanese and Russians, they are too small and powerless to effectively resist.

In 1982, the United Nations created the Working Group on Indigenous Populations (WGIP). The purpose of the WGIP was to develop standards for the protection of indigenous peoples. In the decades that followed, the WGIP and then other United Nations bodies worked with indigenous leaders as well as representatives of national governments to draft a declaration concerning the rights of indigenous peoples. On September 13, 2007, the United Nations General Assembly adopted "The Declaration on the Rights of Indigenous Peoples." Here we quote only a few of the more important points relative to indigenous rights directly related to their political status and landholdings.

Several articles address the political rights of indigenous peoples: "Indigenous peoples have the right of self-determination [and] by virtue of that right . . . freely determine their political status" (Article 3); "the right to autonomy or self-government in matters relating to their internal and local affairs" (Article 4); and "the right to promote, develop and maintain their institutional structures and . . . in the cases where they exist, juridical systems or customs, in accordance with international human rights standards" (Article 34).

Other articles address the issues of land, resources, and economic development: "Indigenous peoples have the right to the lands, territories and resources which they have traditionally owned, occupied or otherwise used or acquired" (Article 26); "the right to be secure in the enjoyment of their own means of subsistence and development, and to freely engage in all their traditional and other economic activities" (Article 20); "the right to determine and develop priorities and strategies for the development or use of their lands or territories and other resources" (Article 32); and "the right to the conservation and protection of the environment and the productive capacity of their lands or territories and resources" (Article 28).

Finally, the declaration states that "indigenous peoples shall not be forcibly removed from their lands or territories" (Article 10), and it gives peoples "the right to . . . restitution or . . . fair and equitable compensation, for lands, territories and resources which they have traditionally owned or otherwise occupied or used, and which have been confiscated, taken, occupied, used or damaged without their free, prior and informed consent" (Article 28).

The United Nations General Assembly adopted the declaration with 143 countries voting in favor, 11 countries abstaining, and 4 countries—the United States, Canada, Australia, and New Zealand—voting against. Later these four countries adopted it.

Although Botswana, India, and Brazil voted in favor of the declaration, the actions of these governments since 2007 in regard to the San, the Dongria Kondh, and the Kayapo are clearly violations of the declaration.

The declaration is a nonbinding resolution, meaning it is not international law. It is merely a statement as to what should be, not what shall be. Tourism is an important source of revenue in Botswana, Orissa is one of the poorest states in India and needs the job that the refinery and mine will create, and Brazil badly needs electricity for its rapidly expanding economy.

Not only did Peru support the declaration, but Peruvian representatives played an important role in drafting the declaration. However, in February 2009, the Peruvian government signed oil leases for portions of the Amazon basin occupied by native groups. In protest, members of several indigenous groups armed with bow and arrows, blocked the main road, while others with canoes blockaded a major river. The response? The Peruvian Navy destroyed the river blockade, and the police, using helicopters and assault rifles, attacked the road block, leaving at least 30 dead. In defending these attacks, President Alan Garcia told the Peruvian people, "The lands of the Amazon belong to you, to you sons, to all the nation, to all Peruvians not just to a small group lives there." What Garcia was saying with is that the economic needs of the 28 million people of Peru were more important than the rights of the 300,000 or so indigenous peoples of the Amazon.

The vast majority of world leaders may agree in principle with the ideas set forth in the declaration. Unfortunately, the vast majority of leaders of underdeveloped and developing countries also agree with President Garcia. The recognition of the rights of their indigenous peoples is a luxury they do not feel their countries can afford.

Vanishing Knowledge

Anthropologists are especially concerned with the rights of indigenous peoples for several reasons. First, because of our interest in cultural diversity, we are more aware than most people of what has happened to non-Western cultures in the past several centuries. Second, we identify with indigenous peoples partly because so many of us have worked among them. Third, our professional training gives us a relativistic outlook on the many ways of being human, so we can appreciate other peoples' customs and beliefs as viable alternatives to our own. Finally, the fieldwork experience often affects our attitudes about our own societies—deep immersion in other cultural traditions leaves some of us not so sure about our commitment to our own.

Whether an anthropologist or not, one can appreciate the rights of any group of people to have their lives, property, and resources secure from domination by powerful outsiders. The most important factors in considering the rights of indigenous peoples to be left alone are ethical ones. Don't people everywhere have the right to live their lives free from the unwanted interference of those more powerful and wealthy than themselves? Does any government, regardless of its "problems," have the right to dispossess people from land they have lived on and used for centuries?

Ethical concerns for the human rights of indigenous peoples, combined with a respect for their cultural traditions, are the primary reasons for granting their rights to survive as living communities. But if the ethical arguments alone are not compelling, other arguments are based on more practical concerns. For example, the long-term welfare of all humanity may be jeopardized by the loss of cultural diversity on our planet. Think about the cultural heritage of humanity as a whole. Consider *all* the knowledge accumulated by *all* humanity over hundreds of generations. Imagine, in other words, human culture—here defined as the sum of all knowledge stored in the cultural traditions of all humans alive today.

Some of the knowledge in present-day human culture has been widely disseminated in the past few centuries by means of written language. We may call it *global knowledge* (not meaning to imply that it is "true" or "universally known"). Although some global knowledge will be lost or replaced, much of the knowledge stored in writing (or, more recently, on computer disks or "the cloud") will be preserved and added to over the coming decades and centuries. Other knowledge in human culture is *local knowledge*—it is stored only in the heads of members of particular cultures, many of which are endangered. Most local knowledge will disappear if those cultural traditions disappear—even if the people themselves survive.

How much of this local knowledge is knowledge that may in the future prove useful to all humanity? No one knows. But no one can doubt that the rest of the world has much to learn from indigenous cultures. In fact, much of what had been only the local knowledge of some indigenous culture has been incorporated into global knowledge, as a consequence of contact with the West and other colonizing peoples. We conclude this book with a small sample of some of the medical and adaptive wisdom of indigenous peoples, whose local knowledge has already contributed so much to the world.

Medicines We Have Learned

"The Medicine Man Will See You Now," proclaimed a headline in a 1993 edition of *Business Week*. The accompanying article described a California pharmaceutical company that sends ethnobotanists and other scientists into rain forests to learn from indigenous shamans. Companies as well as scholars are beginning to understand that the traditional remedies long used by preindustrial peoples often have genuine medical value. In fact, many of the important drugs in use today were derived from indigenous knowledge. Here, we provide only a few examples of the medicines originally discovered by indigenous peoples that now have worldwide significance. An enjoyable source of more examples is the 1993 book *Tales of a Shaman's Apprentice,* by Mark Plotkin.

Malaria remains a debilitating, although usually not fatal, sickness in tropical and subtropical regions. Its main treatment is quinine, a component of the bark of the cinchona tree. Europeans in the seventeenth century learned of the value of quinine from Peruvian Indians.

The Madagascar periwinkle has long been used in folk medicine to treat diabetes. Researchers first became interested in the plant as a substitute for oral insulin, but it seems to have little value for this purpose. During their investigation, however, scientists discovered that extracts from periwinkle yielded dramatic successes in treating childhood leukemia, Hodgkin's disease, and some other cancers. Drugs based on the plant—notably vincristine and vinblastine—remain the major treatments for these otherwise fatal diseases.

Muscle relaxants are important drugs to surgeons. A popular one is curare, made from the chondodendron tree. Taken in large amounts, curare can paralyze the respiratory organs and lead to death. This property was recognized by South American Indians, who used it as arrow poison for hunting birds, monkeys, and other game, and from whom medical science learned of the drug's value.

The ancient Greeks and several North American Indian tribes used the bark of willows for relief from pain and fever. In the nineteenth century, scientists succeeded in artificially synthesizing this compound that today we call *aspirin*.

There is no way of knowing how many plants used by surviving indigenous peoples could prove medically effective. The potential is great. According to pharmacologist Norman Farnsworth, about one-fourth of all prescribed drugs in the United States contain active ingredients extracted from higher plants. The world contains more than 250,000 species of higher plants. Although as many as 40,000 of these plants may have medical or nutritional values that are undiscovered by science, only about 1,100 of these have been well studied. Botanists and medical researchers are coming to realize that indigenous peoples already have discovered, through centuries of trial and error, that certain plants are effective remedies for diseases. The future

GLOBAL CHALLENGES AND OPPORTUNITIES

The Question of Development

Puram Elephant festival, Trissur, Kerala, India.

What is the purpose of the global economy? Judging by the frenzied behavior of many, if not most, of the peoples of the world, it appears to be to satisfy an insatiable demand for material goods and narcissistic pleasures. Is "wealth" only measured in material goods? Does the country or people with the most toys "win"? It certainly appears that way. When we think of development, we almost invariably think only in terms of economic development. To us, the economic development of a country, a state, or a region is easily measured; it is a matter of dollars and cents. We need only to look at the gross national product (GNP) or the per-capita incomes. If we compare countries in terms of their growth of GNP, then we can determine which are the most economically successful—the winners.

However, are the gross production figures the only—or even the best—measure of development? Are per-capita incomes the best measure of the standard of living of the society?

Nobel Prize–winning economist Amartya Sen argues that growth in the GNP alone is not a particularly good indicator of development. As a child in India, he lived through the great famine of 1943, during which 3 million people died. Perhaps not surprisingly, one of his interests as an economist is famines. He has discovered that famines were not solely or even primarily the result of food shortages. Instead, famines are frequently the result of market forces that increase the cost of food while depressing incomes to the point that families can no longer purchase adequate food. Just as famines are not necessarily the result of food shortages, the growth in the GNP of a country does not in itself result in increased prosperity. The GNP might be growing with little economic benefit to many, if not most, of the people.

Sen also questions how we measure standards of living. Is it merely a question of relative income? The Indian state of Kerala is an excellent example that per-capita income figures alone are not always the best measure of quality of life. Covering only 24,000 square miles along the southwest coast of India, Kerala is home to 33 million people. Depending primarily on agriculture, Kerala is a poor state, even by Indian standards. In terms of gross domestic product (GDP), Kerala averages only about $1,000 per capita, $200 less than India as a whole, and only 1/26 that of the United States. By such economic measures alone, residents of Kerala would appear to have a very poor standard of living. If we look at Kerala in terms of health, education, and other social issues, however, we see a far different picture.

In terms of health, the people of Kerala are better off than most other peoples in India and in countries with much higher incomes. Their infant mortality rate is among the lowest in the developing world. Their life expectancy is 72 years—11 years longer than the average for India, and only 4 years shorter than the United States.

Even more impressive are their achievements in education. Well-maintained schools are scattered throughout the state, and education is virtually universal. As a result, 90 percent of the people are literate—an achievement that places Kerala on the same level as the far more prosperous peoples of Spain and Singapore.

Social discrimination is less of a problem than in other parts of India and most of the world. Protests against the caste system began in Kerala in the middle of the nineteenth century, and in no other part of India has this system been so expunged from social consciousness. Although there are sizable Muslim and Christian minorities in the state, there have not been the religious conflicts that have beset most of India.

However, possibly the major factor that distinguishes Kerala from other parts of India and most parts of the world is its relative equality in income and opportunity. In the 1960s, the state government abolished landlordism and redistributed the land to 1.5 million tenant families. Kerala also has a relatively high minimum wage. This wage has discouraged industrial development, and, as a result, Kerala has an unemployment rate of 25 percent. Because most families have land on which they can garden, however, they are shielded from destitution.

Sen is not arguing that Kerala is a utopian paradise. What he is arguing is that the relative health, education, and social harmony of a community are far better measures of a people's development than material wealth. The relative quality of life of a people cannot be measured by wealth alone, and the people of Kerala have made their choice.

Indigenous peoples, such as these Indonesian "medicine men," commonly have an extensive and potentially important knowledge of the curative powers of plants. How much medical knowledge of healers in indigenous cultures will be lost?

value of their medical wisdom to all of humanity is largely unknown, but probably great.

Adaptive Wisdom

Many preindustrial peoples have lived in and exploited their natural environments for centuries. Earlier in this chapter, we discussed the problems of technology in attempting to overcome hunger, and some of the important traditional agricultural alternatives used by indigenous peoples such as the Kayapo and Lacandon Maya. They have learned to control insect pests and diseases that attack the plants on which they depend, and to do so without using expensive and often dangerous artificial chemicals. They have often learned how to make nature work for them while minimizing the deterioration of their environments. They have, in short, incorporated much adaptive wisdom into their cultural traditions. Following are possible benefits that all humanity might gain by preserving the ecological knowledge of indigenous peoples.

Preservation of Crop Varieties

In all cultivation systems, natural selection operates in the farmers' fields. Like wild plants, crops are subject to drought, disease, insects, and other natural elements, which select for the survival of the individual plants best adapted to withstand these hazards. In addition, crops are subject to human selection. For example, crop varieties most susceptible to drought or local diseases are harvested in smaller quantities than drought- and disease-resistant varieties. Perhaps without knowing it, the cultivator replants mainly those varieties best adapted to survive the onslaughts of drought and local diseases. This tuning of plant varieties to the local environment, with all its hazards and fluctuations, goes on automatically so long as the crops harvested from the fields are replanted in the same area. Thanks to the unintentional and intentional selection by hundreds of generations of indigenous cultivators around the world, each species of crop (e.g., beans, potatoes, wheat) evolved a large number of *land races,* or distinct varieties adapted to local conditions.

Over the course of human history, several thousand species of plants have been used for food but less than a hundred of these were ever domesticated. Of all the plants that have been domesticated, today only a handful provide significant amounts of food for the world's people. In fact, only four crops—wheat, rice, maize, and potato—provide almost half of the world's total consumption of food.

Since around 1950, plant geneticists and agricultural scientists have developed new varieties of wheat, corn, rice, and potatoes capable of giving higher yields if they receive proper amounts of water and fertilizers. These new strains were developed by crossing and recrossing native land races collected from all over the world. The aim was to achieve a "green revolution" that would end world hunger by increasing production. Many new varieties are hybrids, which means that farmers must receive a new supply of seeds yearly from governmental or private sources.

Ironically, having been bred from the genetic material present in their diverse ancestors, the new strains now threaten to drive their ancestors to extinction. As farmers in Asia, Africa, and the Americas plant the seeds of artificially bred varieties, the traditional varieties—the land races that are the product of generations of natural and human selection—fall into disuse and many have disappeared.

Why should we care? Increasingly, agricultural experts are realizing the dangers of dependence on a few varieties. If crops that are nearly identical genetically are planted in the same area year after year, a new variety of pest or disease will eventually evolve to attack them. The famous Irish potato famine of the 1840s, which we discussed earlier, was directly related to the genetic uniformity of the potato because all the potatoes in Ireland were apparently descended from only a few plants. The United States has also suffered serious economic losses: The corn blight of 1970 destroyed about 15 percent of the American crop. Losses would have been less severe had most American farmers not planted a single variety of corn.

Many plant breeders are alarmed at the prospect of losing much of the genetic diversity of domesticated plants. Today, they are searching remote regions for surviving land races that contain genes that one day might prove valuable. (The seeds are stored in seed banks for future study.) The searchers have been successful, although no one knows how much of the genetic diversity of crops such as wheat and corn has already disappeared.

The knowledge of indigenous peoples is an important resource in the effort to preserve land races. In many parts of the world—the Andes, Central America, Amazonia, the Middle East, and elsewhere—cultivators still grow ancient varieties of crops. They know where these varieties yield best, how to plant and care for them, how to prepare them for eating, and so on. In the Andes, for instance, over 3,000 potato varieties survive among the indigenous people. Many have specific ecological requirements, and some are even unique to a single valley. Research is now under way to determine how well specific land races will grow in other areas to help solve food supply problems elsewhere. It is important to preserve the genetic information encoded in these varieties for future generations.

Indigenous peoples who still retain the hard-won knowledge of their ancestors and who still use the often-maligned "traditional crop varieties" are important informational resources in the effort to save the genetic diversity of crops on which humanity depends.

"Undiscovered" Useful Species

In addition to their familiarity with local crop varieties that have potential worldwide significance, many indigenous peoples cultivate or use crop species that are currently unimportant to the rest of the world. One example is amaranth, a grain native to the Americas that was of great importance to the Indians in prehistoric times. The great Mesoamerican civilizations made extensive use of the plant in their religious rituals. This led the Spanish conquerors, in their anxiety to root out heathenism, to burn fields of amaranth and prohibit its consumption. Otherwise, it—like maize, potatoes, beans, squash, and other American crops—might have diffused to other continents. Amaranth remains an important food to some indigenous peoples of highland Latin America, who retain knowledge of its properties and requirements. Its unusually high protein content is just starting to make it an attractive grain to some modern consumers in other parts of North America and might someday make it valuable throughout the rest of the world.

Other plants used by native peoples have the potential to become important elsewhere. Quinoa, now grown mainly in Peruvian valleys, has twice the protein content of corn and has long been recognized as a domesticate with great potential. The tepary bean, now grown mainly by the O'odham of the American Southwest, can survive and yield well during extreme droughts, which might make it cultivatable in other arid regions of the world. Another legume, the winged bean, has long been cultivated by the native peoples of Papua New Guinea, and it has helped nourish people in 50 other tropical countries.

Humans use plants for more than food. Indigenous peoples have discovered many other uses for the plants found in their habitats. Scientific researchers today are attesting to the validity of much native knowledge about the use of plants as sources of fuel, oils, medicines, and other beneficial substances, including poisons. Forest peoples of Southeast Asia use the toxic roots of a local woody climbing plant as a fish poison. The root is so powerful that a mixture of 1 part root to 300,000 parts water will kill fish. From the indigenous tribes, scientists learned of the toxicity of these roots, which allowed them to isolate the rotenoid now used as an insecticide spray for plants and as dips and dusting powders for livestock.

Scientists no doubt will rediscover many other useful plants that today they know nothing about—if the tropical forests in which most endangered plant species are found last long enough. Their task will be easier if the original discoverers—indigenous peoples—are around to teach them what their ancestors learned.

Cultural Alternatives

There is another kind of practical lesson we might learn from surviving indigenous peoples. Industrialized humans have developed technologies that discover, extract, and transform natural resources on a scale undreamed of a century ago. To North Americans and many other citizens of the developed world, *progress* is almost synonymous with "having more things." Yet whether our economies can continue to produce ever-increasing supplies of goods is questionable. Many of us are frightened by the thought that economic growth might not continue. The fear that we will be forced to accept a stagnation or even a decline in our levels of material consumption no doubt contributes to the interest today's undergraduates have in careers they believe are most likely to earn high incomes for themselves and their future families.

On the other hand, some individuals and groups in the affluent, developed world have questioned the value of what most of their fellow citizens call "economic progress." They think the environmental and familial costs of the unceasing drive to accumulate and to succeed in a highly competitive environment are not worth the benefits. Some of them believe material affluence cannot bring happiness because it is gained at the high cost of the emotional gratifications that spring from community relationships, from supportive family and friendship ties, and adherence to what some call spiritual values (see the Global Challenges and Opportunities box).

Most readers of this book are the beneficiaries of economic progress. At the same time, we should be careful not to become the victims of the mentality of progress—of that unceasing desire to earn more, to have more, to succeed more. If the industrial bubble does not burst in our lifetime, then most of us who live in the developed world will spend our lives in a continuous effort to increase our consumption of goods. We will do so despite the fact that our efforts will never be sufficient to get us all we want because no one can consume goods as fast as companies can turn them out and advertisers can create new desires for them. We will do so despite the fact that many of our marriages and families will be torn apart by the effort and many of us will suffer psychologically and physically from stress-related disorders. Sadly, most of us pursue our dollars and goods unthinkingly because we remain ignorant of any alternative way of living.

The world's remaining indigenous peoples provide us with such alternatives. They do not and did not live in a primitive paradise. Subjugation of neighboring peoples, exploitation by the wealthy and powerful, degradation of women, warfare, and other ideas and practices many of us find abhorrent existed among some preindustrial peoples, just as they do today. Yet, we also find other cultural conditions that some of us long to recover: closer family ties, greater self-sufficiency, smaller communities, more personal and enduring social relationships, and "more humane," "more moral" values. No anthropologist can tell you whether life is *better* or worse in preindustrial communities; indeed, we cannot agree on the meaning of better. We do know that humanity is diverse. We know that this diversity means that human beings—ourselves included—have many alternative ways of living meaningful and satisfying lives. In the end, it is these cultural alternatives provided by indigenous peoples that might have the greatest value to humankind.

Perhaps a people themselves are the only ones qualified to judge the quality of their lives, to decide what it will take to lend meaning and dignity to their existence. We hope we have convinced you that there are many ways of being human, and we hope you have learned to appreciate some of the alternative ways of living experienced by various human populations. We hope you will agree that some of these alternatives are worth preserving, both in their own right and for the long-term well-being of all humanity.

SUMMARY

1. **Define applied anthropology and discuss its importance today in understanding the cultures of other peoples.** Anthropological expertise is useful for solving human problems because the way anthropologists look at people and cultures (our worldview) differs somewhat from the views of other professionals. Applied anthropologists have conducted research relevant to both global and local-level problems.

2. **Define medical anthropology.** Medical anthropology is the study of all aspects of health and health care for the purpose of improving the health of the people of the world.

3. **Compare the differences between Western or scientific medicine and most traditional systems of healing.** Explanation of illness usually falls into two broad categories: natural causation, which accounts for illness as a physiological consequence of some experience of the individual; and supernatural causation, which accounts for illness as the consequences of some supernatural experience. Western or scientific medicine sees and treats illness as the result of natural causes, while many traditional medical practices are based on the belief that illness is at least in part the result of supernatural causes.

4. **Identify the unfavorable consequences of rapid population growth.** Population growth has many unfavorable consequences. It contributes to serious environmental problems, low economic productivity, urban sprawl and shantytowns, political conflicts, and even war. This is the main paradox of population growth: the high fertility of a country's citizens is mainly responsible for it, yet their high fertility contributes to many of their nation's problems.

5. **Explain why the population growth rates are high in the poorer regions of the world.** High fertility in the LDCs is likewise a consequence of the overall economic and social environment that constrains reproductive behavior. Ethnographic studies suggest that children are a net economic asset rather than a liability in the rural areas of the Third World. Children are productive family members at a young age. They seek jobs with local people to supplement the family income. When older, they go to the cities or to foreign countries and send money back home. They provide old-age security for their parents. Under such conditions, high fertility exists because large families are beneficial.

6. **Describe the two explanations for world hunger.** Population growth is often believed to be the major cause of world hunger. This is the scarcity explanation of hunger, which holds that overpopulation leads to chronic malnutrition and periodic massive starvation. The alternative is the inequality explanation. It holds that land and other food-producing resources are in fact sufficient to provide an adequate diet for the whole world. Hunger is caused by the way local and world economies allocate resources. These two explanations of hunger are compatible: population growth contributes to hunger by increasing the scarcity of food production resources, yet prevalent inequalities in access to productive resources aggravate the scarcity and prevent people from adjusting to it.

7. **Identify some of the possible solutions for hunger.** Technology transfer is a viable solution to hunger in the LDCs, according to many. But there are numerous problems with this solution. Temperate agricultural methods often do not work well in tropical climates and soils. New technologies sometimes harm rather than help the poorest families. Peasants often do not adopt new technologies and crop varieties because they perceive them not worth the costs, or because they cannot afford to assume the risks of failure. Mechanized agriculture requires so much energy to produce food that it may not be affordable to Third World farmers and may not be sustainable in the long run. Agricultural scientists, anthropologists, and others have been researching alternative farming methods long used by traditional peoples of the world. Traditional methods such as intercropping and resource management hold promise for increasing food production sustainably. It is likely that a combination of solutions will be necessary to alleviate problems of hunger and poverty.

8. **Discuss how globalization is changing the lives of indigenous peoples and destroying the cultural traditions of these peoples.** Smaller indigenous foraging, farming, and herding peoples have existed until the present day in isolated and remote regions of the world. They have survived primarily because they had nothing their more powerful neighbors wanted. Globalization and the global economy are today threatening the continued existence of these peoples. The forests and jungles that many depend on are being cut for timber and/or farmland and ranchland. Mining and energy development is destroying their land and polluting their water. The construction of hydroelectric dams is flooding their valleys. The national governments who claim dominion over them are ignoring their rights in the name of development.

9. **Analyze the potential importance of the cultural knowledge of indigenous peoples.** Ethical considerations alone are a sufficient reason these peoples should be allowed to remain in their communities, on their traditional lands, living in the ways of their ancestors, if that is their choice. Pragmatic considerations are also important because these people still retain a vast body of

knowledge—knowledge that is of great potential value to all humanity. Science has already adapted several important medicines and treatments from indigenous peoples. Many other plants with medical value will probably be discovered, if the tropical forests and the cultural knowledge of their indigenous inhabitants last long enough. Adaptive wisdom is to be found in the traditions of indigenous peoples. Land races of important crops still survive and might contain genetic materials from which useful foods might someday be bred. Crops that today are used primarily by indigenous peoples—such as amaranth, quinoa, tepary bean, and the winged bean—might eventually have worldwide significance. Nonfood plants are also important as insecticides, oils, fibers, and other products. Indigenous people also provide us with alternative cultural models that should reduce our anxieties about the likelihood of eventual decline in our material living standards. The diversity of the human species shows that we can live meaningful and wholly satisfying lives without the technologies and huge quantities of consumer goods we consider necessary to our economic welfare. The remaining preindustrial cultures allow us to see that there is more than one narrow road to personal fulfillment, cultural health, and national dignity and prestige.

Glossary

accommodation Creation of social and political systems that provide for and support ethnic group differences together with local autonomy.

acculturation Cultural changes that occur whenever members of two cultural traditions come into contact.

aesthetic Qualities that make objects, actions, or language more beautiful or pleasurable, according to culturally relative and variable standards.

agriculture (cultivation) Purposeful planting, cultivation, care, and harvest of domesticated food plants (crops).

ambilocal residence Residence form in which couples choose whether to live with the wife's or the husband's family.

ancestral rituals Rituals intended to worship, honor, or beseech the deceased ancestors of a kin group.

animism Belief in spiritual beings.

anthropological linguistics Subfield that focuses on the interrelationships between language and other aspects of a people's culture.

anthropology Academic discipline that studies all of humanity from a broad biological and cultural perspective.

applied anthropology Subfield whose practitioners use anthropological methods, theories, and concepts to solve practical, real-world problems; practitioners are often employed by a governmental agency or private organization.

archaeology Investigation of past cultures through excavation of material remains.

art Any human action that modifies the utilitarian nature of something for the primary purpose of enhancing its aesthetic qualities; or actions, objects, or words valued largely for their aesthetic pleasure or symbolic communication.

artificial countries Multinationality countries created by external powers; usually applied to former colonies.

assimilation Merging of the members of one ethnic group into another, with the consequent abandonment of the former group's identity.

authority Recognized right of an individual to command another to act in a particular way; legitimate power.

avunculocal residence Residence form in which couples live with or near the mother's brother of the husband.

balanced reciprocity Exchange of products or services considered to have roughly equal value; social purposes usually motivate the exchange.

band Small foraging group with flexible composition that migrates seasonally.

big men Political leaders who do not occupy formal offices and whose leadership is based on influence, not authority.

bilateral kinship Kinship system in which individuals trace their kinship relationships equally through both parents.

bilocal residence Residence form in which couples move between the households of both sets of parents.

biological determinism Idea that biologically (genetically) inherited differences between populations are important influences on cultural differences between them.

biological (physical) anthropology Major subfield of anthropology that studies the biological dimensions of humans and other primates.

body arts Artificial artistic enhancement or beautification of the human body by painting, tattooing, scarification, or other means.

body painting Decoration of the body by painting designs.

body piercing Decoration of the body by piercing holes in parts of the body for the attachment of ornaments.

bound morphemes Morphemes attached to a free morpheme to alter its meaning.

brideservice Custom in which a man spends a period of time working for the family of his wife.

bridewealth Custom in which a prospective groom and his relatives are required to transfer goods to the relatives of the bride to create or validate the marriage.

capitalism Market economy; emphasizes capital accumulation through profit making as the key to economic growth and maximum material welfare.

cargo cults Melanesian revitalization movements in which prophets claim to know secret rituals that will bring wealth (cargo).

caste Stratification system in which membership in a stratum is in theory hereditary, strata are endogamous, and contact or relationships among members of different strata are governed by explicit laws, norms, or prohibitions.

chiefdoms Centralized political systems with authority vested in formal, usually hereditary, offices or titles.

civilization Form of complex society in which many people live in cities.

clan Named unilineal descent group, some of whose members are unable to trace how they are related but who still believe themselves to be kinfolk.

class System of stratification in which membership in a stratum can theoretically be altered and intermarriage between strata is allowed.

classifications of reality (cultural constructions of reality) Ways in which the members of a culture divide up the natural and social world into categories, usually linguistically encoded.

cognatic descent Form of descent in which relationships may be traced through both females and males.

cognatic descent group Group of relatives created by tracing relationships through both females and males.

Columbian Exchange Exchange of people, diseases, domesticated animals and plants, and other cultural knowledge between the peoples of the Old World and the New World.

communal organizations Religious organizations in which the members of a group cooperate to perform rituals intended to benefit all.

comparative methods Methods that test hypotheses by systematically comparing elements from many cultures.

comparative perspective Insistence by anthropologists that valid hypotheses and theories about humanity be tested with information from a wide range of cultures.

composite bands Autonomous (independent) political units consisting of several extended families that live together for most or all of the year.

configurationalism Theoretical idea that each culture historically develops its own unique thematic patterns around which beliefs, values, and behaviors are oriented.

conflict theory of inequality Theory holding that stratification benefits mainly the upper stratum and is the cause of most social unrest and other conflicts in human societies.

consultant (informant) Member of a society who provides information to a fieldworker, often through formal interviews or surveys.

controlled comparisons Methodology for testing a hypothesis using historic changes in societies.

court legal systems Systems in which authority for settling disputes and punishing crimes is formally vested in a single individual or group.

courts of mediation Court systems in which the judges attempt to reach compromise solutions, based on the cultural norms and values of the parties involved, that will restore the social cohesion of the community.

courts of regulation Court systems that use codified laws, with formally prescribed rights, duties, and sanctions.

cross-cultural comparisons Methodology for testing a hypothesis using a sample of societies drawn from around the world.

cultivation Planting, caring for, and harvesting domesticated plants.

cultural anthropology (social anthropology, sociocultural anthropology) Subfield that studies the way of life of contemporary and historically recent human populations.

cultural construction of gender Idea that the characteristics a people attribute to males and females are culturally, not biologically, determined.

cultural construction of kinship Idea that the kinship relationships a given people recognize do not perfectly reflect biological relationships; reflected in the kinship terminology.

cultural construction of reality See **classifications of reality.**

cultural determinism Notion that the beliefs and behaviors of individuals are programmed by their culture.

cultural identity Cultural tradition a group of people recognize as their own; the shared customs and beliefs that define how a group sees itself as distinctive.

cultural integration Interrelationships among the various components (elements, subsystems) of a cultural system.

cultural knowledge Information, skills, attitudes, conceptions, beliefs, values, and other mental components of culture that people socially learn during enculturation.

cultural relativism Notion that one should not judge the behavior of other peoples using the standards of one's own culture.

cultural universals Elements of culture that exist in all known human groups or societies.

culture (as used in this text) The socially learned knowledge and patterns of behavior shared by some group of people.

culture shock The feeling of uncertainty and anxiety an individual experiences when placed in a strange cultural setting.

descent group A group whose members believe themselves to be descended from a common ancestor.

diachronic Describing changes in a culture over time.

dialects Variations in a single language based on factors such as region, subculture, ethnic identity, and socioeconomic class.

domestication Process by which people control the distribution, abundance, and biological features of certain plants and animals in order to increase their usefulness to humans.

dowry Custom in which the family of a woman transfers property or wealth to her and/or her husband's family upon her marriage.

ecclesiastical organizations Religious organizations in which full-time priests perform rituals believed to benefit believers or the whole society, usually in large buildings dedicated to religious purposes or deities; found in complex societies.

egalitarian society Form of society in which there is little inequality in access to culturally valued rewards.

enculturation (socialization) Transmission (by means of social learning) of cultural knowledge to the next generation.

endogamous rules Marriage rules requiring individuals to marry some member of their own social group or category.

ethnic boundary markers Any overt characteristics that can be used to indicate ethnic group membership.

ethnic cleansing Elimination or removal of an unwanted ethnic group or groups from a country or a particular geographic region; usually involves genocide and/or relocation of the population.

ethnic group Named social group based on perceptions of shared ancestry, cultural traditions, and common history that culturally distinguish that group from other groups.

ethnic homogenization Attempt to create a single ethnic group in a particular geographic region.

ethnocentrism Attitude or opinion that the morals, values, and customs of one's own culture are superior to those of other peoples.

ethnogenesis Creation of a new ethnic group.

ethnographic fieldwork Collection of information from living people about their way of life; *see also* **fieldwork**

ethnographic methods Research methodologies used to describe a contemporary or historically recent culture.

ethnography Description of a specific culture.

ethnohistoric research Study of past cultures using written accounts and other documents.

ethnohistory *See* **ethnohistoric research**.

evolutionary psychology (sociobiology) Scientific approach emphasizing that humans are subject to similar evolutionary forces as other animals; associated with the hypothesis that human behavior patterns enhance genetic fitness.

exogamous rules Marriage rules prohibiting individuals from marrying a member of their own social group or category.

extended family Nuclear families related through culturally variable kinship ties.

feud Method of dispute settlement in self-help legal systems involving multiple but balanced killings between members of two or more kin groups.

fictive kinship Condition in which people who are not biologically related behave as if they are relatives.

fieldwork Ethnographic research that involves observing and interviewing a community in order to document and describe their way of life.

forced assimilation Social absorption of one ethnic group by another ethnic group through the use of force.

forensic anthropology Specialization within physical anthropology that analyzes and identifies human remains.

form of descent Principle through which a people trace their descent from previous generations.

free morphemes Morphemes that can be used alone.

functional theory of inequality Theory holding that stratification is a way to reward individuals who contribute most to society's well-being.

functionalism Theoretical orientation that analyzes cultural elements in terms of their useful effects to individuals or to the persistence of the whole society.

gender crossing Custom by which a person of one sex is allowed to adopt the roles and behavior of the opposite sex, with little or no stigma or punishment.

gender (sex) roles Rights and duties individuals have because of their perceived identities as males, females, or another gender category.

gender stratification Degree to which males and females are unequal in dimensions such as status, power or influence, access to valued resources, eligibility for social positions, and ability to make decisions about their own lives.

gendered (sexual) division of labor Kinds of productive activities (tasks) assigned to women versus men in a culture.

generalized reciprocity Giving of products or service without expectation of a return of equal value at any definite future time.

genocide Deliberate attempt to eliminate the members of an ethnic category or cultural tradition.

global economy Integrated global market in which goods and services are bought and sold globally with prices determined by supply and demand.

global trade Economic exchange of goods and products between the different peoples of the world via established trade networks.

globalization Flow of cultural knowledge, directly or indirectly, between the different peoples of the world.

globalization of production Process of corporations headquartered in one country relocating their production facilities to other countries to reduce production costs and remain globally competitive.

grammar Total system of linguistic knowledge that allows the speakers of a language to send meaningful messages that hearers can understand.

group marriage Several women and several men married to one another simultaneously.

herding (pastoralism) Tending, breeding, and harvesting the products of livestock, which are taken to seasonally available pasturelands and water.

hierarchical nesting Occurs when an ethnic group is part of a larger collection of ethnic groups, which together constitute a higher level of ethnic identity.

historic archaeology Field that investigates the past of literate peoples through excavation of sites and analysis of artifacts and other material remains.

historical particularism (historicism) Theoretical orientation emphasizing that each culture is the unique product of all the influences to which it was subjected in its past, making cross-cultural generalizations questionable.

historicism *See* **historical particularism**

holistic perspective Assumption that any aspect of a culture is integrated with other aspects, so that no dimension of culture can be understood in isolation.

homeland Geographic region over which a particular ethnic group feels it has exclusive rights.

horticulture Methods of cultivation in which hand tools powered by human muscles are used and in which land use is extensive.

household Dwelling or compound inhabited by biological relatives or fictive kin who cooperate and share some resources; in some contexts, a kin group of one or more nuclear families who live in the same physical space.

human variation Physical differences among human populations; an interest of physical anthropologists.

humanistic approach Orientation that mistrusts attempts to explain cultural differences and similarities and cultural changes in favor of achieving an empathetic understanding of particular cultures.

hunting and gathering (foraging). Harvest of wild (undomesticated) plants and animals.

ideologies Ideas and beliefs that legitimize and reinforce inequalities in stratified societies.

incest taboo Prohibition against sexual intercourse between certain kinds of relatives.

incipient courts Court systems in which judicial authorities meet, frequently informally, in private to discuss issues and determine solutions to be imposed. Evidence is not formally collected, and the parties involved in these cases are not formally consulted.

indigenous peoples Culturally distinct peoples who have occupied a region longer than peoples who have colonized or immigrated to the region.

individualistic organizations Religious organizations based on personal relationships between specific individuals and specific supernatural powers.

industrialism Development of technology to harness the energy of fossil fuels to increase productivity, profits, and the availability of consumer commodities.

inequality Degree to which individuals, groups, and categories differ in their access to culturally valued rewards.

inequality explanation of hunger Notion that hunger is not caused by absolute scarcity but by the unequal distribution of resources and how these resources are used.

influence Ability to convince people they should act as you suggest.

initiation rituals Rites of passage whose purpose is to incorporate males and/or females into new roles or into new social groups.

innovation Creation of a new cultural trait by combining two or more existing traits.

intellectual (or cognitive) approach The notion that religious beliefs provide explanations for puzzling things and events.

intensive agriculture Systems of cultivation in which plots are planted annually or semiannually; usually uses irrigation, natural fertilizers, and (in the Old World) plows powered by animals.

interpretive anthropologists Contemporary theorists who analyze cultural elements by explicating their meanings to people and understanding them in their local context; generally emphasize cultural diversity and the unique qualities of particular cultures.

interviewing Collecting cultural data by systematic questioning; may be structured (using questionnaires) or unstructured (open-ended).

key consultant (informant) Member of a society who is especially knowledgeable about some subject and who supplies information to a fieldworker.

kin group Group of people who culturally view themselves as relatives, cooperate in certain activities, and share a sense of identity as kinfolk.

kin terms Labels that an individual uses to refer to his or her relatives of various kinds.

kindred All the bilateral relatives recognized by an individual.

kinship terminology Logically consistent system by which people classify their relatives into labeled categories ("kinds of relatives").

language Shared knowledge of sounds, words, meanings, and grammatical rules used to send and receive messages.

law Kind of social control characterized by the presence of authority, intention of universal application, obligation, and sanction.

levirate Custom whereby a widow marries a male relative (usually a brother) of her deceased husband.

lineage Unilineal descent group larger than an extended family whose members can actually trace how they are related.

linguistic relativity hypothesis See **Sapir-Whorf hypothesis**.

market Exchange by means of buying and selling, using money.

market economy Economy organized by market principles: prices determined by supply and demand; individuals and families rely on the market for livelihood; free market allocation of resources, products, and services; self-regulation and decentralization of decision making.

market globalization Process through which the world's national economies become integrated into a single global exchange system organized by market principles.

marriage alliances Relationships created between families or kin groups by virtue of intermarriage between them.

material culture Artifacts and other physical, visible manifestations of culture, including art, architectural features, tools, consumer goods, clothing, and writing.

materialism Scientific theoretical orientation claiming that the main influences on cultural differences and similarities are technology, environment, and how people produce and distribute resources.

matrifocal family Family group consisting of a mother and her children, with a male only loosely attached or not present at all.

matrilineal descent Form of descent in which individuals trace their primary kinship relationships through their mothers.

matrilocal residence Residence form in which couples live with or near the wife's parents.

medical anthropology Specialization that researches the connections between cultural beliefs and habits and the spread and treatment of diseases and illnesses.

money Objects that serve as media of exchange in a wide range of transactions of goods, services (including labor), or both.

monogamy Each individual is allowed to have only one spouse at a time.

morpheme Combination of phonemes that communicates a standardized meaning.

morphology Study of the units of meaning in language.

multiple-gender identities Definitions of sexual identities beyond the female and male duality, including third and fourth genders such as man–woman or woman–man.

myths Stories that recount the deeds of supernatural powers and cultural heroes in the past.

nationality Ethnic group that claims a right to a discrete homeland and to political autonomy and self-determination.

negative reciprocity Reciprocal exchange motivated largely by the desire to obtain products or services.

neoevolutionism "New evolutionism," or the mid-twentieth-century rebirth of evolutionary approaches to studying and explaining culture.

neoliberalism (laissez-faire) Belief that economic freedom results in the best results for society as a whole; mistrust in government interference with free markets.

neolocal residence Residence form in which a couple establishes a separate household apart from both the husband's and the wife's parents.

New World Landmasses of North and South America.

nomadism Seasonal mobility, often involving migration to high-altitude areas during the hottest and driest parts of the year.

nonunilineal descent Form of descent in which individuals do not regularly associate with either matrilineal or patrilineal relatives, but make choices about whom to live with, whose land to use, and so forth.

norms Shared ideals and/or expectations about how certain people ought to act in given situations.

nuclear family Family consisting of a married couple and their offspring.

Old World Landmasses of Europe, Asia, and Africa.

origin myth Collective history of an ethnic group that defines which subgroups are part of it and its relationship to other ethnic groups.

paleoanthropology Specialization within biological anthropology that investigates the biological evolution of the human species.

participant observation Main technique used in conducting ethnographic fieldwork, involving living among a people and participating in their daily activities.

passive assimilation Voluntary social absorption of one ethnic group by another ethnic group.

pastoralism Adaptation in which the needs of livestock for naturally occurring pasture and water greatly influence the movements of groups.

patrilineal descent Form of descent in which individuals trace their most important kinship relationships through their fathers.

patrilocal residence Residence form in which couples live with or near the husband's parents.

patterns of behavior Within a single culture, the behavior most people perform when they are in certain culturally defined situations.

peasants Rural people integrated into a larger society politically and economically.

performance arts Forms of art such as music, percussion, song, dance, and theater/drama that involve sound and/or stylized body movements.

phoneme Smallest unit of sound that speakers recognize as distinctive from other sounds; when one phoneme is substituted for another in a morpheme, the meaning of the morpheme alters.

phonology Study of the sound system of language.

polyandry One woman is allowed to have multiple husbands.

polygamy Multiple spouses.

polygyny One man is allowed to have multiple wives.

postmarital residence pattern Household in which the majority of newly married couples establish their own residence.

postmodernists Followers of the philosophical viewpoint emphasizing the relativity of all knowledge, including science; focus on how the knowledge of a particular time and place is constructed, especially on how power relations affect the creation and spread of ideas and beliefs.

prehistoric archaeology Field that uses excavations and analysis of material remains to investigate cultures that existed before the development of writing.

priest Kind of religious specialist, often full-time, who officiates at large-scale, bureaucratically organized rituals that keep the population in proper relationship to deities or cosmic forces.

primatology Part of biological anthropology that studies primates, including monkeys and apes.

psychological approach Idea that the emotional or affective satisfactions people gain from religion are primary in interpreting religion.

ranked society Society that has a limited number of high-ranking privileged social positions; groups are ranked relative to one another.

rapport Working relationship between the researcher and the members of the community he or she is studying.

reasonable-person model Model used in legal reasoning that basically asks how a reasonable individual should have acted under these circumstances.

recall ethnography Attempt to reconstruct a cultural system at a slightly earlier period by interviewing older individuals who lived during that period.

reciprocity Exchange of products or objects between two or more individuals or groups.

redistribution Collection of products or money from an organized group or society, followed by a reallocation to the group by a central authority.

refugees Individuals and families who temporarily take up residence in another region or country to escape famine, warfare, or some other life-threatening event.

relocation Forced removal of the members of a particular ethnic group from one geographic region to another.

revitalization movement Religious movement explicitly intended to create a new way of life for a society or group.

rite of passage Rituals celebrating, causing, and/or symbolically marking the stages of life as defined by their culture.

ritual Organized, stereotyped, symbolic behaviors intended to influence supernatural powers.

role Rights and duties that individuals receive because of their perceived personal identity or membership in a social group.

Sapir-Whorf hypothesis Idea that language profoundly shapes the perceptions and worldview of its speakers.

scarcity explanation of hunger Holds that there are not enough land, water, and other resources to feed all the people of a country or region an adequate diet, given current technology.

scarification Scarring of the skin to produce designs on the body.

scientific approaches General approaches suggesting that human cultural differences and similarities can be explained in the same sense as biologists explain life and its evolution.

seasonal rituals Form of communal religious organization in which group cooperation is required to ensure the seasonal changes that restore or maintain life.

secular ideology Ideology that does not rely on the will of supernatural powers but justifies inequality on the basis of its society-wide benefits.

segregation The enforced separation of ethnic groups, in which the dominant ethnic group places legal restrictions on the actions of the members of the other group.

self-help legal systems Informal legal systems in societies without centralized political systems, in which authorities who settle disputes are defined by the circumstances of the case.

semantic domain Class of things or properties perceived as alike in some fundamental respect; hierarchically organized.

sexual dimorphism Physical differences based on genetic differences between females and males.

shaman Part-time religious specialist who uses his special relationship to supernatural powers for curing members of his group and harming members of other groups.

shamanistic organizations Religious organizations in which certain individuals (shamans) have relationships with supernatural powers that ordinary people lack.

simple bands Autonomous or independent political units, often consisting of little more than an extended family, with informal leadership vested in one of the older family members.

social anthropology See **cultural anthropology**.

social control Mechanisms by which behavior is constrained and directed into acceptable channels, thus maintaining conformity.

social Darwinism View that the degree of success in achieving social rewards is determined by the inherent (inborn) characteristics of individuals and groups.

social distance Degree to which cultural norms specify that two individuals or groups should be helpful to, intimate with, or emotionally attached to one another.

socialism Economy in which government makes decisions about product prices, wages and employment, what is produced, and accumulation of income and wealth.

socialization Process of social learning of culture by children.

social welfare capitalism Capitalist economy in which a legitimate function of government is protection of workers and society from the harmful impacts of free markets; involves extensive regulations of business and worker protections.

sociobiology See **evolutionary psychology**.

sociocultural anthropology See **cultural anthropology**.

sociolinguistics Specialty within cultural anthropology that studies how language is related to culture and the social uses of speech.

sociological approach Emphasizes effects of religion on maintaining the institutions of society as a whole by instilling common values, creating solidarity, controlling behavior, and so forth.

sodalities Formal institutions that cut across communities and serve to unite geographically scattered groups; may be based on kin groups (clans or lineages) or on non-kin-based groups (age grades or warrior societies).

sorcery Performance of rites and spells for the purpose of causing harm to others by supernatural means.

sororate Custom whereby a widower marries a female relative of his deceased wife.

state Centralized, multilevel political unit characterized by the presence of a bureaucracy that acts on behalf of the ruling elite.

stereotyping Having preconceived mental images of a group that bias the way one perceives group members and interprets their behavior.

stratified society Society with significant and variably inherited differences in access to wealth, power, and prestige; inequality is based mainly on unequal access to productive and valued resources.

subculture Cultural differences characteristic of members of various ethnic groups, regions, religions, and so forth within a single society or country.

subnationalities Dependent subgroups within a larger nationality that lack the concept of a separate homeland and make no claim to any

inherent right to political autonomy and self-determination.

surplus Amount of food (or other goods) a worker produces in excess of the consumption of herself or himself and her or his dependents.

synchronic Describing a culture at one period in time.

symbols Objects, behaviors, sound combinations, and other phenomena whose culturally defined meanings have no necessary relationship to their inherent physical qualities.

tattooing Decorating of the body with designs by cutting and placing colored pigments under the skin.

technology-transfer solution Notion that developing nations can best solve their hunger problems by adopting the technology and production methods of modern mechanized agriculture.

tone languages Languages in which changing voice pitch within a word alters the entire meaning of the word.

totemism Form of communal religious organization in which all members of a kin group have mystical relationships with one or more natural objects.

transhumance Pastoral pattern involving migration to different elevations to respond to seasonal differences in the availability of pasturelands.

transnational corporation Company that produces and sells most of its products or services outside its "home" country.

transnationals Members of an ethnic community living outside their country of origin.

tribe Autonomous political unit encompassing a number of distinct, geographically dispersed communities held together by sodalities.

tribute Rendering of products (usually including food) to an authority such as a chief.

unilineal descent Descent through "one line," including patrilineal and matrilineal descent.

unilineal descent group Group of relatives formed by tracing kinship relationships through only one sex, either female or male, but not both.

unilineal evolutionism Nineteenth-century theoretical orientation that held that all human ways of life pass through a similar sequence of stages in their development.

unilineally extended families Group of nuclear families formed by tracing kinship relationships through only one sex.

values Shared ideas or standards about the worthwhileness of goals and lifestyles.

vision quest Attempt to enlist the aid of supernatural powers by intentionally seeking a dream or vision; example of individualistic religious organizations.

visual arts Arts produced in a material or tangible form, including basketry, pottery, textiles, paintings, drawings, sculptures, masks, carvings, and the like.

witchcraft Use of psychic powers alone to harm others by supernatural means.

worldview Ways people interpret reality and events, including how they see themselves relating to the world around them.

Notes

Chapter 1—The Study of Humanity

Subfields of Anthropology
A short article summarizing the capacities of humans versus chimpanzees is Balter (2008). Information about archaeological work at Fredericksburg is from a November 11, 2012, article in the *New York Times* by Theo Emery titled "Construction Site Offers Fleeting Glimpse of the Civil War Past." Material on cannibalism in Jamestown is from Joseph Stromberg, "Starving Settlers in Jamestown Colony Resorted to Cannibalism," *Smithsonian,* www.smithsonianmag.com/history-archaeology/Starving-Settlers-in-Jamestown-Colony-Resorted-to-Eating-A-Child-205472161.html, accessed May 6, 2013.

Cultural Anthropology Today
The examples of fieldworkers studying North America are drawn from Lane (2009), Johnson (2007), and Luhrmann (2012).

Chapter 2—Culture

Tylor's definition of culture is from Tylor (1871, 1).

Defining Culture
The material on the Yanomamo and Semai is drawn from Chagnon (1983) and Dentan (1968), respectively. Most general concepts (e.g., ethnic identity, subculture) are from our general knowledge of the literature. Information about mass killings under the subheading ". . . Socially Learned . . ." was summarized from a wide variety of news sources.

Cultural Knowledge
Edward Hall's two early books (1959, 1966) were among the first to systematically discuss the importance of nonverbal communication in everyday social interaction. Turner (1967) applied the concepts of multivocality and condensation to ritual symbols. The example of symbolic behavior from Micronesia is from Jim Peoples's own research. Information on Navajo witchcraft comes from Kluckhohn (1967). Reichel-Dolmatoff (1971) describes shamanism among the Tukano. Information on Hanunoo ethnobotanical classification is from Conklin (1957). Discussion of the cultural construction of race was put together by ourselves, but is familiar to most anthropologists and in accord with the AAA website on race (www.aaanet.org/resources/A-Public-Education-Program.cfm).

The Origins of Culture
On the early bone flutes in Germany, see Conard, Malina, and Munzel (2009); on the first known beads in Morocco, see Bouzouggar and Barton et al. (2007); on the use of silcrete and fire to harden stone used for microliths, see Brown et al. 2012 and Brown, Marean, et al. (2012). The use of abalone shells to process ochre is reported by Hensilwood et al. (2012). All interpretations and speculations about the origins of culture are ours.

Biology and Cultural Differences
The phrase "wired for culture" is from Pagel (2012). The example of lactose intolerance is well known, but Arjamaa and Vuorisalo (2010) place it in the context of coevolution. Murdock (1945) was the first to provide a systematic list of cultural universals, but more thorough coverage is provided in D. Brown (1991).

Chapter 3—Culture and Language

The Power of Language
Information on the five distinguishing features of human language is from Hockett's (1960) seminal discussion. Ideas about their applications and extensions are our own.

How Language Works
The examples of Thai aspiration and Nupe tones are taken from Fromkin and Rodman's (1988) textbook. The author's (J.P.) own knowledge is the basis for the discussion of the Kosraen language. Information on Native American words incorporated into English is taken from Nestor (2003) and Weatherford (1991). An authoritative website with words compiled by Mark Rosenfelder is www.zompist.com/indianwd.html (accessed May 16, 2013). Data for Global Challenges and Problems are taken from SIL International's website Ethnologue.com, Crystal (2003), Dalby (2003), Sampat (2001), and Walsh (2005).

Communication and Social Behavior
Hall (1959, 1966) originated many ideas about proxemics. Chagnon (1983) discusses the Yanomamö name taboo. We thank Kathryn Meyer and Gary deCoker for help with the example of Japanese honorifics.

Language and Culture
The Aztec 52-year calendar cycle is described by Berdan (2005) and Smith (2012). A concise description of the Sapir-Whorf hypothesis is in D. Brown (1991). We consulted reviews by Leavitt (2006), Lucy (1997), and P. Brown (2006). Levinson (2003) describes the Guugu Yimithirr. Deutscher (2010) is a readable book covering the effects of language on perceptions and worldviews.

Chapter 4—Cultural Diversity and Globalization

Cultural Change and Diversity
This section has been adapted from Foster (1962), Steward (1955 and 1977), White (1959), Service (1962 and 1971), and Sahlins and Service (1960).

The World Before Globalization

The main sources relied on for this section were Fagan (2002) and Wenke (1990).

Globalization Sections

The overview of globalization was derived from Stavrianos (1983), Wolf (1982), and Diamond (1999). Additional information for the period from the fifteenth through the eighteenth centuries was taken from Braudel (1979a, 1979b) and Frank (1998). The discussion of the Columbian Exchange is from Crosby (1972). Additional data on the Americas are drawn from Stannard (1992), Kehoe (1992), Thornton (1987), and Wolf (1969); and on Africa from Davidson (1969), Oliver and Fage (1962), Mintz (1986), and Miracle (1966, 1967).

The Global Economy

For general information on the global economy, we have drawn from several studies: Giddens (2000), Hines (2000), Hutton and Giddens (2000), Klein (1999), Robbins (1999), and general reading. The portion on the development of free trade is in large part from the website of the World Trade Organization (www.wto.org). Information on shipping is from an article in the *Washington Post National Weekly Edition* (September 3–9, 2001) and the Shipping-Facts website (www.marisec.org/shippingfact/worldtradeindex.htm). The information on information technology is from general reading.

The basic inspiration for the portion on the ways in which the global economy directly and indirectly is affecting global culture is from Berger (1997). However, we have defined different categories in some cases and elaborated on others. For data on wealth distribution, see Wealth Distribution Statistics 1999 compiled by the United Nations (www.geocities.com) and the World Council of Churches (2000). For data on immigration issues, we drew heavily from the *Migration News* (www.migration.ucdavis.edu). Additional current data on economic, social, migration, and other issues are taken from news reports in the *Washington Post, Christian Science Monitor*, the BBC News website (www.news.bbc.co.uk), and television and radio news reports. The data on the number of Facebook subscribers are from the "Newsroom" page of Facebook's website (http://newsroom.fb.com/Key-Facts), and the data on the number of automobile registrations are from the website of Wardsauto (http://wardsauto.com/print/ar/world_vehicle_population_110815). The portion on capitalism was inspired by Robbins (1999) and Mahbubani (2012), supplemented by general readings.

Global Challenges and Opportunities

The portion on the Gurifuna or Black Caribs is from Marshall (1973) and Sweeney (2007). Information on the Saramaka is from Price and Price (1980), Price (2012), and Orellana (2008).

Chapter 5—The Development of Anthropological Thought

The Emergence of Anthropology

K. R. Howe (2003) discusses the idea that the Polynesians were a lost tribe of Israel. Unilineal evolutionary theory is best known from the works of Tylor (1865, 1871) and Morgan (1877). The times and places of the founding of the first anthropology programs in the United States are from Black (1991).

Anthropological Thought in the Early Twentieth Century

The best single source of writings on Boas is a collection of his articles (1966). Configurationalism is best known from Benedict (1934). The critique of historical particularist assumptions is taken from Harris (1968). Malinowski's ideas about the functions of institutions, behaviors, and beliefs were first presented in a 1944 book, reprinted as Malinowski (1960). Good sources on structural-functionalism are Radcliffe-Brown (1922, 1965) and Nadel (1951). Kuwayama (2004) provides part of the material used in Global Challenges and Opportunities.

The Rebirth of Evolutionism in the Mid–Twentieth Century

See Leslie White (1949, 1959). Steward's most influential articles appear in two volumes (1955, 1977).

Anthropological Thought Today

The general discussion of controversies over the scientific and humanistic approaches is based on our own knowledge and interpretations.

Scientific Approaches

Dawkins (1976) and E. O. Wilson (1975, 1978) were instrumental works that popularized sociobiology. Books by Marvin Harris (1977, 1979, 1985, 1999) were influential in the development of modern materialist thought. Harris's work and M. Cohen (1977) emphasized the importance of population pressure. Sanderson (1999, 2007) provides nice summaries of current evolutionary theory and defends it from both old and new critics.

Humanistic Approaches

On interpretive anthropology, good sources are early works by Geertz (1973, 1980).

Either, Or, or Both?

Discussion of controversies over the 2010 long-range plan of the AAA is drawn from two articles in the online *New York Times* by Nicholas Wade: "Anthropology as a Science? Statement Deepens a Rift" (December 9, 2010), and "Anthropology Group Tries to Soothe Tempers After Dropping the Word 'Science'" (December 13, 2010) (both accessed March 8, 2013). On its website, the AAA responds in "AAA Responds to Public Controversy over Science in Anthropology."

Chapter 6—Methods of Investigation

Ethnographic Methods

The discussion of ethnographic field methods is based on the authors' own field experiences and numerous informal discussions with colleagues about the problems and issues they encountered during their field research. The discussions of particular field research problems with the Navajo are from Sasaki (1960, viii) and Kluckhohn (1944, 7). The discussion of suicide in the Trobriand Islands is derived from Malinowski (1926). The problems of collecting genealogies among the Yanomamö are recounted by Chagnon (1983). The discussion of how to evaluate a particular historical account was influenced by Naroll (1962). See also Hickerson (1970) on the ethnohistoric method and Fogelson (1989) for a discussion of interpretation of historical events. The data on Captain Cook is from Sahlins (1981, 1995) and Obeyesekere (1992).

Comparative Methods

For information on cross-cultural research, see Ember and Ember, "A Basic Guide to Cross-Cultural Research" and the Human Relations Area Files (see www.yale,edu/hraf.htm). The cross-cultural test of the sorcery and social control hypothesis is from B. Whiting (1950). The basic discussion of controlled comparisons is drawn from Eggan (1954). Data on matrilineal and patrilineal societies are from Allen (1984) and Bailey (1989).

Global Challenges and Opportunities

The historical discussion was from general reading. The quote and statements of White on Zia are from White (1967). The discussion of the Native American Protection and Repatriation Act as well as the discussion of international repatriation is from the National NAGPRA website (www.nps.gov/nagpra), while the discussion of the UN Declaration on the Rights of Indigenous People is from the UN website (www.un.org/esa/socdev/unpfi/documents/DRIPS_en.pd). The information on the Pitjantjatjara cases is from Brown (2003, 33–34). The discussion on the San is from the WIMSA website (www.wimsanet.org) and Stephenson (2003). The Protocols for Native American Archival Materials can be found at www2.nau.edu/libnap-p/protocols.html; the Hopi Protocols are available at www.nptao.arizona.edu/research/docs/Hopi. See the website of the American Anthropological Association for its Code of Ethics (www.aaanet.org/committees/ethics/ethics.htm).

Chapter 7—Culture and Nature: Interacting with the Environment

Hunting and Gathering

Dobyns (1983) provided most of the information on the distribution of foragers in North America used in Figure 7.1. Denevan (1992) and Krech (1999) discuss the use of fire to provide habitat for game animals among prehistoric Native Americans. Information on specific foragers is taken from the following sources: BaMbuti (Turnbull 1962), Hadza (Woodburn 1968), Netsilik (Balikci 1970), Western Shoshone (Steward 1938, 1955), Ju/'hoansi (Lee 1969, 1979, 2003), Northwest Coast (Ferguson 1984; Piddocke 1965; Suttles 1960, 1962, 1968) and Cheyenne (Hoebel 1978). Information on the recent endangering of the Ju/'hoansi is from Lee (2003); on the Hadzabe from the *Japan Times*, June 19, 2007, p. 7. Comparative information on foraging working hours is from Sahlins (1972) and Kelly (1995).

Domestication

Bowles (2011) uses archaeological, ethnographic, and historic evidence to conclude that early farming was not more productive than foraging. Bocquet-Appel (2011) uses prehistoric burial evidence to claim that mortality generally increased and fertility increased after agriculture. Smith (1995) is a readable book covering the origins of farming in various world regions. Diamond (1999) summarizes dates and places of plant and animal domestication and provides reasons for both developments. Sources consulted on the origins of plant domestication are Barton et al (2009), Crawford (2009), Denham et al. (2003), Dillehay et al. (2007), D. Fuller et al. (2009), Pickersgill (2007), Pope et al. (2001), T. D. Price (2009), vonHoldt (2010), and Zeder (2008).

Historian Alfred Crosby (1972, 1983) pioneered the study of the extraordinary impacts of the transfer of crops and livestock between the Old World and New World. Mann (2011) updates and extends Crosby's work on the Columbian Exchange, which includes pathogens.

Horticulture

M. Cohen (1989) provides an overview of evidence about the health of prehistoric foragers. Sources used to draw the North American portion of the map on the distribution of horticulture are Dobyns (1983) and Doolittle (1992). Material on shifting cultivation is from Conklin (1957), Freeman (1970), and Ruddle (1974). See Bradfield (1971) on dry land gardening among the Pueblo (mainly the Hopi).

Intensive Agriculture

Differences between extensive and intensive agriculture are described in Boserup (1965) and Grigg (1974). Material on intensive agriculture in the New World is drawn from our general knowledge and from Donkin (1979). On peasant revolts, see E. Wolf (1969). Johnson and Earle (1987) analyze the relationship between intensification and cultural evolution. G. Clark (2007) argues that the overall quality of human life did not improve until after the Industrial Revolution.

Pastoralism

Porter (1965) discusses the subsistence risk reduction benefit of pastoralism. Schneider (1981) shows the negative relationship between the distribution of the tsetse fly and cattle pastoralism in Africa. A short source on the Karimojong is Dyson-Hudson and Dyson-Hudson (1969).

Industrialism

Most material in this section is drawn from our general knowledge of the Industrial Revolution and its consequences. Strauss, Rupp, and Love (2013) provided the inspiration and data on power and energy slaves.

Globalization and the Environment

For specific information, Economy (2004) is an excellent source on China's water pollution problems. Economy (2007) provided numerical data on Chinese pollution and resource use. Recent information about China's environmental damage is drawn from two *New York Times* articles by Edward Wong: "Cost of Environmental Damage in China Growing Rapidly amid Industrialization" (March 29, 2013) and "On Scale of 0 to 500, Beijing's Air Quality Tops 'Crazy Bad' at 755" (January 12, 2013). Factual information for the discussion in the Globalization Challenges and Opportunities insert were taken from several sources. Three *New York Times* articles available online provided the information on the G-8 meeting in July 2009: (1) July 8, 2009, "Poorer Nations Reject a Target on Emission Cuts," by Peter Baker; (2) July 10, 2009, "Where Iron Is Bigger Than Oil or Gold," by Betinna Wassener; and (3) July 15, 2009, "U.S. Officials Press China on Climate," by Keith

Bradsher. On the Copenhagen meetings in December 2009, we consulted "5 Nations Forge a Climate Deal, but Many Goals Remain Unmet" by John Bowder, *New York Times*, December 18, 2010; and "Countries Submit Emissions Goals," by John Bowder, *New York Times*, February 2, 2010. Four entries from Johansen (2009) were helpful in summarizing the impacts of global warming: (1) "Agriculture and Warming" (pp. 10–16); (2) "Bangladesh, Sea Level Rise in" (pp. 83–84); (3) "China and Global Warming" (pp. 144–149); and (4) "Gulf of Mexico: Prospective Climate Changes" (pp. 319–321). Battista and Naylor (2009) discuss potential food shortages from global warming. Lobell, Schlenker, and Costa-Roberts (2011) conducted the statistical study on the global decline in wheat and maize production due to climate change.

Chapter 8—Exchange in Economic Systems

Information in the chapter opening vignette is from NPR: "Starbucks Order Gives Ohio Mug Maker a Jolt" (broadcast June 12, 2012). An article in the *New York Times* also contributed: "For Ohio Pottery, a Small Revival," by Stephanie Strom (June 12, 2012, online edition accessed July 15, 2012).

Economic Systems
Sahlins (1965) first distinguished the three forms of exchange.

Reciprocity
Lee (1979, 2003) describes Ju/'hoansi sharing and *hxaro*. Kelly (1995) generalizes some of Lee's points to other foragers. Malinowski (1922) describes Trobriand *wasi*. The Maring discussion is from Rappaport (1968) and Peoples (1982).

Redistribution
Alkire (1977), Sahlins (1958), D. Oliver (1989), and Peoples (1985) describe tribute in Micronesia and Polynesia.

Market Exchange
Neale (1976) remains a good general source on money, although many features in the text are our own idea. Schneider (1981) describes some African monies. Pospíšil (1978) discusses the multiple uses of money among Kapauku. Distinctions between market exchange and market economies are from our own general knowledge, as is that between the two forms and ideas of capitalism that we call *neoliberalism* and *social welfare capitalism*. Ho (2009) conducted the ethnographic interviews with Wall Street investment bankers, but she is not responsible for our interpretations and conclusion.

Globalization and Markets
General information in this section is from our own knowledge and opinions. Shapouri et al. (2002) provide a quantitative estimate of the energy balance of ethanol. Levitt (2011) provides information of the impact of ethanol production and speculation on Mexican corn tortilla prices. Information on corn also came from two news sources: (1) *New York Times*, "Cost of Corn Soars, Forcing Mexico to Set Price Limits," by James C. McKinley, January 19, 2007 (online edition accessed June 13, 2012) and (2) *Washington Post*, "A Culinary and Cultural Staple in Crisis," by Manuel Foig-Franzia, January 26, 2007 (online, accessed June 13, 2012). Information on the collapse of the Bangladesh clothing factory is from a variety of news sources. The *New York Times* reported specific facts in three articles: (1) "Building Collapse in Bangladesh Leaves Scores Dead," April 24, 2013, by Julfikar Ali Manik and Jim Yardley (online, accessed May 27, 2013); (2) "Retailers Are Pressed on Safety at Factories," by Steven Greenhouse, May 11, 2013 (online, accessed May 27, 2013); (3) "Report on Deadly Factory Collapse in Bangladesh Finds Widespread Blame," by Jim Yardley, May 23, 2013 (online, accessed May 27, 2013).

For the "Globalization Challenges and Opportunities" feature, M. Brown (2003) discusses issues of ownership of native cultures. Information on the 2009 West Sedona sweat lodge tragedy is from "Death at Sweat Lodge Brings Soul Searching," by John Dougherty, *New York Times*, October 11, 2009.

Chapter 9—Marriages and Families

Some Definitions
2010 U.S. Census Bureau data are from the website *Households and Families 2010*, available at www.census.gov/prod/cen2010/briefs/c2010br-14.pdf (accessed May 30, 2013).

Incest Taboos
Tylor (1888) first proposed the "marry out or die out" theory. "Familiarity breeds disinterest" was originally the idea of Westermarck (1926). On Taiwan, see A. Wolf (1970). On Israeli kibbutz, see Shepher (1971). On Lebanese cousin marriages, see McCabe (1983).

Marriage
Information on the Musuo is from Hua (2001). The material on Nayar "marriage" is from Gough (1959). Hart, Pilling, and Goodale (1988) describe Tiwi marriage and other aspects of Tiwi culture. J. Goodale (1971) provides information about Tiwi wives.

Marriage in Comparative Perspective
Goldstein (1987) and LeVine (1988) describe Tibetan polyandry and its advantages to husbands and the wife. Chagnon (1983) discusses the importance of marriage alliances among the Yanomamö. The challenges of Tierney (2000) do not alter Chagnon's conclusions about marriage alliances. Kuper (1963) describes Swazi bridewealth. See Lee (1979, 240–242) on Ju/'hoansi brideservice. See Goody and Tambiah (1973) and Harrell and Dickey (1985) on dowry. Material on Indian "dowry deaths" is from our general knowledge and a report in the *Columbus Dispatch* (July 25, 2004, p. A13). Specific information in Globalization Challenges and Opportunities insert is drawn from the following sources: Bernstein (1983); CIA *The World Factbook* (www.cia.gov/library/publications/the-world-factbook/index.html, retrieved June 9, 2013); James Brooke, "Japan Farms: An Old Man's Game," *New York Times*, November 7, 2003; Kunio (1988); Joji Sakurai, "Japan Looks to Foreign Brides to Save Its Villages," *Delaware Gazette*, May 19, 1997, p. 12; Zielenziger (2007).

Same-Sex Marriage and the Culture Wars
Factual information about the acceptance or rejection of same sex marriage by states is from the website of the National Conference of State Legislatures, updated May 2013 (www.ncsl.org/IssuesResearch/Human-Services

/SameSexMarriage/tabid/16430/Default.aspx, retrieved June 9, 2013).

Other specific information is from news sources:

- Tim Padgett, "Gay Family Values," *Time*, July 16, 2007, pp. 51–52.
- Sheryl Gay Stolberg and Dalia Sussman, "Same-Sex Marriage Should Be States' Call, Most in Poll Say," *New York Times*, June 7, 2013 (online edition, accessed June 9, 2013).
- Erik Eckholm, "Gay Marriage Measure Advances in Rhode Island," *New York Times*, April 24, 2013 (online edition, accessed June 9, 2013).
- Nate Silver, "How Opinion on Same-Sex Marriage Is Changing, and What It Means," *New York Times*, March 26, 2013 (online edition, accessed June 6, 2013).
- David Von Drehle, "How Gay Marriage Won," *Time*, April 8, 2013, pp. 16–24.
- Adam Liptak, "Supreme Court Bolsters Gay Marriage with Two Major Rulings," *New York Times*, June 26, 2013 (online edition, accessed June 27, 2013).
- Jeremy W. Peters, "Effects of Ruling on Same-Sex Marriage Start Rippling Out Through Government," *New York Times*, July 9, 2013 (online edition, accessed July 11, 2013).
- Frank Newport, "Religion Big Factor for Americans Against Same-Sex Marriage." Gallup Politics, December 5, 2012, available at http://www.gallup.com/poll/159089/religion-major-factor-americans-opposed-sex-marriage.aspx.

Postmarital Residence Patterns
We use the frequencies of different residence patterns reported in Pasternak (1976, p. 44). Ember and Ember (1971, 1972) and Pasternak (1976) have discussed the influences on residence patterns.

Family and Household Forms
Murdock (1949) first suggested how forms of postmarital residence produce various forms of the family and household. Pasternak, Ember, and Ember (1976) suggest an economic hypothesis for why extended families exist.

Chapter 10—Kinship and Descent
Unilineal Descent
Information on the frequencies of patrilineal and matrilineal descent are from Aberle (1961) and Divale and Harris (1976). Firth (1936, 1965) describes the functions of Tikopian lineages and clans. See Eggan (1950) on Hopi matrilineal descent. Information for Globalization Challenges and Opportunities is from our general knowledge and from *China Daily* (November 5, 2003), Fong (2004), Jackson and Howe (2006), and Yan (2006).

Nonunilineal Descent
Cognatic descent in Polynesia is discussed in Firth (1968), Howard and Kirkpatrick (1989), and D. Oliver (1989). The Samoan *'aiga* is described in M. Ember (1959), Holmes and Holmes (1992), and D. Oliver (1989).

Influences on Kinship Systems
We consulted Aberle (1961); Alexander (1974); Divale (1974); Divale and Harris (1976); C. Ember (1974); Ember and Ember (1971); Ember, Ember, and Pasternak (1974); and Holden and Mace (2003).

Cultural Construction of Kinship
The diagrams portraying the terminological systems are from our own knowledge. Aberle (1961) and Pasternak (1976) provide statistical data on the general but imperfect correlation between forms of descent and terminological systems.

Chapter 11—Gender in Comparative Perspective
Sex and Gender
Holden and Mace (1999) conducted the comparative study suggesting that small variations in sexual dimorphism depend on female contributions to subsistence.

Cultural Construction of Gender
The Hua material is from Meigs (1988, 1990). Quantitative data on occupational distributions for 2011 are from the United States Bureau of Labor Statistics (www.bls.gov/cps/wlf-table11-2011.pdf, retrieved July 14, 2013). The BLS also reports the changing percentages of women who earn more income than their husbands (www.bls.gov/cps/wlf-table25-2011.pdf, retrieved July 14, 2013).

Multiple-Gender Identities
The primary sources of generalized information on Native American peoples are Roscoe (2000) and Nanda (2000). Information on the Zuni is from Roscoe (1991). Hoebel (1978) discusses Two Spirits among Cheyenne. Epple (1998) interprets nadleehi among Navajo. Nanda (1999) provides factual material on hijra.

The Gendered Division of Labor
Table 11.1 was constructed from data in Murdock and Provost (1973). On female hunting among BaMbuti and Agta, see Turnbull (1962) and Estioko-Griffin (1986), respectively. On the possibility that strenuous exercise inhibits ovulation, see Graham (1985). The influence of female child care responsibilities on the division of labor was first made forcibly by J. Brown (1970a). The discussion of why female contributions to subsistence tend to decline with intensification uses information in C. Ember (1983), Martin and Voorhies (1975), Boserup (1970), Burton and White (1984), and White, Burton, and Dow (1981). The Kofyar material is from Stone, Stone, and Netting (1995).

Gender Stratification
The general discussion in this section relies on material in di Leonardo (1991), Leacock (1978), Morgen (1989), Rosaldo and Lamphere (1974), Quinn (1977), and Sacks (1982). The information about Andalusia is from Gilmore (1980, 1990). The suggestion that women's status improves with age in many cultures is from J. Brown (1988). Sanday (2002) challenges the common definition of matriarchy. Information on the Iroquois is from Albers (1989), Stockard (2002), and J. Brown (1970b). Lepowsky (1993) describes gender egalitarianism among Vanatinai. On BaMbuti and Aka, see Turnbull (1962) and Hewlett (1992). The idea that women's control over key resources frequently leads to high overall status is discussed in Sanday (1973, 1981). Friedl (1975, 1978) was one of the first to argue that women's status in hunting and gathering cultures is positively related to the importance of women's ability to control the distribution of the

products they produce. Yoruba material is from Barnes (1990). The U.S. Bureau of Labor Statistics publishes *Women in the Labor Force: A Databook,* available at www.bls.gov/cps/wlf-databook (retrieved July 16, 2013). Data on women's employment through 2011 are taken from Tables 7, 24, and 25 in this source. Schlegel (1972) and Whyte (1978) discuss why matrilineality and matrilocality tend to give women high status, all else equal. Information on Chinese wives is from M. Wolf (1972) and our general knowledge. Information shared in the Global Challenges and Opportunities feature is from Adrian (2003), CIA (2010), and Vogel (1991).

Chapter 12—The Organization of Political Life

Forms of Political Organization

The definitions and ideas concerning political structure were influenced by Steward (1955), Service (1962), Cohen and Service (1978), Krader (1968), and Fried (1967). Ethnographic examples were taken from the following sources: Comanche from Hoebel (1940) and Wallace and Hoebel (1952); Tahiti from Goldman (1970); and Inca from D'Altroy (1987), Mien (1988), LaLone and LaLone (1987), LeVine (1987), and Metraux (1969).

Social Control and Law

For the basic definition of law as well as many of the concepts about legal systems, we relied on Hoebel (1954), Pospíšil (1958), Fallers (1969), Bohannan (1968), Newman (1983), and Gluckman (1972, 1973). Ethnographic examples were taken from the following sources: Comanche from Hoebel (1940), Cheyenne from Llewellyn and Hoebel (1941), Nuer from Evans-Pritchard (1940), Jivaro from Harner (1973), and Barotse from Gluckman (1972, 1973).

Global Challenges and Opportunities: Multinational Corporations Versus the Nation-states

The general information on economic size of multinational corporations is based on news reports over the past few years and the websites of the United Nations (www.un.org), the World Bank (www.worldbank.org), the International Monetary Fund (www.imf.org), and the World Trade Organization (www.wto.org).

The discussion of free trade and WTO is based in large part on Chomsky (2000), "The MAI Shell Game: The World Trade Organization (WTO)" from the Public Citizen Global Trade Watch website (www.tradewatch.org); "The WTO in Brief" from the World Trade Organization website (www.wto.org); and "Is Globalization Shifting Power from Nation States to Undemocratic Organizations?" from the Globalisation Guide website (www.globalisationguide.org). Many of the general ideas in the portions on multinational corporations are from Phillip (2008) as well as news reports. The part on Apple and other multinationals and corporate taxes are from Duhigg and Kocieniewski (2012), Drucker (2010), Emer-Dewitt (2012), and websites of Apple Inc. (www.apple.com) and the U.S. Public Interest Research Group (http://usprig.org/reports/usp/picking-tab).

Chapter 13—Social Inequality and Stratification

Equalities and Inequalities: Three Systems

Fried (1967) first introduced the classification of societies into egalitarian, ranked, and stratified. Woodburn (1982) discusses reasons for egalitarianism among foragers. Information on Tikopia is from Firth (1936). Berreman (1959) long ago noted the similarity of race relations in the American South to caste systems. For the Globalization Challenges and Opportunities feature, we used information from the following sources: Chang (2009); *New York Times* online editions of June 2, 6, 9, 13, and 22, 2010 (retrieved June 22, 2010).

Castes in Traditional India

The traditional Indian caste system and its relationship to Hinduism are discussed in Dumont (1980), Hiebert (1971), Mandelbaum (1970), and Tyler (1973).

Classes in Industrial Societies: The United States

Information on 2011 income quintiles came from United States Census Bureau, (2013), Table F.2, "Share of Aggregate Income Received by Each Fifth and Top 5 Percent of Families," www.census.gov/hhes/www/income/data/historical/families/(retrieved June 15, 2013). Quantitative information on the distribution of wealth in the United States for 2010 is from Economic Policy Institute (2012).

Maintaining Inequality

This narrative came from our general knowledge and opinions.

Theories of Inequality

Davis and Moore (1945) originated the functionalist theory. Conflict theory goes back to Marx (1967, original 1867). Dahrendorf (1959) was important in formulating conflict theory in sociology. Lenski (1966) remains an excellent source, comparing and evaluating the functionalist and conflict theories. Information on CEO-to-worker income ratios is from an online paper by Mishel and Sabadish (2013; retrieved July 21, 2013).

Chapter 14—Religion and Worldview

Defining Religion

Tylor (1871) defined religion as animism. Shore (1989) summarizes Polynesian *mana*. The Hopi information is from Frigout (1979) and our general knowledge.

Theories of Religion

The Trobriand magic example is from Malinowski (1954). Frazer's intellectual theory is from Frazer (1963). Geertz (1965) argued that religion provides meaning. The anthropomorphic theory is Guthrie's (1993). Malinowski (1954) argues that magic and religion alleviate anxieties during times of stress and uncertainty. Dobu beliefs about the fate of the dead are discussed in Fortune (1932, 179–188). Kwaio pollution is described in Keesing (1982). The theory that ritual behavior creates social solidarity goes back to Durkheim (1915).

Supernatural Explanations of Misfortune

The distinction between imitative and contagious magic is Frazer's (1963). Fortune (1932) describes Dobu sorcery. The witchcraft examples are from Kluckhohn (1967, Navajo); M. Wilson (1951, Nyakyusa); Evans-Pritchard (1976, Zande); Offiong (1983, Ibibio); Middleton (1965, Lugbara), and Knauft (1985). Kluckhohn (1967) hypothesizes that Navajo witchcraft beliefs reduce overt, socially disruptive hostilities.

Varieties of Religious Organization

Wallace (1966) formulated and named the kinds of "cult" organizations. The vision quest material is from Lowie (1954, 1956) and our general knowledge. Middleton (1965) describes the Lugbara ancestral cult. V. Turner (1967) describes women's fertility rituals among the Ndembu. Farrer (1996) is a readable ethnography of Mescalero Apache girls' puberty rituals.

Revitalization Movements

A general description of cargo cults is in Worsley (1968). Lawrence (1964) describes several Garia movements. On Handsome Lake's movement among the Seneca, see Wallace (1969). Stewart (1980) and E. Anderson (1996) describe peyotism among Native Americans. Specific information for Globalization Challenges and Opportunities came from the following sources: "In France, Politicians Make Halal Meat a Campaign Issue," National Public Radio broadcast, March 16, 2012; *World Almanac and Book of Facts 2007*, pp. 711–712; Lewin, "Muslims' Footbaths Set Off Debate," *Columbus Dispatch*, August 12, 2007, p. G2; "Belgium: Toward a Ban on Veils," *Time*, May 17, 2010, p. 13.

Chapter 15—Art and the Aesthetic

Many of the ideas for this chapter came from Hunter and Whitten (1975), R. Anderson (1989), and Toni Fratto (1978). On Shaker art, we consulted the classic study by Andrews and Andrews (1937) and a more recent study by Kirk (1997). Other sources of general information used in this chapter were Lipman and Winchester (1974), Hobson (1987), and Harvey (1937). Specific information on art in particular cultures is drawn from Colton (1959, Hopi); Connelly (1979, Hopi); Hoebel (1978, Cheyenne); and Hail (1983, Plains Indians).

Forms of Artistic Expression

The general discussion of body arts is based primarily on Brain (1979). Nuba body paint is from Faris and from a conversation with Faris. Information on Polynesian tattooing is from Gell (1993), Hage et al. (1995), and Simmons (1983). A 1998 research paper by undergraduate Maureen McCardel of Ohio Wesleyan University also was helpful on Polynesian tattooing.

Close (1989) provides a good summary of the archaeological debate over style versus function. Material on the Northwest Coast art is from our general knowledge, with specific points drawn from R. Anderson (1989), Boas (1955), Furst and Furst (1982), and Holm (1965, 1972). The comparative information on style in visual arts is from Fischer (1961).

We drew from the studies of Kaeppler (1978) and Lomax (1962, 1968). Good sources on *voudon* are Metraux (1972) and W. Davis's (1985) controversial book. We drew information on !Kung healing from Lee (2003) and Shostak (1983) and on Tumbuka healing from Friedson (1998). A source of case studies on various performances and healing is Laderman and Roseman (1996). An informative and heavily illustrated source for students on Native American dance is Heth (1993). For a discussion of the individual in art, see Warner (1986).

Art and Culture

Information on the use of sand paintings and song/chants in Navajo curing ceremonials is taken from Sandner (1991), Reichard (1950, 1977), and Parezo (1991). BaMbuti *molimo* is described in Turnbull (1962).

Global Challenges and Opportunities

This box is based on general reading together with Tanner (1975) and Haile (1980).

Chapter 16—Ethnicity and Ethnic Conflict

There is a vast body of literature in anthropology and sociology on ethnicity and related issues. Because the entire chapter draws on the sources given here, we have not divided these notes into sections. Our ideas on the nature and significance of ethnicity have been most strongly influenced by the studies of Barth (1958, 1969), Vincent (1974), Khlief (1979), Glazer and Moynihan (1963, 1975), Bennett (1975), Himes (1974), DeVos and Romanusci-Ross (1975), R. Cohen (1978), Tax (1967), Nietschmann (1988), Horowitz (1985), Huntington (2011), and Jackson and Hudman (1990a, 1990b). For discussions of international legal and political issues, see Alfredsson (1989) and Swepton (1989).

For additional data on particular ethnic groups and historical events, we have drawn on a number of sources: *CIA World Factbook* (2012), Canfield (1986), Ember and Ember (2001), Gerner (1994), Hajda and Beissinger (1990), Foster (1980), Bodley (1999), E. Wolf (1982), Stavrianos (1998), Davidson (1969), Carmack (1988), Kehoe (1992), McAlister (1973), Handler (1988), Price (1979), Harrison (2007, 2009), and the Library of Congress online Country Studies (http://countrystudies.us), as well as general news accounts and discussions with colleagues and students from Angola, Saudi Arabia, Oman, Bangladesh, Indonesia, Pakistan, and Malaysia. Most of the information on current ethnic conflicts is taken from current news reports, the website of the BBC (www.bbc.co.uk/news/world/) being the primary source.

Ideas and information on migration and transnational groups are from general reading, and Al-Ali and Koser (2001), Tsakiri (2005), Hirsch (2012), Semple (2012), and the websites of the Ministry of Overseas Indian Affairs (www.moia.gov.in) and the Immigration Policy Institute (www.migrationinformation.org).

Chapter 17—World Problems and the Practice of Anthropology

Applied Anthropology

The ideas about the unique contributions of anthropology to problem solving are our own.

Health

The discussion of western and traditional medicine is based on Murdock (1980). The data on Navajo healing and health are from Wyman (1983), Kunitz (1983), Csordas (2000), and Lewton (2000).

Population Growth

The economic interpretation of high birthrates in the Punjabi villages was presented by Mamdani (1973). The 1982 study of the same area is reported in Nag and Kak (1984). Data on large Javanese and Nepalese families appear in B. White (1973) and Nag, White, and Peet (1978). Nardi (1981, 1983), Shankman (1976), and Small (1997) discuss the importance of remittances in Samoa and Tonga. Freed and Freed (1985) discuss why Indian couples think they need more than one son.

World Hunger

The inequality explanation of hunger is stated and defended in lay terms in Lappé and Collins (1977, 1986). Data on the Irish famine are from O'Grada (1989), Kinealy (1995), and Woodham-Smith (1991). The discussion of the effects of the "green revolution" on Javanese peasants is from Franke (1974). Johnson (1971) discusses risk minimization among peasants. The quantitative data on the energetic efficiency of various food systems are compiled from information given in Pimentel et al. (1973, 1975) and Pimentel and Pimentel (1979).

The potential value of traditional farming methods for the modern world is described in Altieri (1987) and Wilken (1987). The advantages of intercropping and other traditional methods are covered in Innis (1980), Gliessman and Grantham (1990), and Harrison (1987). Traditional resource management is covered by Alcorn (1981) and Posey (1983, 1984, 1985). Nations and Nigh (1980) discuss the potential of Lacandon Maya shifting cultivation.

Anthropologists as Advocates

The anthropologist as advocate is best discussed by Peterson (1974). The early roles of anthropologists in American Indian rights issues are discussed in Mark (1987). For Boas and the issue of racism, see Stocking (1974); and for Mead, see Mark (1999).

For the best general discussion of the evolution of European attitudes to indigenous peoples, see Berkhofer (1978). Germany's policies toward the Herero are discussed in Bodley (1999). S. Davis (1977) discusses the impact on indigenous tribes of Brazil's efforts to develop the Amazon basin. On San relocation, see Hitchcock (1999); Hitchcock, Biesele, and Lee (2003); and the websites of BBC news (http://news.bbc.co.uk/ 2/hi/africa) and Survival International (www.survival-international.org/tribes/bushmen). The quote about government policy is from the Botswana Tourism Board (http://botswanatourism.con.bw/attractions/central_kalahari_gam), and the quote of the Bushman Welfare Minister is from Survival International (www.survivalinternational.org/news/5705).

The Dongria Kondh materials are from the websites of Survival International (www.survivalinternational.org/tribes/dongria) BBC World News (http://news.bbc.co.uk/2/hi/asia) and Rahman (2010), while the quote of the Supreme Count is from NDTV (www.ndtv.com/article/india/in-multi-billion-dollar-vedanta-battle). The Kayapo and Belo Monte dam materials are from T. Turner (1989), A. Goodale (2003), Fearnside (2006), Swifkes (2008), BBC News (http.newsvote.bbc.co.uk/2/hi/Americas), the *Huffington Post* (www.huffingtonpost.com/bianca-jagger/belo-monte-dam), and Amazon Watch (http.amazonwatch.org/news). See also the Piaracu Declaration (www.irn.org/pdf/xingu/Piaracu Declaration). The information concerning the U.S. treatment of Native American societies is from general reading. The quote on Black Mesa is from Lacerenza (1988). On the conflict between the Peruvian government and the tribes of the Amazon, see BBC News (http://news.bbc.co.uk/2/hi/americas). The statement of President Garcia is from the website of Tribe (http://tribes.tribe.net/amazonistas).

The *Business Week* issue referred to is from March 1, 1993. The examples of medicines learned about from indigenous peoples are taken from Lewis and Elvin-Lewis (1977). Farnsworth (1984) argues that many more plants will be discovered to have medical uses. A good discussion of the insights of "traditional medicine" is in Fabrega (1975). The discussion of the erosion of the genetic diversity of major food crops is from our general knowledge and Harlan (1975). The material on amaranth is from Sokolov (1986). Information on "The Declaration on the Rights of Indigenous People" was taken from the United Nations website (www.un.org) and from the BBC News website (http://news.bbc.co.uk).

Global Challenges and Opportunities

Ideas in this feature are taken from Sen (1984, 1987) and Kapur (1998).

Bibliography

Aberle, David F. 1961 "Matrilineal Descent in Cross-Cultural Perspective." In *Matrilineal Kinship,* edited by David M. Schneider and Kathleen Gough, pp. 655–727. Berkeley: University of California Press.

Adams, Richard N. 1982 *Paradoxical Harvest.* Cambridge: Cambridge University Press.

1988 "Energy and the Regulation of Nation States." *Cultural Dynamics* 1:46–61.

Adler, Daniel S. 2009 "The Earliest Musical Tradition." *Nature* 460:695–696.

Adrian, Bonnie 2003 *Framing the Bride: Globalizing Beauty and Romance in Taiwan's Bridal Industry.* Berkeley: University of California Press.

Al-Ali, Nadje and Kalid Koser 2001 *New Approaches to Migration? Transnational Communities and the Transformation of Home.* Oxford: Routledge.

Albers, Patricia C. 1989 "From Illusion to Illumination: Anthropological Studies of American Indian Women." In *Gender and Anthropology: Critical Reviews for Research and Teaching,* edited by Sandra Morgen, pp. 132–170. Washington, D.C.: American Anthropological Association.

Alcorn, Janice 1981 "Huastec Non-Crop Resource Management." *Human Ecology* 9:395–417.

Alexander, Richard 1974 "The Evolution of Social Behavior." *Annual Review of Ecology and Systematics* 5:325–383.

Alfredsson, Gudmundur 1989 "The United Nations and the Rights of Indigenous Peoples." *Current Anthropology* 30:255–259.

Alkire, William H. 1977 *An Introduction to the Peoples and Cultures of Micronesia.* 2nd ed. Menlo Park, Calif.: Cummings.

Allen, Michael 1984 "Elders, Chiefs, and Big Men: Authority Legitimation and Political Evolution in Melanesia." *American Ethnologist* 11:20–41.

Altieri, Miguel A. 1987 *Agroecology: The Scientific Basis of Alternative Agriculture.* Boulder, Colo.: Westview.

Anderson, Edward F. 1996 *Peyote: The Divine Cactus.* 2nd ed. Tucson: University of Arizona Press.

Anderson, Richard L. 1989 *Art in Small-Scale Societies.* 2nd ed. Englewood Cliffs, N.J.: Prentice Hall.

Andrews, Edward Deming, and Faith Andrews 1937 *Shaker Furniture: The Craftsmanship of American Communal Sects.* New Haven, Conn.: Yale University Press.

Arjamaa, Olli, and Timo Vuorisalo 2010 "Gene-Culture Coevolution and Human Diet." *American Scientist* 98:140–147.

Aveni, Anthony 1995 *Empires of Time.* New York: Kodansha America.

Bailey, Garrick 1989 "Descent and Social Survival of Native Horticultural Societies of the Eastern United States." Paper presented at the American Anthropological Association meetings, Washington, D.C.

Balikci, Asen 1970 *The Netsilik Eskimo.* Garden City, N.Y.: Natural History Press.

Balter, Michael 2008 "Why We're Different: Probing the Gap Between Apes and Humans." *Science* 319:404–405.

Barnes, Sandra T. 1990 "Women, Property, and Power." In *Beyond the Second Sex,* edited by Peggy Reeves Sanday and Ruth Gallagher Goodenough, pp. 253–280. Philadelphia: University of Pennsylvania Press.

Barth, Fredrik 1958 "Ecological Relationships of Ethnic Groups in Swat, North Pakistan." *American Anthropologist* 60:1079–1089.

1969 *Ethnic Groups and Boundaries.* Boston: Little, Brown and Company.

Barton, Loukas et al. 2009 "Agricultural Origins and the Isotopic Identity of Domestication in Northern China." *Proceedings of the National Academy of Sciences* 106(14):5523–5528.

Battisti, David S. and Rosamond L. Naylor 2009 "Historical Warnings of Future Food Insecurity with Unprecedented Seasonal Heat." *Science* 323:240–244.

Benedict, Ruth 1934 *Patterns of Culture.* Boston: Houghton Mifflin.

Bennett, John, ed. 1975 "The New Ethnicity: Perspectives from Ethnology." *1973 Proceedings of the American Ethnological Society.* St. Paul, Minn.: West.

Berkhofer, Robert F., Jr. 1978 *The White Man's Indian: Images of the American Indian from Columbus to the Present.* New York: Knopf.

Bernstein, Gail 1983 *Haruko's World: A Japanese Farm Woman and Her Community.* Stanford, Calif.: Stanford University Press.

Berreman, Gerald D. 1959 "Caste in India and the United States." *American Journal of Sociology* 66:120–127.

Black, Nancy Johnson 1991 "What Is Anthropology?" In *Introduction to Library Research in Anthropology,* edited by John Weeks, pp. 1–5. Boulder, Colo.: Westview.

Boas, Franz 1955 *Primitive Art.* New York: Dover.

1966 *Race, Language and Culture.* New York: Free Press (original 1940).

Bocquet-Appel, Jean-Pierre 2011 "When the World's Population Took Off." *Science* 333:560–561.

Bodley, John H. 1999 *Victims of Progress*. 4th ed. Palo Alto, Calif.: Mayfield.

1968 *Justice and Judgement Among the Tiv*. London: Oxford University Press.

Boserup, Ester 1965 *The Conditions of Agricultural Growth*. Chicago: Aldine.

1970 *Women's Role in Economic Development*. New York: St. Martin's.

Bouzouggar, Abdeljalil, Nick Barton, et al. 2007 "82,000-Year-Old Shell Beads from North Africa and Implications for the Origins of Modern Human Behavior." *Proceedings of the National Academy of Sciences* 104:9964–9969.

Bower, Bruce 2010 "Evolution's Bad Girl". *Science News (January 16, 2010)*:22–25.

Bowles, Samuel 2011 "Cultivation of Cereals by the First Farmers Was Not More Productive Than Foraging." *Proceedings of the National Academy of Sciences* 108(12):4760–4765.

Bradfield, Maitland 1971 "The Changing Pattern of Hopi Agriculture." Royal Anthropological Institute of Great Britain and Ireland Occasional Paper, no. 30. London: Royal Anthropological Institute.

Brain, Robert 1979 *The Decorated Body*. New York: Harper & Row.

Braudel, Fernand 1979a *The Structures of Everyday Life. Civilization & Capitalism 15th–18th Century*, vol. 1. New York: Harper & Row.

1979b *The Wheels of Commerce. Civilization & Capitalism 15th–18th Century*, vol. 2. New York: Harper & Row.

Brown, Donald E. 1991 *Human Universals*. New York: McGraw-Hill.

Brown, Judith K. 1970a "A Note on the Division of Labor by Sex." *American Anthropologist* 72:1073–1078.

1970b "Economic Organization and the Position of Women Among the Iroquois." *Ethnohistory* 17:131–167.

1988 "Cross-Cultural Perspectives on Middle-Aged Women." In *Cultural Constructions of "Woman,"* edited by Pauline Kolenda, pp. 73–100. Salem, Wisc.: Sheffield.

Brown, Kyle S., Curtis W. Marean, et al. 2012 "Fire as an Engineering Tool of Early Modern Humans." *Science* 325:859–862.

Brown, Kyle S., et al. 2012 "An Early and Enduring Advanced Technology Originating 71,000 Years Ago in South Africa." *Nature* 491:590–593.

Brown, Michael F. 2003 *Who Owns Native Culture?* Cambridge, Mass.: Harvard University Press.

Brown, Penelope 2006 "Cognitive Anthropology." In *Language, Culture, and Society*, edited by Christine Jourdan and Kevin Tuite, pp. 96–114. New York: Cambridge University Press.

Burton, Michael L., and Douglas R. White 1984 "Sexual Division of Labor in Agriculture." *American Anthropologist* 86:568–583.

Canfield, Robert L. 1986 "Ethnic, Regional, and Sectarian Alignments in Afghanistan." In Ali Banuazizi and M. Weiner (eds.), *The State, Religion, and Ethnic Politics: Afghanistan, Iran, and Pakistan*, pp. 75–103. Syracuse: Syracuse University Press.

Carmack, Robert, ed. 1988 *Harvest of Violence*. Norman: University of Oklahoma Press.

Central Intelligence Agency 2010 *The World Factbook*. www.cia.gov/library/publications/the-world-factbook/index.html.

Chagnon, Napoleon A. 1983 *Yanomamö: The Fierce People*. 3rd ed. New York: Holt, Rinehart & Winston.

Chang, Leslie T. 2009 *Factory Girls: From Village to City in Changing China*. New York: Spiegel & Grau.

Chomsky, Noam 2000 "Control of Our Lives." Lecture, February 26, 2000, Albuquerque, N.M. (www.zmag.org).

Clark, Gregory, 2007 *A Farewell to Alms: A Brief Economic History of the World*. Princeton, N.J.: Princeton University Press.

Close, Angela E. 1989 "Identifying Style in Stone Artifacts: A Case Study from the Nile Valley." In "Alternative Approaches to Lithic Analysis," edited by Donald Henry and George Odell. *Archaeological Papers of the American Anthropological Association* 1:3–26.

Cohen, Mark Nathan 1977 *The Food Crisis in Prehistory*. New Haven, Conn.: Yale University Press.

1989 *Health and the Rise of Civilization*. New Haven, Conn.: Yale University Press.

Cohen, Ronald 1978 "Ethnicity: Problem and Focus in Anthropology". *Annual Review of Anthropology* 7.

Cohen, Ronald, and Elman Service 1978 *Origins of the State: The Anthropology of Political Evolution*. Philadelphia: Institute for the Study of Human Issues.

Colton, Harold S. 1959 *Hopi Kachina Dolls*. Albuquerque: University of New Mexico Press.

Commission for the Creation of Yanomami Park (CCPY) 1989a "The Threatened Yanomami." *Cultural Survival Quarterly* 13:45–46.

1989b "Brazilian Government Reduces Yanomami Territory by 70 Percent." *Cultural Survival Quarterly* 13:47.

Committee for Human Rights, American Anthropological Association 2001 "The Yanomami of Brazil: Human Rights Update," http://www.aaanet.org/committees/cfhr/rptyano 10.htm.

Conklin, Harold 1957 "Hanunoo Agriculture." FAO Forestry Development Paper, no. 12. Rome: Food and Agriculture Organization of the United Nations.

Connelly, John C. 1979 "Hopi Social Organization." In *Handbook of North American Indians*, vol. 9, edited by William Sturtevant, pp. 539–553.

Conrad, Nicholas J., Maria Malina, and Susanne C. Munzel 2009 "New Flutes Document the Earliest Musical Tradition in Southwestern Germany." *Nature* 460: 737–740.

Crawford, Gary W. 2009 "Agricultural Origins in North China Pushed Back to the Pleistocene-Holocene Boundary." *Proceedings of the National Academy of Sciences* 106(18):7271–7272.

Crosby, Alfred W. 1972 *The Columbian Exchange*. Westport, Conn.: Greenwood.

1986 *Ecological Imperialism: Biological and Cultural Consequences of 1492.* Westport, Conn.: Praeger.

Csordas, Thomas J. 2000 "The Navajo Healing Project." *Medical Anthropology Quarterly* 14(4):463–475.

Dahrendorf, Raff 1959 *Class and Class Conflict in Industrial Society.* Berkeley: University of California Press.

Dalby, A. 2003 *Language in Danger: The Loss of Linguistic Diversity and the Threat to Our Future.* New York: Columbia University Press.

D'Altroy, Terence N. 1987 "Transitions in Power: Centralization of Wanka Political Organization Under Inka Rule." *Ethnohistory* 34:78–102.

Davidson, Basil 1961 *The African Slave Trade: Precolonial History 1450–1850.* Boston: Atlantic–Little Brown.

1969 *Africa in History.* New York: Macmillan.

Davis, Kingsley, and Wilbert E. Moore 1945 "Some Principles of Stratification." *American Sociological Review* 10:242–249.

Davis, Shelton H. 1977 *Victims of the Miracle.* Cambridge: Cambridge University Press.

Davis, Wade 1985 *The Serpent and the Rainbow.* New York: Warner Books.

Dawkins, Richard 1976 *The Selfish Gene.* Oxford: Oxford University Press.

Denevan, William M. 1992 "The Pristine Myth: The Landscape of the Americas in 1492." *Annals of the Association of American Geographers* 82:369–385.

Denham, T.P. et al. 2003 "Origins of Agriculture at Kuk Swamp in the Highlands of New Guinea." *Science* 301:189–193.

Dentan, Robert Knox 1968 *The Semai: A Nonviolent People of Malaya.* New York: Holt, Rinehart & Winston.

Deutscher, Guy 2010 *Through the Looking Glass: Why the World Looks Different in Other Languages.* New York: Metropolitan Books.

DeVos, George, and Lola Romanusci-Ross, eds. 1975 *Ethnic Identity: Cultural Continuities and Change.* Palo Alto, Calif.: Mayfield.

di Leonardo, Micaela, ed. 1991 *Gender at the Crossroads of Knowledge.* Berkeley: University of California Press.

Diamond, Jared 1999 *Guns, Germs, and Steel.* New York: Norton.

Dillehay, Tom, Jack Rossen, Thomas Andrus, and David Williams 2007 "Preceramic Adoption of Squash, Peanut, and Cotton in Northern Peru." *Science* 316:1890–1893.

Divale, William T. 1974 "Migration, External Warfare, and Matrilocal Residence." *Behavior Science Research* 9:75–133.

Divale, William T., and Marvin Harris 1976 "Population, Warfare, and the Male Supremacist Complex." *American Anthropologist* 78:521–538.

Dobyns, Henry F. 1976 *Native American Historical Demography: A Critical Bibliography.* Bloomington: Indiana University Press.

1983 *Their Numbers Become Thinned.* Knoxville: University of Tennessee Press.

Donkin, Robin 1979 *Agricultural Terracing in the Aboriginal New World.* Tucson: University of Arizona Press.

Doolittle, William E. 1992 "Agriculture in North America on the Eve of Contact: A Reassessment." *Annals of the Association of American Geographers* 82:386–401.

Dozier, Edward P. 1970 *The Pueblo Indians of North America.* Prospect Heights, Ill.: Waveland Press (reissued 1983).

Dumont, Louis 1980 *Homo Hierarchicus: The Caste System and Its Implications.* Chicago: University of Chicago Press.

Durkheim, Émile 1915 *The Elementary Forms of the Religious Life.* London: Allen and Unwin.

Dyson-Hudson, Rada, and Neville Dyson-Hudson 1969 "Subsistence Herding in Uganda." *Scientific American* 220:76–89.

Economy, Elizabeth C. 2004 *River Runs Black: The Environmental Challenge to China's Future.* Ithaca, N.Y.: Cornell University Press.

2007 "The Great Leap Backward?" *Foreign Affairs* (September/October).

Economic Policy Institute 2012 *The State of Working America.* 12th edition. Cornell University Press (.stateofworkingamerica.org/).

Eggan, Fred 1950 *Social Organization of the Western Pueblos.* Chicago: University of Chicago Press.

1954 "Social Anthropology and the Method of Controlled Comparison." *American Anthropologist* 56:743–61.

Ember, Carol 1974 "An Evaluation of Alternative Theories of Matrilocal Versus Patrilocal Residence". *Behavior Science Research* 9:135–149.

1983 "The Relative Decline in Women's Contribution to Agriculture with Intensification." *American Anthropologist* 85:285–304.

Ember, Melvin 1959 "The Nonunilinear Descent Groups of Samoa." *American Anthropologist* 61:573–577.

Ember, Melvin, and Carol R. Ember 1971 "The Conditions Favoring Matrilocal Versus Patrilocal Residence." *American Anthropologist* 73:571–594.

1972 "The Conditions Favoring Multilocal Residence." *Southwestern Journal of Anthropology* 28:382–400.

Ember, Melvin, and Carol R. Ember, eds. 2001 *Countries and Their Cultures,* 4 vols. New York: Macmillan Reference USA.

Ember, Melvin, Carol R. Ember, and Burton Pasternak 1974 "On the Development of Unilineal Descent." *Journal of Anthropological Research* 30:69–94.

Epple, Carolyn 1998 "Coming to Terms with Navajo Nadleehi: A Critique of Berdache, "Gay," "Alternate Gender," and "Two Spirit." *American Ethnologist* 25:267–290.

Estioko-Griffin, Agnes 1986 "Daughters of the Forest." *Natural History* 95:36–43.

Evans-Pritchard, E. E. 1940 *The Nuer.* Oxford: Clarendon.

1976 *Witchcraft, Oracles, and Magic Among the Azande.* Abridged ed. Oxford: Clarendon Press.

Ewers, John 1955 "The Horse in Blackfoot Indian Culture." Bureau of American Ethnology, Bulletin 159. Washington, D.C.: U.S. Government Printing Office.

Fabrega, H., Jr. 1975 "The Need for an Ethnomedical Science." *Science* 189:969–975.

Fagan, Brian 2002 *Archaeology: A Brief Introduction.* 8th ed. Englewood, Cliffs, N.J.: Prentice Hall.

Fallers, Lloyd A. 1969 *Law Without Precedent.* Chicago: University of Chicago Press.

Farnsworth, Norman R. 1984 "How Can the Well Be Dry When It Is Filled with Water?" *Economic Botany* 38:4–13.

Farrer, Claire F. 1996 *Thunder Rides a Black Horse.* 2nd ed. Prospect Heights, Ill.: Waveland Press.

Fearnside, Phillip M. 2006 "Dams in the Amazon: Belo Monte and Brazil's Hydroelectric Development of the Xingu River Basin." *Environmental Management* 20(10):1–13.

Ferguson, R. Brian 1984 "A Reexamination of the Causes of Northwest Coast Warfare." In *Warfare, Culture, and Environment,* edited by R. Brian Ferguson, pp. 267–328. Orlando, Fla.: Academic Press.

Fine, Gary Allan 2007 *Authors of the Storm: Meteorologists and the Culture of Prediction.* Chicago: University of Chicago Press.

Firth, Raymond 1936 *We, the Tikopia.* Boston: Beacon.

1965 *Primitive Polynesian Economy.* New York: Norton.

1968 "A Note on Descent Groups in Polynesia." In *Kinship and Social Organization,* edited by Paul Bohannan and John Middleton, pp. 213–223. Garden City, N.Y.: Natural History Press.

Fischer, John 1961 "Art Styles as Cultural Cognitive Maps." *American Anthropologist* 63:80–84.

Fogelson, Raymond D. 1989 "The Ethno-history of Events and Nonevents." *Ethnohistory* 36:133–147.

Fong, Vanessa 2004 *Only Hope: Coming of Age Under China's One-Child Policy.* Stanford, Calif.: Stanford University Press.

Fortune, Reo 1932 *Sorcerers of Dobu.* New York: Dutton.

Foster, Charles R., ed. 1980 *Nations Without a State: Ethnic Minorities of Western Europe.* New York: Praeger.

Frank, Andre Gunder 1998 *ReOrient: Global Economy in the Asian Age.* Berkeley: University of California Press.

Franke, Richard W. 1974 "Miracle Seeds and Shattered Dreams in Java." *Natural History* 83:10–18, 84–88.

Fratto, Toni Flores 1978 "Undefining Art: Irrelevant Categorization in the Anthropology of Aesthetics." *Dialectical Anthropology* 3(2): 129–38.

Frazer, Sir James George 1963 *The Golden Bough.* Abridged ed. Toronto: Macmillan (original 1911–1915).

Freed, Stanley A., and Ruth S. Freed 1985 "One Son Is No Sons." *Natural History* 94:10–15.

Freeman, Derek 1983 *Margaret Mead and Samoa.* Cambridge, Mass.: Harvard University Press.

Fried, Morton 1967 *The Evolution of Political Society.* New York: Random House.

Friedl, Ernestine 1975 *Women and Men: An Anthropologist's View.* New York: Holt, Rinehart & Winston.

1978 "Society and Sex Roles." In *Anthropology 98/99,* edited by Elvio Angeloni, pp. 122–126. Guilford, Conn.: Dushkin.

Friedson, Steven 1998 "Tumbuka Healing." In *The Garland Encyclopedia of World Music,* vol. 1, edited by Ruth M. Stone, pp. 271–284. New York: Garland.

Frigout, Arlette 1979 "Hopi Ceremonial Organization." In *Handbook of North American Indians,* vol. 9, *Southwest,* edited by Alfonso Ortiz, pp. 564–576. Washington, D.C.: Smithsonian Institution.

Fromkin, Victoria, and Robert Rodman 1988 *An Introduction to Language.* 4th ed. New York: Holt, Rinehart & Winston.

Fuller, D. et al. 2009 "The Domestication Process and Domestication Rate in Rice: Spikelet Bases from the Lower Yangtze." *Science* 323: 1607–1610.

Furst, Peter T., and Jill L. Furst 1982 *North American Indian Art.* New York: Rizzoli International.

Geertz, Clifford 1965 "Religion as a Cultural System." In *Anthropological Approaches to the Study of Religion,* edited by Michael Banton, pp. 1–46. Association of Social Anthropologists Monographs, no. 3. London: Tavistock.

1973 *The Interpretation of Cultures.* New York: Basic Books.

1980 *Negara.* Princeton, N.J.: Princeton University Press.

1983 *Local Knowledge: Further Essays on Interpretive Anthropology.* New York: Basic Books.

Gell, Alfred 1993 *Wrapping in Images.* Oxford: Clarendon Press.

Gerner, Deborah J. 1994 *One Land, Two Peoples: The Conflict over Palestine.* Boulder, Colo.: Westview.

Giddens, Anthony 2000 *Runaway World: How Globalization Is Reshaping Our Lives.* New York: Routledge.

Gilmore, David D. 1980 *The People of the Plain.* New York: Columbia University Press.

1990 *Manhood in the Making.* New Haven, Conn.: Yale University Press.

Gladwell, Malcolm 2001 "The Mosquito Killer." *New Yorker* (July 2), 42–51.

Glazer, Nathan, and Daniel P. Moynihan 1963 *Beyond the Melting Pot.* Cambridge: Harvard University Press.

Glazer, Nathan, and Daniel P. Moynihan, eds. 1975 *Ethnicity: Theory and Experience.* Cambridge, Mass.: Harvard University Press.

Gliessman, Stephen, and Robert Grantham 1990 "Agroecology: Reshaping Agricultural Development." In *Lessons of the Rain Forest,* edited by Suzanne Head and Robert Heinzman, pp. 196–207. San Francisco: Sierra Club Books.

Gluckman, Max 1972 *The Ideas in Barotse Jurisprudence.* Manchester: Manchester University Press.

1973 *The Judicial Process Among the Barotse*. Manchester: Manchester University Press.

Goldman, Irving 1970 *Ancient Polynesian Society*. Chicago: University of Chicago Press.

Goldstein, Melvyn C. 1987 "When Brothers Share a Wife." *Natural History* 96(3):38–49.

Goodale, Ava Y. 2003 "The Kayapo Indians' Struggle in Brazil." www.action-bioscience.org/environment/goodale.html.

Goodale, Jane C. 1971 *Tiwi Wives*. Seattle: University of Washington Press.

Goodenough, Ward H. 1961 "Comment on Cultural Evolution." *Daedalus* 90:521–528.

Goody, Jack, and S. J. Tambiah 1973 *Bridewealth and Dowry*. Cambridge: Cambridge University Press.

Gough, E. Kathleen 1959 "The Nayars and the Definition of Marriage." *Journal of the Royal Anthropological Institute* 89:23–24.

Graham, Susan Brandt 1985 "Running and Menstrual Dysfunction: Recent Medical Discoveries Provide New Insights into the Human Division of Labor by Sex." *American Anthropologist* 87:878–882.

Grigg, David 1974 *The Agricultural Systems of the World*. Cambridge: Cambridge University Press.

Guthrie, Stewart 1993 *Faces in the Clouds: A New Theory of Religion*. Oxford: Oxford University Press.

Hage, Per, Frank Harary, and Bojka Milicic 1995 "Tattooing, Gender and Social Stratification in Micro-Polynesia." *Journal of the Royal Anthropological Institute (N.S.)* 2:335–350.

Hail, Barbara 1980 *Hau, Kola: The Plains Indian Collection of the Haffenrefer Museum*. Bristol, R.I.: Haffenreffer Museum of Anthropology, Brown University.

Hajda, Lubomyr, and Mark Beissinger, ed. 1990 *The Nationalities Factor in Soviet Politics and Society*. Boulder, Colo.: Westview.

Hall, Edward T. 1959 *The Silent Language*. Greenwich, Conn.: Fawcett.

1966 *The Hidden Dimension*. Garden City, N.Y.: Doubleday.

Handler, Richard 1988 *Nationalism and the Politics of Culture in Quebec*. Madison: University of Wisconsin Press.

Harding, Susan Friend 2000 *The Book of Jerry Falwell: Fundamentalist Language and Politics*. Princeton, N.J.: Princeton University Press.

Harkin, Michael E., and David Rich Lewis, 2007 *Native Americans and the Environment*. Lincoln: University of Nebraska Press.

Harlan, Jack R. 1975 "Our Vanishing Genetic Resources." *Science* 188:618–621.

Harner, Michael J. 1973 *The Jívaro*. Garden City, N.Y.: Doubleday-Anchor.

Harrell, Stevan, and Sara A. Dickey 1985 "Dowry Systems in Complex Societies." *Ethnology* 24:105–120.

Harris, Marvin 1968 *The Rise of Anthropological Theory*. New York: Crowell.

1977 *Cannibals and Kings*. New York: Random House.

1979 *Cultural Materialism*. New York: Vintage Books.

1985 *Good to Eat*. New York: Simon & Schuster.

1999 *Theories of Culture in Postmodern Times*. Walnut Creek, Calif.: Altamira Press.

Harrison, Paul 1987 *The Greening of Africa*. New York: Penguin.

Harrison, Selig S. 2007 "The Pashtun time bomb." *New York Times* August 1.

2009 "Pakistan's Ethnic Fault Line." *Washington Post*, May 11.

Hart, C. W. M., Arnold R. Pilling, and Jane C. Goodale 1988 *The Tiwi of North Australia*. Belmont, Calif.: Wadsworth.

Harvey, Paul 1937 *The Oxford Companion to Classical Literature*. Oxford: Clarendon Press.

Hepner, George F., and Jesse O. McKee 1992 *World Regional Geography: A Global Approach*. St. Paul, Minn.: West.

Heth, Charlotte, general ed. 1993 *Native American Dance*. Washington, D.C.: Smithsonian Institution.

Hewlett, Barry S. 1992 *Intimate Fathers*. Ann Arbor: University of Michigan Press.

Hickerson, Harold 1970 *The Chippewa and Their Neighbors: A Study in Ethnohistory*. New York: Holt, Rinehart & Winston.

Hiebert, P. G. 1971 *Konduru: Structure and Integration in a Hindu Village*. Minneapolis: University of Minnesota Press.

Himes, Joseph S. 1974 *Racial and Ethnic Relations*. Dubuque, Ia.: Brown.

Hines, Colin 2000 *Localization: A Global Manifesto*. London: Earthscan Publications.

Hirsch, Michelle 2012 U.S. Educated Immigrants Return to Their Homelands. *Fiscal Times*, May 14.

Hitchcock, Robert K. 1999 "Resource Rights and Resettlement Among the San of Botswana". *Cultural Survival Quarterly* 22 (4):51–55.

Hitchcock, Robert K., Megan Biesele, and Richard B. Lee 2003. "The San of Southern Africa: A Status Report, 2003." www.aaanet.org/committees/cfhr/san.htm.

Ho, Karen 2009 *Liquidated: An Ethnography of Wall Street*. Durham, N.C.: Duke University Press.

Hobson, Christine 1987 *The World of the Pharaohs*. New York: Thames and Hudson.

Hockett, Charles F. 1960 "The Origin of Speech." *Scientific American* 203:88–96.

Hoebel, E. Adamson 1940 *The Political Organization and Law-Ways of the Comanche Indians*. American Anthropological Association, Memoir 54. Menasha, Wisc.: American Anthropological Association.

1954 *The Law of Primitive Man*. Cambridge, Mass.: Harvard University Press.

1978 *The Cheyennes*. 2nd ed. New York: Holt, Rinehart & Winston.

Holden, Clare Janake, and Ruth Mace.1999 "Sexual Dimorphism in Stature and Women's Work: A Phylogenetic Cross-Cultural Analysis." *American Journal of Physical Anthropology* 111:27–45.

2003. "Spread of Cattle Led to the Loss of Matrilineal Descent in Africa: A Coevolutionary Analysis." *Proceedings of the Royal Society of London B:* 270:2425–2433.

Holm, Bill 1965 *Northwest Coast Indian Art: An Analysis of Form.* Seattle: University of Washington Press.

1972 *Crooked Beak of Heaven.* Seattle: University of Washington Press.

Holmes, Lowell D., and Ellen Rhoads Holmes 1992 *Samoan Village Then and Now.* 2nd ed. Fort Worth, Tex.: Harcourt Brace Jovanovich.

Horowitz, Donald L. 1985 *Ethnic Groups in Conflict.* Berkeley: University of California Press.

Howard, Alan, and John Kirkpatrick 1989 "Social Organization." In *Developments in Polynesian Ethnology,* edited by Alan Howard and Robert Borofsky, pp. 47–94. Honolulu: University of Hawaii Press.

Howe, Kerry 2003 *The Quest for Origins: Who First Discovered and Settled the Pacific Islands?* Honolulu: University of Hawaii Press.

Hua, Cai 2001 *A Society Without Fathers or Husbands: The Na of China.* New York: Zone Books. (Translated by Asti Hustvedt)

Hunter, David E., and Phillip Whitten, eds. 1975 *Encyclopedia of Anthropology.* New York: Harper & Row.

Huntington, Samuel P. 2011 *The Clash of Civilizations and the Remaking of World Order.* New York: Simon & Schuster.

Hutton, Will, and Anthony Giddens, eds. 2000 *Global Capitalism.* New York: New Press.

Innis, Donald Q. 1980 "The Future of Traditional Agriculture." *Focus* 30:1–8.

Izady, Mehrdad R. 1992 *The Kurds.* Washington, D.C.: Taylor & Francis.

Jackson, Richard, and Neil Howe 2006 "The Greying of the Middle Kingdom: The Demographics and Economics of Retirement Policy in China." *European Papers on the New Welfare,* Paper no. 4, http://eng.newwelfare.org/?p=91 (retrieved October 14, 2007).

Jackson, Richard, and Lloyd E. Hudman 1990a *Cultural Geography: The Global Discipline.* St. Paul, Minn.: West.

1990b *Cultural Geography: People, Places and Environment.* St. Paul, Minn.: West.

Jenike, Brenda Robb 2003 "Parental Care and Shifting Family Obligations in Urban Japan." In *Demographic Change and the Family in Japan's Aging Society,* edited by John W. Traphagan and John Knight, pp. 177–201. Albany: State University of New York Press.

2004 "Alone in the Family: Great-grandparenthood in Urban Japan." In *Filial Piety: Practice and Discourse in Contemporary East Asia,* edited by Charlotte Ikels, pp. 217–242. Stanford, Calif.: Stanford University Press.

2006 "From the Family to the Community: Social and Cultural Meanings of Elder Care in Aging Japan." Paper delivered for Japan in Transition Conference, Lawrence University (Appleton, Wisc.).

Johansen, Bruce E. 2009 *The Encyclopedia of Global Warming Science and Technology.* Santa Barbara: ABC-CLIO.

Johnson, Allen W. 1971 "Security and Risk-Taking Among Poor Peasants: A Brazilian Case." In *Studies in Economic Anthropology,* edited by George Dalton, pp. 143–150. American Anthropological Association Special Publication, no. 7. Washington, D.C.: American Anthropological Association.

Johnson, Allen W., and Timothy Earle 1987 *The Evolution of Human Societies.* Stanford, Calif.: Stanford University Press.

Johnson, Ericka 2007 Dreaming of a Mail Order Husband: Russian-American Internet Romance. Durham, N.C.: Duke University Press.

Julien, Catherine J. 1988 "How Inca Decimal Administration Worked." *Ethnohistory* 35:257–279.

Jurmain, Robert, Lynn Kilgore, Wenda Trevathan, and Russell L. Ciochon 2008 *Introduction to Physical Anthropology.* 11th ed. Belmont, Calif.: Wadsworth.

Kaeppler, Adrienne L. 1978 "Dance in Anthropological Perspective." *Annual Review of Anthropology* 7:31–49.

Kalb, Laurie Beth 1994 *Crafting Devotions: Tradition in Contemporary New Mexico Santos.* Albuquerque: University of New Mexico Press.

Kapur, Akash 1998 "The Indian State of Kerala Has Everything Against It—Except Success." *Atlantic Monthly,* September, 40–45.

Keesing, Roger M. 1982 *Kwaio Religion.* New York: Columbia University Press.

Kehoe, Alice B. 1992 *North American Indians: A Comprehensive Account.* 2nd ed. Englewood Cliffs, N.J.: Prentice Hall.

Kelly, Robert L. 1995 *The Foraging Spectrum: Diversity in Hunter-Gatherer Lifeways.* Washington, D.C.: Smithsonian Institution.

Khlief, Bud B. 1979 "Language as Identity: Toward an Ethnography of Welsh Nationalism". *Ethnicity* 6(4):346–357.

Kinealy, Christine 1995 *This Great Calamity: The Irish Famine 1845–52.* Boulder, Colo.: Roberts Rinehart.

Kirk, John T. 1997 *The Shaker World: Art, Life, Belief.* New York: Abrams.

Klein, Naomi 1999 *No Logo.* New York: Picador.

Kluckhohn, Clyde 1944 *Navajo Witchcraft.* Boston: Beacon.

Knauft, B.M. 1985 *Good Company and Violence: Sorcery and Social Action in a Lowland New Guinea Society.* Berkeley: University of California Press.

Krader, Lawrence 1968 *Formation of the State.* Englewood Cliffs, N.J.: Prentice Hall.

Kraybill, Donald B. 1989 *The Riddle of Amish Culture.* Baltimore, Md.: Johns Hopkins University Press.

Krech, Shepard 1999 *The Ecological Indian: Myth and History.* New York: Norton.

Kunio, Sato 1988 "Wives for Farmers: A Critical Import." *Japan Quarterly,* July–September, 253–259.

Kunitz, Stephen J. 1983 *Disease Change and the Role of Medicine.* Berkeley: University of California Press.

Kuper, Hilda 1963 *The Swazi: A South African Kingdom.* New York: Holt, Rinehart & Winston.

Kuwayama, Takami 2004 *Native Anthropology.* Melbourne: Trans Pacific Press.

Lacerenza, Deborah 1988 "An Historical Overview of the Navajo Relocation." *Cultural Survival Quarterly* 12 (3) (www.culturalsurvival.org./publications/cultural-survival-quarterly/united-states/historical-overview-navajo-relocation).

Laderman, Carol, and Marina Roseman, eds. 1996 *The Performance of Healing.* New York: Routledge.

LaFlesche, Francis 1905 *Who Was the Medicine Man?* Hampton, Va.: Hampton Institute Press.

1925 "The Osage Tribe: Rite of Vigil." In *39th Annual Report of the Bureau of American Ethnology (1917–18),* pp. 523–833. Washington, D.C.: Government Printing Office.

1928 "The Osage Tribe: Two Versions of the Child-Naming Rite." In *43rd Annual Report of the Bureau of American Ethnology (1925–1926),* pp. 23–164. Washington, D.C.: U.S. Government Printing Office.

LaLone, Mary B., and Darrell E. LaLone 1987 "The Inka State in the Southern Highlands: State Administrative and Production Enclaves." *Ethnohistory* 34:47–62.

Lane, Carrie 2009 "Man Enough to Let My Wife Support Me: How Changing Models of Career and Gender Are Reshaping the Experience of Unemployment." *American Ethnologist* 36:681–692.

Lappé, Frances Moore, and Joseph Collins 1977 *Food First.* New York: Ballantine Books.

1986 *World Hunger: Twelve Myths.* New York: Grove Press.

Lawrence, Peter 1964 *Road Belong Cargo.* Manchester: Manchester University Press.

Leacock, Eleanor 1978 "Women's Status in Egalitarian Society: Implications for Social Evolution." *Current Anthropology* 19:247–275.

Leacock, Eleanor, and Nancy Lurie, eds. 1971 *North American Indians in Historical Perspective.* New York: Random House.

Leavitt, John 2006 "Linguistic Relativities." In Christine Jourdan and Kevin Tuite, *Language, Culture, and Society,* pp. 47–61. New York: Cambridge University Press.

Lee, Richard B. 1969 "!Kung Bushman Subsistence: An Input-Output Analysis." In *Environment and Social Behavior,* edited by Andrew P. Vayda, pp. 47–79. Garden City, N.Y.: Natural History Press.

1979 *The !Kung San.* Cambridge: Cambridge University Press.

2003 *The Dobe Ju/'hoansi.* 3rd ed. Belmont, Calif.: Wadsworth.

Lenski, Gerhard E. 1966 *Power and Privilege.* New York: McGraw-Hill.

Lepowski, Maria 1993 *Fruit of the Motherland: Gender in an Egalitarian Society.* New York: Columbia University Press.

LeVine, Terry Yarov 1987 "Inka Labor Service at the Regional Level: The Functional Reality." *Ethnohistory* 34:14–46.

Levinson, Stephen 2003 *Space in Language and Cognition: Explorations in Cognitive Diversity.* Cambridge: Cambridge University Press.

Levitt, Tom 2011 "Mexico's Poor Suffer as Food Speculation Fuels Tortilla Crisis." *The Ecologist,* Sept. 13 (online edition retrieved June 13, 2012).

Lewis, Walter H., and Memory P. F. Elvin-Lewis 1977 *Medical Botany.* New York: Wiley.

Lewton, Elizabeth L. 2000 "Identity and Healing in Three Navajo Religious Traditions: Sa'ah Naaghai Bik'eh Hozho." *Medical Anthropology Quarterly* 14(4):476–97.

Lieberman, Philip 2007 "The Evolution of Human Speech." *Current Anthropology* 48:39–53.

Lipman, Jean, and Alice Winchester 1974 *The Flowering of American Folk Art.* New York: Viking.

Llewellyn, Karl, and E. Adamson Hoebel 1941 *The Cheyenne Way.* Norman: University of Oklahoma Press.

Lobell, David B., Wolfram Schlenker, and Justin Costa-Roberts 2011 "Climate Trends and Global Crop Production Since 1980." *Science* 333:616–620.

Lomax, Alan 1962 "Song Structure and Social Structure." *Ethnology* 1:425–451.

1968 "Folk Song Style and Culture." American Association for the Advancement of Science Publication, no. 88. Washington, D.C.: American Association for Advancement of Science.

Love, Thomas 2008 "Anthropology and the Fossil Fuel Era." *Anthropology Today* 24(2): 3–4.

Lowie, Robert H. 1954 Indians of the Plains. Garden City, N.Y.: American Museum of Natural History.

1956 *The Crow Indians.* New York: Holt, Rinehart & Winston (original 1935).

Lucy, John A.1997 "Linguistic Relativity." *Annual Review of Anthropology* 26:291–312.

Luhrmann, T. M. 2012 *When God Talks Back: Understanding the American Evangelical Relationship with God.* New York: Vintage Books.

Mahbubani, Kishore 2012 "Western Capitalism Has Much to Learn from Asia." *Financial Times,* Feb. 7 (http://blogs.ft.com/the-a-list/2012/02/07/western-capitalism)

Malinowski, Bronislaw 1922 *Argonauts of the Western Pacific.* New York: Dutton.

1926 *Crime and Custom in Savage Society.* London: Routledge & Kegan Paul.

1954 *Magic, Science and Religion.* Garden City, N.Y.: Doubleday.

1960 *A Scientific Theory of Culture and Other Essays.* New York: Oxford University Press (original 1944).

Mamdani, Mahmood 1973 *The Myth of Population Control: Family, Caste, and Class in an Indian Village.* New York: Monthly Review Press.

Mandelbaum, David G. 1970 *Society in India.* 2 vols. Berkeley: University of California Press.

Mann, Charles 2011 *1493: Uncovering the New World Columbus Created.* New York: Knopf.

Mark, Joan 1987 *A Stranger in Her Native Land: Alice Fletcher and the*

American Indians. Lincoln: University of Nebraska Press.

1999 *Margaret Mead: Coming of Age in America.* New York: Oxford University Press.

Marshall, Bernard 1973 "The Black Caribs: Native Resistance to British Penetration into the Windward Side of St. Vincent 1763–1773." *Caribbean Quarterly* 19(4):4–19.

Marshall, Mac 1979 *Weekend Warriors.* Palo Alto, Calif.: Mayfield.

Martin, M. Kay, and Barbara Voorhies 1975 *Female of the Species.* New York: Columbia University Press.

Marx, Karl 1967 *Capital,* vol. 1. New York: International Publishers (original 1867).

Mayo, Katherine 1927 *Mother India.* New York: Harcourt, Brace.

McAlister, John T., ed. 1973 *Southeast Asia: The Politics of National Integration.* New York: Random House.

McCabe, Justin 1983 "FBD Marriage: Further Support for the Westermarck Hypothesis of the Incest Taboo." *American Anthropologist* 85:50–69.

McDonald, Kim 1995 "Unearthing Sins of the Past." *Chronicle of Higher Education,* Oct. 6, A12, A20.

Mead, Margaret 1928 *Coming of Age in Samoa.* New York: Morrow.

Meigs, Anna S. 1988 *Food, Sex, and Pollution: A New Guinea Religion.* New Brunswick, N.J.: Rutgers University Press.

1990 "Multiple Gender Ideologies and Statuses." In *Beyond the Second Sex,* edited by Peggy Reeves Sanday and Ruth M. Gallagher Goodenough, pp. 99–112. Philadelphia: University of Pennsylvania Press.

Metraux, Alfred 1969 *The History of the Incas.* New York: Pantheon Books.

1972 *Voodoo in Haiti.* New York: Schocken Books.

Middleton, John 1965 *The Lugbara of Uganda.* New York: Holt, Rinehart & Winston.

Milner, G. B. 1969 "Siamese Twins, Bird, and the Double Helix." *Man* 4:5–23.

Mintz, Sidney W. 1986 *Sweetness and Power: The Place of Sugar in Modern History.* New York: Penguin Books.

Miracle, Marvin P. 1966 *Maize in Tropical Africa.* Madison: University of Wisconsin Press.

1967 *Agriculture in the Congo Basin.* Madison: University of Wisconsin Press.

Mishel, Lawrence and Natalie Sabadish 2013 "CEO Pay in 2012 Was Extraordinarily High Relatively to Typical Workers and Other High Earners." www.epi.org/publication/ceo-pay-2012-extraordinarily-high/(retrieved July 21, 2013)/

Morgan, Lewis Henry 1877 *Ancient Society.* New York: World.

Mulroy, Kevin 2004 Seminole Maroons. In *Handbook of North American Indians,* vol. 14, pp. 465–477. Washington, D.C.: Smithsonian Institution.

Murdock, George Peter 1949 *Social Structure.* New York: Free Press.

1980 Theories of Illness. Pittsburgh: University of Pittsburgh Press.

Murdock, George P., and Caterina Provost 1973 "Factors in the Division of Labor by Sex: A Cross-Cultural Analysis." *Ethnology* 12:203–225.

Nadel, S. F. 1951 *The Foundations of Social Anthropology.* London: Cohen & West.

Nag, Moni, and Neeraj Kak 1984 "Demographic Transition in a Punjab Village." *Population and Development Review* 10:661–678.

Nag, Moni, Benjamin N. F. White, and R. Creighton Peet 1978 "An Anthropological Approach to the Study of the Economic Value of Children in Java and Nepal." *Current Anthropology* 19:293–306.

Nanda, Serena 1999 *Neither Man nor Woman: The Hijras of India.* Belmont, Calif.: Wadsworth.

2000 *Gender Diversity: Cross-Cultural Variations.* Prospect Heights, Ill.: Waveland Press.

Nardi, Bonnie 1981 "Modes of Explanation in Anthropological Population Theory." *American Anthropologist* 83:28–56.

1983 "Goals in Reproductive Decision Making." *American Ethnologist* 10:697–714.

Naroll, Raoul 1962 *Data Quality Control—A New Research Technique.* New York: Free Press.

Nations, James, and Robert Nigh 1980 "The Evolutionary Potential of Lacandon Maya Sustained-Yield Tropical Forest Agriculture." *Journal of Anthropological Research* 36:1–30.

Neale, Walter C. 1976 *Monies in Societies.* San Francisco: Chandler and Sharp.

Nestor, Sandy 2003 *Indian Placenames in America: Volume 1: Cities, Towns and Villages.* London: McFarland.

Newman, Katherine S. 1983 *Law and Economic Organization: A Comparative Study of Pre-industrial Societies.* Cambridge: Cambridge University Press.

Nietschmann, Bernard 1988 "Third World War: The Global Conflict over the Rights of Indigenous Nations." *Utne Reader,* Nov./Dec., 84–91.

Obeyesekere, Gananath 1992 *The Apotheosis of Captain Cook: European Mythmaking in the Pacific.* Princeton, N.J.: Princeton University Press.

Offiong, Daniel 1983 "Witchcraft Among the Ibibio of Nigeria." *African Studies Review* 26:107–124.

O'Grada, Cormac 1989 *Ireland Before and After the Famine: Explorations in Economic History 1800–1925.* Manchester: University of Manchester Press.

Oliver, Douglas L. 1989 *Oceania: The Native Cultures of Australia and the Pacific Islands.* Honolulu: University of Hawaii Press.

Oliver, Roland, and J. D. Fage 1962 *A Short History of Africa.* Baltimore: Penguin.

Orellana, Marcos A. 2008 "Saramaka v Suriname." *American Journal of International Law* 102(4):841–847.

Ortiz, Alfonso 1969 *The Tewa World.* Chicago: University of Chicago Press.

Pagel, Mark 2012 *Wired for Culture: Origins of the Human Social Mind.* New York: Norton.

Parezo, Nancy J. 1991 *Navajo Sandpainting: From Religious Act to Commercial Art*. Albuquerque: University of New Mexico Press.

Pasternak, Burton 1976 *Introduction to Kinship and Social Organization*. Englewood Cliffs, N.J.: Prentice Hall.

Pasternak, Burton, Carol R. Ember, and Melvin Ember 1976 "On the Conditions Favoring Extended Family Households." *Journal of Anthropological Research* 32:109–123.

Peoples, James G. 1982 "Individual or Group Advantage? A Reinterpretation of the Maring Ritual Cycle." *Current Anthropology* 23:291–309.

1985 *Island in Trust*. Boulder, Colo.: Westview.

2007 "Materialist Particularity in Nuclear Micronesia." In *Studying Societies and Cultures: Marvin Harris's Cultural Materialism and Its Legacy*, pp. 104–127. Boulder, Colo.: Paradigm.

Petersen, Glenn 2009 "Kanengamah and Pohnpei's Politics of Concealment". *American Anthropologist* 95(2): 334–352.

Peterson, John 1974 "The Anthropologist as Advocate." *Human Organization* 33:311–318.

Pickersgill, Barbara 2007 "Domestication of Plants in the Americas: Insights from Mendelian and Molecular Genetics." *Annals of Botany* 1–16, http://aob.oxfordjournals.org/cgi/content/abstract/mcm193v1 (retrieved September 22, 2007).

Piddocke, Stuart 1965 "The Potlatch System of the Southern Kwakiutl: A New Perspective." *Southwestern Journal of Anthropology* 21:244–264.

Pimentel, David, et al. 1973 "Food Production and the Energy Crisis." *Science* 182:443–449.

1975 "Energy and Land Constraints in Food Protein Production." *Science* 190:754–761.

Pimentel, David, and Marcia Pimentel 1979 *Food, Energy and Society*. New York: Wiley.

Plofkin, Mark 1993 *Tales of a Shaman's Apprentice*. New York: Viking.

Pope, Kevin O., Mary E. D. Pohl, et al. 2001 "Origin and Environmental Setting of Ancient Agriculture in the Lowlands of Mesoamerica." *Science* 292:1370–1373.

Porter, Philip W. 1965 "Environmental Potentials and Economic Opportunities—A Background for Cultural Adaptation." *American Anthropologist* 67:409–420.

Posey, Darrell 1983 "Indigenous Ecological Knowledge and Development of the Amazon." In *The Dilemma of Amazonian Development*, edited by Emilio Moran, pp. 225–257. Boulder, Colo.: Westview.

1984 "A Preliminary Report on Diversified Management of Tropical Forest by the Kayapo Indians of the Brazilian Amazon." *Advances in Economic Botany* 1:112–126.

1985 "Indigenous Management of Tropical Forest Ecosystems: The Case of the Kayapó Indians of the Brazilian Amazon." *Agroforestry Systems* 3: 139–158.

Pospíšil, Leopold 1958 *Kapauku Papuans and Their Law*. Yale University Publications in Anthropology, no. 54. New Haven, Conn.: Yale University Press.

1978 *The Kapauku Papuans of West New Guinea*. 2nd ed. New York: Holt, Rinehart & Winston.

Price, Richard 2012 "*Saramaka People v Suriname*: A Human Rights Victory and Its Messy Aftermath." *Cultural Survival*, July 30 (www.culturalsurvival.org/news/saramaka-people-v-suriname (retrieved Feb. 25, 2013).

Price, Richard, ed. 1979 *Maroon Societies: Rebel Slave Communities in the Americas*. Baltimore, Md.: Johns Hopkins University Press.

Price, Sally and Richard 1980 *Afro-American Arts of the Suriname Rainforest*. Berkeley: University of California Press.

Price, T. Douglas 2009 "Ancient Farming in Eastern North America." *Proceedings of the National Academy of Sciences* 106(16): 6427–6428.

Radcliffe-Brown, A. R. 1922 *The Andaman Islanders*. Cambridge: Cambridge University Press.

1965 *Structure and Function in Primitive Societies*. New York: Free Press.

Rappaport, Roy 1968 *Pigs for the Ancestors*. New Haven, Conn.: Yale University Press.

Reichard, Gladys A. 1950 *Navaho Religion*. Princeton, N.J.: Princeton University Press.

1977 *Navajo Medicine Man Sandpaintings*. New York: Dover.

Reichel-Dolmatoff, Gerardo 1971 *Amazonian Cosmos*. Chicago: University of Chicago Press.

Ridley, Matt 2010 *The Rational Optimist: How Prosperity Evolves*. New York: HarperCollins.

Robbins, Richard H. 1999 *Global Problems and the Culture of Capitalism*. Boston: Allyn & Bacon.

Rosaldo, Michelle Z., and Louise Lamphere, eds. 1974 *Women, Culture, and Society*. Stanford, Calif.: Stanford University Press.

Roscoe, Will 1991 *The Zuni Man-Woman*. Albuquerque: University of New Mexico Press.

2000 *Changing Ones: Third and Fourth Genders in Native North America*. New York: St. Martin's.

Rostow, W. W. 1978 *The World Economy: History and Prospect*. Austin: University of Texas Press.

Ruddle, Kenneth 1974 *The Yukpa Autosubsistence System: A Study of Shifting Cultivation and Ancillary Activities in Colombia and Venezuela*. Berkeley: University of California Press.

Sacks, Karen 1982 *Sisters and Wives*. Urbana: University of Illinois Press.

Sahlins, Marshall 1958 *Social Stratification in Polynesia*. Seattle: University of Washington Press.

Sahlins, Marshall and Elman Service, eds.1960 *Evolution and Culture*. Ann Arbor: University of Michigan.

1965 "On the Sociology of Primitive Exchange." In *The Relevance of Models for Social Anthropology*, edited by Michael Banton, pp. 139–236. London: Tavistock.

1972 *Stone Age Economics*. New York: Aldine.

1981 *Historical Metaphors and Mythical Realities: Structure in the Early History of the Sandwich Island Kingdom.* Ann Arbor: University of Michigan Press.

1995 *How "Natives" Think: About Captain Cook, for Example.* Chicago: University of Chicago Press.

Sampat, Payal 2001 "Last Words." *World Watch Institute*, May/June, 34–40.

Sanday, Peggy R. 1973 "Toward a Theory of the Status of Women." *American Anthropologist* 75: 1682–1700.

1981 *Female Power and Male Dominance.* Cambridge: Cambridge University Press.

2002 *Women at the Center: Life in a Modern Matriarchy.* Ithaca, N.Y.: Cornell University Press.

Sanderson, Stephen K 1999 *Social Transformations.* Expanded ed. New York: Rowman & Littlefield.

2007 *Evolutionism and Its Critics.* Boulder, Colo.: Paradigm.

Sandner, Donald 1991 *Navajo Symbols of Healing.* Rochester, Vt.: Healing Arts Press.

Sapir, Edward 1964 "The Status of Linguistics as a Science." In *Edward Sapir*, edited by David G. Mandelbaum, pp. 65–77. Berkeley: University of California Press (original 1929).

Sasaki, Tom 1960 *Fruitland, New Mexico: A Navaho Community in Transition.* Ithaca, NY: Cornell University Press.

Schlegel, Alice 1972 *Male Dominance and Female Autonomy.* New Haven, Conn.: HRAF Press.

Schneider, Harold K. 1981 *The Africans.* Englewood Cliffs, N.J.: Prentice Hall.

Semple, Kirk 2012 "Many U.S. Immigrants' Children Seek American Dream Abroad." *New York Times*, Apr. 15.

Sen, Amartya 1984 *Resources, Values and Development.* Cambridge, Mass.: Harvard University Press.

1987 *The Standard of Living.* Cambridge: Cambridge University Press.

Service, Elman 1962 *Primitive Social Organization: An Evolutionary Perspective.* New York: Random House.

1971 *Cultural Evolutionism: Theory in Practice.* New York: Holt, Rinehart and Winston.

Shankman, Paul 1976 *Migration and Underdevelopment: The Case of Western Samoa.* Boulder, Colo.: Westview.

Shapouri, Hosein, James A. Duffield, and Michael Wang 2002 *The Energy Balance of Corn Ethanol: An Update.* U.S. Department of Agriculture. Agricultural Economics Report No. 813, www.transportation.anl.gov/pdfs/AF/265.pdf (retrieved September 15, 2007).

Sheper-Hughes, Nancy 1992 *Death Without Weeping: The Violence of Everyday Life in Brazil.* Berkeley: University of California Press.

Shepher, Joseph 1971 "Mate Selection Among Second Generation Kibbutz Adolescents and Adults: Incest Avoidance and Negative Imprinting." *Archives of Sexual Behavior* 1:293–307.

Shore, Bradd 1989 "Mana and Tapu." In *Developments in Polynesian Ethnology*, edited by Alan Howard and Robert Borofsky, pp. 137–173. Honolulu: University of Hawaii Press.

Shostak, Marjorie 1983 *Nisa: The Life and Words of a !Kung Woman.* New York: Vintage.

Simmons, Dave 1983 "Moko." In *Art and Artists of Oceania*, pp. 226–243. Palmerston North, New Zealand: Dunmore Press.

Small, Cathy 1997 *Voyages.* Ithaca and London: Cornell University Press.

Smith, Bruce 1995 *The Emergence of Agriculture.* New York: Scientific American Library.

Smith, Michael 2012. *The Aztecs.* 3rd ed. West Sussex, U.K.: Wiley-Blackwell

Sokolov, Raymond 1986 "The Good Seed." *Natural History* 95:102–105.

Stavrianos, Leften S. 1998 *The World Since 1500: A Global History.* 8th ed. Englewood Cliffs, N.J.: Prentice Hall.

Stephenson, David 2003 "San Reach Landmark IPR Benefit-Sharing Accord for Diet Pill." *Cultural Survival Quarterly* 27(3), www.culturalsurvival.org/publications/cultural-survival-quarterly.

Steward, Julian H. 1938 *Basin-Plateau Sociopolitical Groups.* Bureau of American Ethnology Bulletin 120. Washington, D.C.: U.S. Government Printing Office.

1955 *Theory of Culture Change.* Urbana: University of Illinois Press.

1977 *Evolution and Ecology: Essays on Social Transformation*, edited by Jane C. Steward and Robert F. Murphy. Urbana: University of Illinois Press.

Stewart, Omer C. 1980 "The Native American Church." In *Anthropology on the Great Plains*, edited by W. Raymond Wood and Margot Liberty, pp. 188–196. Lincoln: University of Nebraska Press.

Stockard, Janice E. 2002 *Marriage in Culture.* Fort Worth, Tex.: Harcourt.

Stocking, George W. Jr., 1974 *The Shaping of American Anthropology, 1883–1911.* New York: Basic Books.

Stone, Arthur A., Joseph E. Schwartz, Joan E. Broderick, and Angus Deaton 2010 "A Snapshot of the Age Distribution of Psychological Well-Being in the United States". *Proceedings of the National Academy of Sciences* 107 (22): 9985–9990.

Stone, M. Priscilla, Glenn Davis Stone, and Robert M. Netting 1995 "The Sexual Division of Labor in Kofyar Agriculture." *American Ethnologist* 22:165–186.

Strauss, Sarah, Stephanie Rupp, and Thomas Love, eds., *Cultures of Energy.* Walnut Creek, CA: Left Coast Press.

Sturm, Cirse, and Kristy J. Feldhousen-Giles 2008 "The Freedmen." In William Sturtevant (gen. ed.), *Handbook of North American Indians; Indians in Contemporary Society* 2:275–284.

Suttles, Wayne 1960 "Affinal Ties, Subsistence, and Prestige Among the Coast Salish." *American Anthropologist* 62:296–305.

1962 "Variations in Habitat and Culture on the Northwest Coast."

In *Man in Adaptation: The Cultural Present*, edited by Yehudi A. Cohen, pp. 128–141. Chicago: Aldine.

1968 "Coping with Abundance: Subsistence on the Northwest Coast." In *Man the Hunter*, edited by Richard B. Lee and Irven DeVore, pp. 56–68. Chicago: Aldine.

Swanson, Guy 1960 *The Birth of the Gods.* Ann Arbor: University of Michigan Press.

Sweeney, James L. 2007 "Caribs, Maroons, Jacobins, Brigands, and Sugar Barons: The Last Stand of the Black Caribs on St. Vincent." The African Diaspora Archaeological Network. March newsletter.

Swepton, Lee 1989 "Indigenous and Tribal Peoples and International Law: Recent Developments." *Current Anthropology* 30:259–264.

Tanner, Clara Lee 1975 *Southwest Indian Craft Arts.* Tucson: University of Arizona Press

Tax, Sol, ed. 1967 *Acculturation in the Americas.* New York: Cooper Square.

Thornton, Russell 1987 *American Indian Holocaust and Survival: A Population History Since 1492.* Norman: University of Oklahoma Press.

Tierney, Patrick 2000 *Darkness in El Dorado.* New York: Norton.

Tsakiri, Elisa 2005 "Transnational Communities and Identity." *Refugee Survey Quarterly* 24(4):102–104.

Turnbull, Colin M. 1962 *The Forest People.* New York: Simon & Schuster.

Turner, Terence 1989 "Kayapo Plan Meeting to Discuss Dams." *Cultural Survival Quarterly* 13:20–22.

Turner, Victor 1967 *The Forest of Symbols.* Ithaca, N.Y.: Cornell University Press.

Tyler, Stephen A. 1973 *India: An Anthropological Perspective.* Pacific Palisades, Calif.: Goodyear.

Tylor, Edward B. 1865 *Researches into the Early History of Mankind and the Development of Civilization.* London: J. Murray.

1871 *Primitive Culture.* London: J. Murray.

1888 "On a Method of Investigating the Development of Institutions, Applied to Laws of Marriage and Descent." *Journal of the Royal Anthropological Institute* 18:245–272.

United States Bureau of the Census 2007 *Income, Poverty, and Health Insurance Coverage in the United States, 2007.* Current Population Reports P60-233,www.census.gov /prod/2007pubs/p60-233.pdf.

Valeri, Valerio 1985 *Kingship and Sacrifice: Ritual and Society in Ancient Hawaii.* Chicago: University of Chicago Press.

Vincent, Joan 1974 "The Structuring of Ethnicity." *Human Organization* 33:375–379.

Vogel, Ezra F. 1991 *The Four Little Dragons: The Spread of Industrialization in East Asia.* Cambridge: Harvard University Press.

Wallace, Anthony F. C. 1966 *Religion: An Anthropological View.* New York: Random House.

1969 *The Death and Rebirth of the Seneca.* New York: Vintage Books.

Wallace, Ernest, and E. Adamson Hoebel 1952 *The Comanches: Lords of the South Plains.* Norman: University of Oklahoma Press.

Walsh, Michael 2005 "Will Indigenous Languages Survive?" *Annual Review of Anthropology* 34:293–315.

Warner, John Anson 1986 "The Individual in Native American Art: A Sociological View." In *The Arts of the North American Indian: Native Traditions in Evolution*, edited by Edwin L. Wade, pp. 171–202. New York: Hudson Hills Press.

Wax, Emily 2007 "An Ancient Indian Craft Left in Tatters." *Washington Post National Weekly Edition*, June 11–17, p. 21.

Weatherford, Jack 1991 *Native Roots: How the Indians Enriched America.* New York: Fawcett Columbine.

Wenke, Robert 1990 *Patterns in Prehistory: Humankind's First Three Million Years.* 3ed. New York: Oxford University Press.

Westermarck, Edward 1926 *A Short History of Marriage.* New York: MacMillan.

White, Benjamin N. F. 1973 "Demand for Labor and Population Growth in Colonial Java." *Human Ecology* 1:217–236.

White, Douglas R., Michael L. Burton, and Malcolm M. Dow 1981 "Sexual Division of Labor in African Agriculture: A Network Autocorrelation Analysis." *American Anthropologist* 83:824–849.

White, Leslie 1949 *The Science of Culture.* New York: Grove Press.

1959 *The Evolution of Culture.* New York: McGraw-Hill.

1962 *The Pueblo of Sia New Mexico.* Smithsonian Institution Bureau of American Ethnology, Bulletin 184. Washington D.C.: Government Printing Office.

Whiting, Beatrice 1950 *Paiute Sorcery.* Viking Fund Publications in Anthropology 15. New York: Viking.

Wilken, Gene C. 1987 *Good Farmers: Traditional Resource Management in Mexico and Central America.* Berkeley: University of California Press.

Wilson, E. O. 1975 *Sociobiology: The New Synthesis.* Cambridge, Mass.: Harvard University Press.

1978 *On Human Nature.* Cambridge, Mass.: Harvard University Press.

Wilson, Monica 1951 *Good Company.* Oxford: Oxford University Press.

Wolf, Arthur 1970 "Childhood Association and Sexual Attraction: A Further Test of the Westermarck Hypothesis." *American Anthropologist* 72:503–515.

Wolf, Eric 1969 *Peasant Wars of the Twentieth Century.* New York: Harper & Row.

1982 *Europe and the People Without History.* Berkeley: University of California Press.

Wolf, Margery 1972 *Women and the Family in Rural Taiwan.* Stanford, Calif.: Stanford University Press.

Woodburn, James 1968 "An Introduction to Hadza Ecology." In *Man the Hunter*, edited by Richard B. Lee and Irven DeVore, pp. 49–55. Chicago: Aldine.

1982 "Egalitarian Societies." *Man* 17:431–451.

Woodham-Smith, Cecil 1991 *The Great Hunger; Ireland 1845–1849.* London: Penguin Books.

World Bank 1999 *World Development Report 1998/9.* New York: Oxford.

World Council of Churches 2000 "There Are Alternatives to Globalization." Dossier prepared by the Justice, Peace and Creation team.

Wormsley, William E. 1993 *The White Man Will Eat You!* Fort Worth, Tex.: Harcourt Brace Jovanovich.

Worsley, Peter 1968 *The Trumpet Shall Sound.* New York: Schocken Books.

Wyman, Leland C. 1983 "Navajo Ceremonial System." In Alfonso Ortiz (ed.), *Handbook of North American Indians,* vol. 10, *Southwest,* pp. 536–557,. Washington, D.C.: Smithsonian Institution, Yan, Yunxiang 2006 "Girl Power: Young Women and the Waning of Patriarchy in Rural North China." *Ethnology* 45(2):105–123.

Zeder, Melinda 2008 "Domestication and Early Agriculture in the Mediterranean Basin: Origins, Diffusion, and Impact." *Proceedings of the National Academy of Sciences* 105(33):11,597–11,604.

Zielenziger, Michael 2007 *Shutting Out the Sun.* New York: Vintage Books.

People and Cultures Index

A
Aborigines of Australia, 64, 93, 94
Acadians, 67
Aceh people, 383, 384
Acoma people, 147
African Americans, 51, 368, 370–371, 381–382
Afrikaans, 370
Agta people, 254
Aka people, 264
Albanians, 378
Aleut people, 348
Amish, 58, 348
Andean civilizations, 72–73, 149–150
Arikara people, 403
Ashkenazi Jews, 369
Azande people, 326, 327
Aztec civilization
   agriculture, 149, 150
   blood sacrifice, 324–325
   calendars, 63
   compared to Inca, 72–73
   conquest of, 74, 77–78, 305
   Cortés and, 92
   inequalities, 300
   marketplaces, 176
   Sahagún and, 120
   state religion, 336

B
Balochi people, 377
BaMbuti pygmies, 137, 254, 264, 296, 358
Bangladesh, 161, 183, 186–187, 377, 378
Bantu people, 35
Basque separatists, 366, 385
Bengalis, 377
Black Caribs, 84, 85
Boers, 370
Bosniaks, 369, 378, 380, 383
Brazil/Brazilian people, 35, 78, 160–161, 162, 402–404
Bretons, 350
Bunyoro, 305, 307
Burakamin people, 35

C
Cajuns, 67
Caribs, 84
Chechens, 384
Cherokee people, 371, 383
Cheyenne people, 128, 140, 250, 275–276, 287–288, 362, 371
China/Chinese culture
   agriculture, 150
   ancestor veneration, 333
   autonomous regions, 383
   bridewealth and dowry, 209
   ethnic identity, 369
   factory production, 158
   global warming and, 160
   globalization and inequality, 300, 301
   greenhouse gases, 160
   indigenous products, 185
   kinship terminology, 235
   languages of, 59
   leaders as descendants of gods, 307, 337
   music, 43
   as newly industrialized nation, 160–162
   patrilineality in, 224–225
   pollution, 160–161, 162
   Polo and, 91
   religious pluralism, 340
   residence patterns, 213
   separatist movements, 384
   trade with Europeans, 79
   writing, 50
Comanches, 272, 274–275, 276, 285, 339
Croats, 369, 378, 382–383
Crow people, 239, 249, 330

D
Djuka people, 85
Dobu people, 323, 325
Dongria Kondh people, 401–402
Dutch, 75, 85, 370

E
Egyptians, 50, 150, 192, 278, 337, 348, 350
English people, 75, 78, 79, 80, 84, 85
Eskimo people, 348

F
Fijians, 104
French, 75

G

Garia people, 338
Garifuna, 84, 85
Gebusi people, 326
Greeks, 97, 348, 357, 359
Guatemalans, 369–370, 381, 384
Guugu Yimithirr, 64
Gypsies, 381

H

Hadzabe people, 137, 141–142, 296
Han people, 196, 224, 340
Hanunoo people, 34
Hasidic Jews, 348
Havasupai, 403
Hawaiians, ancient, 192, 336
Hidatsa people, 403
Hijra of Hindu India, 251–252
Himalayan people, 205
Hispanic Americans, 51
Hmong people, 11, 58
Hopi people
  agriculture, 147
  body arts, 348
  ethnic groups, 371
  gender hierarchy, 261–262
  globalization of indigenous products, 184
  hairstyles, 230
  language, 63, 368–369
  matrilineal society, 228–229
  mining, 403
  research protocols, 122
  rituals, 319
  seasonal rituals, 335
  women's control over key resources, 264
Hua of Papua New Guinea, 245–246
Huguenots, 370

I

Ibibio people, 84, 326
Igbo people, 377
Inca civilization
  agriculture, 150
  compared to Aztecs, 72–73
  conquest of, 74, 77–78, 92, 305
  incest taboo, 192
  inequalities, 300
  leaders as descendants of gods, 278
  Machu Picchu, 280
  overview of, 279
  Vega and, 120
India/Indian culture
  castes in traditional India, 299–302
  children in, 392–393
  division of, 376
  dowry, 208
  factory production, 158
  as newly industrialized nation, 160–161, 162
  religious pluralism, 340
Inuits, 97, 141, 142, 169, 213, 296, 352, 383
Irish, 35, 395–396
Iroquois, 93, 103–104, 261–264, 338–339, 371
Israelites, ancient, 206, 207, 208

J

Jamaican people, 332
Japan/Japanese culture
  Europeans and, 82
  homogenaity, 35
  honorifics, 56–57
  language, 51
  marriage and family, 202–203
  popular culture, 59
  primogeniture in, 202, 205
  Shinto, 96
Jews, 193–194, 373, 383–384
Jivaro people, 286–287
Ju/'hoansi people, 137–141, 169, 233, 264, 296, 332, 355

K

Kalahari people, 141
Kanen-Bornu kingdom, 76
Kapauku people, 174, 281
Karen Padaung, 348
Karimojong people, 153
Kayapo people, 348, 399, 402–404
Khoisan people, 35
Kikuyu culture, 42
Kiowa people, 339
Klamath-Modoc tribe, 184
Kofyar people, 259
Kongo kingdom, 76
Korean culture, 56–57, 59, 235, 331
!Kung. *See* Ju/'hoansi people
Kurds, 377–378
Kwaio people, 323
Kwakiutl, 97, 98

L

Lacandon Mayans, 399
Ladinos, 381
Lakota people, 250
Lipan-Apache, 339
Lugbara people, 326, 333

M

Maasai, 154, 204, 349
Macedonians, 378, 382–383
Mandan people, 403
Maori, 351, 359
Maring people, 170, 233

Maroons, 84, 85
Marquesas, 351
Mayan people, 50, 63–64, 120, 150, 324–325
Melanesians, 73, 264, 297
Mennonites, 348
Mescalero Apaches, 184, 334
Mesoamerican civilizations, 72–73
Mexican Americans, 372
Micronesia, 51, 55, 56, 73, 173, 220
Micronesian culture, 257
Minangkabau people, 261
Mohave people, 249
Montenegrins, 382–383
Mormons, 200–201
Musuo people, 196

N
Na people. *See* Musuo people
Naga people, 376
Nandi people, 196
Native Americans
   1910 census, 129
   Anglo Americans and native culture, 185
   assimilation into Anglo society, 251
   beadwork and quillwork, 359, 360, 362
   clothing styles, 369–370
   domesticated animals, 144
   domesticated crops, 143–144
   enslavement by the Portuguese, 78
   ethnic identity, 384
   ethnogenesis, 370
   European conquest, 74–75
   as foragers, 137
   foragers in the Pacific Northwest, 140, 142
   foragers on the Great Plains, 140, 142
   forced assimilation, 381
   intensive agriculture, 149–150
   languages of, 58
   Old World diseases, 141
   ranked societies, 297
   revitalization movements, 338–340
   under Spanish rule, 68, 77
   traditional arts and market economy, 360–361
   two spirits, 247–251
   vision quest, 330
   visual arts, 352
   words adopted from, 54–55
Navajo people
   art and healing, 357–358
   Christianity, 390–391
   ethnic groups, 371
   globalization of indigenous products, 184
   health and healing, 390–391
   humor, 123–124
   language, 368–369
   mining and, 403
   multiple gender identities, 248–249, 250
   pastoralism, 78
   service as "code talkers," 119
   shamans, 332
   supernatural powers, 34
   witches/witchcraft, 326, 327–328
Naxi people. *See* Musuo people
Nayar people, 197–198
Ndembu people, 32, 333
Netsilik people, 141
New Guinea tribes, 334
Nuba, 349, 350
Nuer people, 196, 285–286, 287, 351
Nyakyusa people, 326

O
Oba of Benin, 120
Ojibwas, 142
Omani people, 72, 75
Osage people, 340, 348

P
Pakistan/Pakistani culture, 150, 209, 376, 377
Papua New Guineans, 170, 171, 349, 359
Pitjantjatjara people, 121, 122
Plains Indians. *See* Native Americans
Polynesia/Polynesian culture
   chiefdoms, 278
   cognatic descent, 231–232
   cultural evolution, 93
   globalization and, 73
   Morgan on, 96
   polytheism, 97
   religion and worldview, 317
   respect language, 56
   tattooing, 350–351
   tribute payments, 173
Portuguese, 74, 75, 78
Powhatan people, 7
Pueblo peoples, 147, 184, 207, 335, 360, 361–362
Punjabis, 377
Pushtun people, 377, 383
Pygmies, 35

Q
Quebecois, 67

R
Romans, 154, 357
Russians, 75

S
Sahrawi people, 378
Samoans, 232, 351
San people, 69, 122, 400–401

Sara people, 348
Saramaka of the Guianas, 85
Scotch-Irish, 373
Semai people, 29
Seminoles, 370
Seneca people, 338–339, 403
Serbs, 369, 378, 380, 382–383
Shakers, 358
Sikhs, 348, 366, 369, 376
Sindhi people, 377
Sioux people, 249
Slovenians, 378, 382–383
Somali people, 58, 148, 378
Songhai Empire, 76
Suya people, 348
Swazi people, 207

T
Tahitian society, 277
Taiwan/Taiwanese culture, 193, 266, 267, 268
Tamil people, 377
Tasmanians, 73, 80, 82, 370
Tibetans, 378, 384
Tikopia, 227–228, 297
Tiwi people, 198–199
Toltecs, 150
Trobriand Islanders, 100, 118, 169–170, 320
Tukano people, 34, 261
Tumbuka-speaking peoples, 355–356
Tungus people, 331
Turkana people, 153
Turks, 340, 380–381

U
Ulster-Scots, 373
Uyghur people, 340, 384

V
Vanatinai, 263, 264
Vietnamese culture, 42

W
Wasco people, 403
Western Shoshone, 103, 138, 139
Winnebago people, 251, 288
Wishram people, 403

Y
Yanomamö, 29, 57, 124, 206, 208, 233, 261, 402
Yap people, 174–175
Yoruba people, 264–265

Z
Zapotec people, 50
Zia Pueblo people, 120
Zulu people, 57, 206–207, 305
Zuni people
  agriculture, 147
  Benedict on, 98
  gender hierarchy, 261–262
  globalization of indigenous products, 184
  multiple gender identities, 249–250
  religion and worldview, 319
  seasonal rituals, 335
  shamans, 332

Subject Index

A

AAA (American Anthropological Association), 9, 10, 36, 112, 122
Aboriginal and Torres Straits Islander Heritage Act, 121
Aborigines of Australia, 93, 94
Academic knowledge, globalization of, 83–84
Accommodation, 382–383, 384
Ad hoc legal systems, 281. *See also* Self-help systems
Adaptation, 134
Adaptive wisdom, 407–408
Adoption, 191–192
Adrian, Bonnie, 266, 267
Afghanistan, 377
Africa
  civilizations in, 71–72
  European expansion, 75, 76, 82
  Industrial Revolution, 80
  map, 72
  Old World crops, 142, 144
  slave trade, 75
Age, division of labor by, 137
"Age of Enlightenment," 78
Agricultural collectives, 193–194
Agriculture
  in Africa, 76
  animal domestication, 70
  definition of, 135
  development of, 5–6
  global warming and, 162
  intensive agriculture, 148–152
  intercropping, 398–399
  plant domestication, 69–70
  technology transfer, 396–398
  traditional resource management practices, 399
  world hunger and, 398–399
'Aiga, 232–233
Air conditioning, 157
Al Qaeda, 28, 366, 377
Albanian Liberation Army, 378
Alexander, Richard, 234
Allen, Michael, 129
Allocation of resources, 135, 139–140, 148
Altamira Gathering, 403
Altruism, 105

Ambilineal descent. *See* Cognatic descent
Ambilocal residence, 212
American Anthropological Association (AAA), 9, 10, 36, 112, 122
American Mug and Stein Company, 166
American Sign Language, 50
American South, 298
American Southwest, 147
Americans United for the Separation of Church and State, 341
Americas, 72–75, 81. *See also* Central America; North America; South America
Ancestor focused, 231
Ancestor veneration, 333
Ancestral rituals, 333
Ancient civilizations, 150–151
Ancient Society (Morgan), 93
Andean civilizations, 72–73
Anderson, Richard, 345
Animal domestication, 70. *See also* Domestication of plants and animals
Animism, 95, 96, 316
Annual Report (AAA), 9
Anthropological linguistics, 8–9
Anthropologists as advocates, 399–405, 407–409
Anthropology
  applications of, 9–10
  British functionalism, 99–100
  careers in, 10
  current state of, 11–13, 103–111
  definition of, 2
  differences in, 112–113
  in the early 20th-century, 95–101
  emergence of, 91–95
  fieldwork, 100–101
  globally, 102, 103
  historical particularism, 95–99
  humanistic approach to, 107–111
  introduction to, 2
  late 19th-century unilineal evolutionism, 93–95
  lessons of, 16–18
  neoevolutionism, 101–103
  perspectives, 13–16
  scientific approach to, 104–107

Anthropology (*continued*)
  scientific vs. humanistic approach to, 108–109, 111–112
  subfields of, 2–9
Anthropomorphism, 321
Antislavery movement, 307
Apocalyptic messages, 337
Apple Inc., 283–284
Applied anthropology, 9–10, 388
Arab League, 373
Arabic language, 59
Arbitrariness of language, 49, 50
Arbitrary meanings, 32
Archaeology, 6–7
Argonauts of the Western Pacific (Malinowski), 100
Arii, 277
Armed force, and maintenance of inequality, 305–306
Arranged marriages, 195, 206
Art and the aesthetic
  culture, 356–359, 362–363
  definition of, 345–346
  forms of artistic expression, 347–356
  gender, 358–359
  introduction to, 345–346
  pervasiveness of art, 346–347
  secular and religious art, 357–358
  social functions of art, 359, 362–363
Artificial countries, 376
Artificial hormones in beef, 283
Artistic expression, forms of
  body arts, 347–351
  performance arts, 354–356
  visual arts, 351–354
Arts and Crafts movement, 361
Aryan Nation, 36
Ascending generations, 235
Asia. *See also specific nations*
  civilizations in, 71
  European expansion, 75, 82
  Industrial Revolution, 79–80
  map, 72
  Old World crops, 142, 144
Aspirin, 405
Assimilation, 380–381, 382, 384
Association of Southeast Asian Nations, 163
Association on American Indian Affairs, 399
Atolls, 161
Atzlan, 372
Aum Shinrikyo, 27
Australia, 73, 80, 82, 121
Authority, 273–274
Automobiles, 158
Autonomous regions, 23, 383, 384–385
Avunculocality, 212, 229–230
Avunculocally extended households, 215, 216

B

Bahuchara Mata, 251
Balanced reciprocity, 169–171, 176
Balboa, 74
Baldwin Holding Unlimited, 284
Bands, 138–139, 273–275
Bangladesh, 161, 183, 186–187, 378
Barbarism stage of cultural evolution, 93
Barnes, Sandra, 265
Barotse judicial system, 288–289
Barter, 171
Basketry, 352
Basque separatists, 385
Bathurst Islands, 198
Beadwork and quillwork, 359, 360, 362
Beards, 348
Behavior
  individual, 39–40
  patterns of, 23, 29–30, 244
  as symbols, 32–33
Belgium, 340, 382, 384
Benedict, Ruth, 98
Benin, Kingdom of, 120
Berdache, 359
Berlin Conference, 80
Bible, Christian, 207, 307, 323
Biblical creation story, 92
Biblical myths, 317
The Big Bang Theory, 176
Big men, 273–274, 297
Bilateral descent, 231, 233
Bilocal residence, 212
Bilocally extended households, 215, 216
Biological anthropology, 3–5
Biological determinism, 41–43, 254
Biological fatherhood, 244
Biological relatives, 221
Birthrate in Japan, 203
Birthrates, 391–392
Bison, 140
Black Power movement, 36
Black September Organization, 366
Blood sacrifice, 324–325
Boas, Franz, 17, 95–98, 101, 399
Bodhi Tree, 319
Body arts
  body painting, 348–349
  overview of, 356
  physical alterations, 347–348
  tattooing and scarification, 349–351
Body painting, 348–349
Body piercing, 348
Bosnia, 378
Boston Marathon attack, 15, 366

Bound morphemes, 53
Bourgeoisie, 311
Brahmins, 299
Brain, Robert, 350
Brazil, 35, 78, 160–161, 162, 402–404
Brazilian Institute of Environment and Renewal Natural Resources, 403
Breadwinning, 252
BRIC nations, 160–161
Bride photos, 266, 267
Brideservice, 208, 263
Bridewealth, 201, 204, 207–208, 233–234
British East India Company, 79
British functionalism, 99–100
Bronze Age, 92
Brothers and sisters, terminology, 235, 236–238, 239
Brown, Judith, 256
Buddhism, 99, 319, 336, 341, 369
Bureaucrats/bureaucracies, 278, 279, 335
Bush, George W., 211
Business cycles, 178
Business Week, 405
Butterfly hairstyle, 348

C

Calendrical rituals, 319
Canada, 121, 375, 382, 383, 384
Cannibalism, 7
Cannon Mills, 183
Cape of Good Hope, 74, 75
Capital accumulation, 178
Capitalism, 176–180
Capitalist class, 311
Careers in anthropology, 10
Cargo cults, 338, 340, 341
Carlisle Indian School, 381
Carvings, 352, 354
Caste systems, 298
Castes in traditional India, 295, 299–302
Cataract Canyon, 403
Catholic Church, 211, 337, 358, 373
Cattle, 99, 108, 207, 233–234, 286
"Cattle camps," 153
Cave paintings, 352
Central America, 143–144
Central Kalahari Game Reserve (CKGR), 400–401
CEO compensation, 310
Ceramics, 353
Cereal crops, 258
Chagnon, Napoleon, 124
Changing Ones (Roscoe), 248
Charitable donations, 168
Cheney, Dick, 210
Chief executive officers, compensation of, 310

Chiefdoms, 274, 277–278, 336
Chiefs, 276, 297
Child care compatibility, 255, 256–257
Childhood familiarity hypothesis, 193–194
Children, costs and benefits of in LDCs, 392–394
Chili peppers, 143
Chimpanzees, 3–4, 38, 47, 244
China/Chinese culture
  ethnic identity, 369
  globalization and inequality, 300, 301
  kinship terminology, 235
  leaders as descendants of gods, 307, 337
  patrilineality in, 224–225
  religious pluralism, 340
  separatist movements, 384
Chinampas, 149–150
Chinatowns, 58
Chinese Communist Party, 224
Christian missionaries, 390
Christianity, 77, 129, 316–317, 338, 341, 369
Chronic hunger, 394
Circumcision, female. *See* Female genital mutilation
Circumcision, male, 16
Citigroup, 284
Civilization stage of cultural evolution, 93
Civilizations
  agriculture and, 150–152
  development of, 5, 70–71
  ethnic conflict and, 366
  ethnic identity, levels of, 371
  ethnicity and ethnic conflict, 372
CKGR (Central Kalahari Game Reserve), 400–401
Clan mother, 229
Clans, 226
Clark, Gregory, 152
The Clash of Civilizations and the Remaking of World Order (Huntington), 372
Class, 295, 298, 302–305
Climate change. *See* Global warming
Clinton, Bill, 209
Clinton, Hillary, 247
Clothing styles, 359, 362, 369–370
CNN, 7
Coal mining, 159
Code of Ethics, 122
Code of Hammurabi, 289
"Code talkers," 119
Coevolution, 42
Cognatic descent, 231–233
Cognitive interpretations of witchcraft and sorcery, 327
Cohabitation, 195
Cohesion of society, 323
Collins, Joseph, 395

Colonialism
  in Africa, 80
  in Asia, 79–80
  British India, 376, 377
  in Oceania, 80
Columbia University, 97
Columbian Exchange, 73, 74
Columbus, Christopher, 74, 91, 368
Coming of Age in Samoa (Mead), 97
Commoners, 173, 336
Communal nurseries, 193–194
Communal organizations, 329, 330, 332–335
Communally organized rituals, 334–335
Communication
  international, 83
  nonverbal, 32–33
  social behavior and, 55–57, 60
Communication satellites, 83
Communist Revolution in China, 209
Comparative methods, 126
  controlled comparisons, 128–130
  cross-cultural comparisons, 127–128
Comparative perspective, 14
Composite bands, 273–274
Condensation, 32
Configurationalism, 98
Conflict theory of inequality, 309, 310–312
Confucianism, 235, 268
Congo Free State, 82
Conscious purposes of rituals, 319
Conservation International, 401
Constitutional amendment, 209–210
Constructions, 31
Consultants, identification and interviews, 123–124
Consumers, 183
Consumption, 166
Contagious principle, 325
Container ships, 83, 158. *See also* Transportation
Context and situation, 29
Contract archaeology, 7
Control, and religion, 322–323
Controllability of money supply, 174
Controlled comparisons, 128–130
Conventional symbols, 32
Cook, James, 126
Cooperation, patterns of, 135
Coral reefs, 161
Corn blight, 407–408
Corn production, 181–182
"Corn riots," 182
Corporate anthropology, 10
Corporate culture, 180
Corporate taxes, 283–284
Corporations, 183

Correlation, vs. causation, 127–128
Corry, Stephen, 399
Cortés, Hernán, 74, 92
Cosby, Alfred, 73
Council for Scientific and Industrial Research (CSIR), 122
Council of Forty-Four, 276, 287–288
Court systems, 287
Courts of mediation, 287, 288–289
Courts of regulation, 287, 289–291
Cousins, terminology, 237
Create Jobs for USA Fund, 166
Crisis rituals, 319
CRM (Cultural resource management), 7
Crop varieties, preservation of, 407–408
Crops, 5
Cross cousins, 223
Cross-cultural comparisons, 127–128, 130, 233
Cross-gender occupation or work roles, 249
Cross-generational marriage, 198–199
CSIR (Council for Scientific and Industrial Research), 122
Cultivation. *See* Agriculture
Cults, 27, 329
Cultural alternatives, 408–409
Cultural anthropology, 7–8, 11–13, 91, 120
Cultural barriers, 124
Cultural construction of gender, 244–247
Cultural construction of kinship, 229, 234
  cultural integration and, 238–240
  Eskimo, 236
  Hawaiian, 236–237
  Iroquois, 237
  kinship terminology, 235
  logic of, 235–236
  Omaha, 237–238
  varieties of kinship terminology, 236–238
Cultural construction of relatives, 220–221
Cultural constructions and language, 53–55
Cultural constructions of reality, 33–36
Cultural determinism, 39–40
Cultural diversity, 17, 23, 42
Cultural evolution, 102
Cultural identity, 23–24
Cultural imperialism, 26, 267
Cultural integration, 238
Cultural interpretations of historical events, 125–126
Cultural knowledge
  components of, 31
  definition of, 22
  individual behavior, 39–40
  norms, 30–31
  overview of, 28–29
  social context of speech, 56–57
  values, 31
Cultural materialism, 106–107

Cultural patterns, 220
Cultural relativism, 14, 96, 97–98, 111, 124–125
Cultural resource management (CRM), 7
Cultural Survival, 399
Cultural universals, 43–44
Culture, 17
Culture change, 67–68
Culture shock, 125
Culture wars, 209–211
Culture(s). *See also* Cultural knowledge
   vs. biological differences, 41–43
   cultural knowledge, 30–37
   definition of, 23–30, 67
   human life and, 38–39
   introduction to, 21–23
   as knowledge, 28–29
   language and, 60–64
   language as a reflection of, 61–62
   origins of, 37–38
   as patterns of behavior, 29–30
   as shared by a group of people, 23–25
   as socially learned, 25–28
   symbols, 32–33
Curare, 405
Curing ceremonies, 357–358
Curses, 281
Czechoslovakia, 384

D

Da Gama, Vasco, 74
Daibutsu-den, 336
Dalby, Andrew, 59
Dams, 402–404
Darwin, Charles, 42, 92–93
Dawkins, Richard, 105
De facto endogamy, 200
"Deadbeat dads," 266
"The Declaration on the Rights of Indigenous Peoples," 404
Declaration on the Rights of Indigenous Peoples, 121
Defense of Marriage Act (DOMA), 209, 210
Deforestation, 146
Deng Xiaoping, 224–225
Denmark, 383
Dentan, Robert, 29
Descending generations, 235
Descent groups, 223, 226–227, 268
"Developed" nations, 13
Development, question of, 406
Development anthropology, 9
Diachronic, 116
Dialects, 50–51
Diamond, Jared, 144
Dichotomous gender category, 244
Dionysian, 98

Discourse, control of, 57
Discrete elements of language, 48–49, 50
Disney, 225
Displacement property of language, 49, 50
Divisibility of money, 174
Division of labor, 135, 137. *See also* Sexual division of labor
DNA sequences, 5
Dogs, domestication of, 144
DOMA (Defense of Marriage Act), 209, 210
Domestication of plants and animals
   advantages and costs of, 145–146
   movement of crops and livestock, 144–145
   New World crops, 143–144
   New World livestock, 144
   Old World crops, 142–143
   Old World livestock, 144
   origins of, 142–145
"Double Irish," 283
Dowry, 208–209
"Dowry deaths," 208
Dreaming of a Mail-Order Husband, 11
Dry land gardening, 147
Durkheim, Émile, 323–324

E

"East Africa cattle complex," 154
East Liverpool, Ohio, 166
Eastern Europe, 378, 380
"Eat local" movement, 145
Ecclesiastical organizations, 329, 330, 335–337
Ecological tourism, 185
Economic classes, 303
Economic crisis, 284
Economic freedom, 179
Economic immigrants, 374
Economic inequality, 86, 178
Economic Policy Institute, 304–305
Economic systems. *See* Exchange and economic systems
Economy, global, 12–13
Educational anthropology, 9
Efficiency, 178
Egalitarian societies, 276, 295, 296–297
Eggan, Fred, 128
Ego, 214, 222, 235–236
Ego focused, kindred as, 231, 232
Egypt, 150
Electricity, 156
Elites, and maintenance of inequality, 305–308, 312
Emasculation, 251
Enculturation, 25–28
The End of Alms (Clark), 152
Endangered cultures, recording, 97
Endangered languages, 59
Endogamous rules, 199–200

Endogamy, 200, 298
Energy and society, 156–157
Energy slaves, 157
Energy sources, 181
English language, 59, 225
English theater, 359
Enlightenment, 93, 110
Environmental regulations, 159
Equal opportunity, 31
Equilibrium, 100
Eskimo kinship terminology, 236, 238, 239–240
Essentialization, 262
Estioko-Griffin, Agnes, 254
Ethanol, 181–182
"Ethnic art," 361–362
Ethnic boundary markers, 368–370
Ethnic cleansing, 379, 382, 383
Ethnic communities, transnational, 374–375
Ethnic conflict, responses to
   accommodation, 382–383
   homogenization, 379–381
   results, 383–385
   segregation, 381–382
Ethnic conflicts, 373
Ethnic groups, 366
   attributes of, 367–370
   definition of, 367
   ethnic boundary markers, 368–370
   fluidity of, 370–371
   situational nature of ethnic identity, 367
   types of, 371–372
Ethnic homogenization, 379, 382
Ethnic identity, 367, 371, 384
Ethnic stereotyping, 118–119
Ethnicity, 36
Ethnicity and ethnic conflict
   civilizations, 372
   ethnic groups, 366–372
   responses to ethnic conflict, 379–385
   stateless nationalities, problem of, 372–373, 376–379
Ethnocentrism, 14, 109, 125–126
Ethnogenesis, 370
Ethnographic Atlas (Murdock), 126, 128
Ethnographic fieldwork. *See* Fieldwork
Ethnographic methods, 130
   ethnohistory, 125–126
   fieldwork, 116–118
   fieldwork as a rite of passage, 124–125
   problems and issues in, 118–119, 123–124
Ethnography, 8, 116
Ethnohistoric research, 116, 130
Ethnohistory, 125–126
Ethnologue, 58–59
Ethnology, definition of, 116

Europe, 72, 340. *See also specific nations*
European expansion
   Africa, 75
   Americas, 74–75
   Asia, 75
   consequences of, 80–87
   cultural consequences of, 76–78
   earliest, 73–78
European Union, 163, 283
Evans-Pritchard, E. E., 327
Evolution, 92–93
Evolutionary psychology, 104–106, 234
Exchange and economic systems
   globalization and markets, 181–183, 186–187
   market, 174–181
   overview of, 166–167, 168
   reciprocity, 167–172
   redistribution, 172–173
Exchange of products, 167
Exogamous rules, 199
Expectations, 29
Exploitation, 311
Expressions of culture, 30
Extended families, 191
Extended households, 215–216
Extramarital relationships/sex, 105, 197

F

Facebook, 87, 284
Facial expressions, 55
Facial hair, 348
Factory farming, 157, 159
Factory production, 13, 158
Fallow land, 146
Familial legal systems, 281, 285
"Familiarity Breeds Disinterest" hypothesis, 193–194
Family disruption hypothesis, 192–193
Family values, 31
Family violence, 266
Famines, 406. *See also* Hunger, world
Farm wives, 203
Farnsworth, Norman, 405
Farrer, Claire, 334
Fathers, in matrilineal societies, 229
Fathers and mothers, terminology, 236–237, 239
Federal Reserve Board, 304
Federally Administered Tribal Territories, 377
Feedback relationships, 106
Feet binding, 348
Female genital mutilation, 15–16
"Female husband," 196
Female infanticide, 205
Female preference for marrying high-status males, 106

Feminist movement, 243
Fertile Crescent, 142
Fertility maintenance, 254–256
Feuds, 286
Fictive kinship, 191
Fieldwork
   Boas on, 97–98
   consultants, identification and interviews, 123–124
   definition of, 130
   as ethnographic method, 116–118
   Malinowski on, 100–101
   overview of, 8
   power relationships in, 111
   problems and issues in, 118–119, 123–124
   as a rite of passage, 124–125
   role and rapport, development of, 119, 123
   tradition of, 100–101
Figapa, 245–246
Financial assets, 304
Financial crisis of 2007-2009, 181, 309–310
First brother distinction, 235
First Carib War, 84
Firth, Raymond, 227–228
Fischer, John, 353
Fitness, 105
Flute, prehistoric, 37
Folk classifications, 34
Folkways, 30
Fong, Vanessa, 225
Food, natural reality and, 34
Food crops, 142
Food First (Lappé and Collins), 395
Foraging and culture
   bands, 138–139
   definition of, 135
   division of labor by age and sex, 137
   egalitarian societies, 296–297
   in evolution of modern humans, 70
   gender stratification, 264
   generalizations, 155
   map of, 136
   overview of, 137–140
   reciprocal sharing, 139
   resource allocation, 139–140
   seasonal congregation and dispersal, 137–138
   seasonal mobility, 137
Forced assimilation, 380–381, 382, 384
Forced conversions to Christianity, 77
Forced resettlement, 379–380
Ford, Henry, 158
Foreign aid, 170–171
Forensic anthropology, 5
Form, 13
Form of descent, 221

Formal groups, 219
Fort Berthold Reservation, 403
Fossil fuels, 156–157, 160, 181
Fossils, 4–5
Founder, 222
Fourth World peoples, 400. *See also* Indigenous peoples
Fourth-gender identity, 248, 249
"Fracking," 181
France, 272, 340
Fraternal polyandry, 205
Fratto, Toni, 345
Frazer, James, 321, 325
Fredericksburg, Virginia, 7
Free black communities, 81
Free markets, 176, 179
Free morphemes, 53
Free trade, 282–283
Freed, Ruth, 393
Freed, Stanley, 393
Freight transportation, 158
Fried, Morton, 294–295
Functional theory of inequality, 308, 309–310, 312
Functionalism, 99–100

G

Gandhi, Indira, 376
Garcia, Alan, 404
Garment factory safety, 183, 186–187
GATT (General Agreement on Tariffs and Trade), 82, 282
Gaza Strip, 373
GDP (gross domestic product), 282, 406
Geertz, Clifford, 110, 321
Gell, Alfred, 351
Gender
   art and, 358–359
   cultural construction of, 244–247
   division of labor, 252–259
   Hijra of Hindu India, 251–252
   Hua of Papua New Guinea, 245–246
   multiple gender identities, 247–252
   North American constructions of, 246–247
   sex and, 243–244
   two spirits, 247–251
Gender crossing, 247
Gender stratification
   descent and postmarital residence, 268
   in industrial societies, 268–269
   influences on, 264–267
   introduction to, 259–261
   over the course of a woman's life, 260–261
   universality, 261–264
   women's contribution to material welfare, 264
   women's control over key resources, 264–267

Gendered division of labor
  among foragers, 137
  compatibility with child care, 256–257
  components of, 260
  fertility maintenance, 254–256
  gender stratification, 259–269
  within households, 197
  introduction to, 252–253
  major patterns, 253–254
  relative strength, 256
  reproductive roles, 256
  variability, 257–259
Genealogy, 214
General Agreement on Tariffs and Trade (GATT), 82, 282
Generalized medium of exchange, 175
Generalized reciprocity, 168–169
Genesis, 206, 207, 208
Genetic diversity, 407–408
Genocide, 379–380, 382, 383
Geographic location names, 54–55
Germanic subfamily of languages, 53–54
Gia, 263
Gifts, exchange of, 170, 172
Gilmore, David, 260
Gingrich, Newt, 309
Glazer, Nathan, 367
Global anthropology, 102, 103
Global capitalism, 182–183
Global economy, 82, 158, 374–375
Global factory, 159
Global industrialism, 159–163
Global knowledge, 405
Global trade, 81, 202
Global warming, 160–162
Globalization
  benefits of, 86–87
  cultural change and diversity, 67–68
  cultural consequences of, 76–78
  definition of, 12–13, 68
  early European expansion, 73–78
  economic inequality and, 299, 300, 301
  environment and, 159–163
  ethnic conflict and, 366
  of factory production, 158–159
  indigenous products, 184–185
  Industrial Revolution, 78–80
  inequality in China, 300, 301
  language and, 58–59
  language extinction, 58
  localization and, 266, 267
  of markets, 181–183, 186–187
  process of, 12, 13
  Western culture, 26, 27
  the world prior to, 68–71

Gluckman, Max, 288–289
GNP (gross national product), 406
God/gods, 316–317
Gods, leaders as descendants from, 278
The Golden Bough (Frazer), 321
Goodale, Jane, 198, 199
Goodall, Jane, 3
Google, 284
Gorillas, 4, 47, 244
Gossip, 280
Government bailouts, 178
Government regulation
  of business, 282
  of economies, 179
  of environmental impacts, 160–161
Grammar, 50
Grand Canyon National Park, 403
Grandfathers and grandmothers, 235
Great Britain
  Barotse and, 288–289
  expansion into North America, 78
  expansion into Oceania, 80
  India and, 376
  industrialization, 156
  Ireland and, 396
  religious diversity, 340
  trade with China, 79
  Working Group on Human Remains, 121
Greenhouse gases, 160, 162
Greenland, 383
Grocery stores, 157
Gross domestic product (GDP), 282, 406
Gross national product (GNP), 406
Group marriage, 200, 201
Guardian spirits, 330
Guatemala, 381, 384
Guerrilla wars, 378
Guthrie, Stewart, 321

H
Hairstyles, 348
Haiti, 67
Halal, 340
Hall, Edward, 55
Hamilton, William, 105
Hamlets, 148
Handsome Lake, 338–339, 341
Hart, C. W. M., 198
Hawaii, 126, 209
Hawaiian kinship terminology, 236–237, 238–239
Head shaping, 348
Healers, 332, 390
Health and health care, 173, 180, 389–391
Heat-treating materials, 38
Herding. *See* Pastoralism

Herodotus, 91
The Hidden Dimension (Hall), 55
Hierarchical nesting, 367
High-touch cultures, 55–56
Hindi language, 59
Hinduism, 99, 108, 251, 299–302, 307, 318–319, 341, 376
Hip-hop and rap, 51
Hispaniola, 74
Historic archaeology, 7
Historical particularism, 95–99
Historicism. *See* Historical particularism
Hitchcock, Robert, 401
Ho, Karen, 180–181
Hockett, Charles, 48
Hoebel, E. Adamson, 281
Holistic perspective, 14
Holy People, 357–358
Homeland, 371
Homo sapiens, 4, 37–38, 47, 55, 68, 107, 136
Homogenization, 379–381
Homosexuality, 249
Honor. *See* Prestige
Honorifics, 56–57
Hopi Cultural Preservation Office, 122
Horsemeat, 108
Horses, 140, 144, 146
Horticulture/horticultural societies
  chiefdoms, 277
  cultural consequences of, 147–148
  egalitarian societies, 297
  in evolution of modern humans, 70
  gender stratification, 264
  gendered division of labor, 254, 257–259
  generalizations, 156
  Hopi people, 228
  Hua of Papua New Guinea, 245–246
  matrilineal descent, 234
  overview of, 146–148, 155
  principal regions of, 147
  varieties of, 146–147
House styles, 359
Household forms and family, 214–216
Household tasks, 197
Households, 191, 213
Housing crisis, 213
HRAF (Human Relations Area File), 126
Hua, Cai, 196
Huipil, 369
Human cultural diversity, 9
Human diversity, 9
Human Relations Area File (HRAF), 126
Human Rights Council, 400
Human variation, 4
Humanistic approach to anthropology, 107–111

Hunger, world
  agricultural alternatives, 398–399
  scarcity vs. inequality, 394–396
  technology transfer, 396–398
Huno, 279
Hunting, gender and, 254–256
Hunting and gathering societies
  bands, 138–139, 273–275
  decline of, 140–142
  definition of, 135
  division of labor, 137
  egalitarian societies, 296–297
  in evolution of modern humans, 69–70
  foraging and culture, 137–140
  generalized reciprocity, 169
  map of, 136
  overview of, 155
  quality of life, 141
  reciprocal sharing, 139
  resource allocation, 139–140
  seasonal congregation and dispersal, 137–138
Huntington, Samuel, 366, 372
Hutton, James, 92
Hxaro, 170
Hydraulic fracturing, 181
Hydroelectric dams, 402–404
Hypothesis, 127–128

I

Ideologies, 306–307
Imitative principle, 325
Immigrants, 58, 341, 374–375
Inbreeding avoidance hypothesis, 193, 194
Incest taboo, 118, 192–195, 197, 199
Incipient court systems, 287–288
Incising, 353
Income distribution, 304
Income inequality, 304
Indian Arts and Craft Act, 361
Indian caste system, 199–200
Indian Forest Conservation Act, 401
"Indian Market," 360
Indian Schools, 251, 381
"Indian schools," 58
Indigenous peoples
  adaptive wisdom, 407–408
  anthropologists, changing relationship with, 120–122
  cultural alternatives, 408–409
  current state of, 400–404
  definition of, 78
  medicines, 405, 407
  relationship between indigenous peoples and anthropologists, 120–122
  vanishing knowledge, 404–405

Indigenous products, globalization of, 184–185
Individual behavior, 39–40
Individualistic organizations, 329–330
Individuality and art, 359, 362–363
Indonesia, 383
Indunas, 289
Indus River valley, 150
Industrial Revolution, 68, 78–80, 81, 93, 157, 360
Industrial societies
   class in, 302–305
   gender stratification in, 268–269
Industrialism, 156–159
Inequality. See also Social inequality and stratification
   benefits of inequality, 312–313
   conflict theory, 310–312
   definition of, 294
   functionalist theory, 309–310
   maintenance of, 305–308
   theories of, 308–313
Inequality explanation of hunger, 394–396
Infant betrothal, 198
Infanticide, 205
Influence, 273–274
Informal sanctions, 280
Informants, 123–124
Initiation rituals, 334, 359
Inmarriage, 199
Institutionalized gender crossing, 247–248
Instruments, 106
Intellectual property rights, 121–122
Intellectual/cognitive theory of religion, 320–321
Intensification, 107
Intensity, 13
Intensive agriculture, 70
   cultural consequences of, 150–152
   gendered division of labor, 257–259
   generalizations, 156
   introduction to, 148–149
   overview of, 155
   principal regions of, 149
   varieties of, 149–150
Interactions with nature, 134
Inter-American Court of Human Rights, 85
Intercropping, 398–399
Intercultural communications, 17–18
Interest, 175
Intermarriage, 199
Internet, 103
Interpretive anthropology, 109–110
Interracial marriage, 200
Interviews, 117
Investment banks, 180–181
IRA (Irish Republican Army), 366, 373, 383
Ireland, 205, 283–284

Irish Free State, 373
Irish language, 59
Irish potato famine, 35, 395–396, 407
Irish Republican Army (IRA), 366, 373, 383
Iron Age, 92
Iroquois kinship terminology, 237, 238–239
Irrigation, 149, 150
Islam
   art, 358
   beliefs about supernatural powers, 316–318
   compared to other monotheistic religions, 129
   as ethnic boundary marker, 369
   monotheism, 95
   in Pakistan, 376
   postmarital residence patterns, 268
   religious diversity in the U.S., 340–341
Israel, 193–194, 373, 383–384
Ivan the Terrible, 75

J
Jamestown, Virginia, 7
Jati, 299
Jews. See Israel
Jim Crow laws, 381–382
Johnson, Samuel, 346
Judaism, 129, 316–317
Judeo-Christian worldview, 92, 95, 210, 307–308, 355

K
Kachinas, 319, 358
Kaeppler, Adrienne, 355
Kagalagadi Transfrontier Park, 401
Kak, Neeraj, 392–393
Kakora, 245–246
Kalani'opu'u, King, 126
Kannapolis, North Carolina, 183
Kashmir, 376
Keller, Helen, 50
Kelly, Robert, 141
Kelso, William, 7
Kerala, India, 406
Key consultants/informants, 123
Kibutzism, 193–194
Kin groups, 190, 191, 198
Kin terms, 234–235
Kindred, 231, 232
Kinesics, 55
Kinship and descent. See also Marriages and families
   avunculocality, 212, 229–230
   cultural construction of kinship, 229, 234–240
   cultural construction of relatives, 220–221
   cultural variation in, 220–221
   forms of, 233
   influences on, 233–234

introduction to, 219–221
nonunilineal descent, 230–233
normative expectations, 220
study of, 219–220
unilineal descent, 221–223, 226–230
variety and change in, 240
ways of tracing, 220
Kinship diagrams, 213–214
Kinship terminology, 235
Kiser, Taft, 7
Kluckhohn, Clyde, 119, 327–328
Knowledge, vanishing, 404–405
Knowledge of the environment, 106
Koreatowns, 58
Kosciuszko, Tadeusz, 368
Kosovo, 378
Kottak, Conrad, 35
Kroeber, Alfred, 17, 97
Kshatriyas, 299
Kur, 286
Kut, 331
Kuwayama, Takami, 103
Kwanza, 11

L

Labor market, international, 13
Labor tax, 279
Labrets, 348
Lacevenza, Deborah, 403
Lactose tolerance, 42–43
LaFlesche, Francis, 123
Laissez-faire, 179–180
Lake Mohonk Conference, 399
Land ownership, 148
Land races, 407
Landa, Diego de, 120
Language. *See also* Anthropological linguistics
  cultural constructions and, 53–55
  culture and, 60–64
  definition of, 47
  as ethnic boundary marker, 368–369
  globalization and, 58–59
  humanists on, 107
  humanity and, 47–48
  mechanics of, 50–53
  migrations, 58–59
  political speech, 57, 60
  power of, 48–50
  properties of, 48–50
  as a reflection of culture, 61–62
  of ritual, 319
  social behavior and, 55–57, 60
  worldviews and, 62–64
Language extinction, 58

Language in Danger (Dalby), 59
Language preservation, 59
Lappé, Frances Moore, 395
Latino communities, 58
Law, 281
LDCs (lesser developed countries), 388, 392–394
Leaders as descendants of gods, 307, 336–337
Leaky, Richard, 4
Lebanon, 194
Lee, Richard, 141
Legal sanctions, 281
Legal systems, 281
  court systems, 287
  courts of mediation, 288–289
  courts of regulation, 289–291
  incipient court systems, 287–288
  overview of, 290
  self-help systems, 281, 285–287
Legalese, 61
Leighton, Alexander and Dorothea, 391
Leopard-skin chiefs, 285–286
Lepowsky, Maria, 263
Lesser developed countries (LDCs), 388, 392–394
Levirate, 206
Lhamana, 249
Life after death, belief in, 323
Likombwa, 289
Lineage, 226
Lingua franca, 59
Linguistic communities, 58
Linguistic relativity hypothesis, 62–63
Lip discs, 348
Liquidated (Ho), 180–181
Livestock, 142, 146, 152–155
Loa, 355
Local autonomy, 383, 384
Local knowledge, 69, 405
Local stereotyping, 119
Lomax, Alan, 356
Long-haul trucking industry, 158
Lono (god), 126
Loss of jobs, 182–183
Lowie, Robert, 97
Low-touch cultures, 55–56
Lyell, Charles, 92

M

Maasai, 204
Macedonia, 378
Machu Picchu, 280
Madagascar periwinkle, 405
Magic, 321, 328
Malagasy Republic, 258
Malaria, 405

Male circumcision, 16
Male unfaithfulness to wives, 105
Malinowski, Bronislaw, 99, 100, 102, 106, 118, 162, 322
Mamdani, Mahmood, 392
"Man Enough to Let My Wife Support Me," 11
Mana, 317, 336
Manahune, 277
Mandarin language, 59
Man-woman gender identity, 248
Mao Zedong, 224
Maps
　ancient civilizations, 151
　foragers, 136
　horticulture, 147
　intensive agriculture, 149
　major states and regions, 72
　pastoralism, 152
Maquiladoras, 182
Marital exchanges, 207
Market
　definition of, 167, 168
　market economies, 176–180
　market exchange, 175–176
　money, 174–175
　productivity, 180–181
Market economies, 167, 176–180, 360–362
Market exchange, 175–176
Market globalization, 182–183
Market norms, 176, 181
Market principles, 176–177
Markets, globalization of, 181–183, 186–187
Marquesas, 351
Marriage alliances, 206–207
Marriages and families
　brideservice, 208, 263
　bridewealth, 201, 204, 207–208, 233–234
　defining marriage, 195–196
　dowry, 208–209
　family and household forms, 214–216
　functions of marriage, 196–197
　incest taboo, 118, 192–195, 197, 199
　introduction to, 190–192
　in Japan, 202–203
　kinship diagrams, 213–214
　marital exchanges, 207
　marriage, 195–199
　marriage alliances, 206–207
　marriage rules, 199–200
　number of spouses, 200–201
　polyandry, 205
　polygyny, 201, 204–205
　postmarital residence patterns, 211–213
　same-sex marriage, 209–211
　unusual forms of marriage, 197–199
　variation in beliefs and practices, 199–201, 204–209
"Marry Out or Die Out" (Tylor), 192
Martinez, Maria, 361
Marx, Karl, 178, 311
Massachusetts, 209
Material culture, 30
Materialism, 106–107, 108–109
Matriarchy, 229, 261
Matriclans, 226, 228–229
Matrifocal family, 214–215
Matrifocal households, 214–215
Matrilineage, 226, 333
Matrilineal descent, 128–130, 221, 222–223, 233, 234, 268
Matrilineal descent groups, 223, 226, 228–229
Matrilineal principle, 223
Matrilineality, vs. matriarchy, 229
Matrilocal residence, 212, 228, 268
Matrilocally extended households, 215–216
Mattel, 183
Max Planck Institute for Psycholinguistics, 63
Mayberry-Lewis, David, 399
Mayberry-Lewis, Pia, 399
McCabe, Justin, 194
McCarthy, Joe, 328
McDonald's restaurants, 159
McVeigh, Timothy, 27
Mead, Margaret, 17, 97, 399
Meaning, religion and, 321
Mecca, 318
Media of exchange, 174
Mediator legal system, 281, 285
Medical anthropology, 10, 389
"The Medicine Man Will See You Now," 405
Medicines, 405, 407
Mediterranean area, Old World crops in, 142
Mediums, 331
Meigs, Anna, 245, 246
Melanesian cargo cults, 338
Melanin, 4
Men's house, 195, 334
Mesoamerica, 143
Mesoamerican civilizations, 72–73
Mesopotamia, 150
Messiahs, 337
Metals, 152
Methodological principles, 15
Mexico, 143, 149, 182
Microliths, 38
Micronesia, 173
Microsoft, 284
Middle East, 194
Middleton, John, 333
Migrant workers, in China, 301

Migration, international, 13, 26
Migrations, 67, 70, 85, 340, 374–375
Military technology, 79
Milk, 42–43
Mining, 401–402
Minorities. *See* Indigenous peoples
Miscommunication, 17–18, 55
Misfortune, supernatural explanations for, 325–328
Misinformation from consultants/informants, 123–124
Mississippi, 34
Mixed race, 34
Mobility, 137, 154, 296
Modern Family, 190
Moko, 351
Molimo, 358
Monetary objects, 174–175
Money, 174–175
Monogamy, 200
Monotheism, 95, 96, 97, 128, 129, 316
Monumental architecture, 71
Moral principles, 15
Moral relativism, 15–16
Mores, 30
Morgan, Louis Henry, 93–94, 95, 96, 236
Mormons, 200–201
Morocco, 378
Morphemes, 53
Morphology, 52–53
Mortality, awareness of, 323
Moses, 206
Mother's brother, 238
Motivation, and inequality, 310
Mountford, Charles, 121
Moynihan, Daniel, 367
Multicultural movement, 362–363
Multimedia potential of language, 49
Multinational corporations, 282–284
Multiple gender identities, 247–252
Multivocality, 32
Murdock, George Peter, 126, 389
Muscle relaxants, 405
Museums, 7
Museums, 120–121
Music, 355
Music therapy, 356
Musical instruments, 37, 358
Myths and worldviews, 317–318, 320, 374

N
NAC (Native American Church), 340, 390–391
Nadleehi, 249
NAFTA (North American Free Trade Agreement), 163
Nag, Moni, 392–393
NAGPRA (Native American Grave Protection and Repatriation Act), 121

Name taboo, 57, 124
Nanda, Serena, 249, 252
National Association for the Practice of Anthropology (NAPA), 10
National Historic Preservation Act, 7
National Park Service, 7
Nationalist movements, 377–378
Nationalities, 371–372
Native American Church (NAC), 340, 390–391
Native American Grave Protection and Repatriation Act (NAGPRA), 121
Native Anthropology (Kuwayama), 103
Natural causation, 389–390
Natural environments and cultures
  domestication of plants and animals, 142–146
  global warming, 160, 161
  globalization, 159–163
  horticulture, 146–148
  hunting and gathering societies, 136–142
  industrialism, 156–159
  intensive agriculture, 148–152
  interactions with nature, 134–136
  pastoralism, 152–155
  in preindustrial times, 155–156
Natural gas, 181
Natural reality, 34
Natural resources, 159
Natural selection, 42–43, 92–93, 105
Navaho Witchcraft (Kluckhohn), 119
The Navajo Door (Leighton), 391
Neanderthal, 5, 92
Neck elongation, 348
Negative reciprocity, 171
Neoevolutionism, 101–103
Neoliberalism, 179–180
Neolocal residence, 212, 213
Nephews and nieces, terminology, 238
Net worth, 304–305
Networks, 219
New Guinea, 142–143
New World, 71
New World crops, 143–144
New World livestock, 144
New York Stock Exchange, 177
New York Times, 7, 185
New Zealand, 80, 82
Newly industrialized nations, 160–161, 162
Nile valley, 150
Nixtamalización, 182
Nlum, 355
Nobles, 173, 310–311, 336
Nomadism, 152
Nomads of the Australian Desert (Mountford), 121

SUBJECT INDEX 455

Nonoverlapping membership, 219
Nonunilineal descent, 230–233
Nonverbal communication, 32–33, 55–56
Normative expectations of kin relationships, 220
Norms, 30–31, 39–40
North America, 143–144, 207, 246–247
North American Free Trade Agreement (NAFTA), 163
Northern Ireland, 373, 383
Northern Kentucky University, 10
Northwest Coast, American, art of, 353–354
Nose piercing, 348
Nu, 245–246
Nuclear families, 190, 191, 196
Nunavut, 383

O

Obama, Barack, 34, 60
Obeyesekere, Gananath, 126
Oboler, Regina Smith, 196
Occupational roles, and gender, 246–247
Occupations, 299–302, 303
Oceania, 73, 76, 80, 82
Offshore production, 158–159, 162
Oil prices, 181
Oklahoma City bombing, 27
Old World, 71, 72–73
Old World crops, 142–143
Old World livestock, 144
Olympic Games, 366
Omaha kinship terminology, 237–238, 239
On the Origin of Species (Darwin), 92
One-child policy, 224–225
Only Hope (Fong), 225
Opium War, 79
Organization of African Unity, 163, 378–379
Organization of American States, 163
Origin myths, 320–321, 367–368
Ornamentation, 352–353
Osh-Tisch, 250
"Other"
   conflation of different groups as, 97
   ethnocentrism of, 91
   European expansion, 92
   fieldwork bias, 262
   global anthropology, 102–103
   materialism, 109
   religion and worldview, 104
   rituals of, 320, 328
   unilineal evolutionism, 94
Outline of Cultural Materials, 126
Outmarriage, 192, 199
Outsourcing, 283
Overpopulation, 394
Owsley, Douglas, 7

P

Paganism, 328
Pagel, Mark, 38
Paintings, 352–353, 354
Pakistan, 150
Paleoanthropology, 4–5, 93
Palestine, 373
Palin, Sarah, 247
Panama, 383
Parallel cousins, 223
Paramilitary groups, 366
Parasaito, 203
Parfleches, 359
Parker, Enoch, 339
Parthenon, 71, 357
Participant observation, 101, 117, 118
Passive assimilation, 381, 382, 384
Pastoralism, 70, 135, 152–156, 184–185, 201, 233
Patriarchy, 261
Patriclans, 226, 227
Patrilineage, 226, 333
Patrilineal descent, 128–130, 221–222, 233–234, 239, 245, 268
Patrilineal descent groups, 226, 227–228
Patrilineal principle, 223, 226
Patrilineality, 224–225
Patrilocal residence, 212, 222, 268
Patrilocally extended households, 215
Patterns of behavior, 23
Patterns of cooperation, 135
Patterns of Culture (Benedict), 98
Peabody Coal, 403
"Peace in the Family" hypothesis, 192–193
Peace of Paris, 84
Peasants, 151–152
Pec, 286
Pellagra, 182
Pentecostal churches, 390–391
Per capita incomes, 406
Perceptions, language and, 62–64
Performance arts, 354–356, 359
Permanent settlements, 148
Personal pronouns, 57
Peru, 404
Petroglyphs, 352
Peyote religion, 339–340, 341, 381
Pfizer, 284
Phenotypes, 369
Philippines, 383
Phonemes, 51
Phonology, 51
Physical alterations, 347–348
Physical anthropology. *See* Biological anthropology
Physical characteristics, as ethnic boundary markers, 369

Pictographs, 352
Pig feast, 170
Pilling, Arnold, 198
Pitch of a voice, 51–52
Pizarro, Francisco, 74, 92
Plant domestication, 69–70
Plotkin, Mark, 405
Plows, 149
Plural formation, 53
Political institutions, gender stratification and, 261
Political life, organization of
    bands, 138–139, 273–275
    chiefdoms, 274, 277–278, 336
    forms of, 272–279
    Inca Empire, 279
    legal systems, 281, 285–291
    social control and law, 280–281
    states, 150, 274, 278–279, 282–284
    tribes, 274, 275–276
Political organization, agriculture and, 150–151
Political power, 303
Political refugees, 374
Political speech, 57, 60
Politicians, religious faith of, 307–308, 309
Politicization of laws, 290
Polity, 272
Polo, Marco, 91
Polyandry, 200, 201, 205
Polygamy, 200
Polygyny, 200, 201, 204–205, 263
Polytheism, 95, 96, 97, 104, 128, 316
Popular culture, 59, 84–85
Population growth, 145, 225, 391–394
Portability of money, 174
Portman, Rob, 210
Portuguese, 74
Posey, Darrell, 399, 403
Pospíšil, Leopold, 281
Postindustrial economies, 166
Postmarital residence patterns, 211–213, 268
Postmodernism, 110–111
Postpartum sex taboo, 201
Potlatches, 98
Pottery, 166, 347, 352, 361–362
Power, 294, 298
Power, language of, 57, 60
Power relationships, 110–111
Precipitation patterns, 162
Predispositions, 105–106
Prehistoric archaeology, 5
Preindustrial times, nature and culture in, 155–156
Presentation of self, 57
Prestige, 98, 294, 298, 303
Prices, 175

Priests/priesthood, 335, 337
Primatology, 3
Primitive Culture (Tylor), 21, 94
Primogeniture, 202, 205
Private property, 31
Problems, in human-environment interaction, 135
Production of goods, 79
Productive property, 212
Productive resources, 303, 310–311
Productivity, 180–181
Productivity of horticulture, 147
Productivity of intensive agriculture, 149
Productivity of language, 49, 50
Products, 135, 166
Products of culture, 30
Proletariat, 311
Prophets, 337
Protestants, conservative, 211
Protestants, in Ireland, 373
"Protocol for Research, Publication and Recordings," 122
"Protocols for Native American Archival Materials," 122
Proto-culture, 38
Proto-Germanic languages, 54
Provincially Administered Tribal Areas, 377
Proxemics, 55
Psy, 59
Psychological theory of religion, 322–323
Puberty rites, 334
Public goods, 173
Public resources, 173
Pueblos, 228
Puerto Rico, 383, 384
Punishments, 324. *See also* Sanctions

Q
Al Qaeda, 28, 366, 377
Quebec, 382, 384
Quinine, 405
Quotas, 82

R
Raatira, 277
Race, 34–36
Racial classifications, 35–36
Racial pride, 36
Radcliffe-Brown, A. R., 99–100
Railroads, 158
Rana Plaza, 186
Ranked societies, 295, 297
Rappaport, Roy, 170
Rapport, development of, 119, 123
Rational thought, development of, 321
Reality, constructions of, 33–36
Reasonable-person model, 288–289

Rebellion, 305–306
Recall ethnography, 118
Reciprocal feasting, 170
Reciprocal sharing, 139, 296
Reciprocity, 29
   balanced reciprocity, 169–171
   bridewealth and, 207–208
   definition of, 167, 168
   generalized reciprocity, 168–169
   negative reciprocity, 171
   social distance and, 171–172
Red River War of 1875, 274
Redistribution, 167, 168, 172–173
Refugees, 379
Regional subcultures, 24
Reincarnation, 299, 301, 307
Relative strength, and sexual division of labor, 255, 256
Relativism, 15–16
Relativistic perspective, 14–16
Religion and worldview
   definition of, 36–37, 316–319
   as ethnic boundary marker, 369
   Frazer on, 321
   gender stratification, 261–262
   inequality, maintenance of, 306–307
   intellectual/cognitive approaches, 320–321
   origins of religious beliefs, 94–95
   psychological approaches, 322–323
   religions vs. worldviews, 36
   revitalization movements, 337–342
   rituals and symbols, 318–319
   sociological approaches, 323–325
   supernatural explanations of misfortune, 325–328
   theories of, 319–325
   varieties of religious organizations, 328–337
Religious art, 357–358
Religious diversity, 340, 341
Religious healing, 331
Religious organizations, 328
   communal organizations, 329, 330, 332–335
   definition of, 329
   ecclesiastical organizations, 329, 330, 335–337
   individualistic organizations, 329–330
   shamanistic organizations, 329, 330, 331–332
Religious pluralism, 340
Religious structures, 335–336
Relocation, 379–380, 382, 383
Repatriation of cultural property, 121
Representation, 103
Repression, 305
Reproductive roles, 255, 256
Research methodologies
   comparative methods, 126–130
   ethnographic methods, 116–126

Resource allocation, 135, 139–140, 148, 178
Resource availability, 273
Resources, 135
Resources, access to in stratified societies, 298
Respect language, 56
Revelation, 337
Revitalization movements, 337
   fate of, 340–342
   Melanesian cargo cults, 338
   Native American movements, 338–340
Rewards, 324
Rice production, 203
Rickets, 182
Rights and duties of group membership, 29
Rising Fire, 288
Rites of passage, 333–334
Rites of solidarity, 335
Ritual bathing, 302, 318
Ritual calendar, 229
Ritual duties, 228
Rituals, religious, 261–262, 318–319, 322
Rock art, 352
Role and rapport, development of, 119, 123
Role reversal, 266–267
Roles, 29, 219
Roman Empire, 54
Romance languages, 54
Romantic love, 195
Romney, Mitt, 60, 309
Root crops, 258
Roscoe, Will, 248
Royal Dutch Shell, 282
Rural life in Japan, 202–203
Rural-to-urban migration, 202–203
Russia, 160–161, 384

S

SAE (Standard American English), 51
Sahagún, Bernardino de, 120
Sahlins, Marshall, 126, 171
Salaryman, 203
Salem witch trials, 320
Salvage archaeology. *See* Contract archaeology
Same-sex marriage, 209–211
Same-sex relationships, 249, 250–251
San Francisco, 209
Sanctions, 280–281, 284, 285
Sand paintings, 357–358
Sanday, Peggy Reeves, 261, 264
Sandy Hook Elementary School shooting, 28
Santa Fe, New Mexico, 185, 360
Santorum, Rick, 309
Sapa Inca, 279
Sapir, Edward, 62

Sapir-Whorf hypothesis, 62–63
Sasaki, Tom, 119
Savagery stage of cultural evolution, 93
Scapegoats, 327
Scarcity explanation of hunger, 394–396
Schlegel, Alice, 268
Science, 110, 321
Science, 162
Scientific approach to anthropology, 104–107
Scientific medicine and traditional healing, 389–391
Sea levels, rises in, 161, 162
Seasonal congregation and dispersal, 137–138
Seasonal mobility, 137, 152
Seasonal rituals, 335
Secular art, 357–358
Secular ideologies, American, 307–308
Sedentary groups, 146, 148
Sedona, Arizona, 185
Segmentary organization, 227
Segregation, 298, 381–382
Self-determination, 371
Self-help systems, 281, 285–287
Self-identity, 243
Selfishness, 105
Self-sufficiency, 168, 171
Semantic domain, 61
Sen, Amartya, 406
Separatist movements, 369, 377, 384–385
Sepoy Mutiny, 79
September 11, 2001, terrorist attacks, 15, 27–28, 377
Serbo-Croatian dialect, 369
Seven Years War, 84
Sewing, 353
Sex, gender and, 243–244
Sexual access, 197
Sexual dimorphism, 244
Sexual division of labor. *See* Gendered division of labor
The Sexual Life of Savages (Malinowski), 100
Shakespeare, William, 359
Shamanistic organizations, 329, 330, 331–332
Shamans, 331–332, 355
Shechem, 207
Shell beads, 37–38, 171
Shifting cultivation, 146
Shinto, 96, 318, 319
Shudras, 299
Siddhartha, 319
SIL International, 58
Silcrete, 38
The Silent Language (Hall), 55
Silk Road, 71, 91, 154
Simple bands, 273, 274
Six-Day War, 373
Slash and burn cultivation. *See* Shifting cultivation

Slave trade, 75, 76, 80
Slavery, 75, 300
Slovenia, 378
Smallpox, 74
Social anthropology. *See* Cultural anthropology
Social behavior, language and, 55–57, 60
Social bonds, 170
Social context, 219
Social context of speech, 56–57
Social control, 280–281, 328
Social Darwinism, 42
Social discrimination, 406
Social distance and reciprocity, 171–172
Social fathers, 244
Social functions of art, 359, 362–363
Social functions of religion, 323–324
Social identity, 29, 239, 243
Social inequality and stratification, 178
    benefits of inequality, 312–313
    caste societies, 295
    castes in traditional India, 299–302
    class, 295
    class in the United States, 302–305
    egalitarian societies, 295, 296–297
    equalities and inequalities, 294–299
    ranked societies, 295, 297
    stratified societies, 295, 298–299
    systems of, 295
    theories of inequality, 308–313
Social justice, 178
Social learning, 197
Social norms, 176, 181, 280, 290
Social patterns, 238
Social rank, 228
Social reality, 34–36, 244
Social solidarity, 323
Social stratum, 298
Social welfare capitalism, 179
Socialism, 178, 179
Socialization, 25–28
Socialized medicine, 179–180
Society, definition of, 67
Sociobiology, 104–106
Sociocultural anthropology. *See* Cultural anthropology
Sociolinguistics, 56
Sociological approaches to religion, 323–325
Sociological interpretations of witchcraft and sorcery, 327–328
Sodalities, 275–276
Soetoro, Ann Dunham, 34
Solidarity, rites of, 335
Somaliland, 378
Sons, preference for, 224–225
Sorcery, 127–128, 325–328

Sororal polygyny, 205, 208
Sororate, 206–207
Souls, 333
Sound systems, variations in, 51–52
South Africa, 122
South America, 78, 143–144
Souvenir market, 361
Soviet Union, 82, 366, 377, 378, 383
Space, in nonverbal communication, 55–56
"Spanglish," 11
Spanish expansion, 74–75, 77–78
Spanish language, 59
Special interests, 173
Speech, and social context, 56–57
Spirit helpers, 331
Spiritual powers, associations with, 249, 250
Srebrenica, 380
St. Vincent, 84
Standard American English (SAE), 51
Standard of value, 174
Standards of living, measurement of, 406
Starbucks, 166
Stateless nationalities, problem of, 372–373, 376–379
States, 150, 274, 278–279, 282–284
Status, 294
Status groups, 303
"Status of women," 260. *See also* Gender stratification
Steam engines, 157–158
Stereotyping, ethnic, 118–119
Stevenson, Matilda Cox, 249
Steward, Julian, 102–103, 106
Stone Age, 92
Stone money, 174–175
Store of value, 174
Stratified societies, 295, 298–299
Strip mining, 401–402
Structured interviews, 117
Subcultures, 24–25
Subnationalities, 371–372
Subsistence agriculture, 151
Subsistence risk reduction, 153
Suez Canal, 79
Sun Dance, 381
Sun God, 279
Supernatural beings, 316–317
Supernatural causation, 389–390
Supernatural explanations of misfortune, 325–328
Supernatural forces or substances, 317
Supernatural mandate for the elite, 307
Supernatural powers, 316–317
Supernatural sanctions, 280–281
Superstition, 320
Supply and demand, 175, 177
Suriname, 85

Surplus, 150
Survey of Consumer Finances, 304
Survival International, 399
Sweat lodge ceremony, 185
Switzerland, 340
Symbolic significance of money, 174
Symbolic value of products, 166–167, 170
Symbolic/ritual behavior, 318–319
Symbols
   cultural knowledge, 39
   evidence of in prehistory, 37
   interpretive anthropology, 109
   male-female differences, 244
   nonverbal communication, 55
   overview of, 31, 32–33
   religious, 318–319
Synchronic, 116
Syncretism, 338

T

Taboos, 57, 325
Tabu, 277–278
Tales of the Shaman's Apprentice (Plotkin), 405
Taliban, 377
Tangible assets, 304
Tanzania, 141
Tariffs, 82
Tasmania, 73, 80, 82
Tattooing and scarification, 349–351
Tax systems, 172
Tea Party, 181
Technological determinism, 101–102
Technology, 87, 101–102, 106
Ten Commandments, 323
Ter, 286
Terms of address, 56
Terrorism, 27–28, 366, 376–377
Textiles, 156, 300, 352
Textiles, production of, 79
Theory, 104
"Third World" nations, 13
Third-gender identity, 248, 249
Time magazine, 210
Time-Warner, 225
Timing of rituals, 319
Tito, Josip, 383
Tiwi Wives (Goodale), 199
Todai-ji, 336
Tone languages, 52
Tools, 92, 106
Torii, 318
Totem poles, 354
Totemic clans, 226
Totemism, 334–335

Tourism, 361
Trade partnerships, 169–170
Traditional healing and scientific medicine, 389–391
Traditional medicine, 390
Traditional resource management practices, 399
Trail of Tears, 380
Trances, 331–332
Transfer payments, 172
Transfer pricing, 283–284
Transhumance, 152
Transnational communities, 374–375
Transportation, 157–158
Transsexualism, 247
Transubstantiation, 358
Transvestism, 249, 250
Tribal ceremonies, 276
Tribal peoples, 400. *See also* Indigenous peoples
Tribal war chiefs, 276
Tribes, 274, 275–276
Tribute, 173
Trucking industry, 158
Truman, Harry, 384
Turner, Victor, 32
Two spirits, 247–251
Tylor, E. B., 21, 94–97, 102, 104, 192, 316
Tzeltal language, 63–64

U

Uncles and aunts, terminology, 235, 236, 237
"Underdeveloped" nations, 13
Undergraduate degrees in anthropology, 10
Unequal distribution of resources, 394
Unilineal descent, 221–223, 226–230
Unilineal descent groups, 223, 226–228
Unilineal evolutionism
   comparative methods and, 126
   compared to current anthropological thought, 103–104
   vs. historical particularism, 96, 98
   matrilineal descent, 221, 222–223
   overview of, 93–95
   patrilineal descent, 221–222
Unilineally extended families, 226
United Arab Emirates, 141
United Kingdom, 340, 373, 383, 385
United Nations, 16, 121, 378–379, 404
United States
   class in, 302–305
   cultural heterogeneity, 272
   distribution of income, 304
   forced assimilation, 381
   ideologies, 306–307
   immigrants, 374–375
   inequality, maintenance of, 305–308
   religious diversity, 341
   repatriation of cultural property, 121
   secular ideologies, 307–308
   trade with Europeans, 79
Universal application, intention of, 281
Universal Declaration of Human Rights, 16
Universities/colleges, 83
University of Michigan, Dearborn, 341
University of Pennsylvania, 95
University of Rochester, 95
Unlineal descent group, 226, 233
Unskilled labor, 158
Unstructured interviews, 117
Unta, 286
Untouchables, 300
U.S. Census Bureau, 129, 304
U.S. Census form, 35
U.S. Forest Service, 7
U.S. political system, 172–173
U.S. Supreme Court, 210
USA Today, 7
Useful species, 408

V

Vaishas, 299
Values, 31, 39–40, 244
"Vanishing Indian," myth of, 120–121
Varanasi, 318–319
Varnas, 299
Vega, Garcilaso de, 120
Vegetarianism/veganism, 99
Vendanta Resources, 401–402
Vietnam War, 291
Villages, 146, 148
Vimbuza, 355
Virginia Tech shooting, 28
Vision quest, 330
Visual arts, 351
   art of the Northwest Coast, 353–354
   form, 352
   market economy and, 360–362
   ornamentation, 352–353
   overview of, 356
Volga Germans, 379
Voluntary organizations, 219
Voodoo, 355
Voodoo dolls, 325
Voting Rights Act of 1965, 34
Voudon religion, 355

W

Wage rates, 183, 186
Wallace, Anthony, 329
Walmart, 282
Warfare, 105, 233, 258–259, 263

Warrior societies, 276
Wasi, 170
Wealth, 70, 294, 298, 303–305, 307–308
Wealth ratio, 305
Weather, and rituals, 319
Wedding showers and gifts, 207
Welsh language, 59
West Bank, 373
West Indies, 77–78
Westermarck, Edward, 193–194
Western culture, 26, 27
Western Sahara, 378
Westernization, 26, 27
Wet rice regions, 149
We-wha, 250
WGIP (Working Group on Indigenous Populations), 404
White, Benjamin, 393
White, Leslie, 101–102, 103, 106, 120, 156
Whiting, Beatrice, 127
Whorf, Benjamin, 62–63
Wicca, 328
"Wife stealing," 285
Willow bark, 405
Wilson, Edward O., 105
Wilson, John, 339–340
WIMSA (Working Group of Indigenous Minorities in South Africa), 122
Winkte, 249
"Wired for culture," 38
Witch hunts, 328
Witchcraft, 325, 326–328
Wolf, Arthur, 193
Woman Chief, 249, 250
Woman-man gender identity, 248
Women. *See also* Gender; Gender stratification; Gendered division of labor
  benefits of polygynous marriages, 204–205
  contribution to material welfare, 264
  control over key resources, 264–267
  economic independence, 265–266
  entering the workforce, 265
Woodburn, James, 296
Words and meanings, 52–53
Workers in developing countries and regions, 183, 186–187
Workers in rich countries, 183
Working class, 311
Working Group of Indigenous Minorities in South Africa (WIMSA), 122
Working Group on Human Remains, 121
Working Group on Indigenous Populations (WGIP), 404
World Bank, 162, 402
World Food Programme, 394
World Hunger (Lappé and Collins), 395
World problems and the practice of anthropology
  anthropologists as advocates, 399–405, 407–409
  applied anthropology, 388
  health and health care, 389–391
  population growth, 391–394
  world hunger, 394–399
World religions, 342
World Trade Organization (WTO), 82, 282–283
World views. *See* Religion and worldviews
World War II, 379
Worldviews, 31, 36–37, 40, 62–64. *See also* Religion and worldviews
WTO (World Trade Organization), 82, 282–283
Wuya, 229

X
Xenophobia, 105

Y
Yale University, 126
Yan, Yun-xiang, 224
Yanomamö, 206, 208
Yiddish language, 369
Yugoslavia, 82, 378, 382–383, 384